Higher Education Law in America

- ❖ Campus Security
- ❖ Copyright Law
- ❖ Employment
- ❖ Hazing
- ❖ Athletics
- ❖ Cheating
- ❖ Privacy Issues
- ❖ Freedom of Speech
- ❖ Discrimination

Center for
Education & Employment Law

Center for Education & Employment Law
P.O. Box 3008
Malvern, PA 19355

> "This publication is designed to provide accurate and authoritative information in regard
> to the subject matter covered. It is sold with the understanding that the publisher is not
> engaged in rendering legal, accounting or other professional services. If legal advice or
> other expert assistance is required, the service of a competent professional person
> should be sought." -*from a Declaration of Principles jointly adopted by a Committee of
> the American Bar Association and a Committee of Publishers and associations.*

Library of Congress Cataloging-in Publication Data

Higher Education Law in America.
     p. cm.
  Includes index.
  ISBN 978-1-933043-76-0 (pbk.)
  1. Universities and colleges – Law and legislation – United States. I. Center for Education &
Employment Law.
  KF4225 .H54 2000
  378.73–dc21

                             00-055074

ISBN 978-1-933043-76-0

Cover Design by Amy Jacoby

Other Titles Published
By Center for Education & Employment Law:

Deskbook Encyclopedia of American School Law
Deskbook Encyclopedia of Employment Law
Deskbook Encyclopedia of Public Employment Law
Federal Laws Prohibiting Employment Discrimination
Legal Update for Teachers: The Complete Principal's Guide
Private School Law in America
Statutes, Regulations and Case Law Protecting Individuals with Disabilities
Students with Disabilities and Special Education
U.S. Supreme Court Education Cases
U.S. Supreme Court Employment Cases

TABLE OF CONTENTS

TABLE OF CONTENTS

CHAPTER THREE
Athletics and Student Activities

CHAPTER FOUR
Freedom of Speech and Religion

TABLE OF CONTENTS

TABLE OF CONTENTS

CHAPTER SEVEN
Employment Discrimination

TABLE OF CONTENTS

CHAPTER EIGHT
Intellectual Property

CHAPTER NINE
Liability

TABLE OF CONTENTS

CHAPTER TEN
University Operations

CHAPTER ELEVEN
School Finance

APPENDIX A

APPENDIX B

TABLE OF CONTENTS

INTRODUCTION

Higher Education Law in America provides an encyclopedic compilation of federal and state court decisions in the area of college and university law. We have reviewed hundreds of federal and state court decisions involving higher education law and have included the most important ones in this deskbook. The chapters have been arranged topically, and the cases have been presented in an easy-to-use manner.

Each chapter contains explanatory passages at the beginning of each section to help you develop an overall understanding of the legal issues in that particular area. The case summaries have been written in everyday language, and at the start of each case is a brief note highlighting the holding or the significant issues discussed within. Further, the case summaries themselves contain boldface type to emphasize important facts, issues and holdings.

We feel that *Higher Education Law in America* will help you understand your rights and responsibilities under state and federal law. It has been designed with professional educators in mind, but also has tremendous value for lawyers. We hope you will use this book to protect yourself and to gain greater wisdom and understanding. Hopefully, we have succeeded in making the law accessible to you regardless of your level of understanding of the legal system.

Jim Roth, Esq.
Senior Legal Editor
Center for Education & Employment Law

ABOUT THE EDITORS

James A. Roth is editor of *Legal Notes for Education* and *Special Education Law Update,* and a co-editor of *Students with Disabilities and Special Education Law.* He is a graduate of the University of Minnesota and William Mitchell College of Law, and is admitted to the Minnesota Bar. Mr. Roth is an adjunct faculty member at Hamline University, St. Paul, Minnesota, and an adjunct program assistant professor at St. Mary's University of Minnesota, Twin Cities Campus.

Thomas D'Agostino is a managing editor at the Center for Education & Employment Law and is the editor of *Higher Education Legal Alert.* He is a co-author of *Keeping Your School Safe & Secure: A Practical Guide.* He graduated from the Duquesne University School of Law and received his undergraduate degree from Ramapo College of New Jersey. He is a past member of the American Bar Association's Section of Individual Rights and Responsibilities as well as the Pennsylvania Bar Association's Legal Services to Persons with Disabilities Committee. Mr. D'Agostino is admitted to the Pennsylvania Bar.

Curt J. Brown is the Group Publisher of the Center for Education & Employment Law. Prior to assuming his present position, he gained extensive experience in business-to-business publishing, including management of well-known publications such as *What's Working in Human Resources, What's New in Benefits & Compensation, Keep Up to Date with Payroll, Supervisors Legal Update,* and *Facility Manager's Alert.* Mr. Brown graduated from Villanova University School of Law and graduated magna cum laude from Bloomsburg University with a B.S. in Business Administration. He is admitted to the Pennsylvania Bar.

Carol Warner is the editor of *EducationTechNews.com* and two monthly newsletters: *School Safety & Security Alert* and *Legal Update for Teachers.* She is also a contributing editor for *HigherEdMorning.com* and *Higher Education Legal Alert.* Before joining the Center for Education & Employment Law, she was an editor for two employment law newsletters: *What's Working in Human Resources* and *What's New in Benefits & Compensation.* Carol is a graduate of The New York Institute of Technology and holds a Bachelor of Arts in English with an emphasis in professional writing.

Elizabeth A. Wheeler is editor of the monthly newsletter *Private Education Law Report* and the *Private School Law in America* deskbook. She's also a contributing editor for the newsletters *Higher Education Legal Alert* and *School Safety & Security Alert.* A graduate of Macalester College and Capital

University Law School, she's a member of the Massachusetts bar. Before joining the Center for Education & Employment Law, she was a legal editor for a South Boston publisher, where she edited employment law and education law newsletters.

How to Use Your Deskbook

We have designed *Higher Education Law in America* in an accessible format for both professional educators and attorneys to use as a research and reference tool toward prevention of legal problems.

Research Tool

As a research tool, our deskbook allows you to conduct your research on two different levels – by topics or cases.

Topic Research

◆ If you have a general interest in a particular **topic** area, our **table of contents** provides descriptive chapter headings containing detailed subheadings from each chapter.

➢ For your convenience, we also include the chapter table of contents at the beginning of each chapter.

Example:
For more information on liability, the table of contents indicates that a discussion of instructor misconduct takes place in Chapter Nine, under Intentional Conduct, on page 386:

CHAPTER NINE
Liability

II. INTENTIONAL CONDUCT.............................386
➡ A. Instructor Misconduct 386
B. Employee Misconduct...............................388
C. Third-Party Misconduct.............................389

How to Use Your Deskbook

◆ If you have a specific interest in a particular **issue**, our comprehensive **index** collects all of the relevant page references to particular issues.

> **Example:**
> For information on hazing, the index shows the topic is covered under a section discussing fraternities and sororities:
>
> Student activities
>   Fraternities and sororities, 118
> →   Hazing, 126-128
>   Injuries, 124-126
>   Operation and school supervision, 118-121
>   Organizational liability, 121-124
>
>   Tax issues, 470-475

Case Research

◆ If you know the **name** of a particular case, our **table of cases** will allow you to quickly reference the location of the case.

> **Example:**
> If someone mentioned a case named *Godinez v. Siena College,* looking in the table of cases, which has been arranged alphabetically, the case would be listed under section "G" and would be found on p. 404 of the text.
>
> **G**
>
>   Glenn v. Univ. of Southern California, 402
>   Glover v. Jackson State Univ., 366
> →   Godinez v. Siena College, 404
>   Gonzaga Univ. v. Doe, 41, 43
>   Gonzales v. North Carolina State Univ., 75
>   Goodwin v. Creighton Univ., 83

How to Use Your Deskbook

✓ Each of the cases summarized in the deskbook also contains the case citation, which will allow you to access the full text of the case if you would like to learn more about it. See *How to Read a Case Citation,* p. 499.

◆ If your interest lies in cases from a **particular state**, our **table of cases by state** will identify the cases from your state and direct you to their page numbers.

Example:
If cases from California are of interest, the table of cases by state, arranged alphabetically, lists all of the case summaries contained in the deskbook from that state.

CALIFORNIA

Adoma v. Univ. of Phoenix, Inc., 243
Alpha Delta Chi-Delta Chapter v. Reed, 169
Ass'n for a Cleaner Environment v. Yosemite Community College Dist., 423

✓ Remember, the judicial system has two court systems — state and federal court — which generally function independently from each other. See *The Judicial System,* p. 495. We have included the federal court cases in the table of cases by state according to the state in which the court resides. However, federal court decisions often impact other federal courts within that particular circuit. Therefore, it may be helpful to review cases from all of the states contained in a particular circuit.

Reference Tool

As a reference tool, we have highlighted important resources which provide the framework for many legal issues.

◆ If you would like to see specific wording of the **U.S. Constitution**, refer to **Appendix A**, which includes relevant provisions of the U.S. Constitution such as the First Amendment (freedom of speech and religion) and the Fourteenth Amendment (which contains the Equal Protection Clause and the Due Process Clause).

How to Use Your Deskbook

◆ If you would like to review **U.S. Supreme Court decisions** in a particular subject matter area, our topical list of U.S. Supreme Court case citations located in **Appendix B** will be helpful.

The book also contains a glossary, which provides definitions of legal terms and certain statutes. The glossary can be found on p. 501.

We hope you benefit from the use of *Higher Education Law in America.* If you have any questions about how to use the deskbook, please contact James Roth at jroth@pbp.com.

TABLE OF CASES

TABLE OF CASES

TABLE OF CASES

TABLE OF CASES

TABLE OF CASES

TABLE OF CASES

TABLE OF CASES

TABLE OF CASES BY STATE

TABLE OF CASES BY STATE

CHAPTER ONE

Student Rights

I. THE CONTRACTUAL RELATIONSHIP

The relationship between private institutions of higher learning and their students is contractual. Contract terms are established by the written materials distributed over the course of a student's enrollment. Public institutions of higher learning are government entities which have constitutional due process obligations to provide students notice and an opportunity to be heard.

A. Breach of Contract

◆ *A New York university did not breach a contract by refusing to let a student complete his MBA degree studies after he was convicted of insider trading.*

While he was pursuing his MBA degree, the student worked as a certified public accountant. He was convicted of violating insider trading laws by providing material, nonpublic business information to his brother – a securities trader. But the student did not tell the university about his criminal activity. After he graduated, the university learned about the conviction and decided not to certify him as qualified for an MBA. In a federal court action, the student claimed the university breached an implied contract by not following its rules and procedures. Appeal reached the U.S. Court of Appeals, Second Circuit. It held **academic decisions are best left to educators**. Judicial review of such

1

decisions is limited to a determination of whether the institution acted in good faith. Courts are not to disturb these decisions unless educators acted arbitrarily, irrationally, or in bad faith. In this case, the university disallowed the student's MBA certification on the basis of a bylaw making it the duty of each faculty member to determine standards of academic achievement for degrees.

As the student had admitted his crime, university faculty members had reasonably concluded his conduct was not befitting a member of the academic business community. The court held it could not be shown that the university acted arbitrarily, irrationally, or in bad faith. The judgment was affirmed. *Rosenthal v. New York Univ.*, 482 Fed.Appx. 609 (2d Cir. 2012).

◆ *A federal court of appeals affirmed the dismissal of a former student's breach of contract action against a New York medical school.*

After the student failed a required course, the medical school disenrolled him. As a result, he could not take a required medical licensing exam, and he sued for breach of contract. **Under New York law, an "implied contract" is created when a student is admitted to an institution.** Contract terms are created by the institution's written materials, and it must act in good faith when dealing with a student. On the other hand, the student must satisfy school requirements and follow its procedures. In this case, the student claimed the medical school fabricated his failing grade. A federal court found he presented no evidence from which a reasonable jury could conclude his grade was fabricated. In fact, he emailed his instructor to acknowledge the failing grade. On appeal, the U.S. Court of Appeals, Second Circuit, affirmed the judgment for the medical school. It held the student could not show a breach of contract based on fabricating a failing grade and dismissing him. *Dasrath v. Ross Univ. School of Medicine*, 494 Fed.Appx. 177 (2d Cir. 2012).

◆ *A New York court found no breach of contract based on a college's decision to expel a student who admitted setting a fire on campus.*

After the student admitted committing arson on campus, he was arrested and charged with criminal violations. The college expelled him, and he filed a state court action for breach of contract in which he said he had falsely confessed to arson. After the case was dismissed, the student appealed. **A state appellate division court explained that an implied contract is formed when a student is admitted to a higher education institution.** Students must comply with terms prescribed by the institution. Judicial review of a university disciplinary action is limited. Courts will not disturb the discipline unless there is evidence that the institution acted arbitrarily, or did not substantially comply with its own rules and regulations. In this case, the student failed to identify any specific contract terms were violated. He did not point to any internal rule, regulation or code that was not followed. To succeed on his breach of contract claim, there had to be a more specific showing with respect to what the college did to breach the contract. Since the student relied on vague assertions of breach and did not identify any rule, regulation or code that was violated, his breach of contract claim had been properly dismissed. *Jones v. Trustees of Union College*, 937 N.Y.S.2d 475 (N.Y. App. Div. 2012).

◆ *An Ohio court rejected a former student's breach of contract claim based on his dismissal from a medical college program.*

In his first year of medical school, the student failed two classes and his grade point average fell below 1.5. The school declined a request to remediate the classes and placed him on academic probation. After the student failed two more classes, he was dismissed from the program. He claimed the school breached a contract by changing the sequence of his courses, refusing to let him remediate the failed classes, and refusing to let him register as a special status student. A state court found the university exercised professional judgment. On appeal, the Court of Appeals of Ohio found no breach of contract. Instructor permission was required for a student to enroll as a special status student, and a professor had denied the student's request to take the class via distance learning. As the lower court had found, the student failed to meet the conditions set for him, including raising his grade point average to at least 2.5, completing a particular course, avoiding outside employment without pre-approval, and attending monthly status meetings. There was evidence that he had violated these conditions. **There was competent evidence that the university exercised its professional judgment in good faith.** Rejecting all the student's arguments, the court held for the university. *Jefferson v. Univ. of Toledo*, No. 12AP-236, 2012 -Ohio- 4793 (Ohio Ct. App. 2012).

◆ *A federal district court rejected a breach of contract claim against a California university that dismissed a student from a psychology program.*

Due to poor performance, the university dismissed the student from a graduate clinical psychology child studies program. He waited more than two years after losing an appeal within the university to file a federal district court action for breach of contract. According to the student, the university breached a contract by falsely accusing him of program violations, failing to allow him to challenge the accusations against him, dismissing him, and refusing to refund his tuition. As the court explained, California law required the filing of actions based on breach of an oral or implied contract within two years. On the other hand, the time limit for filing a claim for breach of a written contract is usually four years. In support of his written contract claim, the student offered his application to the university, an admission letter, the university's general catalogue and a clinical training agreement. But the court held these documents did not prove there was a written contract, **as none of them "express[ed] the obligation sued upon." The catalogue did not say that the university was contractually bound and did not create any implied contract provisions**. The clinical training agreement addressed only site-based clinical training and did not address any conditions of enrollment or dismissal, or otherwise create a contract. As a result, the university was entitled to judgment. *Bazzi v. Antioch Univ.*, No. CV 11-00482 DDP, 2012 WL 123542 (C.D. Cal. 1/13/12).

◆ *A Pennsylvania nurse anesthesia student unsuccessfully claimed his university breached its contract with him by dismissing him from the program.*

A Pennsylvania university dismissed a nurse anesthesia student from the clinical portion of his program, stating he consistently needed help and was not at an acceptable level. The university nursing department chair said the student was insubordinate and gave patients medicines he had been told not to provide. Administrators said the student's performance in the clinical portion of the program imperiled patient safety. After being placed on probation, he filed an unsuccessful internal appeal and was dismissed from the program. In a federal court lawsuit against the university and others, the student alleged breach of contract, breach of the covenant of good faith and fair dealing, denial of due process and tortious interference with contract. The court held for the university, and appeal reached the U.S. Court of Appeals, Third Circuit.

On appeal, the court held the relationship between private institutions and their students is a contractual one. Evidence showed the student's performance was deficient, and his deficiencies were documented. His inability to assure administrators that he could work safely with patients justified dismissal and was consistent with terms of the student handbook permitting dismissal "if an error of commission or omission jeopardize[d] the safety and/or welfare of the patient." The court rejected the student's claim that he was denied due process by the refusal of his request to have counsel attend his internal appeal. Private institutions need not offer their students the constitutional due process protections that must be provided by public institutions. *Kimberg v. Univ. of Scranton*, 411 Fed.Appx. 473 (3d Cir. 2010).

◆ *The New York Court of Appeals found issues of fact relating to the question of whether New York University's dental school denied a student a degree because of academic reasons or based on purely financial considerations.*

The student sued New York University and university officials in the state court system for breach of contract based on failure to award him a degree. The circumstances leading to the denial of a degree were not disclosed in court proceedings. A state supreme court ruled for the university and dismissed the complaint, but a state appellate division court reversed the decision and ordered the university to award a degree, with any authorizations needed for the dental boards. The university and officials appealed to the New York Court of Appeals, the state's highest court. It held **there was a factual dispute as to whether the decision to deny a degree was based on purely financial considerations or whether there were academic considerations involved in the decision**. The court said further proceedings were needed to determine whether a contract existed between the parties and whether they had met their duties under any such contract. *Eidlisz v. New York Univ.*, 15 N.Y.3d 730, 932 N.E.2d 876, 906 N.Y.S.2d 520 (N.Y. 2010).

◆ *A Pennsylvania public university had certain due process obligations to its students, but its student handbook did not constitute a binding contract.*

A student claimed she was unfairly dismissed from a clinical practicum for violating safety rules. She had to withdraw from another practicum and, instead of waiting a year to retake them, she completed the requirements at a private university. The student sued the State System of Higher Education for breach of contract, alleging the university did not follow the procedures set out in its handbook when it dismissed her from the practicum. After deciding the handbook constituted a binding contract between the parties, the state Board of

Claims held it had no authority over state contracts to provide education.

On appeal, the Commonwealth Court of Pennsylvania held the claim was properly dismissed because the board lacked jurisdiction (authority) to hear the dispute. **But the board incorrectly found a public institution's handbook forms a binding contract with a student.** Instead, the court held the board lacked jurisdiction over the claim because the handbook was not a contract. While private institutions have a contractual relationship with students, Pennsylvania public institutions have a due process obligation to provide students notice and an opportunity to be heard. **The court held a public university handbook did not constitute a contract** and affirmed the decision. *Tran v. State System of Higher Educ.*, 986 A.2d 179 (Pa. Commw. Ct. 2009).

◆   *An expelled graduate student had no constitutional right to stay in the Indiana University School of Optometry.*

The student claimed two professors assigned him poor grades for purely arbitrary reasons and that a third professor refused to let him take an exam. As a result, the university did not allow him to take required clinical rotations. The student failed a clinical rotation and was dismissed from the program. He sued the university board and several employees in a federal district court, which dismissed the case. On appeal, the U.S. Court of Appeals, Seventh Circuit, found **students generally have no federal constitutional right to remain in a graduate institution**. An exception applies if the student can show an implied contract. But to claim an implied contract was formed, the student must identify some promise from the university that was not honored. This promise could be made in a catalogue or some other written material.

The student said the promises he was relying on had been posted around campus in university bulletins and flyers. But he did not specify what they were, instead claiming the specific promises would be unearthed during the pretrial investigation and information-sharing procedure called "discovery." As a result, the court held the case had been properly dismissed. Repeating language from the lower court decision, the court held that allowing the case to proceed without specific facts would "sanction a fishing expedition costing both parties, and the court, valuable time and resources." *Bissessur v. Indiana Univ. Board of Trustees*, 581 F.3d 599 (7th Cir. 2009).

◆   *Virginia's highest court rejected a claim by female students that a college for women that transitioned to a coeducational facility breached a contract.*

The college was established in 1891. It remained a predominantly female institution until 2006, when its trustees decided to make it coeducational. A group of students sued the college in a state court, claiming the college breached a contract that included a promise of a four-year education at a women's college. They relied on an academic catalogue, which stated that the college offered "an education fully and completely directed toward women." The students claimed they chose the college specifically because it provided a single-sex environment. The college filed a motion seeking documentation on the existence of a contract to keep the college from going coed. The students produced letters of offers of admission, emails and other correspondence.

The trial court dismissed the complaint, and the students appealed to the

Supreme Court of Virginia. On appeal, the students repeated their claim that a contract was formed when they accepted offers of admission, paid tuition and registered for classes. The court rejected the claims, explaining that **to be a legally binding contract, an agreement must be definite as to all terms, identify the subject matter involved, and state essential commitments and agreements relating to the subject matter**. In addition, contract terms must be "clear, definite and explicit." The court found no language in any document indicating a clear promise by the college to remain predominantly female for the duration of their studies. As the students failed to prove the existence of a contract that would require the college to remain all-female while the students were enrolled there, the court affirmed the judgment. *Dodge v. Trustees of Randolph-Macon Woman's College*, 276 Va. 1, 661 S.E.2d 801 (Va. 2008).

◆   *A Florida university could change its academic requirements without being in breach of contract, as long as it did not act arbitrarily or capriciously.*

The student failed five required courses in his first year of an osteopathic medical program. The university then changed a handbook provision to require all students to pass both the Comlex Level II and Comlex Level I exams. The student did not pass the Level II exam, and he was dismissed from the program for failing to meet a six-year deadline for completing his coursework. He sued the university in a state court for breaching an implied contract created by the handbook. The court denied the university's motion for a directed verdict, and a jury found he should get $819,000. Appeal reached a Florida district court of appeal, which found the relationship between the university and student was contractual. There was an implied condition that students would conform to university rules and regulations. **The handbook gave the dean discretion to revise or modify policies at any time.** The university could change its academic requirements, as long as it did not act arbitrarily or capriciously. The denial of the motion for a directed verdict was reversed. *Jallali v. Nova Southeastern Univ.*, 992 So.2d 338 (Fla. Dist. Ct. App. 2008).

◆   *The Supreme Judicial Court of Maine held a handbook reservation clause, which allowed a college to unilaterally change the terms of its handbook without notice to students, defeated a student's breach of contract claim.*

A college appeals board found a male student guilty of sexual assault. The board prohibited him from living in campus housing, eating in college dining halls, and being on campus after 11:00 p.m. It placed him on permanent disciplinary probation. The student sued the college in a state court for breach of contract. The court found the college did not breach any contractual obligation to the student and held for the college. The student appealed, arguing the college breached its contract because the decision by the college to allow the female student to appeal did not meet his reasonable expectations. He said the disciplinary process described in the student handbook did not authorize the female student's appeal to the dean's hearing board. On appeal, the Supreme Judicial Court of Maine held **a reservation clause in the handbook allowed the college to unilaterally change handbook terms without notice to the students**. As a result, the court affirmed the judgment for the college. *Millien v. Colby College*, 874 A.2d 397 (Me. 2005).

B. Fraudulent Misrepresentation

In Byrd v. Lamar, *846 So.2d 334 (Ala. 2002), Alabama's highest court held a student could sue two university employees for intentionally trying to deceive him, where there was evidence he relied on their misrepresentations. In another Alabama case, a party could be held liable for fraud even where a misrepresentation was "made by mistake and innocently," if another party acted on the misrepresentation and suffered harm. See* Craig v. Forest Institute of Professional Psychology, *713 So.2d 967 (Ala. Civ. App. 1997).*

◆ *Recent graduates of a New York law school did not state valid claims for deceptive acts and practices based on published employment and salary data.*

According to the students, the law school did not disclose that employment data it published about its graduates included temporary and part-time positions. It reported mean salaries based on salary information submitted by a deliberately small and selective subset of graduates. The challenge reached a state appellate division court. It found no question that the information published by the law school left some consumers with "an incomplete, if not false, impression of the school's job placement success." But the court held "statistical gamesmanship" did not support a valid state-law claim. This was because **the law school made no express representations about the employment data regarding whether the work was full-time or part-time**. Moreover, it had disclosed that the representations about salary data were based on small samples of self-reporting graduates. While these disclosures were found "less than candid and incomplete," the court found no state-law violation based on "publishing truthful information and allowing consumers to make their own assumptions about the nature of the information." A fraudulent misrepresentation claim also failed because the information disclosed was not actually false, even if it was incomplete. *Gomez-Jiminez v. New York Law School*, 103 A.D.3d 13, 956 N.Y.S.3d 54 (N.Y. App. Div. 2012).

◆ *A federal court allowed a class action to proceed against a New Jersey law school based on claims that it posted misleading and incomplete graduate employment information on its website in violation of state laws.*

In refusing to dismiss the case, the court acknowledged the different result in *Gomez-Jiminez v. New York Law School*, above. The court disagreed with the New York court's finding that persons could not have reasonably relied on the alleged misrepresentations and could have learned about employment prospects through the exercise of due diligence. Instead, the New Jersey court questioned whether a reasonable student looking to go to law school would consider that published data included non-law and part-time work. As a result, the court allowed consumer fraud claims based on New Jersey and Delaware law to proceed. In so doing, **the court held the students did not have to show they reasonably relied on a misrepresentation**. Instead, they had to show the law school knowingly concealed a material fact with the intent of having them rely on the concealment, causing a loss. *Harnish v. Widener Univ. School of Law*, No. 2:12-cv-00608 (WHW), 2013 WL 1149166 (D.N.J. 3/20/13).

◆ *No legal violation occurred in connection with a District of Columbia graduate student's failure to obtain a desired doctoral degree.*

A part-time graduate student at Howard University (HU) lost some credits due to a time lapse. Although HU had procedures to restore credits earned within 10 years, she did not follow them. After the student took a semester of leave, some of her old credits became permanently unusable and some more recently earned credits became unusable. Because the credits were not restored, she was dismissed from the program. In a federal district court action, the student claimed HU breached a contract by failing to provide an adviser and allowing her to continue to register for courses after seven years, even though HU rules stated that students are to be dismissed after seven years in those circumstances. But the court found no contract existed. **Though the student claimed graduate school rules and regulations formed a contract, the court held they were simply a way for HU to communicate expectations to its students.** As there was no evidence that HU intended its rules to create binding obligations, the breach of contract claim failed. A constructive fraud claim was also rejected, as the student did not prove a confidential relationship with her adviser. *Mosby-Nickens v. Howard Univ.*, 864 F.Supp.2d 93 (D.D.C. 2012).

◆ *A federal district court denied a request to hold off on deciding a case filed against a California college until an appeals court had a chance to review it.*

A group of students claimed the college advertised "a quality education at an affordable price." However, they asserted they paid tuition rates that were among the highest in the country and that their degrees did not prepare them for anything but low-wage and low-skill jobs. Among the claims were breach of contract, negligent misrepresentation, fraud, breach of an implied covenant of good faith and fair dealing, and violations of state consumer protection laws. A federal district court held all claims should be resolved via arbitration except for the state consumer protection law claims. They could not be arbitrated because they sought to enforce a public right by blocking the college from deceiving other consumers. The college appealed the decision to deny its motion to compel arbitration with respect to the public injunctive relief claims. It then filed a motion asking the district court to hold off on deciding the public injunctive relief claims until after the appeals court had ruled on its appeal. After balancing the four factors utilized by courts when considering a request for injunctive relief, the court held a stay should be denied. **In the court's view, the public interest in promoting consumer protection justified a denial of the request to stay the proceedings**, and it did not find the college was likely to prevail on the merits of the case. *Ferguson v. Corinthian Colleges*, No. SACV 11-0127 DOC (AJWx), 2012 WL 27622 (C.D. Cal. 1/5/12).

◆ *A federal court dismissed a breach of contract claim against Harvard Extension School by an applicant who misrepresented the fact that he had already attended other institutions and held numerous degrees.*

The extension school's online application required applicants to list all prior colleges and universities attended – even if they did not want to transfer credits and even if they withdrew from a program. Not listing a prior institution attended was a serious enough misrepresentation to trigger disciplinary action. In a federal district court action by the applicant, **the court found no agreement between the parties, much less an agreement to accept him or award him a degree. There was no promise of enrollment or a degree as the applicant claimed**, but only "correspondence regarding certain course requirements." In addition, the court held "the decision to grant or deny admission to a student is a quintessential matter of academic judgment," that would not be "second guessed by the courts." *Getso v. Harvard Univ. Extension School*, No. 10 Civ. 4624, 2011 WL 135012 (S.D.N.Y. 1/13/11).

◆   *The Court of Appeals of Ohio rejected fraud claims by two students in a surgical technician program.*

At the time the students completed their classroom work, the college told them that no externship sites were available. When the students were finally placed in externships, both of them were asked to consider transferring into different programs. They both left the college and later filed a state court action against it for breach of contract, fraud and violation of a state consumer sales practices act. The students claimed the college knew it was enrolling more students than it could place in hospital externships. According to the state court of appeals, **the placement delay may have reflected poor planning, but it did not support a claim based on knowing or false representation**. On the other hand, the court reversed a lower court decision to reject claims under the state consumer sales practices act. To constitute a violation of the act, conduct does not need to rise to the level of fraud, negligence or breach of contract. In this case, a fact issue was present as to whether the college unfairly or deceptively represented that externships would be available during the final term of the program. The judgment was reversed in part, and the case was returned to the trial court for further proceedings. *Hacker v. National College of Business and Technology*, 186 Ohio App.3d 203, 927 N.E.2d 38 (Ohio Ct. App. 2010).

◆   *A Texas chiropractic student failed to convince a court that a college made misrepresentations about its graduation requirements.*

Among other requirements, the college required students to complete 10 trimesters of work. The student completed her 10 trimesters, but the college refused to award her a degree because she failed a clinical exit examination. According to the student, the college told her before she took the examination that her application for graduation had already been approved. She also said a college official told her before she took that examination that she should not worry about passing it. The student sued the college in a state court, raising a claim under a state consumer protection statute. She added claims for fraud, negligent misrepresentation and equitable estoppel. The court ruled for the college, and the student appealed. The Court of Appeals of Texas held all four of the claims had a common element of reliance, meaning she could not prevail unless she showed she relied on misrepresentations by the college. However, **the student did not show she relied on any alleged misrepresentation made by college officials and could not prevail on any of her claims**. As a result, the trial court judgment was affirmed. *Wood v. Texas Chiropractic College*, No. 01-07-00952-CV, 2008 WL 2854268 (Tex. Ct. App. 7/24/08).

◆ *A student did not show breach of contract or fraudulent misrepresentation by a college that accused him of selling copies of an upcoming examination.*

After an investigation and hearing, the college concluded the student had engaged in academic misconduct and dismissed him from the program. He sued the college for breach of contract, fraudulent misrepresentation, and fraudulent nondisclosure. The student filed a separate breach of contract claim against the teacher of the class in which he was accused of cheating. A jury ruled in his favor on the fraudulent misrepresentation claim against the college and awarded him $20,000 in damages. But the court set aside the verdict, and the jury found against the student on the breach of contract and fraudulent nondisclosure claims. On appeal, the Supreme Court of Missouri reversed the judgment on the breach of contract claim, and upheld the decision to set aside the fraudulent misrepresentation verdict. Any misrepresentation regarding the disciplinary hearings did not harm the student because he did almost nothing to prepare for them. **As the student did not show he relied on representations that the college would follow certain due process procedures at his appeal hearing, he could not prove fraudulent misrepresentation.** *Verni v. Cleveland Chiropractic College*, 212 S.W.2d 150 (Mo. 2007).

◆ *The Indiana Court of Appeals held a student had to show a university acted with a dishonest purpose in order to prove bad faith.*

An Indiana student who was pursuing a doctorate in economics received an "Unsatisfactory" grade in a thesis research course. Despite receiving an extension, the student did not complete tasks assigned by an economics policy committee, and he was dismissed from the program. After exhausting internal appeals, the student sued the university and a professor for breach of contract, negligence and defamation. A state court held the university's actions constituted academic judgment that it would not disturb, absent bad faith. It granted the student permission to assert a claim of bad faith, but then dismissed the amended complaint. On appeal, the state court of appeals held **courts do not rigidly apply contract law principles to education disputes, even though the relationship between students and educational institutions is contractual.** Courts recognize that implied contracts exist between students and universities, and the nature of contractual terms varies. To prove bad faith, the student had to show more than bad judgment or negligence. Instead, he needed to show the university acted with a dishonest purpose. As the amended complaint did not support such a claim, the court held for the university. *Gordon v. Purdue Univ.*, 862 N.E.2d 1244 (Ind. Ct. App. 2007).

◆ *A federal district court in New York refused to dismiss students' claims that a university engaged in deceptive business practices and breached a contract when it made changes to its drama program, including a change in its name.*

Current and former students sued the university, claiming the changes were deceptive business practices and in breach of contract. To address the contract claim, the court referred to a catalogue the university published every other year to promote the drama program. The catalogue included a policy relating to changes, which said course offerings, academic requirements, degree programs, tuition, fees and faculty were subject to change at any time.

The court held "the relationship between a university and its students is contractual." It would be inappropriate to grant judgment to the students on the claim that the change in the name of the program was a breach of contract. Although the catalogue clearly stated that degree programs were subject to change, it also emphasized the prestige and uniqueness of the program and promised students they would receive diplomas bearing the previous name. The court found a factual question as to whether the catalogue was likely to mislead a reasonable consumer and as to whether it fully disclosed the university's right to change the program name. *Deen v. New School Univ.*, No. 05 Civ. 7174 KMW, 2007 WL 1032295 (S.D.N.Y. 3/27/07).

C. Educational Malpractice

Courts have been reluctant to recognize educational malpractice claims. In Leiby v. Univ. of Akron, *No. 2004-10094, 2006 WL 1530152 (Ohio Ct. App. 6/6/06), an Ohio court rejected a student's educational malpractice claim based on his contention that his diplomas were "worthless." It held Ohio does not recognize claims for educational malpractice, as they lack readily acceptable standards of care, cause or injury. Educational malpractice claims are further disfavored due to public policy considerations, such as increased litigation and judicial deference for academic decisions. In* Ross v. Creighton Univ., *957 F.2d 410 (7th Cir. 1992), the U.S. Court of Appeals, Seventh Circuit, found at least 11 states have rejected educational malpractice claims.*

◆ *A Missouri court rejected a claim asserting that a law school failed to act on a faculty irresponsibility complaint against a professor.*

A University of Missouri (UM) law professor cancelled some classes and changed the times and places for class meetings. A student then emailed her to object to an assignment and restrictions she placed on outside research. She forwarded his emails to the dean and the associate dean for academic affairs, stating that she found the emails threatening. The professor asked the deans to remove him from her class, alert police and begin an honor code investigation. The student withdrew from the professor's classes, filed faculty irresponsibility charges against her, and later filed a lawsuit against UM for breach of contract.

When the case reached the state court of appeals, it noted Missouri courts have not found a contractual relationship exists between a student and a higher education institution. Other courts have held brochures, policy manuals and other advertisements can form the basis of a contractual relationship. But to show a breach, a student must point to an identifiable contractual promise that was not honored. **Changing a class time did not mean the university failed to provide a guaranteed service.** The court also rejected a claim that failure to follow procedures in handling the faculty irresponsibility charge constituted a breach of contract. As this claim questioned "the reasonableness of the educator's conduct in providing educational services," the court found it was an educational malpractice claim that was not recognized in Missouri. As a result, the court held the case was properly dismissed. *Lucero v. Curators of the Univ. of Missouri*, No. WD 74768, 2013 WL 519460 (Mo. Ct. App. 2/13/13).

◆ *The University of Minnesota did not have to refund tuition paid by a former student who failed to complete a final project and never received her degree.*

Although the student had already completed the minimum number of course credits for completing the program, she was told to take two additional courses intended to help cure the deficiencies identified in her final project. The student never completed the project and was not awarded a degree. She sued the university in a state court for some $6,700 in tuition refunds as well as the removal of an F from her transcript. Although the student asserted contract claims, the court held they were educational malpractice claims and dismissed them. On appeal, the state court of appeals held **courts do not entertain claims that require "an inquiry into the nuances of educational processes and theories."** While the student claimed the university breached a contract by making her take additional courses, the court deferred to the university's argument that she needed the coursework to prepare her final project. The court rejected her claim that the university unjustly kept her money without awarding a degree. The request to have a failing grade removed from her transcript was properly denied, since assigning grades was within the university's discretion. *Zinter v. Univ. of Minnesota*, 799 N.W.2d 243 (Minn. Ct. App. 2011).

◆ *The Supreme Court of Connecticut recognized at least two situations where courts will entertain a claim for breach of a contract for educational services in* Gupta v. New Britain General Hospital, *239 Conn. 574 (Conn. 1996).*

A Yale University School of Medicine handbook granted students three opportunities to pass the U.S. Medical Licensing Examination before dismissal. **That was a distinct contractual promise independent of the medical school's obligation to offer a reasonable educational program.** As a result, a student who was dismissed after two unsuccessful attempts at passing Step 1 of the USMLE would receive a trial to consider his breach of contract claim. Breach of contract may be found if the educational program failed in some fundamental respect, like not offering any of the courses necessary to become certified in a particular field. *Morris v. Yale Univ. School of Medicine*, No. 05CV848 (JBA), 2006 WL 908155 (D. Conn. 4/4/06).

II. DISCIPLINARY ACTIONS

Courts will not disturb disciplinary decisions unless the institution acted arbitrarily, or did not substantially comply with its own rules and regulations.

A. Due Process

1. Hearings and Procedural Safeguards

As noted in Tran v. State System of Higher Educ., *986 A.2d 179 (Pa. Commw. Ct. 2009), this chapter, public institutions of higher learning are government entities with certain due process obligations to their students. The Due Process Clause of the Fourteenth Amendment requires state entities to provide notice and an opportunity to be heard when individual liberty or property interests are at stake. Due process includes the notion of fundamental fairness and notice and an opportunity to be heard at some point during disciplinary procedures. By contrast, private institutions have a contractual relationship with students, and are not bound by constitutional requirements.*

All institutions must comply with the procedural protections they promise to their students. A federal district court explained that informal procedures may minimize the risk of lawsuits in higher education disciplinary cases. These include: 1) use of an impartial decisionmaker; 2) providing notice of the charges and the evidence against the student; 3) an opportunity for the student to appear before the decisionmaker; 4) an opportunity for the student to suggest witnesses; 5) avoiding the imposition of sanctions against witnesses; and 6) permitting the student to either voluntarily accept discipline or the ruling of the decisionmaker. A. v. C. College, 863 F.Supp. 156 (S.D.N.Y. 1994).

◆ *A university did not violate the due process rights of a student when it revoked her doctoral degree after finding she had plagiarized her dissertation.*

After the student received a doctorate in education, university officials began disciplinary action for plagiarism. She selected an informal conference with the school's dean to resolve the matter, after being told that if she did so, she was subject to the full range of sanctions authorized by the student code. According to the student, an associate dean told her the university had never revoked a degree through the informal route. But after a 45-minute conference, the dean considered the evidence and revoked the student's degree. It was found that the dissertation had 27 instances of plagiarism. In a federal action, the student sued the university for due process violations. Appeal reached the U.S. Court of Appeals, Sixth Circuit, which rejected her claim based on insufficient notice that her degree could be revoked. It held that the oral notice of this possibility, which she had acknowledged receiving, was sufficient. In the court's view, the fact that the associate dean told her no degree had been previously revoked was not problematic. **Since the court found the informal conference provided the student an adequate opportunity to present her case, the court held for the university.** *Jaber v. Wayne State Univ. Board of Governors*, 487 Fed.Appx. 995 (6th Cir. 2012).

◆ *No due process violation occurred when Temple University suspended a student who threatened a professor via email.*

While enrolled in a bachelor's degree program at Temple, a student claimed he received an unfair grade. He sent the professor an email threatening "a curse against [the professor's] life and family forever." Another email told the professor the student wanted "justice on [him] spiritually and physically" and warned him to "[c]ooperate to prevent things from escalating." In response to the emails, the university charged the student with student conduct code violations. After a hearing, the university suspended him, required him to attend anger management classes, and placed him on probation. The student sued the university in a federal court for due process violations. On appeal, the U.S. Court of Appeals, Third Circuit, explained that **due process requires officials to provide students facing suspensions notice of the charges, an**

explanation of the evidence, and a chance to present their side of the story. In this case, the student received adequate due process. He received notice of the witnesses against him and was not wrongfully deprived of his right to confront the professor, who was not at the hearing. Instead, the court found "the emails spoke for themselves." The decision for the university was affirmed. *Osei v. Temple Univ.*, No. 1104033, 2013 WL 870376 (3d Cir. 3/11/13).

◆ *A Washington court held a student was properly dismissed from a nursing program after she admitted giving classmates prescription medications.*

When confronted, the student admitted giving classmates Flexeril and Ritalin. After meeting with a community college official, she was dismissed from the program. Instead of appealing, she filed a state court complaint against the community college for negligent dismissal, violation of her due process rights and related claims. The court ruled against her, and she appealed. The state court of appeals held her state-law due process claims were barred by her failure to exhaust available administrative remedies. By refusing to file an internal appeal with the school, she deprived it of the chance to correct any errors it may have made. With respect to her federal procedural due process claim, the student received all the process she was due. **When an institution bases a disciplinary decision on facts admitted by a student, no further hearing is needed.** Rejecting a claim that the student was entitled to "specific treatment" outlined in the student handbook, the court affirmed the judgment. *Buechler v. Wenatchee Valley College*, 298 P.3d 110 (Wash. Ct. App. 2013).

◆ *A Nevada student who was dismissed for plagiarism raised a viable due process claim, according to a federal district court.*

A professor accused the student of plagiarizing text in a draft dissertation. An academic integrity appeal panel held a hearing, but the student said she was denied an opportunity to have an advisor's assistance. The panel found the student committed academic misconduct and did not avail herself of multiple opportunities to correct the plagiarism. The panel recommended removing the student from her Ph.D. program. In a lawsuit against the university, she raised claims for breach of contract, negligence, infliction of emotional distress, defamation and due process violations. A federal court found the student claimed officials had prevented her return to school while also blocking her from admission to another institution. As this asserted a deprivation of her constitutionally protected property and liberty interests, the court held her case could proceed. **By alleging the lack of an advisor had prevented her from effectively representing herself at the hearing, the student made a valid claim** that university procedures violated her rights. *Gamage v. State of Nevada*, No. 2:12-cv-00290-GMN-VCF, 2013 WL 1182084 (D. Nev. 3/19/13).

◆ *A federal district court held Temple University's decision to expel a student could not stand because of the failure to provide him adequate due process.*

Temple police officers arrested and charged the student with aggravated assault on a police officer. Based on the incident, Temple charged the student with violating its code of conduct and instituted disciplinary proceedings. At the hearing, panel members received a hearing summary from one officer. None of the student's witnesses showed up. He asked for a continuance, which was denied. The officer testified but was not closely questioned. By contrast, the student's testimony was vigorously questioned, to the point of arguing. The panel refused to ask some of the questions he wanted to ask witnesses. At one point, a panel member told the student's attorney to "shut up." The panel took about 20 minutes to decide he was guilty, and it recommended expulsion.

The student sued the university and several officials for breach of contract, retaliation, and violation of his due process and equal protection rights. A federal court held the university violated the student's due process rights in several ways. The panel accorded the officer "significant respect" and did not closely question him, but the student was questioned in a confrontational and argumentative manner. **In the court's view, the university did not fairly review the recommendations of the hearing panel and the review board.** An official improperly met with a witness after the hearing. While the court found a due process violation, it held the university officials were entitled to qualified immunity. It ordered the student's reinstatement or a new hearing within 60 days. *Furey v. Temple Univ.*, 884 F.Supp.2d 223 (E.D. Pa. 2012).

◆ *A public university has adequate procedures for academic discipline if it provides notice of lack of progress and the decision is careful and deliberate.*

After a poor performance review, a medical student claimed an evaluating physician made a racist remark about her communication skills. The evaluator later denied this, and the program director met with the student to discuss her performance problems. Within weeks, he recommended placing the student on immediate academic probation with the requirement that she undergo a psychiatric evaluation as a condition of readmission. After failing her licensing examination a third time, the student was released from the program. She filed a federal district court lawsuit against the university and 15 individuals.

In pretrial activity, the court held that racially charged statements can be direct evidence of unlawful bias. However, the statement in this case did not qualify, because it was an "isolated and ambiguous" remark and the evaluator was not directly involved in the decision to put the student on probation. There was no due process violation, as the university had substantial documentation supporting its reasons for action. **A public university provides adequate procedures for academic discipline if a student has been fully informed of the faculty's dissatisfaction with the student's academic progress** and "the decision to dismiss was careful and deliberate." That was the case here. Under Sixth Circuit precedent, a formal hearing was not required for academic discipline, as academic decisions required an expert evaluation of cumulative information and were not readily adapted to judicial decisionmaking. The university and staff were entitled to judgment. *Peavey v. Univ. of Louisville*, 834 F.Supp.2d 620 (W.D. Ky. 7/183/11).

◆ *Texas Tech University (TTU) did not violate a student's due process rights by expelling him after finding he had pointed a gun at a classmate.*

TTU initiated disciplinary proceedings based on information that the student had pointed a pistol at his ex-girlfriend at his off-campus home. TTU'S student conduct board advised him in writing of a hearing date with the factual basis of a complaint against him. The notice also specified the particular student code violations he was being charged with, named the board members, offered him a chance to challenge their partiality, and explained how he could submit his own evidence, call witnesses and get an advisor. At the hearing, the student presented his position but chose not to call witnesses. The board found he had pulled a gun on a fellow student. It expelled him from the university.

The student sued TTU and certain officials for violating his due process rights, but a federal district court held he received all the process he was due. On appeal, the U.S. Court of Appeals, Fifth Circuit, held **students who are subject to discipline by a public institution are entitled to notice of the charges, an explanation of the evidence supporting the charges, and an opportunity to tell their side of the story**. On the other hand, the court said students facing discipline are not entitled to an opportunity to secure counsel, confront and cross-examine witnesses, or call their own witnesses. Based on the record, the court held TTU provided him with more than the minimum process due under the Constitution, and it affirmed the judgment. *Willis v. Texas Tech Univ. Health Sciences Center*, 394 Fed.Appx. 86 (5th Cir. 2010).

◆ *A New Jersey university provided adequate due process to a dentistry school student who was dismissed for cheating.*

A test proctor reported that the student was looking at a classmate's paper during an examination. As a result, the dental school advised the student to appear at a hearing to face charges of cheating. At the hearing, the proctor and four classmates said they thought the student had cheated. A professor said he had caught him cheating on a different exam. The student cross-examined the medical school's witnesses, called his own witnesses and had an active dialogue with the hearing body about the evidence. After the hearing, he submitted documents indicating his back condition was responsible for any unusual movements he made during his exams. The hearing body rejected this evidence, found the student had cheated, and recommended his dismissal.

Administrators accepted the expulsion recommendation, and the student sued the university in a federal district court for violating his due process rights. Appeal reached the U.S. Court of Appeals, Third Circuit, which found **a low risk of wrongfully depriving the student of his protected property interests, as the university had provided extensive procedural protections**. Since university procedures protected the student's interests and did not violate his due process rights, the court held for the university. *Le v. Univ. of Medicine & Dentistry of New Jersey*, 379 Fed.Appx. 171 (3d Cir. 2010).

◆ *Finding a two-year student suspension "arbitrary and capricious," a state court ordered the University of Minnesota to reconsider the discipline.*

The student was accused of sexually assaulting another student. No criminal charges were filed, but he was charged with a student conduct code violation. At a hearing, the Campus Committee on Student Behavior (CCSB) refused to consider evidence that the student would lose more than $200,000 in financial assistance if he was suspended. The CCSB found he had violated university rules and engaged in threatening, harassing or assaultive conduct, and decided he should be suspended for two years. An appeal committee found the student should have a new hearing because the exclusion of the financial evidence violated his due process rights. A university provost reinstated the CCSB's decision, and the student appealed to the state court of appeals. It noted **courts generally defer to university decisions involving student discipline**. But the decision in this case was held "arbitrary and capricious," because the university had no standards or guidelines for sanctions the provost could impose.

CCSB procedures required a fair hearing and required the committee to let accused parties offer relevant, reliable information. The excluded evidence was relevant and would have helped the CCSB make a reasoned decision. Finding the provost had relied on vague and unsupportable statements, the court ordered the university to hold a new hearing on the issue of sanctions. *Berge v. Univ. of Minnesota*, No. A10-131, 2010 WL 3632518 (Minn. Ct. App. 7/21/10).

◆ *A Florida state law school student was entitled to appropriate notice and a hearing prior to expulsion based on falsified admission records.*

A Florida law school learned that two employees in its admissions office fabricated documents and registration records to help an applicant get into law school. One was close friends with the applicant's family. Administrators met twice with the applicant, but they did not offer him a formal hearing before expelling him based on "fabricated admission and registration records." A state district court of appeal reviewed the expulsion decision, where the applicant claimed a right to a notice and a hearing prior to the action. The court agreed. Under the state's administrative procedure act, agency decisions that are based on disputed facts must be reversed if the aggrieved party was not given a hearing.

State universities such as the law school were subject to the provisions of the administrative procedure act. In addition, **Florida universities and colleges must adopt rules to ensure due process and fairness for student discipline.** In this case, the meetings did not satisfy the hearing requirement because the applicant did not receive notice of the charges against him before they were held. As the school improperly denied his statutory right to notice and a hearing under the state administrative code, the court reversed the order of expulsion and ordered a hearing. *Morris v. Florida Agricultural and Mechanical Univ.*, 23 So.2d 167 (Fla. Dist. Ct. App. 2009).

◆ *Students at public institutions have a protected property interest in due process under the Fourteenth Amendment to the Constitution.*

In a Michigan case, the Constitution required less than the student code called for, and the university was not obligated to strictly abide by the code's provisions. A student was accused of stalking and harassing a professor. She received a hearing before a disciplinary board that found she violated the university statement of student rights and code of student conduct.

At the hearing, the student was not allowed to cross-examine the professor. A hearing board then ordered her expulsion. Appeal reached the Court of Appeals of Michigan, which held the student received notice of the hearing and a written statement outlining the charges against her. She was allowed to call witnesses, state her version of the facts and record the hearing. The university offered an appeal process, and the student was allowed to continue her studies. Even if the university did not technically comply with all the requirements of its student code, it provided due process in this case. **Nothing about the university's decision would have been made any more accurate or fair by adding the further procedural protections insisted upon by the student.** Since the steps the university took to provide due process were adequate, the court affirmed the decision for the university. *Lee v. Univ. of Michigan-Dearborn*, No. 284541, 2009 WL 1362617 (Mich. Ct. App. 5/12/09).

◆   *The U.S. Court of Appeals, Sixth Circuit, held an Ohio medical college did not violate a student's due process rights during his disciplinary hearing.*

The student was arrested for a felony drug crime. The college notified him by letter that it was suspending him until investigations and hearings on his drug charge were completed, and advised him of his right to an investigation. The student decided not to schedule an investigation until the pending criminal charges were resolved. The student was not permitted on campus until the completion of a disciplinary hearing. A few months later, the student pled guilty to a felony drug charge, then asked for a hearing. The college sent him a written notice to appear before its student conduct and ethics committee to answer questions about his arrest. The student was not entitled to be represented by an attorney at the hearing because the criminal proceedings had ended. However, the college allowed his attorney to be present. At the hearing, the officer who had arrested the student testified. The committee questioned the officer, but denied the student's attorney an opportunity to do so. The college expelled the student for violating its zero-tolerance drug policy. The student sued the college in a federal district court for due process violations.

The court dismissed the case. On appeal, the Sixth Circuit stated **the student's interest in pursuing an education was a protected property interest. Due process is flexible, and its basic requirements are notice and an opportunity to be heard. Additional procedures vary based on the circumstances of each case.** The court held the college provided the student sufficient notice of the disciplinary charges against him and the procedures that would follow. As college procedures were fundamentally fair, the judgment was affirmed. *Flaim v. Medical College of Ohio*, 418 F.3d 629 (6th Cir. 2005).

◆   *A South Carolina student who was recently dismissed from his academic program was still a "student" when he received an on-campus parking ticket.*

While his dismissal was on appeal, the student agreed to conduct probation for 15 months. Later, the student argued with a university police officer over a parking citation. The officer issued him a notice of policy violation for harassment. The university then denied the student's academic dismissal appeal and expelled him. In a state court, he argued he was no longer a student at the time of the citation incident and thus did not have to obey university policies. The state court of appeals noted the student had agreed to conduct probation and held himself out as a student. There was no change in his status between the date of the agreement and the parking violation. The court rejected the contention that the university handbook definition of "continuing student relationship" was vague. **The academic appellate process was under way at the time of the parking violation, and the dismissal became final at a later time.** *Carter v. Univ. of South Carolina*, 602 S.E.2d 59 (S.C. Ct. App. 2004).

2. Private Schools

Students at private institutions lack the due process rights available to students at public institutions. Private higher education institutions need only ensure they observe their own rules for student discipline and refrain from arbitrary, bad faith or unlawful actions. **When it comes to academic decisions by private institutions, court review is very limited.**

◆ *A private university provided an Oklahoma student adequate procedural protections to consider charges that she had cheated on her assignments.*

A University of Tulsa (UT) student was charged with academic misconduct because her work resembled that of a classmate. She met with an assistant dean, who explained the charge to her. The student also received a chance to discuss the charge with a professor and tell her side of the story. After a second offense, she received similar interviews and was warned in writing that a third offense would lead to dismissal. The student was charged a third time, and TU dismissed her. The student sued TU in a federal court. It observed that private institutions are not state actors and generally cannot violate the Constitution.

Given the student-university relationship, the Tenth Circuit requires private universities to afford certain protections in disciplinary proceedings. These include **notice and a hearing that gives a student a meaningful opportunity to participate.** When private schools provide these protections, federal courts in the Tenth Circuit will defer to their factual findings if they are supported by substantial evidence. Courts could only reverse a student dismissal that was arbitrary. Although the student argued she was not afforded adequate notice or hearings, the court disagreed and upheld the discipline. *Ye Li v. Univ. of Tulsa*, No. 12-CV-641-TCK-FHM, 2013 WL 352116 (N.D. Okla. 1/29/13).

◆ *A Pennsylvania student could not advance a breach of contract claim in a federal court based on a school handbook definition of plagiarism.*

One of the student's professors accused her of plagiarism for using work she performed in another class. A university academic code defined plagiarism as "giving the impression you have written or thought something that you have in fact borrowed from someone else." Based on the professor's finding, the student was expelled. In a federal court, she claimed the university expelled her despite the fact that she committed no plagiarism and did not provide her any opportunity to challenge the action. The court dismissed the due process claim, noting that private institutions are not held to constitutional standards. Private entities need only provide the procedures promised in their written materials and procedures that are "fundamentally fair." In addition, the student's breach of contract claim failed. **In Pennsylvania, a private institution and its students have a contractual relationship.** A contract is based on college guidelines, policies, and handbooks. Even if the university had misconstrued the term "plagiarism," the court found the passage was a definition and not a promise. Since there was no promise to provide a hearing and the student did not show university procedures were unfair, the case was dismissed. *Hart v. Univ. of Scranton*, No. 3:11-CV-1576, 2012 WL 1057383 M.D. Pa. 3/28/12).

◆ *A person who took an online human nutrition class was unable to pursue constitutional claims against a private institution with no state affiliation.*

The person made negative posts about his instructor and the university in response to assignments for students to discuss the effect of the class and the university on their post-graduation plans. He said he planned to "run ... without ever looking back" and to "get out of City U ASAP" following his graduation. The person said the nutrition course was a "flub" or a "fluff" course. The instructor was offended, and she told him he would be assigned a poor grade and brought before a disciplinary committee. He was also told not to have any contact with the instructor. The person sued the university in a federal district court, claiming violation of his speech and due process rights. The university sought dismissal, arguing it could not be held liable for constitutional violations because it is a private institution. **The court stated that constitutional claims against a private actor cannot succeed unless there is some nexus between the challenged action and the state** that is so close that the action could "fairly be treated as that of the state itself." But the university did not exercise any powers usually reserved to a state. Nor did it act in concert with or with the help of state officials or act closely with a state. As the university was not a state actor and had no close connection with a state, the case was dismissed. *Becker v. City Univ. of Seattle*, 723 F.Supp.2d 807 (E.D. Pa. 2010).

◆ *A Tennessee court found evidence to support a jury verdict against an optometry college for dismissing a student in breach of their contract.*

In the student's third year of his optometry program, college faculty recommended he avoid dismissal for poor grades by voluntarily withdrawing and then reapplying. He did and was conditionally re-admitted with the requirement that he earn at least a C in every course. After receiving a D in one class and failures in two classes he was auditing, the student was dismissed. After some negotiations, the college president offered to revise his transcript to reflect withdrawal instead of a dismissal, and to write a letter of good standing. The student agreed, and the college sent the letter and revised transcript to other optometry schools at his request. However, the student was unable to transfer and sued the college in a state court for breach of contract and negligence.

A jury found that even though the college violated its own policies, it did not violate the withdrawal agreement with the student. On appeal, **the state court of appeals found the evidence supported the jury's finding that the college violated its policy when it dismissed the student for failing audited classes**. While the student argued there should be a new trial so he could further pursue his claims, the court found the verdict for the college was not inconsistent and was supported by the evidence. As a result, the court refused to disturb the verdict. *Rutherford v. Southern College of Optometry*, No. W2008-02268-COA-R3-CV, 2009 WL 5064972 (Tenn. Ct. App. 12/28/09).

◆ *A registered sex offender could not bring federal claims against a private Kentucky university and its staff because they were not state actors.*

In a federal district court lawsuit asserting violations of the U.S. and Kentucky Constitutions, the offender claimed the university and staff members wrongfully banned him from attending classes on campus. He acknowledged that he was subject to a state sex offender registration act, but he said he was in compliance with it. The offender claimed that in barring him from campus, the university failed to follow its own guidelines for student conduct and discipline.

The court explained that federal claims filed under 42 U.S.C. § 1983 may survive only against persons who acted with the authority of the state, or "under color of state law." **Private actors can be sued for constitutional violations only if their actions are "fairly attributable to the state."** The university was a private, for-profit corporation, and there was no indication it was publicly funded or that the state controlled its operations. The court held that as the offender failed to state a claim for violation of his rights under the Constitution, he could not proceed with his Section 1983 claims. *McGlothin v. Strayer Univ.*, No. 09-231-JMH, 2009 WL 1956463 (E.D. Ky. 7/6/09).

◆ *A federal court held a Maryland university did not breach a contract by interfering with a student's ability to complete his thesis.*

The student pursued a doctorate degree at a private university. He fulfilled the requirements for his degree except his thesis. Under a university policy, students were allowed a maximum of seven years from the date they enrolled to obtain a degree. The university extended the deadline for the student several times. After the last extension, the university denied the student further access to the office space. The student sued the university in a federal district court, alleging it breached a contract by sabotaging his ability to complete the thesis, among other things. He contended his enrollment in the university established an implied contract. **The court agreed that the relationship between a student and a private university is largely contractual in nature. Such a contract requires a university to act in good faith, and to act fairly.** There was evidence that the university reasonably accommodated the student above and beyond any reasonably imagined contractual requirement. Courts intervene into academic decisions only if a student completes all academic requirements and the school's refusal to grant a degree is "arbitrary and capricious." As nothing suggested the university acted arbitrarily, there was no breach of contract. *Onawola v. Johns Hopkins Univ.*, 412 F.Supp.2d 529 (D. Md. 2006).

The Fourth Circuit later affirmed the decision in a brief memorandum. *Onawola v. Johns Hopkins Univ.*, 221 Fed.Appx. 211 (4th Cir. 2007).

B. Academic Dismissals

Courts have traditionally left grading policies to the special expertise of educators, and do not substitute their judgment for that of university faculty on academic matters unless they are arbitrary and capricious, irrational, made in bad faith, or contrary to constitutional or statutory law. The Tennessee Court of Appeals held it was simply not equipped to review university academic policies. Lord v. Meharry Medical College School of Dentistry, *No. M2004-00264-COA-R3-CV, 2005 WL 1950119 (Tenn. Ct. App. 8/12/05). In* Susan M. v. New York Law School, *556 N.E.2d 1104 (N.Y. 1990), New York's highest court restated the general rule that courts do not substitute their judgment for that of educators regarding degree requirements and academic dismissals.*

1. Poor Performance

◆ *Virginia Commonwealth University (VCU) gained the dismissal of a lawsuit by a student who was dismissed from a physical therapy program.*

Although the student began the program with a 3.85 average, she struggled in a clinical instruction course. An instructor said she was defensive, confrontational and argumentative – and had poor listening and communication skills. In separate letters, the department chair and a dean informed the student of her dismissal for academic reasons and failing the clinical course. One said dismissal was based on her "lack of academic progression and professional behavior." The student sued VCU in a federal court for due process and equal protection violations. In the court's view, the decision to dismiss her was based on her failure in the clinical course. It held that under the circumstances, she received all the process she was due. **The student knew professionalism was a requirement for the course, and the letters made it very clear that she was dismissed for an academic reason.** Next, the court rejected the equal protection claim. Although the student vaguely declared that other students performed poorly but were not dismissed, she did not explain how they were similarly situated or otherwise support her equal protection claim. Rejecting the remaining claims, the court dismissed the complaint. *Nofsinger v. Virginia Comwlth. Univ.*, No. 3:12-CV-236, 2012 WL 2878608 (E.D. Va. 7/13/12).

◆ *Two former Texas law school students were unable to convince a federal court that they were wrongfully dismissed for earning poor grades.*

Texas Southern University dismissed the students for failing to maintain grade averages of at least 2.0. In a federal district court, they claimed their due process rights were violated because a professor did not adequately explain their poor grades. Under this theory, the students were deprived of a fair chance to appeal the grades. The court rejected this argument. It held **courts "strongly disfavor claims that require judges to second-guess judgments about the academic quality of a student's work."** There was no question that the students were dismissed for academic reasons and were given an oral hearing when they petitioned for grade changes. The grading at issue did not depart from academic norms, and the claims failed. *Chan v. Board of Regents of Texas Southern Univ.*, No. H-12-0325, 2012 WL 5832494 (S.D. Tex. 11/16/12).

◆ *There was no breach of contract when a community college followed its handbook in dismissing a student from a medical imaging program.*

During an examination, a college official corrected the student for not staying in an assigned area, not participating in the exam and making repetitive mistakes. A few months later, the college disciplined him for "failure to maintain a professional demeanor." After a third disciplinary incident involving "inconsiderate treatment and failure to perform," the student was placed on an academic readmission plan. Although he met its requirements and was readmitted to the program, he performed a lumbar spine procedure without supervision or permission, and was immediately and permanently dismissed from the program. In the student's action for breach of contract, a state court awarded the college judgment without a trial. On appeal, the state court of appeals found it well-settled under Ohio law that a contract is formed between a student and institution when a student enrolls, pays tuition, and attends class. This contract is typically found in a handbook, catalogue, or other guideline.

Case law precedent required a court to defer to a higher education institution's decisions unless there was "such a substantial departure from accepted academic norms as to demonstrate that the person or committee responsible did not actually exercise professional judgment." See *Regents of the Univ. of Michigan v. Ewing*, 474 U.S. 214 (1985), this chapter. As the college followed its handbook procedures and did not depart from any accepted academic norm, the court upheld the judgment. *Tate v. Owens State Community College*, No. 10AP-1201, 2011 WL 2685664 (Ohio Ct. App. 7/12/11).

◆ *Rutgers Law School was entitled to dismiss a student for failing to maintain a required minimum grade point average (GPA).*

After being placed "on warning" for low grades during her first year of law school, the student was told she had to earn a minimum GPA of 2.0. She took a three-month leave of absence and then petitioned the school for readmission. The petition was denied, but she was informed that she could return as a student and repeat the entire first-year curriculum. The student did so, and she successfully completed her first two years of study. But she finished the third year with a GPA of 1.58 and was again dismissed. Over six years, the student petitioned for readmission six times but was denied each time. She sued the law school for due process violations, breach of contract, disability discrimination and other claims. **A federal court found no evidence of arbitrary and capricious action with respect to the dismissal and readmission petitions.** A contract claim failed because the student did not show the law school failed to follow its code of student conduct. Her remaining claims were also rejected. *Mucci v. Rutgers*, No. 08-4806, 2011 WL 831967 (D.N.J. 3/3/11).

◆ *A federal court dismissed a Nevada dental-school student's due process claim based on the denial of his attempt to appeal an academic decision.*

The dental school twice suspended the student for failing examinations pertaining to Part I of the National Board of Dental Examinations, which are prerequisites to a fourth year of dental school. In his complaint, the student claimed the dental school could not suspend him without a hearing. When the dental school sought dismissal, the court issued an order clarifying that **the U.S. Supreme Court has held a formal hearing is only required for suspensions based on misconduct, not for academic suspensions**. See *Board of Curators v. Horowitz*, 435 U.S. 78 (1978), this chapter. There was no need for a hearing unless the student could prove he was not fully informed of relevant academic requirements. Although the claim was dismissed, the court gave the student permission to allege facts supporting his theory that he was not fully informed of academic requirements. The court refused to dismiss a contract claim at this point, as he made out a preliminary case for breach of contract based on procedures in dental school handbooks and the state higher education code. *Salus v. Nevada ex rel. Board of Regents of Nevada System of Higher Educ.*, No. 2:10-cv-01734-GMN-GWF, 2011 WL 4828821 (D. Nev. 10/10/11).

◆ *A former Pennsylvania law school student was able to avoid dismissal of her challenge to her dismissal for deficient academic performance.*

After the law school informed the student she was not in good academic standing, she sought reinstatement and appealed to the school's academic rules committee. Her request was denied, and a federal court then considered her claims of breach of contract, unjust enrichment and due process violations.

According to the student, her professors did not evaluate her as required by a student handbook. She further claimed a dean who engaged in confidential conversations with her should not have presided at her hearing. But the court held none of these facts supported a due process claim. Evidence indicated **the law school notified the student that she had failed to remain in academic good standing, and provided her with an opportunity to appear before the academic rules committee**. As this was all the process she was due, her due process claim failed. As for the student's contract claim, she pointed to a handbook provision declaring that the academic rules committee must seek evaluations from each faculty member when a student sought reinstatement. The court decided that might be a sustainable claim, and gave her permission to amend her complaint to provide more specific information about her contract dispute. Finally, the court rejected a claim that the law school was unjustly enriched when it accepted her tuition and then dismissed her. *Bradshaw v. Pennsylvania State Univ.*, No. 10-4839, 2011 WL 1288681 (E.D. Pa. 4/5/11).

◆ *A New York medical student who was dismissed for poor academic performance failed to convince a court that he was entitled to reinstatement.*

In his third year of medical school, the student was dismissed from the program. He initiated a state court lawsuit to force his reinstatement. A trial court denied his petition, and he appealed to a state appellate division court. It explained that **judicial review of academic decisions is limited**. Such decisions are not to be disturbed by courts unless they are arbitrary and capricious, irrational, made in bad faith, or contrary to constitutional or statutory law. In this case, the record showed that the student's academic performance was deficient and that he had failed a clerkship while he was on academic probation. As the university's decision to dismiss him was properly based on academic considerations, the lower court's decision to uphold the dismissal was affirmed. *Gilbert v. State Univ. of New York at Stony Brook*, 73 A.D.3d 774, 899 N.Y.S.2d 853 (N.Y. App. Div. 2010).

◆ *The dismissal of a student who failed to timely complete a thesis did not violate his due process or contract rights.*

The student received an unsatisfactory grade on a Ph.D. candidacy exam and did not timely complete his thesis. He continued to take classes for two years, after which he was "retroactively removed" from the program. The student sued the university and a committee chair in a federal district court for due process violations. The court held the claims against the university and the chair in his official capacity were barred by the Eleventh Amendment. **In a disciplinary context, due process requires that a student receive notice and an opportunity to be heard.** However, less is required for academic dismissals, where no formal hearing is required. The university easily met this standard when it notified the student he had failed the exam, told him he had violated rules regarding students who failed the exam, and met with him to tell him he had not timely completed his thesis. These actions more than satisfied due process requirements. The court also rejected a breach of contract claim.

On appeal, the U.S. Court of Appeals, Fourth Circuit, found no error in the district court's finding that the student was dismissed for academic, rather than disciplinary reasons. Removal from the program had been based on his failure to timely complete his thesis after he failed a candidacy exam. As a result, the court found the student ineligible to remain in the program. **Since he was removed for academic, rather than for disciplinary reasons, the district court properly found the decision was due a heightened level of deference and "subject to greatly reduced procedural requirements."** *Brown v. Rector and Visitors of the Univ. of Virginia*, 361 Fed.Appx. 531 (4th Cir. 2010).

◆ *An expelled graduate student had no constitutional right to stay in the Indiana University School of Optometry.*

The student failed a clinical rotation and was dismissed from the program. He sued the university board and several employees in a federal district court, which dismissed the case. On appeal, the U.S. Court of Appeals, Seventh Circuit, found **students generally have no federal constitutional right to remain in a graduate institution**. An exception applies if the student can show an implied contract. But to claim an implied contract was formed, the student must identify some promise from the university that was not honored. This promise could be made in a catalogue or some other written material.

The student said the promises he was relying on had been posted around campus in university bulletins and flyers. But he did not specify what they were, instead claiming the specific promises would be unearthed during the pretrial investigation and information-sharing procedure called "discovery." As a result, the court held the case had been properly dismissed. Repeating language from the lower court decision, the court held that allowing the case to proceed without specific facts would "sanction a fishing expedition costing both parties, and the court, valuable time and resources." *Bissessur v. Indiana Univ. Board of Trustees*, 581 F.3d 599 (7th Cir. 2009).

◆ *The decision to dismiss a graduate student from a master's program was not a retaliatory response to a prior lawsuit he filed against the university.*

The student filed a second suit against the university, claiming he was dismissed in retaliation for the earlier suit. A state court ruled against him, and he appealed to the Court of Appeals of Massachusetts. It noted the lapse of more than two years between the time the first suit was filed and the time the student was dismissed. This gap indicated there was no causal connection between the two events. **The retaliation claim also failed because the student failed to show the university's reasons for dismissing him were pretextual.** There was no evidence that he was making progress toward completion of his degree. *Nguyen v. Univ. of Massachusetts at Boston*, 72 Mass.App.Ct. 1107, 889 N.E.2d 981 (Table) (Mass. App. Ct. 2008). Later, the Supreme Judicial Court of Massachusetts refused to review the student's appeal.

◆ *The District Court of Appeal of Florida held a university did not exercise its discretion arbitrarily by dismissing a student.*

The student attended a master's program in social work. After he received a failing grade in a field practicum course, the university dismissed him. The student was granted two unsuccessful appeals. He sued the university in a state court, alleging it denied him due process. The state court of appeal found no evidence to support the student's claims. **The court held university authorities have wide discretion in determining whether a student has met academic requirements. Courts will not interfere unless school authorities acted in bad faith or exercised their discretion arbitrarily.** The student's field instructor indicated he needed improvement in 10 out of 38 areas evaluated. The field director also noted his difficulties with staff and clients at the agency where he performed his field practicum. The student's clients were unhappy with his performance and demeanor and did not want to participate in any more sessions with him. For all these reasons, the court of appeal held the university did not act in bad faith or exercise its discretion arbitrarily when it dismissed the student. It affirmed the judgment. *Karlan v. Florida Int'l Univ. Board of Trustees*, 927 So.2d 91 (Fla. Dist. Ct. App. 2006).

◆ *The Supreme Court of Alaska held a university did not violate a student's due process rights by dismissing him and denying him readmission.*

The student did not get along with a field instructor who supervised his field course work toward a social work degree. Although the field instructor did not recommend a failing grade, a faculty liaison professor assigned him an incomplete grade that was later changed to failure. An academic review panel upheld the grade, and the university later denied his reapplication. The student sued the university in the state court system, alleging due process violations for allegedly not following its own rules and failing to provide him with proper notice and an opportunity to be heard. The student added discrimination claims based on his gender and a disability. The court held the professor gave the student adequate notice of his academic deficiencies. She warned him several times about ongoing lateness and inferior work. The state supreme court affirmed the decision, agreeing that the university had provided the student with due process. **A person has no due process interest in admission to a professional school in the absence of dishonesty or publication of the reason for denying admission.** *Hermosillo v. Univ. of Alaska, Anchorage*, No. S-10563, 2004 WL 362384 (Alaska 2004).

◆ *The U.S. Supreme Court upheld a university's decision to dismiss a student from an advanced academic program based on poor performance.*

A student enrolled in the University of Michigan's "Inteflex" program – a special six-year course of study leading to both an undergraduate and medical degree. He struggled with the curriculum and failed the NBME Part I, receiving the lowest score in the brief history of the Inteflex program. The university's medical school executive board reviewed the student's academic career and decided to drop him from registration in the program. It denied his request to retake the NBME Part I. The student sued the university in a federal court, claiming due process violations. The evidence showed that the university had a practice of allowing students who had failed the NBME Part I to retake the test up to four times. The student was the only person ever refused permission to retake the test. Nonetheless, the court held that his dismissal did not violate the Due Process Clause. The U.S. Supreme Court agreed. The **Due Process Clause was not offended because "the University's liberal retesting custom gave rise to no state law entitlement to retake NBME Part I."** *Regents of Univ. of Michigan v. Ewing*, 474 U.S. 214, 106 S.Ct. 507, 88 L.Ed.2d 523 (1985).

◆ *Academic dismissals do not require the procedural requirements of* Goss v. Lopez, *419 U.S. 565 (1975). In disciplinary cases, officials need only provide notice of the charges and an opportunity to respond. Institutions have broader discretion in dealing with academic discipline than in misconduct cases.*

Several faculty members expressed dissatisfaction with a Missouri medical student's progress, and she was placed on probationary status. Faculty complaints continued, and a university council warned the student that absent "radical improvement," she would be dismissed. She was allowed to take a set of oral and practical examinations as an "appeal" from the council's decision.

Subsequent reports regarding the student were negative, and she was dropped from the program upon the council's recommendation. She sued the student in a federal district court for due process violations. Her case reached the U.S. Supreme Court, which held **she received all the process she was due**. The procedures leading to the student's dismissal, under which she was fully informed of faculty dissatisfaction with her progress, and the consequent threat to her graduation and continued enrollment did not violate the Fourteenth Amendment. **The court explained that dismissals for academic reasons do not necessitate a hearing before the school's decision-making body.** *Board of Curators v. Horowitz*, 435 U.S. 78, 98 S.Ct. 948, 55 L.Ed.2d 124 (1978).

2. Cheating and Plagiarism

The Court of Appeals of Indiana has recently held that courts use different paradigms to analyze the student-university relationship. In Amaya v. Brater, *below, the court explained that Indiana has adopted the "most pervasive and enduring theory" – that the parties have a contract and that "catalogues, bulletins, circulars, and regulations" form the terms.*

A recent New York decision recited the general rule that judicial review of academic discipline by educational institutions is very limited. In Kickertz v. New York Univ., *30 Misc.3d 1220(A), 924 N.Y.S.2d 310 (Table) (N.Y. Sup. Ct. 2011), the court held that if an institution "substantially complies" with its written guidelines, courts will not disturb their decisions.*

◆ *Deferring to a university's decision to dismiss a medical student for cheating, an Indiana court noted the university's duty to the public.*

An Indiana University (IU) medical school handbook provision prohibited cheating and the appearance of cheating. Three professors observed a student looking at a neighbor's exams, resulting in a dismissal hearing. A committee gave the student letters from the professors explaining their belief that he cheated. After the hearing, the committee determined that test proctors could distinguish between glances at a clock and glances at a neighbor's test. The committee recommended dismissal, and the student sued the dean and others in a state court for breach of contract. When the case reached the state court of appeals, it held **Indiana court review of academic decisions is limited to determining if the institution acted "illegally, arbitrarily, capriciously, or in bad faith."** The court refused to consider the student's arguments absent some evidence that IU had acted arbitrarily or in bad faith. Since he offered no such evidence, the court found IU medical school officials made a "rational determination arrived at after much deliberation." IU offered the student many opportunities to be heard and explain himself. As a result, UM was entitled to judgment. *Amaya v. Brater*, 981 N.E.2d 1235 (Ind. Ct. App. 2013).

◆   *A New York Appellate Division Court upheld Union College's decision to suspend a student who was caught cheating three different times.*

During his freshman year at Union, the student admitted plagiarizing a lab report in a biology class. He received a zero and did not challenge the penalty. Two years later, Union charged the student with two more acts of plagiarism. An internal committee found him guilty of the two charges. After exhausting his internal appeal rights, the student sought a state court order to annul the decisions. Appeal reached a state appellate division court, which explained that **court review of a disciplinary decision was limited to whether the college substantially followed its disciplinary rules and was based on a rational interpretation of the evidence.** The student admitted he had failed to properly cite material in his written assignment and also admitted collaborating with a partner to produce the report. Union guidelines would have allowed expulsion under these circumstances, and the court upheld its decision. *Shah v. Union College*, 97 A.D.3d 949, 948 N.Y.S.2d 456 (N.Y. App. Div. 2012).

◆   *A New York Appellate Division Court reinstated a state college's decision to dismiss a student from a nursing program for cheating.*

One of the student's classes required a position paper that made up 25% of the grade. After he submitted his paper, the instructor discovered it matched one submitted by a different student in an earlier semester. After disciplinary proceedings, the college dismissed the student from the program. He sued the college in a state court, which found dismissal was too severe a penalty. It instructed the college to reduce the discipline. On appeal, a state appellate division court explained that **a penalty imposed by a college is to be upheld unless it is shocking to one's sense of fairness.** That standard was not met in this case, because the student received notice that he could be dismissed. Despite this, he denied plagiarism and did not provide a plausible explanation for the similarity between his paper and the other student's. As a result, the court held the case should have been dismissed. *Idahosa v. Farmingdale State College*, 97 A.D.3d 580, 948 N.Y.S.2d 104 (N.Y. App. Div. 2012).

◆   *Vanderbilt University followed proper procedures and gathered enough evidence to support its decision to expel a student for cheating.*

The student correctly answered only one of 15 questions on a physics test. It was discovered that 13 of his answers matched those of a classmate who sat next to him but took a different version of the test. At a hearing, a university official stated that the chance of randomly matching 13 of 15 test answers with a classmate was less than one in two billion. A university honor council found the student guilty of cheating on the test. Following an unsuccessful internal appeal, he sued the university in a federal court. Appeal reached the U.S. Court of Appeals, Sixth Circuit. It first rejected an argument that the university lacked clear and convincing evidence of cheating. The student's answers were nearly identical to those of the classmate, and could not be explained by his test notes. In the court's view, this adequately supported the cheating charge. **There was no breach of contract based on the university's appeal procedures and no violation of the university student handbook based on the official's statement.** The university handbook did not bar opinion testimony nor limit the type of testimony that could be offered. As a result, the university was entitled to judgment. *Anderson v. Vanderbilt Univ.*, 450 Fed.Appx. 500 (6th Cir. 2011).

◆ *An Ohio university did not breach a contract with a law school student who was suspended for violating its honor code.*

After an investigation, a university honor council found probable cause that the student violated the honor code by receiving test questions prior to an exam and then giving them to a classmate. A seven-student panel found the student violated five honor code provisions. In response to a three-term academic suspension, the student filed a federal action against the university. The case reached the U.S. Court of Appeals, Sixth Circuit, which held the university did not breach its contract by limiting the student's request to introduce certain evidence. This also defeated his claims for breach of the duty of good faith and fair dealing. In the court's opinion, none of the tort claims were viable. Nor was a claim for breach of a fiduciary duty. It held **a "fiduciary relationship" is not properly applied to the university-student relationship**. A negligence claim could not proceed because it was based entirely on an alleged breach of contract. As none of the student's claims had any merit, the court held for the university. *Valente v. Univ. of Dayton*, 438 Fed.Appx. 381 (6th Cir. 2011).

◆ *A California court denied a private law-school student's challenge to her discipline after a judicial board found she cheated on an assignment.*

In her final semester, the student submitted material she had found online for a group assignment. A few days before she was to graduate, the university notified her of an investigation for plagiarism and academic dishonesty. The student refused to "plea bargain," but two of her classmates accepted offers to admit wrongdoing for reduced penalties. A judicial board upheld the charges and voted to deny credit to the student for the class. She challenged her suspension in a state court for violating state Education Code Section 94367.

The section prohibited private universities from disciplining students based solely on speech that would be protected by the state and federal constitutions if it had occurred off campus. The court denied a request to halt additional penalties, and the student appealed. The state court of appeal explained that **Section 94367 covered only speech rights and created no right to seek redress from an institution**. Moreover, the punishment was not increased because of a letter to the dean. The letter explained that the suspension was justified based on her lack of remorse and other relevant reasons. As a result, the court denied the requested order. *Yu v. Univ. of La Verne*, 196 Cal.App.4th 779, 126 Cal.Rptr.3d 763 (Cal. Ct. App. 2011).

◆   *A New York court upheld a plagiarism charge against a student despite the inability of university officials to identify the source of the plagiarized item.*

A history professor concluded that the student had plagiarized a paper. The case was referred to a committee on academic honesty, which found the student had plagiarized the paper and recommended a one-semester suspension. After an internal appeal, a state trial court rejected the student's case. A state appellate division court later held that **identifying the source of plagiarism was not a prerequisite to a finding of plagiarism under the university academic honesty code**. Evidence supported the university's conclusion that the student used secondary sources in the paper. He submitted the paper just 10 days after he had selected his topic. The professor said the manner in which the paper linked complex documents suggested the analytical ability of a professional historian. The student received all the process he was due, and the university's decision was upheld. *Katz v. Board of Regents of the Univ. of the State of New York*, 85 A.3d 1277, 924 N.Y.S.2d 210 (N.Y. App. Div. 2011).

◆   *A University of Washington (UW) student who admitted that she doctored an exam failed to win a federal court order requiring her reinstatement.*

The court held that people who claim failure to accommodate a disability generally bear the burden of requesting accommodations. In this case, the student did not seek accommodations before disciplinary proceedings. **As the university had a legitimate, nondiscriminatory reason for suspending her from the program, and she did not show that the charge of cheating was a pretext for disability bias, the court denied her request for a temporary restraining order against UW.** *Blower v. Univ. of Washington*, No. C10-1506MJP, 2010 WL 3894096 (W.D. Wash. 9/27/10).

◆   *A New York court held a university did not act arbitrarily or otherwise improperly when it decided to expel a student for plagiarism.*

The student was repeatedly told to remove plagiarized portions of her master's thesis from drafts she prepared. Eventually, she was expelled for plagiarism. After a state trial court denied the student's request to set aside the expulsion, she appealed. A New York Appellate Division Court held **the school substantially complied with applicable procedures for dealing with students accused of plagiarism**. It was acceptable for the professor who reported the plagiarism to serve on a committee that considered the charges. It was also acceptable for an associate dean to serve on two committees that were involved in the expulsion decision. *Dequito v. The New School for General Studies*, 68 A.D.3d 559, 890 N.Y.S.2d 56 (N.Y. App. Div. 2009).

◆   *The Supreme Court of Vermont rejected a medical student's claim that a university violated state law by dismissing him for falsifying documents.*

In the student's fourth year of the medical program, a faculty member discovered he had falsely reported completing a rotation at another medical school. At a hearing of the committee on fitness, the student admitted lying about the rotation. The university later discovered he had engaged in other misconduct and had falsely reported at his hearing that he graduated *magna cum laude* from an undergraduate institution. It was further learned he had falsified reports of completing rotations at other schools and had impersonated an employee of his undergraduate institution. Based on this information, the college held a second hearing, where the student said his misconduct was caused by his disabilities.

The university dismissed the student, and he sued it in a state court. The case reached the state supreme court, which held the university had legitimate interests in enforcing its standards, protecting patients and producing students who could successfully practice medicine. As the student did not meet the medical school's essential eligibility requirements, his disability discrimination claims failed. His dishonesty and fraud were unacceptable, regardless of their cause. **It would fundamentally alter the nature of the medical school to require the school to accept dishonest behavior. Nor did the student timely meet his duty to seek an accommodation.** Accordingly, the decision for the university was affirmed. *Bhatt v. Univ. of Vermont*, 958 A.2d 637 (Vt. 2008).

◆ *A Georgia university did not breach a contract with a medical student by expelling him for dishonesty and plagiarism.*

In a state court lawsuit, the student claimed he was expelled because he had criticized university employees. He further alleged the university breached its contract with him by failing to follow its own hearing procedures. A state trial court held for the university, its dean and an associate dean. The Court of Appeals of Georgia rejected arguments regarding the university's hearing procedures. **The student received information about the charges before his hearing.** Although he complained that the hearing was not transcribed, the student handbook did not require this. The student received proper notice regarding an honor council hearing. A faculty member tried to talk to him about the hearing and sent him a letter notifying him of an investigation. Although the hearing did not take place within 21 days of the charge, this was not an absolute requirement. The university followed all applicable handbook guidelines, and the court affirmed the decision on the breach of contract claim. The student did not show that a person who searched him for a tape recorder prior to his hearing acted with university authorization. This defeated his assault and battery claims, because he did not show an attempt "to commit a violent injury." *Kuritzky v. Emory Univ.*, 294 Ga.App. 370, 669 S.E.2d 179 (Ga. Ct. App. 2008).

◆ *A Texas student who cheated on a paper was not denied due process when he was dismissed for failing to maintain a 2.0 grade point average.*

A course instructor concluded the student and a classmate had violated a rule against collaborating on a paper and assigned both students zero grades. The student's final grade for the course slipped to failing. He pursued an honor court complaint against the classmate and asked for a time extension to file a request for a grade change. After the semester ended, the university notified the student of his dismissal for failure to meet school academic requirements. After an unsuccessful appeal within the university, he sued the university and others in a state court for defamation, breach of contract, fraud and violation of due process. The court granted summary judgment against him. On appeal, the Court of Appeals of Texas rejected the student's claim that he had a property interest in university rules and regulations. **Under Supreme Court precedents, students lack a substantive interest in specific academic procedures. The student lacked a "right" to have his paper graded fairly.** This claim had merit only if the university acted irrationally in assigning the grade. Assigning a zero grade for cheating was logical punishment that did not violate due process rights, and the court affirmed the judgment. *Jackson v. Texas Southern Univ.*, 213 S.W.3d 437 (Tex. Ct. App. 2007).

◆   *An engineering student failed to convince a Florida court that a university failed to follow appropriate disciplinary procedures before expelling him.*

The student failed a required engineering class three times. While enrolled in the class for a fourth time, the course professor determined that his paper was missing after an open-book examination. The professor partially graded all the returned examinations and placed them in an envelope in his office. When he returned to his office later that day, he found the student's paper had been placed with all the others. The paper indicated an expected time of return but did not show the time it was actually handed in. Still, the professor left part of his examination ungraded, hoping the student would contact him to discuss the discrepancy. The student never contacted the professor about the exam. As the professor's suspicions were elevated, he arranged for the final examination to be videotaped. The tape showed the student receiving a note from another student during the exam. After the exam, the professor met with the student and later filed a formal complaint of academic misconduct against him. The university expelled the student, and he brought a state court action for due process violations. **The court held evidence showed the university provided adequate due process and followed appropriate disciplinary procedures before it expelled the student.** Since there was substantial evidence to support the charges of academic misconduct, the court affirmed the expulsion. *Colorado v. Florida Int'l Univ.*, 967 So.2d 372 (Fla. Dist. Ct. App. 2007).

◆   *A Pennsylvania court upheld a college's decision to sanction a student who was found guilty of plagiarizing a paper for a biology course.*

A student enrolled in an investigative laboratory biology course in which the professor assigned her to work with two classmates on a lab experiment. Parts of the student's paper were identical to a classmate's, and the professor suspected plagiarism. The school investigated, and an honors committee panel found a "reasonable likelihood" that she had violated the honor code. A college judicial board held a hearing and found the student guilty of plagiarism. The board imposed a failing grade for the course and stripped her of an honor she had won in another course. It also ordered her to perform community service and placed her on academic probation for the rest of her time at the school. The student sued the classmates, college and professor in state court for breach of contract, defamation, infliction of emotional distress and negligence.

The court dismissed her complaint. On appeal, the Superior Court of Pennsylvania found the parties had a contractual relationship governed by a student handbook. Although the student claimed the college breached the contract by failing to follow its procedures for misconduct claims, **the record showed she was provided all the procedural protections of the handbook**. The court rejected the breach of contract claim against the professor. The student's vague assertions that he was biased were insufficient. The court rejected the defamation claims against all the defendants, as their statements were opinion, fact, or lacked defamatory intent. As the negligence and emotional distress claims were properly dismissed, the court affirmed the judgment. *Reardon v. Allegheny College*, 926 A.2d 477 (Pa. Super. Ct. 2007).

◆ *Due process requires that an individual with a constitutionally protected interest receive notice and a meaningful opportunity to be heard.*

In a case involving a student accused of repeated violations of a student code of conduct, the Court of Appeals of Michigan **held due process requires that an individual receive notice and a meaningful opportunity to be heard. To prove a constitutional risk of bias, an individual must show the risk or probability of unfairness was too high to be tolerated.** The court held the student in this case did not prove an unacceptable risk of bias. Members of the university honor council and an *ad hoc* committee only submitted recommendations to an executive committee. The court rejected the student's contention that two honor council members who were classmates could not be impartial. As familiarity with a case does not disqualify a decisionmaker, the judgment was affirmed. *Imitiaz v. Board of Regents of Univ. of Michigan*, No. 253107, 2006 WL 510057 (Mich. Ct. App. 3/2/06).

C. Nonacademic Dismissals

In Schulman v. Franklin & Marshall College, *538 A.2d 49 (Pa. Super. Ct. 1988), the court held courts should not interfere with internal disciplinary matters unless they are biased, prejudicial or lacking in due process.*

◆ *The University of Minnesota provided all the procedure that was due a male student before expelling him for violating its student conduct code.*

The male had sex with an intoxicated female student at a fraternity party. The university charged him with violating its student conduct code. A hearing panel chair emailed a university attorney to say it was important to spell out the charges. Based on this, the male asked the chair to recuse herself. She declined, and a panel found the male should be expelled. A state court rejected the claim that the chair's email required recusal. The email did not harm the integrity of the proceedings. **The court also rejected the claim that the male was denied a fair hearing because the panel did not have a student majority.** University procedures required only that a reasonable effort be made to have a student majority – not that the panel be composed mostly of students. The court also rejected the contention that the university panel used the wrong standard when determining whether the female had consented. Nor did university procedures fail to provide a chance for a fair review. Finally, the university provost did not abuse his discretion by upholding the panel decision. *Brisbois v. Univ. of Minnesota*, No. A11-1720, 2012 WL 2505826 (Minn. Ct. App. 7/2/12).

◆   *A federal court dismissed an action by a Georgia technical college student who fought other students in a college library and a welding shop.*

After the second fight, a college vice president met with the student and warned him he would be suspended if there was another incident. But he immediately confronted a shop instructor, who called security to escort him off campus. The college then suspended the student for student code violations based on repeated classroom disruption, profanity and threatening behavior. He sued the college president and a dean in a federal court for due process violations. It found no fundamental right to obtain an education and learn a trade. There is an exception to the general rule requiring pre-suspension hearings. In *Goss v. Lopez*, this chapter, **the Supreme Court allowed a suspension prior to any hearing where a student's "presence poses a continuing danger to persons or property or an ongoing threat of disrupting the academic process."** *Wells v. Columbus Technical College*, No. 4:11-CV-79(CDL), 2012 WL 1300276 (M.D. Ga. 4/16/12).

◆   *A New York dental college that did not comply with its own guidelines was subject to a court order reversing the expulsion of a student accused of forgery.*

The night before her graduation, a group practice director emailed the student that her status for graduation was "uncertain." Fifteen minutes before the graduation ceremony, he told the student she had insufficient Practice Model Values (PMV) credits to graduate. PMV credits were earned by performing procedures on patients. These procedures generated revenue for the college, and students needed to generate a certain dollar amount before they could graduate. The student was told she was about $1,900 short on her PMV requirement. She stated that in a state of panic and at the suggestion of a college official, she created false patient billing records and paid the shortfall. Based on this conduct, the college dismissed the student with no chance to be reinstated.

In her action against the college, a state court explained that judicial review of disciplinary decisions is limited. But it held **the college did not comply with its published guidelines**. It did not allow the student to cross-examine her accusers. In addition, an assistant dean advised the student's faculty adviser that he could not ask questions, present evidence or make any objections on her behalf. The court annulled the college's decision to expel the student. *Kickertz v. New York Univ.*, 99 A.D.3d 502, 952 N.Y.S.2d 147 (N.Y. App. Div. 2012).

◆   *A Kentucky university did not violate a nursing student's rights when it dismissed her for posting comments on her MySpace page such as: Babies "are demons sent to us from hell to torture us for the whole eternity."*

The student was assigned to follow a patient through the birthing process, and chronicled the experience on her MySpace page. There, she called babies "demons from hell" and referred to a patient's newborn as "the new Creep." The university dismissed the student for violating its honor code and a confidentiality agreement associated with the course. She sued the university in a federal court for violating her speech rights. Resolving the case on contract grounds, the court held the post did not violate the confidentiality agreement, as nothing in it could lead to the discovery of the mother's identity. It also held the post did not violate the professionalism provision of the honor code and ordered the university to reinstate the student. On appeal, the U.S. Court of Appeals, Sixth Circuit, vacated the judgment because the district court had ruled on contract grounds, even though the student had presented only constitutional claims. While the appeal was pending, the student was reinstated, completed her coursework, obtained her degree and left the university. In later proceedings, the court rejected the speech-rights claim. It held the student lacked constitutional rights to post information about a childbirth in a public forum. In fact, she had agreed not to do so. Limitations imposed on revealing information about the birth were related to legitimate pedagogical concerns.

The university's judgment that patient information should be kept private was entitled to deference. The terms "confidentiality" and "professionalism" in the honor code and confidentiality agreement were not overly broad or vague. According to the court, **the student broke her promise not to publicly disclose information about the birth mother, and the university had good reason to ban her from doing so**. In academic dismissal cases, less process was due than for disciplinary dismissals, defeating her claims. *Yoder v. Univ. of Louisville*, No. 3:09-CV-00205, 2012 WL 1078819 (W.D. Ky. 3/30/12).

◆ *A New York appellate court dismissed a former student's appeal from a disciplinary decision, finding it was moot because he had graduated.*

While enrolled at the university, the student was charged with violating a disciplinary code provision. The charge was resolved by administrative agreement, but he later decided to challenge university disciplinary procedures. In a state court action, the student sought to modify or annul the agreement. A trial court held for the university, and he appealed a state appellate division court found the student had already graduated and the university had never enforced the sanction imposed for the disciplinary proceedings. **Since the parties were no longer involved in a controversy, the court held the case was moot and it dismissed the appeal**. *Freeman v. State Univ. of New York at Potsdam*, 83 A.D.3d 1243, 920 N.Y.S.2d 737 (N.Y. App. Div. 2011).

◆ *A Kansas community college violated a student's rights by dismissing her from its nursing program for posting a photo of a placenta on Facebook.*

According to the student, her instructor granted her request to pose for a picture with some classmates and a placenta specimen. After the photo was posted on Facebook, the students were summarily dismissed from the program. During the dismissal process, they were not allowed to argue that they had received the instructor's permission to take the pictures. A community college official announced their guilt in a meeting before their second-level appeal, and the students were told not to bother with a third level of appeal. The student sought a federal district court order that would require her reinstatement.

The court held no privacy rights were implicated in the posted photo, since there was no way that the patient whose placenta was taken could be identified. Although college officials "seemed very concerned" that the placenta was recently taken from a patient, the court found this factor irrelevant. A college code of conduct did not regulate student photography of classroom or clinical events. In addition, **the code of conduct did not ban the transmission of photos to others, including via social media sites such as Facebook**. In fact, the posting of the photo did not violate any student code provision. It was unreasonable for the instructor to assume that photos posted on Facebook would not be viewed once she granted permission to take them. The court held the appeal process was unfair and biased, and it barred the college from dismissing the student. *Byrnes v. Johnson County Community College*, No. 10-2690-EFM-DJW, 2011 WL 166715 (D. Kan. 1/19/11).

◆ *Missouri's court of appeals upheld a lower court decision refraining to order a university to reinstate a student expelled for misappropriating funds.*

The student was class treasurer for the University of Missouri's medical school. He transferred $3,500 to his personal account and spent the money. He then tried to withdraw another $2,000. When the university discovered this, it called the student to a hearing before its honor council. He testified he took the money for "necessary but non-emergent" dental surgery. Although the student repaid the money before the hearing, the council found he violated the honor code. It made nine disciplinary recommendations but did not recommend expulsion. Another hearing was held, this one before a committee on student promotions (CSP). The CSP voted to recommend expulsion, and the student sued the university and some of its officials for due process violations. After a trial, the judge found for the university. On appeal, the Court of Appeals of Missouri found the student's claims boiled down to an allegation that the deans were biased against him. But it held the trial court testimony contradicted this claim. Both university tribunals had found the student violated the honor code, disagreeing only on the penalty to impose. As the student did not show a violation of his rights, the court affirmed the judgment. *Korte v. Curators of Univ. of Missouri*, 316 S.W.3d 481 (Mo. Ct. App. 2010).

◆ *No constitutional violation or other legal violation occurred when an Ohio medical student was dismissed from a university.*

After the student failed four exams in his second year, a medical school committee placed him on academic leave and required him to complete a program that focused on counseling and communication skills. He took a paid research position at the university while on leave, but he later claimed that he was not paid for all the hours that he worked. While repeating his second year at the medical school, the student was again referred to the committee, based on a female student's harassment claim, other unspecified complaints about his behavior in a lab, and his failure to remediate an exam. This time, the committee required him to remediate the exam and submit to a fitness-for-duty exam. After the latter exam showed he had "strong narcissistic traits and an inability to perceive or admit to his own mistakes," the committee decided he should be dismissed from the school. When the committee's decision was upheld in an internal appeal, the student withdrew from the medical school and then filed a state court action for breach of contract and unpaid wages.

After the court held for the university, the student appealed to the Court of Appeals of Ohio. **There was no evidence that the medical school owed him written notice of the grounds for dismissal, or a hearing and record of committee proceedings, as he claimed.** Nor was the school required to make sure the student was present when the reasons for the proceedings against him were explained. As for his claim for unpaid wages, he conceded he was never told in clear terms what work he would be paid for, or how or when he would be paid. As a result, he did not show he had a contract of employment with the university, and the judgment for the university was affirmed. *Obukhoff v. Case Western Reserve Univ.*, No. 93381, 2010 WL 1254589 (Ohio Ct. App. 4/1/10).

◆ *Because she did not show a likelihood of irreparable injury, a California paralegal student was not entitled to reinstatement after being suspended.*

A student at West Valley College (California), was suspended after she was involved in several confrontations with teachers, administration and staff. She sued the college in a federal district court and requested a temporary restraining order (TRO) that would require the college to reinstate her immediately. According to the student, she was arrested in violation of her civil rights and suspended without due process. She claimed violation of her equal protection and speech rights. After dismissing the student's request for a TRO because of lack of notice to the college, the court denied a request for a preliminary order that would cancel her suspension and immediately reinstate her to classes.

The court noted evidence that the student habitually failed to a leave a campus restroom when asked by a custodian. She was charged with becoming belligerent, yelling obscenities at the custodian, and harassing and threatening other staff members. There was further evidence that she resisted arrest when police were called to remove her from campus. **Since the semester had ended, the court found no immediate reason to issue an order that would reinstate the student.** Even if she could prevail on the merits of her claims, she could pursue her program at another institution. As the hardship of reinstating a "repeatedly disruptive student" to the college was greater than the hardship to the student, the court denied her application for preliminary relief. *Mou v. West Valley College*, No. C 09-1910 JF (RS), 2009 WL 1858049 (N.D. Cal. 6/29/09).

◆ *A Pennsylvania university permissibly dismissed a student from its medical program following an extended leave of absence.*

A medical student asked for a leave of absence based on his belief that his telephone conversations were being monitored. He also said someone at the school was intercepting his electronic conversations and posting them on a listserve. The request was granted, but when he extended it by filing three additional requests, the school told him he would not be allowed to return without documentation showing fitness to continue his studies.

After the student failed to provide the documentation, a school committee voted to dismiss him. He sued the school and several officials for defamation and invasion of privacy. The student also said the school breached a contract by failing to follow procedures outlined in the school's code of ethics. The court ruled against him, and he appealed to the U.S. Court of Appeals, Third Circuit. The court held the invasion of privacy and defamation claims were barred by a one-year statute of limitations. The student failed to establish his contract claims, as they were limited to actions that took place during his dismissal hearings. In addition, the student could not pursue a claim of tortious interference with contract because the school was not a party to a contract. **There was insufficient evidence that he was improperly dismissed from**

school or that anyone had intercepted his electronic conversations and posted them on a listserve. As the court found no evidence showing the school had violated its code of ethics, the judgment for the school was affirmed. *Motise v. Parrish*, 297 Fed.Appx. 149 (3d Cir. 2008).

◆   *A federal court denied an expelled student's Second Amendment claims against the University of Nebraska.*

The university expelled the student for carrying a concealed weapon on campus. He was told to complete anger management courses before he would be allowed to re-enroll. Instead, the student sued the university in a federal court for due process and Second Amendment violations. The court held college students are entitled to due process in the form of adequate notice, specific charges, and a hearing. But the student did not claim he was denied adequate notice, and so failed to allege a due process violation. Instead of dismissing the claim, the court granted him 30 days to amend his complaint in a way that clearly stated a due process claim. **The court found that the right to bear arms under the Second Amendment is limited, and that states can ban the carrying of a concealed weapon.** As the student's simple allegation of a Second Amendment violation was insufficient, the court gave him 30 days to either make a clearer statement or face dismissal. *Swait v. Univ. of Nebraska at Omaha*, No. 8:08CV404, 2008 WL 5083245 (D. Neb. 11/25/08).

III. STUDENT PRIVACY RIGHTS

A. The Family Educational Rights and Privacy Act

The Family Educational Rights and Privacy Act (FERPA), 20 U.S.C. § 1232g, was enacted in 1974 to grant eligible students access to their education records and to protect records from access by unauthorized persons.

FERPA applies to any educational institution receiving federal funds. It contains detailed requirements regarding the maintenance and disclosure of student records. These requirements become applicable only upon a student's attendance at an institution. FERPA, at 20 U.S.C. § 1232g(d), requires institutions to allow students to inspect and review their education records.

FERPA applies only to "education records," which are records "directly related to a student" that are "maintained by an educational agency or institution or by a party acting for the agency or institution." FERPA regulations state when personally identifiable information may be disclosed without consent by a parent or eligible student. "Personal identifiers" may indirectly identify students without stating names. This includes a student's date and place of birth, mother's maiden name, or "information that, alone or in combination," may allow identification by a person in the community.

On December 2, 2011, the U.S. Department of Education revised FERPA regulations to permit a limited directory information policy in which institutions specify the parties or purposes for which information is disclosed.

The amended regulations include student email addresses in the term "directory information" and create new sanctions for the improper redisclosure of protected data. Records that originate from a school, or are created by nonschool entities, may become education records if they are "maintained" by an institution. Notes used only as a personal memory aid and kept in the sole possession of the maker are outside FERPA's coverage.

FERPA regulations declare that as states develop and refine their information management systems, it is critical to act to protect personally identifiable information on students. A FERPA regulation at 34 C.F.R. Part 99.31(a)(1) requires educational institutions to "use reasonable methods to ensure that school officials obtain access to only those education records in which they have legitimate educational interests." Institutions may disclose education records to another institution without consent, even after a student has enrolled or transferred, for reasons related to enrollment or transfer.

FERPA allows educational agencies to enter into agreements with organizations that conduct studies and redisclose personally identifiable information from education records. Parts of the 2011 regulations restrict the redisclosure of personally identifiable information by requiring agreements to include provisions for destroying all personally identifiable information by contractors or other third parties when the information is no longer needed for the purposes for which the study was done. Further disclosures must be in accordance with agreements to other parties and only for specified purposes.

To assure that information that is "redisclosed" by an educational agency or institution remains protected by FERPA, the amended regulations declare an intent to enforce the act not only against the educational agency, but against a third-party recipient of the information. A FERPA enforcement tool is the Secretary of Education's declared ability to issue a cease and desist order, and to terminate federal funding eligibility "under any applicable program."

If the Secretary finds that a third party outside an educational agency or institution has violated FERPA regulations, the offending educational agency or institution may not allow the third-party violator access to personally identifiable information from education records for at least five years.

Under 34 C.F.R. Part 99.36, personally identifiable information from an education record may be disclosed to parents and other appropriate parties in connection with "health and safety emergencies." A student's social security number or student identification number is personally identifiable information that may not be disclosed as directory information under 34 C.F.R. Part 99.3.

◆ *A Florida court said FERPA permitted a college to withhold the name of a student from an adjunct professor after the student complained about him.*

The adjunct learned a student had emailed his department chair to report him for making humiliating remarks to students and using unorthodox teaching methods. According to the chair, the student's name could not be disclosed under FERPA. When the adjunct's contract was not renewed, he claimed the email was a factor, and he sued the college. A state court dismissed the case.

On appeal, a Florida District Court of Appeal explained that state law tracked FERPA's definition of "education records," which were exempt from disclosure. Although the adjunct was the primary subject of the email in this case, the court found the email also had information directly related to its student author. In ruling for the college, **the court rejected the argument that** the email could not **"relate directly both to a student and a teacher."** If a record had information directly related to a student, it was irrelevant under FERPA that it might also directly relate to a teacher or other person. Because the plain language of FERPA supported the trial court's decision, the court affirmed the judgment for the college. *Rhea v. District Board of Trustees of Santa Fe College*, 109 So.3d 851 (Fla. Dist. Ct. App. 2013).

◆   *A federal database on postgraduate student earnings proposed by the U.S. Department of Education (DOE) would have violated student privacy rights.*

The Higher Education Act requires for-profit institutions to offer training programs to prepare students for employment. Concerned by high default rates on loans to students attending for-profit institutions, the DOE proposed new regulations to help the institutions comply with the employment requirement. Private universities sued the DOE to challenge the regulations, and a federal court agreed with them in part. One provision, 34 C.F.R. § 668.6(b)(1)(v), required for-profit institutions to disclose median loan debts by students who completed a program. A provision at 34 C.F.R. § 668.6(a)(1)(i)(C)(2) required for-profit institutions to report the amounts graduates received from private education loans, financing plans, and amounts still owed to institutions. The court also struck a "debt measures" provision that took post-graduation income and debt repayment rates into account. In the court's view, **a federal law titled "database of student information prohibited," generally made it illegal to create new federal databases of personally identifiable information about higher education students** unless certain exceptions applied. As no exception applied, the court held for the universities. *Ass'n of Private Sector Colleges and Univ. v. Duncan*, No. 11-1314 (RC), 2013 WL 1111438 (D.D.C. 3/19/13).

◆   *An applicant who was rejected for admission to a Ph.D. program was not entitled to data relating to Ohio State University (OSU) admission practices.*

After being denied admission to OSU's School Psychology Ph.D. program, the applicant filed a disability discrimination lawsuit in a federal court. As the case proceeded, she asked the court to order OSU to divulge documents relating to all program applicants when she applied for admission. This included applications, recommendation letters, curricula vitae and decision forms for a master's program. But **as she never applied to the master's program, the court found these documents irrelevant**. The question of whether the applicant would have been accepted into a master's program shed no light on her claim that she was unlawfully denied admission to the Ph.D. program. The court denied her request for the information. *Sjostrand v. Ohio State Univ.*, No. 2:11-cv-00462, 2012 WL 4442773 (S.D. Ohio 9/25/12).

◆   *A student who claimed that a university violated FERPA could not sue under 42 U.S.C. § 1983 to enforce individual "rights" under the act.*

A student attended a private university in Washington, intending to teach in the state's public school system after his graduation. At the time, the state required new teachers to obtain an affidavit of good moral character from the dean of their college or university. When the university's teacher certification specialist overheard a conversation implicating the student in sexual misconduct with a classmate, she commenced an investigation of the student and reported the allegations against him to the state teacher certification agency. She later informed the student that the university would not provide him with the affidavit of good moral character required for certification as a Washington teacher. The student sued the university and the specialist under state law and under 42 U.S.C. § 1983, alleging a violation of FERPA. A jury awarded the student over $1 million in damages. The case reached the U.S. Supreme Court, which ruled that **FERPA creates no personal rights that can be enforced under Section 1983**. Congress enacted FERPA to force schools to respect students' privacy with respect to educational records. It did not confer upon students enforceable rights. As a result, the Court reversed and remanded the case for further proceedings. *Gonzaga Univ. v. Doe*, 536 U.S. 273, 122 S.Ct. 2268, 153 L.Ed.2d 309 (2002).

◆   *Using students to correct other students' work and call out the grades in a public school classroom did not violate FERPA.*

An Oklahoma parent sued a school district and various administrators under FERPA after learning that students sometimes graded other students' assignments and called out the results in class. A federal court held this practice did not violate FERPA because calling out grades did not involve "education records" within the meaning of the statute. The Tenth Circuit reversed, but the U.S. Supreme Court noted that **student papers are not "maintained" within the meaning of FERPA when students correct them and call out grades**. Moreover, correcting a student's work can be as much a part of the assignment as taking the test itself. The momentary handling of assignments by students was not equivalent to the storing of information in a records room or a school's permanent secure database. *Owasso Independent School Dist. No. I-011 v. Falvo*, 534 U.S. 426, 122 S.Ct. 934, 151 L.Ed.2d 896 (2002).

◆   *FERPA did not prevent an Ohio community college from disclosing prior complaints against an instructor accused of sexually harassing a student.*

In the student's federal district court action against the college, he sought class rosters from classes taught by the instructor for the four years prior to the harassment she claimed. She also sought "every document relevant to any student complaint/concern" about her. The college denied the request, arguing it could not be disclosed under FERPA. The court found some prior student complaints could be relevant to the present claims. Complaints similar in nature to the student's would support charges that the college and supervisor were aware of prior misconduct. However, the court concluded that the request should be limited to prior complaints of alleged sexual harassment. There was insufficient evidence to show that class rosters were relevant to the student's claims. **Any such student complaints were records that related directly to university employees and only indirectly to students**, and they were not "student records" within the meaning of FERPA. FERPA's limitations on disclosure did not apply to the request for student complaints of sexual harassment. *Briggs v. Board of Trustees Columbus State Community College*, No. 2:08-CV-644, 2009 WL 2047899 (S.D. Ohio 7/8/09).

◆ *As FERPA creates no individually enforceable rights, a disabled student could not pursue an action for wrongful disclosure of his condition.*

A Massachusetts university baseball coach told the team that the student had bipolar disorder. The student sued the university in a federal district court for violations of FERPA. The court determined it was unclear as to whether the coach's statement violated the nondisclosure rules of FERPA. **Even if it did, the student had no right of action in court to redress such a violation, because FERPA does not create any individually enforceable rights.** Violations of FERPA are redressed by the Secretary of Education, who may direct in certain circumstances that funds be withheld from the educational institution. Accordingly, the court dismissed the FERPA claim. *Zona v. Clark Univ.*, 436 F.Supp.2d 287 (D. Mass. 2006).

◆ *A federal district court refused to dismiss a newspaper's open records act claims relating to a University of Oklahoma investigation of student-athletes.*

The *Dallas Morning News* asked the University of Oklahoma to provide employment records relating to some student-athletes by a particular employer. The university responded by providing documents with some information blocked from them. The university claimed the blocking was required by FERPA. The newspaper sued the university in a federal district court for open records act violations. The court refused to dismiss the claims, finding the newspaper had adequately alleged wrongful denial of access to additional records. **The newspaper also claimed that even if FERPA applied, the university withheld more information than the statute authorized.** Because the newspaper had stated a valid claim, the court denied the university's dismissal motion. *Dallas Morning News v. State of Oklahoma*, No. CIV-06-1104-M, 2007 WL 1237771 (W.D. Okla. 4/27/07).

◆ *Student applicant information was not protected by FERPA where it was not personally identifiable.*

The University of Wisconsin System received a request for records of applicants applying for admission to the system's 11 undergraduate campuses, its law school and its medical school over a six-year period. The system partially complied with the request, but withheld information on standardized test scores, race and gender because it believed the information was protected by FERPA and because it believed the release of such information would require it to create new records. The case reached the state supreme court, which held **FERPA did not prevent disclosure of the requested data, as it was not personally identifiable information**. Also, the court noted that the system would not have to create new records to comply with the request. It only had to block personally identifiable information from records it already maintained. The system had to provide the requested information. *Osborn v. Board of Regents of Univ. of Wisconsin System*, 647 N.W.2d 158 (Wis. 2002).

◆ *University disciplinary records were held to be "education records" under FERPA and thus could not be disclosed to the press.*

A student newspaper at an Ohio university sought student disciplinary records from the University Disciplinary Board for an article about crime trends on campus. After a lawsuit, the Ohio Supreme Court held that student disciplinary records were not "education records" under FERPA. As a result, the university had to hand over the records, without name, Social Security number and student identification number. Another newspaper then requested disciplinary records from two Ohio universities. The U.S. Department of Education (DOE) asked a federal court for an order to prevent the universities from disclosing the disciplinary records. The court agreed with the DOE that disciplinary records are "education records" under FERPA, and issued an injunction to prevent the release of the information. The Sixth Circuit Court of Appeals affirmed, noting that **as the disciplinary records related to students and were kept by the universities, they were education records under FERPA**. An order preventing release of the information was appropriate. *U.S. v. Miami Univ.*, 294 F.3d 797 (6th Cir. 2002).

◆ *FERPA does not create a student right to learn how grades are assigned.*

A federal district court held that **neither FERPA nor a Texas school policy provided a means for a student to obtain information on how a grade was assigned. At most, the student in this case was only entitled to know whether the assigned grade was recorded accurately** in the records. *Tarka v. Cunningham*, 741 F.Supp. 1281 (W.D. Tex. 1990).

B. State Law Privacy Rights

While there is no private right of action under FERPA for damages under Gonzaga Univ. v. Doe, *this chapter, state laws modeled on FERPA may create enforceable privacy rights for students. Students may also bring common law claims based on enrollment contracts with educational institutions.*

◆ *A federal court denied a request to seal the record in a sex assault case, finding the public had a right to know about the incident.*

A University of Montana student was subjected to disciplinary proceedings after being accused of sexually assaulting another student at an off-campus residence. He asked a federal court to stop the university proceedings, claiming breach of contract and violations of Title IX and the Equal Protection Clause.

After the court allowed the student to proceed anonymously and sealed the case, the university found he violated the student conduct code and expelled him. The court then agreed to dismiss the case, since the only relief sought was an order to stop those proceedings. It then decided the case should no longer be maintained under seal, as the public had a right to inspect and copy judicial records. Although the student argued the case file should remain sealed because it might influence criminal proceedings, the court explained that the local prosecutor was ethically obligated to ignore the outcome of the disciplinary proceedings. **While there was good reason not to disclose the identities of the students, there was no good reason to keep other information from the public.** As a result, the court ordered that the file be unsealed, but with any identifying information relating to students blocked. *Doe v. Univ. of Montana*, No. CV 12-77-M-DLC, 2012 WL 2416481 (D. Mont. 6/26/12).

◆ *A federal district court held the University of San Francisco did not violate the ADA with respect to testing accommodations for a law school student diagnosed as having Attention Deficit Hyperactivity Disorder (ADHD).*

As a result of his disabilities, the student requested and received testing accommodations, including an isolated environment and extended time. But the student complained about testing accommodations for a summer study abroad program, including an indication to other students that he was receiving the accommodations. He sued the university in a federal district court for invasion of privacy, violations of state information practices and public records acts, breach of contract, disability discrimination, infliction of emotional distress, unfair business practices, negligence and various other claims.

The court dismissed the invasion of privacy claim because the student did not show the receipt of testing accommodations constituted a private fact. He did not claim the university disclosed any medical information or information relating to the nature of his ADHD. **The fact that the student took exams in a different room from others "necessarily caused disclosure to the students in his classes."** As the state information practices act and the state public records act applied only to public entities, those claims failed. Although the student said the university breached a promise to maintain the confidentiality of his disability records, he failed to allege the existence of a contract, defeating his breach of contract claim. The court dismissed the disability discrimination claims under the ADA, Rehabilitation Act and state law. **A failure to provide accommodations on a limited number of occasions was not sufficient to establish a legal violation.** Instead, the question was whether the program, when viewed as a whole, "is readily accessible to and usable by individuals with disabilities." In this case, the student did not allege problems with accommodations on more than a limited basis. In general, the accommodations the university provided were sufficient. The court found the remaining claims lacked merit and dismissed the action. *Tecza v. Univ. of San Francisco*, No. C 09-03808 RS, 2010 WL 1838778 (N.D. Cal. 5/3/10).

◆ *A California university did not violate a state privacy statute by failing to safeguard the privacy of student exams.*

A University of California student accused university officials of failing to safeguard student exams by leaving them unguarded and in plain view in hallways. He sought to inspect and copy his personal records and exams, and to correct information contained in his personal records. The student further claimed the destruction of personal records, including his exams, violated the California's Information Practices Act (CIPA). The CIPA limits the disclosure of personal information about individuals by state agencies and requires them to maintain complete and accurate records.

The case reached the Court of Appeal of California, which held **student exams were not covered by the CIPA because they were not stored or maintained by the university**. The CIPA applied only to "records" containing "personal information." In turn, CIPA defined "records" as "any file or grouping of information about an individual that is maintained by an agency." Student exams were typically returned to students or held by individual instructors, and they did not contain personal information. CIPA defined "personal information" as information that "identifies or describes an individual," such as by physical description, Social Security number or home address. Since exams containing only a name or student number did not constitute "personal information" under the CIPA, the court held for the university. *Moghadam v. Regents of Univ. of California*, 169 Cal.App.4th 466, 86 Cal.Rptr.3d 739 (Cal. Ct. App. 2008).

◆ *A private Georgia university did not violate the state's Open Records Act by refusing to grant a student's request to see the records of other students.*

The student stated she had been sexually assaulted on campus. She asked the university for records of other students who were victims of rapes and sexual assaults on campus. The university refused the request, and the student sued the university in a Georgia trial court, alleging it violated the state's Open Records Act. The court found the school's police force performed public functions in the enforcement of state laws. It held the records sought by the student were subject to the act and allowed her to view them. The university appealed to the Court of Appeals of Georgia.

The court explained the state Open Records Act generally required that all "public records" be open to inspection by the general public. It held the act was intended to encourage public access to information and promote public confidence in government through access to public records. The university was a nonprofit corporation, not a government agency. Campus officers were not public officials based on the state's decision to authorize them to perform certain duties. The court found the records were not "public records" because they were not prepared, maintained or received in the course of the operation of a public office or agency. The court reversed the judgment, as the documents maintained by the school police were not covered by the Act. *Mercer Univ. v. Barrett and Farahany, LLP*, 610 S.E.2d 138 (Ga. Ct. App. 2005).

C. Computer Privacy

◆ *The remote search of a dormitory computer did not violate a Wisconsin student hacker's reasonable expectation of privacy in the computer.*

A California-based Qualcomm computer system administrator informed the University of Wisconsin – Madison that someone had hacked Qualcomm's network through a computer connected to the university's network. A university investigator confirmed the report and discovered the hacker had also gained access to the university network. Concerned that the university's 60,000-account email system was in immediate jeopardy, the investigator accessed the computer from a remote location. After viewing the computer's temporary directory, the investigator confirmed the unauthorized activity. The investigator and university went to the hacker's dorm room and unplugged the computer from the network. The hacker arrived and gave the investigator permission to run a few commands. The test confirmed that the computer had been used to hack the networks. Federal agents obtained a warrant and seized the computer. The hacker was indicted on multiple offenses. A federal district court denied his motions to suppress evidence gathered via the remote search.

On appeal, **the U.S. Court of Appeals, Ninth Circuit, held the student hacker had a reasonable privacy expectation in his personal computer,**

which was not eliminated by attaching it to the university's network. The investigator's actions were not taken for law enforcement purposes, and a search warrant was not needed because he was acting in his role as a system administrator. University policy authorized the investigator to rectify emergency situations that threatened the integrity of campus computers or communication systems. His actions were justified because he needed to act at once to protect the system. As the investigator's actions were taken to secure the university's email server, the court held the evidence obtained during the searches was admissible. *U.S. v. Heckencamp*, 482 F.3d 1142 (9th Cir. 2007).

◆ *A student who allegedly saved child pornography on university computer-lab computers was not entitled to privacy under the Fourth Amendment.*

A Maine student left an image on a university computer screen that a university employee considered pedophilic. University authorities investigated the incident and discovered similar images on the hard drives of other computer-lab computers. The university contacted the police, and the student was indicted for receiving child pornography in violation of 18 U.S.C. § 2252A(a)(2). The prosecution obtained two hard drives from the university that allegedly contained illegal images, as well as the university's computer usage logs, which indicated when the student used the computers. The student filed a motion to have the hard drives and logs suppressed as the product of searches that violated his Fourth Amendment right against unreasonable searches and seizures. A federal court judge ruled the student had no right to privacy in this matter and denied the motion to suppress. **To assert a right under the Fourth Amendment, a defendant must show that he believes he had a right to privacy and that society would find his expectation objectively reasonable.**

Because the usage logs were maintained for the benefit of the university, they could not be suppressed. The judge cited *Smith v. Maryland*, 442 U.S. 735 (1970), in which the Supreme Court held a telephone customer had no legitimate expectation of privacy in telephone numbers he had dialed. As for the hard drives, the student pointed to no university computer privacy policies, no statements made about the use of the computer lab, no practices concerning access to and retention of hard drive contents. **The student was simply using university computers under circumstances where images on the monitor were visible to others.** *U.S. v. Butler*, 151 F.Supp.2d 82 (D. Me. 2001).

IV. GRADING AND CURRICULUM

Courts typically use restraint when considering academic matters. In Univ. of Pennsylvania v. EEOC, *493 U.S. 182 (1990), the U.S. Supreme Court stated that courts should avoid second-guessing legitimate academic judgments.*

◆ *Columbia University alumni failed to force the elimination of a women's studies program or the addition of a corresponding "men's studies" program.*

In a federal class action lawsuit, two male alumni accused the U.S. Department of Education and Columbia officials of violating the Establishment Clause by "aiding the establishment of the religion of feminism" at the university. They also claimed a violation of their due process rights, their equal protection rights and Title IX of the Education Amendments of 1972. The alumni requested declaratory relief, injunctive relief and nominal damages.

To support their claims, the alumni asserted the women's studies program harmed them by propagating negative information about males. They also said they were harmed by the absence of a men's studies program. According to the court, they did not assert any injury in fact. Neither of the males enrolled in the women's studies program and they had no firsthand exposure to it. At most, the injury they suffered was subjective – not an objective, concrete harm. **Because they did not suffer an injury in fact, the alumni did not have standing to raise their claims relating to the women's studies program.** Similarly, they did not suffer concrete and particularized injury from the absence of a men's studies program at the university. As a result, they could not pursue the case. Later, the U.S. Court of Appeals for the Second Circuit affirmed the dismissal of the action. *Den Hollander v. Institute for Research on Women & Gender at Columbia Univ.*, 372 Fed.Appx. 140 (2d Cir. 2010).

Dissatisfied with the outcome of the case, one of the alumni filed another lawsuit raising essentially the same claims. He again claimed the university could not provide public funding to the Women's Studies Program because it promoted feminism. A federal magistrate judge recommended that judgment be granted to Columbia and the other defendants. Since each of the issues had been decided in the first action, they could not be relitigated. The court rejected the alumnus' other arguments and adopted the recommendation for dismissal. *Den Hollander v. Members of the Board of Regents of the State of New York*, No. 10 Civ. 9277(LTS)(HBP), 2011 WL 5222912 (S.D.N.Y. 10/31/11).

◆ *A New Jersey court rejected a student's claim that a professor conspired with her boyfriend to assign her low grades and waste her financial assistance.*

After the student transferred from another college, she received grades of "C-" in three of four courses for a semester. She filed an appeal within the college. Following review of her academic record, the college placed her on academic probation for a semester. Acting without a lawyer, the student sued the college in the state court system, asserting that one of her professors there "asked a lot of personal questions" and conspired with her boyfriend to assign her low grades, causing her to waste grant and loan money. She also asserted a claim of unlawful discrimination based on national origin. A state trial court dismissed the complaint, and the student appealed.

A New Jersey Appellate Division Court noted that **New Jersey courts typically defer to the academic decisions of higher education institutions**. In this case, the claims involved a challenge to the student's grades, but decisions in that regard were not subject to judicial review. Though she claimed she had a language-based disability, she did not specifically allege that the college discriminated against her based on a disability. There were no facts supporting a disability bias claim. Finally, the court held the student did not state a viable claim of unlawful discrimination based on national origin. As a result, the judgment for the college was affirmed. *Partovi v. Felician College*, No. DC-022681-09, 2011 WL 867275 (N.J. Super. Ct. App. Div. 3/15/11).

◆ *The University of Washington (UW) did not breach a contract with a student when it set conditions on her participation in a foreign studies program.*

Soon after arriving in Cuba to participate in the program, the student began missing required classes and excursions. She complained of medical problems, and Cuban doctors recommended that she return to the U.S. based on the belief that she had a psychiatric condition. She returned to the U.S. but soon asked for permission to continue the program. UW officials insisted upon an updated medical clearance form. When the student failed to submit one, she was not allowed to return to Cuba. Because the student never provided the requested form, she was not allowed to participate in another international studies program. She sued UW and its officials in a state court for discrimination, retaliation, breach of contract, negligence and emotional distress.

Appeal reached the state court of appeals, which found no contractual breach based on sending the student home. The Cuban doctors had recommended that the student be sent home. UW had no contractual obligation to allow her to complete credits for the Cuba program through independent study. Nor did UW breach a contract by declining to assign numerical grades to the Cuba program courses. **As nothing in the UW handbook required it to assign students numerical grades, the court held for UW.** *Ju v. Univ. of Washington*, 156 Wash.App. 1017 (Wash. Ct. App. 2010). The student's petition for review was denied by the Supreme Court of Washington in 2011.

◆ *A federal court refused to dismiss an Arizona student's claim that a university refused to grant him incomplete grades based on his back ailment.*

After being withdrawn from three classes, the student appealed and was allowed to re-enroll in two of them. He emailed a complaint to an administrator about the university's previous refusal to give him incomplete grades, and he later claimed retaliation for sending the email. The student sued the university in a federal district court for disability discrimination, retaliation, breach of contract and infliction of emotional distress.

The court decided a factual issue was present as to whether the student had a disability within the meaning of the law. There was also a factual issue regarding whether the law required the university to accommodate his back condition by granting his request for incomplete grades. While the court refused to dismiss the disability bias claims, the university was entitled to judgment on the retaliation claim. This was because the university provided legitimate reasons for its actions. For example, **the university threatened to dismiss the student because he behaved abusively toward administrators, and it restricted him from taking a course because it was not designed for doctoral students**. The court granted dismissal of a contract claim and the emotional distress claim as nothing indicated extreme and outrageous conduct. *Yount v. Regent Univ.*, No. CV-08-8011-PCT-DGC, 2009 WL 995596 (D. Ariz. 4/14/09).

◆ *New York Law School did not breach an implied contract with a student by assigning him a grade of "C" for a particular course.*

After transferring to New York Law School, the student claimed he was disadvantaged by being placed in a Legal Writing II course instead of Legal

Writing I. After being assigned a C grade, he said the law school breached an implied contract with him by arbitrarily assigning the grade. To support his breach of contract claim, the student relied on statements on a law school website. In the student's state court action, the trial court held **New York courts generally do not intervene in grading disputes because doing so would "inappropriately involve the courts in the very core of academic and educational decision making."** Through its student handbook, the law school clearly informed all students that it used a letter grading system, not a pass-fail system. The court granted the law school's motion to dismiss the case.

On appeal, the New York Supreme Court, Appellate Division, held "only specific promises set forth in a school's bulletins, circulars and handbooks which are material to the student's relationship with the school, can establish the existence of an implied contract." While academic judgments are not beyond all judicial review, "that review is limited to the question of whether the challenged determination was arbitrary and capricious, irrational, made in bad faith or contrary to Constitution or statute." As the lower court found no promise to the student that a pass/fail grading system would be used, the court affirmed the judgment for the law school. *Keefe v. New York Law School*, 71 A.D.3d 569, 897 N.Y.S.2d 94 (N.Y. App. Div. 2010).

◆ *A federal appeals court rejected several claims raised by a California university student who was dissatisfied with a grade.*

After expressing dissatisfaction with a grade he received, the student was given an opportunity to appear before a faculty panel. After the panel issued a decision against him, he sued the university in a federal district court for violation of his constitutional rights under 42 U.S.C. § 1983. The student claimed due process and equal protection violations and added a conspiracy claim under 42 U.S.C. § 1985. The court held for the university. On appeal, the U.S. Court of Appeals, Ninth Circuit, held the substantive due process claim failed because **the student did not show the university's academic assessment was arbitrary**. The procedural due process claim failed because he was given the chance to appear before the faculty panel. **The panel considered his concerns and made its decision after careful deliberation.** The equal protection claim also failed, because the student did not claim he was treated differently than similarly situated individuals. The conspiracy claim was based on conclusory allegations without factual support. Accordingly, the court affirmed the judgment for the university. *Negrete v. Trustees of the California State Univ.*, 260 Fed.Appx. 9 (9th Cir. 2007).

◆ *A Vanderbilt University student deserved a chance to convince a jury that his professor was negligent in his method of returning graded papers.*

The student's organic chemistry professor placed graded answer sheets for the class in a stack on a table outside the classroom. Students had to go through the stack to find their answer sheets. The professor allowed students to resubmit their answer sheets for re-grading if they believed he incorrectly marked them. The student found a correct answer marked incorrect and returned the paper for re-grading. The professor believed he changed the answer and reported him to Vanderbilt's honor council. The honor council conducted a hearing and found the student guilty of cheating. He received a failing grade for the class and was suspended. The student sued Vanderbilt in a federal court for negligence.

The case reached the Sixth Circuit, which found **Vanderbilt owed its students a duty not to engage in conduct posing an unreasonable and foreseeable risk of harm**. A jury could conclude the burden on the professor to use another method for returning tests was minimal and find the harm to students was foreseeable. The gravity of harm created by the professor's method was severe. A wrongful conviction by a disciplinary committee could ruin a student's chances of getting into graduate school. The professor breached the university's duty of care by acting in a way that posed an unreasonable and foreseeable risk of harm. A jury would have to decide whether Vanderbilt was liable. *Atria v. Vanderbilt Univ.*, 142 Fed.Appx. 246 (6th Cir 2005).

CHAPTER TWO

Discrimination Against Students

I. DISABILITY DISCRIMINATION

A. Eligibility for Disability Law Protection

The Americans with Disabilities Act (ADA), 42 U.S.C. Sections 12101, et seq., *and Section 504 of the Rehabilitation Act, 29 U.S.C. § 794, are federal laws protecting the rights of disabled individuals. Section 504 states the general rule that "no otherwise qualified individual with a disability" shall, "solely by reason of her or his disability, be excluded from the participation in, be denied the benefits of, or be subjected to discrimination under any program or activity receiving Federal financial assistance."*

The ADA is based on the anti-discrimination principles of Rehabilitation Act Section 504. While Section 504 applies only to recipients of federal funding, the ADA applies to a broader class of employers, public accommodations and facilities, including institutions of higher education. In 2008, Congress broadened certain ADA provisions to correct Supreme Court decisions that interpreted the Act differently than Section 504 of the Rehabilitation Act. Congress found that the ADA was enacted with the intent to "provide a clear and comprehensive national mandate for the elimination of discrimination against individuals with disabilities," and to provide broad coverage.

ADA employment regulations published by the federal government in 2011 noted that the focus of Congress was on whether covered entities have complied with their obligations under the ADA and whether discrimination has occurred, not on whether an individual meets a disability definition. Questions of whether an individual meets this definition should not demand extensive analysis. According to the regulations, Congress wanted an easier, more streamlined analysis that results in more people being covered under the law.

While Congress expected the ADA's definition of "disability" would be interpreted consistently with how courts were interpreting the definition of "handicapped individual" under Rehabilitation Act Section 504, it declared "that expectation has not been fulfilled." Sutton v. United Air Lines, Inc., 527 U.S. 471 (1999) *and* Toyota Motor Mfg., Kentucky, Inc. v. Williams, *534 U.S. 184 (2002), were singled out as cases in which the Supreme Court interpreted the term "substantially limits" more restrictively than Congress intended.*

The 2008 Amendments addressed the term "disability," which is defined as "a physical or mental impairment that substantially limits one or more major life activities" of an individual. At the time of the Amendments, ADA regulations defined "substantially limits" as "significantly restricted." This required "a greater degree of limitation" than Congress intended.

"Disability" in the amended ADA is to be construed in favor of broad coverage of individuals, "to the maximum extent permitted by the terms of this Act." Congress specified that "substantially limits" is to be interpreted consistently with its findings and purposes. U.S. Public Laws 110-325 (S. 3406), 110th Congress, Second Session. "ADA Amendments Act of 2008." 29 U.S.C. Section 705, 42 U.S.C. Sections 12101-03, 12106-14, 12201, 12205a.

◆ *A federal court held that having unsteady hands was not a disability under the ADA, defeating a New York student's discrimination and retaliation claims.*

A medical center proctor refused to let the student participate in a required phlebotomy exercise because she observed his hands shaking. The department chair and student met to discuss a number of incomplete reports and the decision to bar him from the phlebotomy exercise. When the student tried to submit missing reports, it was found that he had falsified them, and he was expelled for violating the student code. In a federal court, he accused the university of violating the ADA and retaliating against him by disciplining him after he complained of discrimination. **The court rejected the discrimination claim, finding the student did not have a disability under the ADA.** He also failed to show the university regarded him as having a disability. As for the retaliation claim, the court found the university had a legitimate, nondiscriminatory reason for its decision to discipline the student. He did not present any evidence beyond his personal belief to show a pretext for unlawful retaliation. As a result, the court held for the university. *Widomski v. State Univ. of New York*, No. 09-CV-7517 (KMK), 2013 WL 1155439 (S.D.N.Y. 3/20/13).

◆ *A federal court refused to dismiss a lawsuit filed by a California podiatry student with panic attacks who sought testing accommodations.*

Although the institution granted the student some testing accommodations, she failed part of the American Podiatric Medical Licensing Examination three times. Under the institution's rules, a third failure resulted in dismissal. The student challenged her dismissal by filing a grievance, and she was allowed to take the examination a fourth time. Again, she failed. She sued the institution in a federal court, seeking a preliminary order to grant her inactive student status so she could keep trying to pass the examination. In ruling for the student, the court explained that **Congress had recently amended the ADA to make it clear that the term "disability" should be interpreted broadly**. A 1997 New York case had found test-taking is a major life activity. Since the factors for injunctive relief favored the student, the court issued an order in her favor. In doing so, the court noted that the institution would not be harmed by allowing her to take the examination again. *Doe v. Samuel Merritt Univ.*, No. C-13-00007 JSC, 2013 WL 428637, 2013 WL 497903 (N.D. Cal. 2/8/13).

◆ *An Ohio medical student with disabilities and a history of academic struggles earned a chance for a trial on her disability discrimination claims.*

Despite tutoring, a University of Cincinnati (UC) medical school student failed half of her first-quarter classes and was placed on academic probation. In her second year, she was recommended for dismissal for not meeting academic requirements. Health providers suspected she had attention deficit disorder and other disabilities. An appeals board decided against dismissing her because the conditions were treatable. But during the student's third year, she failed an exam and was denied a retake. This time, the board turned down her appeal, finding her history of depression meant she lacked the stability to be a doctor.

In a federal disability discrimination lawsuit, the court found the student was disabled because her attention deficit disorder substantially limited her ability to learn. **The university was not required to provide an accommodation that required it to fundamentally alter its program.** But in this case, a UC official stated that he denied the student's request to retake the exam because of her "pattern of academic and psychiatric difficulties" – not because it might alter UC's program. Since a jury could find her request to retake the exam was reasonable and would not have altered UC standards, the court refused to award UC judgment without a trial. *Peters v. Univ. of Cincinnati College of Medicine*, No. 1-10-CV-906, 2012 WL 3878601 (S.D. Ohio 9/6/12).

◆ A federal appeals court held the 2008 ADA amendments should not be applied retroactively to events occurring before the Act's effective date in 2009.

Upon enrolling at an Oklahoma university, a student supplied a copy of a neuropsychological evaluation to officials and asked for accommodations such as extended time for tests and assignments, permission to use a note-taker, advance copies of syllabi, and special consideration for spelling errors. After three semesters, he said his professors denied him accommodations and that some of his classes were not readily accessible. Faced with failure in two clinical classes, the student withdrew from the university and sued it in a federal district court for disability discrimination in violation of the ADA and Section 504. But the court held he did not show he had a disability as defined by the ADA. On appeal to the U.S. Court of Appeals, Tenth Circuit, the student argued the 2008 ADA amendments were in effect when he filed his case.

As the amendments were not "mere clarifying legislation," the court held they were inapplicable in this case. **There was no question that the student had physical and mental impairments, but the court held he did not show he was substantially limited in any major life activity**, such as learning. The only evidence of substantial limitation was an affidavit and report from the neuropsychologist, which indicated the student functioned in the average intellectual range. This did not prove he was substantially limited in a major life activity, and the lower court correctly held did not show he was disabled under federal law. *Rhodes v. Langston Univ.*, 462 Fed. Appx. 773 (10th Cir. 2011).

◆ *A federal court refused to grant a Washington community-college student pretrial judgment based on her claims of discriminatory discipline.*

According to the college, the student made statements that she had bipolar disorder, but never provided medical documentation of a disability or requested an accommodation. After she reportedly disrupted the campus and threatened other students, the college held hearings to consider disciplining her. A hearing officer found the student violated conduct-code provisions and suspended her for one term. At a follow-up hearing, the student displayed more aggression, and the college confirmed the suspension. It was stated that the student could re-enroll if she provided medical documentation and an active treatment plan. In a federal court, she sued the college for ADA and Section 504 violations. Among the student's claims was that the college improperly conditioned her return on a mental-health evaluation for a disorder it had no knowledge she had. Later, the college dropped the medical documentation requirement and sought assurances that her disruptive behavior had been addressed. Although the student asked the court for a default judgment, the court found the request was without merit. It held **the student had yet to show a qualifying disability under the ADA**. *Robinson v. Tacoma Community College*, No. C11-5151BHS, 2011 WL 1883821 (W.D. Wash. 5/17/11).

◆ *A federal appeals court upheld the dismissal of a New York medical school student who waited to fail several classes before seeking accommodations.*

Despite a decelerated schedule, the student failed several exams. Facing dismissal, he told a school committee he had Attention Deficit Hyperactivity Disorder. But the medical school dismissed him due to the significant number of failures he accumulated before seeking accommodations. The student sued the medical school and school officials in a federal district court, claiming his dismissal violated the ADA, Section 504 and state laws. The court held he failed to show he was substantially limited in a major life activity. Although the student relied on diagnostic tests, **the test results did not indicate he was substantially limited in a major life activity**. On appeal, the U.S. Court of Appeals, Second Circuit, held the student's request for accommodations had been unreasonable. His numerous exam failures required dismissal from the program. The court affirmed the judgment on the federal claims, but vacated judgment on the state law claims so they could be refiled in a state court. *Brief v. Albert Einstein College of Medicine*, 423 Fed.Appx. 88 (2d Cir. 2011).

◆ *Utah university officials did not violate federal law when they cut off financial aid to a Vietnam veteran with post-traumatic stress disorder.*

The student filed an administrative complaint with the federal Department of Education (DOE), accusing the university of discriminating against him by refusing to waive a credit limit following his withdrawal from school. He said his failure to complete a semester of school was caused by his disability, and he claimed the university was required to waive the credit limit as a disability-related accommodation. The DOE investigated the claim, but did not seek medical documentation of a disability. The DOE found the university violated the ADA and the Rehabilitation Act by failing to accommodate the student.

The student filed a federal district court action for disability discrimination and violation of his religious free exercise rights. The court found he did not show he had a disability under the ADA or Rehabilitation Act. He was never definitively diagnosed with post-traumatic stress disorder. **A ruling by the Veterans' Administration that the student was eligible for a program for veterans with service-related disabilities did not prove a disability under the ADA or Rehabilitation Act.** The requirements for participation in the programs were different. Nor did the DOE investigation establish a qualifying disability. Even if the DOE had found the student was disabled, its conclusion would not be binding on the court. As the student failed to prove he had a qualifying disability, and he did not allege sufficient facts indicating a burden to his practice of religion, the court rejected all of his claims. *Brown v. Southern Utah Univ.*, No. 2:08-CV-542-TC, 2010 WL 1417861 (D. Utah 4/6/10).

◆   *Harassment-related claims filed by a student against Penn State University and several officials were dismissed by a federal district court.*

A female student complained that her Taiwanese male lab manager began to harass her as soon as she started to work in the lab. He refused to help her move a heavy cylinder, and it fell on her hand. She broke two fingers and was impaired in her ability to complete her research and teaching. About a month later, the student complained about the lab manager to university police. An administrative directive ordered the two to have no contact with each other. When the student complained to her advisor about the lab manager, the advisor suggested there would be trouble for her if a report was made. He then scheduled her comprehensive exam for a date she believed was too soon in light of her injury. A panel decided to fail the student, and she was excluded from the Ph.D. program. She filed a federal court action against Penn State and several officials. The court dismissed the student's disability discrimination claim under Section 504 of the Rehabilitation Act because she did not adequately allege she had a disability under the act. **Federal disability laws do not cover temporary illnesses or impairments.** The court also dismissed claims based on failure to accommodate and equal protection violations. *Yan v. Penn State Univ.*, No. 4:10-CV-00212, 2010 WL 3221828 (M.D. Pa. 8/13/10).

◆   *In one of the first cases to interpret the 2008 ADA Amendments Act, the Sixth Circuit noted Congress' expansion of the term "substantially limits."*

A Kentucky medical student with a reading disorder had obtained testing accommodations throughout his educational career. However, when it was time for him to take the United States Medical Licensing Examination, the National Board of Medical Examiners (NBME) denied his request for accommodations.

The student sued the NBME in a federal district court, claiming ADA violations and seeking an order that would require the NBME to grant the accommodations. The court denied the request, finding his reading disorder was not a "disability" under the ADA. After the court's decision, the ADA Amendments Act of 2008 took effect. The student sought review by the U.S. Court of Appeals, Sixth Circuit. The court first agreed that the amended ADA applied to the case, as the student sought prospective relief. **To prove he had a disability under the ADA, the student had to show he was substantially limited in a major life activity.** The evidence showed he read "in a slow and labored fashion when compared to the general public." Reading is a major life activity under the ADA. Congress specifically found in the 2008 amendments that courts have interpreted the phrase "substantially limits" too narrowly. In finding the student was not disabled, the district court had relied on one of the Supreme Court decisions that was invalidated by the ADA Amendments Act. As the amended act applied, the district court would have to reconsider the case, which was returned to it for this purpose. *Jenkins v. National Board of Medical Examiners*, No. 08-5371, 2009 WL 331638 (6th Cir. 2/11/09).

◆ *A federal appeals court rejected a student's claim that he was entitled to sanctions in a discrimination case against a Florida university.*

The student failed four courses in his first two semesters of college and was placed on academic probation. He was then diagnosed with Attention Deficit Hyperactivity Disorder. A university Student Advancement Committee (SAC) allowed the student to retake his examinations, but he failed one of them and was required to repeat his first year of study. After failing two more courses, the university dismissed the student, and he sued the university in a federal district court for disability discrimination. In pretrial activity, the court ordered the university to provide information relating to students who failed courses and appeared before the SAC. It also ordered disclosure of information relating to action taken against these students. In response, the university compiled a chart identifying students by year of enrollment, enrollment status, courses failed, the SAC's recommendation and the action taken.

After a jury found the student did not have a disability, he asked the court to find the university had compiled misleading data. The court denied his request, and he appealed to the U.S. Court of Appeals, Eleventh Circuit. It held the absence of the requested information did not hurt the student's case. **To prevail in a discrimination case, he needed a meaningful comparison between himself and others who had to retake exams.** He did not seek this information, and the university could not be faulted for failing to provide it. Since the lack of more detailed information did not prevent the student from pursuing his case, the court affirmed the judgment for the university. *Hirsch v. Nova Southeastern Univ.*, 289 Fed.Appx. 364 (11th Cir. 2008).

B. Reasonable Accommodation

The ADA and Section 504 of the Rehabilitation Act require colleges and universities to provide persons with disabilities "reasonable accommodations" that do not eliminate or substantially modify program requirements.

An accommodation is "reasonable" if it is necessary to provide a disabled person the opportunity to obtain program benefits that would be available if not for a disability. If an accommodation would fundamentally alter the nature of an education program, it is not "reasonable" and federal law does not require the institution to offer it. Higher education institutions are not required to provide accommodations that would undercut their academic integrity.

◆ *A New York dentistry student who failed a required examination four times was not entitled to further accommodations under federal law.*

When the student informed the dentistry college of his reading disorder, he was allowed time and a half to complete his examinations. Even with the extra time, he failed a required examination four times and was dismissed from the program. In a federal court action, the student claimed the college did not accommodate his disability under the ADA and Section 504. After losing at the district court level, he appealed to the U.S. Court of Appeals, Second Circuit. In a brief order, the court found no error in the lower court findings. It held the student's proposal for more opportunities to pass the examination after having failed it four times had only a tenuous relationship to his reading disability. Moreover, **the college's refusal to create an exception to its graduation requirements was entitled to great deference**. As the college did not fail to accommodate the student's disability, the judgment was affirmed. *Lipton v. New York Univ. College of Dentistry*, 507 Fed.Appx. 10 (2d Cir. 2013).

◆ *A federal bias case against a Michigan university that denied a student's request to keep a guinea pig in on-campus housing could proceed.*

Due to the student's depression and heart condition, a therapist prescribed an emotional support animal. The student presented a letter from her therapist to the university, but her request for an accommodation was denied because the guinea pig was not a trained service animal. After moving off campus, the student sued the university and several university officials, claiming violations of state and federal law. The court held the student's move off campus did not make the case moot. While the Fair Housing Act and state-law claims against the university were barred by immunity, claims against individual defendants for injunctive relief could proceed. Claims under the Rehabilitation Act for failure to accommodate were not to be dismissed, as **the student adequately asserted the university acted in bad faith by denying her request for accommodation**. But the complaint did not support a claim that she was treated differently than other students in university housing. In fact, it appeared that the student was treated the same as others who sought to live on campus. The dismissal motion was granted in part and denied in part. *Velzen v. Grand Valley State Univ.*, 902 F.Supp.2d 1038 (W.D. Mich. 2012).

◆ *A Massachusetts college did not reasonably accommodate a disabled student by offering to reimburse her rental costs for campus housing.*

The student had depression and attention deficit disorder. Due to problems with her roommate, she asked the college to either give her a single room or remove the roommate. The college denied the request and offered the student a new roommate or a room that was a converted study lounge. She declined both options and moved off campus. As requested by the student, the college reimbursed her for the rent she had paid in advance. In a federal lawsuit, she claimed the college violated federal law by denying her requests for accommodation, failing to engage in an interactive process and discriminating against her based on a mental disability. The court refused to dismiss the accommodation claim. Whether the reimbursement was a reasonable accommodation could not be resolved via a pretrial dismissal motion.

But the court found **the college engaged in the interactive process contemplated by federal law by attempting to mediate the student's problems with her roommate**. It also provided her temporary single housing while it considered her accommodation request. As a result, the court dismissed the claim of failure to engage in an interactive process. As nothing indicated the student's accommodation request would have been handled differently had she been physically disabled, the court dismissed the claim for discrimination based on a mental disability. *Blankmeyer v. Stonehill College*, No. 12-1-378-RWZ, 2012 WL 5378721 (D. Mass. 11/2/12).

◆ *A federal court rejected a Pennsylvania student's disability discrimination claim because he did not show the accommodations he sought were necessary.*

To accommodate the student's disabilities, the college provided him accommodations such as extra time for tests, note-takers, additional time for assignments and priority scheduling. His other requests for accommodations were denied, including an exception to certain course requirements, provision of direct feedback to his life coach and tutoring by a student with a particular background. The student encountered many problems, including an accusation of plagiarism and a confrontation with another student after he sent a Facebook friend request to the other student's 13-year-old sister. The student withdrew from the college and sued it in a federal court for failure to accommodate him under federal law and breach of contract. After a trial, the court held the college provided the student with sufficient accommodations. **As for the additional accommodations that were denied, he did not show they were necessary or reasonable.** The student withdrew voluntarily, and the court found no merit to his breach of contract and remaining claims. *Reichert v. Elizabethtown College*, No. 10-2248, 2012 WL 1205158 (E.D. Pa. 4/10/12).

◆ *A Florida university did not unlawfully fail to provide disability-related accommodations to a law school student with post-traumatic stress disorder.*

When the student's GPA slipped below 2.0 on a four-point scale, the university placed her on academic probation. She met with an assistant dean to ask for accommodations and informed the university for the first time that she had post-traumatic stress disorder and frequent panic attacks. The dean granted the student's request for some accommodations, but she was denied extended breaks during exams. When the semester ended, her GPA was under 2.0. An academic standing committee decided the student could not remain in the law school, and she sued the university in a federal district court for violating the ADA and Section 504. The court found the law school reasonably accommodated her requests while preserving the integrity of its testing practices. On appeal, the U.S. Court of Appeals, Eleventh Circuit, found that the law school had reasonably accommodated the student's disability.

While the student claimed a right to a private testing room, she did not produce evidence showing her disability made this necessary. Also, she had never previously raised this argument. **In the court's view, there was insufficient evidence to support a claim that her academic unfitness was a pretext for disability discrimination**, and the university was awarded judgment. *Forbes v. St. Thomas Univ.*, 456 Fed.Appx. 809 (11th Cir. 2012).

♦ *A Wisconsin student was unable to convince a federal court that Carroll University violated the law by failing to accommodate her learning disorders.*

After completing one semester in a physical therapy program, the student was diagnosed with ADD. The university allowed her extra time for tests and quizzes and separate testing rooms. But the university denied the student's request for a tutor. She had continuing problems finding classmates to work with her. When an academic advisor intervened, it was learned that classmates believed the student monopolized faculty time, was sarcastic, and did not contribute to a group project. After the student had a confrontation with a classmate and her GPA slipped below 3.0, she was dismissed from the program. In a federal court, the student sued the university, claiming it did not reasonably accommodate her and did not stop classmates from harassing her.

The court held the university was not required to provide a tutor, as this was a service of a personal nature that Section 504 does not require. There was no failure to accommodate the student by refusing to allow her to reschedule exams and quizzes. No evidence indicated her inability to find a partner was disability-related. A claim regarding failure to provide help with time-management, organizational, communication and study skills was rejected because there was no evidence that the student ever asked for such help. The claim that the university failed to take reasonable steps to stop peer harassment failed because there was no evidence that it was based on her disability. As a result, the court awarded judgment to the university. *Carlson v. Carroll Univ.*, No. 09-C-551, 2011 WL 5921445 (E.D. Wis. 11/28/11).

♦ *A Kansas community college student with multiple sclerosis could not proceed with his claim that the college negligently hired an instructor.*

According to the student, one of his instructors grabbed a computer mouse from him and squeezed his neck "with considerable force." The student filed a federal district court lawsuit against the college and instructor for violating the ADA. He said the college illegally denied his request for accommodations and added claims of negligent hiring, retention and supervision. According to the student, the instructor had been convicted of assault before the college hired him. As for the student's claim that he was denied accommodations for his disability, the court found he did not specify what type of assistance he asked for. He also failed to show he was denied services, programs or activities. Instead, the facts showed that the student was provided access to class and given information about parking for people with disabilities. Since Title II of the ADA applies only to entities, no viable claim existed against the instructor.

No facts suggested how the college failed to accommodate the student's disability. But the court allowed him additional time to amend his complaint in order to state his claim with greater specificity. Therefore, it denied the college's motion to dismiss the ADA Title II claim. It also refused to dismiss a claim of outrage against the instructor. **The college had no duty to uncover**

the instructor's criminal history, defeating the claims for negligent hiring, supervision and retention. *Jacobson v. Johnson County Community College*, No. 110cv-2132-JAR-JPO, 2011 WL 4971422 (D. Kan. 10/19/11).

◆ *A New York student with epilepsy was unable to advance a federal action on the basis of a professor's condescending statements.*

According to the student, the professor condescendingly stated that because of his epilepsy, he would fail the course. The student claimed his meeting with the professor triggered a seizure, causing him to yell and lose the ability to function. As a result of this disruption, the dean instructed the student to complete his classes remotely by phone and mail. In his federal lawsuit, the student said he should have been "provided with help" because he was "unable to use computers." But the court found that even if he had a disability, he raised no inference that he was denied the opportunity to participate in college programs or was discriminated against based on his disability. Instead, the student only "amorphously" claimed that the college should have provided him help. Significantly, **he did not request an accommodation by directly asking for help or by putting the college on notice that he needed it**. As a result, the student could not show he was wrongfully denied an accommodation, resulting in dismissal of the action. *Forde v. Empire State College*, No. 10 Civ. 9446(CM)(THK), 2011 WL 4376499 (S.D.N.Y. 9/19/11).

◆ *Indiana University did not violate federal law by dismissing a student from a social work program for failure to complete a practicum requirement.*

The student tried to complete her practicum at four different agencies, but none of them worked out. One of the agencies terminated her placement because she allowed patients and staff members to push her wheelchair. As a result of her inability to complete the practicum requirement, the student was removed from the School of Social Work. She sued the university in federal court, which held for the university. On appeal to the U.S. Court of Appeals, Seventh Circuit, the student argued she could have completed the practicum requirement with a home-based modification she had proposed. The court rejected this argument. **Federal disability laws require educational institutions to reasonably accommodate students with disabilities, but they need not make any modification that would result in a fundamental alteration to the program.** The practicum required students to interact directly with other professionals, and the court found the student would be unable to meet this requirement through her proposed accommodation. There was no merit to the retaliation claim, because the failing grade was assigned before the student filed her initial complaint. As a result, the judgment was affirmed. *Klene v. Trustees of Indiana Univ.*, 413 Fed.Appx. 919 (7th Cir. 2011).

◆ *A Virginia federal court dismissed a disability discrimination lawsuit filed by an unsuccessful medical school applicant.*

The student's undergraduate grades and MCAT test score were far below the median grades and scores for students accepted by Virginia Commonwealth University (VCU) School of Medicine. He unsuccessfully applied to the medical school four times. VCU declined his request for accommodations such as adjustment of his grades and test scores, and he sued VCU in a federal district court for disability discrimination. The court found the student could not show he was "otherwise qualified" as defined by federal law. VCU did not violate its legal duty to grant the student reasonable accommodations. His requests were unreasonable. **VCU was not required to lower its academic standards by adjusting his GPA or disregarding his MCAT scores.** The court held for VCU because there was no disability discrimination and VCU had no duty to grant the accommodations sought. *Manickavasagar v. Virginia Comwlth. Univ. School of Medicine*, 667 F.Supp.2d 635 (E.D. Va. 2010).

◆ *Since a Maryland college had a legitimate reason to dismiss a doctoral candidate, it did not violate the Americans with Disabilities Act.*

Although the student had excellent grades, faculty members were concerned that he lacked "awareness of [his] impact on others" and did not recognize "power differentials." He was accepted for a teaching internship at a Montana university. In his first semester there, he asked out an undergraduate in his class, in violation of a college handbook. The undergraduate later told her professor she was afraid to come to class because of the student. Loyola dismissed the student, and he sued Loyola in a federal court for disability discrimination. **The court held that even if he had a disability, there was no evidence that his ability to learn was substantially limited as compared to the average person.** He performed well academically both before and after he was diagnosed with ADHD. The student had twice denied in writing that he was disabled. The court dismissed the case. *Herzog v. Loyola College in Maryland, Inc.*, No. RDB-07-02416, 2009 WL 3271246 (D. Md. 10/9/09).

◆ *By allowing a disabled student a chance to substitute courses, Purdue University met its duty to reasonably accommodate him under federal law.*

A foreign language committee proposed that the student complete two lower-level courses in a different language rather than attempt a higher-level Spanish course he had dropped. Following this recommendation, the student enrolled in a lower-level French course. He was then caught cheating in the lower-level French class, and he withdrew from it to avoid being expelled. The student transferred to another Purdue campus, where he was allowed to take Latin and an East Asian studies course to fulfill his foreign language requirement. He graduated a year later than planned and then sued the university in a federal court, alleging that failure to accommodate his disability forced him to attend school an extra year. **The court held the university met its duty to reasonably accommodate the student when it allowed him to substitute the French course for advanced Spanish.** *Strahl v. Trustees of Purdue Univ.*, No. 4:07-cv-61-AS, 2009 WL 1085736 (N.D. Ind. 4/22/09).

◆ *California law did not entitle people with learning and reading disabilities to accommodations on standardized tests.*

The Association of American Medical Colleges (AAMC) administers the Medical College Admission Test (MCAT) as part of the medical school application process. The AAMC evaluates requests for accommodations under ADA standards. Four individuals with reading-related disabilities and/or

Attention Deficit Hyperactivity Disorder were denied MCAT testing accommodations, and they sued the AAMC for disability discrimination under state laws defining the term "disability" more broadly than the ADA does. The AAMC argued it would be wrong to apply the more generous state standard to these accommodation requests because the MCAT is a national test that requires consistent standards. A state superior court disagreed and ordered the AAMC to apply state law to the requests. The Court of Appeal of California held **the state's Unruh Civil Rights Act does not apply to practices that apply equally to all. AAMC test time limits were neutral and applied to all test-takers.** The students did not claim the AAMC applied its policy in an intentionally discriminatory way. Accommodations were not required by the state Disabled Persons Act, which focuses on physical access. As neither act required performance-related accommodations for MCAT applicants, the court reversed the judgment. *Turner v. Ass'n of American Medical Colleges*, 167 Cal.App.4th 1401, 85 Cal.Rptr.3d 94 (Cal. Ct. App. 2008).

◆ *A New York graduate institute did not make reasonable attempts to accommodate a student with lupus in a Ph.D. distance learning program.*

The institute denied the student's request to transfer to a different residency group because it was oversubscribed. It also denied her permission to fulfill her residency requirement by video-conferencing. The student sued the institute in a federal district court. The case reached the U.S. Court of Appeals, Second Circuit, which held the institute did not violate the ADA or Rehabilitation Act by denying the request for a different group. However, a jury might find that the institute failed to properly evaluate the student's request for a delay in the start of her program and to fulfill her residency requirement through video-conferencing. **The court found evidence that the institute had failed to engage in an interactive process of finding an accommodation for her.** The case was returned to the district court for further proceedings. *Hartnett v. Fielding Graduate Institute*, 198 Fed.Appx. 89 (2d Cir. 2006).

◆ *The U.S. Court of Appeals, Eighth Circuit, held a Missouri student failed to prove a university violated the ADA by refusing requested accommodations.*

The university allowed the student to attend as an unclassified graduate student in the American Studies Department. He attempted 12 credit hours the next semester but earned none and was disqualified from federal financial aid. The university barred him from entering its campus after learning he had threatened a professor. The student sued the university in a federal district court for violating the ADA, and the case reached the Eighth Circuit. The court found the university offered him many accommodations, such as changes in his academic status and classes. He failed to specify which accommodations had been rejected and why he needed them. **An accommodation is reasonable only if it is related to a disability.** As the student failed to substantiate his case with sufficient evidence that the university did not provide certain requested accommodations, and that reasonable accommodations would have qualified him for admission into the graduate school, the court affirmed the judgment for the university. *Mershon v. St. Louis Univ.*, 442 F.3d 1069 (8th Cir. 2006).

◆ *The U.S. Supreme Court held that institutions do not have to make accommodations that fundamentally alter the nature of the programs offered.*

A nursing school applicant with severe hearing impairments claimed she was denied admission in violation of Section 504. The school explained the hearing disability made it unsafe for the applicant to practice as a registered nurse. Even with a hearing aid, she had to rely on her lip-reading skills, and patient safety demanded the ability to understand speech without reliance on lip-reading. Agreeing with the nursing school, **the Supreme Court held the term "otherwise qualified individual with a disability" means an individual who is qualified in spite of his or her disability**. While an institution may need to make minor curricular modifications to accommodate a disability, the applicant was able to take only academic courses. **No accommodations were required since clinical study would be foreclosed due to patient safety concerns.** The Court held Section 504 did not require a major curricular modification such as allowing the applicant to bypass clinical study. The denial of admission was upheld. *Southeastern Community College v. Davis*, 442 U.S. 397, 99 S.Ct. 2361, 60 L.Ed.2d 980 (1979).

C. Liability Issues

Compensatory damages may be awarded in failure-to-accommodate cases if the institution acts knowingly, voluntarily, and deliberately in violation of an individual's rights. A Maryland federal court held that ADA claimants who alleged an unlawful failure to accommodate a disability could recover damages if they showed an institution acted with "deliberate indifference."

◆ *Finding a key piece of evidence had been excluded by a lower court, a federal appeals court reinstated a Nebraska medical student's claims.*

After the university denied the student's requests for interpreters, he sought a federal court order that would allow him to use interpreters and require the university to pay for them. The court denied the request, noting that both the ADA and Section 504 only required an institution to do what was "necessary" to avoid discrimination. In this case, the student did not establish the accommodations he requested were necessary. The court cited Supreme Court cases advising courts to "show great respect for the faculty's professional judgment" when an "accommodation involves an academic decision." As the accommodations were unnecessary, the court held for the university. On appeal, the U.S. Court of Appeals, Eighth Circuit, explained that **an individual with a disability is in the best position to decide what accommodations will be effective**. As the student's statement was supported by independent corroborating evidence, the court found the lower court had wrongfully excluded it. As the district court erred by allowing pretrial judgment, the decision was reversed and the case was returned to the lower court. *Argenyi v. Creighton Univ.*, 703 F.3d 441 (8th Cir. 2013).

◆ *A Louisiana court held a state university violated the ADA by failing to provide adequate restroom access in the student union. An attorneys' fee award for the prevailing students was upheld by the state's highest court.*

A student had difficulty entering a restroom in the student union because the doorway was too narrow for her wheelchair. After a struggle, she was able to enter, but she urinated on herself and was hurt while trying to exit. The student sued the university in a state court for violating the ADA and state law. Rejecting the university's defenses, the court held the student was entitled to ADA protection and found the university had discriminated against her. On appeal, the Court of Appeal of Louisiana found **the university admitted the restroom door was too narrow. It had unlawfully discriminated against the student by not complying with applicable access requirements.** Moreover, providing wheelchair access would not have created an undue financial burden.

In 2007, the student was awarded judgment. After the university agreed to bring itself into compliance with accessibility requirements, more than a year passed without the creation of an accommodation plan. When the plan was finally done, it addressed about 15,000 access problems on campus. The students then sought their attorneys' fees, costs, and expenses. The court held in their favor but reduced the requested number of billable hours by 20%, set an hourly rate of $240, and declined to enhance the award as requested. The state court of appeal amended the award by increasing the number of billable hours to the amount requested and setting the hourly rate at $265. It further enhanced the fee award, finding the case was "rare and exceptional" based on the results achieved and the protracted and highly-contested shape of the litigation. When the case reached the state supreme court, it found no abuse of discretion by the trial court and reinstated the lower court's judgment. *Covington v. McNeese State Univ.*, No. 2012–C–2182, 2013 WL 1878905 (La. 5/7/13).

◆   *A Pennsylvania student stated valid claims of disability discrimination and breach of contract against a private university that dismissed him.*

The student was accepted to the university's doctorate of psychology program despite his diagnosis of Attention Deficit Hyperactivity Disorder. He struggled academically and was placed on academic probation in his first year. Professors considered his behavior strange and sometimes misunderstood him. After being on and off academic probation throughout his career, the student failed an examination. A professor emailed him that if he wanted to continue, he had to submit a written request by a specified deadline. By the time he responded, he had already been dismissed from the program.

In a federal district court lawsuit, the student alleged breach of contract and disability discrimination. The court refused to dismiss the case during pretrial activity, finding the facts presented were sufficient to make out a federal disability discrimination claim. The U.S. Supreme Court has stated that a student is "otherwise qualified" under Section 504 if he or she "is able to meet all of the program's requirements" despite having a disability. In this case, **the student showed he was "otherwise qualified" because he was in good academic standing when he was dismissed. Also, he failed a retake exam by only one point.** He also alleged that five similarly situated nondisabled peers were allowed to continue despite failing their retake exams. As the facts presented by the student supported his claims, the court refused to dismiss the lawsuit. *North v. Widener Univ.*, 869 F.Supp.2d 630 (E.D. Pa. 2012).

◆ *A federal court held an Ohio student could proceed with her claim that a school violated the ADA by failing to provide her effective tutoring services.*

The student had epilepsy, attention deficit hyperactivity disorder, anxiety and depression. She obtained an individual accommodation plan from the university's accessibility office that granted accommodations such as tutoring, drinks in the classroom, use of a tape recorder and extended test time. But when the student took a test, her professor was unaware of the plan. She later claimed a tutoring session was ineffective, and she failed the course. When the university dismissed her from the program, the student filed an ADA complaint in a federal district court, claiming that she was denied effective tutoring. The court issued a temporary restraining order directing the university to reinstate the student. In later proceedings, it considered a request to extend the order. While the court found support for the argument that post-secondary institutions do not have to offer tutoring to accommodate students with disabilities, there was also support for the idea that **institutions must provide tutoring services if they are provided to the general student population**. The university in this case maintained such a policy. Since the student showed she would be irreparably harmed if the extension was not granted, the court extended the temporary order. *Sellers v. Univ. of Rio Grande*, 838 F.Supp.2d 677 (S.D. Ohio 2012).

◆ *A federal court held a Maryland college had to provide accommodations for a disabled student who needed help getting to class when a construction project temporarily blocked access to parking for persons with disabilities.*

According to a student, security staff refused to transport her to her car during the construction project, as promised by the college dean. She fell and hurt herself while leaving campus and later sued the college and its officials in a federal court for ADA violations. The court held that the student alleged facts sufficient to support a claim of unlawful failure to accommodate. **The college had a duty to accommodate students with disabilities, even if the temporary lack of accessible parking was not a separate violation of law.** The court held the student could proceed with her compensatory damage claims. It found claimants who allege an unlawful failure to accommodate a disability can recover damages if they show the institution acted with "deliberate indifference." This required showing the institution acted "knowingly, voluntarily, and deliberately." Since the student met this standard, her damage claims could go forward. *Adams v. Montgomery College (Rockville)*, 834 F.Supp.2d 386 (D. Md. 2011).

◆ *A Washington student with bipolar/manic depressive disorder was unable to show college officials violated disability laws when they suspended her.*

College officials held a hearing to determine if the student had violated its student conduct code during an off-campus incident. She informed the college during the hearing that she had a disability. After the college found the student had violated the conduct code, it suspended her for one quarter. She sued the college in a federal court for disability discrimination, retaliation, harassment, breach of contract and violation of her due process rights. **The court held the**

student did not establish a link between her suspension and her disability. She was suspended due to her conduct, not her disability. This defeated her ADA and Rehabilitation Act disability claims. The due process and state law claims were barred by the Eleventh Amendment, and as the remaining claims failed, the court dismissed the case. *Robinson v. Green River Community College*, No. C10-0112-MAT, 2010 WL 3947493 (W.D. Wash. 10/7/10).

◆ *No legal violation occurred when a law school dismissed a student with learning disabilities who failed to maintain a minimum grade average.*

Oklahoma City University Law School placed a student on academic probation for failing to maintain a 4.5 GPA on a 12-point scale. She was then dismissed after earning a D grade in a class despite receiving accommodations for her dyslexia and attention deficit hyperactivity disorder. In a federal district court action against the university and law school, the student claimed she was dismissed due to her learning disabilities, in violation of the Americans with Disabilities Act (ADA), Rehabilitation Act and state law. After the court held against her, the student appealed to the U.S. Court of Appeals for the Tenth Circuit. **According to the court, the evidence showed she was dismissed due solely to her poor academic performance, not because of a disability.** The decision was entitled to deference, and the judgment was affirmed. *Doe v. Oklahoma City Univ.*, 406 Fed.Appx. 248 (10th Cir. 2010).

◆ *A federal court refused to order an Ohio law school to reinstate an expelled student until his lawsuit over the dismissal was decided.*

In a federal district court action, the student claimed the law school failed to reasonably accommodate him by giving him only half the extra exam time his doctor recommended, denying him another semester to pull up his GPA, and imposing an arbitrary cumulative 2.0 GPA requirement. He asked the court to order the school to reinstate him pending the resolution of his lawsuit. It refused. To receive a preliminary injunction, the student had to show he was likely to win his case. **The court found the expulsion decision was entitled to deference. It appeared the cause behind the student's dismissal was his lack of effort – not any failure to provide him reasonable accommodations.** The court found this conclusion was backed up by the fact that he got higher grades on the exams he took without accommodations. *Oser v. Capital Univ. Law School*, No. 2:09-cv-709, 2009 WL 2913919 (S.D. Ohio 9/8/09).

◆ *A Nevada community college and the University of Nevada, Las Vegas, failed to accommodate a student's hearing impairment.*

The student claimed the community college and university failed to provide her accommodations to ensure equal access in the classroom. A federal district court ruled against her, and she appealed to the U.S. Court of Appeals, Ninth Circuit. It found evidence that the student had complained about the quality of interpreter services several times. A jury should be presented with factual disputes about whether the student was provided a qualified interpreter and adequate note-taking services. Evidence indicated that officials had acknowledged a problem with the provision of note-taking services. The student also alleged she was wrongfully denied real-time captioning services for a global economics class. As experts for the parties disagreed as to whether it would be proper to provide a combination of services, this question had to be decided by a jury. **A jury would also have to resolve the question of whether the student could show deliberate indifference by the institutions, which would determine her eligibility for an award of damages.** The case was returned to the district court. *Button v. Board of Regents of Univ. and Community College System of Nevada*, 289 Fed.Appx. 964 (9th Cir. 2008).

♦   *The U.S. Supreme Court held a university should receive a final ruling on whether it had to pay the costs of a deaf student's interpreter.*

A deaf graduate student at a Texas university requested a sign-language interpreter. The university refused to pay for an interpreter because he did not meet university financial assistance guidelines. The student sued the university in a federal district court under Section 504. He sought an order requiring the appointment of an interpreter at the university's expense for as long as he remained there. The court granted his request for a preliminary order requiring the university to pay for the interpreter. The university appealed to the U.S. Court of Appeals, Fifth Circuit, which affirmed the preliminary order but vacated the stay pending administrative action. The university complied with the order by paying for the interpreter.

The student completed his graduate program. The U.S. Supreme Court granted review to address the university's argument that the lower courts should make a final ruling on who was to pay for the interpreter. The student argued that the case was now moot in view of his graduation. **The Court vacated the appeals court's decision and remanded the case for a trial to allow the university a full opportunity to argue for recoupment of its payments for the interpreter.** *Univ. of Texas v. Camenisch*, 451 U.S. 390, 101 S.Ct. 1830, 68 L.Ed.2d 175 (1981).

♦   *A student obtained a federal court order requiring a California community college district to improve its campus wheelchair access.*

According to the student, he was encountering multiple barriers to the use of his wheelchair every day on campus. He sought a court order to require the district to comply with ADA Title II access requirements. The court entered a permanent order requiring the community college district to make several improvements, including accessible desks and workstations in all classrooms. It ordered the district to hire an access expert, approved by the student, to oversee placement of accessible desks and workstations. **The district was banned from charging students with disabilities fees for accommodations such as parking spaces or elevator keys.** It was further required to establish a schedule for a wheelchair-accessible shuttle to take students with disabilities to areas of the campus that lacked accessible paths of travel. An access expert was to oversee the removal of physical access barriers and submit status reports on barrier removal every three months. The district was also required to publicize its modified policies relating to access in written materials, and to make those materials available to students with disabilities at student orientations. *Huezo v. Los Angeles Community College Dist.*, No. CV 04-09772 MMM (JWJx), 2008 WL 4184659 (C.D. Cal. 9/9/08).

◆ *A federal court in Nebraska restated the rule that employees and administrators are not individually liable for violations of federal laws protecting disabled individuals, since they do not "operate" an institution.*

The court noted that other federal courts have held **university employees and administrators do not "operate" a university in a way that exposes them to liability under the Americans with Disabilities Act and the Rehabilitation Act.** The student did not allege facts to support his claim for intentional infliction of emotional distress. He did not show intentional or reckless conduct that was so outrageous and extreme as to go beyond all possible bounds of decency. *White v. Creighton Univ.*, No. 8:06 CV 536, 2006 WL 3419782 (D. Neb. 11/27/06).

The court later granted the university's motion for pretrial judgment, finding absolutely no evidence to counter the university's explanation that the student was dismissed due to his academic performance. *White v. Creighton Univ.*, No. 06CV536, 2008 WL 64692 (D. Neb. 1/3/08).

◆ *The non-disabled parent of a disabled student could sue a university under Section 504 to vindicate her rights.*

A job applicant sued the University of Missouri in a federal district court, alleging it did not hire her due to her son's disability. The university argued Section 504 did not allow the applicant to claim discrimination on the basis of another person's disability. But the court held Section 504 extends to all persons aggrieved by violations. **Courts have held individuals and entities who are injured by discrimination on the basis of a disability may sue under Section 504, even though they are not themselves disabled.** Congress intended to prohibit discrimination against any disabled individual who would benefit from a federally funded program or activity. *Feurer v. Curators of Univ. of Missouri*, No. 4:06CV750 HEA, 2006 WL 2385260 (E.D. Mo. 9/17/06).

II. SEX DISCRIMINATION AND HARASSMENT

Title IX of the Education Amendments of 1972 prohibits recipients of federal funding from denying program participation or benefits based on gender. States have enacted their own laws prohibiting discrimination on the basis of gender to comply with federal law. If a public institution is involved, students may attach equal protection claims to discrimination complaints.

A. Discrimination

◆ *The Eleventh Circuit held a Georgia medical college did not discriminate against a male applicant who was rejected for enrollment five times.*

After being denied admission to the Medical College of Georgia (MCG) five times, the applicant sued MCG in a federal court for denial of due process, gender discrimination and retaliation. A federal court dismissed the case, and the applicant appealed. Before the Eleventh Circuit Court of Appeals, he asserted a fundamental right to purchase a medical school education. The court held there is no fundamental right to public education, let alone a fundamental right to a public medical school education. The court rejected the argument that MCG discriminated against men in violation of Title IX by applying undergraduate math grades toward the minimum grade average required for admission. Although he claimed MCG retaliated against him for asking it to review his fourth rejection, **the court found a strong and reasonable inference that MCG denied his application because he was unqualified.** The court held the case had been properly dismissed. *Bowers v. Board of Regents of the Univ. System of Georgia,* 509 Fed.Appx. 906 (11th Cir. 2013).

◆ *A New York nursing school student who blamed his academic failure on his professors will not be able to pursue his federal case for lack of merit.*

According to the student, he failed examinations because of inaccurate test questions, lack of time and arbitrariness by professors. In a lawsuit against the college, the student claimed professors discriminated against him based on race and gender. He further alleged deprivation of a right to an education without due process and breach of contract. A federal court referred the case to a magistrate judge, who rejected the race and gender discrimination claims. In the magistrate judge's view, **the complaint did not allege facts from which discriminatory intent or motivation could reasonably be inferred.** Instead, the complaint consisted of conclusory allegations, such as the claim that his professors "blatantly discriminated against all white males." In fact, the student did not allege facts suggesting white males were treated differently than other students. Rather, his generalized complaints about his professors apparently referenced their treatment of all students. Allegations of generic teaching failures did not support the claims, and the magistrate judge recommended dismissing the case. *Manolov v. Borough of Manhattan Community College,* No. 12 Civ1919(GBD)(FM), 2012 WL 6703570 (S.D.N.Y. 12/20/12).

◆ *An applicant to a Pennsylvania university could proceed with a federal action claiming that she was denied admission based on her gender.*

Between 2002 and 2007, the applicant sought admission to the University of Pennsylvania School of Veterinary Medicine six times. Her grades and GRE scores were at the low end of the range accepted by the school, but she said that during her interviews there had been improper discussions relating to her status as a mother with young children and a husband in the military. During post-denial interviews, an associate dean of admissions allegedly encouraged her to continue to apply. The applicant sued the university in a federal court, claiming she was denied admission in violation of Title IX. **The court refused to dismiss the Title IX claim, based on direct evidence that admissions committee members considered the applicant's status as a mother with young children and a husband in the military** when they rejected her 2004 and 2006 applications. An interviewer allegedly asked her whether she would be able to handle the program if her husband was deployed. The court sought to further consider if the applicant was rejected because she was a mother of young children with a husband in the military. But the court dismissed the retaliation and fraudulent misrepresentation claims. *Tingley-Kelley v. Trustees of the Univ. of Pennsylvania,* 677 F.Supp.2d 763 (E.D. Pa. 2010).

◆ *A New York police academy student was allowed to pursue some of her discrimination claims against a community college.*

Soon after beginning the program, the student complained about unequal treatment based on gender. She said the college responded by dismissing her from the academy. After an internal appeal failed, the student filed two administrative charges with the state human rights division. She asserted gender discrimination and retaliation against the community college for providing negative, false and misleading information to prospective employers.

After the human rights division consolidated the complaints, the college agreed to pay the student $1,000 in settlement of her claims. It also agreed to provide her positive references. The student later claimed the college violated the settlement agreement by continuing to provide prospective employers negative references. She sued the college in a federal district court for gender discrimination, retaliation and constitutional rights violations. The court held the settlement did not bar the action. It rejected the college's argument that her Title IX discrimination and retaliation claims failed because she no longer had a "direct, educational relationship" with it. **The court held the lack of a current relationship with the college did not bar her claims based on negative references.** A valid preliminary claim for retaliation could be based on the negative references. As the college was a state actor, the court refused to dismiss the constitutional claims. *Jordan v. Corning Community College*, No. 11-CV-6182, 2011 WL 4402752 (W.D.N.Y. 9/22/11).

◆ *An Oregon doctoral student was unable to show retaliation based on her gender, resulting in dismissal of her Title IX sex discrimination lawsuit.*

The student acted as spokesperson for several graduate students and wrote a two-page memo to the dean of their college listing 15 suggestions for improving the program. On the list was a request that qualified women be hired into tenured faculty positions and that "the college model a balance of gender appointments that reflected the proportion of student gender population ratios." Some eight months after writing the memo, the chair of the student's dissertation committee resigned, and she was unable to find a faculty member for her dissertation proposal. She asserted her advisor's resignation was the start of sexist retaliation against her for her memo, and sued the university in a federal court for retaliation in violation of Title IX. But the court held for the university, finding the student could not connect "perceived complaints about gender inequality" to the refusal of any professor to serve as her dissertation committee chair. Other courts have held **a general allegation of unfairness does not qualify as a complaint of discrimination under Title IX.** As a result, the university was entitled to pretrial judgment. *Emeldi v. Univ. of Oregon*, No. 08-6346-HO, 2010 WL 2330190 (D. Or. 6/4/10).

◆ *A Massachusetts appeals court held that state law required the National Board of Medical Examiners (NBME) to provide extra time for a student to pump breast milk during a licensing examination.*

The student was the mother of a four-month-old. The NBME balked when she asked for an extra 60 minutes of break time per test day so she could pump breast milk. It offered alternative accommodations, including permission to pump breast milk in a private room during the allocated break time. The student rejected the alternatives and sued the board in a state court, which denied her request for preliminary relief. On appeal, the state court of appeals recited evidence that a nursing mother of a four-month-old infant should express breast milk at least every three hours and that the failure to do so can lead to medical problems. Nursing mothers required regular trips to the restroom because they consume additional calories and liquids to maintain an adequate milk supply.

Without more time, the student was at a significant disadvantage compared to her peers. **The NBME's test structure unfairly subjected breastfeeding women to greater hardships than other test-takers.** The court vacated the lower court's decision and entered an order requiring the NBME to grant the student an additional 60 minutes of break time per test day. The state's highest court affirmed the judgment without opinion. *Currier v. National Board of Medical Examiners*, 450 Mass. 1102, 875 N.E. 863 (Table) (Mass. 2007).

◆   *The Supreme Court held that a university for women could not justify a policy that denied men the opportunity to enroll for credit.*

The policy of the Mississippi University for Women, a state-supported university, was to limit its enrollment to women. The university denied otherwise qualified males the right to enroll for credit in its School of Nursing. A male who was denied admission sued in federal court claiming that the university violated the Fourteenth Amendment's Equal Protection Clause. The court agreed, and appeal reached the U.S. Supreme Court. The Court held **the university's discriminatory admission policy against men was not substantially and directly related to an important governmental objective**. The school argued that women enrolled in its School of Nursing would be adversely affected by the presence of men. However, the record showed that the nursing school allowed men to attend classes in the school as auditors, thus fatally undermining the school's claim that admission of men would adversely affect women students. The Court held that the policy of the university, which limited enrollment to women, violated the Equal Protection Clause. *Mississippi Univ. for Women v. Hogan*, 458 U.S. 718, 102 S.Ct. 3331, 73 L.Ed.2d 1090 (1982).

◆   *The U.S. Supreme Court held the categorical exclusion of women from the Virginia Military Institute (VMI) denied equal protection to women.*

The U.S. Attorney General's office filed a complaint against the state of Virginia and VMI on behalf of a female high school student seeking admission to the state-affiliated, male-only college. A federal court found that because single-gender education conferred substantial benefits on students and preserved the unique military training offered at VMI, the exclusion of women did not violate the Equal Protection Clause. The case eventually reached the U.S. Supreme Court. It stated that parties seeking to defend gender-based government action must demonstrate an exceedingly persuasive justification that is genuine and not invented as a response to litigation.

Virginia had failed to show an exceedingly persuasive justification for excluding women from VMI. There was evidence that some women would be able to participate at VMI, and the lower courts had improperly found that most women would not gain from the adversative method employed by the college. **The remedy proposed by Virginia left its exclusionary policy intact and afforded women no opportunity to experience the rigorous military training offered at VMI.** *U.S. v. Virginia*, 518 U.S. 515, 116 S.Ct. 2264, 135 L.Ed.2d 735 (1996).

B. Harassment

1. Sexual Harassment by Employees

Title IX liability standards for sexual harassment were established by the U.S. Supreme Court in Franklin v. Gwinnett County Public Schools, *503 U.S. 60, 112 S.Ct. 1028, 117 L.Ed.2d 208 (1992),* Gebser v. Lago Vista Independent School Dist., *524 U.S. 274, 118 S.Ct. 1989, 141 L.Ed.2d 277 (1998), and* Davis v. Monroe County Board of Educ., *526 U.S. 629, 119 S.Ct. 1661, 143 L.Ed.2d 839 (1999). Title IX liability based on the conduct of an employee requires proof that an official with authority to take corrective action actually knew of the conduct, but remained deliberately indifferent to it. In addition, the student must show the harassment was so severe, pervasive and objectively offensive that it caused a deprivation of educational benefits.* **Since Title IX applies only to federal funding recipients, there is no individual liability under the Act.** *For this reason, in* Krumlauf v. Benedictine Univ., *No. 09 C 7641, 2010 WL 3075745 (N.D. Ill. 8/4/10), a federal district court dismissed Title IX sexual harassment claims filed against an Illinois university instructor.*

◆   *Southern Illinois University responded to a student's harassment claims against a professor in a manner sufficient to avoid liability under federal law.*

According to the student, the professor harassed him and improperly touched him three different times. Upon his first report to the university, he said a supervisor discouraged any report because of the professor's status as a major donor to the university. Later, he said the department chair said the donor could not be held accountable for his actions. After the student changed his major, he lost his job at the university. A supervisor said the decision was motivated by his poor job performance. In a federal court action against the university, the student asserted Title VII and Title IX violations. The court held for the university, and appeal reached the U.S. Court of Appeals for the Seventh Circuit. It found no basis for employer liability, noting that **at every step, the university promptly and adequately responded to reported harassment**.

The university was also credited with quickly moving the student away from the professor to another work area. It immediately investigated when the student filed a formal complaint, reprimanded the professor and banned him from campus after he did not complete required training. Even if officials discouraged a complaint, this did not create liability because the university still promptly investigated. The university was entitled to judgment on the Title VII and Title IX claims, as the student did not show it was deliberately indifferent to his reports. *Milligan v. Board of Trustees of Southern Illinois Univ.*, 686 F.3d 378 (7th Cir. 2012).

◆ *An Illinois music student failed to prove a Title IX violation because she did not show deliberate indifference by university officials to her complaints.*

The student sued the professor and university in a federal district court, accusing the university of violating Title IX by failing to adequately respond to the professor's sexually harassing behavior. The university filed a motion for pretrial judgment. The court explained that to prevail on her Title IX claim against the university, the student needed to show that she was subjected to sex-based and unwelcome harassment that was severe or pervasive enough to create a hostile or abusive atmosphere. Because she based her claim on the conduct of an instructor, she also had to show the university had actual notice of the misconduct and was deliberately indifferent to it. The court held the claim against the university failed because the student did not show the university acted with deliberate indifference. **Each time the university received a report of improper conduct, it responded promptly by taking investigatory action.** By the time the student first presented her claim, the university had decided to discharge the professor. The motion for pretrial judgment was granted. *Hunt v. Forbes*, No. 07-1095, 2010 WL 1687863 (C.D. Ill. 4/26/10).

◆ *A federal court found no merit to a South Carolina student's harassment lawsuit, as she had consented to a relationship with the alleged harasser.*

The student attended a Halloween party at her instructor's apartment. Over the next three days, she sent him over 100 text messages. Three days after the Halloween party, the two began a sexual relationship that lasted the rest of the semester. Three weeks after the instructor posted the student's course grade, she told the college for the first time that he had been sexually harassing her. She said that up until that time, she had pretended his conduct toward her was welcome because she feared he would otherwise sabotage her course grade.

The college discharged the instructor, and the student sued him and the college in a federal district court for civil rights violations, battery, harassment, stalking, intentional infliction of emotional distress and assault. After the court held for the college, it held **no reasonable jury could return a verdict for the student against the instructor**. It noted she had initiated the relationship and had sent him more than 950 text messages. The student had continued the relationship even after her grade was posted. Under the circumstances, no reasonable jury could find the instructor's conduct was unwelcome. Similarly, the student's claims of assault, battery and intentional infliction of emotional distress were barred because she consented to the conduct. *Ray v. Bowers*, No. 2:08-CV-3512-PMD, 2009 WL 4893209 (D.S.C. 12/17/09).

◆ *The suspension of a California college student was not a retaliatory response to her allegation that she was sexually assaulted by one of her teachers.*

The student filed a formal discrimination complaint with the college, claiming a math teacher sexually assaulted her. An outside investigator found insufficient evidence to support the claim. The student later made the statement "pray for me that the devil doesn't triumph over me." College officials interpreted this as a threat, placed her on probation and suspended her indefinitely. In a federal district court action against the college, the student claimed unlawful retaliation under Title IX and discrimination based on her post-traumatic stress disorder (PTSD) in violation of the Americans with Disabilities Act (ADA). **The court held the Title IX claim failed because the student did not establish a causal connection between her complaint and the discipline issued two years later.** She did not link her PTSD to any conduct by the college. As a result, the ADA claim failed. There was no merit to the student's claim that the college discriminated based on her religion when it interpreted her comment as a threat. *Thomsen v. City College of San Francisco*, No. C 08-3333-SBA, 2008 WL 5000221 (N.D. Cal. 11/21/08).

◆ *An Arizona student lacked evidence to support a sexual harassment claim.*
   The student claimed an instructor sexually harassed her and created a hostile environment by telling sexual jokes to students. She said he suggested in front of a class that she should use oral sex for birth control and accused students who were late for class of "fooling around ... with their boyfriends." As the student was married, she interpreted the latter comment as an accusation of adultery. She withdrew from school and filed a federal lawsuit charging the college and instructor with sexual harassment in violation of Title IX and other federal laws. The court held that to prove sexual harassment, the student had to show she was subjected to sexual advances, requests for sexual favors, or other sexual conduct. She also had to show the conduct was unwelcome and was so severe or pervasive that it altered the conditions of her education and created an abusive educational environment. But aside from the student's allegations, no evidence supported these claims. **Even if her claims were true, she did not show misconduct so severe or pervasive that it created a sexually hostile or abusive educational environment.** As the college could not be held liable unless the instructor was acting pursuant to a policy or custom, the claims against the college failed. *Currie v. Maricopa County Community College Dist.*, No. CV-07-2093-PHX-FJM, 2008 WL 4905980 (D. Ariz. 11/13/08).

◆ *A North Carolina court affirmed a decision to award monetary damages to two students who successfully claimed that a professor sexually harassed them.*
   A student research assistant claimed a professor sexually harassed her for almost 10 years. She then refused to take a class he taught, but because the class was required, she was forced to discontinue her studies. After the student reported the professor's misconduct to the university sexual harassment officer, she learned that he had harassed other employees and students in the past. The university then conducted an investigation, which revealed that the professor had sexually harassed at least eight other women. There was evidence that the university did not take any corrective action despite being informed of at least one of the cases. The university allowed the professor to resign with a year's pay and a neutral letter of reference. Two students filed separate claims against the university, alleging negligent retention and supervision of the professor. They added claims for negligent infliction of mental and emotional distress.
   An administrative commission found for the students and awarded them $150,000 each. The university appealed to the Court of Appeals of North Carolina, arguing that there was no evidence of negligence. The court held the university's failure to properly respond to the earlier harassment incidents caused injury to the students. It rejected the university's argument that it could

not investigate one of the past cases because a student did not file a formal complaint. Whether she had filed a formal complaint or not, the university knew about the allegations. **The university should have asked for a written complaint, documented the oral complaint, and investigated the charges.** Doing so might have prevented the later harassment. The decision to award the students monetary damages was affirmed. *Gonzales v. North Carolina State Univ.*, 659 S.E.2d 9 (N.C. Ct. App. 2008); *Wood v. North Carolina State Univ.*, 189 N.C.App. 789, 661 S.E.2d 55 (Table) (N.C. Ct. App. 4/15/08).

◆ *An Arkansas student failed to show university officials were legally responsible for sexual harassment by a professor.*

The student visited the professor's home to prepare a grant proposal. She said they had dinner and that the professor kissed her, held her down on his bed, and told her he wanted to have sex with her. The student said he later tried to contact her, resulting in "emotionally distressing meetings." She complained to university officials, who forced the professor to resign within a week. The student sued the university and officials in a federal district court for Title IX and constitutional violations. The court refused to dismiss monetary damage claims against the officials, and they appealed to the U.S. Court of Appeals, Eighth Circuit. **The court noted the officials had no direct contact with the professor during the relevant time period.** The student did not present sufficient evidence that they did not respond to her complaints or act to prevent sexual harassment. The university had a strong, published policy against sexual harassment. **The student did not prove the officials were deliberately indifferent to sexual harassment. As a result, they could not be held liable for damages.** The court returned the case to the district court with directions to separate the claims against the professor and dismiss the remaining federal claims against the officials. *Cox v. Sugg*, 484 F.3d 1062 (8th Cir. 2007).

◆ *An Oklahoma college did not violate Title IX as it was not deliberately indifferent to a complaint about a professor's sexual behavior.*

A student claimed a professor touched her inappropriately and made sexual comments in front of her peers and while they were alone. She sued the college under Title IX, claiming it knew the professor sexually harassed others before she enrolled there. A federal court found the college did not know about any prior incidents. On appeal, the U.S. Court of Appeals, Tenth Circuit, found the courts have differed on whether notice sufficient to trigger liability may consist of prior complaints or must consist of notice regarding current harassment in the recipient's programs. There was evidence that the professor had dated two students close to his age, but the court held this did not provide the college with knowledge that he posed a substantial risk of sexual harassment to students. Other student complaints of inappropriate sexual behavior against the professor occurred almost 10 years earlier. Those complaints involved significantly different behavior, including inappropriate touching and name-calling. **The court rejected the student's contention that the college was deliberately indifferent to her allegations, and affirmed the judgment for the college.** *Escue v. Northern Oklahoma College*, 450 F.3d 1146 (10th Cir. 2006).

2. Sexual Harassment by Peers

In Fitzgerald v. Barnstable School Committee, *555 U.S. 246, 129 S.Ct. 788, 172 L.Ed.2d 582 (2009), the U.S. Supreme Court allowed students who assert Title IX harassment actions to include "parallel and concurrent" gender discrimination claims against their educational institutions under the Equal Protection Clause of the Fourteenth Amendment via 42 U.S.C. Section 1983.*

Section 1983 is a federal statute that creates no rights itself, but is used to enforce rights created by federal laws and the U.S. Constitution. For additional harassment cases involving student-athletes, please see Chapter Three, Section I.D. of this volume.

◆ *Bucknell University did not have to delay its investigation of sexual assault charges against a student until criminal charges against him were resolved.*

A female student accused the male student of physical and sexual assault, and a hospital found she had suffered bruising. After the local district attorney filed criminal charges against the male student, the female filed an internal charge against him at Bucknell. The male filed his own student complaint, accusing the female of sexually assaulting him and filing false charges against him. Bucknell's policy called for delaying internal action until the conclusion of criminal hearings. But it decided to conduct its own hearing in advance of the criminal case. In response, the female asked a federal court to issue a preliminary order that would force Bucknell to delay its internal hearing. She said that forcing her to attend the university hearing would violate her due process rights. In addition to other constitutional violations, the female claimed Bucknell violated Title IX by allowing the male to keep harassing her.

The court first explained that the Fourteenth Amendment governs only state conduct. Since Bucknell is a private entity, the female had to show some kind of state action to proceed with her constitutional claims. The court found no basis for doing so. **Although Title IX applied to Bucknell because it received federal funding, the female did not show it ignored discrimination against her or acted unreasonably.** As a result, the court denied the request for an order requiring Bucknell to delay its internal proceedings. *Stefanowicz v. Bucknell Univ.*, No. 10-CV-2040, 2010 WL 3938243 (M.D. Pa. 10/5/10).

◆ *A Delaware university created a hostile environment and violated Title IX by failing to adequately respond to the assault of a student.*

According to the student, a male student at the university assaulted her after she refused to have sex with him. Her injuries required hospitalization, and she reported the incident to campus police. After both parties made statements, the university did not stop the male from attending classes. The student said the university's director of residential life and judicial affairs said she should change her schedule and transfer from any classes she had with the male. She missed a semester due to fear of the male, and sued the university in a federal court. According to the student, the university charged her with several violations of the student code, including assault and battery. She said this was done to stop her from complaining about the incident. **The court held the student's complaint adequately alleged a Title IX violation against the**

university. But she could not proceed with a Title IX claim against any individual, because the statute does not authorize such claims. Due process claims against the university and its director were blocked by immunity, but a due process claim against the director could go forward. The court granted the university's motion to dismiss an abuse of process claim. *Terrell v. Delaware State Univ.*, No. 09-464 (GMS), 2010 WL 2952221 (D. Del. 7/23/10).

◆   *The estate of a New York student who killed herself seven months after she was raped on campus could advance several claims against the college.*

According to the student's mother, the college violated Title IX and was liable for negligence, infliction of emotional distress, fraud, deprivation of federally secured rights and wrongful death. She filed a federal district court action against the college, which considered a motion by the college for dismissal. The court found the complaint alleged that the college refused to take any action following the rape, instead deferring entirely to a criminal investigation. It held the mother raised a sufficient claim that the college was deliberately indifferent to the assault and her daughter's attempts to report it.

To prove a Title IX violation, "deliberate indifference" must be shown. A key is whether the defendant acted reasonably under the circumstances. In this case, the complaint alleged a valid equal protection claim based on collaboration by the college with a local police detective to conceal reports of sexual assault. The court also refused to dismiss a fraud claim that was based on the college's alleged misrepresentation of campus safety to help recruit students. The claim of intentional infliction of emotional distress survived pretrial dismissal, as the court found a jury should decide whether the college's reliance on a police investigation conducted by one of its own employees was outrageous enough to support the claim. *McGrath v. Dominican College of Blauvelt, New York*, 672 F.Supp.2d 477 (S.D.N.Y. 2009).

◆   *A University of Georgia student presented sufficient evidence of a sexual assault by student-athletes in a dorm room to advance to a trial.*

The student went to a student-athlete's dorm room, where she consented to sex. Two teammates then sexually assaulted the student. She filed criminal charges against the student-athlete and teammates and withdrew from school. The student-athletes were charged with disorderly conduct under the university's code of conduct and suspended from athletics. A university judiciary panel decided not to punish the student-athletes. The student sued the university in a federal district court for violating Title IX. The court held for the university, and the case reached the U.S. Court of Appeals, Eleventh Circuit.

The court held student-on-student harassment may violate Title IX. **A university may be held liable for Title IX violations if it acts with deliberate indifference to known acts of harassment that are so severe, pervasive and objectively offensive that they bar a victim's access to an educational opportunity or benefit.** The student claimed the university had accepted the student-athlete even though it knew of his history of similar misconduct at other schools. The court found the university did not sufficiently respond to the student's allegations. Within 48 hours of the incident, the university made a preliminary report of the incident. However, it exercised almost no control over the student-athlete and failed to enforce its harassment policies. As the student presented evidence of discrimination that effectively barred her access to an educational opportunity or benefit, the court reversed the judgment. *Williams v. Univ. of Georgia*, 441 F.3d 1287 (11th Cir. 2006).

III. RACE AND NATIONAL ORIGIN DISCRIMINATION

The Equal Protection Clause of the Fourteenth Amendment, Title VI of the Civil Rights Act of 1964, 42 U.S.C. § 1981 and state anti-discrimination laws all prohibit discrimination against individuals in educational settings. Title VI provides that no person shall on the ground of race or color be excluded from participating in any program receiving federal financial assistance.

A. Affirmative Action

In 2013, the U.S. Supreme Court held a University of Texas student admission plan was subject to strict judicial scrutiny. "Strict scrutiny" is a searching examination under which a state must show the reasons for any racial classification were "clearly identified and unquestionably legitimate." A **reviewing court must be satisfied that no workable race-neutral alternative is available.** *The judiciary is charged with ensuring that the means chosen by a university to implement a diversity plan are "narrowly-tailored" to meet its purposes. "Narrow tailoring" involves a careful judicial inquiry into whether a university could achieve sufficient diversity without racial classifications.*

◆   A student admission plan implemented by the University of Texas was subject to strict judicial scrutiny.

In *Hopwood v. Texas*, 78 F.3d 932 (5th Cir. 1996), the Fifth Circuit struck down the use of race-based admissions criteria by the University of Texas (UT) law school. UT then started using a "holistic metric" to assess applicants. State legislators passed a law that Texas resident seniors in the top 10% of their high school classes would be automatically admitted to any state university. In 2003, the Supreme Court held colleges could consider race in admissions when this was necessary to promote diversity and to achieve a "critical mass" of minority students. UT then adopted a policy including race as a factor in admissions.

White applicants sued UT in a federal court, claiming equal protection violations. The court held for UT, and the Fifth Circuit affirmed this result. It held UT admissions decisions were entitled to deference and a presumption of good faith. On appeal, the Supreme Court held diversity in higher education encompasses an array of qualifications and characteristics of which racial or ethnic origin are only a part. **Strict scrutiny requires a university to clearly demonstrate a constitutionally permitted purpose and the necessity of making a racial classification.** Official action that treats a person differently on account of race or ethnic origin is "inherently suspect." If a university establishes a goal of diversity, the university still has to prove it implemented its goals in a narrowly tailored way. "Narrow tailoring" requires a court to verify that the university had to use race to achieve the educational benefits of diversity. A university has to show each applicant was evaluated as an individual, not by race or ethnicity. It is up to the courts to determine whether this was done. Since the lower courts did not apply strict scrutiny, the Court vacated the judgment and returned the case to the Fifth Circuit. *Fisher v. Univ. of Texas at Austin*, 133 S.Ct. 2411 (U.S. 2013).

◆ *A Michigan voter initiative barring public institutions from preferential treatment based on race, sex, color, ethnicity and national origin came under review by all judges of the U.S. Court of Appeals, Sixth Circuit.*

A 2006 voter initiative became an amendment to the state constitution that prohibited the consideration of race, sex, color, ethnicity and national origin in admissions decisions by state universities and colleges. A federal district court rejected an equal protection challenge to the amendment, and the challengers appealed to the Sixth Circuit. A three-judge panel held the amendment violated the Equal Protection Clause, but a majority of the active judges of the Sixth Circuit voted to vacate the decision and rehear the case. The full Sixth Circuit then voted to reverse the district court decision. It held a law deprives minority groups of equal protection when it has a racial focus that targets a policy or program that primarily benefits a minority and reallocates political power or reorders the decision-making process in a way that places special burdens on the ability of a minority group to achieve its goals via the decision-making process. The court held **the amendment violated the Equal Protection Clause by reordering the political process in a way that placed special burdens on racial minorities**. It reversed the lower court's decision to uphold the constitutionality of the amendment. *Coalition to Defend Affirmative Action v. Regents of the Univ. of Michigan*, 701 F.3d 466 (6th Cir. 2012).

◆ *A federal appeals court upheld a California constitutional provision enacted to block public entities from granting race and gender preferences.*

Proposition 209 was a 1996 voter initiative intended to bar the state from granting preferential treatment on the basis of characteristics including race, sex, color, ethnicity or national origin. After it went into effect as a state constitutional amendment, the state's public university system stopped considering race and sex in admissions. Over the next year, the number of minority freshmen at two state universities dropped by more than 50%. A group of high school and college students sued state and university officials in a federal district court for equal protection violations. The case was dismissed, and appeal went to the U.S. Court of Appeals, Ninth Circuit. It held that the equal protection claims were foreclosed by its decision in *Coalition for Economic Equity v. Wilson*, 122 F.3d 692 (9th Cir. 1997). The court held the earlier decision considered the scenario involved in this case and upheld the provision at issue. **There was no merit to the students' theory that the provision created an "unequal political structure" that prevented them from using normal democratic processes.** Nor was the earlier ruling inconsistent with more recent Supreme Court cases regarding affirmative action. As a result, the judgment for state and university officials was affirmed. *Coalition to Defend Affirmative Action v. Brown*, 674 F.3d 1128 (9th Cir. 2012).

♦ *While achieving a diverse student body may be a worthy goal, the means to achieve that goal must comply with the Equal Protection Clause. The U.S. Supreme Court allowed race to be used as a "plus" factor in admissions.*

The University of Michigan had an admissions policy for its law school that used race as a "plus" factor for underrepresented minorities. The policy was flexible, utilized an individualized assessment system, and did not create quotas. The policy was challenged as unconstitutional by white students who were not accepted for enrollment. The case reached the U.S. Supreme Court, which upheld the policy. **The Court first noted that the goal of achieving diversity in the student body was a compelling governmental interest.** As a result, the policy would not violate the Equal Protection Clause if it was narrowly tailored to achieving that goal. Since the law school's policy did not set impermissible quotas, and since **it utilized an individualized assessment system by using race/ethnicity as a "plus" factor when evaluating individual applicants for admission**, it was constitutional. The Court also noted that race-conscious admissions policies should be limited in time so that racial preferences can be ended as soon as practicable. *Grutter v. Bollinger*, 539 U.S. 306, 123 S.Ct. 2325, 156 L.Ed.2d 304 (2003).

♦ *The Supreme Court found unconstitutional the University of Michigan's undergraduate admissions policy, which awarded applicants in underrepresented minority groups 20 points out of 100 needed for admission.*

Applying the same strict scrutiny analysis it used in *Grutter*, above, the Court held the undergraduate policy was not narrowly tailored to achieve the compelling governmental interest in a diverse student body. **The undergraduate admissions policy did not assess points on an individualized basis**, but rather awarded them to all minority applicants. The failure to review each applicant individually doomed the policy under the Equal Protection Clause. *Gratz v. Bollinger*, 539 U.S. 244, 123 S.Ct. 2411, 156 L.Ed.2d 257 (2003).

♦ *In 1978, the Supreme Court held a special admissions program at a California medical school that reserved close to one-sixth of the school's openings each year for minority students violated the Equal Protection Clause.*

The Medical School of the University of California at Davis had two admission programs for its entering class of 100 students. Under the regular procedure, candidates whose overall undergraduate grade point averages fell below 2.5 on a scale of 4.0 were summarily rejected. The special admissions policy, designed to assist minority or other disadvantaged applicants, reserved 16 of the 100 openings each year for medical school admission based upon criteria other than that used in the general admissions program. Special admission applicants did not need to meet the 2.5 or better grade point average of the general admission group, and their Medical College Admission Test scores, measured against general admission candidates.

A white male brought suit to compel his admission to medical school after he was twice rejected for admission, even though candidates with lower grade point averages and lower test score results were being admitted under the special admissions program. The plaintiff alleged that **the special**

admissions excluded him from medical school on the basis of his race in violation of the Equal Protection Clause of the Fourteenth Amendment, the California Constitution, and Title VI of the 1964 Civil Rights Act. The California Supreme Court concluded that the special admissions program was not the least intrusive means of achieving the state's goals of integrating the medical profession under a strict scrutiny standard. On appeal, the U.S. Supreme Court held that while the goal of achieving a diverse student body is sufficiently compelling to justify considerations of race in admissions decisions under some circumstances, **the special admissions program, which foreclosed consideration to persons such as the plaintiff, was unnecessary to achieve this compelling goal and was invalid under the Equal Protection Clause.** Since the school could not prove that the plaintiff would not have been admitted even if there had been no special admissions program, the Court ordered that he be admitted to the medical school. *Regents of the Univ. of California v. Bakke*, 438 U.S. 265, 98 S.Ct. 2733, 57 L.Ed.2d 750 (1978).

◆ *The University of Washington (UW) Law School's admission policy did not discriminate against applicants on the basis of race.*

UW's law school had no racial quotas, targets or goals for admission or enrollment, but considered race, ethnicity and other diversity factors as a "plus" in admission decisions. The school also relied on nonracial diversity factors. Several white applicants who were denied admission to the law school sued the university in a federal district court for race discrimination. The court denied summary judgment to the applicants, and they appealed. The Ninth Circuit Court of Appeals relied on *Grutter v. Bollinger*, above. It found the law school acted in good faith to implement its admissions process and satisfied the factors described in *Grutter*. **The school did not establish quotas, targets or goals for admission or enrollment of minorities, nor did it direct the admission of a certain number of minority applicants.** As the law school followed the guidelines in *Grutter* by conducting a "highly-individualized, holistic review of each applicant's file," the court affirmed the judgment. *Smith v. Univ. of Washington Law School*, 392 F.3d 367 (9th Cir. 2004).

◆ *The Supreme Court held that a university could avoid liability for a race-based admission policy if it could show that an applicant would have been denied admission absent the policy.*

An African immigrant of Caucasian descent applied for admission to the Ph.D. program in counseling psychology at a Texas public university. The university considered the race of its applicants at some stage of the review process and denied admission to the applicant. He sued for money damages and injunctive relief, asserting that the race-conscious admission policy violated the Equal Protection Clause. The university moved for summary judgment, arguing that even if it had not used race-based criteria, it would not have admitted the applicant because of his GPA and his GRE score. A federal district court granted summary judgment to the university, but the Fifth Circuit Court of Appeals reversed. The case reached the U.S. Supreme Court, which noted that its decision in *Mt. Healthy City Board of Educ. v. Doyle*, 429 U.S. 274 (1977), made clear that **if the government has considered an impermissible** criterion in making an adverse decision to the plaintiff, it can still avoid liability by demonstrating that it would have made the same decision absent the forbidden consideration. Therefore, if the state could show that it would have made the decision to deny admission to the applicant absent the race-based policy, it would be entitled to summary judgment on the claim for damages. With respect to the claim for injunctive relief, it appeared that the university had stopped using a race-based admissions policy. However, that issue had to be decided on remand. *Texas v. Lesage*, 528 U.S. 18, 120 S.Ct. 467, 145 L.Ed.2d 347 (1999).

B. Discrimination and Equal Protection

Title VI of the Civil Rights Act of 1964 prohibits discrimination based on race, color or national origin in any program that receives federal funds. Title VI is based on equal protection principles, and many discrimination complaints allege violations of Title VI, the Equal Protection Clause, and analogous state laws. In Alexander v. Sandoval, *532 U.S. 275 (2001), the Supreme Court noted that the courts require proof of intentional discrimination in Title VI cases.*

◆ *A federal district court rejected a Missouri student's claim that a community college discriminated against her by assigning her low grades.*

According to the student, she appealed her grades to the academic appeals committee, but the committee denied her appeal for race-related reasons. She said that her instructors' supervisor wrongfully failed to remedy racist acts by instructors. In a federal court action, the student claimed the community college failed to properly discipline staff members, engaged in faulty hiring, and covered up discrimination. **The court explained that individual defendants cannot be held personally liable for violating Title VI.** As for claims against the community college appeals committee, the court found a committee of this nature could not be sued under Title VI. Finally, the court held the Title VI claim against the community college could not proceed, as the student could not show intentional harassment on the basis of her race or nationality. She made no viable claim that the college had a policy of discrimination or did anything to further discrimination against her. As a result, the case was dismissed. *Tatum v. St. Louis Community College*, No. 4:12CV2218 CDP, 2013 WL 171072 (E.D. Mo. 1/16/13).

◆ *A federal district court in Nebraska rejected an unsuccessful applicant's claim that she was denied admission to law school due to racial discrimination.*

Creighton University law school rejected the applicant in 2010-11 based on her low Law School Admissions Test (LSAT) score and a credential assembly service report used to predict law school grades. No one with an LSAT as low as the applicant's had been admitted to the law school since 2003. Alleging the existence of an unlawful quota system, the applicant sued the university in a federal court for race discrimination. She sought an order requiring her admission, and $10 million in damages. The court found the law school's admissions criteria did not include race, national origin, religion, gender, disability, sexual orientation, marital status or age. The applicant's

LSAT score and a related index were far lower than those of anyone who had been admitted for 2010-11. No evidence supported her claim that the law school denied her application based on race. **As the evidence showed the student was denied admission because her academic credentials did not meet objective standards, the court held for the university.** *Goodwin v. Creighton Univ.*, No. 8:10CV423, 2011 WL 2680481 (D. Neb. 7/8/11).

◆ *A federal court dismissed most of the claims by an African-American student who said he was tackled by a private university safety officer.*

According to the student, the safety officer stopped him as he walked with a white student, then tackled him, kneed him and pepper-sprayed him. He claimed the attack was based on racial profiling, as the officer left the white student alone. In a federal district court action asserting 16 claims, the court noted the complaint did not say why the student was stopped, or what he and his friend were doing at the time, or whether he might have been doing something that the friend was not. **The court dismissed a claim under the Equal Protection Clause and other constitutional provisions, as none of the named defendants were state actors.** But the court allowed the student to refile the claim and provide more factual details. *Johnson v. Univ. of San Diego*, No. 10CV0504-LAB (NLS), 2011 WL 4345842 (S.D. Cal. 9/16/11).

◆ *A former Columbia University student who committed plagiarism did not show the resulting decision to expel him was unlawfully motivated.*

The plagiarism charge was referred to a disciplinary committee, which voted to expel the student. Although he admitted to plagiarism, he claimed he was expelled because of his race and because he had refused to submit to an administrator's sexual advances and filed a complaint about them. In a federal district court lawsuit against the university, the student alleged retaliation under Title IX, race discrimination and breach of contract. After the court held for the university, appeal went before the U.S. Court of Appeals, Second Circuit.

On appeal, the court explained that to prove a retaliation claim, the student had to show he engaged in a protected activity of which the university was aware. Even if he could make this showing, the school could defeat the claim by offering a legitimate, nondiscriminatory reason for its decision. There was no evidence to support the conclusion that the student was really expelled for a reason other than plagiarism. Since he could not show the university gave a pretextual reason for dismissing him, the race discrimination claim failed. **Evidence did not show the university was in breach or that the student performed his contractual duties**, and the judgment was affirmed. *Shelton v. Trustees of Columbia Univ.*, 369 Fed.Appx. 200 (2d Cir. 2010).

◆ *A Kentucky family medicine training program participant was unable to pursue claims against a university after she was released from the program.*

A participant in the University of Louisville's family medicine training program exhibited behavioral problems and was placed on academic probation. A program director referred her to an assistance program, and a psychiatric evaluation was recommended for her. Meanwhile, the participant's pending grievance alleging race discrimination was resolved against her due to lack of evidence of discrimination. When the participant failed to set up a psychiatric appointment, she was released from the family medicine training program.

In a race discrimination case against the university, the participant asserted violations of federal law, breach of contract, defamation, libel, slander, wrongful discharge, breach of the covenant of good faith and fair dealing, and fraud and deceit. The court found several federal claims failed because the program was a private corporation whose actions could not be deemed to have been taken by the state. **There was no indication any action was taken with an intent to discriminate against the participant.** Finally, since she did not show assistance program personnel acted outside their duties or with actual malice, they were entitled by statute to immunity. *Peavey v. Univ. of Louisville*, No. 3:09-CV-00484-R, 2010 WL 2836093 (W.D. Ky. 7/16/10).

◆ *An Illinois law school applicant failed to show she was denied admission for discriminatory reasons in a federal district court case.*

After being denied admission to seven law schools in northern Illinois, the applicant filed separate lawsuits against all seven, claiming discrimination on the basis of gender, age, race and disability. A judge dismissed her case against the University of Chicago because she did not provide a basis for her allegation that gender, age, race or disability played any role in the decision to deny her application. Different judges dismissed her claims against the DePaul College of Law and Northwestern University School of Law, finding a legal doctrine called *collateral estoppel* barred claims that were previously rejected. The court held the applicant's claims would fail even if *collateral estoppel* did not bar them. Neither the ADA nor the Rehabilitation Act required law schools to alter their acceptance standards as a disability-related accommodation, and Northwestern was not required to admit her based on her admittedly inferior qualifications. In addition, **the applicant alleged only that she is a black woman and Northwestern admitted a low percentage of black applicants**. Her conclusory allegations did not support an inference of intentional discrimination, resulting in dismissal of the action. *Jackson v. Northwestern Univ. School of Law*, No.10 C 1986, 2010 WL 5174389 (N.D. Ill. 12/15/10).

◆ *A white student who was beaten by his African-American roommate failed to prove Tennessee State University (TSU) was responsible for his injuries.*

According to the student, the roommate called him a "cracker" and often used the word "nigger." While the student and his father met with a university director to discuss the roommate's conduct, they did not raise race as an issue, and they did not request a change in roommate assignments. Soon after one of the meetings, the roommate beat the student with a clothes iron in their dorm room. TSU police arrested the roommate, who promptly moved out of the dorm but finished the semester at TSU. According to the student, TSU did not officially suspend the roommate for several months, and he continued to appear on campus. When the student returned to TSU for his sophomore year, his grades slipped and he lost a scholarship. In the student's federal district court action against the university, he asserted race discrimination in violation of Title VI of the 1964 Civil Rights Act. **The court held TSU did not have knowledge of severe and pervasive harassment because the student did not**

inform TSU about any racial tensions. Nor was TSU's conduct unreasonable under the circumstances. After the attack, the roommate was arrested and forced out of his dorm room. TSU's motion for pretrial judgment was granted. *Maislin v. Tennessee State Univ.*, 665 F.Supp.2d 922 (M.D. Tenn. 2009).

◆ *A student of Asian ancestry was unable to prove that a California community college librarian discriminated against her based on her race.*

According to the student, the librarian falsely accused her of using library computers for personal reasons and on some occasions forced her to leave the library. Although the student filed a complaint against the college asserting the librarian bullied and harassed her, she did not allege race discrimination. After an investigation, the community college declined to find bullying by the librarian. The student transferred to another college, but again encountered the librarian, who had also been transferred. In a federal district court, the student sued the community college district and librarian for race discrimination. The court found insufficient evidence of discrimination based on race. **Undisputed evidence showed the librarian treated all students poorly.** The student did not counter this evidence, and one of her own witnesses stated that the librarian's behavior was not based on race. As a result, the court held for the librarian and community college district. *Santos v. Peralta Community College Dist.*, No. C-07-5227 EMC, 2009 WL 3809797 (N.D. Cal. 11/13/09).

◆ *A Florida university did not unlawfully discriminate against an unqualified intern by declining to hire him for a paid position.*

As a non-student and a volunteer, the intern received no pay or benefits, although he tried to secure paid positions. His applications were denied, since one was open only to students and the other was filled before he applied for it. In a federal district court action, the intern accused the university of race discrimination. The court agreed with the university, noting he was ineligible for the first position as a non-student. As for the other position, he did not show he was as well qualified for the job as the person chosen for it. **The university said the intern performed poorly, and this was a legitimate, nondiscriminatory reason for the decision not to hire him.** Because he did not show this reason was a pretext for unlawful discrimination, his claim of race discrimination failed, and the case was dismissed. *Cummings v. Univ. of Florida*, No. 1:04cv430-SPM/AK, 2008 WL 4534262 (N.D. Fla. 9/30/08).

◆ *A Georgia university properly suspended an African-American nursing student for selling stolen textbooks to the university's bookstore.*

A nursing student was accused of violating the university code of conduct by re-selling four stolen textbooks to a university bookstore. A disciplinary hearing was held, and she was suspended for two years. The student claimed race discrimination, as five white students who were accused of theft were not penalized as harshly as she was. The student sued the university in a federal district court, asserting due process and equal protection violations. She added discrimination and breach of contract claims. The court held for the university, and the student appealed. The U.S. Court of Appeals, Eleventh Circuit, upheld the dismissal of the due process and equal protection claims and rejected a Title

VI race discrimination claim. As the court explained, **Title VI bars recipients of federal funding from discriminating on the basis of race in any federally funded program**. Applying an equal protection analysis, the Eleventh Circuit rejected the claim that the suspension was motivated by intentional race discrimination. As white students disciplined by the university were not similarly situated to the student, the different punishment did not prove racial discrimination. According to the court, differences in individual circumstances justified imposing less severe punishment on the white students. *Carr v. Board of Regents of the Univ. System of Georgia*, 249 Fed.Appx. 146 (11th Cir. 2007).

◆ *A federal appeals court held the University of Colorado did not violate a student's rights under federal disability and civil rights laws.*

The student, a native of Zaire, attended the university's pre-med program. She claimed to have an unspecified disability due to injuries she suffered while working for the university. She claimed four professors failed to honor letters of accommodation issued by the university's office of disabilities services, and did not provide other accommodations. The student sued the university in a federal district court, alleging it discriminated against her based on disability.

The court found the student failed to present evidence that the university denied her request for accommodation, as the professor provided her extra time to sit for an exam. On appeal, the U.S. Court of Appeals, Tenth Circuit, held the student's disability discrimination claim failed. She later admitted that the professor refused to grant her extra time on the final examination because she fell asleep and not because she had test-taking anxiety. Her race discrimination claim failed. Although the student claimed she was treated differently than similarly situated "blond students," other students were not similarly situated because they did not fall asleep during the final examination. The court affirmed the judgment for the university. *Buhendwa v. Univ. of Colorado at Boulder*, 214 Fed.Appx. 823 (10th Cir. 2007).

C. National Origin

Because Title VI covers only entities that receive federal funding, there is potential Title VI liability for entities that discriminate on the basis of race, color or national original, but no liability is possible for individuals.

◆ *An Indiana student of Korean descent stated a valid equal protection claim based on intensive scrutiny for plagiarism due to his race and orientation.*

A final paper submitted by the student was reviewed for plagiarism by three professors. One of them veered from usual practices by running it through a plagiarism-checking program. After the check showed part of the paper had been plagiarized, the student was expelled. He claimed two students in the program – non-Asians, one a woman – turned in papers with more plagiarism than his paper. A program director refused to reconsider the expulsion, and the other students were not disciplined. In a federal district court action, the student claimed professors subjected his paper to increased scrutiny because of race and sexual orientation. The professors and director sought dismissal of the due process and equal protection claims. As they were sued in their individual capacities, the court held the Eleventh Amendment did not bar the due process and equal protection claims. Nor did they have qualified immunity on the equal protection claim, because **the student alleged a violation of a clearly established equal protection right not to be arbitrarily subjected to different standards of plagiarism review than other students based on race, national origin, sex or orientation**. The due process claims failed because he was not deprived of a protected interest and was given a fair chance to respond to the charges. *Park v. Trustees of Purdue Univ.*, No. 4:09-CV-87 JVB, 2011 WL 1361409 (N.D. Ind. 4/11/11).

◆ *Columbia University's decision to deny admission to a woman who failed to demonstrate English language proficiency was not based on her ancestry.*

At age 50, the woman sought admission to the special education program offered at the Teachers College of Columbia University. The college required an English language proficiency examination for non-native speakers. After the woman scored 190 on a test that had a minimum passing grade of 500, the college told her she could take a different exam at the university, or take an exam that was administered only in Australia. After she took and failed the in-house exam, the woman filed an administrative complaint with the U.S. Department of Education's Office for Civil Rights (OCR), claiming age discrimination. The OCR rejected her claim as untimely but she sued Columbia in a federal district court for "civil conspiracy to commit humiliation," tortious interference with her rights, age and race discrimination and other claims.

A federal magistrate judge recommended dismissal of the federal claims. He also said it would be appropriate not to consider the remaining state claims. A federal district court agreed with the magistrate that the age discrimination claims were barred because the woman did not file a timely administrative complaint. **It also agreed to reject her national origin discrimination claim because none of the allegations in her complaint related to her Romanian ancestry.** As the remaining claims lacked merit, the court adopted the magistrate's report and recommendation. *Strujan v. Teachers College Columbia Univ.*, No. 08 Civ. 9589(WHP)(HBP), 2010 WL 3466251 (S.D.N.Y. 9/3/10).

◆ *A federal court held a Texas university expelled a foreign student for nondiscriminatory reasons and dismissed the student's claims.*

Two professors used a plagiarism detection service and determined the student had plagiarized his papers. He received a failing grade for both courses. A week after meeting with the dean, another student reported to the police that the student had talked about his plagiarism charge and then said, "I understand why people shoot up or bomb schools in America." The dean of students suspended the student from campus, and the college then decided to expel him for plagiarism. The same day, students from a study group in the library went to university police and said the student had talked about a bomb threat.

A university judicial appeals board found the student should be suspended from campus for a year. Separately, the university charged him with academic dishonesty for plagiarism and lying, and held two hearings – one for each paper. Both ended with the board finding plagiarism, and the student was expelled. In a federal court, the student alleged due process and discrimination violations. The court held the expulsion was an academic decision and that the student could not show it was made arbitrarily. Instead, the court found it was properly made by faculty exercising professional judgment. **A national origin discrimination claim failed as the university had valid, nondiscriminatory reasons for suspending and expelling him.** There was no evidence of pretext, as the student had made a threatening statement and plagiarized two term papers. *Mawle v. Texas A&M Univ.-Kingsville*, No. CC-08-64, 2010 WL 1782214 (S.D. Tex. 4/30/10).

◆ *A student who was dismissed from Howard University for poor academic performance was unable to proceed with a federal case against the university.*

University rules specified that students who received more than nine credit hours of grade C or below should be dropped from their courses. University rules allowed graduate faculty to recommend the dismissal of any student who was not performing satisfactorily. In four semesters, the student did not achieve any grade higher than C, and his advisor did not approve his thesis proposal. After he was dismissed for poor academic performance and unwillingness to listen to his academic advisor, he sued the university and several faculty members in a federal court for national origin and disability discrimination. **Claims asserted against the individual defendants could not proceed because none of the laws under which they were brought permitted claims against individuals.** The student did not show the reason the school provided for the dismissal – poor academic performance – was really a pretext for unlawful discrimination. *Mwabira-Simera v. Howard Univ.*, 692 F.Supp.2d 65 (D.D.C. 2010).

◆ *An Iranian dental school student with D grades could not proceed with a national origin discrimination case against Marquette University.*

After compiling a D grade average, the university dental school dismissed the student. He filed a state circuit court action against Marquette, alleging national origin discrimination. To support his claim, he alleged that a Caucasian student was treated more favorably than he was. The court dismissed the complaint, finding he did not show he was similarly situated to the other student. **On appeal, the Court of Appeals of Wisconsin held the student failed to show he was similarly situated to the Caucasian student in all relevant respects.** The Caucasian student completed his first year of studies with no unsatisfactory grades, while the Iranian student did not. In addition, the Caucasian student offered a medical explanation when his grades began to slip. Marquette was not made aware of any medical problems suffered by the Iranian student at a relevant time. As he did not show he was similarly situated to the other student, the judgment was affirmed. *Amir v. Marquette Univ.*, 322 Wis.2d 572, 776 N.W.2d 287 (Table) (Wis. Ct. App. 2009).

◆ *A federal district court denied a trial for a student who did not provide enough information to support his race and national origin claims.*

According to the student, two architecture professors complained about his accent, criticized his proposal based on preconceived racial beliefs, and created a hostile learning environment. They eventually dropped him from the class. But when the student took the same class from a different professor, he again failed. After the university expelled the student, he sued the university and architecture professors in a federal district court. **It found the student "utterly fail[ed] to make the minimal showing necessary to avoid dismissal."** Under the rules for filing federal cases, legal papers are supposed to provide plain, short statements that give notice of the claims and grounds for asserting them. Since the student merely made "labels and conclusions" and not a factual basis sufficient to avoid dismissal, he was unable to proceed with the case. The court dismissed the action, saying it refused to "second-guess an educational institution's application of its own academic standards and procedures" without a valid allegation it had acted with an illegal motive. *Wanko v. Catholic Univ. of America*, No. 08-2115 (RJL), 2009 WL 3052477 (D.D.C. 9/22/09).

◆   *A Texas federal district court dismissed a Cameroon native's race and national origin discrimination claims against an associate professor.*

The student sought a doctoral degree in English. She claimed an associate professor questioned her about her country of origin and academic profile. The professor allegedly threatened to ruin the student's transcript and delay her graduation. She brought grading and discrimination complaints against the professor under a university policy. The English department dismissed the accusations as unfounded. Another professor in the English department accused the student of plagiarism. The university honesty panel, which included the associate professor, concluded the student had plagiarized and she received an F for that class. The student was later expelled after another charge of plagiarism by the same professor. The student sued the university, professor, and others in a federal district court for discrimination and retaliation under Title VI. The court held **Title VI claims may only be brought against entities that receive federal funding, not individuals. It dismissed the Title VI claim against the associate professor.** *Bisong v. Univ. of Houston*, Civil Action No. H-06-1815, 2006 WL 2414410 (S.D. Tex. 8/18/06).

IV. AGE DISCRIMINATION

In addition to state laws, the Age Discrimination Act of 1975 (42 U.S.C. § 6101, et seq.) provides the basis for claims of age discrimination by students. Similar to Title IX claims, however, the Age Discrimination Act applies only to programs or activities receiving federal funding. The Age Discrimination in Employment Act (ADEA) has broad coverage in employment cases.

◆   *Calling a 20-year-old student's age discrimination case "patently absurd," a federal court dismissed his action against a New Hampshire law school.*

After falling two points short of the required score for early admission, the student was invited to apply for admission the next year. Instead, he sued the law school, claiming he was denied admission based on age and that the law school violated his equal protection rights. A federal court held the student did not comply with Age Discrimination Act notice and exhaustion requirements, requiring the dismissal of that claim. As for the equal protection claim, the court noted the law school was a private, non-governmental entity. It held **the** receipt of federal financial assistance did not make the law school a public actor for Equal Protection purposes. There was no showing that the government had influenced the decision being challenged in the lawsuit. As a result, the court dismissed the action. *Prete v. Roger Williams Univ. School*, No. 12-cv-474-JL, 2012 WL 6203083 (D.N.H. 12/12/12).

◆ *A New York student could not proceed with her discrimination claim due to her untimely filing and other procedural errors.*

During her time at the university, the student wanted to live with her son in on-campus housing. After her requests were denied, she sued the university, accusing it of unlawfully discriminating against her based on her familial status. A federal court found a claim relating to study abroad was untimely. As for the rest of the time that she was enrolled at the university, **she was not eligible for housing because she was a part-time student**. The university made its housing available only to students who were enrolled on a full-time basis. After the court held for the university, the student sought to overturn the judgment. But the court held she did not meet the standard applicable to motions for relief from judgment, and her motion was denied. *Whitaker v. New York Univ.*, No. 09 Civ. 8410(LTS), 2012 WL 2369510 (S.D.N.Y. 6/20/12).

◆ *A New York student did not convince a federal court that a community college gave preferential treatment to younger, minority students.*

The community college's student handbook specified nursing students must earn at least a C in required classes and repeat any failed required class. Three failed classes meant dismissal unless a student obtained a waiver. The student failed three classes, but obtained a waiver based on recent deaths in her family. She then used a paper towel instead of sterile gauze while giving an injection and was promptly expelled. The student claimed the college gave younger, minority students preferential treatment by bending rules for them, but not for her. She sued the community college and several of its officials under Title VI, asserting discrimination based on her Caucasian race and "advanced years." But the court rejected her claims, based on the absence of admissible evidence to support them. **Even if the inadmissible hearsay she relied on was true, it did not prove to the court that the community college did not follow its handbook.** *Maya v. Bronx Community College*, No. 09 Civ. 3605(CM)(DCF), 2011 WL 2732519 (S.D.N.Y. 7/6/11).

◆ *A Washington student's lawsuit against a university failed because state law prohibited age discrimination in employment but not education.*

Faculty members grew concerned about the student's lack of progress after six semesters of a graduate psychology program. She received two extensions but refused to sign a contract intended to help her prepare for her exams. After a "not negotiable" deadline was set, the student filed an age discrimination complaint. Meanwhile, a deadline passed without her taking required exams, and faculty members assigned her an F for the course. Her grade average dropped below the program minimum, and she was disenrolled.

In a state court, the student accused the university of breach of contract, age discrimination and retaliation. After the case was dismissed, the state court of appeals found no merit to a contract claim based on breach of a duty to provide clear guidelines for academic expectations. These requirements were set out in a graduate school program description and were otherwise made clear to the student. The court held Washington law allows employee claims for age discrimination but not student claims. **Work as a teaching assistant did not make the student an employee**, as she argued. There was no merit to a retaliation claim based on the filing of an age discrimination complaint. As the university had a legitimate, nondiscriminatory reason to disenroll the student, the judgment was affirmed. *Becker v. Washington State Univ.*, 164 Wash.App. 1016 (Wash. Ct. App. 2011).

◆   *A federal court rejected a claim that Alabama State University violated the federal Age Discrimination Act by removing him from campus housing.*
       When the student was 41 years old, the university removed him from campus housing for unspecified reasons. He sued the university in a federal district court for violating the Age Discrimination Act, a federal law that bars discrimination on the basis of age in programs and activities that receive any form of federal financial assistance. **The court dismissed the case for failing to comply with an Age Discrimination Act requirement that he first file an administrative complaint.** An Age Discrimination Act provision requires claimants to provide written notice to the Secretary of Health and Human Services, the Attorney General of the United States and the person against whom the action is directed before filing suit. As the student admitted that he did not file an administrative complaint, the court granted the university's motion to dismiss the case. *McGhee v. Alabama State Univ.*, No. 2:09-cv-0092-MEF, 2009 WL 1684604 (M.D. Ala. 6/12/09).

◆   *A 31-year-old Louisiana student raised a discrimination claim against a university after he was excluded from the varsity football team.*
       According to the student, the head football coach would not let him try out for the team because he was too old. In response, he sued university officials in a federal district court for age discrimination. Following negotiations, the university signed a commitment to resolve the action. After six years, the student refiled the case, which later reached the Fifth Circuit Court of Appeals. It explained that two requirements had to be met in an age discrimination case. First, **the student had to exhaust his administrative remedies.** Second, he needed to provide written notice of his intention to sue to the Secretary of Health and Human Services, the United States Attorney General and the defendant. **Since the student was unable to show he met these requirements, the case had been properly dismissed.** *Parker v. Board of Supervisors Univ. of Louisiana-Lafayette*, 296 Fed.Appx. 414 (5th Cir. 2008).

◆   *The claim that a California college librarian subjected a student to harassing and discriminatory conduct was ordered to proceed.*
       A Merritt College student claimed a college librarian harassed her at least five times. She said the librarian falsely accused her of using a library computer for personal use. After complaining to the dean of the library and other college employees, the student sued the college in a federal district court for violating

the state's Fair Employment and Housing Act (FEHA). She added federal age and race discrimination claims against the college and librarian under 42 U.S.C. § 1981, along with state law claims of intentional infliction of emotional distress, breach of contract and negligent misrepresentation. The court first dismissed the FEHA claim against the college, as the statute covers only discrimination in employment. The Section 1981 claims were also dismissed, because they were based on age discrimination, which Section 1981 does not address. However, **the court refused to dismiss the Section 1981 claim of race discrimination against the librarian in her individual capacity**. The court dismissed the remaining state law claims so the student could re-file them in a state court. *Santos v. Merritt College*, No. C-07-5227 EMC, 2008 WL 131696 (N.D. Cal. 1/11/08).

◆   *The U.S. Court of Appeals, Second Circuit, held Cornell University had a valid reason to expel a student that was not based on her age or gender.*

The female student attended Cornell's veterinary program. She twice failed required exams, and the university expelled her. The student sued the university in a federal district court, alleging discrimination based on her gender and because of her age in violation of the Age Discrimination Act. The court held the student did not prove the motivation to expel her was based on gender or age discrimination and dismissed the claims. The student appealed to the Second Circuit. The court found she had failed to exhaust her administrative remedies before she filed suit. **The court agreed with the district court's finding that the student failed to prove the university had expelled male students who twice failed required exams. It affirmed the judgment.** *Curto v. Edmundson*, 392 F.3d 502 (2d Cir. 2004).

CHAPTER THREE

Athletics and Student Activities

I. ATHLETIC PROGRAMS

A. Eligibility of Participants

There is no recognized constitutional right to participate in interscholastic athletics or other extracurricular activities. The possibility of obtaining a college athletic scholarship is also not protected. The National Collegiate Athletic Association (NCAA) has broad powers to enforce its rules.

◆ *A Michigan student-athlete was unable to pursue due process claims against a university based on the loss of eligibility for four football games.*

The student's father, who served as varsity football coach at the university, arranged for a below-market-rate lease on an apartment located near campus and also paid for the rental. In a separate action, the university accused the coach of violating NCAA rules. But a jury held for the father/coach, and the case against him was dismissed. Meanwhile, university officials informed the student that he had violated NCAA rules by obtaining the below-market rental rate. Although the university informed him he was ineligible to play football, the NCAA reinstated his eligibility and he transferred. In a federal district court action against the university, the student asserted due process violations.

The court considered the university's dismissal motion and noted that the student had missed four games and less than one month of the season. His scholarship status was not affected, nor was he deprived of a right to continue his education. There was no merit to the student's claim to a due process "right" to play football. **The Sixth Circuit does not recognize a constitutionally protected property interest in athletic participation.** While the student

93

asserted a liberty interest in his good name and reputation, he lost this claim by failing to ask the university for a name-clearing hearing. Moreover, university officials were entitled to qualified immunity. As a result, the court dismissed the student's case. *Awrey v. Gilbertson*, 833 F.Supp.2d 738 (E.D. Mich. 2011).

A separate action filed by the student's father against university officials, is summarized in Chapter Five, Section IV.B. of this volume. *Awrey v. Gilbertson*, No. 10-14242-BC, 2011 WL 2312175 (E.D. Mich. 6/9/11).

◆ *A federal court rejected a student-athlete's request for reinstatement of his admission to a Connecticut university after he was arrested on felony charges.*

As a Florida high school senior, the student was arrested and charged with aggravated stalking of a minor. At the time, he had accepted a partial lacrosse scholarship from Quinnipiac University in Connecticut. He said the arrest was based on a "horseplay" incident in which he "fake raped" a younger male. But the high school suspended him, and he did not graduate with his class. After receiving a diploma through an online program, the student pleaded guilty to misdemeanor battery. He was sentenced to probation, community service and counseling, and was also required to report to a probation officer in person.

Florida officials granted him a temporary travel permit, and he enrolled at Quinnipiac. But the Florida Department of Corrections (DOC) sent Quinnipiac a letter saying the student was a "sexual predator or sexual offender." Quinnipiac rescinded his admission pending an investigation. The DOC sent another letter explaining that the first letter had been sent in error, and the student sued Quinnipiac in a federal court for breach of contract. The court denied his request for a preliminary order requiring his reinstatement, finding claims that he would otherwise fall behind his peers and lose his lacrosse scholarship purely speculative. Inability to play lacrosse during the current semester resulted from the student's own actions. He was still unable to travel with the team in several states. As the student could reapply to the university for the next semester and might miss just one semester, the court denied the request for an injunction. It held **Quinnipiac made a reasonable decision to rescind his admission pending an investigation.** *Stockstill v. Quinnipiac Univ.*, No. 3:10-cv-265 (VLB), 2010 WL 2011152 (D. Conn. 5/19/10).

◆ *No contract was breached when a Duke University golf coach dismissed a student from the golf team and revoked his access to university golf facilities.*

According to the student, Duke University head golf coach Rod Myers promised him lifetime access to Duke's state-of-the-art training facilities when he recruited him as a high school golfer. While the student accepted an offer to attend Duke and play on the golf team, he was not awarded a scholarship. After Myers died, his successor dismissed the student from the team and revoked his access to Duke's golf facilities. The student sued the successor coach and Duke in a federal district court for breach of contract and related claims. A federal magistrate judge rejected the contract claim, explaining that **student policy manuals are not binding contracts**. The manuals upon which the student relied to support his breach of contract claim could be unilaterally altered at any time. The magistrate judge rejected a claim that the university and the coach breached a covenant of good faith and fair dealing. **Without a contract, a** covenant of good faith and fair dealing does not exist, and the student could not claim tortious interference with any contract. *Giuliani v. Duke Univ.*, No. 1:08CV502, 2009 WL 1408869 (M.D.N.C. 5/19/09).

◆ *A soccer player who was subject to an athletic conference transfer rule failed to demonstrate that the rule violated federal antitrust laws.*

After the player learned that other University of Southern California (USC) student-athletes received fraudulent academic credits, she transferred to the University of California, Los Angeles (UCLA). Both USC and UCLA were members of the Pacific 10 Athletic Association (PAC 10). USC opposed the transfer and sought sanctions against the player under a PAC 10 transfer rule, which would bar her from competing for UCLA during her first year there. In a federal district court, the player sued USC, USC officials and the PAC 10, asserting that USC enforced PAC 10 sanctions against her, but not others. She alleged retaliation and claimed the transfer rule conflicted with the Sherman Act, which prohibits contracts or conspiracies that restrain trade or commerce.

After the court dismissed the case, the player appealed to the U.S. Court of Appeals, Ninth Circuit. It held her antitrust claim required proof that the transfer rule produced significant anticompetitive effects in relevant geographic and product markets. The player claimed the relevant geographic market in this case was the Los Angeles area, and the relevant product market was the UCLA women's soccer program. The Ninth Circuit rejected this interpretation, noting that the player was recruited by similar soccer programs outside the area. In any event, the claim failed because the PAC 10 transfer rule only applied to member schools. **As the player admitted she was the only USC athlete to suffer sanctions under the transfer rule, she conceded that the rule did not affect all relevant consumers, foiling her antitrust claim.** *Tanaka v. Univ. of Southern California*, 252 F.3d 1059 (9th Cir. 2001).

◆ *In the following case, the California Supreme Court held student-athletes have lower privacy expectations than the general student population.*

In 1986, the NCAA instituted a drug testing program for six categories of banned drugs including steroids and street drugs. In order to participate, all students had to sign a consent form at the start of each school year allowing the drug tests. Two Stanford athletes instituted an action in a California trial court, alleging that the drug testing program violated their right to privacy. The case reached the Supreme Court of California, which held that student-athletes have lower expectations of privacy than the general student population. Competitive events involved close regulation and scrutiny of student-athletes. **Required physical examinations (including urinalysis) and the special regulation of sleep habits, diet, fitness and other activities that intrude significantly on privacy interests are routine aspects of a college athlete's life not shared by other students or the population at large.** Further, the court noted that drug testing programs involving student-athletes have routinely survived Fourth Amendment privacy challenges. The court held the NCAA had an interest in protecting the health and safety of student-athletes involved in NCAA-regulated competition. *Hill v. NCAA*, 26 Cal.Rptr.2d 834 (Cal. 1994).

◆ *A drug testing program was struck down where it was not voluntary, and where the college athletes did not have a diminished expectation of privacy.*

The Supreme Court of Colorado held the university did not articulate an important governmental interest for the program. **Unlike cases involving high school athletes, college students did not have a diminished expectation of privacy under the Fourth Amendment that justified government searches in the absence of an important governmental interest.** Random, suspicionless urinalysis was unconstitutional. Student-athletes did not consent to participation in the program because there could be no voluntary consent where the failure to consent resulted in denial of a governmental benefit. As the program did not ensure confidentiality and was mandatory, the court held for the athletes. *Univ. of Colorado v. Derdeyn*, 863 P.2d 929 (Colo. 1993).

B. NCAA Rules

The National Collegiate Athletic Association (NCAA) is a voluntary, nonprofit association which regulates college athletics, defines eligibility for players and imposes sanctions for violating its rules. NCAA rules limit student eligibility for interscholastic competition to a five-year period and prevent athletic participation for one year after a transfer between member institutions. The NCAA's core course requirement excludes from consideration for initial eligibility all courses taught below regular high school instructional levels.

◆ *Two student-athletes, who lost their scholarships to play football at NCAA Division I institutions due to career-ending injuries, made an unsuccessful challenge to two NCAA rules. One rule prohibited multiyear scholarships, and the other capped the number of scholarships available to a member institution.*

Two NCAA Division I football players suffered career-ending injuries while they were in college. Their injuries prevented them from playing football, and their institutions refused to renew their scholarships. The students claimed NCAA rules prevented them from obtaining scholarships that would have covered the full costs of their college education. One of the rules limited the number of scholarships available to a team. The other rule concerned the NCAA's prohibition on multi-year scholarships.

In an Indiana federal court, the students asserted the NCAA regulations had an anti-competitive effect on the market for student-athletes that violated the Sherman Antitrust Act. The court dismissed the case, and the players appealed to the U.S. Court of Appeals, Seventh Circuit. It held the proposed "market" between universities and student-athletes for bachelor's degrees was not legally recognized. Moreover, **the students did not identify a labor market for collegiate student-athletes**. Since the lower court did not abuse its discretion in dismissing the case, the court affirmed the judgment for the NCAA. *Agnew v. NCAA*, 683 F.3d 328 (7th Cir. 2012).

In February 2012, the NCAA announced a majority of NCAA institutions had voted to allow Division I schools the option of offering multi-year scholarships. The rule change did not affect the students in the *Agnew v. NCAA* case, summarized above.

◆ *The U.S. Supreme Court has held that the NCAA is not a recipient of federal funds and is therefore not subject to suit under Title IX.*

The case was filed by a college graduate who had played two years of intercollegiate volleyball at a private college before enrolling in postgraduate programs at two other colleges. Because she had exhausted only two years of her athletic eligibility, she sought a waiver from the NCAA's Postbaccalaureate Bylaw, which allows postgraduate student-athletes to compete in intercollegiate sports only at the institution where they received an undergraduate degree. The student sued the NCAA in a Pennsylvania federal court after it denied her requests for a waiver. She claimed that the NCAA discriminated against her on the basis of gender in violation of Title IX. The complaint asserted that the NCAA granted more waivers to male postgraduate students than it did to females. The case reached the U.S. Supreme Court, which noted that Title IX covers entities that receive federal financial assistance – whether direct or indirect – whereas those entities that only benefit economically from federal financial assistance are not covered. **Because the NCAA only benefited economically from institutions that received federal financial assistance, it could not be sued under Title IX.** *NCAA v. Smith*, 525 U.S. 459, 119 S.Ct. 924, 142 L.Ed.2d 929 (1999).

◆ *An assistant football coach who was forced to give up his job due to rules violations was unable to advance various claims against the NCAA.*

Officials at the University of Kentucky (UK) confronted the coach with evidence of NCAA rules violations. He agreed to step down and later claimed that he did so based on assurances that no further action would be taken against him. However, UK conducted an internal investigation and turned over its findings to the NCAA. In turn, the NCAA held a hearing to consider charges of improper recruiting practices, such as improperly inducing prospective athletes and high school coaches, and fraudulently assisting student-athletes in the form of preparation of their work. The NCAA sanctioned UK for the rules violations. It also imposed an eight-year restriction on the coach and any NCAA member seeking to hire him for an athletic-related position. He sued the NCAA, UK and the Southeastern Conference in a federal district court.

The court dismissed the action, and the coach appealed. The U.S. Court of Appeals, Sixth Circuit, held his antitrust claim was properly dismissed. Since the coach did not advance a commercial claim, he failed to allege an antitrust injury. **NCAA rules were not commercial and were designed to promote and ensure competitiveness among its members.** The coach admitted his own misconduct had caused any injury he suffered, defeating his fraud claim. A breach of contract claim was disallowed as against public policy. The court noted that if not for the coach's own misconduct, he would still have his job, and affirmed the judgment. *Bassett v. NCAA*, 528 F.3d 426 (6th Cir. 2008).

◆ *A federal district court denied a Kansas student-athlete's request for an order to prevent the enforcement of an NCAA athletic eligibility rule.*

The student transferred to the University of Kansas (KU) in 2004 after beginning college at another school. He eventually made the KU football team. The NCAA denied a request for a waiver of the NCAA's five-year eligibility rule. After an unsuccessful appeal, the student sued KU and the NCAA in a federal district court for civil rights violations. He petitioned a court for an order preventing the university from enforcing the NCAA's eligibility ruling.

The court found the five-year eligibility period begins to run when a student-athlete initially registers and attends the first day of classes in a regular term of an academic year for a full-time program of studies. The NCAA may waive the eligibility rule for reasons beyond the control of the student or institution which deprive the student of the opportunity to participate for more than one season within the five-year period. **An NCAA member school may grant a one-year extension of the five-year period for a female student-athlete for reasons of pregnancy.** The student contended that he missed the chance to participate in football when his girlfriend became pregnant some time before he enrolled at KU. He said he decided not to attend college so he could work and care for his daughter. The court rejected the student's gender discrimination claim. It also found no merit to his claim that he would be unable to complete his education and lose any chance to be recruited by a professional football team. The student's financial aid package was not an athletic grant, and the threat of losing a professional career was speculative. The court denied the student's request for relief, finding it was in the public interest to allow the NCAA to enforce its own rules without court intervention. *Butler v. NCAA*, Civ. Act. No. 06-2319 KHV, 2006 WL 2398683 (D. Kan. 8/15/06).

◆ *A federal court held a student's religious courses and computer classes were not "core courses" under the NCAA academic eligibility requirements.*

The NCAA sets eligibility requirements for Division I competition, which mandate that students take at least 13 high school "core courses" and that students achieve a specified minimum grade point average in those courses as well as a specified minimum score on either the SAT or ACT. The higher a student's test score, the lower the required GPA needed. An 18-year-old black student, who excelled at basketball, graduated from a private, Catholic high school. He was heavily recruited by colleges and universities, and selected a private Illinois university. The NCAA ruled the student was not qualified to compete in Division I play during his freshman season, and he sued the NCAA.

A federal district court held the high school religion courses **were taught from a particular religious point of view – based on a Christian ideology**. The court also determined that, based on the syllabi **for the computer classes, at least 50% of the course instruction included keyboarding or word processing**, which took the classes outside core status. As a result, the student did not have even a negligible chance of success on the merits of his claim, and he was not entitled to injunctive relief. The court refused to overrule the NCAA's eligibility determination, and the student was not allowed to play basketball as a freshman. *Hall v. NCAA*, 985 F.Supp. 782 (N.D. Ill. 1997).

◆ *A wrestler who transferred from a Rhode Island university had to sit out for one year because he was not in good academic standing.*

The student, a talented wrestler, failed a course during his first semester at Nebraska and did not repeat the course before transferring to Brown. The NCAA notified him he would be prohibited from wrestling the next academic year because he had not successfully repeated the course. The student sued the NCAA in a federal district court, seeking an injunction to restrain the NCAA from preventing him from wrestling. The court denied the injunction. **NCAA regulations prevent athletic participation for one year after transfer.** There is an exception to this rule for students in good academic standing who would have been eligible to participate had they remained at their previous institution. As the student had failed the course, he would have been ineligible at both Nebraska and Brown. He could not bring constitutional claims against the NCAA, as it is private entity. *Collier v. NCAA*, 783 F.Supp. 1576 (D.R.I. 1992).

C. Students with Disabilities

In PGA Tour v. Martin, *532 U.S. 661 (U.S. 2001), the U.S. Supreme Court recited a general rule that the Americans with Disabilities Act (ADA) requires an individualized inquiry to determine whether a requested modification is reasonable and necessary for a disabled individual, and whether the modification would fundamentally alter the nature of the competition.*

◆ *A deceased student-athlete's claims against several colleges that stopped recruiting him survived his death.*

The student had learning disabilities but was recruited for football by several NCAA Division I schools. The NCAA ruled that a number of his high school special education classes did not satisfy its core course requirement and declared him ineligible during his freshman season. He filed a federal district court action against the NCAA, the ACT/Clearinghouse and several universities. After the student died, his estate continued the litigation. After years of court activity, the student's mother revealed that he had been in and out of drug treatment and mental health programs and that his death resulted from an apparent drug overdose. The court sanctioned the mother and her attorneys, finding that the failure to disclose this information was willful and in bad faith.

On appeal, the U.S. Court of Appeals, Third Circuit, held the alleged discrimination took place during the 1995-96 school year, when the student was declared ineligible by the NCAA. Evidence of substance abuse in 1995-96 was minimal and was irrelevant for liability purposes. **A determination of whether a person is a "qualified individual with a disability" under the ADA is made "from the time at which the alleged discriminatory decision was made."** The district court's contrary ruling was reversed. The mother could not use posthumously revealed information to her own advantage, but an order sanctioning the mother's attorneys for failing to disclose the student's full medical history was reversed. The case was returned to the district court for a determination of whether the NCAA and universities had violated the ADA and Rehabilitation Act. *Bowers v. NCAA*, 475 F.3d 524 (3d Cir. 2007).

◆ *The University of North Carolina at Greensboro did not violate federal disability laws when it dismissed a disabled student from its golf team.*

The student earned a partial golf scholarship and was the fourth best player on the team in his freshman year. The next year, the student's father informed the golf coach of his diagnosis with Obsessive-Compulsive Disorder, and explained that the condition caused him to repeat ritualistic behaviors and have negative thoughts. The coach suggested that the student red-shirt for the season and he agreed to allow him to attend therapy sessions that sometimes conflicted with team practices. The student began having attendance problems and did not play in any more tournaments. The coach did not excuse the absences as a disability-related accommodation because the student did not register with the university office of disability services. At the end of the season, the coach removed him from the team for misconduct and rules violations. As a result, the student lost his scholarship. He transferred to another college where he played on the golf team, and sued the university in federal court for violating the Americans with Disabilities Act and Section 504 of the Rehabilitation Act.

The court granted the university's motion for pre-trial judgment, because the student failed to show he had a "disability" within the meaning of the Rehabilitation Act. **Although he had a mental impairment, he did not show it substantially limited his ability to perform any major life activity.** He was typically on time for appointments, completed course work and was able to follow school rules. The student's condition had improved significantly as a result of therapy and medication. The coach's red-shirt offer did not prove he regarded the student as disabled. University officials met to discuss his condition and consulted with its counseling and testing center. This conduct did not prove a perception of disability. *Costello v. Univ. of North Carolina at Greensboro*, No. 1:03CV01050, 2006 WL 3694579 (M.D.N.C. 12/14/06).

◆ *A college football player with a disability could be prohibited from continuing to play.*

A University of Kansas physician discovered that a student had a congenital condition that put him at an extremely high risk for suffering severe and potentially permanent injuries, including quadriplegia. The university disqualified the student from participating in intercollegiate football. Although the student obtained opinions from three other doctors stating that his risk of injury was no greater than any other player's, the university denied his request to rejoin the football team. He filed a lawsuit against the university in a federal court, claiming it had violated Section 504 of the Rehabilitation Act.

The court denied the university's motion to dismiss the lawsuit, and the student sought an order to require his reinstatement to the football team. Because Section 504's definition of a person with a disability involves a consideration of whether the individual is impaired in some major life activity, the court considered whether intercollegiate athletic participation was a major life activity. **The court agreed that playing football was related to the major life activity of learning, but it held that his disqualification did not substantially limit his ability to learn.** The university had not revoked the student's athletic scholarship, and he retained the opportunity to participate in the football program in a role other than player. The court accepted the conclusion of the university's physicians that there was a reasonable basis for his exclusion from the team. The court denied the student's motion. *Pahulu v. Univ. of Kansas*, 897 F.Supp. 1387 (D. Kan. 1995).

D. Discrimination and Harassment

1. Gender Equity in Athletics

Title IX of the Education Amendments of 1972 (20 U.S.C. § 1681, et seq.*) prohibits sex discrimination in education programs, including interscholastic, intercollegiate, club and intramural athletics. It applies only to programs that receive federal financial assistance. One of the most important Title IX implementing regulations is 34 C.F.R. § 106.41(c). It states that*:

A [federal funding] recipient which operates or sponsors interscholastic, intercollegiate, club or intramural athletics shall provide equal athletic opportunity for members of both sexes. In determining whether equal opportunities are available the Director will consider, among other factors:

(1) Whether the selection of sports and levels of competition effectively accommodate the interests and abilities of members of both sexes; (2) The provision of equipment and supplies; (3) Scheduling of games and practice time; (4) Travel and per diem allowance; (5) Opportunity to receive coaching and academic tutoring; (6) Assignment and compensation of coaches and tutors; (7) Provision of locker rooms, practice and competitive facilities; (8) Provision of medical and training facilities and services; (9) Provision of housing and dining facilities and services; (10) Publicity.

Unequal aggregate expenditures for members of each sex or unequal expenditures for male and female teams if a recipient operates or sponsors separate teams will not constitute noncompliance with this section, but the Assistant Secretary [for Civil Rights of the U.S. Department of Education] may consider the failure to provide necessary funds for teams for one sex in assessing equality of opportunity for members of each sex.

A "three-part test" approved by the Office for Civil Rights (OCR) affords educational institutions three ways to demonstrate Title IX compliance. Compliance with Title IX may be shown by demonstrating: (1) **substantial proportionality** (the number of men and women in intercollegiate athletics is proportionate to their enrollment at the institution); or (2) **the institution has a "history and continuing practice of program expansion" for the underrepresented sex. If a university cannot satisfy the first two options, a third method allows it to show it "fully and effectively accommodates" the interests of women.** See 44 Fed.Reg. 71,413 (1979).

◆   *A federal court held cheerleading is not a sport, so Quinnipiac University could not count cheerleaders toward the total it needed to establish it provided female students equitable opportunities to participate in varsity athletics.*

Quinnipiac University eliminated varsity women's volleyball, men's golf, and men's track and field teams. At the same time, it announced a new women's cheerleading squad. Women's volleyball players and their coach sued the university, claiming the changes would violate Title IX. After a hearing, the district court issued a preliminary injunction that stopped the university from cutting women's volleyball. **It found Quinnipiac had artificially increased women's team rosters and decreased men's rosters to make it look like it was complying with Title IX.** After a trial, the court found Quinnipiac violated

Title IX. Appeal reached the U.S. Court of Appeals, Second Circuit. First, the court agreed with the district court's decision to exclude cheerleaders from the total number of student-athletes for Title IX compliance purposes.

Neither the NCAA nor the federal Department of Education has recognized cheerleading as a varsity sport. Cheerleaders did not have team locker rooms, and Quinnipiac did not hold off-campus recruiting for the team. There was no uniform set of rules for cheerleading competitions. Finally, a 3.62% disparity between female athletic participation and the percentage of females in the entire student body was not too small to show females were denied equitable opportunities to participate in varsity athletics. *Biediger v. Quinnipiac Univ.*, 691 F.3d 85 (2d Cir. 2012).

◆ *An Indiana university tennis coach may proceed with her claim that she was fired while another coach was only reprimanded for similar misconduct.*

Over an 18-year period, the coach often complained about lack of equity in the school's athletic programs. Her contract was renewed via a letter describing her performance as "exemplary." The coach then told her associate athletic director she might have violated NCAA rules. When he asked for her practice log, she texted three student-athletes, asking them to misrepresent when the practices were held. Later, the coach sent players another text asking them to run a practice. When the university learned of the texts, it released her from employment. In a federal court, the coach sued the university for violating Title IX and her First and Fourteenth Amendment rights. In the court's view, the coach produced enough evidence to avoid pretrial judgment on her Title IX claim. **She showed another coach had violated the same NCAA rule and was reprimanded but not discharged.** The court also refused to dismiss the First Amendment claim. There was no Fourteenth Amendment due process violation because the coach received a hearing. Her defamation claims failed because of a state immunity law. *Bull v. Board of Trustees of Ball State Univ.*, No. 1:10-cv-00878-JMS-TAB, 2012 WL 1564061 (S.D. Ind. 5/2/12).

◆ *A federal district court approved a settlement between women's softball players and a West Virginia university to resolve a Title IX dispute.*

The softball players claimed the university did not provide the women's softball team with facilities and equipment equal to those provided to the men's baseball team. To resolve a complaint filed with the U.S. Department of Education's Office for Civil Rights, the parties entered into an agreement. But the players later claimed the university failed to implement the promised changes. They sued the university in a federal district court, which directed the parties into mediation. After the parties reached an agreement, they submitted it to the court for approval. In the court's view, the agreement offered a long-term solution to the dispute by specifying the renovation of the university's on-campus sports facility so that softball could be played there. In the meantime, the softball team could use a high school facility near the university. **Finding the proposed agreement was "fair, adequate and reasonable," the court approved it.** *Harrison v. Board of Governors of West Virginia Univ.*, No. 2:08-cv-00078, 2011 WL 3269636 (S.D. W.Va. 7/29/11).

◆ *The U.S. Court of Appeals, Fourth Circuit, held a Virginia university did not violate Title IX or other laws when it cut a number of athletic programs.*

To remedy a 10% disparity between its undergraduate student population against its population of varsity athletes, James Madison University planned to cut seven men's teams and three women's teams. Opponents of the cuts, including athletes, coaches, alumni and fans, formed an organization to oppose the action. The group sued the U.S. Department of Education (DOE) and others, claiming DOE guidelines violated Title IX, the Constitution and the Administrative Procedure Act (APA). When the university rejected the group's request to hold off on the cuts, the group added claims against it and university officials. After a federal district court dismissed the lawsuit, appeal reached the Fourth Circuit. It upheld the three-part federal test for Title IX compliance first published in 1979 (above). **According to the court, Title IX permitted consideration of proportionality between participation and enrollment.** It found nothing in the test mandated statistical balancing. Instead, it creates a presumption that compliance is achieved when statistical balance is reached.

The court held that eliminating gender bias in collegiate athletics served an important government objective. It did not violate the Constitution to consider gender when decreasing athletic offerings to create a better balance. Neither the initial policy interpretation nor subsequent clarifications were subject to APA notice and comment requirements, as they were interpretive guidelines that did not create new law. For the same reason, the test did not require presidential approval. State law claims against the university were barred by the Eleventh Amendment, and an equal protection claim failed because the group did not show it was subject to disparate treatment or discrimination. Rejecting the group's additional arguments, the court upheld the judgment and found the university was motivated by the desire to achieve proportionality. *Equity in Athletics, Inc. v. Dep't of Educ.*, 639 F.3d 91 (4th Cir. 2011).

◆ *Central Michigan University (CMU) was entitled to immunity for a breach-of-contract claim by a student who lost her athletic scholarship.*

CMU offered a student an athletic scholarship to play basketball. She declined other scholarship offers and enrolled at CMU. She later claimed CMU's first-year coach harassed her, said she was not her "type" of person and repeatedly tried to force her to transfer. After missing some practices, the coach told her she was dismissing her from the team and that she would lose her scholarship. The student sued CMU, the coach and other CMU officials in a federal district court for breach of contract and violation of her due process and equal protection rights. She added claims of defamation, interference with contract, intentional infliction of emotional distress, negligent hiring and negligent supervision. **The court dismissed the breach of contract claims against CMU and individual officials on the basis of sovereign immunity.** However, the court granted the student an opportunity to further develop her negligent hiring and supervision claims, explaining that she could not win on these claims unless she showed the athletic director's conduct was gross negligence. This claim was not dismissed at this stage of the case. The court further directed the parties to file supplemental briefs regarding the student's defamation claims. *Heike v. Guevera*, 654 F.Supp.2d 658 (E.D. Mich. 2009).

A year later, the student and a teammate filed a second action in the same court, alleging violations of Title VI of the 1964 Civil Rights Act, the Equal Protection Clause of the Fourteenth Amendment and other laws. They claimed the CMU defendants discriminated against them based on their races (Caucasian/Native American and Caucasian) and their sexual preference by not renewing their scholarships. The court agreed with the university that **nothing had prevented the women from bringing these claims in the first case.** Since the dismissal of the first lawsuit constituted a final decision on the merits of a dispute involving the same parties, and both cases were based on the same facts, the second action had to be dismissed. *Heike v. Cent. Michigan Univ. Board of Trustees*, No. 10-11373-BC, 2011 WL 2602004 (E.D. Mich. 7/1/11).

◆ *A federal district court agreed to let female student-athletes at Delaware State University proceed with their Title IX case as a class action.*

Delaware State University (DSU) decided to eliminate its women's equestrian team at the end of the 2009-10 academic year. In response, 15 of the team's 21 members filed a lawsuit against the university, accusing it of violating Title IX by failing to provide female student-athletes with equal opportunities to participate in varsity intercollegiate athletics. Team members sought court orders that would block DSU from eliminating the team. DSU agreed not to eliminate the team until the end of the 2010-11 year. A new group of eight student-athletes sought permission to have the case proceed as a class action. **Applying the test used by federal courts for class certification, the court held the team members could adequately represent a class of persons with an interest in the lawsuit.** They could represent other student-athletes regarding whether DSU was meeting its Title IX obligations. If it was held that DSU was out of compliance with Title IX, the class could represent others regarding whether proposed corrective actions would bring DSU into compliance. As a result, the motion for class certification was granted. *Foltz v. Delaware State Univ.*, 269 F.R.D. 419 (D. Del. 2010).

◆ *Female wrestlers at the University of California, Davis (UCD) were not required to give the university prior notice before filing a Title IX lawsuit.*

UCD effectively ended female wrestling participation by requiring females to beat male wrestlers in their weight classes under men's rules. Three female wrestlers sued UCD and several university officials in a federal district court for Title IX and equal protection violations. The court held their equal protection claims were subsumed by Title IX. It then held the students failed to give UCD notice and a chance to cure any Title IX deficiencies before they filed suit.

On review, the U.S. Court of Appeals, Ninth Circuit held the Title IX notice requirement was based on a misapplication of *Gebser v. Lago Independent School Dist.*, 534 U.S. 274 (1998), Chapter Two, Section II. B.1. *Gebser's* **notice requirement applied only when an alleged Title IX violation was based on an institution's deliberate indifference.** No notice requirement applied to Title IX claims based on an affirmative institutional decision, such as cases alleging inequality of athletic opportunity. The court rejected UCD's argument that it was entitled to judgment because it was in compliance with Title IX. Nor did UCD prove a continuing practice of program expansion. Finally, the court held that the students' equal protection claims should proceed. In *Fitzgerald v. Barnstable School Committee*, 555 U.S. 246 (2009), the Supreme Court held Title IX does not bar parallel and concurrent equal protection claims. As a result, the judgment was reversed, and the case was returned to the district court. *Mansourian v. Regents of the Univ. of California*, 602 F.3d 957 (9th Cir. 2010).

2. Sexual Harassment

As explained in Chapter Two, Title IX of the 1972 Education Amendments prohibits all federal funding recipients from denying program participation or benefits based on gender. The courts have interpreted Title IX as barring sexual harassment, and most student harassment claims arise under Title IX.

◆ *A federal court held a student did not produce enough evidence to pursue Title IX and other claims against the University of South Carolina.*

After accepting a soccer scholarship, the student complained that the university's husband-wife varsity coaches improperly touched her and suggested she was having a lesbian relationship with a teammate. When the coaches told the student her scholarship would end, she transferred to a different college. In her lawsuit against the university, a federal court held the university had Eleventh Amendment immunity from her federal and negligence claims. Next, **the court found that the university was not liable under Title IX, as it had no notice of harassment at any relevant time**. After learning of the student's claims, the university did not act with deliberate indifference. Nor was there sufficient evidence of harassment severe enough to support a Title IX claim. As for the student's tort claims, the court held the student could not show infliction of emotional distress. It held the conduct of the coaches was not "so extreme and outrageous as to exceed all possible bounds of decency." As a result, the university was granted pretrial judgment. *DeCecco v. Univ. of South Carolina*, No. 3:11-cv-2300-CMC, 2013 WL 168221 (D.S.C. 1/16/13).

◆ *A federal court rejected Title IX claims by a California student who said she was sexually assaulted by three members of the men's basketball team.*

The student said the team members sexually assaulted her in an on-campus apartment. She did not immediately report the incident, and her friends relayed her story to an assistant coach of the women's team. Within a day, the information was provided to the university athletic director and a vice president of student affairs. Two days after the friends' report, the university issued a campus-wide safety alert and forwarded the charge to local police. University officials also offered the student counseling and a victim advocacy program.

The student sued the university in a federal court for violating Title IX. The court rejected a claim that the university failed to investigate a prior assault involving the same men. There was evidence that the university investigated the incident promptly, provided counseling services, encouraged the student to file criminal charges and punished the men. The court rejected a claim that the university retaliated against the student for reporting the incident by temporarily barring social interaction between the men's and women's teams. On appeal, the U.S. Court of Appeals, Ninth Circuit, held the student did not show university officials acted with "deliberate indifference" or that their response was "clearly unreasonable in light of the known circumstances." Officials had no knowledge that any of the individuals who assaulted the student were involved in the prior attack. The court rejected the claim that the university acted unreasonably by declining to expel the assailants. **The student was not entitled to the precise remedy she preferred.** As the steps taken by the university in response to the assault were not clearly unreasonable, her Title IX claim failed. Nothing suggested the university acted with a retaliatory motive, defeating the retaliation claim. As a result, the judgment was affirmed. *Doe v. Univ. of the Pacific*, 467 Fed.Appx. 685 (9th Cir. 2012).

◆   *A federal district court in Massachusetts declined to dismiss most of the sexual harassment claims filed against a college by a student.*

The student joined the college's all-female equestrian team, which was coached by a 67-year-old male who the student soon accused of frequent and ongoing sexual harassment. A sexual harassment complaint was filed against the coach by another student, and the college issued him a "final warning." But the student said she then accepted offers to sleep at his house because she was having problems with a roommate. She said the coach touched her and forced her to stay in his hotel room on an overnight team trip. The student withdrew from college and sued both the college and coach in a federal district court for violations of Title IX and state law. She added claims against the coach for assault and battery and false imprisonment, and negligence and breach of contract claims against the college. **The court held the college could be held liable under Title IX if it had knowledge of a risk of abuse to students based on prior complaints about the coach.** There was evidence of a valid complaint against him, and this was held sufficient to support a Title IX claim.

The court refused to dismiss state-law sexual harassment claims, but dismissed the assault and battery claims. It held such acts went far beyond the scope of the coach's employment. False imprisonment claims based on the charge that he trapped the student in his home and hotel room were allowed to go forward because it was conceivable that he was acting in the interest of the college when he did so. The court refused to dismiss the negligent retention and supervision claims, noting the college had been put on notice of the coach's sexual misconduct, yet failed to limit or even monitor his activities. Finally, the court granted dismissal of the breach of contract claim. *Bloomer v. Becker College*, No. 09-11342-FDS, 2010 WL 3221969 (D. Mass. 8/13/10).

◆   *An Alabama community college was not liable for the rape of a student-athlete by one of her basketball coaches.*

In her state court lawsuit, the student claimed the community college hired her assailant to act as an assistant, even though he had been jailed "relating to the death of a child." A teammate claimed he touched her inappropriately on two occasions. The player stated she initially viewed the assistant as a father figure and spent time at his home. He also gave her rides. But the assistant later raped the student in a motel room after an away basketball game. She sued the college in a state court for violating Title IX and other federal laws. The court held for the college and officials, and the student appealed to the state supreme court. The court rejected claims that the college did not properly investigate the touching incidents or the inappropriate relationship between the student and assistant. Evidence showed the touching incident was promptly investigated. **While the head basketball coach's failure to strictly follow investigation procedures might have been negligent, it did not prove deliberate indifference.** The court also rejected the student's argument that the head coach should have seen the assistant was sexually harassing her and should have unilaterally initiated procedures under the college's sexual harassment policy. This argument failed because she admitted she did not consider her relationship with him to be sexual. The judgment against the student was affirmed. *J.B. v. Lawson State Community College*, 29 So.3d 164 (Ala. 2009).

◆   *The Supreme Court recognized a retaliation claim under Title IX, finding coaches are often in the best position to vindicate the rights of student-athletes.*

An Alabama high school teacher discovered the girls' basketball team did not receive the same funding or access to equipment and facilities as did boys' teams. He began complaining to supervisors, but said the school district did not respond. The teacher said he was given negative evaluations and was removed as girls' coach. He sued the school board in a federal court, claiming the loss of his coaching contract constituted unlawful retaliation in violation of Title IX.

Appeal reached the U.S. Supreme Court, which held Title IX covers retaliation against a person for complaining about sex discrimination. "Retaliation is, by definition an intentional act," and it is a form of discrimination, since the person who complains is treated differently than others. A program that retaliates against a person based on a sex discrimination complaint intentionally discriminates in violation of Title IX. Without finding that actual discrimination had occurred, the Court held the teacher was entitled to bring his case before the district court and attempt to show the board was liable. A private right of action for retaliation was within the statute's prohibition of intentional sex discrimination. Title IX did not require the victim of retaliation to also be the victim of discrimination. **The text of Title IX gave the board sufficient notice that it could not retaliate against the teacher after he complained of discrimination.** The Court found a reasonable school board would realize it could not cover up violations of Title IX by retaliating against teachers. It returned the case to the district court, where the teacher would be allowed to try to prove retaliation by the school board. *Jackson v. Birmingham Board of Educ.*, 544 U.S. 167, 125 S.Ct. 1497, 161 L.Ed.2d 361 (2005).

◆   *A federal appeals court reinstated claims that the University of Colorado (CU) violated Title IX by encouraging student-athletes to commit rape.*

Two female students claimed that a football player and a female tutor for the athletic department planned a football recruiting event to provide recruits an opportunity to have sex with intoxicated female students. They further claimed recruits and players sexually assaulted them, and they sued CU for violating Title IX. The students contended the university had control over recruits and players, but failed to control or eliminate the risk. The court held the university could not be deliberately indifferent to acts it knew nothing about. The students could not prove CU was liable without showing it had actual knowledge and was deliberately indifferent to the misconduct.

On appeal, the U.S. Court of Appeals, Tenth Circuit, explained that CU could not be liable under Title IX unless it showed the assaults resulted from its deliberate indifference. **Deliberate indifference could be established by proving a failure to train regarding obvious risks.** In this case, there was evidence that CU and its head football coach were deliberately indifferent to the need to provide training and undermined efforts to prevent harassment. Evidence showed that player-hosts received little or no direction regarding proper behavior or level of responsibility. In addition, the coach prevented a female player from remaining on the team after she complained of harassment, and hired an assistant coach who had been accused of assaulting a woman. As a jury could find the coach knew of a serious risk of sexual harassment, the judgment was reversed. *Simpson v. Univ. of Colorado*, 500 F.3d 1170 (10th Cir. 2007). CU reportedly agreed to pay one of the students $2.5 million to settle the case. A settlement called for a payment of $385,000 to the other student.

◆   *The University of Washington (UW) may have inadequately responded to a sexual assault allegation against a key player for the UW football team.*

A female student claimed the player forced his way into her dorm room and raped her shortly after she broke off their relationship. The student made no report until months later. A UW associate athletic director (AAD) learned of the assault and suggested that the student leave her position as an assistant equipment manager. He also warned her that team members would probably harass her if they learned of her report. The student refused to give up her job, and UW officials including a Title IX compliance officer decided to conduct mediation. After the player denied the allegation, the AAD refused to suspend him. A UW ombudsman asked the student if she was "making everything up" and had her sign a form saying she considered the matter closed. The student suffered from anxiety and depression, and she underwent counseling. She then sued UW in a state court for Title IX violations. After the court ruled for UW, the Court of Appeals of Washington reversed the judgment, finding a jury should consider the evidence. UW officials had knowledge of the incident, and **UW could be held liable if it responded to the student's reports in a way that was "clearly unreasonable in light of all the known circumstances."** *S.S. v. Alexander*, 143 Wash.App. 75, 177 P.3d 724 (Wash. Ct. App. 2008).

◆   *The informal atmosphere of collegiate athletics includes profanity, slang, and sarcasm that does not always create a hostile educational environment.*

A University of North Carolina women's varsity soccer team member claimed a coach asked players about their sexual activities, commented about their legs and breasts and called one player a "slut." The coach met with the student in his hotel room and asked her about her social life and who she was sleeping with. She told him it was not his business, and he soon kicked her off the team. After the university investigated the student's complaint, the coach apologized to her and promised to refrain from further discussing sexual matters with players. However, the student sued the university in a federal district court, alleging he had created a hostile sexual environment. The court held for the university. A three-judge panel of the U.S. Court of Appeals, Fourth Circuit, found no jury could find the coach's remarks created a hostile environment. *Jennings v. Univ. of North Carolina*, 444 F.3d 255 (4th Cir. 2006).

All the judges of the Fourth Circuit agreed to reconsider the appeal, and decided the student had stated a valid discrimination claim under Title IX based on a hostile environment. She made a sufficient showing that she was subjected to severe or pervasive sexual harassment. **The evidence indicated the coach's comments were not "of a joking and teasing nature," but were degrading and humiliating.** The student also showed the coach's conduct negatively affected her ability to participate in soccer. The fact that she was disappointed at being cut did not defeat her Title IX claim. There was enough evidence to show the university had actual notice of a hostile environment. *Jennings v. Univ. of North Carolina*, 482 F.3d 686 (4th Cir. 2007).

3. Race Discrimination

Higher education institutions may be subject to liability for intentional discrimination based on race, color or national origin under Title VI of the Civil Rights Act of 1964, and the Equal Protection Clause. Some claims have also been filed against universities under 42 U.S.C. Section 1981, which prohibits race discrimination in the making and enforcement of contracts.

In Cureton v. NCAA, *198 F.3d 107 (3d Cir. 1999), the U.S. Court of Appeals, Third Circuit, held the National Collegiate Athletic Association (NCAA) was not subject to a Title VI claim. It held the NCAA was not a direct recipient of federal funds and did not exert sufficient authority over its member institutions to make it liable for Title VI violations.*

◆ *A Delaware court dismissed a white student's discrimination claims but held she had a viable claim for retaliation for reporting alleged racism.*

After accepting a volleyball scholarship from the university, the student had a dispute with her African-American roommate. The students accused each other of racism. Although the white student was told she would have to move to another dormitory, her mother objected, and the African-American student had to move instead. According to the student, the African-American volleyball coach then stopped talking to her and kept her out of games. He later told her that her scholarship was being cut for budgetary reasons. The student failed a drug test and then left the university. In a federal court, she sued the university for race discrimination and retaliation. It held **the student could not show officials treated her differently from African-Americans or that she was deprived of access to educational benefits in a significant way.** In the court's opinion, there was no evidence that race was a factor in the challenged actions. But the student's mother had complained that the coach was a racist. It appeared to the court that the coach had denounced the student to the team and "went to considerable lengths to make Elliott's life as a volleyball player miserable." Since there was evidence of retaliation, the court refused to dismiss the claim. *Elliott v. Delaware State Univ.*, 879 F.Supp.2d 438 (D. Del. 2012).

◆ *An NCAA eligibility rule survived a challenge by California student-athletes who claimed the rule unfairly excluded financially disadvantaged minority students from obtaining Division I athletic scholarships.*

NCAA Division I Bylaw 14.5.4.2 disqualified student-athletes from athletic scholarships and sports participation if they transferred from two-year colleges to four-year Division I colleges under certain circumstances. A group of seven students sued the NCAA and the University of California system's president in a federal court, claiming the bylaw violated their right to equal protection. In reviewing the case, the court found that the NCAA classifies college applicants as "qualifiers" or "non-qualifiers" – meaning they do or do not qualify for athletic scholarships or participation under NCAA rules.

Nonqualifiers from four-year and two-year institutions alike were eligible to compete and receive athletic scholarships after a transfer to a Division I institution if they completed one year in residence, earned a minimum number of credits, and attained a minimum GPA. Eligibility requirements were stricter for non-qualifiers transferring from a two-year school to a Division I school. After August 2009, the NCAA required students transferring under these circumstances to pass the equivalent of one math class and two English classes. According to the student-athletes, the bylaw put an unfair barrier between them and a Division I athletic scholarship. But the court held **the rule supported the legitimate purpose of assuring nonqualifiers had the academic tools to succeed at a Division I institution**. The rule's different transfer requirements were rationally related to that purpose. As hardship alone did not state an equal protection claim, the court dismissed the case. *Davis v. National Collegiate Athletic Ass'n*, No. C 11-01207 WHA, 2011 WL 2531394 (N.D. Cal. 6/24/11).

◆ *Three African-American student-athletes were allowed to pursue a federal race discrimination case against a California community college.*

The student-athletes claimed an assistant football coach unfairly criticized them and verbally abused them. They also said the head coach favored less-skilled white players over African-American players and gave the white players more playing time. According to the student-athletes, the athletic director was told about the assistant coach's racially hostile conduct but did not take steps to stop it. They claimed they were cut from the team to make room for less skilled white players. In a federal court lawsuit, the student-athletes claimed they were subjected to a racially hostile educational environment in violation of Title VI of the Civil Rights Act of 1964. They also claimed racial discrimination under Title VI, violation of 42 U.S.C. § 1981 and violation of 42 U.S.C. § 1983. Although the community college sought dismissal, the court declined to do so. **The charges relating to a hostile environment were sufficient to show an environment that interfered with the education of the student-athletes.** They adequately alleged race discrimination as well as a contractual violation in being cut from the team. The Section 1983 claim survived because the complaint alleged sufficiently that the college violated equal protection by treating African-American student-athletes differently than white student-athletes. *Boyd v. Feather River Community College Dist.*, No. 2:11-CV-0231 JAM-EFB, 2011 WL 5024547 (E.D. Cal. 10/20/11).

◆ *An Ohio university did not violate the rights of a coaching applicant by declining to hire him until after an offer to another candidate fell through.*

Another candidate was chosen for the coaching job, but he did not respond to a request for a preemployment criminal background check. The college then rescinded its offer to him and extended an offer to the coach. Although he began coaching and returned for a second season, the coach sued the college and various officials because he was not the college's first choice for the job. He claimed unlawful discrimination under Title VI, discrimination and retaliation under 42 U.S.C. § 1981, and a claim of retaliation for exercising his speech rights. The court explained that to prevail on a Title VI claim, the coach had to show he was engaged in protected activity that was known to the college, and that materially adverse action was taken against him based on the protected activity. **The court held the Title VI claim failed because the coach did not show the college took "materially adverse action" against him.** Rejecting all the other claims, the court adopted the report and recommendation of the magistrate judge and held for the college. *Moberly v. Univ. of Cincinnati Clermont College*, No. C-1-08-569, 2010 WL 3489003 (S.D. Ohio 8/31/10).

◆ *Former University of Arkansas basketball coach Nolan Richardson was unable to prove his discharge was based on race.*

Richardson became Arkansas' first African-American head coach in 1985, and his team won the NCAA men's basketball championship in 1994. In 2000, a sportswriter wrote an article in which he said Richardson had called Arkansas fans "redneck SOBs." Fans complained about the comment. A former board member contacted the athletic director (AD) and told him Richardson should be fired for the statement. Shortly after that, the AD allegedly asked the columnist if he would write a column equating Richardson's comment with a white person calling the coach a "nigger." The columnist said he wanted to avoid controversy and later told Richardson about the conversation. After losing a game against Kentucky in 2002, Richardson said "if they go ahead and pay me my money, they can take the job tomorrow." The university chancellor felt the statement was damaging to basketball recruiting and recommended firing Richardson. When he refused to retire, the university discharged him.

Richardson sued the university in a federal court for violating Title VII. The court found he failed to prove the university fired him because of his race, and he appealed to the U.S. Court of Appeals, Eighth Circuit. The court held he would have to show a specific link between the alleged discrimination and the decision to discharge him. The court held that when the university discharged Richardson – two years after his remark to the columnist – Richardson and the AD had already made amends and Richardson had signed a new contract. **This evidence severed any possible link between the remark and the discharge.** *Richardson v. Sugg*, 448 F.3d 1046 (8th Cir. 2006).

◆ *Two African-American student-athletes could pursue their race discrimination lawsuit against the NCAA under Proposition 16.*

The NCAA used Proposition 16 to determine which first-year college students could play Division I and II sports. The rule used a combination of high school grades in NCAA-approved "core courses" and scores on such standardized tests as the SAT and the ACT to determine eligibility. Two African-American students who signed national letters of intent to play sports at Division I schools failed to meet the NCAA's test score requirements. They were not allowed to play intercollegiate athletics their freshman year.

The students sued the NCAA in a federal district court, alleging the NCAA intentionally discriminated against them on the basis of race in violation of Title VI of the Civil Rights Act of 1964 and 42 U.S.C. § 1981, and violated the Americans with Disabilities Act (ADA) and Section 504 regarding one of the athletes. One athlete proved causation by claiming the design of Proposition 16 discriminated against her because of a disability. But the claims failed because an NCAA rule change allows student-athletes who do not qualify for their initial year of eligibility to recoup that lost year with good grades. As a result, the athlete was not denied a year of eligibility by failing to meet the qualifying requirements, and lacked standing to bring ADA and Section 504 claims. The court dismissed the race discrimination claims, but on appeal, the Third Circuit held **the students sufficiently alleged race discrimination** to survive pretrial dismissal. Their claim that the NCAA considered race when it adopted Proposition 16 could proceed. However, the Title VI, ADA, and Section 504 claims were properly dismissed. *Pryor v. NCAA*, 288 F.3d 548 (3d Cir. 2002).

E. Injuries

Collegiate athletes assume the risks inherent in sports competition. The Supreme Judicial Court of Massachusetts explained that to hold a university liable for injuries to a student-athlete during a competitive athletic event, there must be a showing of willful, wanton or reckless conduct by participants. In Gauvin v. Clark, 404 Mass. 450, 537 N.E.2d 94 (Mass. 1989), the court said players engaging in sports agree to undergo some physical contacts which could amount to assault and battery without their consent. For that reason, college hockey participants only had a duty to refrain from reckless misconduct. This standard applies to non-contact sports, but may not apply to cheerleading injuries.

◆   *The New York Court of Appeals held a college baseball pitcher assumed the risk of being hit by a line drive when he participated in an indoor practice.*

Coaches told the pitcher he would pitch from an artificial mound inside a nylon cage. He observed other pitchers throwing to batters inside the cage without an L-screen, which protects pitchers from balls batted back at them. After about six pitches, the pitcher was hit in the jaw by a batted ball. He sued the university and a coach in the state court system. After a trial court held for the university, the case reached the state's highest court. It explained that a legal doctrine called **assumption of the risk bars recovery for injuries to participants in sporting and amusement activities, if the participant is aware of the risks, appreciates their nature, and voluntarily assumes them**.

An educational institution can be liable for injuries to a student-athlete if it does not take reasonable care to protect him from risks that are "unassumed, concealed, or enhanced." In this case, the student was aware of the risk of getting hurt playing baseball. He had played for more than 13 years in varying conditions. He knew it was dangerous to pitch without an L-screen and had observed the conditions before the incident. Since the university met its duty to make conditions as safe as they appeared to be, the court held for the university. *Bukowski v. Clarkson Univ.*, 19 N.Y.3d 353, 971 N.E.2d 849 (N.Y. 2012).

◆ *A Florida court reinstated a negligence claim filed by an injured wrestler against the president of a university wrestling club.*

The student was hurt while participating in a wrestling club practice at Florida Atlantic University (FAU). After the accident, he sued FAU and the president of the wrestling club. The student said the president did not inspect wrestling equipment, failed to correct a dangerous condition in the gym where the accident happened, and did not adequately fasten wrestling mats together. Applying Florida law, **a state trial court held the claim against the president was barred because he was acting as an agent of FAU at the time of the accident**. On appeal, a state district court of appeal found genuine issues of fact relating to whether the president was acting as FAU's agent at the time of the accident. As a result, the court of appeal held the trial court should not have granted pretrial judgment against the student on his negligence claim. The trial court judgment was reversed, and the case was returned to that court for further proceedings. *Florida Atlantic Univ. Board of Trustees v. Lindsey*, 50 So.3d 1205 (Fla. Dist. Ct. App. 2010).

◆ *A spectator assumed the risk of injury at a Syracuse University hockey game and could not recover damages from the university for his injuries.*

Near the end of the game, the spectator was in an area of the rink where the players would exit the ice. Some players stopped to talk to him, and one of them got into a fight with another fan. The spectator tried to pull them apart, but fell over a barricade and broke his ankle. He later sued both universities and the individuals involved in the fight in a New York supreme court. He claimed Syracuse failed to provide enough supervision at the game. The court found the spectator had voluntarily involved himself in the fight. In so doing, he assumed the risk of getting hurt. He appealed to a state appellate court. It held the university owed spectators a duty of reasonable care to maintain safety. **There was no duty to protect spectators from unexpected and unforeseeable assaults.** There had never been a fight between a spectator and a hockey player at the facility before, and the fight was not preceded by escalating hostilities. The confrontation was not reasonably foreseeable, and it was quickly stopped by university staff. As the university acted reasonably, the judgment was affirmed. The court held **the spectator could not recover damages from them because he assumed the risk of injury by intervening**. Under a rule called the "danger invites rescue" doctrine, a person is not barred from recovery for attempting a rescue based on a reasonable belief that the party in need of rescue was about to suffer a serious injury. A jury would have to decide whether the spectator acted reasonably and could rely on the "danger invites rescue" doctrine. *O'Connor v. Syracuse Univ.*, 66 A.D.3d 1187, 887 N.Y.S.2d 353 (N.Y. App. Div. 2009).

The Court of Appeals of New York denied a motion for appeal. *O'Connor v. Syracuse Univ.*, 14 N.Y.3d 766, 898 N.Y.S.2d 92 (N.Y. 2010).

◆   *New Hampshire parents may proceed with an action against Dartmouth College for the wrongful death of a student who was injured in a ski class.*

The student took an introductory ski class at a college-owned and operated facility. Instructors knew she was inexperienced, but told her to ski down a trail alone while they accompanied other students. She followed their directions but veered off course and hit a tree, fracturing her skull. The student became paraplegic and later died. Her parents sued the college in a federal district court for negligence and wrongful death. Dartmouth filed a motion to dismiss the case, relying on the state's "Ski Statute," which barred claims for injuries occurring due to risks inherent in skiing. The court found the negligence **claim was essentially one for "negligent instruction." There was no reason to categorize negligent instruction as an inherent risk of skiing.** New Hampshire's highest court had held in an earlier case that the Ski Statute did not bar a claim of negligent instruction. As a result, the statute's provisions regarding inherent risks did not bar the action. The court also rejected Dartmouth's argument that the action was time-barred. *Porter v. Dartmouth College*, Civil No. 07-cv-28-PB, 2007 WL 3124623 (D.N.H. 10/24/07).

Over two years after the case was filed, attorneys realized the parents had never sought appointment as their child's administrators. Dartmouth filed a motion to dismiss the case. Two weeks later, the parents obtained letters of administration from a state probate court. The federal district court allowed them to proceed despite their delay in securing the letters of administration. The parents had cured their mistake, and the college was not harmed by the delay. *Porter v. Dartmouth College*, 678 F.Supp.2d 15 (D.N.H. 2010).

◆   *A New York Appellate Division court preserved negligence claims raised by a student who injured her back while swimming for a university team.*

The student said her injury was caused by the training methods used by her coach, and that he continued to use the same methods even after she complained of back pain. She sued the university and the coach in a state court for negligent hiring and supervision. The university and coach argued that the student was an experienced swimmer who assumed the risk of hurting her back. The court denied them pretrial judgment, and appeal went to the state appellate division. On appeal, the appellate court held the lower court should have awarded pretrial judgment to the university on the negligent hiring and supervision claims. It explained that **when an injured plaintiff seeks to recover damages based on actions taken by an employee within the scope of employment, the doctrines of negligent hiring and negligent supervision do not apply**. However, the court upheld the ruling in favor of the student on her claim that the coach negligently continued to employ particular training methods even after she complained of back pain. A question of fact was also present as to whether she had assumed the risk of injury. *Segal v. St. John's Univ.*, 69 A.D.3d 702, 893 N.Y.S.2d 221 (N.Y. App. Div. 2010).

◆   *A New York court allowed a student-athlete to proceed with a claim that Iona College failed to keep MRSA bacteria out of its athletic facilities.*

The student-athlete claimed he contracted an MRSA infection at Iona's athletic facilities. He filed a state court action against Iona asserting the college had a duty to keep its facilities free of MRSA bacteria and to routinely screen for the presence of MRSA bacteria. The student asserted Iona had a duty to provide medical care and to instruct him regarding precautionary measures to help him avoid infection, and that the college had actual or constructive notice of MRSA bacteria in its facilities but negligently failed to remove it.

After the court dismissed the claims, the student appealed to the New York Supreme Court, Appellate Division. **The court held the trial court properly dismissed the claim that Iona had a duty to maintain MRSA-free facilities.** Such an obligation exceeded any recognized duty under law. However, the court held the lower court should not have dismissed the claim that Iona knew that its athletic facilities were not MRSA-free but failed to properly address the situation. The claim could proceed in further court activity. *Zaffarese v. Iona College*, 879 N.Y.S.2d 348 (N.Y. App. Div. 2009).

◆   *An Ohio cheerleading coach was not liable for catastrophic injuries to a cheerleader who fell while participating in a human pyramid maneuver.*

Not all the cheerleaders had performed the maneuver on the day of the fall and some had never seen it. A substitute spotter failed to catch the cheerleader, and she fell to the ground from about 15 feet. She suffered catastrophic injuries, including paraplegia. In a state court lawsuit against the university, the cheerleader claimed her injuries were caused by her coach's negligence. The case reached the Court of Appeals of Ohio, which held **an injury from a fall was an inherent risk of cheerleading and that the cheerleader voluntarily assumed that risk**. The risk of injury could be managed but not eliminated. Further, the court found the coach did not act intentionally or recklessly in causing the student's injuries. *Crace v. Kent State Univ.*, 185 Ohio App.3d 534, 924 N.E.3d 906 (Ohio Ct. App. 2009).

◆   *A Georgia court held an insurer was required to provide a defense to an athletic association sued by a college athlete for failing to provide disability insurance.*

An assistant athletic director (AAD) at the University of Georgia coordinated a disability insurance program for student-athletes. He obtained a coverage quote for a student from an insurance broker, but he failed to send the broker a coverage request form with the student's signature. The student was seriously hurt while playing for the football team and became disabled for life from playing any contact sports. The insurer refused to backdate coverage, and the student was denied $500,000 that would have been payable under the policy. He sued the university athletic association and AAD in a state court for breach of fiduciary duties, breach of contract, and negligence. The association notified its liability carrier of the lawsuit and asked for defense and indemnity.

The carrier refused to provide a defense, claiming that two policy exceptions relieved it of any duty to defend the action. The association then sued the carrier in the state court system. The court ruled for the association, and the carrier appealed. The Court of Appeals of Georgia affirmed the determination that the policy required the carrier to provide a defense to the suit. Moreover, **the connection between the student's injury and his claims was too attenuated to apply a bodily injury exclusion**. The conduct of the insured parties was not causally related to the injury, and the conduct that gave rise to the student's claims occurred before he was injured. Therefore, the exception did not apply. The court affirmed the judgment for the university association, noting a question remained as to whether the carrier was required to cover the loss. *Fireman's Fund Insurance Co. v. Univ. of Georgia Athletic Ass'n*, 288 Ga.App. 355, 654 S.E.2d 207 (Ga. Ct. App. 2007).

◆   *Texas law barred a spectator's lawsuit against a state university based on his fall from bleachers at a baseball game.*

The spectator fell about six feet to the ground from the top row of the bleachers. In his state court lawsuit against the host institution, he claimed the seat backing gave way as a result of metal fatigue. State law immunized governmental entities from liability for injuries resulting from the recreational use of their premises, unless the injury resulted from gross negligence or from willful or wanton conduct. The court denied the university's motion for dismissal, and an appeal followed. The Court of Appeals of Texas stated that under the state recreational use statute, the university could not be held liable unless it was grossly negligent or acted willfully or wantonly. The statute applied to "recreational activity," which included any activity associated with enjoying the outdoors. This **broad language justified the conclusion that the statute applied to the conduct of sitting on bleachers and watching a game**. Because the recreational use statute applied, and the spectator did not allege or prove gross negligence, willful conduct or wanton conduct by the university, the court dismissed the action. *Sam Houston State Univ. v. Anderson*, No. 10-07-00403-CV, 2008 WL 4901233 (Tex. Ct. App. 11/12/08).

◆   *The Supreme Court of California held a community college was not liable for injuries to a student who was hit by a pitch during a baseball game.*

During a preseason road game against another community college, the host team's pitcher hit the student in the head with a pitch, cracking his batting helmet. The student said he was intentionally hit in retaliation for an earlier pitch thrown by a pitcher for his team that hit an opposing batter. The student staggered, felt dizzy, and was in pain, but his manager and first base coach told him to stay in the game. He was later told to sit on the bench, but his injuries were not immediately treated. The student sued the host community college in a state superior court. The case was dismissed, but the Court of Appeal of California reversed the judgment, finding the college owed the student a duty of supervision. The Supreme Court of California agreed to review the case.

The court held the college players were co-participants, and its coaches and managers had supervisory authority over the game. **Co-participants had a duty not to act recklessly, outside the bounds of the sport. Coaches and instructors had a duty not to increase the risks inherent in sports participation.** Colleges derive economic and marketing benefits from a major sports program. These benefits justified finding that a host school owed a duty to home and visiting players to not increase the risk inherent in the sport. The court found the host college did not fail in its duty to supervise and control the pitcher. **Being hit by a pitch was an inherent risk of baseball. The failure to provide umpires did not increase the inherent risk.** The host college had no duty to provide medical care, as the student did not submit evidence of injury.

Colleges are not vicariously liable for the actions of their student-athletes during competition. The court reversed the judgment. *Avila v. Citrus Community College Dist.*, 38 Cal.4th 148, 131 P.3d 383 (Cal. 2006).

◆   *A Connecticut student-athlete's signed waiver of liability did not protect a university from liability for negligence.*

The student was a pitcher on the university baseball team. During a batting practice he was behind an L-screen, which is a safety device placed in front of pitchers. The screen has an opening so the pitcher can throw the ball to the batter. A batter hit a ball that struck the student on the head. He sued the university in a state court for negligence. The student claimed the screen was defective, damaged, worn and improperly repaired. The university contended the student had voluntarily and knowingly signed a waiver releasing it from liability caused by or arising out of his athletic participation.

The court found the university's release form did not expressly refer to negligence. In *Wagenblast v. Odessa School Dist.*, 110 Wash.2d 845, 758 P.2d 968 (Wash. 1988) – a case involving minors – the court found **"exculpatory releases from any future university district negligence are invalid because they violate university policy."** The superior court found that waiver agreements that do not explicitly refer to negligent conduct should not bar negligence claims by students – adults or minors – who engage in sports activities that present a risk of injury. The court denied the university's motion for dismissal on the student's negligence claim against the university. *Zides v. Quinnipiac Univ.*, 40 Conn.L.Rptr. 745 (Conn. Super. Ct. 2006).

◆   *A Massachusetts cheerleader was allowed to proceed with a negligence action against her university after being severely injured at practice.*

The cheerleader fell during a maneuver that required two cheerleaders to stand on the shoulders of two others, who launched her about 10 feet up to the shoulders of cheerleaders on the upper tier. Although she was experienced, the cheerleader had never tried this maneuver before. The coach talked her through the exercise and placed spotters at the front and sides of the pyramid – but none in the rear. He spent about five minutes instructing the spotters. The squad attempted the stunt when the coach was not there. The cheerleader fell from the top of the pyramid, suffering serious neck fractures that caused her to become disabled. She sued the university in a Massachusetts superior court, alleging negligence by the coach. The university argued it could not be held liable for negligence under *Gauvin v. Clark*, 404 Mass. 450, 537 N.E.2d 94 (Mass. 1989), unless there was evidence of willful or reckless conduct. **The court disagreed and held the university owed the student a duty to exercise reasonable care.** The failure to do so in this case caused her injuries. *Torres v. Univ. of Massachusetts*, 20 Mass.L.Rptr. 310 (Mass. Super. 2005).

◆   *A federal district court held a Vermont student waived any claims against his school for injuries suffered during an intercollegiate hockey game.*

The student signed a "Student Athlete Agreement to Participate in Intercollegiate Sports" before his first season on the team. The agreement stated in part: "I understand the dangers and risks of trying out for and playing and practicing in the above sports." It also indicated "I hereby voluntarily assume all risks associated with participation and agree to hold harmless [the university and coaches] . . . except in the event of their gross negligence."

An opposing player checked the student during a game, causing him to fall backward and strike his head on the ice. He continued to play on the team, but two years later, he suffered a concussion. The student was diagnosed with mild but permanent neuropsychological deficits from the checking incident two years earlier. The university required the student to sign an additional release, but he failed to do so. He left the university the next year to play professional hockey. The student sued the university in a federal district court for negligence. The university contended the participation agreement barred the action and that the student assumed the risk of injury. The student argued the "hold harmless" language of the agreement was ambiguous and unenforceable. **The court held the words "hold harmless" did not make the agreement ambiguous. The agreement clearly demonstrated the intent to relieve the university from liability except in cases of gross negligence.** The court granted the university's motion for summary judgment and dismissed the negligence claim. *Sanders v. Univ. of Vermont*, No. 2:00-CV-424 (D. Vt. 2004).

II. STUDENT ACTIVITIES

In Beach v. Univ. of Utah, *726 P.2d 413 (Utah 1986), the Supreme Court of Utah explained that "colleges and universities are educational institutions, not custodial." It held imposing liability on higher educational institutions for injuries arising from illegally drinking alcohol would require them to "baby-sit" each student. Colleges and universities may limit official recognition of particular organizations and impose restrictions on them.*

A. Operation and School Supervision

◆ *Neither a fraternity nor its local chapter could be held liable for negligence in an action by a student who said she was raped at a fraternity party.*

In a federal district court, the student claimed she was raped by a fraternity member. She claimed the fraternity negligently failed to supervise the party. In pretrial activity, the court observed that the fraternity did not own or control the premises where the party took place. Only two of the three tenants that leased the property were associated with the fraternity. There was also a dispute as to whether the student was even invited. Under state law, owners or possessors of premises had no duty to protect visitors from criminal acts of third parties – unless criminal activity was foreseeable. In this case, **the fraternity did not have any knowledge of prior violent crimes or sexual assaults occurring on the premises**. Nothing suggested that the individual who was charged with the rape had any history of violence, aggressive behavior or history of sexual assault. As the fraternity did not have a duty to protect the student and she was a social guest, her negligence claims against the fraternity could not proceed. *Roe v. St. Louis Univ.*, No. 4:08CV1474 HEA, 2012 WL 5377895 (E.D. Mo. 10/31/12).

◆ *Immunity shielded a Kentucky state university from claims that campus police did not respond properly to a student's assault report.*

An African-American student claimed he was assaulted and called racial epithets by fraternity brothers at a fraternity party. He asserted that campus police took no action against the fraternity or its members. Claiming that university-related groups sanctioned the party, the student sued the university and its president in a federal district court. He asserted interference with a right to contract in violation of 42 U.S.C. § 1981, violation of his due process rights, conspiracy to interfere with civil rights, and state-law claims including assault and battery. But the court held **much of the lawsuit was barred by the Eleventh Amendment to the Constitution**. This amendment generally bars suits brought in federal courts against a state, state agencies, and state officials in their official capacities. As Kentucky public universities and directors are protected by Eleventh Amendment immunity, the federal claims could not go forward. Constitutional claims against the president in his individual capacity failed, as no personal involvement was alleged. The state-law claims against the president were equally flawed, and the court dismissed them. *Jackson v. Murray State Univ.*, 834 F.Supp.2d 609 (W.D. Ky. 2011).

◆ *Washington State University (WSU) was allowed to revoke official recognition of a fraternity for five years for drug and alcohol violations.*

WSU said fraternity members used, possessed, manufactured and/or distributed illegal drugs on fraternity property and at a rental house occupied by fraternity members. WSU cited the fraternity for a number of violations, including supplying alcohol to minors at fraternity-sponsored events. A student conduct board held a hearing, where the fraternity's national executive director admitted underage drinking issues. The board found the fraternity responsible for each charge and withdrew official recognition for five years. In a state court action, the fraternity alleged that WSU failed to follow proper procedures and violated the fraternity's constitutional rights to freedom of association.

Appeal reached the Court of Appeals of Washington. It found **the evidence showed illegal activity was "actively condoned" by fraternity officers**. The fraternity's risk manager, live-in advisor and social chair had all bought illegal drugs, and the fraternity failed to take reasonable steps to stop illegal activity. Fraternities at WSU were expected to follow the law and university policies and to respond promptly if officers, members or guests engaged in illegal behavior. As the evidence supported WSU's decision, and the sanction imposed was not arbitrary and capricious, the court affirmed the discipline. *Alpha Kappa Lambda Fraternity v. Washington State Univ.*, 152 Wash.App. 401, 216 P.3d 451 (Wash. Ct. App. 2009).

◆ *A Florida court ordered a university to reinstate a fraternity that was suspended for violating regulations governing alcohol and reckless behavior.*

The evidence of the fraternity misconduct consisted entirely of videotaped interviews and the testimony of two investigating police officers. A Florida District Court of Appeal found all the evidence consisted of inadmissible hearsay. The university's own rules gave the fraternity the right to question adverse witnesses at a hearing, and it was clearly denied this right. **Without the**

improperly admitted evidence, nothing supported the decision to suspend the fraternity. The court reversed the university's decision and ordered it to reinstate the fraternity. *Alpha Eta Chapter of Pi Kappa Alpha Fraternity v. Univ. of Florida*, 982 So.2d 55 (Fla. Dist. Ct. App. 2008).

◆   *A court rejected a fraternity's claim that a New York university violated federal antitrust law by requiring all students to live in university housing.*

Four people died in a car crash on the campus of Colgate University in 2000. One was an underage member of Delta Kappa Epsilon (DKE). Colgate responded by announcing it would require all its students to live in university-owned housing. Colgate took steps to buy and operate all fraternity and sorority housing and residential services on its campus. Many chapters negotiated for purchase prices in excess of their market values. Colgate offered DKE $725,000 for its fraternity house, but DKE chose not to sell. In response, Colgate withdrew its recognition of the local DKE chapter. DKE sued Colgate in a federal district court for violating the federal Sherman Antitrust Act.

The court held that to prevail, DKE needed to show Colgate had engaged in improper conduct that had the effect of controlling prices or excluding competition, resulting in a high degree of market power. The court determined that the relevant market for purposes of an antitrust claim was the student housing market for all selective colleges nationwide. **Once a student decided to enroll at a particular college, the student agreed to submit to college policies to protect the welfare of its students.** In this case, Colgate created a residential policy that was part of the education it provided. The court held that Colgate's residential policy, which required all students to live in housing it owned, was an exercise of its lawful rights. *Delta Kappa Epsilon (DKE) Alumni Corp. v. Colgate Univ.*, 492 F.Supp.2d 106 (N.D.N.Y. 2007).

◆   *Texas A&M University officials could not be held liable for the collapse of a bonfire stack that killed 12 students and injured 27 others.*

After the tragic collapse of a bonfire stack that killed or injured several students, the students' representatives sued the university and its officials for violating student constitutional rights to bodily integrity. The representatives claimed the university encouraged unqualified students to build the bonfire and failed to provide adequate supervision. A federal district court dismissed the claims against university officials, finding them barred by sovereign immunity.

The U.S. Court of Appeals, Fifth Circuit, found the representatives stated a claim under the "state-created danger" theory, and the case was returned to the district court for more proceedings. The district court again held for the officials, this time on the basis of qualified immunity. The representatives filed another appeal to the Fifth Circuit, which found the officials were entitled to immunity as long as their conduct was objectively reasonable in light of clearly established law. Although the state-created danger theory was a valid theory, it was not clearly established as a basis for recovery at the time of the accident. **Since the theory was not clearly established when the bonfire stack collapsed, the university officials were entitled to qualified immunity.** *Breen v. Texas A&M Univ.*, 485 F.3d 325 (5th Cir. 2007).

◆ *A college could use money from a fund-raising campaign to eliminate single-sex fraternities and sororities.*

A New Hampshire college initiated a five-year fund-raising campaign that raised about $568 million from alumni. Several years later, the board of trustees announced that it was going to use some of the money raised to eliminate single-sex fraternities and sororities. A group of alumni who had contributed to the campaign sued the college to prevent it from using the funds for that purpose. They asserted the college had engaged in misrepresentation in violation of the state Consumer Protection Act, and that the board of trustees had withheld information about its intent to eliminate traditional fraternities and sororities. They also alleged that the board was in a fiduciary relationship to the alumni because there were alums on the board. A state court dismissed the case, and the Supreme Court of New Hampshire affirmed the judgment. First, the board of trustees did not owe a fiduciary duty to the alumni despite the existence of alums on the board. Second, **the alumni failed to show that the board engaged in intentional, fraudulent nondisclosure**. And third, since the fund-raising campaign was not commerce (the transactions were in the nature of a gift), there was no violation of the Consumer Protection Act. *Brzica v. Trustees of Dartmouth College*, 791 A.2d 990 (N.H. 2002).

B. Organizational Liability

◆ *A student who said she was hazed by sorority sisters could pursue a claim that a Connecticut university did not respond appropriately to the incident.*

After sorority members required the student and other pledges to maintain certain poses and perform exercises, she reported hazing to the university. Although the sorority members were excluded from campus and told to have no contact with the student, their suspensions were later reduced and they were permitted to return to classes. According to the student, the sorority members continued to intimidate her on Facebook, by phone and in person. She sued the university in a federal court for negligent infliction of emotional distress. In the court's view, **the student produced evidence that the university undertook to protect her from foreseeable attacks through its anti-harassment and anti-hazing policies**. Because she presented evidence sufficient to indicate she met all the elements of her emotional distress claim, the motion for pretrial judgment was denied. It would be up to a jury to decide whether the university was liable. *Vega v. Sacred Heart Univ.*, 871 F.Supp.2d 81 (D. Conn. 2012).

◆ *Nevada's highest court refused to impose liability on a fraternity in a lawsuit filed by a spectator who had part of his nose bitten off during a fight.*

According to the spectator, an alumnus of another college bit off a piece of his nose during a fight in a tailgating area prior to a college football game. The spectator sued the alumnus, local chapters of a fraternity, its national affiliate and several others in a state court. The court held the case could not proceed due to the family's failure to try to ascertain the identities of certain alumni entities. It also held the fraternities were entitled to judgment. On appeal, the Supreme Court of Nevada agreed with the lower court that the spectator did not exercise reasonable diligence in ascertaining the identity of the alumni entities. In addition, the trial court had properly held that neither the national fraternity nor its local chapters were liable for his injuries. **The spectator did not provide any rationale for making the national fraternity responsible for the safety of a tailgate party, even if it was being hosted by one of its local chapters.** There was no special relationship between the national fraternity and the spectator, and the national fraternity did not owe him a duty to protect him from injuries inflicted by a third party. Similarly, the local fraternity chapters were not liable. The alumnus was not a fraternity member and was not under the control of the fraternity. Moreover, the fight began unexpectedly and ended quickly. The lower court judgment was affirmed. *Sparks v. The Alpha Tau Omega Fraternity*, 255 P.3d 238 (Nev. 2011).

◆   *The family of a Louisiana student who killed herself after being raped could proceed with claims that local police and a fraternity caused her death.*

The student was raped by a member of a fraternity at an off-campus residence. Her family claimed the fraternity and a local police officer continually harassed her in an attempt to dissuade her from reporting the rape. The officer, who was a fraternity alumnus, allegedly told the student the authorities would do nothing if she reported the incident. The family said the officer also told her she would be sued for defamation or slander if she insisted on pressing charges. The student then hanged herself. A trial court threw out the family's negligence claims against the officer and police department, but the Court of Appeal of Louisiana reversed the judgment. **Although state law generally immunizes the government from liability for discretionary actions, an exception applies to acts that constitute malicious, intentional or willful misconduct.** If the allegations about the police officer's actions were true, this exception might apply. *Garza v. Delta Tau Delta Fraternity National*, No. 2006 CA 0698, 2007 WL 914875 (La. Ct. App. 3/28/07).

◆   *An Ohio student lacked evidence to show who might have injured her at a campus event, defeating her negligence claim against a fraternity.*

The student rode on a fraternity float in a homecoming parade. Those riding floats tossed candy to parade watchers. People gathered in front of a fraternity house to watch the parade. Intoxicated fraternity members threw candy at people on the floats. The student was struck in the eye and injured by a thrown piece of candy in front of the house. Believing a fraternity member was responsible, she sued the fraternity in a state court for negligence and loss of consortium, seeking $1.5 million. The court held the fraternity owed the student no duty of care, and she did not prove who caused her injury. On appeal, the Court of Appeals of Ohio held that **to prove negligence, the student needed to show that the fraternity's actions directly and proximately caused her injury**. She failed to make this showing, admitting she did not know who threw the candy that hit her. Evidence showed the group in front of the house included non-members of the fraternity who were also throwing candy at floats. As no evidence indicated a fraternity member threw the candy that struck the student, her case failed. *Muir v. Phi Mu Delta*, No. 6-07-09, 2007 WL 2983152 (Ohio Ct. App. 10/15/07).

♦ *The Phi Kappa Tau fraternity chapter at the University of Mississippi was not liable in negligence for a woman's injuries.*

A fraternity brother provided beer to an underage fraternity member at the fraternity house when school was not in session. The woman was riding on the back of a four-wheeler on the grounds of the house. The fraternity member confronted the driver and threw a bottle that struck the woman in the face. She sued the local and national chapters of the fraternity for negligence in a federal court. The court held the fraternity chapters did not owe the woman any legal duty under state law. She appealed to the U.S. Court of Appeals, Fifth Circuit. The court affirmed the judgment. **As unincorporated associations, the chapters were not liable for the wrongful acts of their members unless they "encouraged, promoted, or subsequently ratified them." There was no evidence that the chapters encouraged or ratified the member's behavior.** There was no duty on the part of the national chapter to supervise the local chapter more closely, as no special relationship existed in this case. *Lewis v. Univ. of Southern Mississippi*, 227 Fed.Appx. 340 (5th Cir. 2007).

♦ *A Texas fraternity and its members were not liable to a student for statements resulting in the withdrawal of his pledge invitation.*

A student who had pledged to join the Phi Gamma Delta Fraternity was accused of sexual misconduct. He denied the allegations, claiming they were part of an extortion scheme to gain money. Phi Gamma withdrew its pledge invitation. A year later, the student pledged to join a chapter of the same fraternity at a different Texas university campus. He was denied admittance based on information communicated between fraternity members at different chapters. The student sued the fraternity and various fraternity members in the state court system for damaging his reputation and subjecting him to increased hazing based on the allegations of sexual misconduct. The court held for the fraternities and their members. The student appealed, arguing that Phi Gamma owed him a duty of care because its members made statements in the course and scope of their fraternity membership. The Court of Appeals of Texas found no evidence indicating the fraternity was incorporated in the state.

As an unincorporated entity, the fraternity did not owe the student any duty of care. Moreover, he was unable to show a member's remarks were made in the course of his official duties as a fraternity historian. **There was no evidence that these comments were communicated to other fraternities at the University of Texas.** The court agreed with the trial court that the hazing claim was untimely filed under a two-year state statute of limitation. The judgment was affirmed. *Waddill v. Phi Gamma Delta Fraternity Lambda Tau Chapter, Texas Tech Univ.*, 114 S.W.3d 136 (Tex. Ct. App. 2003).

♦ *A Kansas fraternity pledge could not sue the fraternity or its members when he passed out after drinking too much.*

A student attended a Pledge Dad night at a fraternity at the University of Kansas. While there, he consumed a large amount of alcoholic beverages. At 2:00 a.m., his pledge dad found him passed out in the living room of the fraternity house and took him to a local hospital emergency room, where his blood alcohol level was measured at .294. The student later sued the national fraternity, the local chapter and five individual members for negligence, and the company that owned the property for premises liability. The court ruled in favor of all the defendants, and the state supreme court agreed. The local chapter was not a legal entity and therefore could not be sued. Individual members could not be liable because **they did not breach any duty they owed him; he voluntarily drank alcohol**. As far as the national fraternity was concerned, there was no special relationship between the student and the fraternity so as to give rise to liability. Finally, the company that owned the property could not be held liable for conditions on the premises at a fraternity party. *Prime v. Beta Gamma Chapter of Pi Kappa Alpha*, 47 P.3d 402 (Kan. 2002).

C. Injuries

◆ *A North Carolina university was not liable for injuries suffered by a 21-year-old student at an off-campus party.*

During a confrontation with a fraternity member, the student was pushed down and became permanently paralyzed. Although the fraternity chapter rented the house where the incident took place, it was off campus. In a state court, the student sued the university, fraternity and others, alleging negligence. The court rejected his claims, and the case reached the North Carolina Court of Appeals. It held neither the university nor the fraternity owed the student a duty of care that might create liability. **University regulations regarding fraternities did not create an obligation to keep students safe.** There was no special relationship between the student and the university. He voluntarily attended a party he was not invited to attend. In addition, the university did not know about the party. Finally, the court disagreed with the student's claim that the individual who caused his injuries was acting as an agent of the university or fraternity. *Mynhardt v. Elon Univ.*, 725 S.E.2d 632 (N.C. Ct. App. 2012).

◆ *A Vermont student was not relieved of a university sexual harassment reporting requirement that was mandated by state law.*

The student reported being drugged and raped at a fraternity party. A university advocate understood she was reporting rape, not harassment. Acting on the advocate's advice, the student reported the incident to the University Center for Student Ethics and Standards, and she and a male student soon agreed in writing not to have any contact with each other. At a disciplinary hearing, the university found the student did not prove her rape charge. She sued the university for failing to promptly investigate harassment. A state court held for the university, finding the student should have used the university's harassment policy. The student appealed to the Supreme Court of Vermont, which held state law required institutions to conduct prompt investigations when they received actual notice of conduct that may constitute harassment. **The law specifies that complainants cannot sue before exhausting an available harassment policy.** Rejecting the student's claim that she gave notice of conduct that could be construed as harassment, the court held the university was not required to automatically treat the complaint as one for sexual harassment. *Allen v. Univ. of Vermont*, 973 A.2d 1183 (Vt. 2009).

◆ *A New Jersey court held a university was not liable for the death of a student who died when he fell from his fourth-floor dorm window after a party.*

A county prosecutor investigated and found that the student had leaned out the window and accidentally fallen. The student's family filed a negligence action against the university in a state court, asserting its alcohol policy was not appropriate and was negligently enforced. A jury found the death was caused by negligence, and it assessed damages of $520,000. As the parties were equally negligent, the court entered a judgment against the university in the amount of $260,000. The university appealed to a state appellate court, where it argued any negligence claim was barred by a state charitable immunity act.

Under the act, the university was immune from negligence claims raised by a person injured while benefiting from the university. But no immunity was available if injury resulted from "willful, wanton or grossly negligent" conduct. The court said providing student housing "falls within the broad range of reasonable educational goals" the university sought to achieve. Students living in dormitories received the benefit of the university's educational works. The student's violation of a university alcohol policy did not alter his status as a beneficiary of the university's works while he lived in the dormitory. **As he was a beneficiary of the university's works, the immunity statute was applicable,** and the judgment for the family was reversed. *Orzech v. Fairleigh Dickinson Univ.*, 985 A.2d 189 (N.J. Super. App. Div. 2009).

◆ *A Maine university officer was unable to prove a fraternity intentionally inflicted emotional distress on him by publicizing his past legal troubles.*

As the director of the University of Maine at Orono office of community standards, the officer reviewed student misconduct charges and oversaw the student discipline process. He sometimes adjudicated cases himself. In 2002, the officer investigated misconduct charges against a fraternity. In response to his investigation, a group of current and former fraternity members hired a private investigator to determine whether he might be biased against their fraternity or against fraternities in general. The investigator discovered the officer had been convicted of "driving while ability impaired," and that a former girlfriend had gotten a temporary restraining order against him. The fraternity assembled court documents and newspaper articles relating to these proceedings and sent them to university officials, the board of trustees and two local newspapers. The officer claimed the disclosure caused him emotional distress, and he sued the fraternity in a district court.

The court found that **as a public official, the officer was required to show the memo contained a false statement that was made with actual malice**. As he did not meet this test, the court ruled for the fraternity. On appeal, the U.S. Court of Appeals, First Circuit, affirmed the judgment. It agreed with the lower court that the officer was properly classified as a public official for purposes of his emotional distress claim. He failed to show the fraternity made a false statement of fact. The officer's legal difficulties relating to domestic violence were documented by the restraining order, and he did not show the fraternity made a false statement about him. As a result, the judgment was affirmed. *Fiacco v. Sigma Epsilon Fraternity*, 528 F.3d 94 (1st Cir. 2008).

◆ *A court upheld a $10,000 jury verdict for a bar patron who said a University of Minnesota police officer performed a "knee-drop" on his head.*

The patron got in a fight at a bar near the University of Minnesota campus. After being ejected from the bar, he accused bar security of starting another fight with him in a parking lot. University police arrived and pinned the patron to the ground. He said that while he was down, an officer violently smashed his knee onto his head. Witnesses later confirmed that the officer had used a "knee-drop" maneuver. The patron avoided criminal conviction for disorderly conduct, then filed a civil case in a federal court against the officer for excessive force. A jury awarded the patron $10,000 plus nearly $220,000 in attorneys' fees. The officer appealed to the U.S. Court of Appeals, Eighth Circuit.

The court rejected the officer's claim that the lower court should have allowed evidence of the patron's prior criminal history. The lower court had properly excluded a statement made by the patron's lawyer during the criminal trial. The statement indicated no one had accepted responsibility for the knee-drop maneuver. The lower court did not abuse its discretion when it told the jury that a criminal defendant does not have to call witnesses. It was not obligated to tell the jury that the officer could have been called as a witness. **Even though it dwarfed the $10,000 damage award, the appeals court upheld the award of $219,648.50 attorneys' fees.** Rejecting the officer's other arguments, the court affirmed the judgment for the patron. *Gill v. Maciejewski*, 546 F.3d 577 (8th Cir. 2008).

D. Hazing

◆ *Indiana's highest court decided to consider whether a freshman could sue a college and fraternity for injuries suffered in a hazing incident.*

While the student was pledging a fraternity, fraternity members tried to place him in a shower. When he resisted, one of the members placed him in a chokehold. The student passed out and suffered physical and mental injuries as a result. He filed a state court personal injury action against the fraternity, local fraternity chapter, and the student who placed him in the chokehold. A trial court held for the college and fraternity. It found the student was not the victim of hazing, finding he instigated the events that led to his injury. On appeal, the student argued the college and fraternity had a duty to protect him from injury.

According to the Court of Appeals of Indiana, there was no breach of the applicable standard of care. While landowners must take reasonable precautions to protect visitors from foreseeable criminal attacks, the court found no indication that harm was foreseeable in this case. And though hazing is a crime in Indiana, the court found the incident was not the result of hazing. **Appeal reached the Supreme Court of Indiana, which agreed to transfer the case to its docket.** *Yost v. Wabash College*, 984 N.E.2d 221 (Ind. 2013).

◆ *A Virginia university did not violate the speech or due process rights of a fraternity by suspending a fraternity chapter for disciplinary reasons.*

The Iota Xi Chapter of the Sigma Chi Fraternity was officially recognized at George Mason University. A university student judicial board met and found the chapter responsible for hazing, providing alcohol to minors and sponsoring a party under conditions that led to sexual assault. As a result, the chapter was suspended for 10 years. The university barred chapter members from associating with fraternal organizations recognized by the university, and it withdrew official recognition of the chapter. The chapter and two members sued university officials in a federal district court for constitutional violations.

The court rejected the chapter's claims, finding **the university provided due process before imposing sanctions. The fraternity had notice of the charges and a meaningful opportunity to be heard.** Withdrawal of official recognition did not stop chapter members from associating with one another, defeating their speech rights claim. On appeal, the U.S. Court of Appeals, Fourth Circuit, held the university did not deprive fraternity members of any liberty interest in free association, as it did not bar anyone from joining other fraternities. Nor did the publication of the hearing outcome in a university newspaper deprive the fraternity or its members of any protected property interest. **There is no constitutional right to be free from stigma such as that allegedly created by the article, and the chapter did not identify any injury from the publication.** The court affirmed the decision to reject the speech claims. Even if marching and singing near the library was protected speech, the university had other adequate reasons to impose sanctions. *Iota Xi Chapter of Sigma Chi Fraternity v. Patterson*, 566 F.3d 138 (4th Cir. 2009).

◆ *A federal appeals court held a decision to suspend three Illinois students for hazing a sorority pledge was not based on their African-American race.*

The university suspended the students for beating a pledge repeatedly over a four-day period. The university suspended them under its student conduct code provision on hazing. One student was suspended for two years, and the others were suspended for three years. They sued the university in a federal district court, claiming race discrimination under Title VI of the Civil Rights Act of 1964 and the Equal Protection Clause. They said the university punished them more severely than it would have punished them if they had been white.

The court held for the university, and the students appealed. The U.S. Court of Appeals, Seventh Circuit, found insufficient evidence of race discrimination to pursue the claims. **The university did not distinguish by race when punishing the hazers.** The court rejected the contention that the university systematically punished hazing more harshly when it was carried out by African-Americans. Other examples of student misconduct could not meaningfully be compared to the students' situation. The court rejected the students' due process claims, which were based on the charge that the university's disciplinary procedures were a sham. The claims failed because the students did not adequately allege deprivation of a protected constitutional property right. *Williams v. Wendler*, 530 F.3d 584 (7th Cir. 2008).

◆ *Although a fraternity had a duty to a Pennsylvania student, it did not breach that duty when local chapter members hazed him.*

A University of Pittsburgh student applied to the Beta Epsilon chapter of the Kappa Alpha Psi fraternity after Kappa lifted a restriction on inducting new members that had been imposed when a Kappa pledge died in Missouri. The student attended a fraternity gathering and was paddled more than 200 times by four fraternity brothers. He went to the hospital the next day and remained there for three weeks with renal failure, seizures and hypertension. He sued Kappa, the local chapter, the chapter advisor and a number of others for negligence. A Pennsylvania trial court held for the defendants, and an appellate court largely affirmed. Here, even though Kappa owed a duty of care to the student, the student failed to show that it breached that duty. For example, he failed to show that the two-year moratorium on new members was merely a symbolic gesture and not a sincere attempt to curb hazing. However, **he was allowed to proceed with his lawsuit against the chapter advisor**. The evidence indicated that the chapter advisor failed to discuss hazing with local chapter members and did not advise them to read the executive orders that imposed sanctions for hazing. *Kenner v. Kappa Alpha Psi Fraternity,* 808 A.2d 178 (Pa. Super. Ct. 2002).

◆   *A university that knew about prior instances of hazing had a duty to protect a student from such behavior.*

Members of a Nebraska fraternity kidnapped a pledge, handcuffed him to a radiator and gave him a large quantity of alcohol. After he became ill, he was taken to a third-floor restroom where he was handcuffed to a toilet pipe. The pledge attempted to escape by exiting a restroom window but fell and suffered severe injuries. He sued the university, claiming it negligently failed to enforce prohibitions against hazing, consumption of alcohol, and physical abuse when it should have known the fraternity was in violation of those prohibitions. The court held for the university. On appeal, the Supreme Court of Nebraska held **the university could be liable to the pledge as an invitee on its property**. Because the university knew of two prior instances of hazing at fraternities on campus and was aware of several incidents involving members of the fraternity, the acts were reasonably foreseeable. The university had a duty to protect the pledge. Whether it breached that duty had to be decided at trial. *Knoll v. Board of Regents of the Univ. of Nebraska*, 601 N.W.2d 757 (Neb. 1999).

CHAPTER FOUR

Freedom of Speech and Religion

I. EMPLOYEES

A. Protected Speech

1. Retaliation

To prove a First Amendment retaliation claim, public employees must show their speech resulted in adverse employment action. In any speech rights claim against a public employer, the employee must show (1) the statements at issue were not made pursuant to professional job duties, (2) that the speech involved a matter of public concern, and (3) that the exercise of protected speech outweighed the employer's interest in efficient workplace operations.

◆ *A University of Colorado professor did not show the university violated his speech rights by firing him after he published a controversial essay.*

In the essay, the professor compared those killed in the World Trade Center on 9/11 to a Nazi officer and convicted war criminal. In response to public outcry, the board of regents voted to investigate his work. A formal investigation yielded findings that his work fell below the relevant academic standards of professional integrity, including two acts of plagiarism and an act of falsification. As a result, the university discharged the professor.

In a state court, the professor accused the university and its board of speech rights violations and retaliation for writing his controversial essay. A trial court held for the university on all claims except the retaliatory termination claim, which went to a jury. The jury found for the professor but awarded him only one dollar in damages. On appeal, the Supreme Court of Colorado held the regents were entitled to absolute immunity because their decision was quasi-judicial. It held the professor was not entitled to reinstatement or front pay regarding his retaliatory termination claim. The bad relationship of the parties made reinstatement inappropriate, and front pay was not warranted because the professor made no attempt to mitigate the salary he lost. **The court found it proper to reject the claim that the university investigated his academic record in bad faith**, as this activity was shielded by qualified immunity. *Churchill v. Univ. of Colorado at Boulder*, 285 P.3d 986 (Colo. 2012).

◆ *A North Carolina university teaching assistant professor (TAP) did not show she was denied a tenure-track position based on her political speech.*

After being encouraged by the director of the school's Middle East Studies Program to apply for a tenure-track position, the TAP introduced a film at a university event. As part of her introduction, she told the student audience she was happy to present the film as it "showed support for the airing of Palestinian cultural perspectives, especially those which promote Palestinian liberation." Program officials felt this conveyed support for the Palestinian cause, and the TAP was later removed from a list of applicants for the tenure-track position.

In a state court action against the university's board of governors, the TAP asserted speech rights violations. The court ruled for the university, and appeal reached the Court of Appeals of North Carolina. It explained that **to prevail, the TAP had to show that her comments were "a substantial or motivating factor" in the decision not to hire her for the tenure-track position**. In the court's opinion, the TAP's claim was nothing more than speculation. She did not provide evidence of a causal connection between the comments and the university's hiring decision. In any event, the university showed it would have taken the same action if she did not make the comments at the film festival. As a result, the court affirmed the judgment. *Ginsberg v. Board of Governors of Univ. of North Carolina*, 718 S.E.2d 714 (N.C. Ct. App. 2011).

◆ *A Georgia university defeated an employee's speech rights case by showing she was fired for insubordination and not for retaliatory reasons.*

University officials fired the employee shortly after she yelled at her supervisor. A university committee upheld the discharge, and she sued the university's board of regents in a Georgia trial court under the state whistleblower statute. According to the employee, she was fired in retaliation for reporting the supervisor's wrongdoing, and not for yelling at him. She said that in the two years before her firing, she had spoken out three times to report that he was breaking rules. The court held for the university, and the employee appealed. The state court of appeals held **the whistleblowers' law prohibited public employers from retaliating against employees** for objecting to or refusing to participate in any practice the employee reasonably believed was in violation of a law, rule, or regulation. But the court of appeals found direct evidence that the employee had been discharged for insubordination, not her speech. As the evidence supported the board's valid, nonretaliatory reason for firing her, the court affirmed the judgment. *Caldon v. Board of Regents of Univ. System of Georgia*, 311 Ga.App. 155, 715 S.E.2d 487 (Ga. Ct. App. 2011).

◆ *An Idaho State University (ISU) professor was unable to convince the state's supreme court that officials retaliated against him based on his speech.*

The professor began working for ISU in 1991. He later began to criticize ISU administrators in a newspaper on a range of topics, declaring his dislike for a former university president and administrators. In a paid advertisement, the professor speculated that ISU was conspiring with another institution to move an engineering program and create a medical school. He said that as a result of his criticisms, ISU retaliated against him by not evaluating his job performance for five years, declining to hire him as a department chair and increasing his salary by the lowest possible increments, among other things. In a state court, the professor sued ISU for retaliation, defamation and breach of contract. The case reached the Supreme Court of Idaho, which held the professor's speech was made as a private citizen. **His speech on the issue of creating a medical school at ISU was a matter of public concern.** But the professor's claim that ISU retaliated against him for exercising his speech rights failed because he did not show he suffered any adverse employment action. ISU was not required to conduct evaluations annually, and he never applied for the department chair he claimed to have been wrongfully denied. The contract claim had been correctly rejected, and the professor was liable for attorneys' fees related to the claim. *Sadid v. Idaho State Univ.*, 151 Idaho 932, 265 P.3d 1144 (Idaho 2011).

◆ *The University of Connecticut's decision to take a deanship away from a professor who railed against official policies did not violate his speech rights.*

In his second term as dean of the engineering school, the professor became an outspoken critic of university policies, including the university's plan to establish a campus in Dubai. He opposed plans to close three schools at the university and was charged with verbally attacking a provost. The professor accused the university of mismanaging construction funds, opposed university supported-funding, criticized the university's handling of a federal audit related to billing practices, and complained about support for faculty researchers.

The university president, provost and many faculty members grew unhappy with the professor's leadership, and he was asked to resign. He refused to resign and was removed from the deanship. The professor sued the university, its president and its provost in a federal district court, asserting First Amendment and due process violations. After the court denied a request for pretrial judgment by university officials, the U.S. Court of Appeals, Second Circuit, held the university's interest in efficient administration justified its decision to remove the professor as dean. The deanship of the engineering school was an executive, policymaking position. For this reason, **the university could expect the person who held the position to refrain from voicing opposition to university policies.** As it was entitled to remove the professor for expressing opposition to several university policies, the court reversed the judgment. The court also rejected the due process claim, as the university was not required to provide additional pre-deprivation process under the circumstances. *Faghri v. Univ. of Connecticut*, 621 F.3d 92 (2d Cir. 2010).

◆ *A tenured Mississippi business professor was unable to show he was removed from his teaching duties in retaliation for his behavior.*

According to the dean of the college of business, the professor's behavior created an environment where students and faculty members felt unsafe. In a letter to the university president, the dean described the professor's "negative and disruptive behavior" and charged him with failing to engage in scholarly or professional activities. The president removed the professor from teaching duties but directed him to continue research activities. The professor stopped doing his research and sued the university and several officials in a federal court for speech rights and due process violations. He claimed the discipline came in retaliation for creating a website critical of the university and for filing a complaint with an accrediting agency. The case reached the Fifth Circuit, which held **he could not show retaliation since he did not suffer "adverse employment action."** All the "tangible accoutrements of his position – except his teaching duties – remained stable." *DePree v. Saunders*, 588 F.3d 282 (5th Cir. 2009).

◆ *A Delaware State University professor and department chair was unable to show he was dismissed in retaliation for engaging in protected conduct.*

After discovering a grade irregularity in the transcript of a student-athlete, the university registrar found the professor had changed incomplete and failing grades to passing grades for 48 students. He was not the professor of record for many grades he changed, but he claimed the authority to do so as department chair. The university president instituted dismissal proceedings against the professor, and after a hearing, a disciplinary committee recommended suspending him for misrepresented and unauthorized grade changes. The president pursued dismissal instead of suspension, and university trustees later voted to dismiss the professor. He claimed the action was in retaliation for his opposition to the university's selection of the president and other incidents.

In a civil rights action filed by the professor, a federal district court held for the board of trustees and president. On appeal, the U.S. Court of Appeals, Third Circuit, explained that as a public employee, the professor could only claim First Amendment protection if he was speaking as a citizen on a matter of public concern. However, he was not speaking as a citizen when he rescinded a speaking invitation and when acting as an advisor to student-athletes. Any speech he engaged in during these activities was unprotected because it related to his official duties. In addition, **the professor failed to show the president's decision to pursue his discharge was motivated by his**

speech. And even if the president was aware of these actions, there was evidence that he still would have pursued dismissal of the professor. As a result, the judgment was affirmed. *Gorum v. Sessoms*, 561 F.3d 179 (3d Cir. 2009).

◆ *A New Mexico university may have retaliated against an employee for his comments about financial dealings between the university and a state agency.*

The employee was the program manager of a university subdivision. A state health department employee told him the department would extend a grant to the school, but insisted the bulk of the funds flow through a nonprofit organization headed by a recent department retiree and the girlfriend of the program manager's supervisor. The manager suspected the employee was trying to avoid a state procurement law requiring a competitive bidding process. He declined the grant offer. The supervisor told the manager to resign or be fired. The manager resigned and sued the university. A federal district court then granted the university's summary judgment motion.

The manager appealed to the U.S. Court of Appeals, Tenth Circuit. It held the statements about the grant were a matter of public concern because it alleged official wrongdoing. **The form and content of the manager's speech indicated he intended to vindicate the public interest, not to benefit himself. The manager's interest in speaking outweighed the university's interest in regulating him.** Since he was entitled to go before a jury to determine whether the university would have reached the same decision regardless of his speech, the court remanded the case. *Baca v. Sklar and the Board of Regents of the Univ. of New Mexico*, 398 F.3d 1210 (10th Cir. 2005).

2. Speech Pursuant to Official Duties

In Garcetti v. Ceballos, 547 U.S. 410, 126 S.Ct. 1951, 164 L.Ed.2d 689 (2006), *the Supreme Court restated the general rule that public employees have limited First Amendment rights to speak as private citizens on matters of public concern.* Garcetti *clarified that* **a public employee's speech made pursuant to official duties is not protected by the First Amendment.** *The Court held "when public employees make statements pursuant to their official duties, the employees are not speaking as citizens for First Amendment purposes."*

◆ *A federal court rejected a University of Virginia researcher's claim that his contract was not renewed because he reported financial misconduct.*

According to the researcher, others misrepresented time spent on a grant project to improperly draw more money than they should. His contract was not renewed due to serious issues concerning his professional relationship with a supervisor. The researcher sued the university in a federal court, claiming he was discharged in retaliation for raising concerns about grant funding. He also raised a False Claims Act claim. First, the court held for the university on the First Amendment claim. It held **the researcher was acting as a government employee and not a private citizen when he reported his concerns about grant funding**. He reported his concerns in the course of his official duties and in his role as an employee of the university. Even if the researcher had spoken as a citizen and not as a public employee, his First Amendment claim would still fail because his speech did not touch on a matter of public concern. But the court denied a motion for pretrial judgment on the False Claims Act, as there was evidence from which a jury could infer that the decision not to renew his contract was motivated at least partially by his report. *Huang v. Rector and Visitors of the Univ. of Virginia*, 896 F.Supp.2d 524 (W.D. Va. 2012).

◆ *A University of Oregon instructor enjoyed no First Amendment protection to threaten his students.*

The instructor had a "voices off" policy for certain parts of his classes so he could teach American Sign Language. A group of students violated the policy and disrupted class. The instructor told the class that while he was in Pakistan, he encountered tribesmen with rifles. He said he treated them with respect to avoid being shot. According to the instructor, the point of the story was that his students needed to respect his "voices off" policy, just as he needed to respect the tribesmen. But when students kept talking, the instructor asked "do you want me to take out a gun and shoot you in the head?" The remark was recorded and later, the instructor's contract was not renewed. He sued the university, its dean and other officials, asserting First Amendment violations.

A federal court found no speech rights violation. The instructor was not speaking as a private citizen and was not speaking about the public concern. The statements were made in his capacity as a public employee. While the instructor tried to link his statement about shooting students to his talk about respect for different cultures, the court held he "simply crossed the line." **There is no First Amendment right to make threats.** A disability rights claim failed, as no evidence showed students violated his policy because of his deafness. *Quint v. Univ. of Oregon*, No. 6:11-CV-6371-TC, 2013 WL 363782 (D. Or. 1/30/13).

◆ *A federal court rejected a former faculty member's claim that she was fired for expressing concerns about a Michigan university's treatment of animals.*

For 27 of her 37 years at the university, the employee sat on a committee that attempted to assure humane treatment of lab animals. She publicly sided with another committee member's charges of non-compliant conditions at the facility, and she spoke out at meetings. After the university discharged her, the employee filed a federal court action for First Amendment violations. The court held she did not show she was speaking as a citizen on a matter of public concern because **the statements at issue were pursuant to her professional responsibilities**. This meant her statements were not protected by the First Amendment. It did not matter to the court that there were members of the public present when the employee was speaking. Nor was the court impressed by the fact that some of her statements were made outside the workplace. As a result, the court held for the university. *Hrapkiewicz v. Board of Governors of Wayne State Univ.*, No. 11-13418, 2012 WL 393133 (E.D. Mich. 2/6/12).

◆ *A Louisiana professor may pursue a claim that he was discharged because he criticized the U.S. Army Corps of Engineers after Hurricane Katrina.*

The professor had worked at the state geological survey since 1992 and co-founded the Louisiana State University (LSU) Hurricane Center in 2000. Soon after Hurricane Katrina hit in 2005, the professor was chosen by a state agency to lead a research group to find the cause of the catastrophic flooding in New Orleans. Later, he made public statements suggesting the flooding was caused by the Army Corps of Engineers' failure to properly engineer and maintain the city's levees. After LSU officials ordered the professor not to make public statements or provide testimony about causes of the levee failures, he continued to make public statements about the case and testified before the Louisiana Legislature and Congress. In 2006, he published a book discussing the case and LSU's efforts to keep him quiet. After LSU demoted the professor, he sued LSU in a federal court. The court refused to dismiss the professor's retaliation claim, rejecting LSU's argument that his comments were made pursuant to his official duties and thus were not protected. Instead, **the court found he was not performing official job duties when he criticized the Army Corps of Engineers**. There was enough evidence of retaliation for the claim to proceed. *Van Heerden v. Board of Supervisors of Louisiana State Univ.*, No. 3:10-CV-155-JJB-CN, 2011 WL 5008410 (M.D. La. 10/20/11).

3. Speech About the Public Concern

In Pickering v. Board of Educ., *391 U.S. 563 (1968), the Supreme Court held a public employee may not be disciplined for speaking on matters of public concern unless the communication was made in reckless disregard for the truth. In* Connick v. Myers, *461 U.S. 138 (1983), the Court held **a public employee's speech upon matters of purely personal interest has no constitutional protection**. In* Rankin v. McPherson, *483 U.S. 378 (1987), the Court held that "the public concern" is determined by the content, form, and context of speech.*

◆ *A University of Toledo interim Associate Vice President (VP) for human resources did not show her speech rights outweighed those of the university.*

The VP objected to an editorial that compared the civil rights movement with the gay rights movement. She wrote a column stating that gay people should not have the same protections as African-Americans. At a university hearing, the VP insisted she had expressed her own views as a private citizen in the column. But the university terminated her employment because she took a public position that directly contradicted university policies and procedures.

In the VP's lawsuit against the university and its officials, she claimed speech and equal protection violations. Appeal reached the U.S. Court of Appeals, Sixth Circuit. After finding the column involved a matter of public concern, the court sought to resolve whether her speech interests outweighed the university's interests. It found that **if a policymaking public employee is discharged due to speech that relates to political or policy views, a presumption exists that the government employer's interest in efficiency outweighs the employee's free speech interests**. That presumption applied in this case. The column implied that LGBT individuals should not be compared with African-Americans when it comes to affording civil rights protections, and this sentiment contravened relevant university policies. A lower court had correctly ruled against the VP on her First Amendment and equal protection claims. *Dixon v. Univ. of Toledo*, 702 F.3d 269 (6th Cir. 2012).

◆   *A University of Arkansas public safety officer was unable to show the denial of a promotion was based upon his speech.*

The officer reported to university officials that the chief of the university's department of public safety was misusing resources. Three years later, state police investigated the chief for misappropriating university resources, resulting in the chief's resignation. Although the officer sought to replace the chief, another candidate was selected for the position, and the officer sued the university board in a federal district court for First Amendment violations.

The court held for the board, and the officer appealed. The U.S. Court of Appeals, Eighth Circuit, explained that **public employee speech is protected only if the employee speaks as a citizen on a matter of public concern**. The speech must also outweigh the government interest in efficient services. While the officer's internal complaints about the chief were protected by the First Amendment, his statement to state police investigators was made pursuant to his job duties and was unprotected. To prevail on his First Amendment claim, the officer needed to show a connection between his internal complaints and the decision not to promote him. **The court found no evidence showing his internal complaints about the chief were a substantial or motivating factor in the decision to deny him the job as chief many years later.** As a result, the district court had proper grounds to deny the First Amendment claim. The district court correctly rejected a claim that the university violated the officer's due process rights, since he presented no evidence of any legitimate claim to a promotion. The judgment against the officer was affirmed. *Davenport v. Univ. of Arkansas Board of Trustees*, 553 F.3d 1110 (8th Cir. 2009).

◆   *A California university did not violate employee speech rights by using a form with a confidentiality provision for reporting violations.*

A nurse reported unsafe and unsanitary practices at a university hospital. She then claimed the university retaliated and discriminated against her, and she sued university regents in a state superior court. But the nurse did not first file an administrative complaint. She claimed she was excused from this requirement because the form the university used for filing complaints violated her First Amendment rights by requiring employees to keep subject matter confidential. The court denied relief, and the nurse appealed. **The Court of Appeal of California explained that the form required confidentiality only until a matter was resolved, and did not prevent any additional reporting.** Because the nurse was not required to submit to the confidentiality provision in order to file a retaliation complaint, she did not prove a speech violation. The court affirmed the judgment. *Jones v. Regents of the Univ. of California*, 164 Cal.App.4th 1072, 79 Cal.Rptr.3d 817 (Cal. Ct. App. 2008).

◆   *A South Dakota university did not violate an untenured physics professor's speech rights by not renewing his contract.*

The professor said the department director ignored his concerns. He then accused the director of lying and badmouthing him. The university informed him by letter his contract might not be renewed, and it scheduled a meeting with the department chair and others. In the meeting, the professor admitted calling his department director "a lying, backstabbing sneak." The university did not renew his contract based on his lack of civility. The professor sued the university in a federal district court, alleging First Amendment violations. The court held that **the professor's speech was unprotected because it was personal, and not a matter of public concern.** The court also rejected the claim for a preliminary order based on the argument that having to pursue a career outside the university would cause the professor irreparable harm. The university would also suffer harm if it had to reemploy him. As forced reemployment would be disruptive to the university, the case was dismissed. *Keating v. Univ. of South Dakota*, 386 F.Supp.2d 1096 (D.S.D. 2005).

◆ *When employees are disciplined or discharged for legitimate reasons, the First Amendment will not protect them from the adverse action.*

An untenured Ohio teacher was not rehired after a number of incidents that led the school board to conclude he lacked tactfulness in handling professional matters. His federal case reached the U.S. Supreme Court. It held that apart from the actions for which the teacher might claim First Amendment protection, the board could have chosen not to rehire him on the basis of several other incidents, and could have reached the same decision had he not engaged in constitutionally protected conduct. **A marginal employee should not be able to prevent dismissal by engaging in constitutionally protected activity and then hiding under a constitutional shield as protection from all other actions that were not constitutionally protected.** *Mt. Healthy City School Dist. v. Doyle*, 429 U.S. 274, 97 S.Ct. 568, 50 L.Ed.2d 471 (1977).

◆ *The U.S. Supreme Court held a reasonable belief of workplace disruption can be enough to outweigh a speaker's rights under the First Amendment.*

In *Waters v. Churchill,* the Supreme Court held public employee termination is permitted where only a likelihood of disruption existed. **It was unnecessary to demonstrate an actual disruption if termination was based on the employer's reasonable belief that a disruption could occur.** *Waters v. Churchill*, 511 U.S. 661, 114 S.Ct. 1878, 128 L.Ed.2d 686 (1994).

B. Religion and Free Speech

The First Amendment's Establishment Clause prohibits Congress from making any law respecting the establishment of a religion. The Free Exercise Clause of the First Amendment bars Congress from making any law that prohibits the free exercise of religion. Since the First Amendment apply only to governmental action, it does not bind private institutions and their employees.

◆ *A tenured North Carolina criminology professor's First Amendment claims against a university required further court consideration.*

After earning strong evaluations from students and peers, the professor became a Christian and spoke out about political and social issues on a website, radio and television broadcasts, and a book that made his conservative leanings clear. Members of the university's board of trustees, faculty, staff and others began making complaints about his expression. When he applied for promotion to full professor, he supported his application by citing the very writings and appearances that caused tension at the university. He was denied the promotion due to deficient scholarly research, productivity and record of service.

In a federal court action against university officials, the professor asserted religious discrimination in violation of Title VII and the First Amendment, and denial of his equal protection rights. The court held for the university, and the professor appealed to the U.S. Court of Appeals, Fourth Circuit. It rejected the Title VII and equal protection claims, as he did not produce sufficient evidence of religious discrimination to pursue them. As for the First Amendment claims, the court held **the professor was speaking as a citizen on matters of public concern in his columns, books and media appearances**. The appropriate test required consideration of whether his speech rights outweighed the university's interests and whether his speech was a substantial factor in an adverse employment decision. As a result, the court returned the case to the district court to further consider the First Amendment claims. *Adams v. Trustees of Univ. of North Carolina-Wilmington*, 640 F.3d 550 (4th Cir. 2011).

◆ *The Supreme Court held the act of certifying a union by the National Labor Relations Board (NLRB) infringed on a Catholic school's rights.*

The right of employees of a Catholic school system to join together and be recognized as a bargaining unit was successfully challenged in a case decided by the U.S. Supreme Court. In this case, the unions were certified by the NLRB as bargaining units, but the diocese refused to bargain. The Court said that the religion clauses of the U.S. Constitution, which require religious organizations to finance their educational systems without governmental aid, also free the religious organizations of the obviously inhibiting effect and impact of unionization of their teachers. The court agreed with the employer's contention that **the very threshold act of certification of the union by the NLRB would necessarily alter and infringe upon the religious character of parochial schools**, since this would mean that the bishop would no longer be the sole repository of authority as required by church law. Instead, he would have to share some decision-making with the union. This, said the Court, violated the religion clauses of the U.S. Constitution. *NLRB v. Catholic Bishop of Chicago*, 440 U.S. 490, 99 S.Ct. 1313, 59 L.Ed.2d 533 (1979).

◆ *A New York university supervisor did not violate the Establishment Clause by allowing employees to decorate their cubicles with religious items.*

An accountant in the university bursar's office began to complain to the bursar about religious displays in the office. In particular, he objected to small angel figurines that his supervisor kept in his cubicle, religious posters hung outside the bursar's office, and an annual office party with a Christmas tree and Menorah display. Prior to filing these complaints, the accountant had a history of poor relationships with supervisors and co-workers. A performance review indicated he needed to improve his attitude and manner. He became involved in conflicts with five co-workers, and was reassigned to the accounting department. His performance problems continued there, and some co-workers asked not to work with him, as they could get things done faster without him.

The accountant complained that he was reassigned in retaliation for his complaints about the religious articles in the workplace. He sued the university in a federal district court for Establishment Clause violations and retaliation. He also claimed he was denied a reasonable accommodation for a mental disability. The court explained that **government action does not violate the Establishment Clause when it has a secular purpose, has a principal or primary effect that neither advances nor inhibits religion, and does not foster excessive entanglement with religion**. The accountant did not show the college acted with a religious purpose when it allowed employees to display religious items. There was no evidence that officials knew about or approved of much of the conduct he cited. The court rejected the retaliation claim, ruling that neither a job transfer nor a negative job evaluation could be considered an "adverse employment action." The accountant's disability discrimination claim was rejected because he did not provide evidence of a disability. *Menes v. City Univ. of New York Hunter College*, 578 F.Supp.2d 598 (S.D.N.Y. 2008).

C. Electronic Communications

In Faculty Rights Coalition v. Shahrokhi, *204 Fed.Appx. 416 (5th Cir. 2006), the Fifth Circuit Court of Appeals held Texas university officials did not violate an adjunct professor's speech rights by limiting his email access. It noted that in* Perry Educ. Ass'n v. Perry Local Educators' Ass'n, *460 U.S. 37 (1983), the Supreme Court held a public school system's internal mail system is not a "state-created forum" for unlimited expression. State agencies may reserve such forums for their intended purposes, as long as their regulations are reasonable and not intended to suppress expression. In* Shahrokhi, *the court found no speech rights violation, as restrictions created by a spam filter and an email access policy were uniformly applied and not content-based.*

◆ *An Idaho faculty association was denied a temporary order it sought in order to force a university to allow faculty members to use a university listserv.*
Idaho State University (ISU) used an email service to create email lists. Users could easily send emails to the entire faculty through the service. Members of ISU's provisional faculty senate wanted to use the service to circulate and vote on a draft constitution. When permission was denied, a faculty association sued ISU and several university officials in a state court for First Amendment violations. The court denied the association's request for a temporary restraining order and preliminary injunction. Using a test applied to decide First Amendment cases, the court considered whether there was speech on a matter of public concern. It had to be found that the speech was a substantial or motivating factor in adverse action. In the court's view, ISU had good reason to prevent the faculty senate from using the service, as it opposed the association's message. The court explained that **when faculty members speak about job-related matters, they speak as public employees**. Because their messages could be seen as reflecting ISU's position, the university could take steps to make sure its own message was not distorted. For this reason, the association was not entitled to a preliminary order. *Idaho State Univ. Faculty Ass'n for the Preservation of the First Amendment v. Idaho State Univ.*, No. 4:12-cv-00068-BLW, 2012 WL 851516 (D. Idaho 3/13/12).

◆   *A California community college district did not violate a professor's rights by ordering him to stop sending incendiary electronic communications.*

The professor sent racially charged emails to a distribution list maintained by the community college district. He questioned the district's endorsement of what he called the "racist event" of "Dia de la raza," and said it was "time to acknowledge and celebrate the superiority of Western Civilization." Another email by the professor stated "[o]ur survival depends on discrimination," and another said "if we don't pull ourselves out of the multicultural stupor, another culture with some pretty unsavory characteristics ... will dominate." The final email linked to his website on the district's server that urged the "preservation of White majority" and said the "persistent inflow of Hispanic immigrants" was a threat to the U.S. The community college did not discipline him, even after some employees complained. Hispanic employees sued the community college district. A federal court denied judgment to the community college president and chancellor, and they appealed, seeking qualified immunity.

On appeal, the U.S. Court of Appeals, Ninth Circuit, explained that the employees were entitled to be free from harassment on the basis of protected status. **Employers who are made aware of unlawful harassment must "take reasonable and appropriate steps to investigate and make it stop."** But in this case, the court held the professor's speech was not unlawful harassment. Hispanic employees objected to the speech based on his viewpoint. **According to the court, the government cannot silence speech because it promotes ideas that are considered offensive.** The court held substantial deference was due for an official decision not to take disciplinary action. As the court expressed doubt that a college professor's expression on a matter of public concern could ever be unlawful harassment, it reversed the district court's decision to deny the officials qualified immunity and returned the case to the lower court. *Rodriguez v. Maricopa County Community College Dist.*, 605 F.3d 703 (9th Cir. 2010).

◆   *A University of Virginia employee's email to a member of a local NAACP chapter regarding the university pay scale was not protected speech.*

The employee used her university email account to send university payroll data to the NAACP. University officials investigated the action. The employee refused to answer questions involving her NAACP membership. Supervisors notified her "she was facing termination." According to the employee, she was not informed of the nature of the claims and a "hearing" amounted to being handed pink slips. She sued the university in a federal district court for First Amendment, due process and state law violations. After issuing a favorable initial ruling to the employee, the court awarded judgment to the university.

On appeal, **the U.S. Court of Appeals, Fourth Circuit, rejected the claim that the email and attachments from the employee's work computer were protected speech**. Instead, the university's interest in providing effective and efficient services to the public strongly outweighed her interest in expression. The employee violated a state policy limiting personal emails from state computers and accounts. This policy supported the university's efforts to disseminate its own message. Even though the employee had an interest in her own communication, it did not outweigh that of the university. Questions by the university regarding her NAACP affiliation did not violate her association rights, as there was a legitimate interest in ascertaining the source of potentially false data about the university pay structure. As a result, the judgment for the university was affirmed. *Bowers v. Scurry*, 276 Fed.Appx. 278 (4th Cir. 2008).

D. Academic Freedom

In Rodriguez v. Maricopa County Community College Dist.*, this chapter, the Ninth Circuit held academic speech requires "breathing room." Courts must defer to university decisions that err on the side of free speech and academic freedom. Another court has held that universities have the right to decide "who may teach, what may be taught, how it may be taught, and who may be admitted to study."* **The right to academic freedom belongs to the institution, not to any individual.** *Thus, courts have held that public university professors lack First Amendment rights to determine what will be taught.*

◆ *Finding an Iowa law school employee made out a claim of political discrimination based on her conservative views, a federal appeals court allowed her to pursue First Amendment claims against the law school dean.*

After being hired as a part-time associate director in a law school writing center, the employee applied for a full-time job teaching writing. Although there were 50 applicants, and she was one of only three candidates to reach a final interview, she believed her conservative political beliefs would preclude her hiring. The employee raised this concern to an associate dean, who then relayed her comments to the law school dean. The dean acted on a committee recommendation to hire another candidate with less teaching experience, who presented himself as a liberal. After being denied four adjunct positions, the employee sued the law school dean for violating her First Amendment rights.

The court held the dean had qualified immunity, and the employee appealed to the U.S. Court of Appeals, Eighth Circuit. It held **the employee had a First Amendment right to be free from political discrimination**. This right was clearly established by *Rutan v. Republican Party of Illinois*, 497 U.S. 62 (1990). Since the employee offered enough evidence for a reasonable jury to find her political affiliation was a motivating factor in the decision not to hire her, the court held the claim against the dean in her individual capacity could go forward. To prevail, the dean had to prove it was more likely than not that she would have made the same hiring decision regardless of the employee's political beliefs. *Wagner v. Jones*, 664 F.3d 259 (8th Cir. 2011).

◆ *Because he was not speaking as a citizen on a matter of public concern, a New York community college professor lost his speech rights case.*

The professor said that when his department chair stepped down, an election was held to choose her successor. The professor supported a candidate who eventually lost. After the election, he claimed the winning candidate retaliated against him for supporting his opponent. Among the professor's claims was that the new chair fabricated student complaints, changed his work assignments and gave him a poor performance review. After the professor lost his job, he filed a federal lawsuit against the community college for First

Amendment speech and association violations. The college sought dismissal, arguing he could not proceed because his speech and employment associations were made pursuant to his job duties and did not involve the public concern.

The court explained that although the First Amendment may protect the right of public employees to speak as citizens on matters of public concern, **public employees must accept some limitations on their free speech rights**. To decide whether public employee speech is protected from retaliation, courts ask whether the employee spoke as a citizen on a matter of public concern, and if so, whether the government entity had a good reason to treat him differently than a member of the general public. In this case, the professor did not show that his support of a particular candidate addressed a matter of public concern. He did not show his participation in the election "reflected anything more than a personal interest." The motion to dismiss was granted. *Flyr v. City Univ. of New York*, No. 09 Civ. 9159(JGK), 2011 WL 1675997 (S.D.N.Y. 4/25/11).

1. Classroom Speech

◆ *Virginia State University (VSU) administrators did not violate a professor's rights by changing a student's grade.*

For a physics course, the professor calculated each student's final grade by averaging the three highest scores on five quizzes. This calculation resulted in an average of 59 for one student. He said the student achieved quiz scores of 16, 66, 89, 21 and 22. Although the score of 59 merited a grade of F, the professor assigned the student a D. The student protested, believing he had earned higher scores on two quizzes, which would have entitled him to an A.

The student handed in faxed copies of the quizzes showing scores of 95, but the professor believed they were doctored and refused to change the grade. The department chairman sided with the student and changed the grade to an A. The professor sued VSU in a federal district court for violating an asserted right to academic freedom. He also said administrators changed the grade to retaliate against him for testifying on behalf of a colleague who had filed a lawsuit against VSU. The professor asked the court to order VSU to change the grade to a D. He also sought monetary damages. The court explained that the U.S. Supreme Court has recognized that the Constitution gives "some measure of academic freedom to academic institutions." Universities have the right to determine "who may teach, what may be taught, how it may be taught, and who may be admitted to study." **The right to academic freedom belongs to universities and not to individual professors.** VSU officials exercised their authority to change the grade without requiring the professor to do so personally. He lacked a constitutional right to academic freedom that would prevent VSU officials from changing the grade. The court granted VSU's motion to dismiss the claim. *Stronach v. Virginia State Univ.*, No. 3:07CV646-HEH, 2008 WL 161304 (E.D. Va. 1/15/08).

◆ *Institutions are entitled to direct their instructors to keep personal discussions about sexual orientation or religion out of their classes.*

An Illinois college instructor gave a gay student religious pamphlets on the sinfulness of homosexuality. One was entitled "Sin City" and told the story of a man who was beaten when he tried to stop a gay pride parade and was arrested by police. It also said a demon urged on a minister who preached that "God loves even gay people." The student complained to college officials and urged them to fire the instructor. In a follow-up letter, the student reported that the instructor had accused him of trying to get her fired.

The college investigated the report and concluded that the instructor had sexually harassed the student based on sexual orientation. It did not offer the instructor a job the following semester, and she sued the college in a federal district court for speech rights violations. The court held for the college and the instructor appealed to the U.S. Court of Appeals, Seventh Circuit. The court relied on *Garcetti v. Ceballos*, this chapter, noting the case signalled the Court's concern that the courts give appropriate weight to a public employer's interests in First Amendment cases. In this case, **the college had an interest in ensuring that instructors stayed on the subject matter of their clinics and classrooms**. The court affirmed the judgment for the college, as it could lawfully direct instructors to keep personal discussions about sexual orientation or religion out of a class or clinic. *Piggee v. Carl Sandburg College*, 464 F.3d 667 (7th Cir. 2006).

◆ *An Ohio university did not violate a lecturer's First Amendment rights by telling her to communicate grading requirements more clearly to her students.*

The lecturer gave incomplete grades to 13 of 17 students in a writing class for improper formatting, improper citations, and/or textual changes to their work. She left it up to each student to determine which reason applied in his or her own case. The lecturer's listserv postings did not specify particular reasons for which students received incomplete grades, and at least one student complained. A supervisor told the lecturer her listserv postings were not sufficiently clear to inform students how to complete the course. She asked her to send each student in the class a letter with individualized instructions for earning a final grade. Five weeks later, several students complained that the lecturer did not provide this information. The supervisor again asked the lecturer to draft letters to each student and emphasized that incomplete grades were a serious problem affecting student academic and financial aid status. The lecturer never responded and did not prepare the letters. She later sued the director of the English department and the supervisor for violating her rights to speech and academic freedom. A federal district court dismissed the case.

On appeal, the U.S. Court of Appeals, Sixth Circuit, rejected the lecturer's claim that an instruction by a supervisor to communicate with students violated the First Amendment. **Any right to academic freedom recognized by the First Amendment applied to the university, not the lecturer. A university is entitled to determine who may teach, what may be taught, how it is taught, and who may be admitted.** Professors have certain protections under the First Amendment, like making decisions about instruction and grading that differ from those of the university. In this case, the university simply asked the lecturer to explain to students exactly what was required to obtain a final grade. As the university did not violate her rights, the court affirmed the judgment. *Johnson-Kurek v. Abu-Absi*, 423 F.3d 590 (6th Cir. 2005).

2. Loyalty Oaths

In Sweezy v. New Hampshire, *354 U.S. 234 (1957), the U.S. Supreme Court declared unconstitutional a university policy aimed at prohibiting the employment of communist party members.*

◆   *An Arizona statute that prohibited even associating with the Communist Party was struck down by the U.S. Supreme Court.*

An Arizona teacher who was a Quaker refused to take an oath required of all public employees under Arizona law. The oath swore that the employees would support both the Arizona and the U.S. Constitutions as well as state laws. The legislation also stated that anyone who took the oath and supported the Communist party or the violent overthrow of government would be discharged from employment and charged with perjury. The teacher sued for declaratory relief in the Arizona courts, having decided she could not take the oath in good conscience because she did not know what it meant.

The U.S. Supreme Court held that political groups may have both legal and illegal aims and that there should not be a blanket prohibition on all groups that might have both legal and illegal goals. Such a prohibition would threaten legitimate political expression and association. The Court held that mere association with a group cannot be prohibited without a showing of "specific intent" to carry out the group's illegal purpose. It went on to say that **the Arizona statute was constitutionally deficient because it was not confined to those employees with a "specific intent" to do something illegal**. The statute infringed upon employee rights to free association by not punishing specific behavior that yielded a clear and present danger to government. The statute was struck down as unconstitutional. *Elfbrandt v. Russell,* 384 U.S. 11, 86 S.Ct. 1238, 16 L.Ed.2d 321 (1965).

◆   *A state could not require teachers to file annual affidavits listing every organization they belonged to in the past five years.*

The Arkansas Legislature established **a statute that required every teacher employed by a state-supported school or college to file an annual affidavit listing every organization to which he or she had belonged in the past five years**. A teacher who had worked for an Arkansas school system for 25 years and who was a member of the NAACP was told he would have to file such an affidavit before the start of the next school year. After he failed to do so, his contract for the next year was not renewed. He filed a class action lawsuit against the school district in a federal district court. The court found that the teacher was not a member of the Communist Party or any organization advocating the violent overthrow of the government. It upheld the statute, finding that the information requested by the school district was relevant. The Supreme Court of Arkansas had upheld the statute's constitutionality in a case brought by other teachers. The U.S. Supreme Court noted that the state had a right to investigate teachers, since education of youth was a vital public interest. It stated that the requirement of the affidavit was reasonably related to the state's interest. However, **requiring teachers to name all their associations interfered with teacher free speech and association rights.**

Because fundamental rights were involved, governmental screening of teachers was required to be narrowly tailored to the state's ends. Because the statute went beyond what was necessary to meet the state's inquiry into the fitness of its teachers, the Court ruled it unconstitutional. *Shelton v. Tucker,* 364 U.S. 479, 81 S.Ct. 247, 5 L.Ed.2d 231 (1960).

◆ *A Washington statute aimed at prohibiting subversives from becoming teachers was too vague to be constitutional.*

Faculty members sued to declare two state statutes unconstitutional. One statute required all state employees to take loyalty oaths, and the other required all teachers to take an oath as a condition of employment. Both oaths dealt with employee loyalty to the U.S. Constitution and to the government. The public employee statute applied to all public employees and defined a "subversive person" as one who conspired to overthrow the government. The Communist Party also was named as a subversive organization. Persons designated as subversives or Communist Party members were ineligible for public employment. The U.S. Supreme Court held that the statutes were vague and overbroad, and violated the Fourteenth Amendment's Due Process Clause. The statutes did not provide sufficient notice of what conduct was prohibited. This constituted a denial of the teachers' due process rights. **The university could not require its teachers to take an oath that applied to some vague behavior in the future**, especially since there were First Amendment freedom of speech and association claims at stake. *Baggett v. Bullitt,* 377 U.S. 360, 84 S.Ct. 1316, 12 L.Ed.2d 377 (1963).

◆ *A loyalty oath could not be administered to two applicants who objected to it on religious grounds.*

As part of state-mandated pre-employment procedures, a California community college district required applicants to sign an oath swearing "true faith and allegiance" and to "support and defend" the United States and California Constitutions. Two Jehovah's Witnesses applied for positions but refused to take the oath due to their religious beliefs. They sued the district under the Religious Freedom Restoration Act of 1993 (RFRA), challenging the validity of the loyalty oath as a condition precedent for employment. A federal court held that **requiring the applicants to take an oath that violated their religious tenets placed an undue burden on their right to free exercise of religion**. The district failed to assert that the loyalty oath furthered a compelling government interest or was the least restrictive means of achieving that interest. Although employee loyalty was a compelling interest, the evidence failed to establish that a loyalty oath effectively achieved this goal. An alternative oath directed to an applicant's actions rather than his or her beliefs would be equally effective and less restrictive. Because the loyalty oath could not be justified under the compelling interest test articulated in the RFRA, the court enjoined the district from administering the loyalty oath to the applicants. *Bessard v. California Community Colleges,* 867 F.Supp. 1454 (E.D. Cal. 1994).

[*Editor's Note*: The U.S. Supreme Court held that the RFRA was unconstitutional as applied to state actions in *City of Boerne, Texas v. Flores,* 521 U.S. 507, 117 S.Ct. 2157, 138 L.Ed.2d 624 (1997).]

II. DEFAMATION

To pursue a defamation claim, a defamed party must allege that false material was "published" to a third party who understands it refers to the defamed party. The defamed party must suffer a loss of reputation and a "tangible injury," which is usually some harm to an economic interest.

Defenses to defamation include truth, privilege, consent and opinion. The defense of privilege defeats many otherwise actionable defamation claims in employment cases. In Fink v. California State Univ. Northridge, *No. B183977, 2006 WL 465947 (Cal. Ct. App. 2/28/06), the Court of Appeal of California held that statements reporting suspected criminal activity to law enforcement officers are privileged and cannot form the basis of a defamation claim.*

A judicial privilege applies to proceedings before government bodies and pursuant to a statute or administrative regulation. The U.S. Court of Appeals, Third Circuit, has limited an absolute privilege to judicial proceedings. Applying Pennsylvania law, the court held internal grievance proceedings are not entitled to the same absolute immunity as regular judicial proceedings. Overall v. Univ. of Pennsylvania, *412 F.3d 492 (3d Cir. 2005).*

◆ *A Minnesota student who was disciplined for an in-class incident did not show the university's investigation of the case supported a defamation claim.*

Due to multiple sclerosis, the student needed help for many daily activities. She brought a note-taker to class without permission, and the university charged her with violating its conduct code. A letter documenting the incident described her as agitated, threatening and apparently under the influence of alcohol. After an appeal, the university revoked its finding that the student violated student conduct code provisions on alcohol. But other conduct code violations were found, and she was banned from classes taught by the teachers involved in the incident. The student sued the university for defamation. Her case reached the state court of appeals, which held the publication requirement of the defamation claim could be satisfied if the student was compelled to make the publication. But the court found she was not obligated to disclose any information about the incident. Although the university had published statements internally during its investigation, it had a qualified privilege to do so. **The university had good reason to share the information among internal parties involved with the investigation.** A privilege is lost when statements are made with actual malice, which was not shown in this case. The decision for the university was affirmed. *De Jong v. Metropolitan State Univ.,* No. A12-0829, 2012 WL 5990306 (Minn. Ct. App. 12/3/12).

◆ *Ill will among employees was not enough to establish "actual malice," defeating a Michigan employee's defamation lawsuit.*

A University of Michigan (UM) researcher had a personality conflict with two supervisors and was fired during her probationary term. She claimed one of them told her she would never work at UM again and threatened to ruin her reputation. When the researcher applied for another UM job, she said a professor told her he initially planned to hire her but could not because her discharge during a probationary period resulted in automatic "do not hire status." The researcher sued UM and the supervisors in a state court for defamation. In pretrial activity, the court found UM had valid cause to fire her for not following lab protocols. But it issued a protective order requiring UM to provide a neutral reference and not to discuss her termination with any outside parties. On appeal, the state court of appeals held the statements were only communicated to the UM human resources department and were privileged communications.

To state a valid defamation claim, the researcher had to show that statements were made with actual malice – defined as making a statement despite knowing it is false or with a reckless disregard for the truth. Ill will or hatred alone is not enough to establish actual malice. The researcher's own testimony suggested that a supervisor believed she had falsified data. The court held the supervisor's dislike for her was not enough to establish actual malice. For this reason, the court affirmed the judgment for UM. *Osak v. Univ. of Michigan Regents*, No. 306239, 2012 WL 5061640 (Mich. Ct. App. 10/18/12).

◆   *A New York court rejected claims that graduate psychology administrators defamed a student by making misleading statements about her dismissal.*

Administrators became concerned with the student's professionalism, ethics and conduct, and they developed a remediation plan for her. She was to write a paper addressing the concerns raised about her performance. Administrators reviewed the paper, ultimately finding it was unsatisfactory. In the process, they shared documents evaluating the student's fitness to continue. After being dismissed from the program, she sued the university and some administrators in a state court for defamation. She claimed statements in the remediation paper evaluation were materially and knowingly false, made in bad faith, with actual malice and in reckless disregard of the truth. The court explained that to show defamation, a person has to prove a false statement was published to a third party without authorization. There must be evidence of fault and special harm.

"Privileged statements" do not support a defamation claim. These include good-faith communications between parties having an interest in the subject matter. In this case, the student did not show that the statements made about her were published to anyone other than individuals involved in evaluating her academic conduct. The statements were protected by privilege, as they were made among faculty members who were evaluating her fitness as a doctoral degree candidate. In addition, she admitted she acted unprofessionally and sometimes lied to her professors. The court dismissed the case. *Lipsky v. Gonzalez*, 39 Misc.3d 1202(A) (N.Y. Sup. Ct. 2013).

◆   *The University of New Hampshire (UH) did not defame a tenured professor when it suspended him a day after he had a tirade over a parking ticket.*

The professor had a poor relationship with a female colleague. On the day of his tirade, the colleague reported his car was parked illegally, and he received a ticket. In the presence of the colleague's assistant and several others, the professor said he could "kill that fucking bitch," and he kicked a trash can. He was arrested and charged with disorderly conduct and stalking. UH placed the professor on leave and suspended him as a department chair. Faculty and staff members were instructed to avoid him and to notify authorities if he was seen on campus. He was later cleared of criminal charges and allowed back on campus. The professor sued UH in a federal court for false arrest, due process violations and defamation based on an email alert. The court held for UH, and the professor appealed to the U.S. Court of Appeals, First Circuit.

The appeals court rejected the professor's false arrest claim, which he based on the theory that he had been unreasonably seized. There was probable cause for the charges of disorderly conduct and stalking. UH did not violate the professor's due process rights by suspending him with pay, limiting his access to the campus and removing him from his post as a department chair. Finally, **the defamation charge failed because his conduct gave UH good reason to alert employees that they should avoid him and advise police if he was seen on campus.** *Collins v. Univ. of New Hampshire*, 664 F.3d 8 (1st Cir. 2011).

◆ *A Michigan court held state law protected educators who criticized student performance from libel claims, defeating a student's claim for defamation.*

American University of Antigua College of Medicine (AUA) put a student on nonacademic probation for unprofessional conduct. He also had a 1.5 grade point average. Later, the student was placed in a clinical experience rotation at a Michigan hospital. There, he said the program was a waste of time, and he was disrespectful and disruptive in class. Among other things, the student used inappropriate language and passwords. AUA eventually initiated proceedings before its grievance and disciplinary committee, but he skipped his hearing.

After being dismissed from medical school, the student sued AUA and the hospital owner in a Michigan court for defamation. A judge found no trial necessary and dismissed the case. On appeal, the Court of Appeals of Michigan held the student could not show any statements about him by AUA or the hospital were false. He also failed to show the statements were not entitled to a "qualified privilege." Instead, **the lower court correctly found the statements were made in good faith, motivated by an interest in the program's integrity, and communicated to proper parties only**. It was important to the court that internal records established AUA was concerned about the student's poor grades and unprofessional conduct. Statements about him were protected, and the court affirmed the judgment. *Woodward v. Trinity Health-Michigan*, No. 292172, 2011 WL 118812 (Mich. Ct. App. 1/13/11).

◆ *A California dental student was unable to show a conspiracy to keep her from earning a degree by misreporting her academic performance.*

Near her expected graduation date, the student had a problem with a patient at a school clinic. After the patient left, the chair of her department made disparaging remarks about the student in front of other faculty members. Four days before graduation, the student was notified that she had failed part of an exam and would not graduate based on a vote by a student academic committee. Believing the department chair had influenced the vote against her, the student sued the university and several instructors and administrators for defamation. She also asserted her official transcript had been altered. A federal district court held the student offered no facts to show any oral or written defamatory statements resulting in errors on her official transcript. Another problem was that defamation claims cannot be based on opinions. **California** courts have found "statements regarding a student's academic competence" to be "non-actionable statements of opinion." Finding the student's defamation claim was based on speculation, the court dismissed it. *Rashdan v. Geissberger*, No. C 10-00634 SBA, Docket No. 10, 2011 WL 197957 (N.D. Cal. 1/14/11).

◆ *As opinions cannot form the basis for a defamation claim, a first-year Texas residency program student could not pursue his case.*

Within a few weeks of entering the program, faculty members advised the director that the student was not performing at the level expected of first-year residents. The faculty terminated his rotation 10 days early, and he was placed in a remediation rotation. Despite the extra feedback and attention he received, the student continued to struggle and was discharged. He sued the medical program officials in a federal district court for defamation, claiming the program director asked him disparaging questions in front of other residents. He said she then wrote in a dismissal letter that he was "unable to complete the simplest task independently" and provided it to the Accreditation Council for Graduate Medical Education. But the court granted the director's request for pretrial judgment. **Generally speaking, a statement is defamatory when it is both false and damaging to the person's reputation.** In this case, the student could not prove the director published the statements. And the statements he attributed to her were expressions of opinion, not assertions of fact needed to support a defamation claim. Noting that only assertions of fact – not expressions of opinion – can qualify as defamatory, the court held for the program director. *Sayibu v. Univ. of Texas Southwestern Medical Center at Dallas*, No. 3:09-CV-1244-B, 2010 WL 5139494 (N.D. Tex. 12/17/10).

◆ *A tenured Illinois professor was allowed to proceed with a defamation case against a university and its vice president in the federal court system.*

At a faculty council meeting, the professor complained that the arrest of student demonstrators on campus was part of a pattern of harassment against students who opposed the war in Iraq. A vice president who oversaw the campus police and student affairs said the professor and students were responsible for the incident. He also claimed the professor had been charged with stalking a student. Although she had been elected to be the chair by members of her department, the university declined to appoint her, and it did not give her a faculty excellence award for which she claimed to be eligible.

In a federal district court action against the vice president and university for defamation and retaliation, the court explained that **as a government official, the vice president had immunity if the defamatory statement was reasonably related to his public duties**. In making this determination, the relevant factors included whether the statements were made in his role as a supervisor, as part of an official duty to speak on behalf of his department, and to defend against allegations of wrongdoing. Based on the papers filed so far, there was little information regarding the vice president's duties. The court refused to dismiss the defamation and law retaliation claims. *Capeheart v. Northern Illinois Univ.*, No. 08 CV 1423, 2010 WL 894052 (N.D. Ill. 3/9/10).

◆   *Pennsylvania law protects state employees from defamation lawsuits, barring a student's claim that she was falsely accused of plagiarism.*

After an instructor assigned the student an F on a paper for plagiarism, her course grade went to a C. Although she denied committing plagiarism, a university judicial board disagreed. Her course grade became an F, and she was dismissed from her doctoral program. Twelve years after being expelled, the student applied for readmission to the program but was rejected. She sued the instructor and university in a federal district court, alleging she was denied readmission due to bias and animosity. She also alleged that the instructor should have been fired for falsely accusing her of plagiarism. The court found the student's constitutional claims were untimely. Her defamation and negligence claims failed, as **the state Sovereign Immunity Act protected a public university and faculty from claims based on civil wrongs committed when employees acted within the scope of their employment.** *Shuqin v. Rafoth*, No. 08-1343, 2009 WL 3834009 (W.D. Pa. 11/16/09).

◆   *A Louisiana university coach who submitted a false resume could not claim defamation or breach of contract based on his subsequent discharge.*

The coach was hired as head basketball coach after he submitted a resume indicating he had earned a degree from the University of Texas at San Antonio (UTSA). In fact, he had attended UTSA but did not graduate. After being hired, the coach filled out forms correctly indicating he had graduated from another university that was not accredited by the Southern Association of Colleges and Schools. After the hiring, a newspaper article mentioned his failure to graduate from UTSA, and the university fired him for lying on his resume. The coach sued the university for defamation and breach of contract, claiming the resume was sent by mistake and that he later submitted correct information. The case reached the Supreme Court of Louisiana. It held the defamation claim failed because the statements indicating the coach had misrepresented his qualifications on his resume were true. **A party cannot recover for defamation based on a true statement.** The breach of contract claim failed, because the university had a valid reason to rescind the contract. Evidence showed the coach would not have been hired if the university had known he did not have a degree from an accredited institution. *Cyprien v. Board of Supervisors for the Univ. of Louisiana System*, 5 So.3d 862 (La. 2009).

◆   *A Kentucky community college did not defame a teacher or retaliate against her in response to her complaints about her work environment.*

The teacher repeatedly refused to administer an opinion poll to her students as requested by a professor. Discussion about whether the poll should be included spread to other faculty members, and the teacher complained to a college dean and the college president about a hostile work environment. When the teacher learned her contract would not be renewed for the next academic year, she posted a cartoon outside her office depicting two hooded figures. One figure was labeled as the college president. The college maintained that the figures represented Ku Klux Klan members, and the dean removed them.

After being placed on a paid leave of absence, the teacher sued the college and five employees for wrongful termination, breach of contract, infliction of emotional distress, and retaliation for exercising her speech rights. A state court dismissed the case. On appeal, the Court of Appeals of Kentucky noted that the college did not terminate the teacher's contract but had instead placed her on leave. She did not allege any harassment until after the decision not to renew her contract had been made. **The court held that the Constitution does not protect defamatory statements. A suggestion that someone is a member of the Ku Klux Klan is defamatory.** In this case, the teacher failed to show she was treated more harshly than similarly situated males. The judgment for the community college was affirmed. *McBrearty v. Kentucky Community and Technical College System*, 262 S.W.3d 205 (Ky. Ct. App. 2008).

◆   *The Supreme Court of Indiana rejected a professor's defamation claims against two students who filed complaints of sexual harassment against him.*

Two female students filed formal complaints of sexual harassment against an Indiana education professor. Pursuant to its anti-harassment policy, the university affirmative action office investigated. After a series of interviews, the investigator found the professor had created a hostile educational environment. The investigator specifically found harassment in one of the complaints, but the second complaint was not timely reported. A three-person panel and a senior executive officer accepted the investigator's recommendation that the professor should not have teaching responsibilities or student contact. He was assigned to a research position for the remainder of his contract. The professor sued the university in a state court for defamation and malicious interference with his employment contract. The case reached the Supreme Court of Indiana.

According to the state supreme court, **there is an absolute privilege for statements made during judicial proceedings, regardless of their truth or the motive behind them.** The rule is intended to allow people to participate in judicial proceedings without fear of being sued for defamation. At least three other states – Maryland, California and New York – have extended the privilege to complaints to school authorities against educators. It was appropriate to extend the privilege in this way so students could raise complaints without fear of retaliatory litigation. *Hartman v. Keri*, 883 N.E.2d 774 (Ind. 2008).

◆   *A Rhode Island university did not defame a student when its security office posted a "crime alert" to inform the campus community about him.*

The student became involved in a late-night fight with another student. He punched the other student and knocked him to the ground, where he hit his head. A witness told the police that the student had a knife during the fight. Police filed criminal charges against the student, and the incident was reported to a university safety and security office. The office investigated and filed an incident report stating that the student was the likely aggressor in the fight. The security office then posted a crime alert at various campus locations, naming the student as the party responsible for the crime. After being dismissed from the university, the student filed a federal court action against the university for defamation and breach of contract. The court held the university had a qualified privilege to publish the alert. On appeal, the U.S. Court of Appeals, First Circuit, held the university enjoyed a qualified privilege with respect to the defamation claim. **The university reasonably believed it had a duty to**

report the crime to the campus community under the federal Clery Act.
The student did not show the university published the alert with spite, ill will
or malice. The court also rejected the breach of contract claim, as the university
complied with student handbook terms relating to the appeal process. *Havlik v.
Johnson & Wales Univ.*, 509 F.3d 25 (1st Cir. 2007).

III. STUDENTS

A. Protected Speech

*The Establishment Clause of the First Amendment to the U.S. Constitution
requires government neutrality with respect to religion and non-religion. The
Free Exercise Clause of the First Amendment prohibits government
interference with the reasonable exercise of religious rights. Public institutions
must refrain from content-based restrictions on speech.*

1. Religious Speech

◆ *Since the First Amendment binds only governmental institutions and
employees, a federal action against Duke University was dismissed.*

Duke University Press owns and operates a lesbian and gay studies journal.
When an author submitted "The Crucible of a Gay Jew: A Resolution to an
Orthodox Duress" for publication as a paid advertisement, the university
rejected it. In a federal court, the author asserted First Amendment violations.
A federal magistrate found the claims to be so insufficient as to make the case
a clearly frivolous action. **A First Amendment violation claim can be
brought only against a government agency or employee.** Because Duke
University is a private institution, the case had to be dismissed. *Kanli v. Duke
Univ.*, No. 1:12CV63, 2012 WL 2366449 (M.D.N.C. 6/21/12).

◆ *A federal court refused to dismiss a lawsuit by a Michigan graduate
counseling student who refused to counsel a homosexual client.*

Near the end of her graduate counseling program, the student took a course
where she would counsel persons who paid a small fee. Before meeting a
client, she read his file and saw he wanted help with a homosexual relationship.
The student refused to counsel him, stating religious reasons. She was expelled
after a hearing where it was found that she violated a student handbook and a
counseling code of ethics by imposing values inconsistent with counseling
goals and discriminating on the basis of sexual orientation. The student filed a
federal district court action for speech rights violations. The court held for the
officials, and appeal reached the U.S. Court of Appeals, Sixth Circuit. It held
that public institutions cannot selectively enforce curricular requirements or
single out students based on their speech. The court found the student had made
the request to avoid imposing her values on homosexual clients and declared
that she was willing to counsel them about other issues. She said the university
discriminated against her because it let other students limit their counseling
roles. For instance, a grieving student had been allowed to avoid counseling a

grieving client. **Because it was possible that a jury could find the student was expelled for her speech, the judgment for the university officials was reversed.** *Ward v. Polite*, 667 F.3d 727 (6th Cir. 2012).

◆   *A federal appeals court rejected claims that a University of California (UC) policy for evaluating high school religion courses was unconstitutional.*

UC's policy for recognizing high school religion and ethics courses required that they "treat the study of religion or ethics from the standpoint of scholarly inquiry, rather than in a manner limited to one denomination or viewpoint." UC justified the policy to assure a multidisciplinary study of religion. An association representing Christian schools and students sued UC officials in a federal district court, asserting speech, free exercise, Establishment Clause and equal protection violations. After the court held for UC, appeal reached the U.S. Court of Appeals, Ninth Circuit, which said the association showed no risk that the policy would suppress protected speech.

The court held the policy did not stop high schools from teaching what they wanted, or prevent high school students from taking the courses they wanted. UC did not punish high schools or students, and the court found no unlawful viewpoint discrimination. Evidence indicated UC approved courses with religious content and viewpoints, even those using religious textbooks as primary texts. UC's refusal to accept four courses offered by a Christian school was reasonable because the courses were not college preparatory, lacked necessary course information or materials, or had other procedural defects. The court rejected an equal protection challenge and affirmed the judgment for UC. *Ass'n of Christian Schools Int'l v. Stearns*, 362 Fed.Appx. 640 (9th Cir. 2010).

◆   *Temple University's sexual harassment policy was worded so broadly that it violated a student's First Amendment rights.*

A Temple policy prohibited "expressive, visual, or physical conduct of a sexual or gender-motivated nature," if the conduct had the "purpose or effect" of unreasonably interfering with another person's "work, educational performance, or status." The policy also barred "sexual or gender-motivated" conduct intended to create "an intimidating, hostile or offensive environment" for others. A graduate student who served in the National Guard claimed the policy inhibited him from expressing his views about women in the military. He sued Temple, its president and two professors in a federal district court for First Amendment violations. While the case was pending, Temple modified the policy. The court considered the old policy and held it was unconstitutional.

On appeal, the U.S. Court of Appeals, Third Circuit, rejected Temple's claim that the case was moot since the old policy had been revised. It then found there is no "harassment exception" to the First Amendment. The policy violated a general rule that **student speech cannot be barred unless it creates a real threat of disruption**. Under the policy, students could be punished even if their actions had no effect on others. Terms such as "hostile," "offensive," and "gender-motivated" were broad enough to ban some protected speech. The policy lacked a requirement that conduct or speech actually create a hostile environment or interfere with the work of others. The phrase "gender-motivated" required inquiry into the motivation of a speaker. It was also unclear whether it was the speaker's gender or the listener's that served as the motivation. A policy prohibition of conduct that "unreasonably interfere[d] with an individual's work" was suspect as well. The court affirmed the judgment. *DeJohn v. Temple Univ.*, 537 F.3d 301 (3d Cir. 2008).

♦   *A federal district court dismissed claims that an assignment to read a religious-related book violated student free exercise rights.*

An orientation program held by the University of North Carolina, Chapel Hill (UNC) required incoming freshmen to read a book that explored Islam. Although the program had an exception for students with religious objections, several students sued UNC in a federal district court for Free Exercise Clause violations. **The court considered UNC's motion for dismissal and noted the book was not a religious reading.** It found the orientation program was an academic exercise. The court said UNC had attempted to engage students in a scholarly debate about a religious subject and encouraged them to express their opinions. Students who objected to reading the book could refrain from doing so. **UNC did not compel the affirmation of any particular religious belief, favor any religious dogma, or punish the expression of any particular religion**. As UNC did not ask students to compromise or give up their religious beliefs, the court dismissed the action. It gave permission for the students to add new allegations. *Yacovelli v. Moeser*, 324 F.Supp.2d 760 (M.D.N.C. 2004).

♦   *A Seventh Circuit panel allowed a theater student to continue with his production of a play that was alleged to be anti-Christian.*

The dispute arose after a theater student at an Indiana university chose to produce a play depicting a homosexual Christ-like character who engaged in sex with his apostles. A group of taxpayers, members of the state General Assembly, and Purdue University board members alleged that the publicly funded university would be violating the Establishment Clause by allowing the performance. A federal district court denied a request to stop the production. **Because the theater was a limited public forum, the university could not discriminate against the viewpoint of performers.** On appeal, the U.S. Court of Appeals, Seventh Circuit, upheld the decision. It found "absurd" the assertion that the First Amendment prevents state universities from providing venues for un-Christian ideas. There was no evidence that the university was hostile to Christianity because it did not tell the student to produce the play. *Linnemeir v. Board of Trustees of Purdue Univ.*, 260 F.3d 757 (7th Cir. 2001).

♦   *Graduation prayers were allowed at Indiana University.*

In a case involving graduation prayers at Indiana University, the Seventh Circuit **found no element of coercion in requiring students to participate in large, impersonal university commencement exercises**. Many students and family members remained seated during the prayer. Adult students were not likely to succumb to peer pressure and could skip the ceremony without severe consequences. The court agreed with the university that the prayers solemnized the ceremony, did not endorse any religion and allowed the university's 155-year-old tradition to continue. *Tanford v. Brand*, 104 F.3d 982 (7th Cir. 1997).

2. Academic Practices

◆   *A Louisiana student charged with harassing his girlfriend was denied a preliminary order in his First Amendment challenge to a code of conduct rule.*

After the student and his girlfriend broke up, she told campus police he was threatening her. University officials investigated and found the student had violated its conduct code. He declined an offer of disciplinary probation for a year with an anger management class requirement. A hearing panel found the student had violated a code provision prohibiting "extreme, outrageous or persistent acts, or communications that are intended or reasonably likely to harass, intimidate, harm, or humiliate another." He sued the university's board and chancellor for First Amendment violations in a federal district court.

After the court denied the student's request for preliminary relief, he appealed to the U.S. Court of Appeals, Fifth Circuit. Like the district court, the court rejected the claim that the code of conduct violated the First Amendment by restricting more protected speech than necessary to achieve a legitimate goal. While state institutions cannot limit protected speech with which they disagree, the court held **state institutions can legally limit speech that intrudes on other students' rights**. And a code provision requiring expression to be "extreme," "persistent" and "reasonably likely" to cause a violation prevented application of the code to speech or conduct that was only offensive. *Esfeller v. O'Keefe*, 391 Fed.Appx. 337 (5th Cir. 2010).

◆   *The U.S. Court of Appeals, Third Circuit, found three challenged university rules were constitutionally overbroad.*

A student at the University of the Virgin Islands (UVI) was charged with violating a student code paragraph that banned "any act which causes or is likely to cause serious physical or mental harm or which tends to injure or actually injures, frightens, demeans, degrades or disgraces any person. This includes but is not limited to violation of the University policies on hazing, sexual harassment or sexual assault." The student sued UVI in a federal court, arguing four student code provisions were unconstitutionally overbroad. The case reached the Third Circuit, which found three of the rules overbroad. **An overbroad rule is assumed to violate First Amendment rights by "chilling" expression.** State universities cannot prohibit offensive or unpopular opinions. UVI did not specify what steps students could take to obtain authorization for signs. The second rule banned conduct "which causes emotional distress" – which the court found was not based on conduct but the reaction to it. All three rules were held unconstitutional as precluding more protected activity than the university could legally prohibit. *McCauley v. Univ. of the Virgin Islands*, 618 F.3d 232 (3d Cir. 2010).

◆   *A federal district court rejected a Texas student's claim that her professor violated her speech rights by banning abortion as a topic for an assignment.*

When the student chose abortion as the topic for her public speaking assignment in a speech communication class, the instructor told her it was off limits. She sued the instructor in a federal district court for violating her First Amendment rights. After rejecting the student's non-speech claims, the court explained that **the instructor could defeat any speech claim by showing he had a legitimate pedagogical reason for restricting her speech**. This was shown based on his statement that the topic of abortion was potentially disruptive and could shift the focus away from the topic of communication skills. Since the instructor had a valid pedagogical reason for banning the topic of abortion in his class, he was entitled to judgment on the speech claim. The student also failed to show his criticism of her was retaliatory. **The decision to grant a specific grade to a student is within the discretion of education professionals and not the judiciary.** All the remaining claims in the case were dismissed. *O'Neal v. Falcon*, 668 F.Supp.2d 979 (W.D. Tex. 2009).

◆   *The University of Tennessee (UT) did not violate the Constitution by suspending a student for displaying anti-war banners in violation of its policy.*

The student hung anti-war banners from UT buildings and painted the words "NO WAR" on them. He was arrested for vandalism, public intoxication and evading arrest. UT's student handbook barred vandalism and acts violating any law. A UT facilities guide allowed notices only on designated bulletin boards and barred political signs. Relying in part on the fact that other graffiti was present on campus, the student insisted he did not know that painting on university buildings or hanging banners on them violated UT policy or state law. He sued UT officials in a federal district court for violating the First Amendment. He also claimed that he was arrested in violation of the Fourth Amendment. Appeal reached the U.S. Court of Appeals, Sixth Circuit, which explained that campus grounds were not public forums. So the university could reasonably restrict speech. **The evidence showed the messages were removed as they were "unusually noticeable and intrusive," not because they expressed a particular viewpoint.** The court rejected the student's Fourth Amendment claim, as well as his claim that UT's policy on vandalism was unconstitutionally vague. The term "vandalism" was readily understood, and UT was not required to make sure all students had specific notice of its policies. *Wilson v. Johnson*, 247 Fed.Appx. 620 (6th Cir. 2007).

◆   *A federal district court upheld the U.S. government's decision to tighten restrictions on American higher education programs offered in Cuba.*

In 1999, federal Cuban Assets Control Regulations (CACR) allowed American colleges and universities to participate in structured educational programs in Cuba. These regulations had no minimum durational requirements, and students could enroll in Cuban educational institutions even if they were not enrolled in an undergraduate or degree program. In 2004, the government added a requirement that educational programs conducted by American schools in Cuba last at least 10 weeks. It also required any student using an institution's license for educational travel to Cuba to be enrolled at that school, and required teachers to be full-time, permanent faculty members. Students, professors and others challenged the regulations.

A federal court held **the regulations did not violate the First Amendment, as they were neutral with respect to content** and supported by the government interest in denying hard currency to Cuba. The court held the amendments did not violate an asserted Fifth Amendment right to international travel. Denying U.S. currency to the Castro government was an important government interest, and courts defer to the political branches of government with respect to foreign affairs. *Emergency Coalition to Defend Educational Travel v. U.S. Dep't of Treasury*, 498 F.Supp.2d 150 (D.D.C. 2007).

3. Retaliation

◆ *A student was unable to show Central Michigan University (CMU) dismissed her in retaliation for exercising her constitutional rights.*

During her master's program in speech-language pathology, the student abruptly cancelled client appointments without obtaining a substitute and without providing adequate notice to supervisors. She was assigned an F grade for patient abandonment, and she was recommended for dismissal from the program. Instead of complying with CMU grievance procedures, she sued the university in a federal court, asserting retaliation for constitutionally protected speech. In pretrial activity, the student claimed she had reported "unethical misconduct" and lack of professionalism by faculty members in emails to her supervisors. The court disagreed, finding **any message she may have intended was "vague and cryptic."** CMU instructors acted according to CMU policy when preparing to dismiss the student. She abandoned her clients. Her instructors lowered her grade because of it, as specified in the relevant handbook provision. As the student failed to make a valid speech claim and instructors properly followed the handbook in lowering her grade, the case was dismissed. *Stephenson v. Cent. Michigan Univ.*, 897 F.Supp.2d 556 (E.D. Mich. 2012).

CMU then sought $141,428 in attorneys' fees and $11,577.82 in costs as sanctions from the student for a baseless filing. **The court held it was not in a position to second-guess good-faith academic decisions by university staff.** Exercising its broad discretion to determine a sanction, the court awarded only fees and costs incurred after the motion for sanctions. This resulted in an award to CMU of $11,582 in attorneys' fees and $59.25 in costs. *Stephenson v. Cent. Michigan Univ.*, No. 11-12681, 2013 WL 306514 (E.D. Mich. 1/25/13).

◆ *Georgia technical college administrators had qualified immunity against a nursing student's due process and speech rights retaliation claims.*

After the college suspended the student from her licensed practical nursing program, she filed a federal district court action for retaliation. She claimed she was suspended for reporting instructors for falsifying attendance records. A federal district court held a jury trial, after which a jury returned a $450,000 verdict for the student. The court overturned the verdict and held college instructors had qualified immunity.

On appeal, the U.S. Court of Appeals, Eleventh Circuit, held the law at the time of the alleged offenses was unclear as to whether the student was entitled to an immediate appeal of her discipline. For this reason, college administrators were entitled to qualified immunity as to the due process claims. As for the student's speech rights claim, the record showed she often disrupted class and was warned that her behavior had to improve or she would face expulsion. Despite being warned, the student was twice reported for misconduct by her instructors, and there was evidence that she pressured a student to sign a petition. Another student said she had threatened him. After the student reported teachers were leaving class early, one of the instructors filed a grievance against her, stating she had bullied her, spread lies about her, called her names and disrupted class. As the court found a lawful motive for suspending the student, it agreed with the lower court that **the administrators were entitled to immunity. They could have reasonably believed the suspension would not violate her First Amendment speech rights.** *Castle v. Appalachian Technical College*, 631 F.3d 1194 (11th Cir. 2011).

◆ *A federal court dismissed a graduate student's lawsuit asserting that the University of Houston (UH) trumped up discipline against him for activism.*

The student opposed department policies and faculty appointments. He founded two student activist groups and interrupted a faculty senate meeting with a fair trade protest. UH twice referred the student for discipline for "obstructing or interfering with university functions or activities." Meanwhile, supervising professors said he was insensitive and derogatory to students in his role as a teaching assistant. After several other students complained about the student, a professor had to regrade much of his teaching assistant work. Disciplinary referrals were made for violations of the UH disciplinary code.

The professor recommended banning the student from departmental positions, and UH followed the recommendation. The student sued UH in a federal district court for retaliation for exercising his speech rights. Claims against UH's former president failed, as he had nothing to do with denying any teaching assistant positions. **The court held UH had immunity under federal law unless the state consented to be sued or Congress validly abrogated its immunity.** As neither was true, the case was dismissed. *O'Brien v. Univ. of Houston*, No. H-08-2337, 2010 WL 890979 (S.D. Tex. 3/8/10).

◆ *A Pennsylvania student unsuccessfully claimed he was arrested in retaliation for accusing an instructor of discrimination.*

A white Jewish student argued with an African-American computer lab instructor over his use of computer lab facilities. A college policy permitted computer use by students enrolled in active, ongoing classes, but prohibited access for personal use. At the time, the student was not enrolled in an active, ongoing class and was using computers for his own use. He wrote a letter to the college president complaining about the denial of lab use. The dispute continued for eight months and resulted in the student's forcible removal from the computer lab by Pittsburgh police officers. He was arrested for trespass, but charges were later withdrawn. The student sued the college and officials including the instructor in a federal district court for speech rights violations and breach of contract. He claimed violation of his First Amendment rights. A federal district court held for the college and officials, and the student appealed.

The U.S. Court of Appeals, Third Circuit, said that **to prevail on a speech rights retaliation claim, the student had to show he engaged in protected speech and the college retaliated against him for making the speech.** The court found his letter was not a matter of public concern and was thus not protected activity. The student's contract claim failed because he had no contract with the college. The college was not required to provide written notice of every regulation governing the use of its facilities to enforce its regulations. The court affirmed the judgment for the college and officials. *Feldman v. Community College of Allegheny*, 85 Fed.Appx. 821 (3d Cir. 2004).

B. Electronic Communications

Use of electronic media does not enhance or detract from speech rights. The same principles apply to cyberspace speech as for other media.

◆   *University of Minnesota officials were entitled to assign a failing grade to a mortuary school student who made Facebook posts about a lab cadaver.*

On a Facebook page, the student referred to the lab cadaver as "Bernie" from the film "Weekend at Bernie's." She also posted a "Death List" and a post about stabbing "a certain someone in the throat." After the posts were reported, the university's office for student conduct and academic integrity filed a formal complaint. It found the student violated the conduct code based on threatening, harassing or assaultive conduct and breaking university rules. As a result, she was assigned a failing grade in her anatomy laboratory class, required to enroll in an ethics course and ordered to write a letter about professional respect.

The student was instructed to undergo a psychiatric evaluation and placed on academic probation. In a state court lawsuit, she challenged the discipline. Her case reached the Supreme Court of Minnesota, where she argued the discipline violated her speech rights. In ruling for the university, the court based its decision on the relevant professional standards at issue. It held **a university did not violate student speech rights in a professional program by imposing sanctions for Facebook posts that violated academic program rules**. This ruling assumed university rules were narrowly tailored and directly related to established professional conduct standards. State law concerning professional conduct for mortuary science licensees and interns made it unprofessional conduct not to treat the body of the deceased with dignity and respect. The court also found the lab rules were narrowly tailored because they allowed "respectful and discreet" speech. In this case, the student was sanctioned for posts that might be viewed by thousands – and for taking those posts to the media. *Tatro v. Univ. of Minnesota*, 816 N.W.2 509 (Minn. 2012).

◆   *A federal court dismissed disability and privacy claims by a Pennsylvania student against a college, but it allowed a conspiracy claim to proceed.*

The student told college officials he had Attention Deficit Hyperactivity Disorder, a seizure disorder and learning disabilities. He began having trouble during his sophomore year of a teacher preparation program, when he argued with a professor about dropping a class. When this incident was reported to a department chair, the college considered expelling the student. He said faculty members and a college provost then conspired to force him from the institution by discontinuing his accommodations, spreading rumors and monitoring his email account. The college charged the student with plagiarism and disputed his professional competency to become a teacher. In a federal court action against the college, he asserted disability discrimination and breach of contract. The court held the student asserted sufficient facts to support a claim of conspiring to violate his civil rights under federal law. A **claim relating to email access failed because the student did not show college officials intercepted any email at the time of transmission**.

A computer-related claim was dismissed because the statute under which it was brought did not apply to an entity that provides the electronic communications service. Finally, the court dismissed the student's invasion of privacy claim, since he did not allege any mental suffering, shame or humiliation. The court dismissed each of the claims, except the conspiracy-based claim. *Reichert v. Elizabethtown College*, No. 10-2248, 2011 WL 3438318 (E.D. Pa. 8/5/11).

◆ *A Michigan student who was discharged before completing his degree and then filed a losing defamation case also lost a court challenge to his dismissal.*

After being dismissed from medical school, the student launched a website with a domain name nearly identical to that of the college. The college sued him in a federal district court, seeking to shut down the site and asserting claims for trademark infringement, unlawful publication of student records and defamation. At a hearing, the student agreed to prevent the public from viewing the website and to mark videos he had posted on YouTube as private. Based on these assurances, the court declined to issue an injunction. The college later said the student reactivated his site without court approval, and it renewed its motion for an order to stop him from publishing information and from using his website domain. It also sought to stop him from publishing student records.

The court explained that preliminary injunctive relief is not typically granted in defamation cases, because courts may not impose prior restraints on speech. Instead, **the typical remedy for defamation is monetary damages**. Since there had been no final finding that information on the student's site was false and defamatory, the court found it would be inappropriate to grant injunctive relief. But the court denied the student's request to dismiss the case. *American Univ. of Antigua College of Medicine v. Woodward*, No. 10-10978, 2010 WL 5185075 (E.D. Mich. 12/16/10).

◆ *Like a traditional classroom, an online university discussion board is not a public forum where students have an absolute right to say what they want.*

A Southern Oregon University (SOU) online class was delivered entirely over the Internet. A student was disrespectful to classmates and the instructor in an online forum. After being warned about his conduct, the student enrolled in another online class and was charged with classroom defiance and disrespect. After a disciplinary hearing, SOU placed the student on probation. He sued SOU in a federal district court for civil rights violations. The court said a university conduct policy which prohibited the display of defiance or disrespect of others was not unconstitutionally vague or overbroad. Some regulation of speech is permissible. In the educational context, it is reasonable to limit speech rights to maintain order and discipline on university property. **The student was not barred from expressing his views. He was only barred from insulting others.** As the SOU policy furthered the important government interest in maintaining decorum and order in an online classroom environment, and students were put on notice of what conduct was prohibited, the policy was upheld as constitutional. **A classroom is not a public forum where students have an absolute right to say whatever they want.** The court denied the student's request for an order and held SOU could limit speech that might lead to disruption of its activities. *Harrell v. Southern Oregon Univ.*, No. 08-3037-CL, 2009 WL 3562732 (D. Or. 10/30/09).

◆ *A student had no constitutional right to use an unflattering picture of Regent University President Pat Robertson as his Facebook profile picture.*

The student used a YouTube clip of Robertson scratching his face with his middle finger on his Facebook profile. At a certain point, it appeared as though Robertson was "flipping the bird." When school administrators learned of the picture, they told the student it violated a prohibition on profane or obscene behavior in the university's standards of personal conduct. The student removed the picture, but he posted a discussion on a public email list declaring "[t]he value the picture serves is to show that Pat Robertson is a very bad man."

A short time later, the university received reports that the student was acting in an "unstable" and "erratic" manner and possibly kept a gun in his car. After he was barred from classes, he sued the university for speech and due process violations. He also raised Title IX and defamation claims. The court rejected the speech and due process claims because Regent is a private entity that is not obligated to comply with the Constitution. The Title IX claim failed because the student was not similarly situated to a female student who was allegedly permitted to have a stun gun on campus. She later agreed to surrender her gun. **The court rejected the student's defamation claim, as he deliberately manipulated television images, and there was no actual malice by university officials.** *Key v. Robertson*, 626 F.Supp.2d 566 (E.D. Va. 2009).

◆ *A California community college policy violated student speech rights by improperly restricting use of its library Internet service.*

A student viewed MySpace.com member profiles on a computer in the college library. A campus police officer accused him of viewing pornography and told him he could not access the site at the library. Although the student was not disciplined, he sued the community college district in a state superior court for violating a state law that gives students the same speech rights on campus they have when not on campus. The court held that the district's policy, which limited library Internet use to "appropriate academic, professional or institutional purposes," violated the state law because it was overbroad. The court ordered the district to revise its Internet use policy. The district revised the policy, and the court entered judgment in the case. Both sides appealed.

The Court of Appeal of California held that the revised policy complied with state law. While the student claimed the law gave students the same speech rights on campus that they enjoyed in their homes, the court held the law guaranteed only the speech rights they enjoyed "off campus." **Speech rights varied, depending on where the speech took place. In this case, the activities took place in a college library, which was like a public library.** For that reason, whether the revised policy met free speech requirements depended on whether it would be permissible if applied to public library users. Relying on a U.S. Supreme Court decision addressing Internet access in public libraries, the court held the revised policy was reasonable and not an effort to suppress expression based on viewpoint. As a result, the trial court had properly limited relief to declaring the old policy invalid and requiring the district to adopt a new one. *Crosby v. South Orange County Community College Dist.*, 172 Cal.App.4th 433, 91 Cal.Rptr.3d 161 (Cal. Ct. App. 2009).

C. Newspapers and Yearbooks

◆   *A New York college had to pay a group of student editors more than $233,000 in legal fees and costs in a federal action that has been ongoing since 1997.*

A student newspaper endorsed a group of candidates, many of whom were also student editors, before a campus election. The college president found the newspaper had improperly used student activity fees to publish what she called a thinly veiled "piece of campaign literature." Since the president found the newspaper endorsement compromised the electoral process, she scheduled a new vote. The student editors sued the university and officials in a federal court, which held the president violated their rights but was entitled to immunity.

On appeal, the U.S. Court of Appeals, Second Circuit, found viewpoint discrimination by the president. It held more consideration of the immunity issue was necessary. Although the U.S. Supreme Court was asked to review the case, it denied the request. When the case returned to the district court, the president asked the court to enter a judgment against herself in the amount of one dollar for each of the student editors, but with no admission of liability on her part. This motion was granted. **As the students were prevailing parties in the case, they were entitled to their attorneys' fees and costs.** But they were not entitled to the punitive damages they sought, and the attorneys' fees award was far less than the $832,000 they sought. *Husain v. Springer*, No. 97 CV 2982(NG)(CLP), 2013 WL 1122718 (E.D.N.Y. 3/15/13).

◆   *The U.S. Court of Appeals, Seventh Circuit, held a university dean was entitled to immunity for prior restraint of the content of a student newspaper.*

The university became interested in the school newspaper, the *Innovator*, after it printed articles attacking the integrity of the dean of the college of arts and sciences. The dean and university president issued statements accusing the *Innovator* of irresponsible and defamatory journalism. The newspaper refused to retract comments that officials insisted were false, or even to print their responses. When the dean of student affairs notified the newspaper's printing company that a university official had to review and approve the newspaper's content before each issue was printed, the students sued the university for speech rights violations. A federal district court refused to dismiss the claims against the dean. The Seventh Circuit held in 2003 that she was not entitled to qualified immunity because the prohibition against censorship within the university setting was clearly established at the time she acted.

In *Hazelwood School Dist. v. Kuhlmeier*, 484 U.S. 260 (1988), the U.S. Supreme Court held that high school officials have broad powers to censor school-sponsored newspapers, if their actions are supported by valid educational purposes. The Court had allowed prior restraint in *Hazelwood* because the student newspaper was prepared as part of a high school journalism curriculum. In this case, the Seventh Circuit found the greater maturity of college students made censorship of college newspapers untenable, and it held in their favor. *Hosty v. Carter*, 325 F.3d 945 (7th Cir. 2003).

The dean then petitioned the Seventh Circuit for reconsideration. The petition was granted, and the court reversed its 2003 decision. The court held the *Hazelwood* standard could apply to a public university. Since public officials need not predict constitutional uncertainties, the dean was entitled to qualified immunity. *Hosty v. Carter*, 412 F.3d 731 (7th Cir. 2005).

◆ *The U.S. Supreme Court has held that, at the collegiate level, the conduct of students and the dissemination of ideas – no matter how offensive – could not be curtailed based solely on the "conventions of decency."*

A graduate student at the University of Missouri was expelled for distributing on campus a newspaper that violated university bylaws since it contained forms of "indecent speech." The newspaper was found objectionable for two reasons. First, on the front cover was a political cartoon of policemen raping the Statue of Liberty and the Goddess of Justice with a caption that read "… with Liberty and Justice for All." Secondly, the issue contained an article entitled "Mother Fucker Acquitted," which discussed the trial and acquittal on an assault charge of a New York youth. The student sued the university in a federal district court, for First Amendment violations. The court denied relief, but the U.S. Supreme Court held the student should be reinstated. It stated that **while a university has an undoubted prerogative to enforce reasonable rules governing student conduct, it is not immune from the sweep of the First Amendment.** *Healy v. James*, 408 U.S. 169 (1972), made it clear that the mere dissemination of ideas – no matter how offensive to good taste – may not be shut off in the name of "conventions of decency" alone. *Papish v. Univ. of Missouri*, 410 U.S. 667, 93 S.Ct. 1197, 35 L.Ed.2d 618 (1973).

◆ *A university violated the First and Fourteenth Amendment rights of a yearbook editor when it confiscated yearbooks for being "inappropriate."*

The editor of Kentucky State University's (KSU's) yearbook during the 1993–1994 school year decided to be innovative and, for the first time, gave the yearbook a theme: "Destination Unknown." The theme reflected the students' uncertainty about life after college and the pending question of whether the university was to become a community college. The yearbook included pictures from KSU events as well as current national and world events. KSU's vice president for student affairs objected to the final product. She opposed the yearbook's cover, theme, the lack of captions under many photos and the inclusion of current events unrelated to KSU. **The vice president and other university officials prohibited the yearbooks from being distributed and confiscated them.** The editor and another student sued the school on behalf of all KSU students in federal court, claiming their First and Fourteenth Amendment rights were violated. The court dismissed the suit, finding that the yearbook was a nonpublic forum because it was not intended to be a journal of expression, but rather a record of the events at KSU for its students.

The students appealed to the U.S. Court of Appeals, Sixth Circuit, which held a high school yearbook is not a public forum and is subject to strict control by school officials. **A college yearbook is a limited public forum.** KSU's policy toward the yearbook gave the student editors control over the publication because it did not allow a faculty/staff advisor to change the yearbook in order to alter the content. In addition, **the language of the university's student publication policy indicated that such publications were intended to be limited public forums**. The policy begins by saying, "The Board of Regents respects the integrity of student publications and the press, and the rights to exist in an atmosphere of free and responsible discussion and of intellectual exploration." The Sixth Circuit remanded the matter to the district court for further proceedings. *Kincaid v. Gibson*, 236 F.3d 342 (6th Cir. 2000).

D. Student Activity Fees

A "facial challenge" to a government law or policy proceeds on the premise that the law or policy always violates the Constitution. On the other hand, an "as-applied challenge" relies on the argument that a policy violated the Constitution as it was applied to a particular party in a certain situation.

◆   *A Wisconsin university was required to grant religious groups equal access to a public forum and did not violate the Establishment Clause by doing so.*

The University of Wisconsin-Madison collected about $400 per semester from each student for non-instructional student services, programs and facilities. About $33 of this went into a General Student Services Fund (GSSF), which funded student organizations. The stated purpose of the GSSF was to give students a way to "engage in dynamic discussions" relating to a number of enumerated topics – including religion – in extracurricular activities.

The Roman Catholic Foundation (RCF) received funding from segregated fees, but the university denied reimbursement for expenditures that supported worship, proselytizing, or religious instruction. The RCF and student members sued the university in a federal court for viewpoint discrimination. The court issued a preliminary order barring the university from enforcing any policy that prevented RCF from being reimbursed for activities on the basis of prayer, worship or proselytizing. Later, the court issued an order denying the group's request for permanent relief, limiting its relief to a declaration and denying damages. It declined to characterize the university's conduct as "content based discrimination." *Roman Catholic Foundation, UW-Madison v. Regents of the Univ. of Wisconsin System*, 590 F.Supp.2d 1083 (W.D. Wis. 2008).

On appeal, the U.S. Court of Appeals, Seventh Circuit, held the district court had correctly interpreted Supreme Court cases in finding the university would not violate the Establishment Clause by funding the RCF programs. *Widmar v. Vincent*, 454 U.S. 263 (1981), and *Rosenberger v. Rector and Visitors of Univ. of Virginia*, 515 U.S. 819 (1995), supported the lower court's conclusion. These and other cases led the court to declare that "**underwriting a religious speaker's costs, as part of a neutral program justified by the program's secular benefits, does not violate the Establishment Clause** even if the religious speaker uses some of the money for prayer or sectarian instruction." *Badger Catholic, Inc. v. Walsh*, 620 F.3d 775 (7th Cir. 2010).

◆ *A federal appeals court refused to hear a case involving the constitutionality of a university policy that was no longer in effect.*

College Standard Magazine (CSM) published a conservative newspaper on the campus of a New York state university. The university student association denied funding to CSM from revenues made up of mandatory student activity fees. A federal district court agreed with CSM's claim that a university policy was facially unconstitutional because it gave the student association "unbridled discretion" when it came to distributing funding. The student association appealed to the U.S. Court of Appeals, Second Circuit, which found nothing in the record to show the university's former policy would be reinstated. The association was asking for a ruling on the constitutionality of a policy that was no longer in effect. **Court powers are limited to deciding actual controversies, and the court held it could not issue an order that could have any effect on the relationship between the parties.** Any ruling on the constitutionality of the old policy would be "strictly advisory." The challenged policy had been repealed, and CSM had conceded an "as-applied" challenge to it. Thus, the court denied the appeal. *College Standard Magazine v. Student Ass'n of the State Univ. of New York at Albany*, 610 F.3d 33 (2d Cir. 2010).

◆ *The U.S. Supreme Court held that the University of Wisconsin could assess a mandatory activity fee to fund student extracurricular programs.*

The University of Wisconsin required all students to pay the university a nonrefundable activity fee to support registered student groups. Students who objected to the collection and use of their student fees to support objectionable political and ideological expression sued university regents in a federal district court, asserting that the program violated their speech rights. The court held that the fee program compelled students to support political and ideological activity with which they disagreed in violation of the First Amendment.

Appeal reached **the U.S. Supreme Court, which found that the university had assessed the fee to facilitate the free and open exchange of ideas among students**. Objecting students could insist upon certain safeguards regarding the compelled support of expressive activities. To insist upon germaneness to the university's mission would contravene the purpose of the program, which was to encourage a wide range of speech. The Court found it inevitable that the fees would subsidize some speech that students would find objectionable, and it declined to impose a constitutional requirement upon the university compelling it to refund fees to students. Viewpoint neutrality was the proper standard for the protection of the First Amendment rights of the objecting students. **The university could require students to support extracurricular speech of other students in a viewpoint-neutral manner**, and the parties had stipulated in this case that the program was viewpoint neutral. The university had wide latitude to adjust its extracurricular speech programs to accommodate students. The Court reversed and remanded the case for further proceedings. *Board of Regents of Univ. of Wisconsin System v. Southworth*, 529 U.S. 217, 120 S.Ct. 1346, 146 L.Ed.2d 193 (2000).

On remand, the district court determined the university's updated fee system, which set forth the criteria groups had to meet before obtaining funding and required the student government to determine which groups received funding, was unconstitutional because it was not viewpoint neutral. Under the new system, the university's student government made funding decisions with little or no oversight. The court further held the criteria used to determine whether a group received funding was too subjective. The university was ordered to establish a viewpoint-neutral funding system. *Fry v. Board of Regents of Univ. of Wisconsin System,* 132 F.Supp.2d 744 (W.D. Wis. 2000).

◆   *The Supreme Court held a university could not withhold authorization for payments to a printer on behalf of a Christian student organization.*

The University of Virginia collected a mandatory $14 student activity fee from full-time students each semester. The fees supported extracurricular activities that were related to the educational purposes of the university. University-recognized student groups could apply for funding by the activities fund, although not all groups requested funds. University guidelines excluded religious groups from student funding as well as activities that could jeopardize the university's tax-exempt status. A university-recognized student group published a Christian newspaper for which it sought $5,862 from the activities fund for printing costs. The student council denied funding because the group's activities were deemed religious under university guidelines. After exhausting appeals within the university, group members filed suit in a federal district court, claiming constitutional violations. The court held for the university.

Appeal reached the U.S. Supreme Court. The Court observed that **government entities must abstain from regulating speech on the basis of the speaker's opinion.** Upon establishing a limited public forum, state entities must respect the forum by refraining from the exclusion of speech based upon content. **Because the university had opened a limited public forum by paying other third-party contractors on behalf of student groups, it could not deny the religious group's claim for funds on the basis of its viewpoint.** Allowing the payment of the group's printing costs amounted to a policy of government neutrality for different viewpoints. The Court distinguished the student fee from a general tax and placed emphasis on the indirect nature of the benefit. The Court reversed the lower court decisions, ruling that access to public university facilities on a neutral basis does not violate the Establishment Clause of the First Amendment. *Rosenberger v. Rector and Visitors of Univ. of Virginia,* 515 U.S. 819, 115 S.Ct. 2510, 132 L.Ed.2d 700 (1995).

E. Student Elections

◆   *A Washington college violated the speech rights of students when it turned them away from an on-campus political rally because of the shirts they wore.*

Although the college announced the rally was open to all college students, faculty and staff members, five students were told they could not attend the event because they were wearing T-shirts with the name of an opposing candidate. The students later sued the college and officials for speech rights violations. A federal district court held it was clear that the college had violated their speech rights. As the law regarding expression in an open forum such as a political rally was clearly established at the time of the violation, the officials did not have immunity. Although the college argued it rented the space to one candidate's campaign, it had encouraged all students, faculty and staff to attend. As a result, **the students could not be excluded from the rally just because they showed support for the other candidate.** *Yates v. Fithian,* No. CV09-01289-RSM, 2010 WL 3788272 (W.D. Wash. 9/23/10).

◆ *A Montana student's constitutional challenge to a university rule limiting campaign spending in student elections failed.*

The student was elected president of the Associated Students of the University of Montana (ASUM). However, he violated an ASUM bylaw that limited candidates from spending more than $100 on their campaigns by spending about $300 on the campaign with his running mate. Although the two were censured, they were allowed to retain their offices. The student exceeded the limit again when he ran for the student senate the next year. This time, he was denied permission to assume office. The student sued university officials in a federal district court, claiming the spending cap violated the Speech Clause of the First Amendment. The district court upheld the cap and ruled against him, finding the spending limitation was reasonable. The student appealed.

The U.S. Court of Appeals, Ninth Circuit, noted that the student had now graduated, but was seeking an order requiring the university to clear all records of disciplinary sanctions based on the spending limit. Therefore, his graduation did not moot the case. **The court held the election was a limited public forum, created by the university to allow students to gain the educational experience of campaigning for a student government position.** Because the election was a limited public forum, the spending limitation was constitutional as long as it was viewpoint neutral and reasonable. The limitation met these requirements, because it did not favor one speaker's message over another's. It was reasonable, as it served the goal of teaching students responsible leadership and behavior. The district court's ruling in favor of university officials was affirmed. *Flint v. Dennison,* 488 F.3d 816 (9th Cir. 2007). In 2008, the U.S. Supreme Court denied a petition to further review the case.

IV. USE OF CAMPUS FACILITIES

A. Students and Student Groups

In Christian Legal Society Chapter of the Univ. of California, Hastings College of Law v. Martinez, *this chapter, the Supreme Court stated the general rule that public university speech regulations are allowed if they are narrowly drawn and serve a compelling state interest. Under the "forum analysis" used by the courts, public institutions may designate particular forums for expression and limit their use, so long as there is no viewpoint discrimination.*

◆ *Ohio students obtained a temporary order preventing the University of Cincinnati (UC) from enforcing a policy placing prior restraints on speech.*

Students who wanted to solicit signatures for a political cause sought a federal court order against UC for policies confining such activities to a "free speech area" on campus. The court granted their request for a preliminary injunction, finding the policies imposed an unconstitutional prior restraint on expressive activity. UC policies had restricted all demonstrations, picketing, and rallies to an area comprising less than 0.1% of the campus. UC also required students to provide UC officials with five to 15 days of notice in advance of all expressive activities on campus and to obtain a permit first. **A restriction on protected speech in a designated public forum must be narrowly tailored and justified by a compelling government interest.** In the court's view, the restrictions here were not narrowly tailored. *Univ. of Cincinnati Chapter of Young Americans for Liberty v. Williams*, No. 1:11-cv-155, 2012 WL 2160969 (S.D. Ohio 6/12/12).

◆ *The U.S. Supreme Court held a California law college could deny official recognition to a Christian student organization that only accepted members who shared the organization's beliefs about religion and sexual orientation.*

Hastings College of Law allowed officially recognized Registered Student Organizations (RSOs) to use college communications channels, office space and email accounts. RSO events were subsidized by student fees. To gain RSO status, groups had to comply with a school nondiscrimination policy. The Christian Legal Society (CLS) did not accept students whose religious convictions differed from its Statement of Faith. The CLS sought an exemption from the nondiscrimination policy, but Hastings denied the request due to noncompliance with the nondiscrimination policy. In a federal district court action, the CLS asserted speech, religious free exercise and due process violations. The court upheld Hastings' policy, and the case eventually reached the U.S. Supreme Court. The Court held regulations on speech are allowed if they serve a compelling state interest. According to the Court, the CLS faced only indirect pressure to modify its policies. The group could still exclude any person for any reason if it decided to forego the benefits of RSO recognition.

Hastings' policy applied to "all comers," which ensured a student was not forced to fund any group that might exclude her. An all-comers requirement helped Hastings "police" its policy without inquiring into the reasons for restricting RSO membership. Social networking sites reduced the importance of RSO channels. As for the CLS's argument that Hastings had no legitimate interest in regulating its membership, the Court held Hastings could "reasonably draw a line in the sand permitting all organizations to express what they wish but no group to discriminate in membership." The policy did not distinguish among groups based on viewpoint and was "textbook viewpoint neutral." *Christian Legal Society Chapter of the Univ. of California, Hastings College of Law v. Martinez*, 130 S.Ct. 2971, 177 L.Ed.2d 838 (U.S. 2010).

◆ *San Diego State University (SDSU) could deny official recognition to groups that did not comply with a viewpoint-neutral nondiscrimination policy.*

SDSU denied official recognition to a Christian fraternity and sorority, stating their membership rules were in conflict with SDSU's nondiscrimination policy. The policy barred recognizing student groups that discriminated based on race, religion, ethnicity, age, gender, or sexual orientation. The fraternity and sorority sued SDSU officials in a federal court for violation of their speech and association rights. The case reached the U.S. Court of Appeals, Ninth Circuit. It held the SDSU student organization program was a limited public forum. This meant exclusion of the fraternity and the sorority was permissible if it was viewpoint neutral and reasonable in view of the forum's purposes. In the court's view, the SDSU policy was reasonable in light of its purpose to promote diversity and nondiscrimination. **The policy was viewpoint neutral because it did not target specific speech or discriminate based on content.**

There was no evidence before the court that SDSU purposely suppressed any viewpoint or that it even restricted expression at all. The court held SDSU merely withheld benefits. But the fraternity and sorority presented evidence that the policy had not been applied evenly. SDSU had officially recognized other religious groups with similar membership restrictions. As SDSU did not explain why some student groups had been recognized despite violating the nondiscrimination policy, further consideration by a lower court was needed. *Alpha Delta Chi-Delta Chapter v. Reed*, 648 F.3d 790 (9th Cir. 2011).

◆   *A federal appeals court rejected claims by a pro-life student rights group that accused university officials of violating its right to free expression.*

A Maryland student organization sought permission to display posters on campus to show "what abortion actually does to unborn children." A university official said the posters would block access to a building, and a university lawyer said the university had a right to prevent the "emotional harassment" of students. The university let the group set up the display in a different area of campus. After being told it would have to use this less-preferred area for a second demonstration, the group sued university officials in a federal district court for speech rights violations. The court held for the university officials, finding the group lacked standing to pursue claims based on code of conduct and sexual harassment policies. On appeal, the U.S. Court of Appeals, Fourth Circuit, held **the group lacked standing to challenge the sexual harassment policy. It did not show a true threat that the policy would be enforced against it.** The group had no standing to challenge the conduct code. University officials deserved qualified immunity, and the judgment was affirmed. *Rock for Life-UMBC v. Hrabowski*, 411 Fed.Appx. 541 (4th Cir. 2010).

◆   *A Texas college could not halt students from participating in a demonstration staged by "Students for Concealed Carry on Campus" (SCCC).*

The SCCC promoted "empty-holster protests" to prompt changes in laws and college rules to allow concealed handguns on campuses. Tarrant County College District (TCC) limited student protests to a "free speech zone." To hold a protest there, students had to ask for permission at least 24 hours in advance. Two SCCC student leaders sued TCC in a federal district court for speech rights violations. The court held TCC interfered with their rights to speak in public by requiring a permit and limiting protests to the free speech zone. TCC could not enforce those rules. TCC removed the permit requirement from its manual and eliminated the free speech zone. It added new rules banning disruptive activities and on-campus speech that was "co-sponsored" by off-campus organizations. The court struck down these rules and held TCC must let students wear empty holsters in classrooms. **Student speech – which** includes wearing something to symbolically communicate a message – can be restricted in classrooms only if the restriction is viewpoint neutral, furthers a substantial governmental interest, is unrelated to suppressing student speech, and does not overly restrict protective activities.

While TCC could ban speech-making and leafleting in classes and halls, it could not show that the wearing of empty holsters was "inherently" disruptive. The court struck TCC's co-sponsorship rule, finding it could not prohibit speech for being affiliated with an off-campus group. *Smith v. Tarrant County College Dist.*, 694 F.Supp.2d 610 (N.D. Tex. 2010).

◆ *A New York university did not violate a fraternity's association rights by declining to recognize it as a student group because it refused to admit females.*

The university denied the fraternity's application for official recognition due to a conflict with the university's nondiscrimination policy. The fraternity sued the university in a federal district court for First Amendment violations. The court held the fraternity qualified as an "intimate association." Forcing it to admit females would burden its associational rights. The university appealed to the U.S. Court of Appeals, Second Circuit, which held the fraternity's interest in intimacy did not merit strict scrutiny. It placed no limit on membership size, and many Jewish men who expressed an interest in the fraternity were invited to join. The fraternity's purposes were inclusive, and it allowed non-members into some functions. **The college had a strong interest in assuring its resources were available to all students.** As the district court applied the wrong standard, its order was vacated. *Chi Iota Colony of Alpha Epsilon Pi Fraternity v. City Univ. of New York*, 502 F.3d 136 (2d Cir. 2007).

◆ *A student Christian organization obtained a preliminary order preventing a law school from revoking its official status.*

The dean of an Illinois law school revoked the official student organization status of the Christian Legal Society (CLS) because the organization excluded those who engaged in or affirmed homosexual conduct. This violated the university's affirmative action/equal opportunity (EEO) policy. The CLS sued the university in a federal district court for First Amendment violations. The court denied its request for an order requiring the university to restore its official status. The CLS appealed to the U.S. Court of Appeals, Seventh Circuit. The court found it unclear whether the CLS had violated any university policy. **It was likely that the university impermissibly infringed on the CLS's right of expressive association, and its speech rights.** The university failed to identify which federal or state law it believed the CLS had violated. CLS membership requirements did not exclude members on the basis of sexual orientation. Rather, the organization required members to adhere to certain standards of sexual conduct. **The university's affirmative action/EEO policy did not apply to CLS because the organization did not employ anyone.** The court reversed the judgment and granted the CLS its requested order. *Christian Legal Society v. Walker*, 453 F.3d 853 (7th Cir. 2006).

◆ *Student rights to association may not be disregarded or limited.*

A group of students desired to form a local chapter of Students for a

Democratic Society (SDS) at a state-supported college. They were, however, denied recognition as a campus organization. The students sued for declaratory and injunctive relief. A federal district court held the college's refusal to recognize the group, in light of the disruptive and violent nature of the national organization, was justifiable. The U.S. Court of Appeals for the Second Circuit affirmed, stating that the students had failed to avail themselves of the due process of law accorded to them and had failed to meet their burden of complying with the prevailing standards for recognition.

The U.S. Supreme Court held that **the lower courts erred in disregarding the First Amendment interest in freedom of association that the students had in furthering their personal beliefs.** It also held that putting the burden on the students (to show entitlement to recognition) rather than on the president (to justify nonrecognition) was also in error. The Court stated that insofar as the denial of recognition was based on the group's affiliation with the national SDS, or as a result of disagreement with the group's philosophy, the president's decision violated the students' First Amendment rights. A proper basis for nonrecognition might have been that the group refused to comply with a rule requiring them to abide by reasonable campus regulations. Since it was not clear that the college had such a rule, and whether the students intended to observe it, the case was remanded to the district court for resolution. *Healy v. James*, 408 U.S. 169, 92 S.Ct. 2338, 33 L.Ed.2d 266 (1972).

◆   *A Texas state university policy that was used to prohibit students from distributing pro-life leaflets was held unconstitutional.*

The university policy required the name of each organization handing out leaflets to be stated on leaflets. After a student anti-abortion group distributed leaflets on campus without doing so, the university acted to stop them. They sued the university in a federal district court for speech rights violations. The court held the policy was unconstitutional, and appeal reached the U.S. Court of Appeals, Fifth Circuit. It found the Supreme Court has held anonymous pamphleteering is a form of advocacy that exemplifies the purpose behind the First Amendment. But public universities can and typically do restrict access to campus facilities. Students often must identify themselves before they can use campus facilities. The Fifth Circuit held that on-campus speech is almost never totally anonymous. **The court held the policy was too far-reaching, as it required each speaker to identify him or herself to every person receiving literature.** *Justice for All v. Faulkner*, 410 F.3d 760 (5th Cir. 2005).

◆   *Where a Washington college allowed secular demonstrations, it could not place restrictions on a demonstration based on religion.*

The dean of a community college allowed an anti-abortion demonstration on campus. His office received a number of complaints, leading him to ask campus security to remove the demonstrators. When they refused to leave, police were called, and a demonstrator was arrested. He later sued the dean and the head of campus security under 42 U.S.C. § 1983 for violating his First Amendment rights. A federal court granted pretrial judgment to the defendants, but the Ninth Circuit Court of Appeals reversed the judgment. The court held a **"no religious instruction or worship" condition imposed by the college**

dean violated the First Amendment as a content-based restriction on speech. Only if that restriction was necessary to achieve a compelling state interest, and was narrowly designed to accomplish that interest, would it be constitutional. The court also held that the dean was not entitled to immunity under Section 1983 because he should have known that placing the "no religion" restriction on the demonstration violated the First Amendment. There also was a question of fact, requiring a trial, as to whether the security head was entitled to immunity. *Orin v. Barclay*, 272 F.3d 1207 (9th Cir. 2001).

◆ *The Establishment Clause does not prevent private citizens from using public facilities for religious purposes.*

The University of Missouri at Kansas City, a state university, made its facilities available for the general use of registered student groups. A registered student religious group that had previously received permission to conduct its meetings in university facilities was informed that it could no longer do so because of a university regulation that prohibited use of its facilities for the purposes of religious worship or teaching. Members of the group sued in federal court, alleging that the regulation violated their First Amendment rights to free exercise of religion and freedom of speech. The court upheld the school's regulation, but the U.S. Court of Appeals, Eighth Circuit, reversed, stating that the regulation was discriminatory against religious speech and that the Establishment Clause does not bar a policy of equal access.

The Supreme Court agreed with the court of appeals' assessment, stating **that the university policy violated the fundamental principle that state regulation of speech must be content neutral**. It is obligatory upon the state to show that the regulation is necessary to serve a compelling state interest and that it is narrowly drawn to achieve that end. The state was unable to do that here. The state's interest in achieving greater separation of church and state than is already ensured under the Establishment Clause was not sufficiently "compelling" to justify content-based discrimination against religious speech of the student group in question. *Widmar v. Vincent*, 454 U.S. 263, 102 S.Ct. 269, 70 L.Ed.2d 400 (1981).

B. Commercial Speech

◆ *A university did not have to allow the KKK to underwrite a radio program.*

A not-for-profit public broadcast radio station operated by the University of Missouri (and a member of National Public Radio) received a request from the state coordinator for the Ku Klux Klan to underwrite a number of 15-second spots on the station's "All Things Considered" program. This would require the station to acknowledge the gift by reading a message from the Klan stating that it was a white Christian organization standing up for the rights and values of white Christians and leaving contact information. The university's chancellor decided that allowing the underwriting would result in a loss of revenue to the station of at least $5 million, and rejected the offer.

The state coordinator and the Klan sued the station manager, asserting that the station could not reject the offer because it was a public forum and could not discriminate by viewpoint. A federal court held **the station did not have to**

accept the Klan's offer. Station employees had the discretion to choose which offers to accept, and the underwriting program could not be deemed a public forum. Further, the decision to reject the offer was not based on viewpoint but on business considerations. The court granted pretrial judgment to the station manager. The Eighth Circuit Court of Appeals affirmed. It noted that the underwriting spots constituted governmental speech and that the government could exercise discretion over what it chose to say. Since the station had the right to reject the proposed spots, the Klan's lawsuit could not succeed. *KKK v. Bennett*, 203 F.3d 1085 (8th Cir. 2000).

◆ *The Supreme Court has held that restrictions on commercial free speech need not be subjected to as rigorous an analysis to determine the restrictions' reasonableness. As long as the restriction is reasonable, it will be upheld.*

The State University of New York (SUNY) prohibited private commercial enterprises from operating in SUNY facilities. Campus police prevented a housewares manufacturer from demonstrating and selling its products at a party hosted in a student dormitory. The manufacturer and a group of students sued SUNY in a federal district court, stating that the policy violated the First Amendment. The court held for SUNY, stating that the student dormitories did not constitute a public forum for purposes of commercial activity, and the restrictions were reasonable in light of the dormitories' purpose. The Second Circuit Court of Appeals reversed, stating that it was unclear whether the policy directly advanced SUNY's interest and whether it was the least restrictive means of achieving that interest. The U.S. Supreme Court granted review and stated that the court of appeals erred in requiring the district court to apply a least restrictive means test. The Court stated that **regulations on commercial speech require only a reasonable "fit" between the government's ends and the means chosen to accomplish those ends**. The Court reversed and remanded the case. *Board of Trustees of the State Univ. of New York v. Fox*, 492 U.S. 469, 109 S.Ct. 3028, 106 L.Ed.2d 388 (1989).

◆ *A student newspaper lost its First Amendment challenge to a Pennsylvania statute sanctioning businesses that advertise alcohol in any school publication.*

The Pitt News filed suit seeking to prevent the enforcement of "Act 199," a 1996 amendment to the state's liquor code that sanctioned advertisers of alcohol products in school newspapers. The U.S. Court of Appeals, Third Circuit, ruled that the newspaper could not sue because it could not demonstrate that its constitutional rights were being violated, and it could not sue on behalf of third parties. **The paper's loss of advertising revenue and subsequent decrease in the length of the publication did not demonstrate that its First Amendment rights were violated.** *The Pitt News v. Fisher*, 215 F.3d 354 (3d Cir. 2000), *cert. denied*, 121 S.Ct. 857 (U.S. 2001).

C. Non-Student Groups

◆ *A federal court revived an evangelical Christian's claim that a Tennessee university violated his rights by limiting his ability to speak on campus.*

A Tennessee Technological University (TTU) dean told the Christian a campus use policy required him to submit a written application in person at least 14 days before he wanted to distribute literature on campus. The Christian sued TTU officials after they threatened to arrest him for noncompliance with the policy. A federal court held TTU's policy was narrowly tailored to serve significant government interests and left ample alternative channels for communication. On appeal, the U.S. Court of Appeals, Sixth Circuit, held the Christian's failure to apply for a permit did not block his claims. His intention to engage in expression supported his claim that the policy chilled his speech.

The court rejected the lower court's conclusion that TTU's policy was a permissible time, place and manner restriction. Instead, TTU's policy of requiring a permit imposed a prior restraint. **Prior restraints must be content-neutral, narrowly tailored, serve a significant government interest, and leave communication alternatives open.** In this case, the TTU policy violated the First Amendment because it was not narrowly tailored to serve a legitimate interest. The 14-day notice requirement was much longer than other notice periods that have been upheld. Also, the court found the policy banned anonymous speech without a good explanation. The lower court decision to dismiss individual university officials based on qualified immunity was held erroneous. According to the court, the Christian had a clearly established right to engage in expression free of unconstitutional interference. The case was returned to the lower court. *McGlone v. Bell*, 681 F.3d 718 (6th Cir. 2012).

◆ *Because they were hostile and disruptive, two disability rights activists were permissibly banned from the campus of a New Jersey university.*

The activists took pictures and videos on campus to document the university's noncompliance with accessible parking requirements. After people complained that the couple harassed, frightened and threatened them, the university issued a trespass notice banning the couple from campus. The activists sued the university in a federal court under the Americans with Disabilities Act (ADA), state laws and federal constitutional provisions. The court held they lacked standing to bring the ADA and state law discrimination claims because they were not disabled. Their retaliation claims failed because they engaged in hostile, harassing, disruptive and aggressive behavior. There was no due process violation because **the activists had no constitutional right to enter the campus**. An equal protection claim failed because they did not show activists who engaged in similar behavior were not barred from campus. There was no evidence that the activists were barred from campus based on protected speech. *Cottrell v. Rowan Univ.*, 786 F.Supp.2d 851 (D.N.J. 2011).

◆ *Tufts College did not violate a private veterinarian's speech rights by excluding her from a lecture because she had failed to pay a bill.*

A veterinarian refused to pay Tufts College for a surgical procedure for a horse. Eight years later, she went to a lecture at the college. A college official recognized her and said she would be arrested if she entered the lecture hall. In a state court action against Tufts, the veterinarian claimed a constitutional right to attend the lecture and asserted defamation, breach of contract, infliction of emotional distress, negligence and other claims. The court held for the college, and the case reached the Supreme Judicial Court of Massachusetts. First, the court found no interference with the veterinarian's constitutional rights by way of threats, intimidation or coercion. The lecture did not take place on public property. At most, the veterinarian had the rights accorded those seeking access to a limited public forum. **Restrictions on speech in a limited public forum need only be reasonable and neutral as to content and viewpoint.** It was reasonable for the college to deny to the veterinarian access until she paid her bill. In addition, the decision to exclude her was content neutral and viewpoint neutral. It did not reflect any judgment on the part of the college about the substance of the veterinarian's speech. The court also upheld the lower court's decision to reject the remaining claims, and the judgment was affirmed. *Roman v. Trustees of Tufts College*, 461 Mass. 707 (Mass. 2012).

◆ *A traveling preacher could not stop Georgia Southern University from enforcing reasonable policies regulating non-students.*

The preacher refused to seek a permit to speak on campus, claiming a constitutional right to speak. After being arrested for trespass, he sued several university officials for constitutional rights violations. A federal district court denied the preacher's request for a preliminary order that would stop the university from enforcing its speech policies. On appeal, the U.S. Court of Appeals, Eleventh Circuit, explained **"the First Amendment does not guarantee access to property just because it is owned by the government."** Instead, the degree of access that must be provided depends on the nature of the property involved. A public university has the purpose of education and can place content-neutral time, place and manner restrictions on speech. The court also upheld university speech policies relating to its sidewalks, pedestrian mall and rotunda. Each of these sites was a limited public forum, and any time, place and manner restrictions regulating them were upheld as viewpoint neutral and reasonable. *Bloedorn v. Grube*, 631 F.3d 1218 (11th Cir. 2011).

◆ *The U.S. Supreme Court held a federal law requiring higher education institutions to provide equal access to military recruiters or forfeit certain federal funding did not violate university speech or association rights.*

Congress enacted the Solomon Amendment to address restrictions put on military recruiting by law schools that disagreed with the U.S. government's policy on homosexuals in the military. The amendment disqualified institutions of higher learning from receiving certain federal funds, if any part of an institution denied access to military recruiters that was equal to that provided other recruiters. An association of law schools and faculties sued the U.S. government in a federal district court, asserting the Solomon Amendment violated the schools' First Amendment speech and association rights. The court denied the association's request for an order preventing enforcement of the Amendment. Congress took note of the court's finding that the law could be interpreted as allowing promotion of nondiscrimination policies by limiting military recruiting to undergraduate campuses. It amended the law to require equal access for military recruiters. The U.S. Court of Appeals, Third Circuit, then held the Amendment regulated speech, and reversed the decision.

On appeal, the U.S. Supreme Court explained that the First Amendment protects rights of association, as well as free speech. The law

schools "associated" with military recruiters only in the sense of their interactions with them. The Solomon Amendment forbade higher education institutions from applying their general nondiscrimination policies to military recruiters. Law schools had to provide the military the same access they provided to all other employment recruiters. The Solomon Amendment did not force the schools to associate with the military. Students and faculty remained free to associate and voice their disapproval of the military's message, and the Court reversed the judgment. *Rumsfeld v. Forum for Academic and Institutional Rights*, 547 U.S. 47, 126 S.Ct. 1297, 164 L.Ed.2d 156 (2006).

◆ *The University of North Dakota (UND) did not violate speech rights by placing restrictions on how individuals can solicit petition signatures.*

UND's code of student life required completing a "special events form" for on-campus events and before soliciting petition signatures in student housing. Petitioners had to sit at designated tables and wait for students to come to them. UND policy prohibited signature collectors from harassing, embarrassing or intimidating people. A group of solicitors obtained UND's permission to collect signatures on campus sidewalks and lawns and inside campus buildings. But a student manager told the group that it could not seek signatures in the building unless the solicitors agreed to stay behind designated tables. One of the solicitors sued UND in a state court for First Amendment violations.

The court held for UND, and the solicitor appealed to the Supreme Court of North Dakota. It rejected the solicitor's claim that he should not have been required to gain UND permission before seeking signatures on UND property. **The First Amendment did not guarantee the solicitor an unrestricted right to use campus property to gather signatures.** Expressive activity on government property is subject to time, place and manner restrictions. UND's policy was content neutral and narrowly tailored to serve the goals of aiding in event planning, protecting the safety of UND property and people on campus, and making sure facilities were used appropriately. UND's ban on harassing, embarrassing or intimidating people asked to sign a petition did not violate the First Amendment. *Riemers v. State*, 767 N.W.2d 832 (N.D. 2009).

◆ *A New York community college lacked a right to regulate the use of its premises by outsiders because it failed to have a policy on facilities use.*

An ordained Baptist minister videotaped himself preaching and handing out religious leaflets on the campus of a New York community college. He was in an outdoor area where students often congregate. A student complained to the assistant dean for administrative services, who asked the minister to stop the videotaping. He refused. The dean then called police, who arrested the minister and charged him with criminal trespass. The charge was later dismissed, but he was cited for simple trespass. The minister sued the college and dean in a federal court for First Amendment violations. **The court explained that the right of a college to limit access depends on the nature of the forum.** If an area is designated as a place for public expression, then speech regulation needs to be "narrowly tailored to serve a significant government interest."

In this case, the college had no regulation authorizing the minister's removal. He had a First Amendment right to preach, hand out leaflets and videotape himself. His conduct did not obstruct the flow of people or vehicles in the area and did not create a disruption. Despite the violation, the Eleventh Amendment barred the minister's claims against the college, which was a state government unit. However, the dean could be sued in his official capacity for equitable relief. *Davis v. Stratton*, 575 F.Supp.2d 410 (N.D.N.Y. 2008).

◆ *An Indiana university did not violate the First Amendment when it prohibited a traveling evangelist from preaching on its campus.*

Traveling preacher James Gilles appeared in public places and preached for many years. His confrontational style led to disturbances, and he was arrested many times. In 2001, Gilles began preaching at Vincennes University without an invitation to be on the campus. His preaching led to a disturbance, and campus police asked him to leave. Following that incident, the university adopted a new policy requiring prior approval by the dean of students for all sales and solicitations on campus. Approved solicitors could solicit only on a walkway in front of the student union. Gilles sued university officials in a federal district court, claiming the policy violated his right to free speech.

The case reached the U.S. Court of Appeals, Seventh Circuit. It held **public universities are not required to make all their facilities equally available to students and non-students. As owners of public property, public universities have the right to ensure the property is used only for lawfully dedicated purposes.** The university had the right to bar access to any outsider, as long as the exclusion was not based on the content of the speaker's message. In this case, the university had placed the area where Gilles sought to speak completely off limits to those who were not invited by a faculty member or student group. Because the university could lawfully bar uninvited guests from using a particular area to speak, the district court's ruling was affirmed. *Gilles v. Blanchard*, 477 F.3d 466 (7th Cir. 2007).

◆ *A federal appeals court reinstated a traveling preacher's claim that a university violated his due process and speech rights.*

James Gilles, the evangelist described in the case above, spoke on the campus of Miami University for about 45 minutes before being interrupted by a security guard who threatened to arrest him if he did not obtain permission to speak on campus. A university policy stated that anyone with "legitimate business" had "the privilege of free access" to public areas of the university's buildings and grounds during times when they were open. The university informed Gilles his speech was not "legitimate business" and that its policy was to permit formal speeches only when the speaker was invited by the school or a recognized student organization. After trying without success to get an invitation to speak, Gilles sued the university in a federal district court for speech and due process violations. The court dismissed his complaint.

On appeal, the U.S. Court of Appeals, Sixth Circuit, noted that the university did not maintain a written policy requiring an invitation to speak. Nor was the policy well understood by the university officials who had the duty to enforce it. **In addition, the policy had no standards by which requests for permission to speak were to be evaluated.** The policy was vulnerable to a due process claim. Because the policy was so ill-defined, the court held it was improper to dismiss the speech claim at this stage. Although the speech claim was "improbable" and recovery was unlikely, the court found dismissal of the claim was premature. The case was remanded for further proceedings. *Gilles v. Garland*, 281 Fed.Appx. 501 (6th Cir. 2008).

◆ *Faculty members at Yale Law School failed to show their rights were violated by the Solomon Amendment.*

Yale Law School faculty members claimed the Solomon Amendment conflicted with Yale's nondiscrimination policy. Accordingly, the school prohibited military interview programs. When the military warned Yale that it could lose federal funding by denying access, Yale exempted military recruiters from its nondiscrimination policy. Members of the law school faculty then sued the Secretary of Defense, claiming the Solomon Amendment violated their First Amendment rights of freedom of speech and freedom of association. After the district court agreed, the U.S. Supreme Court held the Solomon Amendment does not violate the First Amendment in *Rumsfeld v. Forum for Academic and Institutional Rights*, above. With the benefit of that ruling, the Second Circuit Court of Appeals then considered an appeal in the Yale case.

The court held the Supreme Court most likely intended its ruling to include rejection of an academic freedom claim. Even if it did not, **the Solomon Amendment did not restrict the content of teaching or membership of teachers in organizations**. The claim that the amendment violated a right to academic freedom was indirect and speculative. The Second Circuit rejected the claim that the Solomon Amendment violated First Amendment rights to boycott recruiters, noting that the faculty members remained free to disassociate themselves from the recruiters in other ways. A judgment for the Secretary of Defense was issued. *Burt v. Gates*, 502 F.3d 183 (2d Cir. 2007).

CHAPTER FIVE

Employment

I. BREACH OF CONTRACT

Breach of contract claims arise from written contracts, academic custom and usage, faculty handbooks and reliance on written and oral statements implying or modifying an employment contract.

A. Written Contracts

◆ *A former Grambling State University head football coach received a fraction of the amount a jury awarded him in his breach of contract action.*

A state governing board accused the coach of wrongdoing. This included charges that he gave drug tests to players, caused an NCAA investigation by letting a player use his vehicle, ran up the score in a game, and made insensitive remarks about a team affected by Hurricane Katrina. When advised of these charges, the coach was defiant and uncooperative, and he was given two weeks' notice of contract termination. The contract required a 60-day notice of termination, and he sued the university for breach of contract and defamation.

A jury rejected the defamation claim but found the university had breached its contract. It awarded the coach $642,500 in salary, penalty wages, and attorneys' fees. On appeal, the Court of Appeal of Louisiana held the trial court should have allowed into evidence newspaper articles to show the coach had generated bad publicity for the university. The court found evidence that he had been insubordinate, impugned the university's reputation and prompted an investigation. This led the court to find the jury had impermissibly found a lack of just cause for discharge. **Failure to provide the full 60-day notice of contract termination did not justify an award of the entire remaining salary under the contract.** Instead, the court found the coach was entitled to 47 days of pay – about $20,000. It reduced the penalty wages from $54,000 to $38,000. Finally, the court reduced the attorneys' fees to $34,500, leaving a total award of $93,053.80. *Spears v. Grambling State Univ.*, 111 So.3d 392 (La. Ct. App. 2012).

◆   *Howard University did not breach a contract with a probationary professor when it denied his application for tenure.*

In 2003 and again in 2005, the professor received two-year appointments but never received a performance evaluation. In 2006, a tenure committee supported his application. However, his department chair, a college dean and the university president accepted a provost's recommendation to deny it. In an action filed in the District of Columbia court system, the professor said the university breached its contractual obligations to evaluate him and to provide him with specific tenure criteria. In addition, he claimed the university officials breached an implied covenant of good faith and fair dealing by making inconsistent and inaccurate assertions regarding his application. After the trial court held for the university, appeal reached the District of Columbia Court of Appeals. It agreed with the lower court that the breach of contract claim was untimely, because it was not filed within the allotted three years.

A claim regarding the lack of more specific tenure criteria was also rejected as untimely. Although the professor said he could not correct any deficiencies because he was not advised of them, the court disagreed and upheld the trial court's decision to reject the claim for breach of the implied covenant of good faith and fair dealing. **While there were inaccuracies and inconsistencies in the tenure review process, they did not show bad faith or unfair conduct sufficient to support the claim.** As a result, the court affirmed the judgment for the university. *Wright v. Howard Univ.*, 60 A.3d 749 (D.C. 2013).

◆   *Factual issues about the scope of a release signed by a former employee prevented the dismissal of his bias suit against a New York university.*

The employee sued the university for discrimination based on his sexual orientation. The university argued he had waived all his claims by signing a waiver and accepting a $4,651.94 payment at the time of his separation. The employee said that at the time of his separation, he was unaware of potential discrimination claims and did not understand he was giving up any such claims. Instead, he asserted that the payment he received represented compensation for unused vacation and sick time. A state court held for the university, finding the release was "a straightforward, uncomplicated document." A state appellate division court reviewed the case and explained that under state law, **a waiver or release of employment discrimination claims must have been "fairly and knowingly made."** The university had the burden of showing the document was unambiguous with respect to what it covered. According to the court, the university did not meet this burden. It held the employee raised a factual issue on the question of whether a release of discrimination claims was fairly and knowingly made. The relatively small amount of the payment supported the view that the scope of the release was narrower than the university suggested. As a result, the judgment was reversed. *Johnson v. Lebanese American Univ.*, 84 A.D.3d 427, 922 N.Y.S.2d 57 (N.Y. App. Div. 2011).

◆ *A New Hampshire community college did not violate the constitutional rights of an adjunct professor when it declined to hire him on a full-time basis.*

According to the professor, the community college retaliated against him for accusing it of not providing sufficient services to students with disabilities. He said the college violated his due process and equal protection rights by failing to renew his contract and wrongly refusing to hire him on a full-time basis. The professor added state law fraud and whistleblowers' protection act claims. A federal magistrate recommended dismissal of the complaint. **The due process claims failed because the professor did not show he had any property interest in the renewal of his contract.** There was no "promise, policy, rule or practice" entitling him to contract renewal. The equal protection claim failed, as the professor did not claim he was treated differently than others. His retaliation claim failed because he did not show any link between his complaints and the non-renewal of his contract or the refusal to hire him for a full-time job. Having rejected the federal claims, the court declined to rule on the remaining state law claims. *Coleman v. Great Bay Community College*, No. 09-cv-161-SM, 2009 WL 3698398 (D.N.H. 10/30/09).

◆ *A librarian failed to show a Texas university breached its employment contract with her or constructively discharged her from employment.*

The university hired the librarian in 1972 and granted her tenure on the faculty of the library in 1981. Things went smoothly until the university hired a new library director in 1987. The director was not satisfied with the librarian's work performance, and he reassigned some of her duties. In 1993, the director and another official documented the librarian's alleged history of "low quality and quantity of work," rude behavior toward staff and the public, and excessive absenteeism. The director changed the librarian's title, and she complained that he had demoted her. The librarian requested retirement, then sued the university, director and another official in the state court system for breaching her employment contract and constructive discharge. The court held a trial. It refused to instruct the jury to consider the question of breach. Instead, it focused the jury on constructive discharge. The jury found for the university.

On appeal, the state court of appeals found the jury had received improper instructions and reversed the judgment. The university appealed to the Supreme Court of Texas, which reinstated the verdict. Although the librarian claimed she was demoted in breach of her contract, there was no evidence that she ever held any job other than as a tenured librarian. Her contract with the university did not specify any particular job functions. Nor did the librarian show she was constructively discharged from employment. **Constructive discharge does not take place merely because job assignments have changed. Instead, an** employee must show she was subjected to unendurable working conditions. As the librarian did not show this, the court reversed the judgment. *Baylor Univ. v. Coley*, 221 S.W.3d 599 (Tex. 2007).

◆   *Ohio State University (OSU) failed to negate a multi-million dollar verdict for a former basketball coach who was fired for loaning money to a recruit.*

The coach was a former national coach of the year. He began recruiting a seven-foot, three-inch player from the Republic of Serbia who was playing at a community college. The coach learned the recruit had played professionally in Europe. Although the coach knew this made the recruit ineligible to play for OSU, he continued to recruit him in hopes that the NCAA would allow him a waiver. The coach had an assistant deliver $6,000 to the recruit's family.

The recruit never enrolled at OSU, but when the coach disclosed the loan, he was fired for violating NCAA rules and a contract term requiring him to "run a clean and compliant program." The coach sued OSU in a state court for breach of contract. At the time of trial, the NCAA had opened an investigation but had not yet reached any conclusion. The court held the coach breached his contract by making the loan but found the breach was not "material" and did not justify discharge. It rendered a verdict for the coach and entered a judgment for nearly $2.5 million. On appeal, **the Court of Appeals of Ohio held the contract could be terminated only under specific conditions, none of which had occurred at the time OSU acted**. Although the loan could have constituted a material breach of contract if the NCAA determined it was a major infraction of its rules, OSU reached its own conclusion before the NCAA had finished its investigation. The trial court's finding that the loan did not substantially harm OSU was supported by the evidence, and the court affirmed the judgment. *O'Brien v. Ohio State Univ.*, No. 06AP-946, 2007 WL 2729077 (Ohio Ct. App. 9/20/07). The state supreme court denied review in *O'Brien v. Ohio State Univ.*, 117 Ohio St.3d 1406, 881 N.E.2d 274 (Ohio 2008).

◆   *The U.S. Court of Appeals, Third Circuit, held a Pennsylvania college did not breach a professor's employment contract by discharging her.*

The college hired the professor to be its Director of Athletics and Professor and Head of Physical Education and Athletics. She continued to work after her initial 2.5 year term and received salary letters advising her of annual increases. The college faculty handbook provided further guidance as to the terms and conditions of employment for faculty members. The college later discharged the professor, stating it believed the athletic department needed new leadership. It notified her a year and a half before the termination was to be effective. Assuming she was tenured, the professor tried to appeal the decision. The college president refused to accept the professor's claim she was tenured. He explained that she had never been tenured, but instead the professor served at the pleasure of the president as stated in her appointment letter.

The professor wrote to the president again and requested a hearing before a faculty tenure review appeals committee. The president denied the request, and the professor sued the college in a federal district court for breach of contract. **The court noted the professor's appointment letter clearly provided that the term of her position is "at the pleasure of the President**

of the College." This language expressly negated any possibility of tenured status as a faculty member. As the language was unambiguous, the case was dismissed. *Atkinson v. Lafayette College*, 460 F.3d 447 (3d Cir. 2006).

◆ *A South Carolina faculty member could not sue a university for missing office items after he signed a release agreeing not to file further claims.*

The university suspended the faculty member after a student filed a sexual harassment complaint against him. The faculty member was instructed to leave the campus immediately and was not allowed to return pending a criminal investigation. He left behind several volumes of his private library in his locked office, along with teaching materials, maps, and personal mementos. After the faculty member was acquitted of the criminal charge, he sued the university, alleging it wrongfully suspended him. The parties settled the case through mediation. Under the terms of the agreement, the faculty member released the university of any claims arising out of his employment and retained tenure.

The faculty member returned to the university and discovered his property was gone. The university never located the missing items, and he sued it in a state court for negligence. The court determined the release was comprehensive and dismissed the action. The faculty member appealed to the state court of appeals. It held **a valid release barred subsequent claims arising from the same circumstances, even if the parties may not have intended to release a specific claim.** The court held the release in this case clearly precluded future claims arising out of the faculty member's employment. *Abu-Shawareb v. South Carolina State Univ.*, 613 S.E.2d 757 (S.C. Ct. App. 2004).

B. Handbooks

◆ *A California community college dean with many personal problems was unable to show breach of contract and discrimination by the college.*

After signing a new two-year contract, the dean began going to a casino on her lunch breaks. She began missing work, lied about the reasons and charged personal debts on a community college district credit card. When confronted, the dean lied about her misconduct. After being released from employment, she filed a state court action for breach of contract, failure to accommodate her disability, wrongful termination and infliction of emotional distress. A state trial court dismissed her case, and the dean appealed to a California district court of appeal. It rejected her argument that the community college district should have imposed progressive discipline. She said the district could have taken away the credit card after the first instance of misuse and could have given her written notice of the charges against her. But the court found **the community college district's policy required no progressive discipline.**

No evidence supported a disability discrimination claim, as the dean was not fired for taking time off to care for her medical needs. Finally, the court found there was no merit to the dean's emotional distress claim. As a result, the lower court's decision for the community college district was affirmed. *Dadah v. Mount San Jacinto Community College Dist.*, No. E054269, 2013 WL 1080480 (Cal. Ct. App. 3/15/13).

◆ *Washington's highest court upheld a university's decision to suspend a professor after holding the kind of hearing specified in a faculty handbook.*

Soon after receiving tenure, the professor was accused of widespread and repeated verbal abuse of students, staff members and faculty members. He was repeatedly admonished for making demeaning, inappropriate comments about women, gay students and minorities, and for misconduct including carrying a knife in class. After tolerating this conduct for years, the university suspended the professor. Although he sought a hearing that was open to the public, the university stated the faculty handbook required a closed one. After the hearing, the professor was suspended for two semesters. A state trial court denied his request for relief. On appeal, the Supreme Court of Washington held the state Administrative Procedure Act (APA) generally required open hearings.

An APA exception allowed the presiding officer to close a meeting under a provision of law authorizing closure. In this case, the university based its decision to close the hearing on a faculty handbook provision that said disciplinary hearings were generally closed. **The court held the university did not improperly close the hearing because the handbook provision was a "provision of law" under the APA.** It was reasonable to conclude that the state law provision authorizing the establishment of rules relating to peer review proceedings contemplated a faculty handbook rule calling for closure of the hearing. Closing the hearing did not violate the state APA. *Mills v. Western Washington Univ.*, 170 Wash.2d 903, 246 P.3d 1254 (Wash. 2011).

◆ *Two California professors were entitled to a trial to consider if a Christian college discharged them based on marital status.*

The professors taught in the marriage and family counseling department of the college, which was affiliated with the Church of Christ. The church looked to the Bible as its ultimate constitution and required professors to accept the Bible as the word of God. The professors' teaching contracts indicated they were to comply with the faculty handbook. The handbook also stated that faculty members should conduct their on- and off-campus activities and relationships in a Christ-like manner. One of the professors filed for divorce, and a rumor circulated that he was having an affair with the other professor.

The dean asked the divorcing professor to step down from his chair position but allowed him to keep teaching. When the professors announced their wedding, the college refused to renew their teaching contracts. Both professors sued the college in a state court, alleging discrimination on the basis of marital status and breach of contract. The court denied the college pretrial judgment. **The college appealed to the California Court of Appeal, arguing it was entitled to the "ministerial exception," which allows religious institutions to enjoy immunity from examination into religious doctrine.** The court found no evidence that the college cared about marital status. It showed concern only for whether the professors were perceived to be committing adultery. The court said the claim was based on a contract, not marital status discrimination. It held the trial court had to further consider whether the professors fell within the ministerial exception. *Hope Univ. v. Superior Court*, 119 Cal.App.4th 719, 14 Cal.Rptr.3d 643 (Cal. Ct. App. 2004).

C. AAUP Guidelines

*Language from the American Association of University Professors (AAUP) "1940 Statement of Principles on Academic Freedom and Tenure with 1970 Interpretive Comments" has been included in the conditions of employment in some contracts for college faculty members. The AAUP Statement on Tenure provides: "[I]f the decision [on tenure] is negative, the appointment for the following year becomes a terminal one." Accordingly, a federal court held **the general rule in academia is that if a faculty member is denied tenure, he or she completes a terminal year of employment and then leaves the institution.** See* McMahon v. Carroll College, *2007 WL 804149 (E.D. Wis. 3/9/07).*

A 1925 AAUP Conference Statement on Academic Freedom and Tenure provides that the termination of a permanent or long-term appointment due to financial exigencies "should be sought only as a last resort, after every effort has been made to meet the need in other ways and to find for the teacher other employment in the institution. Situations which make drastic retrenchment of this sort necessary should preclude expansions of the staff at other points at the same time, except in extraordinary circumstances." Saxe v. Board of Trustees of Metropolitan State College of Denver, *179 P.3d 67 (Colo. Ct. App. 2007).*

◆ *A university followed the proper procedures when it fired a professor for sexual harassment.*

A tenured anthropology professor at Baylor University took several students on a university-sponsored academic field trip to Guatemala. While there, he engaged in inappropriate sexual contact with female students and made crude sexual remarks to them. A student reported his conduct to university officials upon returning, and an investigation found the student's accusations to be true. When the professor refused to accept a demotion and mandated counseling, a hearing was conducted, after which the tenure committee recommended the professor's termination.

The president fired the professor, who sued for breach of contract and defamation. A jury found the university breached its contract with the professor, but the Texas Court of Appeals reversed. The inclusion of an American Association of University Professors (AAUP) statement in the employment manual did not mean that the manual incorporated the AAUP's termination procedures. **The university had clearly set forth its termination procedures and followed them in this case.** The professor received written notice of the charges against him and had an opportunity to challenge the evidence and confront witnesses at the hearing. The termination was upheld. *Fox v. Parker*, 98 S.W.3d 713 (Tex. Ct. App. 2003).

◆ *A professor could not use the American Association of University Professors (AAUP) guidelines, which had been incorporated into his contract, to modify the intent of the contract.*

A professor and a New Jersey private university entered into five separate employment contracts, each of which incorporated the terms of the university's collective bargaining agreement with the AAUP guidelines. However, the professor's applications for tenure were denied due to his lack of a doctorate degree and his failure to publish. His contract for a sixth academic year stated that his associate professor position was a "non-tenured position." In the following year, he was appointed as an associate dean but continued to teach three credits per semester without additional compensation. He was fired several years later because his overall performance was found to be "significantly below expectations." The professor filed a lawsuit in a New Jersey superior court, alleging that he had acquired *de facto* tenure under the provisions of the AAUP contract. The AAUP contract required that faculty members who had taught for 14 continuous academic semesters be granted tenure. The superior court held for the university, and the professor appealed.

A state appellate division court noted that **the provision requiring tenure for faculty members teaching 14 continuous semesters was a subsidiary provision that should not be interpreted so as to conflict with the principal purpose of the contract**. The court rejected the professor's disproportionate emphasis on the provision to support his tenure claim. The interpretation of the probationary appointments provision urged by the professor unlawfully conflicted with the principal purpose of the university's formal tenure policy, which placed substantive and procedural prerequisites on the acquisition of tenure. The superior court ruling was affirmed. *Healy v. Fairleigh Dickinson Univ.*, 671 A.2d 182 (N.J. Super. Ct. App. Div. 1996).

◆   *Where a part of the AAUP guidelines was excluded from an employment contract, the university did not have to follow the procedures listed in that part.*

A private Louisiana university dismissed a tenured professor for alleged professional incompetence. She sued the university for reinstatement of tenure and employment. She argued that the university, after agreeing to modify her existing employment contract, failed to apply Paragraph Seven of the AAUP guidelines, which provide procedures for the termination of a tenured professor. The trial court held that the college had no obligation to comply with Paragraph Seven, and the professor appealed, arguing Paragraph Seven was implied in her employment contract. The court held **the faculty handbook and contract clearly excluded Paragraph Seven of the AAUP guidelines. As a result, the paragraph did not apply to any procedures established by the university for the termination of tenured professors.** The court further stated that there was no merit to the professor's argument that the college agreed to modify her original employment contract. The court affirmed the trial court's decision. *Olivier v. Xavier Univ.*, 553 So.2d 1004 (La. Ct. App. 1989).

D. Implied Contracts

◆   *A Texas coach did not show Baylor University breached his contract by failing to rehire him. The Supreme Court of Texas also rejected his fraud claim.*

Baylor hired the coach to lead its women's volleyball team in 1989 without a written contract, as was its practice. In 1995, Baylor told its coaches that it planned to begin the practice of entering into written contracts. The volleyball coach said Baylor's general counsel announced it would enter into two-year contracts with its head coaches beginning in 1995-96. However, he never received a written contract. The coach sued Baylor in a state court, claiming it breached an oral promise to enter into a two-year written contract. He added a fraud claim based on a promise. The court held for Baylor, but the state court of appeals reversed the judgment. On appeal, the state supreme court noted the coach had admitted a written contract was never delivered. **Any contract for a period of more than one year must be evidenced by writing.** The court rejected the fraud claim, which was based on benefits the coach would have gained if a contract had been enforced. The court reversed the judgment and held for Baylor. *Baylor Univ. v. Sonnichsen*, 221 S.W.3d 632 (Tex. 2007).

◆   *The Court of Appeals of Wisconsin held Ripon College did not misrepresent information to an applicant for an assistant professor position.*

A college vice-president interviewed the applicant, who asked him about the college's financial condition. The vice-president described the college's endowment, and discussed past and present student enrollment numbers. He told the applicant that the college intended to raise faculty salaries so it could better compete with comparable institutions. The applicant turned down a higher-paying offer from another institution to work at the college. But the position was ended at the end of an academic year, and she sued the college in a state court for misrepresentation. Appeal reached the state court of appeals, which found the information disclosed during the applicant's interview was true. **The court found she was asking the court to impose a duty on the college to provide her with predictions, not facts.** As the college had no duty to predict future economic events, the court held for the college. *Bellon v. Ripon College*, 278 Wis.2d 790, 693 N.W.2d 330 (Wis. Ct. App. 2005).

◆   *The U.S. Court of Appeals, Ninth Circuit, held against an instructor who sued an Oregon community college for misrepresentation.*

The instructor was offered a contract and was assured his position was "as official as it gets." Based on these assurances, he resigned from a prior tenured teaching position. Because of budget shortfalls, the college president refused to recommend the approval of his contract, and the board declined to do so. The college then claimed the contract was not binding without board approval and denied the instructor the secure position he originally had been offered.

The instructor sued the college in a federal district court. **The case reached the Ninth Circuit, which held he could not show the type of justifiable reliance required to establish a claim for misrepresentation.** It then granted a petition for a rehearing. After the rehearing, the Ninth Circuit found the instructor again did not show he justifiably relied on representations. Without the board's approval, no offer was within the community college's powers. *Oja v. Blue Mountain Community College*, 184 Fed.Appx. 597 (9th Cir. 2006).

◆   *A private New Jersey college did not breach its employment contract with an employee by firing her without a hearing for not revealing a criminal embezzlement matter.*

The college hired the employee as its director of graduate programs. She did not reveal that she and her husband were defending federal criminal charges of embezzling over $1 million in employee pension and profit-sharing funds from a previous venture. The college learned of the employee's indictment and guilty plea and suggested she resign. The employee agreed to resign but then changed her mind. The college stated it could discharge her without a hearing or other due process protections because she was an at-will employee. The employee sued the university in a federal district court.

The court dismissed the case, finding the employee was not a full-time faculty member and that there was no employment contract. The professor appealed to the U.S. Court of Appeals, Third Circuit. **Under New Jersey law, the professor was an employee at-will unless she presented evidence to show the parties intended to renew a fixed term contract.** As she did not submit such evidence, the court held she was an employee at-will. The college was not obligated to offer the professor due process when it terminated her employment. Since there was no employment contract at the time of the alleged breach, the court affirmed the judgment. *Fanelli v. Centenary College*, 112 Fed.Appx. 210 (3d Cir. 2004).

◆ *The Supreme Court of New Hampshire upheld a jury verdict which found that reappointment letters created an employment contract.*

A New Hampshire college audio-visual director worked for 11 years under annual reappointment letters describing terms such as his salary, employment period and duties. The college discharged the director prior to the end of the term of a reappointment letter. He sued the college for breach of contract in the state court system, alleging termination without good cause. The case went to trial, which resulted in a verdict for the director. The court denied the college's motion for a directed verdict. The college appealed to the state supreme court. It reviewed the terms of the reappointment letters and held a reasonable jury could find they constituted an employment contract. The fact that they stated 12-month terms was persuasive evidence that the director was not an "at-will" employee. **The reappointment rights section of the College Handbook stated employees could be disciplined for just cause.** As there was sufficient evidence for a jury to find an employment contract existed, the court upheld the verdict. *Dillman v. New Hampshire College*, 838 A.2d 1274 (N.H. 2003).

II. EMPLOYEE MISCONDUCT

Employee misconduct includes a variety of actions such as inappropriate, unethical, or criminal behavior. In addressing such actions, educational institutions may be bound by faculty handbooks or requirements for hearings.

◆ *An Indiana professor was unable to recast his discharge for sexual harassment as a breach of contract matter.*

The professor, who had been on the faculty for 25 years, was charged with several incidents of improper conduct with female students. Students complained that he made derogatory comments about women, used "crude and scary" language, and touched them inappropriately. When confronted with the complaints, the professor insisted he had done nothing wrong. A student then filed a formal internal complaint against him. The university placed the professor on paid leave and conducted an investigation that found he had violated its sexual harassment policy. He declined an option to retire early and was dismissed from the university. In a state court, the professor claimed the university discharged him in breach of his contract. The case reached the state supreme court, which found the professor failed to prove breach of contract. He also failed to show he had a contractual right of entry onto university property. **There was sufficient evidence to show the professor violated the terms of his employment contract, which barred him from engaging in harassing behavior.** In the court's view, his conduct met the employment contract's definitions of harassment. Moreover, the court held the professor received all the process he was due. The decision for the university was affirmed. *Haegert v. Univ. of Evansville*, 977 N.E.2d 924 (Ind. 2012).

◆ *A federal court held a Pennsylvania campus police officer did not have a due process right "to refuse to violate the constitutional rights of others."*

An anti-gay group demonstration on campus prompted some objections by students. A university police chief arrived and found the crowd was acting disorderly. He ordered the officer to "push" away anti-gay demonstrators, but the officer did not believe they were being disorderly, and he told the chief that arresting them might violate their civil rights. He also feared he might be held personally liable if he arrested them without good cause. After a disciplinary hearing, the officer was suspended without pay for five days and warned in writing that he could be discharged if he disobeyed another order. The officer said he was then assigned menial tasks, given poor evaluations, and denied training opportunities. He sued the chief and other university officials in a federal district court, claiming a right to refuse to obey unconstitutional orders.

The court dismissed the officer's speech rights claim, as he had spoken in his capacity as a public employee and not as a private citizen. It also declined to accept the theory that a substantive due process claim can be premised on the refusal to violate the constitutional rights of others. On appeal to the U.S. Court of Appeals, Third Circuit, the officer dropped his First Amendment claim. But like the lower court, **the Third Circuit declined to recognize a fundamental substantive due process right to refuse to violate the constitutional rights of others**. It held paramilitary organizations like university police would not be able to function effectively if the relief he sought was granted. *Armbruster v. Cavanaugh*, 410 Fed.Appx. 564 (3d Cir. 2011).

◆ *A New York university did not commit constitutional violations when it discharged an ethics professor who pled guilty to embezzlement charges.*

The professor had taught at the university for more than 25 years when he pled guilty to third-degree robbery charges based on the embezzlement of almost $80,000 from a church where he served as an accountant. After the plea, he took a leave of absence from the university, but he later sought reinstatement with a full course load. The university instead informed the professor he would be discharged, and an arbitrator upheld the decision. After an unsuccessful state court lawsuit, he sued the university in a federal court for constitutional violations. The court held that the state court had decided all relevant issues, including the professor's claim that he was not provided adequate due process.

On appeal, the U.S. Court of Appeals, Second Circuit, held the applicable collective bargaining agreement provided disciplinary procedures for faculty members who were convicted of felonies. The professor identified no fundamental right with which this provision interfered. He also identified no suspect class under which he could claim any discrimination. **While a hearing is normally provided for tenured faculty, there was no need for one where the professor was suspended without pay after having been convicted of a felony.** A conviction "demonstrates that the deprivation is not arbitrary and serves to assure that the employer's decision is not baseless or unwarranted." As none of the professor's arguments had any merit, the court affirmed the judgment. *Rosa v. City Univ. of New York*, 306 Fed.Appx. 655 (2d Cir. 2007).

◆ *The University of Minnesota could suspend a tenured professor who was found to have submitted false student evaluations for a class.*

Student evaluations were used to determine whether merit-based salary increases should be granted. A department chairperson who reviewed the professor's evaluations became suspicious because of abnormally high ratings. The chairperson was also suspicious because the forms were turned in after the semester was over and because in a prior semester, the professor had asked a secretary to make changes to forms that were already submitted. An investigation showed students in the course did not submit the evaluations. A university committee found the professor had engaged in serious misconduct, and the president suspended him for one year without salary or benefits. A state trial court affirmed the university's decision, and the professor appealed. The Court of Appeals of Minnesota found the evidence sufficient to support the suspension. **The professor was the only person who would benefit from the false evaluations, and he had been in the office on the day the secretary found them.** He was not a credible witness and had engaged in questionable behavior in the past regarding evaluations. As a result, the court upheld the judgment for the university. *Tennyson v. Univ. of Minnesota*, No. A07-1095, 2008 WL 2344257 (Minn. Ct. App. 6/10/08).

◆ *An Ohio university had good reason to discharge an employee who disclosed private information about a student to a newspaper reporter.*

The employee was a program assistant in a research and graduate studies program. When she started work there, she received a letter from the university explaining she must ensure the confidentiality of sensitive and protected record information. The assistant received a copy of the university's policy on student information and acknowledged that she was familiar with policies on student education records. A student who was a candidate for student government participated in the program. The campus newspaper published a story listing grade averages of student candidates. It reported the student's GPA as 2.92. The assistant contacted the newspaper to tell them this was incorrect and revealed that the student's correct GPA was 2.68. The newspaper printed a story with the headline "KSU staff member claims candidate lied about GPA." The student sued the university for disclosing her GPA. After providing a full hearing procedure, the university discharged the assistant for violating the agreement.

The assistant sued the university in a state court. The case reached the Court of Appeals of Ohio. The court held that **the assistant's good reputation did not outweigh the harm she caused by knowingly disclosing confidential**

student information. A good reputation could not mitigate intentional acts and their consequences. The order of removal stated the assistant was removed for violating her agreement, not for violating federal law. As she knew she was violating her agreement, the court affirmed the judgment. *Swigart v. Kent State Univ.*, No. 2004-P-0037, 2005 WL 1077176 (Ohio Ct. App. 5/6/05).

◆ *A North Dakota instructor failed to counter a college's evidence that there was adequate cause to fire her for neglect of duties and incompetence.*

Bismarck State College (BSC) notified a tenured commercial art instructor it intended to dismiss her for disclosing a student's confidential information to a classroom of students. BSC alleged the disclosure violated state higher education board policy and federal law, and it demanded she apologize to the student. BSC later found the instructor's apology inappropriate and told her it considered her behavior to be a neglect of duty. She challenged the sufficiency of this notice. BSC amended the notice to include charges of neglecting teaching responsibilities by ending a class a month early and failing to clean up her classrooms. It also alleged incompetent teaching, an inappropriate pattern of behavior and incompetence. BSC then fired the instructor for cause. An administrative law judge upheld the dismissal, and a state district court affirmed the decision. The Supreme Court of North Dakota found the trial court had properly ordered judgment on the instructor's breach of employment contract claim. She failed to present any facts to show why a jury would not have found adequate cause to fire her. **The instructor presented no facts to support her wrongful termination and conspiracy charges**, and the judgment was affirmed. *Peterson v. North Dakota Univ. System*, 678 N.W.2d (N.D. 2004).

III. TENURE AND PROMOTION DENIALS

A. Tenure and Promotion Cases

Tenured employees are entitled to any employment protections promised by their institutions. A public institution must comply with constitutional requirements for due process. At minimum, this amounts to notice and an opportunity to respond to any charges. Private institutions are not bound by the Constitution, but must afford employees any procedures that they have been promised. If an institution's policy (or a state law or regulation) requires it, an employee may also be entitled to a hearing with the right to confront and cross-examine witnesses, and the right to be represented by counsel.

◆ *New Jersey county college lecturers who did not hold positions conferring academic rank were unable to gain tenure under state law.*

New Jersey law permitted county college faculty members to gain tenure if they completed five years of satisfactory service in tenure-eligible positions and were in academic rank at the time they completed the service requirement. Burlington County College denied a group of lecturers tenure rights, because they were not appointed to positions that conferred academic rank.

The lecturers and a county college faculty association sued the college in a state court, arguing the college had transformed their temporary positions into tenure-eligible ones. They also claimed their duties were the same as those of instructors and other faculty members. The court found the decision of the college trustees was entitled to great deference. Under state law, tenure was available to faculty members "in academic rank" after five years. **The law defined "academic rank" to include an instructor, assistant professor, associate professor and professor.** A faculty member was "any full-time member of the teaching staff appointed with academic rank." The court rejected the lecturers' theory that they held positions that were functionally equivalent to the tenure-eligible position of instructor, and it held they did not qualify for tenure under state law. *Burlington County College Faculty Ass'n v. Burlington County College*, 2010 WL 1427253 (N.J. Super. Ct. App. Div. 4/7/10).

◆   *Board of Regents v. Roth*, 408 U.S. 564 (1972) and *Perry v. Sindermann*, 408 U.S. 593 (1972), help define employee due process rights. *Roth* and *Sindermann* emphasize, first, that there must be an independent source for a liberty or property interest to exist. Such interests are not created by the Constitution, but arise by employment contract or by operation of state tenure laws. Second, if a liberty or property interest is not established, no requirement of due process exists under the Fourteenth Amendment. Third, **if a teacher possesses a liberty or property interest in employment, then due process is required and the teacher may not be dismissed without a hearing**.

A tenured teacher, or an untenured teacher during the term of his or her contract, possesses a property interest in continued employment. An untenured teacher who is not rehired after expiration of his or her contract is entitled to a due process hearing if the decision not to rehire is accompanied by a finding of incompetence or immorality, because the teacher's liberty of employment would be impaired by such a finding. However, probationary employees or at-will employees generally do not enjoy due process protections.

The teacher in *Roth* was hired at a Wisconsin university for a fixed contract term of one year. At the end of the year, he was informed that he would not be rehired. No hearing was provided and no reason was given for the decision. In dismissing the teacher's due process claims, the Supreme Court stated that no liberty interest was implicated. In declining to rehire the teacher, the university made no charge against him such as incompetence or immorality. Such a charge would have made it difficult for the teacher to gain employment elsewhere and thus would have deprived him of liberty. As no reason was given for the non-renewal of his contract, his liberty interest in future employment was not impaired, and he was not entitled to a hearing on these grounds.

The Court declared that because the teacher had not acquired tenure he possessed no property interest in continued employment at the university. To be sure, the teacher had a property interest in employment during the term of his one-year contract, but upon its expiration the teacher's property interest ceased to exist. The Court stated: **"To have a property interest in a benefit, a person clearly must have more than an abstract need or desire for it. He must have more than a unilateral expectation of it. He must, instead, have a legitimate claim of entitlement to it."** *Board of Regents v. Roth*, 408 U.S. 564, 92 S.Ct. 2701, 33 L.Ed.2d 548 (1972).

◆   The *Sindermann* case involved a teacher employed at a Texas university for four years under a series of one-year contracts. When he was not rehired for a fifth year, he brought suit contending that due process required a dismissal hearing. The Supreme Court held that "a person's interest in a benefit is a 'property' interest for due process purposes if there are such rules and mutually explicit understandings that support his claim of entitlement to the benefit that he may invoke at a hearing." Because the teacher had been employed at the university for four years, the Court felt that he may have acquired a protectable property interest in continued employment. The case was remanded to the trial court to determine whether there was an unwritten "common law" of tenure at the university. If so, the teacher would be entitled to a dismissal hearing. *Perry v. Sindermann*, 408 U.S. 593, 92 S.Ct. 2694, 33 L.Ed.2d 570 (1972).

◆   *A Pennsylvania university's decision to deny tenure to an associate professor did not violate any university handbook, policies or procedures.*

The professor accepted a position under a letter of acceptance by which he agreed to abide by university policies and procedures. These policies specified annual performance reviews, a third-year review, and eligibility for tenure in the sixth year. In the event tenure was denied, the seventh year would be the final year of employment. After satisfactory annual performance reviews during the early years of his employment, the professor applied for tenure. A five-member tenure committee made an inconclusive report, and tenure was denied. An appeal to a reconstituted four-member committee resulted in two committee members finding the professor marginally met tenure criteria while the others found he easily met the criteria. After being discharged, the professor sued the university in a state court for breach of contract. He also claimed the five-point scale used for his evaluations violated university policy.

The court rejected his claim that the university had a contractual duty to follow its policies and procedures, and that it failed to do so when it allowed a four-member committee to reconsider the application after a five-member committee did so. On appeal, the Superior Court of Pennsylvania held **it was within the prerogative of the university president to reconstitute the committee with four members**. This decision did not breach any contract with the professor. The same was true of the use of a five-point evaluation scale. The president was not required to agree with the initial committee's conclusion and the court affirmed the judgment for the university. *Robertson v. Drexel Univ.*, 991 A.2d 315 (Pa. Super. Ct. 2010).

◆   *A federal court upheld a decision to revoke the tenure of a faculty member based on charges that he neglected his professional responsibilities.*

University administrators filed a complaint seeking the revocation of the professor's tenure. The complaint referenced a suspension eight years earlier and a letter allegedly written by a university vice president on October 30, 1997. The complaint was supplemented by a statement of misconduct, which did not mention a letter of October 30, 1997. A faculty panel agreed with the charge of neglect for professional responsibilities and noted its decision was based on the professor's conduct after April 1999. During the revocation proceedings, the university did not release any letter dated October 30, 1997, to him. The professor sued the university in a federal court for breach of contract. After dismissing most of his claims, the court held that even if a letter dated October 30, 1997 did exist, it was not relevant to the tenure revocation.

The letter was not mentioned in the statement of misconduct that supported the complaint. **In addition, the panel clearly indicated its decision was based on actions after April 1999.** Therefore, whether or not the letter existed was immaterial, and the university was entitled to judgment. On appeal, the U.S. Court of Appeals, District of Columbia Circuit, affirmed the judgment. It found no binding contract, as the professor did not identify a relevant faculty code provision that was violated. Despite 28 alleged contractual breaches, there was no plausible claim for relief. The judgment was affirmed. *Saha v. George Washington Univ.*, 358 Fed.Appx. 205 (D.C. Cir. 2009).

◆   *A North Carolina university employee was not entitled to priority consideration for a vacant position based on her 10 years of work there.*

The employee worked in the university's Animal Science Department. She left for three years and returned as an administrative billing assistant in the Communication Technologies Department. The university promoted the employee to the position of Telecom Project Manager/Telecom Analyst II. A few months later, she was laid off, but a Telecom Analyst I position soon became vacant. The employee applied for the job, but the university hired a less experienced former employee who had also been let go. The employee filed a complaint with the state office of administrative hearings, alleging she was entitled to priority consideration for the job under North Carolina General Statutes Section 126-7.1. This law provides state employees with more than 10 years of service priority consideration over state employees with less than 10 years of service in the same or a related job classification. A state trial court held the employee was entitled to priority consideration for the job.

The university appealed. The Court of Appeals of North Carolina held the trial court misinterpreted the law. Under the trial court's reading, a state employee with over 10 years of service, regardless of the position, should receive priority consideration over another person with less than 10 years of service in the same or a related position classification. **As the employee did not have more than 10 years in the same or a related classification as the position for which she applied, she was not entitled to priority consideration** for the job. The court reversed the judgment. *Wilkins v. North Carolina State Univ.*, 178 N.C.App. 377, 631 S.E.2d 221 (N.C. Ct. App. 2006).

◆   *A District of Columbia professor did not prove a university interfered with her bid for tenure in a way that breached its duty of good faith and fair dealing.*

The professor worked in a tenure track position for five years, then applied for a tenured associate professor position. The tenure committee voted against tenure because it considered her research weak. A scholarly journal notified the professor that it had rejected a paper she authored due to serious criticism by reviewers. The university again denied the professor's request for tenure based on lack of progress in publishing. The professor sued the university in a District of Columbia court for breach of contract and breach of the covenant of good faith and fair dealing. The court held for the university, and she appealed.

On appeal to the District of Columbia Court of Appeals, the professor stated that she was denied sufficient lab space and that her research grant was arbitrarily cancelled. This made her unable to perform contractual publishing obligations, breaching both her contract and the covenant of good faith and fair dealing. **The court noted all contracts contain an implied duty of good faith and fair dealing. This means neither party may do anything which has the effect of destroying or injuring the rights of the other party under the contract.** The university took steps to make lab space available to the professor, but she failed to progress in her scholarly productivity. The court agreed with the university that courts are reluctant to interfere with tenure decisions. As the professor failed to satisfy the tenure requirements of the faculty handbook, the judgment was affirmed. *Allworth v. Howard Univ.*, 890 A.2d 194 (D.C. 2006).

◆ *A Kentucky tax professor will receive a trial in an action against a university for negligence and fraudulent representation.*

The university hired the professor for an academic year and agreed to pay him a $25,000 supplement funded by an endowment fund. The professor believed his appointment to the endowed professorship was permanent. After he accepted the position, the professor learned his appointment to the endowed professorship was temporary and his future supplemental salary was determined at the discretion of the dean. He left the university and sued it in a Kentucky trial court for negligently or fraudulently misrepresenting the terms of his contract verbally and through emails. The court found no bad faith and dismissed the case. The professor appealed to the state Court of Appeals.

The court found the professor introduced oral communications, emails, and other correspondence that created doubt about the university's good faith. The dean would be entitled to official immunity for negligently performing discretionary acts as long as he acted in good faith. But the hiring process included the non-discretionary aspect of representing or communicating his compensation. **If the dean negligently represented the compensation to the professor, a court could find the university liable.** The court held the trial court's finding that no facts supported a finding of bad faith was premature and reversed the judgment. *Westin v. Shipley*, No. 2003-CA-001548-MR, 2004 WL 2260299 (Ky. Ct. App. 2004). State supreme court review was denied in 2005.

◆ *A California court held a temporary community college instructor was not a regular employee under the college system's academic classification system.*

The instructor taught less than 60% of the hours required for a full-time assignment and was deemed a temporary employee. He submitted three grant requests and worked on them during the intercession so as to not exceed the 60% rule. The college later rescinded one of the grant awards because it believed his work during the intercession might count toward the 60% rule. The college denied a request by the instructor's union for reclassification as a permanent employee and he petitioned a state court for relief. The court held his projects constituted "teaching" and that he exceeded the 60% rule. It ordered the college to reclassify the instructor as a permanent employee, and the university appealed.

The Court of Appeal of California noted the state code established three classifications for community college instructors. Temporary employees could be terminated at the discretion of the governing board. **Pursuant to the code, a temporary employee who teaches full time for a complete school year and is rehired for the next school year will automatically be reclassified as a contract employee.** The court held an instructor teaching adult or community college classes less than 60% of a full-time assignment must be classified as a temporary employee. It distinguished statutory teaching requirements from the research and grant projects, which it characterized as "faculty work." Since these projects could not be considered "teaching" under the statute, the instructor did not exceed the 60% rule and should not be reclassified. The judgment was reversed. *Kamler v. Marin Community College Dist.*, No. A098114, 2003 WL 21493662 (Cal. Ct. App. 2003).

◆ *A professor's position as associate dean was not a protected property interest preserved by her tenured faculty position.*

A University of North Dakota (UND) professor had administrative duties as director of the School of Communication and associate dean of the College of Fine Arts and Communication. After being dismissed from administrative duties, she sued UND, alleging the action violated her protected property interests under tenure law. A federal court dismissed her claim that she had a protected property interest in her administrative positions. Citing the North Dakota State Board of Higher Education Policy Manual, which was included in her employment contract, the district court noted that tenure does not extend to administrative positions. The Eighth Circuit agreed, noting that the professor's administrative position was at will and thus did not evoke a protected property interest. A letter of understanding supplementing her employment contract stated, "Associate Deans have no specific term, but rather serve at the pleasure of the Dean." The court found the professor's position as director of the School of Communication included a three-year contract, but her protected property interest had been satisfied. **UND had fully compensated her for the salary associated with the position even though she did not serve out the full term.** *Rakow v. State of North Dakota*, 208 F.3d 218 (8th Cir. 2000).

B. Claims of Discrimination

◆ *Northwestern University (NU) medical school successfully defended a gender discrimination claim with evidence of increasing female tenure rates.*

NU denied a female professor's tenure application, finding her scholarship was below average, and her teaching and service contributions were minimal. She also did not prove an ability to gain renewal of research awards. In a federal court action against NU, the professor claimed the stated reasons were a pretext for unlawful discrimination. After the court held for NU, she appealed to the U.S. Court of Appeals, Seventh Circuit. It found the professor had relied on stray remarks to support an inference of discrimination. She said someone described her as "a woman scientist who reproduces" with an "emotional need to be heard." In the court's opinion, these remarks were ambiguous and did not support her claim. The fact that a male earned tenure near the time her application was denied did not support her claim. The male had been a lead author on six articles, while the professor was the lead author on one. Also, the male obtained six funding grants while she obtained two. There was evidence that the percentage of tenure-track female faculty members at the NU medical school was increasing and that females were earning tenure at a higher rate than males. **As no evidence indicated any decision-maker was biased against women with regard to tenure, the court held for the university.** *Blasdel v. Northwestern Univ.*, 687 F.3d 813 (7th Cir. 2012).

◆   *A federal court rejected a Mississippi professor's claim that he was denied tenure based on his race and national origin rather than his performance.*

After completing his probationary period, the professor sought tenure. But the department of electrical and computer engineering tenure review committee unanimously voted to deny his application, and his internal review was denied. After making an administrative charge that he was denied tenure based on his race and Cypriot origin, the professor sued the university in a federal court for race and national origin discrimination. The university sought pretrial judgment, claiming nondiscriminatory reasons for the tenure denial. It noted the professor had published only two referenced journal articles and had received no grants based on research as a principal investigator. He countered that a similarly situated faculty member was granted tenure. When the court compared their qualifications, it discovered the faculty member had better evaluations, a better publishing record and strong research projects and grant work. By contrast, the professor misrepresented some of his research projects in applying for tenure. **The court held he did not produce enough evidence to show he was denied tenure based on unlawful discrimination.** As a result, it held for the university. *Lazarou v. Mississippi State Univ.*, No. 1:07-CV-00060-GHD-DAS, 2013 WL 548774 (N.D. Miss. 2/14/13).

◆   *A federal court dismissed an untimely lawsuit by a Long Island University (LIU) instructor who claimed national origin discrimination.*

The instructor worked for seven years at LIU on digital products for faculty relating to plagiarism. She applied for tenure but was twice denied, and she filed a grievance. LIU agreed to extend the instructor's employment for two years and to allow her to reapply for tenure. A dispute arose over how to assess her digital products, and she filed a discrimination complaint against LIU with a federal agency. Later, the instructor sued LIU for discriminatory denial of tenure and constructive discharge. But **the court held the claim for denial of tenure was time-barred**, as she was denied tenure more than 300 days before she filed her administrative complaint. The constructive discharge claim failed because it was not in her administrative charge and nothing else put LIU on notice she might bring this claim. As neither of the claims was viable, the case was dismissed. *Madray v. Long Island Univ.*, No. 10-CV-3841 (ADS)(WDW), 2012 WL 2923500 (E.D.N.Y. 7/16/12).

◆   *A court rejected a University of North Carolina professor's claim that she was denied a promotion and tenure based on her race.*

The professor claimed she was denied tenure and a promotion based on her race, in violation of Title VII of the 1964 Civil Rights Act. A federal district court held for the university, and appeal went to the U.S. Court of Appeals, Fourth Circuit. It held that the professor did not meet a filing deadline for the position she sought. She did not support her allegation it would have been futile for her to submit a timely application package. **Her discrimination claim failed because she did not show she had the necessary qualifications for promotion and tenure.** Moreover, the professor would have failed to prove her case because she did not identify a faculty member outside her protected class with a similar academic record who gained tenure and a promotion. *Weathers v. Univ. of North Carolina at Chapel Hill*, 447 Fed.Appx. 508 (4th Cir. 2011).

◆   *An unsuccessful candidate for a tenure-track position at a New York college did not show he was denied the post because of his national origin.*

Soon after the professor began teaching computer information technology, students began complaining about his demeanor and grading policies. One student claimed the professor shoved him. Near this time, the college posted his temporary position as a tenure-track position. After a run-in with his superiors, the professor was banned from campus and told he would not be rehired. He sued the college in a federal court, claiming he was denied a tenure-track position because of his Chinese ancestry. After the court held for the college, he appealed. The U.S. Court of Appeals, Second Circuit, noted the professor's own admission that his position had been temporary. He also admitted that he was the subject of student complaints and was rude and threatening in his interactions with college officials. Finally, **the applicant chosen for the tenure track position was better qualified than the professor because he had a Ph.D.** As the college had legitimate reasons for its decision, the court held in its favor. *Li v. Morrisville State College*, 434 Fed.Appx. 34 (2d Cir. 2011).

◆   *An Illinois university medical school was entitled to deny tenure to a female research professor based on her poor record of performance.*

The medical school hired the research professor, despite her poor record of publications at another institution. Once hired, it took her three years to publish an article, and she had secured only one grant as the time to apply for tenure approached. The professor's application for tenure was denied based on her low publication rate, limited success with grants, and minimal teaching and service contributions. She sued the university in a federal court, alleging the tenure denial was based on sex. But the court instead found **the university had valid, nondiscriminatory reasons to deny her tenure. The professor could not show these reasons were a pretext for gender bias.** Remarks she offered as evidence of bias had been made years before the tenure decision and were completely unrelated to it. The professor failed to make an indirect case of bias because she was not qualified for tenure. The court held for the university. *Blasdel v. Northwestern Univ.*, 787 F.Supp.2d 759 (N.D. Ill. 2011).

◆   *A professor who was denied tenure and discharged earned a chance to show that a Michigan university breached his employment contract.*

Kettering University terminated the professor's faculty appointment after an investigating committee found he misrepresented grant information, falsely stated he was the primary author of an article and keynote speaker at a conference from which he wrongfully withheld money, failed to accurately list dates on his employment application and made other misrepresentations. He sued the university in a federal court for breach of contract, retaliation and national origin discrimination. The court found none of the comments he relied on to support his national origin discrimination claim mentioned his Iranian descent. The professor did not show the stated reasons for discharge were a pretext. Appeal reached the U.S. Court of Appeals, Sixth Circuit. It agreed with the university that its stated reasons for terminating the professor's employment were not a pretext for unlawful retaliation. But the court held **there were genuine issues of material fact regarding whether the termination was in violation of the "just cause" provisions of the employment contract**. Since the professor raised some doubt as to whether just cause existed to discharge him, the contract claim was returned to the trial court. *Sanders v. Kettering Univ.*, 411 Fed.Appx. 771 (6th Cir. 2010).

◆ *A Tennessee professor who was a Hindu and a native of India failed to prove he was denied a promotion based on his religion or national origin.*

The professor joined Tennessee State University as an assistant professor in 1990. He was granted tenure and promoted to associate professor in 1997. But the university denied the professor's application for full professor, telling him he needed more substantial achievements in research and public service to be promoted. After he was again denied a promotion, the professor sued the university in a state court, claiming he was denied the promotions based on his national origin and religion. He accused the university of violating its faculty handbook policies by allowing a professor to serve on two committees that considered his application and failing to provide timely access to committee recommendations. The court granted a pretrial order for the university. On appeal, the state appeals court noted that the university faculty handbook confirmed its claim that research and public service activities were important considerations in the promotions process. **The university had consistently maintained that the professor was denied promotion due to his deficiencies in these areas.** He failed to submit evidence of public service or research activities, and the record showed he was not qualified for promotion. As a result, the judgment was affirmed. *Marpaka v. Hefner*, 289 S.W.3d 308 (Tenn. Ct. App. 2008). The Supreme Court of Tennessee denied an appeal in 2009.

◆ *A Missouri professor's due process claim against a private college failed because she did not show the college engaged in state action.*

The professor claimed male professors with similar responsibilities in her department were paid about $13,000 more annually than females. The college initially renewed her appointment for the 2006-07 term, but the college president then informed her that she would be placed on leave with pay and that she would not be reappointed for 2007-08. The college denied her grievance without a hearing. She then filed bias charges with state and federal agencies before suing the college's board of trustees for due process violations, retaliation, sex and age discrimination, breach of contract, tortious interference with her contract of employment and violation of the Equal Pay Act. **The court rejected the due process claim because the professor failed**

to show the private college had engaged in any state action. Next, the court granted the motion to dismiss the retaliation claim. The professor had admitted the college took no action relating to her employment after she filed the grievance. The claim of tortious interference with a contractual relationship was also dismissed, as such claims can be filed only against a third party. However, the court retained the discrimination claims. Both Title VII and the state's human rights act allowed punitive damage awards in cases of discrimination with malice or reckless indifference to federally protected rights. *Reed v. Board of Trustees of Columbia College*, No. 07-04155-CV-W-NKL, 2007 WL 4365749 (W.D. Mo. 2007).

◆ *The Supreme Court of Rhode Island refused to overturn a $455,000 jury verdict for a professor who was denied tenure for unlawful reasons.*

After serving in the engineering division for three years, the professor had a falling out with the division's director of undergraduate programs over a grading controversy. The professor eventually changed the grades under protest, but his relationship with the director remained sour. The director asked the professor to interview a minority candidate for a vacant position. The professor claimed the director's secretary told him the interview was being conducted for "affirmative action considerations." The professor refused to conduct the interview, saying he was concerned it might be illegal to interview a candidate for a job that had been set aside. He was denied tenure, and his internal grievance was then denied. In a state court action against the university, the professor claimed the director retaliated against him for opposing discriminatory practices, and he asserted national origin discrimination. A jury sided with the professor with respect to his retaliation claim and awarded him $675,000 in damages. On appeal, the state supreme court upheld the verdict for the retaliation claim. **While a rational jury could have reached a contrary verdict, the court found enough evidence to support the conclusion that the professor was denied tenure because he opposed the university's hiring practices.** *Shoucair v. Brown Univ.*, 917 A.2d 418 (R.I. 2007).

C. Collegiality and Animosity

◆ *A federal court held the University of Washington (UW) denied tenure to an assistant professor based on her lack of collegiality, not discrimination.*

All three of the tenured professors in the assistant professor's department were male. She personalized workplace problems and was humiliated when a student chose to work with another professor on a project. Assessments of the professor noted she felt threatened when her colleagues began projects in her perceived areas of expertise. She reacted angrily when she was not given credit she thought she was due, and she suspected unfairness when she was denied grants. Student evaluations of her teaching were mostly neutral or negative.

Twice, the department director decided not to support the professor's requests for tenure. Although the university provost considered the application, a decision was postponed due to concerns about her teaching effectiveness, concerns about collegiality, and a need for clarification relating to her scholarly achievements. Evidence indicated the professor believed collegiality should not be a factor in the tenure analysis. After her application for tenure was rejected a third time, she sued UW in a federal court for discrimination and retaliation. **The court held gender was not a motivating factor in the tenure decisions.** Even if the director disliked the professor, his recommendations did not cause the denial of tenure. As the professor could not prove unlawful retaliation, the court ordered the entry of judgment for UW. *Bichindaritz v. Univ. of Washington*, No. C10-1371RSL, 2012 WL 1378699 (W.D. Wash. 4/20/12).

◆ *Lack of collegiality was a valid basis upon which to discharge a tenured North Carolina State engineering professor.*

After gaining tenure at North Carolina State University, the professor was given unsatisfactory performance reviews for three straight years. A faculty hearing committee found he was not incompetent, but university trustees discharged him for incompetence of service. Among the university's findings was a lack of collegiality with colleagues that had become so disruptive that the professor's department was unable to operate efficiently. A state court upheld the discharge, and he appealed to the Court of Appeals of North Carolina.

On appeal, the professor claimed that tenured professors cannot be discharged on grounds other than incompetence, misconduct or neglect of duty under the state university code. The court rejected this argument, as the discharge was for incompetence – one of the permissible reasons for discharge under the code. **A university regulation authorized discharge for incompetence when a tenured professor had unsatisfactory reviews for two straight years. Moreover, disruptive behavior may also constitute incompetence.** The professor's due process claim failed because the university followed the relevant code provisions. Since there was "ample evidence" that he disrupted his department to the point that its functions and operations were impaired, the discharge was affirmed. *Bernold v. Board of Governors of the Univ. of North Carolina*, 683 S.E.2d 428 (N.C. Ct. App. 2009).

◆ *A federal district court refused to reverse an Iowa university's decision that a professor with several years of experience should not be granted tenure.*

The professor occupied a tenure-track position, with tenure becoming available in the sixth year of employment. A university promotion and tenure document noted that decisions relating to promotion involved subjective considerations. The university denied the professor's request for an early promotion in his fifth year, and the next year, only 12 of 29 faculty members voted for promotion. After his internal appeals were turned down, he sued the university regents in the state court system, claiming the decision to deny tenure was arbitrary, capricious and an abuse of discretion. The court ruled against him, noting that university officials had expressed concerns about the lack of impact of his scholarship and his low number of publications. On appeal, the Court of Appeals of Iowa noted that **the subjective process of deciding whether to award tenure should be left to the professional judgment of educators**, unless it was shown that they acted in a way that was arbitrary or capricious. As no such showing was made in this case, the court affirmed the judgment for the university regents. *Meltzer v. Board of Regents*, No. 08-0345, 2008 WL 5412225 (Iowa Ct. App. 12/31/08).

◆ *A tenured Arkansas professor did not show any causal connection between his dismissal and his filing of a lawsuit four years earlier.*

The professor claimed he was removed as department chair in violation of his constitutional rights. To settle his lawsuit, the university paid him a nominal sum. After the settlement, friction developed between the professor and the new chair. Following a series of insubordinate acts by the professor, the chair told him he could not teach during a summer session. When the professor went to a class he would have taught and started filming it, he was removed by university security and warned that further disruptions would result in his dismissal. A short time later, he filmed students as they registered for classes and was again removed by security. The professor did not appear at a meeting called by the university chancellor, and he was soon dismissed. In a federal district court action against university officials, the professor accused the chair and university of retaliating against him for filing a lawsuit. He also claimed race discrimination and due process violations.

The court ruled for the university. On appeal to the U.S. Court of Appeals, Eighth Circuit, the university asserted Eleventh Amendment immunity. The professor provided no authority to support his argument that the university could not claim immunity because it did not timely raise this defense. The retaliation claim failed because he did not show a causal connection between a protected activity and his dismissal. In any event, the university had legitimate reasons for its decision. **There was evidence that the professor was insubordinate, refused to attend meetings and acted unprofessionally.** No due process violation occurred, since he did not show university officials acted arbitrarily, and he did not comply with university procedures. As a result, the judgment was affirmed. *Satcher v. Univ. of Arkansas at Pine Bluff Board of Trustees*, 558 F.3d 731 (8th Cir. 2009).

◆ *A federal district court dismissed an Illinois professor's constitutional rights violation claims.*

The professor was disciplined after having confrontations with other faculty members. After a no-confidence vote by the faculty, he lost his position as a member and chair of a college personnel committee. He was also removed from the University Council Personnel Committee position. The professor sued university officials in a federal district court for denial of due process and equal protection rights. The court dismissed the claims against the board and officials on Eleventh Amendment grounds, finding they were not subject to constitutional claims for damages. The claims of deprivation of property and liberty without due process lacked merit. Although the professor had a property interest in his employment as a tenured faculty member, he did not have any interest in membership on committees. As he did not show damage to his good name, reputation, honor or integrity, the court dismissed his claim based on deprivation of a liberty interest. Since the university did not take adverse employment action against the professor, such as termination, demotion, or a loss of pay and benefits, he failed to allege any significant legally cognizable injury, and the case was dismissed. *Ganesan v. NIU Board of Trustees*, No. 02 C 50498, 2003 WL 22872139 (N.D. Ill. 2003).

D. Handbooks and Procedures

◆ *An African-American professor did not convince a federal court that he was not rehired or granted tenure by an Illinois university based on his race.*

The professor filed a complaint against the university in which he asserted he had been denied tenure based on race discrimination. He later sued the university, again asserting race discrimination and denial of tenure because he advocated for a racially diverse faculty. The professor claimed the university retaliated against him and violated contract law by failing to comply with a university faculty handbook when it considered his application for tenure.

A federal court accepted the university's explanation that the professor's research record was weak and he only minimally met teaching requirements. Because he did not show these reasons were false, his race discrimination claim was rejected. But the court declined to grant pretrial judgment to the university on the professor's retaliation claim based on the filing of his complaint. He made a preliminary showing that he engaged in protected activity and suffered a materially adverse action. **There was evidence from which a reasonable jury could conclude that the university did not rehire the professor as an adjunct because he filed the race discrimination complaint.** But the court rejected his breach of contract claim because he did not show the university failed to comply with the faculty handbook. *Montgomery v. DePaul Univ.*, No. 10 C 78, 2012 WL 3903784 (N.D. Ill. 9/7/12).

◆ *A trial court was ordered to re-examine claims that changes to an employment handbook wrongfully deprived professors of vested tenure rights.*

Until 2002, the Metropolitan State College of Denver was a part of the Colorado State Colleges System. At that time, the state removed the college from the system and created a board of trustees to govern it. In 2003, the board issued a new handbook describing the rights of professional personnel at the college. The new handbook superseded one that had been in place since 1994, and it included some changes that did not sit well with tenured professors. For example, it did not afford tenured faculty priority over nontenured faculty in the event of a layoff. In addition, it removed the requirement that the college try to relocate dismissed faculty and eliminated a hearing committee procedure that was used when tenured faculty members sought to challenge their dismissal.

Five tenured professors filed a state court action against the board of trustees, claiming the new handbook breached their employment contracts and violated their due process rights. The court held the new handbook did not breach employment contracts. It also rejected the due process claim, because none of the professors had been subjected to dismissal or layoff under the new handbook. **On appeal, the Court of Appeals of Colorado held the board lacked authority to unilaterally modify handbook provisions that afforded the professors substantive and vested rights.** Provisions in the new handbook relating to priority and relocation in the event of layoffs affected the professors' substantive rights. It was up to the trial court to determine whether those rights were vested. The new handbook violated due process because it allowed the college president to institute and resolve dismissals. *Saxe v. Board of Trustees* *of Metropolitan State College of Denver,* 179 P.3d 67 (Colo. Ct. App. 2007).

In 2008, the Supreme Court of Colorado rejected further appeal of the action. *Saxe v. Board of Trustees of Metropolitan State College of Denver,* No. 07SC301, 2008 WL 698945 (Colo. 2008).

◆ *A private Minnesota university did not breach a professor's contract when it decided not to grant her application for tenure.*

A university faculty handbook called for evaluation of tenure cases by an academic council, which then made tenure recommendations to the university president. The president had final authority regarding all tenure decisions. The academic council recommended denying the professor's application for tenure, and the university president accepted the recommendation. After a hearing, the council reversed itself and recommended tenure. But the president again denied the application, and the professor sued the university and its president in a state court for breach of contract and breach of the covenant of good faith in employment. All the claims were dismissed, and the professor appealed.

Before the Court of Appeals of Minnesota, the professor claimed the faculty handbook created a contract and required it to grant her tenure. She argued that the president was obligated to grant tenure to candidates who met applicable criteria for tenure and were recommended for tenure by the academic council. **The court affirmed the judgment, finding that the handbook set out procedures for candidates seeking tenure but explicitly reserved final tenure decisions for the president.** *Nash-Marshall v. Univ. of Saint Thomas,* No. A07-2028, 2008 WL 3290383 (Minn. Ct. App. 8/12/08).

IV. INVESTIGATIONS, HEARINGS AND PROCEDURES

A. Investigations

Public institutions and administrative agencies are bound to respect the due process rights of public employees during investigations.

◆ *A Minnesota community college did not violate a part-time English instructor's right to due process by declining to renew his contract.*

The instructor's contracts ran from semester to semester. Near the end of his sixth consecutive semester, the college legal affairs director advised him that a student had filed a sexual harassment complaint against him. The director told the instructor to stay away from the bookstore where the student worked, but she did not give him a written notice or a copy of applicable college policies and procedures, or tell him he could submit a written response to the charge. At a later interview, the director failed to give the instructor notices required by state law. After interviewing the instructor, the student and three witnesses, she wrote up a report concluding he had violated the college's sexual harassment policy. After she completed her report, she threw away her notes.

The instructor was informed of the non-renewal of his contract, and he sued the college and various officials in a state court. The case reached the Court of Appeals of Minnesota. It found the instructor **could not show any property interest in continued employment because the terms of his**

contract called only for part-time, temporary employment that ended each semester. The court was not persuaded by his argument that ordering textbooks for the classes he expected to teach showed he had a protected interest in continued employment. No liberty interest in reputation was implicated, as the college did not publicize either the letter informing the instructor he would not be rehired or the investigator's sexual harassment report. The college was entitled to judgment. *Phillips v. State*, 725 N.W.2d 778 (Minn. Ct. App. 2007).

◆ *A Colorado university improperly released an audit report to the media without providing a name-clearing hearing.*

The University of Colorado at Denver (UCD) investigated a managing director for fiscal misconduct. An auditors' report found evidence that he had granted employees paid time off without required approval. The director also gave a subordinate paid time off to prepare for a foreign teaching assignment and falsified an employee's termination date. The director's supervisor told him he would be assigned other duties for 30 days and then discharged. However, the director did not receive a copy of the audit report until two weeks later.

Meanwhile, the UCD newspaper ran an article detailing the report. Another article appeared in a local paper. After the director was discharged, he said the release of the report created a stigma on his reputation and prevented him from applying for jobs he otherwise would have sought. In his federal lawsuit against UCD, the director claimed his due process rights were violated. A federal district court ruled against him, and he appealed. The U.S. Court of Appeals, Tenth Circuit, found enough evidence to create a factual issue as to whether the damaging statements in the audit report were false. The director said he believed he had the authority to grant administrative leave without the approval of his supervisor, and insisted he had made no misrepresentation in allowing an employee to take time off to teach. As to the third incident, the director said the employee worked a full day on each day of her last week of employment. The court found this evidence was important, because **UCD could not prove fiscal misconduct unless it showed the director acted intentionally**. The case was returned to the district court for further proceedings. *Evers v. Regents of the Univ. of Colorado*, 509 F.3d 1304 (10th Cir. 2007).

◆ *An Ohio university football coach was allowed to discover and present information to a trial court before it resolved his breach of contract claim.*

The coach became aware that some of his players were conducting voluntary throwing sessions. He knew players could get hurt unless there was some organization to these workouts. An NFL scout arrived at the university looking for game films and information about a senior quarterback. During the visit, the coach allegedly directed the quarterback while the scout watched. The coach's supervisor reprimanded the coach in writing, stating that such contact with players outside NCAA-approved dates was unacceptable. The university investigated and found the coach violated NCAA rules at a pre-season camp.

After the investigation, the university held a hearing before a five-person faculty committee, then voted to dismiss the coach. He appealed through a grievance process, but the grievance committee rejected the appeal as untimely. The coach sued the university in a state court for breach of contract. The court held for the university, and the coach appealed to the Court of Appeals of Ohio. There, he alleged the trial court should have provided him an opportunity to conduct the pretrial fact-finding process called "discovery." The court agreed, finding **the evidence was not developed in a way necessary to properly determine a motion for summary judgment**. It vacated the judgment and returned the case to the trial court to allow discovery. *Kaczkowski v. Ohio Northern Univ.*, No. 6-05-08, 2006 WL 1312401 (Ohio Ct. App. 5/15/06).

◆ *A private college had to disclose certain records to the EEOC.*

A professor, who had been employed at a Pennsylvania private college for three years, was denied tenure after he was reviewed by the school's Professional Standards Committee. The committee, composed of the dean and five faculty members, recommended that tenure not be granted to the professor. The committee's recommendation was also reaffirmed by the college's grievance committee. The professor then filed a complaint with the EEOC alleging discrimination based on his French national origin. The EEOC issued a subpoena for the committee's records. Although the EEOC offered to accept the records with names deleted, the school refused to disclose them.

The EEOC then filed suit in federal district court to compel the college to comply with the subpoena. The district court ordered disclosure of the records, and the college appealed. The court of appeals affirmed, holding that **although the disclosure might burden the tenure process or invade the privacy of other professors, the records had to be disclosed because they were "relevant" to the EEOC's case**. The college appealed to the U.S. Supreme Court, but its petition for review was denied. *Franklin & Marshall College v. EEOC*, 476 U.S. 1163, 106 S.Ct. 2288, 90 L.Ed.2d 729 (1986).

◆ *The U.S. Supreme Court required a university to comply with an EEOC subpoena seeking peer review information.*

After the University of Pennsylvania, a private institution, denied tenure to an associate professor, she filed a charge with the EEOC alleging discrimination based on race, sex and national origin in violation of Title VII. During its investigation, the EEOC issued a subpoena seeking disclosure of the professor's tenure-review file and the tenure files of five male faculty members identified as having received more favorable treatment. The university refused to produce a number of the tenure-file documents and asked the EEOC to modify the subpoena to exclude "confidential peer review information."

The EEOC successfully sought enforcement of its subpoena through a federal district court. The U.S. Court of Appeals, Third Circuit, rejected a claim that academic freedom required recognition of a qualified privilege or the adoption of a balancing approach that would require the EEOC to demonstrate a showing of need to obtain peer review materials. The U.S. Supreme Court then held **a university does not enjoy a special privilege requiring a judicial finding of necessity prior to access of peer review materials**. It was reluctant to add such a privilege to protect "academic autonomy" when Congress had failed to do so in Title VII. The Court also held "academic freedom" could not be used as the basis for such a privilege. *Univ. of Pennsylvania v. EEOC*, 493 U.S. 182, 110 S.Ct. 577, 107 L.Ed.2d 571 (1990).

B. Hearings and Procedures

◆ *A University of New Hampshire professor who was arrested after a violent outburst could not prove a due process violation or defamation.*

The professor suspected that a faculty member in his department had called police to report parking violations. He received a $100 parking ticket and went into a profane tirade about the faculty member in front of a student and a lab technician. Based on the incident, he was arrested for stalking and disorderly conduct. The professor was suspended and barred from campus. After the criminal charges were dismissed and the suspension and ban were lifted, the professor sued the university for defamation and due process violations. A federal district court rejected all his claims, and the case reached the U.S. Court of Appeals, First Circuit. According to the court, there was probable cause to support the disorderly conduct and stalking charges against the professor.

The university did not violate the professor's due process rights when it suspended him with pay, limited his access to the campus and removed him from his position as a department chair. **Because the suspension was with pay, the court held he was not deprived of a property interest that would require pre-suspension process.** With respect to campus access, the record showed the professor had been allowed on campus at least nine times while he was suspended, and was denied access just once. This did not support a due process claim. With respect to the loss of the department chair position, the professor had received notice of the charges against him and told of the possibility that he could lose the post. Finally, the defamation charge failed because based on the outburst, the university had good reason to advise the community to avoid the professor and tell police if they saw him on campus. *Collins v. Univ. of New Hampshire*, 664 F.3d 8 (1st Cir. 2011).

◆ *University of North Carolina (UNC) employees must follow UNC employment dispute resolution procedures before filing a lawsuit.*

An associate professor completed a probationary year and earned a two-year employment contract. The agreement specified it was "subject to and governed by" UNC's code. A month before his contract was up, the university notified the professor that he would not be rehired. Instead of pursuing an appeal, he sued UNC for wrongful termination. A court dismissed the case, finding it lacked jurisdiction (authority) to hear it. The professor had not exhausted his administrative remedies by completing university appeals before suing. On appeal, the Court of Appeals of North Carolina affirmed the judgment. **North Carolina law required UNC employees to complete university procedures intended to resolve employment disputes before going to court.** As a result, the judgment for UNC was affirmed. *Johnson v. Univ. of North Carolina*, 688 S.E.2d 546 (N.C. Ct. App. 2010).

◆ *Saginaw Valley State University (SVSU) did not violate the due process rights of its head football coach when it did not rehire him.*

SVSU decided not to renew the coach's contract because it suspected him of fraud, and he filed a federal district court action alleging constitutional rights violations. The court found that SVSU had conducted an internal investigation and concluded the coach violated NCAA rules. It had provided him with a name-clearing hearing. In a separate state court action, a jury found SVSU did not breach a contract with the coach. The contract did not automatically renew. Although the court agreed with him that "a person's good name, reputation, honor and integrity are among the liberty interests protected by the Due Process Clause of the Fourteenth Amendment," it held **SVSU was not required to provide a name-clearing hearing before it declined to renew him**. The court found no authority for requiring a public university to initiate such a hearing. As the university offered a hearing when the coach requested one, there was no due process violation. *Awrey v. Gilbertson*, No. 10-14242-BC, 2011 WL 2312175 (E.D. Mich. 6/9/11).

◆ *When a property right to employment exists, due process requires that the employee receive notice and an opportunity to be heard before discipline.*

In two consolidated cases, the U.S. Supreme Court considered what pretermination process must be afforded a public employee who can be discharged only for cause. In the first case, a security guard hired by a school board stated on his job application that he had never been convicted of a felony. Upon discovering that he had in fact been convicted of grand larceny, the school board summarily dismissed him for dishonesty in filling out the job application. He was not afforded an opportunity to respond to the dishonesty charge or to challenge the dismissal until nine months later. In the second case, a school bus mechanic was fired because he had failed an eye examination.

The mechanic appealed his dismissal after the fact because he had not been afforded a pretermination hearing. The Supreme Court held that **because the employees possessed a property right in their employment, they were entitled to a pretermination opportunity to at least respond to the charges against them**. The pretermination hearing need not fully resolve the propriety of the discharge, but should be a check against mistaken decisions. The Court held that in this case, the employees were entitled to a pretermination opportunity to respond, coupled with a full-blown administrative hearing at a later time. *Cleveland Board of Educ. v. Loudermill*, 470 U.S. 532, 105 S.Ct. 1487, 84 L.Ed.2d 494 (1985).

◆ *When the disciplinary action is something less than termination, the protections afforded by due process are not the same as required in* Loudermill.

A police officer employed by a Pennsylvania state university was arrested in a drug raid and charged with several felony counts related to marijuana possession and distribution. State police notified the university of the arrest and charges, and the university's human resources director immediately suspended the officer without pay pursuant to a state executive order requiring such action where a state employee is formally charged with a felony. Although the criminal charges were dismissed, university officials demoted the officer because of the felony charges. The university did not inform the officer that it had obtained his confession from police records, and he was thus unable to fully respond to damaging statements in the police reports. He filed a federal district court action against university officials for failing to provide him with notice and an opportunity to be heard before his suspension without pay.

The court granted pretrial judgment to the officials, but the U.S. Court of Appeals, Third Circuit, reversed and remanded the case. The U.S. Supreme Court stated that the court of appeals had improperly held that a suspended public employee must always receive a paid suspension under *Cleveland Board of Educ. v. Loudermill*, above. The Court held that **the university did not violate due process by refusing to pay a suspended employee charged with a felony pending a hearing**. It accepted the officials' argument that the Pennsylvania executive order made any pre-suspension hearing useless, since the filing of charges established an independent basis for believing that the officer had committed a felony. The Court noted that the officer here faced only a temporary suspension without pay, and not employment termination as in *Loudermill*. The Court reversed and remanded the case. *Gilbert v. Homar*, 520 U.S. 924, 117 S.Ct. 1807, 138 L.Ed.2d 120 (1997).

◆ *A Kentucky community and technical college professor was afforded due process before being demoted for poor job performance.*

The professor received three consecutive negative performance evaluations. After the third, she appealed, but the college president agreed with the evaluations and the college notified her she would be demoted to a temporary, part-time adjunct position. A letter informing the professor of the decision cited her violations of administrative policies and procedures, and her poor job performance. The letter notified her she was on leave without pay and told her she had a right to a pre-demotion hearing. The professor received an administrative hearing where she was represented by counsel and was given the opportunity to show why she should not be demoted. The college allowed her to submit additional information after the hearing, but the college president informed her in writing that she would be demoted. The college then sent the professor a letter advising her of her appeal rights, but later informed her that the demotion was final. This letter outlined reasons for the decision, including job carelessness, poor behavior toward students and staff, and failure to follow security procedures. The letter advised the professor that she had not been discharged and indicated she remained eligible for substitute duties.

The professor sued the college in a state court, claiming it violated her due process rights. The court dismissed her complaint, and she appealed to the Court of Appeals of Kentucky. **The court affirmed the decision, noting that procedural due process is a flexible concept.** Its key components are notice and an opportunity to be heard. In this case, the professor acknowledged that she was given adequate written notice of the charges against her. She also acknowledged that she received a chance to be heard and to present her evidence. As the professor received all the process she was due, the trial court's decision was affirmed. *Bassett v. Board of Regents*, No. 2006-CA-002131-MR, 2007 WL 2687399 (Ky. Ct. App. 9/14/07). In 2008, the Supreme Court of Kentucky denied further consideration of the case.

◆ *An employee on probationary status could not show a California university violated his due process rights.*

The University of California hired the employee under a union contract providing for an initial six-month probationary period. During this time, the university had discretion to fire probationary employees without following collective bargaining grievance procedures. While the employee was still on probation, he was fired for sexual harassment of a co-worker. He sued the university in a federal district court for due process violations. He also argued the university violated his Fourteenth Amendment liberty rights by publicly disclosing the sexual harassment allegation that had been made against him.

The court held for the university, and the employee appealed. The U.S. Court of Appeals, Ninth Circuit, **explained that to be entitled to a notice and a hearing, an employee must have a property interest in employment**. There was no due process violation in this case, as the employee knew he was still in his probationary term and had no property interest in continuing employment. While public employers can violate employee liberty interests by publicly disclosing sexual harassment allegations, the university committed no violation here. The employee could not prove that any co-workers had learned about the sexual harassment charges from the university. As the university had been properly granted pretrial judgment, the court affirmed the judgment. *Whitworth v. Regents of Univ. of California*, 274 Fed.Appx. 559 (9th Cir. 2008).

◆ *The Supreme Court of Nevada was liable to a tenured professor for breach of contract because it discharged him based on outdated evaluations.*

The university gave the professor consecutive unsatisfactory evaluations, which was cause for termination. It filed a complaint against the professor with its administrative code officer and scheduled a hearing. The parties reached a settlement under which the professor agreed to resign at the end of the academic year. The university agreed to cancel the hearing and offer him a non-tenured teaching contract. The professor refused to sign an employment contract without guaranteed language and sued the university for breach of contract in a Nevada trial court. The court prohibited the university from using the unsatisfactory evaluations as a basis for firing the professor. It ordered the university to continue the professor's employment unless it revoked his tenure.

The university filed another administrative complaint against the professor based on the unsatisfactory evaluations, which were now six years old. It decided its own six-month deadline for hearings did not apply to the time of the settlement and its present administrative complaint. After a hearing, the university fired the professor. He sued the university a second time, alleging the prior court order prohibited the university from using the old evaluations as a basis for termination. **The court held for the professor, and the university appealed. The Supreme Court of Nevada held the university breached the settlement by holding the hearing based on an outdated complaint that included the prior evaluations.** The court found the hearing violated the terms of the settlement agreement and held the university breached the agreement when it unilaterally determined it could proceed with a new hearing. *State of Nevada, Univ. and Community System v. Sutton*, 103 P.3d 8 (Nev. 2004).

◆ *The Court of Appeals of North Carolina held state law precluded administrative review of layoff actions involving state university employees.*

Permanent state funding reductions forced the University of North

Carolina at Chapel Hill to eliminate staff positions in various departments. Three employees who were included in the reduction of force pursued grievances that were upheld under university procedures. All three employees filed petitions with the state office of administrative hearings (OAH), alleging they were improperly laid off. A state trial court denied the university's dismissal motions and held the OAH had jurisdiction to determine if just cause supported the layoffs. **The state court of appeals held the OAH only had jurisdiction to hear state employee cases involving demotion, retaliation for opposition to discrimination and disputes relating to veterans preferences.** The state legislature enacted a law that intentionally excluded reductions in force based on procedural violations from OAH jurisdiction. The court directed the trial court to grant the university's dismissal motions. *Univ. of North Carolina v. Feinstein*, 590 S.E.2d 401 (N.C. Ct. App. 2003).

◆ *A New York university was not liable for firing a professor for harassment prior to a hearing.*

Although no grievance or complaint was filed under the university's grievance procedures, the university took the student's information, gathered other information, and decided to fire the professor. When the student failed to appear at the arbitration hearings mandated by the collective bargaining agreement, the termination was rescinded, and the charges against the professor were dismissed. He nevertheless sued the university for failing to follow its own rules when disciplining him. A jury awarded him $25,000 in damages, but the Second Circuit Court of Appeals reversed. Here, **the professor failed to show that the university was required to follow the grievance procedures exclusively when making a finding that an employee had engaged in illegal discrimination.** Because the university's grievance procedures gave it the flexibility to discipline the professor without formal hearings, there was no breach of duty by the university. *Garcia v. State Univ. of New York at Albany*, 320 F.3d 148 (2d Cir. 2003).

◆ *College officials were not entitled to immunity in a lawsuit brought by a teacher accused of misconduct and barred from campus.*

A music instructor at a Nebraska public college taught for 29 years before retiring. He directed a performance group called "Chorale" in addition to teaching, and continued to work in a part-time capacity after he retired until the college eliminated his position. At that time, the college informed him it was banning him from campus, pending an investigation into alleged embezzlement. The college's letter also accused him of permitting Chorale to have inappropriate sexual overtones in their performances. He sued the college and its officials under 42 U.S.C. § 1983, alleging violations of his substantive and procedural due process rights as well as his free speech and freedom of association rights under the First Amendment. The college and officials asserted qualified immunity and sought a dismissal. A federal court dismissed the substantive due process claims, but refused to dismiss the others.

On appeal, the Eighth Circuit Court of Appeals affirmed. **The instructor was entitled to a name-clearing hearing because the accusations of dishonesty and immorality were stigmatizing and were known by faculty**

members at several campuses. He had a liberty interest in his name and reputation, and the college officials were not entitled to qualified immunity after refusing to provide the hearing. Finally, since the college was a public forum, its officials should have determined whether banning the instructor from campus was the least restrictive way to serve a compelling interest. They were not entitled to qualified immunity on the First Amendment claims either. *Putnam v. Keller*, 332 F.3d 541 (8th Cir. 2003).

◆   *An at-large professor might have been qualified for another position so as to avoid a reduction in force.*

A university hired a dean for its college of business and management, but because of a faculty restructuring, gave him an "at-large" executive appointment. Later, the college merged with the college of professional studies, and he was retained as a tenured professor. Finally, a financial crisis caused a reduction in force (RIF), in which he lost his job. He sued the university, claiming that he should have been exempt from the RIF because of his status as an at-large professor. The court ruled for the university, and the D.C. Court of Appeals affirmed in part. Here, **the university had the authority to conduct a RIF and release faculty members**. However, the university never made an initial finding as to whether the professor might have qualified for placement in another department because of his at large status. Thus, that issue had to be remanded to the university. *Hahn v. Univ. of Dist. of Columbia*, 789 A.2d 1252 (D.C. 2002).

◆   *Even if a university violated an employee's procedural due process rights, he did not suffer any harm so as to be entitled to judicial relief.*

A paraprofessional library assistant at a South Carolina university was accused of sexual harassment. Although no formal charges were filed, he was issued several reprimands, which were withdrawn from his file after he challenged them. Several years later, his new assistant accused him of gender discrimination and of making sexual advances toward males in a specific library. The director of the Equal Opportunity Programs (EOPs) office notified him of the allegations but failed to provide him with witness names or details. After yet another complaint, the university temporarily reassigned the employee, then issued him a reprimand and permanently reassigned him, still without providing him with witness names or details of its investigation.

The employee sued the university for violating his due process rights, and a federal court ruled against him. The Fourth Circuit affirmed, noting that even though the EOP office may have violated the employee's procedural due process rights, he could not show that he was deprived of a property interest in employment. **He only had a right to continued employment with the university, not to continued employment in a particular position. Also, he did not suffer a reduction in pay** upon his reassignment. *Parkman v. Univ. of South Carolina*, 44 Fed.Appx. 606 (4th Cir. 2002).

◆   *A Kentucky university police officer whose contract was not renewed could not sue for due process violations.*

A Kentucky university hired a police officer under an annual contract. It later suspended him with pay for his involvement in the dubious arrest of several students. He did not challenge the suspension. When the university refused to renew his contract the following year, he sued it under 42 U.S.C. § 1983, asserting due process and equal protection violations. A federal court ruled in favor of the university, and the Sixth Circuit affirmed. It noted that he could not succeed because **he could not show that he had a legitimate expectation of continued employment with the university**. The university's personnel manual did not create a property interest in employment, nor did it require the university to reappoint him. *Baker v. Kentucky State Univ.*, 45 Fed. Appx. 328 (6th Cir. 2002).

◆ *A North Dakota professor was properly fired where he was able to confront witnesses and challenge evidence in two hearings before his termination.*

A university professor served as chairman of the physics department until his relationships with other faculty members deteriorated and he was removed as chairman. He criticized the department in a number of letters that he sent to university officials and local newspapers. Subsequently, the university received numerous complaints from students about his poor teaching performance. More than 90% of his introductory students transferred out of his class in one semester. The university then sent him a letter of termination that listed six grounds for his firing, including his libelous conduct, his disciplinary record, and his lack of cooperation with faculty members. He obtained a hearing before a special review committee, which ruled in his favor, but the president of the university rejected the committee's findings.

The committee on faculty rights then upheld the dismissal. The professor sued the university in a federal court under 42 U.S.C. § 1983 for violating his First and Fourteenth Amendment rights. The case reached the Eighth Circuit. It noted that while two of the professor's letters addressed matters of public concern, most of them did not. The professor could not claim First Amendment protection for all the letters, and allegedly libelous material in the unprotected letters could be used as a reason for termination. Also, **the professor received due process in that he was given notice of the charges against him and an opportunity to respond**. Thus, his Fourteenth Amendment claim could not succeed. *de Llano v. Berglund*, 282 F.3d 1031 (8th Cir. 2002).

V. WRONGFUL DISCHARGE

"Employment at-will" exists in the absence of an oral or written contract of employment. When an employee works "at will," the law presumes the employment relationship may be terminated by either party at any time and for any reason. But an employer may not discharge an employee for an unlawful reason, such as reporting illegal or fraudulent conduct or agreeing to give testimony that may be adverse to the employer's interests.

◆ *A Maryland university police officer's reporting of misconduct could be protected by a state whistleblower act, even if it was personally motivated.*

The officer became concerned that the arrest of a student by other campus officers violated the Fourth Amendment. He wrote a letter stating that the arrest violated the Fourth Amendment. But instead of sending it to his supervisor, he sent it to a university vice president. He was suspended and, after a hearing, he was discharged for failing to follow the proper chain of command. The officer filed an administrative whistleblower complaint. An administrative law judge (ALJ) found the letter to the vice president was not protected because it was motivated by a "crusade to make changes to the department," rather than to report government abuses. Appeal reached the state's highest court, which explained that **an objective test is used to determine whether a whistleblower has a reasonable belief that he is identifying a legal violation and thus is making a protected disclosure**. The whistleblower does not have to show his disclosure exposes an actual violation. In this case, the court held the ALJ was improperly preoccupied with the officer's motive. The law required only that he had a reasonable belief that he was reporting a violation. As a personal motive was not a reason to deny whistleblower protection, the court ordered the ALJ to reconsider the whistleblower claim under an objective standard. *Lawson v. Bowie State Univ.*, 421 Md. 245, 26 A.3d 866 (Md. 2011).

◆ *A Tennessee court held a professor's demotion did not the trigger the protections of the state Public Protection Act (PPA).*

In his capacity as head of the Department of Philosophy and Religion at a state university, the professor made a highly critical year-end evaluation of a professor who was expecting tenure. But the dean of the college ordered him to delete all his negative comments. When the professor refused, the dean asked him to resign as department head. After he refused, he was stripped of the position, resulting in a significant loss of income. The professor sued the university in a state court, asserting PPA violations for refusing to participate in or remain silent about illegal activities. The court held he did not state a claim under the PPA and awarded judgment to the university.

On appeal, the Court of Appeals of Tennessee held that to prevail in a PPA case, a party had to show a refusal to participate in or remain silent about "illegal activities." This could include firing based on a refusal to participate in or to remain silent about a violation of law. According to the professor, his positions as a department head and professor were separate, and he was fired from only one of them. The court found the removal as department head was a demotion, not a firing. Instead, the PPA required **an act by an employer to end an employment relationship**. As the university had demoted the professor, his retaliation claim could not go forward. *Harman v. Univ. of Tennessee*, No. E2009-02139-COA-R3-CV, 2010 WL 2432049 (Tenn. Ct. App. 6/16/10).

◆ *A New Jersey university's refusal to hire a wrestling coach for a full-time paid position may have been a retaliatory response to his previous complaints.*

After volunteering as an assistant wrestling coach for some time, the coach received a series of one-year appointments as a part-time, salaried coach. Midway through the last of the appointments, the head wrestling coach told the coach he would be resigning and that he would recommend him for the job. The coach was hired as a part-time head coach. During the next season, he complained to the school's athletic director about equipment and facilities.

When university officials decided to eliminate the wrestling program, the coach solicited donations, helped save the program and won honors for his coaching. Near this time, members of the team were illicitly videotaped while showering.

The university's athletic director planned to fire an assistant for failing to promptly report the discovery of the videotape, and the coach complained that female coaches who engaged in misconduct were treated more leniently. The university created a new full-time job for a head wrestling coach/coordinator of student staffing. The athletic director offered the job to another candidate, and the coach sued the university in a federal district court, claiming he was denied the job due to his previous complaints. The court denied the university's motion for pretrial judgment. **Although the university claimed it hired another candidate for legitimate reasons, factual issues existed as to its true motivation for passing over such a successful coach.** *Sabol v. Montclair State Univ.*, No. 06-3214 (DMC), 2008 WL 2354553 (D.N.J. 6/3/08).

◆ *A University of Washington (UW) employee's state-law claim of retaliation was rejected by a federal district court.*

The employee worked in UW's Computing and Communications (C&C) Department. He used his UW email account to send a vulgar email to the United Way. UW issued the employee a letter of counsel, but a month later he received a favorable performance review and a raise. The employee filed a complaint with the UW department of human resources, claiming a co-worker had distributed a harsh critique of his work and that his supervisor failed to address it. He also claimed he was perceived differently by others who learned about the United Way email, and that he was denied an interview for a job based on the critique and email. The employee then resigned to accept another job at UW. He was placed on home assignment for the duration of his two-week notice period. The employee complained that the C&C Department had discriminated and retaliated against him, but the UW complaint resolution office found the complaint unfounded. He then sent harassing emails to several UW officials, leading to the termination of his employment.

The employee sued UW in a federal district court for retaliation. However, the claim was filed under a state law that makes it unlawful to discharge an employee who has opposed unlawful employment practices. **The court granted UW's motion for pretrial judgment, because the employee did not show he opposed any practice forbidden by the state law against discrimination.** He did not show how a critique of his work, or his supervisor's alleged failure to intervene regarding criticism, constituted behavior prohibited by the statute. Even if the employee could show he engaged in protected conduct, his claim would fail because he was fired for sending harassing emails. The court awarded pretrial judgment to UW. *Cooper v. Univ. of Washington*, No. C06-1365RSL, 2007 WL 3356809 (W.D. Wash. 11/8/07).

◆ *The Court of Appeals of Michigan interpreted the term "public body" broadly to allow an employee to pursue a whistleblower action.*

The U.S. Department of Education (DOE) investigated student financial assistance programs at a Michigan college. An administrator who cooperated with the DOE was later discharged. She sued the college in a state court, claiming she was fired for participating in the DOE investigation. The court held for the college, finding the DOE was not a "public body" under a state whistleblower law. The administrator appealed to the Court of Appeals of Michigan, which noted the power to arrest was not the only factor to consider when determining whether an agency was a "law enforcement agency" under the whistleblower law. Instead, it was appropriate to consider the extent of the DOE's overall power to detect and punish legal violations. The DOE has broad investigatory powers, including the power to gain access to people and documents and to issue subpoenas. DOE officials are authorized to execute warrants and make arrests. **In light of the broad powers granted to the DOE, the appeals court concluded the DOE was a "law enforcement agency" within the meaning of the state whistleblower law.** It reversed and remanded the case for further proceedings. *Ernsting v. Ave Maria College*, 274 Mich. App. 506, 736 N.W.2d 574 (Mich. Ct. App. 2007).

◆   *A federal district court held Connecticut College did not cause a director of development emotional distress during termination proceedings.*

After the director of development had worked for the college about two years, a newly hired vice president stated at a meeting that he perceived her position to be a "senior major gift officer" and not director of development. A month later, the acting vice president of development and alumni relations gave the director a negative performance evaluation. The college soon demoted her to a position designated "senior development officer of major gifts." The director's next performance evaluation was critical of her performance and a month later, the college discharged her. The director sued the college in a federal district court for negligently inflicting emotional distress, among other claims. The college moved for dismissal of the emotional distress claim.

The court stated that the time period identified by the director as the basis for her emotional distress claim involved routine employment matters such as job performance evaluations, work assignments, job transfers and title transfers. While these actions may have played a part in the employment action, they did not occur during a "termination process." **A claim for negligent infliction of emotional distress must be based on conduct during the termination itself, not during the time leading up to it.** Since the employee offered insufficient evidence of negligent conduct by the university at a relevant time, the court dismissed the case. *Stitt v. Connecticut College*, No. Civ. A. 3:04 CV577 (CFD), 2005 WL 646218 (D. Conn. 2005).

◆   *The Supreme Court of Iowa held that opposition to a co-worker's discharge was not "protected activity."*

Drake University investigated a security officer for an arrest he made during the annual Drake Relays. The officer was placed on desk duty for three months, then discharged. A university shift sergeant defended the officer's actions and offered to testify on his behalf. The university asked the sergeant to stop discussing the incident with the press, but he continued to talk openly about it. The university then demoted him one rank, resulting in a pay cut. The sergeant resigned and sued the university in an Iowa court, asserting he was constructively discharged for engaging in protected activity. The court awarded the university summary judgment. The state appeals court affirmed.

The state supreme court held that to succeed in a wrongful discharge claim, the sergeant had to establish that his advocacy established a clearly defined public policy that would be undermined by his termination. He would also have to show his termination resulted from his participation in a protected activity and for no other reason. **The court found that opposing a co-worker's wrongful termination was not a "protected activity" under state law.** While public policy protected employees offering truthful testimony at legal proceedings, there was no indication the discharged officer had intended to sue the university. The court affirmed the judgment for the university. *Shoop v. Drake Univ.*, 672 N.W.2d 335 (Iowa 2003).

◆   *An Illinois court denied a professor's claims against a university for defamation, breach of contract and invasion of privacy.*

A divinity school was considering an associate professor for tenure when the administration received complaints about the way he ran his classes. A tenure committee conducted an investigation and learned that students considered him rude and abrasive. They reported he deviated from class topics and was unprofessional. School administrators spoke with the professor several times about these concerns and warned him that failure to change his conduct would result in termination. The professor denied the charges, and the school suspended him. He claimed the charges harmed his professional reputation and that communications to students and faculty about termination constituted defamation. He sued the school for defamation and breach of contract.

The court dismissed the defamation claim and characterized the termination of his contract as a "buy-out," since it paid the professor in full. The professor appealed. The Appellate Court of Illinois rejected contract claims relating to the university handbook, which allowed the interviewing of students about classroom decorum. **The university did not breach his contract by failing to renew it after extending the tenure review process.** Under the faculty constitution, notice of termination was to be given by March 1 of the year, except in cases of moral turpitude. Since the professor did not receive notice by this deadline, he argued colleagues and students would infer he was fired on grounds of moral turpitude. The court rejected his claim and affirmed the judgment. The invasion of privacy claim failed because the professor did not show the university put him in a false light. *Green v. Trinity Int'l Univ.*, 801 N.E.2d 1208 (Ill. App. Ct. 2003).

◆   *A Florida District Court of Appeal held a whistleblower complaint was properly dismissed by the state human relations commission.*

After being discharged, a community college provost filed a complaint with the Florida Commission on Human Relations, accusing college trustees of violating the state whistleblower act. The commission dismissed her complaint because the college was not a "state agency" under state law. The provost appealed to a state district court of appeal. The court found the list of statutory terms for the definition of "state agency" included any official, officer, commission, board or department of the executive branch of state government. For the provost to establish the commission's jurisdiction to investigate her claim, she would have to show the board of trustees was part of the executive branch. However, state law described community colleges as state political subdivisions and emphasized the difference between political subdivisions and state agencies. **As the board of trustees was not a board of the executive branch of state government, the commission lacked jurisdiction to investigate the complaint.** *Caldwell v. Board of Trustees Broward Community College,* 858 So.2d 1199 (Fla. Dist. Ct. App. 2003).

◆ *Project documents did not prevent a university from eliminating an employee's position.*

A university assigned an employee to work on a project updating the university's financial software system for Y2K compatibility. Several months later, the employee's position was eliminated as part of a reorganization and, after he unsuccessfully applied for a number of other jobs, he was fired. He sued the university for breach of contract, asserting that the project work plans amounted to a contract. The university asserted that the work plans did not constitute an employment contract and that, even if they did, it had not breached the contract. A court found in favor of the university, and the California Court of Appeal affirmed. **The work plans did not prohibit the university from conducting the reorganization or from firing the employee when it had no work for him.** *Jenkins v. California Institute of Technology,* No. B153627, 2002 WL 31529092 (Cal. Ct. App. 2002).

◆ *A university employee could not show that he was fired because of complaints he made about co-workers stealing.*

A receiving clerk in the maintenance department at a Florida university complained to university security officers that his supervisor and co-workers were stealing university property. He was then allegedly subjected to certain retaliatory actions, including a glued office lock, a smoke-filled office, and interference with his radio transmissions. He later asked to take a leave, but his request was rejected when the university determined that he had already exhausted his leave time. He took the time off anyway and was fired. **He sued the university for retaliation under the state whistleblower act**, and a state court ruled against him. The Florida District Court of Appeal affirmed. Here, even if the employee's complaint about stealing was protected speech, he failed to show a causal connection between his complaint and his firing. For being absent without leave, he would have been fired regardless of the complaint. Also, as for the retaliatory actions, he was unable to prove that management was either implicated in the attacks or that it condoned them. *Amador v. Florida Board of Regents,* 830 So.2d 120 (Fla. Dist. Ct. App. 2002).

CHAPTER SIX

Employment Practices and Labor Relations

I. PRIVACY RIGHTS

The Fourth Amendment standard of reasonableness applies to searches of public employees as well as their workspaces, offices and computers. Courts reviewing public employee privacy cases typically balance the employee's reasonable expectations of privacy against the government employer's interest in supervision, control and workplace efficiency.

In O'Connor v. Ortega, 480 U.S. 709 (1987), the U.S. Supreme Court held public employees have a reasonable expectation of privacy in their personal workspaces, desks and file cabinets. Acceptable use policies and other workplace rules place limits on reasonable privacy expectations.

In City of Ontario, California v. Quon, *this chapter, the U.S. Supreme Court cautioned courts against departing from established law when interpreting privacy rights in electronic forums such as texting. It said "the judiciary risks error by elaborating too fully on the Fourth Amendment implications of emerging technology before its role in society has become clear."* **A person's constitutional right to privacy is violated only if an alleged invasion occurs where the person has a reasonable expectation of privacy.**

A. Electronic Data and Communications

◆ *A California city did not violate a police officer's rights by reviewing text messages on his department-owned pager to find the cause of excess charges.*

A California police department informed employees that they had "no expectation of privacy or confidentiality when using" department-owned pagers capable of sending and receiving text messages. An officer's monthly pager usage soon exceeded his text message character allotment under the department's contract with the pager service. To find out why, a supervisor investigated. He found many messages on the officer's pager were not work-related and some were sexually explicit. The officer sued the department for Fourth Amendment violations. The U.S. Supreme Court agreed to review the case and noted that a public employer's search was reasonable if justified at its inception and not excessively intrusive in light of the reasons for the search.

The Court determined that the search in this case was justified at its inception, as there were reasonable grounds for investigating pager use. The supervisor had ordered the search to see if the character limit on pagers was sufficient for department needs. As this was a legitimate, work-related reason, the Court found no Fourth Amendment violation. Review of the text messages was not excessively intrusive. Supervisors took care to investigate only pager usage that took place during work hours. **The officer and others had received no assurances of privacy and had limited privacy expectations.** The text-message search did not violate the officer's rights or the rights of those with whom he communicated. The Court noted "the judiciary risks error by elaborating too fully on the Fourth Amendment implications of emerging technology before its role in society has become clear." *City of Ontario, California v. Quon,* 130 S.Ct. 2619, 177 L.Ed.2d 216 (U.S. 2010).

◆ *Officials properly seized an Oklahoma university department head's personal laptop computer as part of a child pornography investigation.*

The case involved a department head at Oklahoma State University (OSU). Another OSU employee reported finding child pornography in a box belonging to the department head. A university dean and associate dean seized the box and turned it over to university police. After legal counsel was consulted, a decision was made to seize the desktop computer in the department head's office. Two members of the university's computer information services security office went to the office and saw a laptop computer on a table near his desk.

The security specialists took the hard drive from the desktop computer and also seized the laptop. The contents were retained by the university's police department. The department head sued university officials, including one of the security specialists, in a federal district court. He claimed the seizure violated the Fourth Amendment. The court relied heavily on the U.S. Supreme Court's ruling in *O'Connor v. Ortega*, above. **It found the search was reasonable, as the purpose was to investigate suspected misconduct involving the possibility that child pornography was being stored on computers located in an on-campus office.** The personal laptop computer was open and running when the security specialists entered the department head's office. The laptop was showing an email program that was supported by the university as well as spreadsheets that looked like they contained university records. Under these circumstances, the search was justified at its inception, and as its scope was reasonable, there was no Fourth Amendment violation. *Soderstrand v. State of Oklahoma*, 463 F.Supp.2d 1308 (W.D. Okla. 2006).

◆ *A Florida high school teacher accused of exchanging sexually explicit emails with students did not have to turn over all his home computers for inspection by his school board for use in an employment termination hearing.*

The board suspended the teacher for misconduct for exchanging emails and instant messages with students that were sexually explicit and made derogatory comments about staff members and school operations. An administrative law judge issued an order allowing a board expert to inspect the hard drives of the teacher's home computers to discover if they had relevant data for use against him in a formal termination hearing.

The teacher appealed, arguing production of the home computer records would violate his Fifth Amendment right against self-incrimination and his privacy rights. **The court noted that computers store bytes of information in an "electronic filing cabinet."** It agreed with the teacher that the request for wholesale access to his personal computers would expose confidential communications and extraneous personal information such as banking records. There might also be privileged communications with his wife and his attorney. The only Florida decision discussing the production of electronic records in pretrial discovery held **a request to examine a computer hard drive was permitted "in only limited or strictly controlled circumstances," such as where a party was suspected of trying to purge data**. There was no evidence that the teacher was attempting to thwart the production of evidence in this case. The court held the broad discovery request violated the teacher's Fifth Amendment rights and his personal privacy. It reversed the administrative order allowing the board to have unlimited access to his home computers. *Menke v. Broward County School Board*, 916 So.2d 8 (Fla. Dist. Ct. App. 2005).

◆ *The Tennessee Court of Appeals applied Florida decisions in finding public school Internet records and emails were not open to public inspection.*

A Tennessee citizen made a written request to a county education board to view and inspect digital records of Internet activity, including emails sent and received, websites visited, and the identity of Internet service providers used during school hours or stored on school-owned computers. A trial court judge reviewed the requested records privately and found they were not accessible under the state Public Records Act (PRA). The citizen appealed to the Court of Appeals of Tennessee, asserting the digital records or documents were open to public inspection because they had been made during business hours or were stored on the school's computers. **The court found the PRA's clear purpose**

favored the disclosure of public records. The PRA defined "public record" to include documents, papers, electronic data processing files and other material "made or received pursuant to law or ordinance or in connection with the transaction of official business by any governmental agency." The PRA did not limit access to records based on the time a record was created or the place the record was produced or stored. The trial court judge had properly inspected documents in private to decide if they were "made or received pursuant to law or ordinance or in connection with the transaction of official business."

The Supreme Court of Florida has rejected arguments that placement of a document in a public employee's file made the document a "public record." The Tennessee PRA definition of "public records" nearly matches the definition used in Florida Law. The court held that while it was not bound by Florida public records cases, it found them well-reasoned and applicable. The trial court did not commit error in privately reviewing the records, and the judgment was affirmed. *Brennan v. Giles County Board of Educ.*, No. M2004-00998-COA-R3-CV, 2005 WL 1996625 (Tenn. Ct. App. 2005).

◆ *A Florida District Court of Appeal held personal email fell outside the current definition of public records.*

The case involved a newspaper's request for emails sent from or received by municipal employees on government-owned computers. The court of appeal held personal email was not "made or received pursuant to law or ordinance." **Although digital in nature, "there was little to distinguish a personal email from personal letters delivered to public employees through a government post office box and stored in a government-owned desk."** The court noted the state supreme court has held "only materials prepared 'with the intent of perpetuating and formalizing knowledge' fit the definition of a public record." The court denied a publisher's request to compel a municipality to release all email sent from or received by two employees on their government-owned computers. *Times Publishing Co. v. City of Clearwater*, 830 So.2d 844 (Fla. Dist. Ct. App. 2002).

◆ *The Second Circuit upheld discipline against a New York state employee for downloading personal tax programs on the state-owned computer he used.*

The state had a policy prohibiting use of state equipment for personal business. The employee came under suspicion of neglecting his duties, and the state authorized an investigation of his computer usage. A list of file names revealed non-standard software was loaded on the computer, and additional searches determined the employee loaded a personal tax preparation program on it. The employee challenged the search of his computer in a federal district court. The court awarded pretrial judgment to the state. On appeal, the U.S. Court of Appeals, Second Circuit, found no Fourth Amendment violation. **Although the employee had a reasonable expectation of privacy in his office computer, the investigatory searches by the state were upheld as reasonable. The searches of his computer were reasonably related to the objectives of the search and not excessively intrusive** in light of the nature of his suspected misconduct. *Leventhal v. Knapek*, 266 F.3d 64 (2d Cir. 2001).

B. Employee Search and Seizure

Searches and seizures conducted by government employers implicate the Fourth Amendment. Because these searches are not carried out to enforce criminal laws, the courts consider them "administrative searches," which may be justified by the need to protect campus safety and ensure order.

◆ *After being criminally prosecuted for stalking a colleague, a professor filed an unsuccessful civil action against the University of New Hampshire.*

The professor was arrested for disorderly conduct and stalking of a colleague who accused him of kicking a garbage can and repeatedly screaming at her. He was also accused of threatening another professor three times and was suspended and banned from campus after having a tantrum about a parking ticket. After the criminal charges were dismissed, the university reinstated the professor, but he filed a federal lawsuit against the university for violating his First, Fourth, Fifth, Ninth and Fourteenth Amendment rights. The court rejected the Fourth Amendment claim, as people can be arrested based on "violations" of a state criminal code. Moreover, the arrest was based on a valid warrant. A warrant is valid if it is supported by probable cause, which was satisfied in this case by a law enforcement officer's belief that the professor had threatened a colleague three times. According to the court, the standard of probable cause is not difficult to meet, requiring only a reasonable belief that a crime has been committed. Since the arrest warrant for stalking was supported by probable cause, there was no violation of the Fourth Amendment and the university was entitled to judgment on the claims of false arrest and stalking.

On appeal, **the U.S. Court of Appeals, First Circuit, rejected the professor's claim that the arrest was an unreasonable seizure and found probable cause for the disorderly conduct and stalking charges**. The university did not violate his due process rights when it suspended him with pay, limited his campus access and removed him from his post as a department chair. Because the suspension was with pay, the professor was not deprived of a property interest that would require pre-suspension process. No defamation was found, as the university had good reason to warn faculty and staff to avoid the professor and tell police if they saw him on campus. As a result, the judgment for the university was affirmed in its entirety. *Collins v. Univ. of New Hampshire*, 664 F.3d 8 (1st Cir. 2011).

◆ *A court upheld a jury's decision to award $1.65 million to a professor whose laboratory contents were cleared out while he was at a conference.*

Upon accepting adjunct work at the University of the District of Columbia (UDC), the professor brought course materials, research data and lab equipment from another institution, where he had created materials and notes for 20 different courses. UDC had renewed his contract annually for several years when he accused it of reneging on a promise to grant him tenure. The professor filed a lawsuit against UDC. During settlement negotiations, UDC's provost told him to vacate his lab because the space was needed for other programs. After several delays, UDC hired a contractor to clear out the lab while the professor was at a conference. No inventory was made and the movers may have "thrown stuff out." The professor found that 90% of his belongings were gone and that some of his property had been thrown into trash dumpsters.

In a lawsuit against UDC, the professor sought compensation for course materials, research data, scientific instruments and other items. Since most of the property was unique or had no fair market value, he offered testimony from a collaborating biomedical engineering researcher and engineering professor to establish its value. He claimed that class materials he developed for 21 different courses had been taken, and that he lost at least 10 ongoing research projects. A jury found UDC liable for trespass, conversion and negligence and set the damages at $1.65 million. UDC sought a new trial, but the District of Columbia Court of Appeals held the valuation testimony was admissible, rejecting UDC's argument that the experts lacked subject-matter knowledge. **The experts had extensive research experience, were familiar with the professor's work, and articulated their methodologies for estimating damages.** As the jury had reasonably found UDC destroyed much of the professor's life work and ruined his career, the damage award was affirmed. *Trustees of the Univ. of the Dist. of Columbia v. Vossoughi*, 963 A.2d 1162 (D.C. Ct. App. 2009).

◆ *Three Ohio university police officers who arrested a school janitor for criminal menacing could not be sued for false arrest.*

The janitor reportedly lost his temper after the co-worker ignored a sign he had posted on a restroom door asking people to use a different bathroom. When the janitor told him to leave, the co-worker refused. Furious, the janitor went to their manager. The co-worker followed the janitor to the manager. The janitor threatened the co-worker, who called university police. The co-worker told the officers he was worried because he believed the janitor was capable of violence.

The officers arrested the janitor and charged him with criminal menacing. The janitor sued the university and nine employees in a federal district court. The court held the officers did not have qualified immunity, and they appealed. The U.S. Court of Appeals, Sixth Circuit, held public officials are protected by immunity unless they violate clearly established federal law. **It is clearly established that arrests based upon probable cause do not violate the Fourth Amendment. Sixth Circuit precedent allows police to base probable cause on credible eyewitness reports.** The co-worker stated the janitor had threatened him, and the manager verified his account. As the officers had probable cause for the arrest, the court reversed the judgment. *Franklin v. Miami Univ.*, 214 Fed.Appx. 509 (6th Cir. 2007).

◆ *The special needs of public employers justify allowing them to avoid the warrant and probable cause requirements of the Fourth Amendment.*

The U.S. Supreme Court held that the search of a public employee's office was reasonable when the measures adopted were reasonably related to the objectives of the search and not excessively intrusive in light of its purpose. The Court held that workplace searches by government employers "should be judged by the standard of reasonableness under all the circumstances."

The Court announced a case-by-case standard for evaluating employee privacy expectations, stating that a public employee's expectation of privacy in the workplace may be reduced by actual office

practices, work procedures or rules. Acceptable-use policies governing employee usage of computers and email are examples of such workplace procedures or rules. *O'Connor v. Ortega*, 480 U.S. 709, 107 S.Ct. 1492, 94 L.Ed.2d 714 (1987).

C. Video Surveillance

A Texas federal district court recently held that video surveillance of areas in which an employee has a reasonable expectation of privacy constitutes a Fourth Amendment "search." Moreover, the court found that video monitoring of employees may be a particularly intrusive form of search that is "a very serious, some say Orwellian, invasion of privacy."

◆ *Texas community college security officers made out a valid challenge to the placement of a hidden camera that recorded them changing clothes.*

Security officers learned that a contractor had put surveillance cameras in hidden areas such as in air vents, behind clocks, and in smoke detectors. They said some cameras could record audio, and that anyone who knew a camera's IP address could access it. The officers sued college officials for Fourth Amendment violations. College officials sought to dismiss the action, arguing the officers had no reasonable expectation of privacy in a room where they changed their clothes. The court rejected this argument. It found employees may have a reasonable expectation of privacy in an office, especially one that is routinely used as a locker room. Federal cases have established that **public employees have a reasonable expectation of privacy in an office against unexpected intrusions by their employers**. Video surveillance of areas in which one has a reasonable expectation of privacy constitutes a Fourth Amendment search, and video monitoring is a particularly intrusive form of search – one which the court called "a very serious, some say Orwellian, invasion of privacy." As case law provided college officials with fair warning that their conduct violated the law, they could not claim immunity, and the case would not be dismissed. *Jones v. Houston Community College System*, 816 F.Supp.2d 418 (S.D. Tex. 2011).

◆ *California officials were immune to invasion of privacy claims based on the videotaping of an employee's wedding and part of her honeymoon.*

A California teacher was married while she was on a disability leave. The School Insurance Program for Employees (SIPE) and her school district hired an investigator to surreptitiously attend her wedding and obtain videotape of her. The investigator went to the wedding and represented himself as a guest. He videotaped the ceremony, reception and the teacher with her husband on their honeymoon sunbathing. The teacher sued the district, SIPE and others in a state court for invasion of privacy and negligence. The court dismissed the case, and the teacher appealed. The state court of appeal held that **state law immunized public employees for injuries caused by instituting or prosecuting any judicial or administrative proceeding within the scope of their employment**, even if an employee acted maliciously. The court rejected the teacher's claim that SIPE and her district "intended to harass her." The investigation was an essential step to a judicial or administrative proceeding and was "cloaked in immunity." The investigation was within the scope of the investigator's employment. For this reason, the district and SIPE were entitled to immunity. *Richardson-Tunnell v. School Insurance Program for Employees (SIPE)*, 157 Cal.App.4th 1065, 69 Cal.Rptr.3d 176 (Cal. Ct. App. 2007).

◆ *A Massachusetts state college did not violate an employee's privacy rights by videotaping her without her knowledge.*

The college learned a former client had entered a building without permission after hours. Without informing the employee, the college installed a hidden security camera in the office in an attempt to record the former client. For three weeks, the employee went to a rear work area, unbuttoned her blouse and applied ointment to a severe sunburn. The area was under video surveillance, but no images of her were recorded. The employee learned about the videotaping and sued the college in a state court for violating her Fourth Amendment privacy rights. The court held the college had qualified immunity.

On appeal, **the Supreme Judicial Court of Massachusetts stated a person's constitutional right to privacy is violated only if an invasion of privacy occurs where a person has a reasonable expectation of privacy**. While the law recognizes some privacy interests in business premises, people cannot have a reasonable expectation of privacy in open places. The office was open to the public, and volunteers and employees could enter at any time. There was no absolute guarantee of privacy, even when the employee locked the front door. Despite her efforts to discreetly conduct personal and private acts in the office, the court held she had no objectively reasonable expectation of privacy there. Accordingly, the court affirmed the judgment for the college. *Nelson v. Salem State College*, 446 Mass. 525, 845 N.E.2d 338 (Mass. 2006).

D. Personnel Records

State data privacy acts protect the confidentiality of public employee personnel files. Common law rules of defamation may also provide a basis for legal action against a school district or its officers for wrongful disclosure of private facts or erroneous factual statements.

1. Media Access

◆ *A Pennsylvania newspaper and reporter had a right to see current and past salary information for certain employees of a state university.*

The reporter asked the State Employees' Retirement System (SERS) for salary information on state university employees. The state right-to-know act provides that "public records" kept by a government agency are accessible for inspection. A "public record" is "any account, voucher or contract dealing with the receipt or disbursement of funds by an agency." But any record or document, which would prejudice or impair a person's reputation or personal security, is not considered a public record. Before SERS responded to the request, it notified the university. The university and employees claimed the salary information was private and protected from release by the Constitution. The State Employees' Retirement Board granted the request, finding the information was a public record. The case reached the Supreme Court of Pennsylvania, which held it was proper to disclose the requested information under the state's right-to-know act. The SERS' fiduciary duties extended to investment matters but were not applicable to requests for salary information.

The court rejected the argument that disclosure was barred by the federal Gramm-Leach-Bliley Act, which protects the privacy of consumer information held by financial services industry institutions. Finally, the court rejected the employees' argument that disclosure would violate their right to privacy. **Although a privacy exception in the right-to-know law excused disclosure that would "prejudice or [impair] a person's reputation or personal security," the exception did not apply because the employees' privacy rights did not outweigh the public interest** in information about the disbursement of state funds. *Pennsylvania State Univ. v. State Employees' Retirement Board*, 594 Pa. 244, 935 A.2d 530 (Pa. 2007).

◆ *The private consideration of applicants for a university president violated the Minnesota Open Meetings Law and Government Data Practices Act.*

The University of Minnesota Board of Regents searched for a new president. Some applicants requested anonymity, and the board voted to screen them privately. The board denied information requests by media organizations about unsuccessful candidates. The organizations sued the board in the state court system for an order forcing disclosure of the information and enjoining the university from holding closed meetings. The court held for the media, and the board appealed. The state court of appeals noted that **the government data privacy act made public all personnel data on current and former applicants for employment by a statewide agency**. The names of applicants were considered "private data," except for finalists. Since the university was a statewide agency, and because the candidates were deemed "finalists," the court held the data practices act applied to procedures for selecting a university president. The only exception to the open meetings law applied to disciplinary proceedings and did not apply in this case. Accordingly, the court affirmed the decision to grant the media organizations' motion. *Star Tribune Co. v. Univ. of Minnesota*, 667 N.W.2d 447 (Minn. Ct. App. 2003).

2. Disclosure to Third Parties

◆ *California State University (CSU) trustees did not violate the state open meetings act by discussing a former chancellor's status in a closed session.*

A former CSU chancellor wanted to return to CSU as a trustee professor. Anticipating his return would result in publicity, he scheduled a closed session of the board of trustees. At the meeting, the board approved his return as a trustee professor. The president of the union representing faculty members sued the board under the state open meetings act, claiming the subject matter required a public session, and seeking an order to disclose what happened in the session. A state superior court rejected the action, and the union appealed.

The Court of Appeal of California held **an open meetings act exception**

applied to meetings held to consider the appointment, employment, evaluation of performance, or dismissal of a public employee. The court held that disclosure in this case would run counter to the policy of shielding employees from unwarranted embarrassment and publicity. The board simply wanted to discuss the former chancellor's vested right to return as a professor, and to address any questions. As the superior court did not commit error, the judgment was affirmed. *Travis v. Board of Trustees of California State Univ.*, 161 Cal.App.4th 335, 73 Cal.Rptr.3d 854 (Cal. Ct. App. 2008).

◆ *The Family Educational Rights and Privacy Act (FERPA) did not prevent an Ohio community college from disclosing prior complaints against an instructor accused of sexually harassing a student.*

In a federal district court action against the college, it was claimed that an instructor's supervisor knew of past misconduct and that the college and supervisor failed to take adequate steps to eliminate the risk he posed. During pretrial activity, the student sought rosters from classes taught by the instructor for the four years prior to the harassment she claimed. She also sought "every document relevant to any student complaint/concern" about the instructor." The college denied the requested information, arguing it could not be disclosed under FERPA. The court disagreed, finding some prior student complaints could be relevant. Complaints that were similar to the student's would support charges that the college and supervisor were aware of prior misconduct. The court concluded that the request should be limited to prior complaints of alleged sexual harassment. **There was insufficient evidence to show that class rosters were relevant to the student's claims**, and FERPA did not bar the request for prior student complaints relating to alleged sexual harassment. *Briggs v. Board of Trustees Columbus State Community College*, No. 2:08-CV-644, 2009 WL 2047899 (S.D. Ohio 7/8/09).

◆ *Michigan law permitted a public university to decline disclosing a record containing personal information, if disclosure would be a privacy invasion.*

The Michigan Federation of Teachers submitted a Freedom of Information Act (FOIA) request to the University of Michigan (UM) for employee names, home addresses, home phone numbers, job titles, pay rates, and work contact information. UM provided most of the information, including home addresses and phone numbers for about 21,000 employees who had given permission to publish this information in a staff and faculty directory. As to the remaining 16,406 employees, UM denied the request on privacy grounds. The Michigan Federation of Teachers and School Related Personnel sued UM in a state court, seeking the remaining addresses and phone numbers. The court held employee home addresses and phone numbers were personal information and not likely to contribute to the public's understanding of how the government works.

The case reached the Supreme Court of Michigan, which explained that **public entities may refuse to disclose a public record, if the record includes information of a personal nature and disclosure "would constitute a clearly unwarranted invasion of an individual's privacy."** The court expanded the definition of "information of a personal nature" to include private or confidential information. Employee home addresses and phone numbers were clearly of a private and confidential nature. Disclosure of this information could subject employees to potential abuses, such as having it used for marketing purposes. Disclosure could also place employees in physical danger if their information fell into the wrong hands. The court held disclosure was unwarranted because it would reveal little or nothing about the conduct of the university and would do nothing to advance the public policy behind the FOIA. *Michigan Federation of Teachers and School Related Personnel v. Univ. of Michigan*, 481 Mich. 657, 753 N.W.2d 28 (Mich. 2008).

◆ *A Missouri college did not violate an untenured professor's right to privacy by confirming to another institution that he was employed there.*

A DeVry University representative called the college's human resources (HR) department, revealed the professor's Social Security number, and asked if he was working full time at the college. The HR department confirmed that he was. The representative told the HR department that the professor was on leave from DeVry and had committed insurance fraud by claiming to be disabled when he was not. DeVry discharged the professor. The college soon reduced its staff and told the professor his contract would not be renewed. The college's long-term disability carrier denied the professor's application for benefits. The professor was told to file another claim seeking benefits for a period during which he was not working and receiving a full salary. The professor continued to teach at the college, but sued the college and several officials in a state court for privacy rights violations. The court found the only evidence that the professor presented was the phone call between DeVry and the HR department. **He did not indicate any confidential information was shared when the HR department confirmed he worked at the college.** The court granted the university's motion to dismiss the case. *Fish v. William Jewel College*, No. 05-00025-CV-W-DW, 2006 WL 2228975 (W.D. Mo. 8/3/06).

II. LABOR RELATIONS

The National Labor Relations Act (NLRA), as amended by the Labor Management Relations Act (LMRA), 29 U.S.C. § 141, et seq., governs unionization and collective bargaining matters in the private sector, including private education. States are also subject to the dictates of the act. The NLRA was passed to protect the rights of employees to organize, or to choose not to organize, and to ensure that commerce is not interrupted by labor disputes. Managerial employees are unprotected by the NLRA.

A. Appropriate Bargaining Units

◆ *The Supreme Court held a public university could require faculty to emphasize undergraduate instruction without bargaining over the new rule.*

The Ohio legislature passed a statute requiring state universities to adopt faculty workload policies and made them an inappropriate subject for collective bargaining. The law was enacted to address the decline in the amount of time faculty spent teaching, as opposed to time spent on research. Any university policy prevailed over the contrary provisions of collective bargaining agreements. One university adopted a workload policy pursuant to the law and notified the collective bargaining agent that it would not bargain over the policy. As a result, the professors' union filed a state court action, seeking an order that the statute violated public employee equal protection rights.

The Supreme Court of Ohio struck down the statute, finding the collective bargaining exemption was not rationally related to the state's interest of encouraging public university professors to spend less time researching at the expense of undergraduate teaching. The U.S. Supreme Court accepted the university's appeal and held that the state supreme court had not applied the correct standard of review under the Equal Protection Clause. In Equal Protection Clause cases that do not involve fundamental rights or suspect classifications, there need only be a rational relationship between disparity of treatment and some legitimate government purpose. In this case, the disputed statute met the rational relationship standard. Ohio could reasonably conclude that the policy would be undercut if it were subjected to collective bargaining. **The state legislature could properly determine that collective bargaining would interfere with the legitimate goal of achieving uniformity in faculty workloads.** The Ohio Supreme Court decision was reversed and remanded. *Cent. State Univ. v. American Ass'n of Univ. Professors, Cent. State Univ. Chapter*, 526 U.S. 124, 119 S.Ct. 1162, 143 L.Ed.2d 227 (1999).

◆ *An exclusive bargaining representative should have the sole voice in discussing employment-related matters with the employer.*

Minnesota Community College faculty members brought suit against the State Board for Community Colleges, claiming a state statute requiring public employers to engage in official exchanges of views only with their professional employees' exclusive representatives on certain policy questions violated their speech rights. Under the statute, public employers were required to bargain only with the employees' exclusive bargaining representative. The statute gave professional employees, such as college faculty members, the right to "meet and confer" with the employer on matters outside the scope of the collective bargaining agreement. The faculty members objected to the "meet and confer" provision, saying that rights of professional employees within the bargaining unit who were not members of the exclusive representative were violated.

The Supreme Court upheld the "meet and confer" provision. **There was no constitutional right to force public employers to listen to member views.** The fact that an academic setting was involved did not give them special constitutional rights to a voice in employer policymaking decisions. Further, the state had a legitimate interest in ensuring that a public employer heard one voice presenting the majority view of professional employees on employment-related policy questions. *Minnesota Community College Ass'n v. Knight*, 465 U.S. 271, 104 S.Ct. 1058, 79 L.Ed.2d 299 (1984).

◆ *In the following unique circumstances, faculty members at a private educational institution could be considered managerial employees.*

Yeshiva University's faculty association petitioned the National Labor Relations Board (NLRB) for certification as their bargaining agent. The NLRB granted certification, but Yeshiva refused to bargain, claiming faculty members were "managerial" and exempt from NLRA coverage. The case reached the Supreme Court, which noted the high degree of control over academic practices exercised by Yeshiva's faculty. Faculty members exercised authority which in any other context would be managerial. They determined teaching methods, grading policies, and the university's admission, graduation and matriculation standards. The Court held schools where faculty do not exercise binding managerial discretion do not fall within the scope of the managerial employee exclusion. **The Court noted that its decision applied only to schools that were "like Yeshiva," not to those where the faculty exercised less control.** *NLRB v. Yeshiva Univ.*, 444 U.S. 672, 100 S.Ct. 856, 63 L.Ed.2d 115 (1980).

◆ *A Michigan court upheld a determination by the State Employment Relations Commission to deny a petition to merge two bargaining units.*

Kendall College of Art and Design is a sub-unit of Ferris State University that retains its academic governance and operates autonomously. The Ferris Faculty Association, which represented full-time faculty members at the university, petitioned to add the Kendall bargaining unit to its bargaining unit. The Kendall unit was composed of full-time and part-time faculty members.

The Michigan Employment Relations Commission denied the petition, and the association appealed. The Court of Appeals of Michigan explained a commission's determination of appropriate bargaining units was factual and could not be disturbed unless there was a lack of competent, material, and substantial evidence. In reaching its decision, the commission focused on Kendall's academic autonomy from the university and the differences between the two educational institutions. The court rejected the association's argument that the commission erred in considering the bargaining history of the Kendall union. **Bargaining history is a relevant factor in considering whether a bargaining unit is appropriate.** The commission acknowledged the need "to avoid fractionalization or multiplicity of bargaining units." As the Kendall bargaining unit served its members well, it was an appropriate bargaining unit. The commission's decision was affirmed. *Ferris Faculty Ass'n v. Ferris State Univ.*, No. 243885, 2004 WL 144671 (Mich. Ct. App. 2004).

◆ *A District of Columbia court returned an NLRB decision recognizing a bargaining unit for college faculty members to the NLRB.*

Approximately 60 full-time faculty members at LeMoyne-Owen College attempted to form a collective bargaining unit. The college denied the request because it considered them managerial employees who were exempt from NLRA coverage. The faculty petitioned the NLRB for recognition as a bargaining unit. The college opposed the petition, citing the Supreme Court's decision in *NLRB v. Yeshiva Univ.*, above, as controlling precedent. The NLRB regional director found the college's faculty were not managerial employees and certified the bargaining unit. The college sought review, arguing the regional director deviated from *Yeshiva* and other precedents. The NLRB found the college committed an unfair labor practice when it refused to bargain with the new bargaining unit. The college petitioned for review of the NLRB's order. The District of Columbia Circuit Court returned the case to the NLRB. While deference is generally afforded to the NLRB's authority to certify bargaining units, **the decision in this case departed from precedent without explanation**. The college made a reasoned argument based on the *Yeshiva* case, and the regional director did not explain why the college's argument should be rejected. *LeMoyne-Owen College v. NLRB*, 357 F.3d 55 (D.C. Cir. 2004).

◆ *The Second Circuit refused to enforce an NLRB order requiring a New York college to bargain with a union because supervisors belonged to the union.*

The Security Department Membership (SDM) is the organization certified by the NLRB to represent Quinnipiac College's security personnel in collective bargaining. Quinnipiac refused to bargain with SDM, maintaining the organization was improperly certified because it included supervisors, who are excluded from collective bargaining under the NLRA. The NLRB conducted a hearing, but held the shift supervisors were not "supervisors" under the act and ordered Quinnipiac to bargain with SDM. The college refused. The NLRB petitioned the U.S. Court of Appeals, Second Circuit to enforce the order.

The NLRA defines "supervisor" as an employee who has the authority to hire, transfer, suspend, lay off, recall, promote, discharge, assign, reward, discipline or responsibly direct other employees, or address grievances. According to the Second Circuit, Quinnipiac's shift supervisors made assignment decisions based on their own expertise and experience, despite the existence of college procedures. Shift supervisors also disciplined employees. Although security directors had to review any disciplinary procedures taken by the shift supervisors, they still amounted to a supervisor's duty. Lastly, the shift supervisors responsibly directed other security employees. In declining to enforce the NLRB's order, the Second Circuit remanded the matter, with the suggestion that the board review the membership of SDM and consider eliminating the shift supervisors from the bargaining unit. *NLRB v. Quinnipiac College*, 256 F.3d 68 (2d Cir. 2001).

◆ *A state labor relations board used incorrect tests to determine whether two employees were "confidential employees" who were ineligible for the union.*

A union sought to represent all classified and specialist employees at an Illinois college. In the representation election, the union won by a single vote. The college challenged the result, asserting that two of the employees should not have been allowed to vote because they were "confidential employees" under the state labor relations act. One was a secretary; the other was a research associate – both reported to an assistant vice president for administrative affairs. An administrative law judge determined that the employees were confidential employees, and the state labor relations board upheld that decision.

The Appellate Court of Illinois reversed and remanded the case, finding that the board used the wrong tests to determine whether the employees were "confidential." Here, **although the college asserted that the employees were going to be performing duties related to the collective bargaining process, they had not yet done so**. Thus, the board should have determined whether there was a reasonable expectation that future job duties would satisfy the definition of a confidential position. *One Equal Voice v. Illinois Educ. Labor Relations Board*, 777 N.E.2d 648 (Ill. App. Ct. 2002).

B. Agency Fees

"Agency-shop agreements" entitle unions to charge "agency fees" to employees who are not union members, but who enjoy the representation of unions. The U.S. Supreme Court has held public sector agency-shop arrangements raise First Amendment concerns that individuals may have to contribute to unions as a condition of public employment. **In Abood v. Detroit Board of Educ., below, the Court held unions cannot use agency fees for ideological purposes that are unrelated to collective bargaining.**

◆ *The U.S. Supreme Court upheld a Washington law requiring public employee unions to obtain affirmative authorization from nonmember employees before using agency fees for election-related purposes.*

Washington law permits public employee unions to charge nonmembers who are in the collective bargaining unit an "agency fee" that is equivalent to full union membership dues. State voters approved an initiative that prohibited unions from spending the agency fees collected from union nonmembers unless the expenditure was "affirmatively authorized by the individual" nonmember. The initiative became Section 760 of the Fair Campaign Practices Act.

The Washington Education Association (WEA) faced separate state court actions claiming it used nonmember agency fees for election-related purposes without the affirmative authorization of union nonmembers. The state supreme court held this authorization requirement violated the First Amendment. On appeal, the U.S. Supreme Court held *Abood* **and later decisions did not require public sector unions to obtain affirmative consent before spending nonmember agency fees for purposes unrelated to collective bargaining.** Section 760 was a "modest limitation" on the extraordinary power of a private union over public employees to prohibit the use of agency fees for election-related purposes. This did not violate the First Amendment, and it would be constitutional for the state to eliminate agency fees. The Court vacated the state court decision, finding Section 760 was a constitutional condition that presented no realistic threat of official suppression of ideas. *Davenport v. Washington Educ. Ass'n*, 551 U.S. 177, 127 S.Ct. 2372, 168 L.Ed.2d 71 (2007).

◆ *In order to justify agency fees, the activities for which the fees are collected must be germane to collective bargaining activity, be justified by the government's interest in labor peace (and the avoidance of free riders), and present only an insignificant burden on employee speech.*

The exclusive bargaining representative of the faculty at a state college in Michigan entered into an agency-shop arrangement with the college requiring nonunion bargaining unit employees to pay a service or agency fee equivalent to a union member's dues. Employees who objected to particular uses by the unions of their service fee brought suit under 42 U.S.C. § 1983, claiming that using the fees for purposes other than negotiating and administering the collective bargaining agreement violated their First and Fourteenth Amendment rights. A federal district court held that certain collective bargaining expenses were chargeable to the dissenting employees. The U.S. Court of Appeals affirmed, and the U.S. Supreme Court granted certiorari.

The Court first noted that chargeable activities must be "germane" to collective bargaining activity and be justified by the policy interest of avoiding "free riders" who benefit from union efforts without paying for union services. It then stated that **the local union could charge the objecting employees for their *pro rata* share of costs associated with chargeable activities of its state and national affiliates, even if those activities did not directly benefit the local bargaining unit.** The local could even charge the dissenters for expenses incident to preparation for a strike, which would be illegal under Michigan law. However, lobbying activities and public relations efforts were not chargeable to the objecting employees. The Court affirmed in part and reversed in part the lower courts' decisions and remanded the case. *Lehnert v. Ferris Faculty Ass'n*, 500 U.S. 507, 111 S.Ct. 1950, 114 L.Ed.2d 572 (1991).

◆ *A union's objection procedures for challenging nonmembers' dues were constitutional.*

Two University of Alaska professors challenged their union's procedures for calculating nonmember dues. Under the collective bargaining agreement, if they declined union membership, they had a choice of either objecting to the use of their dues for unrelated union activities (and paying a reduced agency fee) or requesting arbitration to determine if the nonmember fee was accurate. Under the second option, the arbitrator had the option of raising the amount. A federal court ruled that the union's procedure was constitutional, and the Ninth Circuit Court of Appeals affirmed. Here, the procedures complied with the requirements set forth by the U.S. Supreme Court in *Chicago Teachers Union v. Hudson*, 475 U.S. 292 (1986). **The professors received an adequate explanation of the basis for calculating the agency fee, and they were provided with a reasonably prompt opportunity to challenge the amount of the fee before an impartial decisionmaker.** *Carlson v. United Academics-AAUP/AFT/APEA AFL-CIO*, 265 F.3d 778 (9th Cir. 2001).

◆ *An Illinois local failed to provide adequate procedural protections to non-bargaining unit members who objected to its nonrepresentational activities.*

In federal court, a group of non-bargaining unit members, employed by a university as clerical employees, filed a class action suit against the union. The nonmembers asserted that the union's fair share fee collection procedure failed to provide sufficient safeguards, thereby violating the First and Fourteenth Amendments. The court interpreted the union's response as a pretrial judgment motion and ruled in favor of the union. The employees appealed.

The Seventh Circuit reversed the judgment. Pursuant to the Illinois Educational Labor Relations Act (IELRA), the amount of fair share fees "can neither exceed union dues nor include any costs related to supporting candidates for political office." In *Chicago Teachers Union v. Hudson*, 475 U.S. 292 (1986), the U.S. Supreme Court required a union to satisfy the following three prongs in collecting these fees: (1) provide "an adequate explanation of the basis for the fee"; (2) provide the nonmember with a reasonable opportunity to protest the fee amount; and (3) establish "an escrow account for the amounts in dispute." Here, the union had the university collect 100% of union dues from both members and nonmembers, even though the fair share fee calculated for two of the disputed years amounted to about 85% of full dues. When an objection was filed, the nonmember fees were then held in an escrow account, which could not be accessed by the union. **The collection of fees, based on an advance reduction approach, was not as problematic as the dispute resolution procedure.** Under the IELRA, objectors were deprived of 15% of their funds for a year, a portion of which was not even being disputed. In addition, the fee objections had to be renewed annually. These burdens violated the *Hudson* test. *Tavernor v. Illinois Federation of Teachers*, 226 F.3d 842 (7th Cir. 2000).

◆ *Massachusetts' highest court held expenses related to a two-day strike by university faculty were not germane to collective bargaining.*

Public school teachers and state university instructors sued the Massachusetts Teachers Association (MTA) for charging them agency fees for activities the teachers claimed were not part of doing business as a bargaining representative. The state Labor Relations Commission found the MTA had demanded $26.77 in excess fees from each nonunion member. The Supreme Judicial Court of Massachusetts found most of the MTA's accounting expenses were chargeable. **The union president and vice president's salaries were overhead and therefore chargeable in proportion to the union's overall chargeable activities.** Discussions the union had about a statewide strike to publicize the condition of public education funding were not chargeable.

Expenses related to days when faculty at the University of Massachusetts at Amherst withheld services to protest the lack of funding for their collective bargaining agreement were also not chargeable, even though the university administration approved of and participated in the protest. Because the faculty had withheld services, the two-day action was a strike, and the expenses incidental to it were not chargeable. Nor were the costs of flyers distributed during commencement exercises at the University of Massachusetts at Boston chargeable to nonunion members. However, expenses related to an article that appeared in a union magazine providing pointers on how to communicate during a strike or some other unusual event were chargeable. *Belhumeur v. Labor Relations Comm'n*, 432 Mass. 458, 735 N.E.2d 860 (Mass. 2000).

◆ *Compelled agency fees cannot be used to support political viewpoints.*

In 1977, the U.S. Supreme Court held that the First Amendment prohibited states from compelling teachers to pay union dues or agency fees where their labor unions used the fees for purposes that were unrelated to collective bargaining. Compelled support of collective bargaining representatives implicated free speech, freedom of association, and freedom of religion concerns. However, some constitutional infringement on those rights was justified in the interest of peaceful labor relations. Thus, as long as the union acted to promote the cause of its membership, individual members were not free to withdraw their financial support. However, **compelled agency fees could not be used to support political views and ideological causes that were unrelated to collective bargaining issues**. *Abood v. Detroit Board of Educ.*, 431 U.S. 209, 97 S.Ct. 1782, 52 L.Ed.2d 261 (1977).

C. Collective Bargaining

In NLRB v. Catholic Bishop of Chicago, *this chapter, the U.S. Supreme Court held the First Amendment prevents inquiry by the National Labor Relations Board (NLRB) into a school's religious mission.*

◆ *As the NLRB had no jurisdiction over a church-affiliated Wisconsin college, it could not order the college to bargain with a faculty union.*

The NLRB ordered Carroll College to recognize and bargain with the collective bargaining agent of its faculty. The college appealed to the federal court system, asserting its religious environment and affiliation with the United Presbyterian Church placed it beyond NLRB jurisdiction under *NLRB v. Catholic Bishop of Chicago* and *Univ. of Great Falls v. NLRB*, this chapter. It also said faculty members were managerial employees who were not covered by the National Labor Relations Act. The case reached the U.S. Court of Appeals, District of Columbia Circuit, which stated that the First Amendment religion clauses preclude NLRB review of church-affiliated schools.

The court applied the three-part *Great Falls* analysis to determine whether the college had a "substantial religious character" that exempted it from NLRB review. It found **the college held itself out to students, faculty and the community as providing a religious educational environment**. Second, the college was a nonprofit, and third, it was affiliated with the Presbyterian Church. The court found the college easily satisfied the *Great Falls* test. In assessing religious affiliation, it was unnecessary to show the college was sponsored or controlled by a church. Since the NLRB had no jurisdiction over the college, the NLRB could not order it to recognize and bargain with the union. *Carroll College v. NLRB*, 558 F.3d 568 (D.C. Cir. 2009).

◆ *A Kansas professor's refusal to hold office hours at a particular community college campus justified her discharge for insubordination.*

The college denied the professor's request for mileage reimbursement for her trips between a satellite campus in Leavenworth and its main campus in Kansas City. The disagreement escalated, and she filed a grievance over the college's decision to assign her to the main campus. College trustees denied the grievance but failed to issue a timely decision. The professor believed she was entitled to the relief requested in her grievance and insisted on having her office in Leavenworth, even though she was not assigned to teach any courses there.

A college provost ordered the professor to hold office hours on the Kansas City campus. Although her caseload included online instruction, the provost noted that a relevant master contract required her to hold five office hours per week on campus. When the professor resisted, she was suspended without pay. College trustees discharged the professor for insubordination. A hearing officer found the provost had the sole authority to set class schedules and assign office locations, and held the professor had been insubordinate. She appealed to the state court system, where the Court of Appeals of Kansas rejected her argument that the hearing officer's decision was unsupported. **The college provost had the authority to assign faculty to specific work locations.** The professor failed to show that work locations could be changed only with her consent. The master contract required faculty members who taught online courses to hold at least five office hours per week on campus. There was substantial evidence that the professor refused to comply with the provost's order and was insubordinate. As the record showed she acted in an antagonistic and unprofessional manner, the judgment was affirmed. *Heflin v. Kansas City Kansas Community College,* 43 Kan.App.2d 371, 224 P.3d 1201 (Kan. Ct. App. 2010).

♦ *A union's waiver of employee rights to negotiate an intellectual property policy survived the expiration of a collective bargaining agreement. For that reason, refusal to negotiate the policy was not an improper labor practice.*

A City University of New York (CUNY) policy addressed intellectual property developed by its employees. The policy was not the subject of bargaining between CUNY and the Professional Staff Congress (PSC), which represented CUNY employees. The parties' 1996-2000 collective bargaining agreement expired, and PSC demanded that the intellectual property policy be negotiated. CUNY asserted Article 2 of the expired agreement constituted a waiver by the union to negotiate particular items, including the policy. Article 2 authorized CUNY's board of trustees to alter existing bylaws or policies "respecting a term or condition of employment" after giving PSC notice and an opportunity to consult. PSC filed an improper practice charge with the state public employment relations board (PERB). The parties reached a new agreement covering 2000-2002, which carried forward Article 2 unchanged.

Just before expiration of the 2000-2002 agreement, PSC again sought to negotiate the intellectual property policy. An administrative law judge held CUNY committed an improper practice by refusing to negotiate the policy. The PERB held PSC waived its right to negotiate the intellectual property policy in Article 2. The case reached the Court of Appeals of New York, which held the resolution of improper practice charges was generally within the PERB's discretion. Article 2 granted CUNY the right to unilaterally alter bylaws and policies respecting terms or conditions of employment that did not conflict with the agreement. Article 2 explicitly referred to "terms and conditions of employment," and it was not confined to "management prerogatives." **The court held the intellectual property policy was squarely within the coverage of Article 2, since it was never a part of a collective bargaining agreement and did not conflict with any terms of the current agreement.** Civil Service Law Section 209-a(1)(e) required employers to continue all terms of an expired agreement while a new one was being negotiated. This enhanced the negotiating process by preserving the status quo pending a new agreement. As the PERB had correctly determined the status quo and found the Article 2 waiver remained in effect, the court reinstated its decision. *Professional Staff Congress-City Univ. of New York v. New York State Public Employment Relations Board,* 7 N.Y.3d 458, 857 N.E.2d 1108 (N.Y. 2006).

♦ *A California court rejected a nurse's claim that her dismissal from a student clinic violated her due process and collective bargaining rights.*

A nurse practitioner who worked at a university clinic examined a student and determined she was 24 weeks pregnant. The student wanted to abort the pregnancy, but the nurse recommended against it, saying the pregnancy was too advanced. The nurse later urged the student to put the baby up for adoption and told her that a colleague at the clinic was interested in adopting it. A supervisor learned of the plan and admonished the nurse for unethical conduct. The student later had the baby, and the colleague took it home from the hospital.

The university discharged the nurse, and her grievance was denied. She requested a hearing that was later cancelled by a union representative. A hearing was held in the nurse's absence, and the hearing officer upheld the dismissal. The case reached the Court of Appeal of California, which found the nurse had no right to invoke arbitration. It also rejected her claims that the hearing officer was biased and the proceedings were inherently unfair. The university's failure to provide her with a witness list seven days before the hearing did not prejudice her case. By then, the nurse had already gone through the grievance procedure and knew the identity of the witnesses. Her inability to subpoena witnesses did not render the process unfair. **Since the nurse voluntarily failed to appear for her hearing, she could not now complain it was unfair to hold it in her absence.** *Nelson v. Regents of the Univ. of California*, No. D040623, 2004 WL 339340 (Cal. Ct. App. 2004).

◆ *The D.C. Circuit adopted a test for determining whether a religious institution can exempt itself from NLRB jurisdiction for collective bargaining.*

The University of Great Falls is operated by a Roman Catholic religious order. It refused to recognize or bargain with the Montana Federation of Teachers. The university maintained that the NLRB lacked jurisdiction because it was a religiously run institution, and the Religious Freedom Restoration Act barred the NLRB from ordering it to engage in collective bargaining. The union petitioned the NLRB for relief, and a regional director held the NLRB had jurisdiction. The NLRB upheld that determination, and the university appealed.

The U.S. Court of Appeals, D.C. Circuit, stated that the NLRB had improperly examined the university's religious character. It adopted **a three-part test for determining whether an institution can avail itself of the exemption in *NLRB v. Catholic Bishop of Chicago***, see Chapter Four, Section I.B., where the Supreme Court held the NLRB did not have jurisdiction over religious institutions. Under this test, an institution must: 1) provide a religious educational environment and hold itself out as such, 2) be organized by a nonprofit, and 3) be "affiliated with, or owned, operated or controlled directly or indirectly, by either a recognized religious organization or with an entity, membership of which is determined, at least in part, with reference to religion." Here, the university easily passed that test. As a result, the NLRB did not have jurisdiction, and the university did not have to bargain with the union. *Univ. of Great Falls v. NLRB*, 278 F.3d 1335 (D.C. Cir. 2002).

◆ *A union could use a university's email system to contact members where the collective bargaining agreement did not prohibit it.*

The union representing Oregon University System employees negotiated a collective bargaining agreement that allowed union officers and stewards to "have access to electronic bulletin boards under specified conditions." The union then began using email to transmit information to its members' work computers. The university objected to this practice, claiming that the bargaining agreement did not allow the union to use email in that way. After two arbitrators determined that the university could prohibit union officials from using the email system, the Oregon Court of Appeals determined that the union's use of email neither violated the terms of the bargaining agreement nor breached its duty of good faith and fair dealing. **The bargaining agreement was silent with respect to the union's use of email.** Thus, there was no breach of contract and no bad faith. *Oregon Univ. System v. Oregon Public Employees Union, Local 503*, 60 P.3d 567 (Or. Ct. App. 2002).

◆ *Adjunct faculty members were allowed to join a union in New Hampshire.*

A labor association seeking to represent 147 adjunct faculty members at a New Hampshire state college petitioned for certification by the Public Employees Labor Relations Board (PELRB). The university system opposed the petition, arguing that adjunct faculty are temporary employees who are excluded from bargaining because of their temporary status. A hearing officer granted the petition, allowing instructors who were currently teaching, and those who had taught two of the last three semesters, to join the union. The PELRB upheld that decision, and the adjunct faculty voted for the union.

The case reached the Supreme Court of New Hampshire, which found that there is some expectation that adjunct faculty members will return annually – they are compensated for longevity. The court affirmed the PELRB's decision that **adjunct faculty members are not temporary employees**. Even though their contracts did not include an expectation of continued employment, that did not diminish the adjunct faculty members' **reasonable expectation of continued employment**. The fact that adjunct instructors taught one-third of the college's courses indicated that they were not just "last-minute" hires. The court remanded the case to consider who was eligible for union membership. The PELRB did not provide an explanation for why only adjuncts who were currently teaching or who had taught two of the last three semesters were eligible. *In re Univ. System of New Hampshire*, 795 A.2d 840 (N.H. 2002).

D. Arbitration

◆ *A Michigan court held it was an arbitrator's job to interpret conflicting interpretations of a university faculty collective bargaining agreement (CBA).*

Central Michigan University (CMU) denied a faculty member tenure for two consecutive years. She filed grievances that were referred to arbitration. An arbitrator denied both grievances, finding the faculty member's submissions for publication did not satisfy CBA requirements. A state court judge agreed with the faculty member that the arbitrator had added to the CBA and changed its terms by reading in a quality requirement where none existed. The Court of Appeals of Michigan held that courts reviewing arbitration decisions had authority only to determine if the arbitrator stayed within the boundaries of the CBA. The CBA in this case granted the arbitrator authority to decide promotion disputes and alleged breaches of the CBA. **The lower court was wrong to conclude the arbitrator acted outside his authority by considering the quality of the faculty member's work.** It was the arbitrator's job to decide between conflicting interpretations of the CBA and CMU's department bylaws, and as the arbitrator did not exceed his authority, the court upheld the denial of the tenure grievance. *Cent. Michigan Univ. Faculty Ass'n v. Cent. Michigan Univ.*, No. 293003, 2011 WL 475461 (Mich. Ct. App. 2/10/11).

◆ *Because a settlement voided an earlier pact to arbitrate any employment dispute, a coach could sue Duke University for defamation.*

In 2006, three Duke men's lacrosse team members were accused of rape. The head lacrosse coach resigned, and the parties executed a release to resolve any matters regarding his separation. The release declared an intent to cancel all earlier agreements between the parties but said nothing about arbitrating any future claims that might arise. Two years later, the coach sued Duke and a senior vice president in the state court system for defamation. Duke sought to force him to arbitrate the claims, asserting they were subject to an arbitration agreement in the university's employment policy. The court denied the request, and Duke appealed. The Court of Appeals of North Carolina found the release clearly rescinded all earlier agreements to arbitrate. **There was no doubt that the release stated the intent of both parties to cancel all earlier agreements, and it discharged their duties under previously existing contracts.** The coach was not bound to arbitrate his libel and slander claims and could proceed with his action. *Pressler v. Duke Univ.*, 685 S.E.2d 6 (N.C. Ct. App. 2009).

◆ *An arbitrator wrongfully placed the burden on a Pennsylvania university to show it had good reason to deny tenure to a probationary faculty member.*

The university denied the professor tenure because she failed to demonstrate the requisite scholarly growth. Her professional union filed a grievance on her behalf under the relevant collective bargaining agreement (CBA). After the grievance was denied at all levels, the matter proceeded to arbitration, where an arbitrator held in the professor's favor. He ordered her reinstated as a probationary faculty member who was eligible for reconsideration for tenure. The university appealed to the state court system.

The case reached the Commonwealth Court of Pennsylvania, which noted courts generally defer to the decisions of arbitrators when parties have agreed via a CBA to use arbitration to resolve disputes. **However, an arbitrator's decision is not entitled to deference unless it "draws its essence" from the CBA.** In this case, the CBA did not expressly state which party bore the burden of proof in a grievance proceeding regarding tenure. **The agreement between the university and union specified that tenure candidates had the burden of showing requirements for tenure had been met.** The arbitrator should have consulted this agreement and placed the burden of proof on the professor. The arbitrator's award was vacated, and the case was remanded for additional proceedings. *Slippery Rock Univ. of Pennsylvania v. Ass'n of Pennsylvania State College and Univ. Faculties*, 916 A.2d 736 (Pa. Commw. Ct. 2007).

◆ *The Vermont State Colleges Federation did not unlawfully retaliate against a faculty member by declining to accommodate her scheduling request.*

The faculty member worked part time at a state college. The applicable collective bargaining agreement required the college to give priority to full-time faculty and administrators in scheduling matters. The faculty member filed a grievance when she was not assigned a schedule that accommodated her childcare and commuting needs. She later complained about a new schedule. The department decided not to change the new schedule, and she filed another grievance, this time for retaliation for her earlier grievance. A grievance board found the college was unlawfully motivated by the prior grievance. On appeal, the Supreme Court of Vermont found the faculty member did not present any direct evidence of a discriminatory motive. The court disagreed with the board's findings that the timing of the new schedule was suspicious, and that the college treated her less favorably than others. **The court said the faculty member presented no other evidence to infer the college retaliated because of her earlier grievance.** As the court found no basis to find the college had an unlawful motivation, the judgment was reversed. *Grievance of Rosenberg v. Vermont State Colleges*, 852 A.2d 599 (Vt. 2004).

III. OVERTIME AND WAGE DISPUTES

While wages are typically covered by contract, they may also be subject to the requirements of the Fair Labor Standards Act (FLSA) and state wage laws. Instructors are typically exempt from FLSA overtime coverage, as they are considered professional employees. The FLSA requires employers to pay covered workers the prevailing minimum wage and any earned overtime.

◆ *A Pennsylvania professor who signed a Memorandum of Agreement after mediation to resolve his discrimination case could not later evade its terms.*

After suffering a stroke that limited his daily activities, the professor sought to teach online courses only. This request was rejected, and he sued the university in a federal court for disability discrimination. The parties agreed to mediation, which led to a Memorandum of Agreement (MOA) describing a settlement. The MOA set a formula for an estimated $35,000 in back pay, and the university agreed to cooperate with the professor's disability retirement application. The MOA called for a formal agreement and the professor's employment termination. When the formula was applied, it yielded less than $35,000. Although the university offered to pay the professor $35,000, he balked. The university sought a court order enforcing the MOA.

A federal court held the MOA was an enforceable contract. On appeal, the U.S. Court of Appeals, Third Circuit, explained that contract law applied to the question of whether the MOA was enforceable. The professor argued the MOA was not enforceable because it did not set forth the precise amount of back pay. But **the parties agreed to a formula to calculate back pay, and this was sufficient to create enforceability**. Rejecting the professor's argument that he was forced to sign the agreement, the court affirmed the judgment. *DeHainaut v. California Univ. of Pennsylvania*, 490 Fed.Appx. 420 (3d Cir. 2012).

◆ *An African-American professor and program director did not show that Ohio State University used discriminatory evaluation criteria when it denied him substantial wage increases over a three-year period.*

After being replaced as a program director of social work and enjoying no substantial pay raises for three consecutive years, the professor sued the university in a federal district court. He added a claim for retaliation based on his request for salary-related information, the fact that he had filed an administrative charge of discrimination and his opposition to a pledge declaring that social workers should not discriminate on the basis of sexual orientation. A federal court held for the university and its officials, and the case reached the U.S. Court of Appeals, Sixth Circuit. The court rejected the race discrimination claims, since the professor's replacement as program director was also African-American. With respect to the pay raises, he did not show he was treated differently than similarly situated faculty. **There was no evidence that the university used evaluation criteria that were different than criteria for similarly situated professors.** There was no merit to the professor's retaliation claims, as evidence showed he was removed because he did not develop an undergraduate honors program, a social justice minor or any new courses. The court affirmed the judgment for the university and officials. *Alexander v. Ohio State Univ. College of Social Work*, 429 Fed.Appx. 481 (6th Cir. 2011).

◆ *An Illinois court has found that using state financing to fund construction projects triggers the state's Prevailing Wage Act (PWA).*

A nonprofit corporation operated a Presbyterian ministry at the University of Illinois, Urbana-Champaign. It built a student housing unit at the university that was located on foundation property. The foundation partly financed the project with tax-free bonds issued through the Illinois Finance Authority. The Illinois Department of Labor determined the project was subject to the PWA, which imposes minimum wage requirements on "public work" construction projects. The department ordered the foundation to pay workers certain wages and a fine. The foundation responded by suing the labor department in a state court, asserting the PWA did not apply to the project. The court agreed with the foundation, and the case reached the Appellate Court of Illinois. **The court held "public works" included all projects financed with bonds issued under the Illinois Finance Authority Act.** The act's legislative history made it clear that lawmakers wanted the PWA to apply to entities that benefitted from public financing – even if the entity would not have otherwise been considered a "public body." As the PWA applied to the foundation's construction project, the court reversed the judgment and returned the case to the trial court for further proceedings. *McKinley Foundation at Univ. of Illinois v. Illinois Dep't of Labor*, 936 N.E.2d 708 (Ill. App. Ct. 2010).

◆ *West Virginia's Wage Payment and Collection Act (WPCA) does not protect public institutions through government immunity and does not require employees to exhaust administrative procedures before filing a lawsuit.*

An assistant physics professor became a tenure-track associate at West Virginia University at Parkersburg (WVU-P). He was denied tenure after six years of work because of falling enrollment in physics classes. The professor sued WVU-P in the state court system, asserting he was not paid under faculty overload contracts for performing extra work. In addition to seeking unpaid wages and attorneys' fees, he requested triple the amount of claimed wages under a WPCA liquidated damages provision. A state court held the case was barred by sovereign immunity and the failure to exhaust administrative remedies.

On appeal, the state supreme court of appeals held WPCA remedies were optional and permitted employees or the state labor commissioner to bring "any legal action necessary" to recover unpaid wages. Sovereign immunity did not bar the action. **The legislature intended the WPCA to protect wage claims by both private and public employees.** As the action was not barred, the court returned it to the trial court for further proceedings. *Beichler v. West Virginia Univ. at Parkersburg*, 700 S.E.2d 532 (W.Va. 2010).

◆ *A federal district court approved a class action lawsuit to address wage claims against the University of Phoenix (UP) by enrollment counselors.*

Two UP enrollment counselors brought state and federal claims in a federal district court in California, alleging UP required employees to work off the clock, miscalculated overtime, failed to itemize wage statements and did not provide them meal breaks. Their federal claims under the Fair Labor Standards Act were transferred to a nationwide class action lawsuit in Pennsylvania. The counselors then asked the California court to certify their state law claims as a class action suit for a potential class of more than 1,000 members. **The court agreed to do so as the action involved citizens of different states and there was more than $5 million at stake.** The court found common issues of law in all the claims, and it held the size of the class made individual lawsuits impractical. Three classes of current or former enrollment counselors were certified, including counselors bringing claims for overtime and meal breaks, incorrect pay records, and willful failure to pay overtime. *Adoma v. Univ. of Phoenix, Inc.*, 270 F.R.D. 543 (E.D. Cal. 2010).

◆ *A University of Washington (UW) faculty salary policy that guaranteed raises for "meritorious" faculty did not apply to extension lecturers.*

In 2002, the Washington legislature did not appropriate funds for UW employee pay raises. Faculty members filed a class action against UW in a state court for breach of contract. The class consisted of professors, associate professors, artists, full-time lecturers, senior lecturers and principal lecturers. After the case was settled, a second class action was filed by part-time lecturers who claimed they had been wrongfully excluded from the prior case. UW settled the second action, only to face a third-class action by extension lecturers.

After the trial court certified a class of extension lecturers, it agreed with UW that they were not university faculty and were thus not entitled to salary increases referenced in the faculty salary policy. On appeal, the Court of Appeals of Washington held **a breach of contract claim required proof of "a promise of specific treatment in a specific situation," justifiable reliance on the promise, and a breach of the promise**. But the lecturers could not even show the handbook applied to them. Their appointments were part of a UW educational outreach program that was separate from UW academic faculty appointments. The education outreach program had a separate manual that did not incorporate UW's faculty handbook. As the extension lecturers were not "faculty," the faculty salary policy in the handbook did not apply to them. No promise of a raise was made to them under the faculty salary policy. *Carosella v. Univ. of Washington*, 154 Wash.App. 1038 (Wash. Ct. App. 2010).

◆   *A federal court dismissed a foreign national's claim that increasing his workload without a salary increase was akin to human trafficking.*

A Florida university paid a foreign national $95,000 to serve as an interim program director. When the university director of recruitment and admissions resigned, extra duties were assigned to the foreign national. His request for a salary increase was rejected, in part because the university claimed it was paying attorneys' fees and costs associated with obtaining permanent labor certification in order to retain him. The foreign national sued the university in a federal district court for breach of contract and violation of 18 U.S.C. Section 1589, a law intended to stop forced labor and human trafficking. Section 1589 is part of the Trafficking Victims Protection Act of 2000, which calls trafficking a form of slavery that mainly victimizes women and children.

Section 1589(a)(3) prohibited employers from obtaining labor by abuse of the law or legal process. **The court rejected the foreign national's argument that the university abused any law by expecting him to work for "free" in return for certification.** The real prohibition in Section 1589 is against using a law as a tool of coercion. Given the foreign national's "healthy salary," the court rejected his claims based on financial harm. His contract had an option allowing him to resign. As the foreign national "was not trafficked" to the U.S. and was in the same shoes as others who assumed responsibilities not explicitly mentioned in a job description, the court dismissed the case. *Alvarado v. Univ. Carlos Albizu,* No. 10-22072-CIV, 2010 WL 3385345 (S.D. Fla. 8/25/10).

◆   *A New York university was forced to face a collective FLSA action based on a student's preliminary showing that she was not paid for overtime work.*

A Hofstra University undergraduate assistant was paid a $700 stipend to be a football team manager. Since she held other on-campus jobs, she claimed she was entitled to overtime compensation for all hours worked beyond 40 hours a week. Hofstra's student employment handbook forbade students from working more than 25 hours per week when school was in session and 35 when classes were in recess. No student was to work on campus more than 40 hours a week, and extra care was to be taken to make sure the 40-hour limit was not exceeded when a student worked in more than one department. **The student said Hofstra routinely disregarded these policies and that she worked at least 40 hours per week as the football team manager.** In her federal lawsuit, she accused Hofstra of violating the Fair Labor Standards Act (FLSA), since she regularly worked more than 40 hours a week but was not paid overtime.

The student moved the court to certify a collective FLSA action. She also sought an order requiring Hofstra to provide her with names, addresses, email addresses, Social Security numbers and dates of employment of all students who had worked as undergraduate or graduate assistants in the previous six years. The court held the student was similarly situated to the other undergraduate and graduate assistants, and it conditionally certified a collective action of students who were not paid minimum wage or did not receive overtime pay. The class was limited to students who had worked for Hofstra in the previous three years. *Summa v. Hofstra Univ.,* No. CV 07-3307(DRH)(ARL), 2008 WL 3852160 (E.D.N.Y. 8/14/08).

◆ *A Georgia university did not breach a professor's employment contract when it recalculated his salary following a demotion.*

When the professor acquired tenure, the university paid him an annual salary of $49,537. It then appointed him to an associate vice president position at a salary of $70,000. Over the next three years, the professor entered into a series of one-year contracts, each providing for a pay increase. The university then decided to eliminate the associate vice president position. It notified the professor in writing of its decision and gave him the option of returning to the classroom at an annual salary of $54,341. The professor argued his salary computation was wrong, but his appeal failed. He sued the university in a state court for breach of contract. The court awarded summary judgment to the university, and the professor appealed to the Court of Appeals of Georgia.

The court found the university had compared the professor's salary to those of others in his department. The head of the department earned $59,472 for the same academic year, and the salaries of three associate professors who worked for the university for similar or longer time periods than the professor were less than his. The court found the terms of the professor's contract were unambiguous. **As the contract was clear, the trial court had the discretion to determine its terms.** The court affirmed the judgment. *Homer v. Board of Regents of the Univ. System of Georgia,* 613 S.E.2d 205 (Ga. Ct. App. 2005).

◆ *A California trade school qualified as an institution of higher learning, and its instructors were professionals who did not qualify for overtime pay.*

The school received state accreditation and became a degree-granting institution in 2002. Its instructors held certificates of authorization for service under the Education Code. The state division of labor standards enforcement notified the school its instructors were not exempt from overtime pay under an administrative wage order. The school sought a declaration that its instructors were exempt from overtime pay as professional employees. A state trial court agreed and held the instructors were exempt from the overtime wage order.

The state court of appeal held the school qualified as a "college." It complied with statutory requirements to obtain accreditation. **The "teaching exception" was not limited to institutions granting bachelor's or higher degrees.** The division relied on outdated records and evidence in arguing trade schools did not meet the definition of "higher learning." Instead, the boundaries of California's education system had expanded to include a much broader category of institutions. **Since the professional exemption was not limited to instructors at institutions granting baccalaureate degrees or higher, the school's instructors were entitled to the professional exception**, and the court affirmed the judgment. *California School of Culinary Arts v. Lujan,* 112 Cal.App.4th 16, 4 Cal.Rptr.3d 785 (Cal. Ct. App. 2003).

◆ *A New York court held that a fee required by medical schools from physicians as a condition of employment violated state Education Law.*

Ophthalmologists who worked as full-time assistant professors at Columbia University wanted to continue practicing ophthalmology and remain on the faculty. In exchange for allowing them to change their appointments to part time, Columbia requested that they pay a 10% "Dean's Tax" on all their practice income. When they refused, their appointments were terminated. The doctors sued Columbia in a state trial court, which held in their favor. A state appellate division court held that the **payment of the "Dean's Tax" as a condition of employment constituted illegal fee-splitting**. Because the doctors were no longer employees, and because Columbia was no longer providing them with benefits, facilities or malpractice insurance, the request was a violation of law. The court directed Columbia to review the applications for part-time appointments and affirmed the judgment. *Odrich v. Trustees of Columbia Univ.*, 764 N.Y.S.2d 448 (N.Y. App. Div. 2003).

◆ *Two part-time Washington community college instructors were not entitled to overtime wages.*

Part-time instructors from five community colleges in Washington brought a lawsuit alleging that the colleges violated the state's Minimum Wage Act by failing to compensate them for overtime work. Their wages were determined by multiplying their classroom hours by a negotiated hourly rate that included payment for time spent on course preparation, grading and office hours. However, they asserted that they were not exempt professional employees paid on a salary basis because the colleges docked their pay for time missed after all their accrued sick and annual leave was exhausted. The case reached the Washington Supreme Court, which ruled against them. It noted that as long as **their predetermined wages were not subject to reduction because of variations in the quality or quantity of work performed**, they still could be considered salary-basis employees. Under U.S. Department of Labor regulations adopted by the court, deductions for missed time after accrued sick and annual leave expire do not alter an employee's professional status. *Clawson v. Grays Harbor College Dist. No. 2*, 61 P.3d 1130 (Wash. 2003).

◆ *Probationary campus police officers were not entitled to overtime for attending EMT classes.*

A Massachusetts university hired four probationary campus police officers. As a condition of employment, they had to be certified as emergency medical technicians within one year of their hire date. The officers took the EMT course at the university and completed the course. Although they were not paid for attending EMT classes after work, they were compensated when EMT classes occurred during their regular working hours. They sued the university under the FLSA, seeking overtime pay for time spent working toward their EMT certification. The case reached the U.S. Court of Appeals, First Circuit, which held **the Portal-to-Portal Act permits an employer to avoid paying an employee for activities that are "preliminary or postliminary" to the principal activities the employee is engaged to perform**.

Here, that condition was satisfied because the officers were attending the EMT classes during their probationary period, and they did not perform any EMT-related work until after obtaining certification. Thus, they could be characterized as students during their probationary period for purposes of avoiding overtime compensation. *Bienkowski v. Northeastern Univ.*, 285 F.3d 138 (1st Cir. 2002).

IV. EMPLOYEE LEAVE

A. Generally

The Family and Medical Leave Act of 1993 (FMLA), 29 U.S.C. §§ 2601–2654, makes available to eligible employees up to 12 weeks of unpaid leave per year: 1) because of the birth of a son or daughter of the employee and in order to care for such son or daughter; 2) because of the placement of a son or daughter with the employee for adoption or foster care; 3) in order to care for the spouse, or a son, daughter, or parent, of the employee, if such spouse, son, daughter or parent has a serious health condition; or 4) because of a serious health condition that makes the employee unable to perform the functions of the position of such employee. 29 U.S.C. § 2612.

To be eligible for leave, an employee must have been employed by the covered employer for at least 12 months, and must have worked at least 1,250 hours during the 12-month period preceding the start of the leave. 29 U.S.C. § 2611. If the employer provides paid leave for which the employee is eligible, the employee may elect, or the employer may require the employee, to substitute the paid leave for any part of the 12 weeks of leave to which the employee is entitled under the act. When the need for leave is foreseeable, the employee must provide reasonable prior notice.

An employer may require medical certification to support a claim for leave, and may require, at its own expense, a second opinion. An employer is under no obligation to allow the employee to accrue seniority or other employment benefits during a leave.

◆ *Florida university officials had to justify their refusal to rehire or offer an equivalent job to an employee upon her return from FMLA leave.*

After the employee worked for more than 10 years as an administrative assistant in a university hospital, her supervisor started eliminating her duties without discussing the reasons. The employee claimed the prospect of losing her job caused her to take medication for anxiety, panic attacks and contagious dermatitis. After the university granted her FMLA leave for dermatitis, she was transferred to a temporary position with a drastic reduction in duties upon her return. She then left under circumstances that were later disputed.

In a federal court action against the university, the employee claimed FMLA violations. The court dismissed the case, and appeal reached the U.S. Court of Appeals, Eleventh Circuit. It found no merit to the university's claim that the employee was not entitled to be restored to the same job or given an equivalent position. While the university claimed she could not perform the job and had performance issues, **the court found it suspicious that performance issues were not discussed until after she took FMLA leave**. A reasonable jury could believe the employee's story, making further proceedings regarding reinstatement necessary. But the court held for the university on the claim regarding employment termination. If her separation was deemed a discharge, there were legitimate performance-based reasons for it. *Rodriguez v. Univ. of Miami Hospital*, 499 Fed.Appx. 920 (11th Cir. 2012).

♦ *A Connecticut college employee put his employer on notice that FMLA leave was at issue by asking for time off to care for family members.*

An assistant director of the college's alumni career services had attendance issues because of his wife's degenerative arthritis. He was also the primary caregiver of their young child. When the employee took three days off because his daughter was sick, the college fired him. He sued the college in a federal court for retaliation under the FMLA. In defense, the college argued the employee had never requested FMLA leave. But the court noted an FMLA regulation states that **employees seeking leave for the first time for FMLA-qualifying reasons need not expressly assert rights under the FMLA or even mention the FMLA**. In fact, employers have a duty to ask their employees for more details under those circumstances. As a result, the court refused to dismiss the case. The fact that the employee said he needed time off to care for a family member's medical condition put his supervisor on notice that FMLA leave could be at issue. *McNamara v. Trinity College*, No. 3:12cv363 (JBA), 2013 164221 (D. Conn. 1/15/13).

♦ *An Ohio instructor did not have a valid claim based on his request for a special schedule five years after he first requested FMLA leave.*

Wilberforce University (WU) approved the instructor's request for intermittent FMLA leave for treatment of asthma symptoms. But it denied the special schedule he asked for because it differed considerably from his physician's certification. In a federal court, the instructor claimed interference with his FMLA rights because WU had required him to file a new medical certification and denied his request for a special schedule. In reviewing the case, the court found WU had granted FMLA requests according to the instructor's medical certification. It also held the request for recertification was reasonable.

The FMLA allows employers to require employees to obtain subsequent recertifications on a reasonable basis. FMLA regulations provide that when an employee's medical certification indicates the employee will need intermittent leave for more than six months, the employer can request recertification every six months in connection with an absence. The regulations also say an employer can request a recertification because circumstances have changed – which was the case here. Because the instructor's leave request was inconsistent with the medical certification from his doctor, the leave was not medically necessary for FMLA purposes. As a result, the case could not go forward. *Grisby v. Wilberforce Univ.*, No. 3:10-CV-184, 2012 WL 4957544 (S.D. Ohio 10/16/12).

♦ *A Utah university did not violate the FMLA by eliminating the position of a program manager who disregarded instructions from his supervisor.*

An internal audit indicated "systematic problems, resulting in mistakes on grants" in the manager's department. His supervisor pressed him to prepare a response, but he failed to do so. The supervisor then decided to eliminate the manager's position due to reduced grants. The manager told the supervisor he wanted to take FMLA leave for childcare. But when his leave began, the supervisor went to his office and found he had emptied his drawers and had left no information about the audit. The manager was discharged for his conduct regarding the audit response, and he sued the university for FMLA violations. A federal court held for the university. On appeal, the U.S. Court of Appeals, Tenth Circuit, held the reduction in force did not violate the law. **Evidence showed that the supervisor made that decision before she learned that the manager might take leave.** Nor did the decision to convert the reduction in force to a termination for cause violate the FMLA.

According to the court, the university had produced extensive and undisputed evidence that the manager impeded and obstructed its efforts to respond to the audit report and otherwise do his job while he was on leave. *Sabourin v. Univ. of Utah*, 676 F.3d 950 (10th Cir. 2012).

◆ *A Texas university employee with a record of excessive absences could not show she was fired for requesting and taking FMLA leave.*

A biology lab research assistant received a poor job evaluation, largely due to her unscheduled absences. She requested FMLA leave after being diagnosed with a goiter and hyperthyroidism. A doctor certified the employee to miss up to three days of work a month for four months. The day after he released her to return to work, she called in sick. The employee attended work sporadically over the next six months, and the university fired her for not following directions about reporting absences. She sued university officials in a federal court for FMLA violations. The court noted the employee had ignored multiple instructions to inform supervisors about her absences. It held the FMLA allows intermittent leave. But FMLA regulations required employees to tell their employers the dates they required for leave as soon as practicable.

It was significant to the court that the employee had signed an FMLA acknowledgement stating that she was required to remain in contact with her work area as required by a university policy. The court held **the FMLA "does not allow an employee to violate company job requirements or work rules."** As the employee could not show she was fired for requesting and taking FMLA leave, the court held for the university and its officials. *Harville v. Texas A&M Univ.*, 833 F.Supp.2d 645 (S.D. Tex. 2011).

◆ *A Michigan university employee who did not have medical documentation of a "serious health condition" was unable to claim FMLA protection.*

The employee's duties included data entry. She had carpal tunnel repair surgery and took time off for pain. After a performance review cited the employee's attendance issues, the university eliminated her position, citing budget cuts. The employee sued the university in a federal court for retaliating against her for taking leave protected by the FMLA. The court held that to prevail, she had to show she took FMLA-protected leave and was fired because she took the leave. But the court found that **to invoke FMLA protections, an employee must provide notice and a qualifying reason for requesting the leave**. The employee did not present documentation from her doctor specifying why she was missing work. For this reason, she could not claim to have a "serious health condition" protected by the FMLA. Since her leave requests were unprotected by the FMLA, the court dismissed the case. *Davis v. Wayne State Univ.*, No. 11-10324, 2011 WL 2786186 (E.D. Mich. 7/15/11).

B. Disability Cases

Many employee leave cases combine claims under the Family and Medical Leave Act (FMLA) with disability discrimination claims arising under the Americans with Disabilities Act (ADA), Section 504 of the Rehabilitation Act and state laws protecting individuals with disabilities. For additional disability discrimination cases in employment, see Chapter 7, Section V.

◆   *A Maryland university employee who was not cleared by her physician to return to work was not "qualified" to perform her duties under state law.*

After being injured in two car accidents, the employee took four days off work for knee surgery. She suffered complications that made her return date indefinite. As the employee's paid leave was almost exhausted, a supervisor suggested she apply for FMLA leave. A doctor's note to the university stated she might not be able to return to work and would be reevaluated in six weeks.

Although the employee was instructed to return to work at the end of her leave, she did not and was soon fired for job abandonment. In a federal court, she asserted violations of the FMLA, ADA and state disability law. In pretrial activity, the court held the university had Eleventh Amendment immunity as to her federal claims for monetary damages. To prove her state law disability claims, the employee had to show she was qualified to perform her job at the time of her discharge. But the U.S. Court of Appeals, Fourth Circuit, has held attendance is an essential function of a job, and the court agreed. **As the employee had not been cleared to return to work by her doctor, she was not qualified to perform her job under state law.** Even if she had been qualified, her accommodation claim failed as it was based on a failure to extend her leave – which she had not requested. *Lewis v. Univ. of Maryland, Baltimore*, No. SAG-12-298, 2012 WL 5193820 (D. Md. 10/18/12).

◆   *A federal court dismissed a University of Illinois employee's ADA and FMLA claims based on discrimination for requesting FMLA leave.*

Two years after the employee started work as a university customer service representative, she was diagnosed with kidney cancer. She took FMLA leave, then returned to work part time. After a brief disability leave, the employee returned to work full time. She asked the university to provide her with a part-time schedule and an ergonomic chair, and she claimed the university responded with harassing and retaliatory acts. The employee claimed the university constructively discharged her by manipulating time records, denying her pay and suspending her. She sued the university in a federal court under the ADA and FMLA. However, the court held the ADA claim was untimely filed. It dismissed the FMLA retaliation claim because the employee did not claim she was harassed because she took leave. According to the court, **she did not link any mistreatment to the taking of FMLA leave.** But as the employee might be able to show she was constructively discharged, the court allowed her to amend her complaint to pursue that claim. *Baldwin v. Board of Trustees of the Univ. of Illinois*, No. 10 C 5569, 2012 WL 3292831 (N.D. Ill. 8/8/12).

◆ *A Georgia Technical College instructor could not pursue a federal case for denial of medical leave.*

After leaving work early one day for a medical appointment, the instructor contacted the college human resources director to get medical leave forms. She said the director berated her and accused her of not providing proper notice of her absence. In a federal court, the instructor charged the college with denying her medical leave and unlawfully firing her. The court held the FMLA claim was barred by sovereign immunity. The state constitution immunized the state and its agencies from suit. Although the instructor claimed the college violated the ADA, the court held **she did not assert the existence of a "disability" within the meaning of the statute**. She took only a half day off and was told by her doctor she was temporarily unable to work and was in an "emotionally fragile state." This was not enough to permit a reasonable inference that the instructor had a "disability" within the meaning of the ADA. She did not say she asked for an accommodation or claim that one would have helped her do her job. As a result, the case was dismissed. *Wells v. West Georgia Technical College*, No. 1:11-cv-3422-JEC, 2012 WL 3150819 (N.D. Ga. 8/2/12).

◆ *A federal court held for an Illinois community college in a discrimination and FMLA case filed by an employee with many performance problems.*

Although the employee said she had mononucleosis, she did not provide evidence of this to her employer. She also said she had chronic fatigue syndrome, but she did not have any medical documentation to support the diagnosis. After several performance-related incidents, including incorrectly changing a student's grade, the community college offered the employee a "Final Job Warning and Employee Action Plan." She rejected its terms and was fired. In a federal court lawsuit, the employee asserted ADA and FMLA violations. After reviewing the evidence, the court noted the employee had many performance problems and had refused to accept the Employee Action Plan Agreement. It held no reasonable jury could find the reasons for discharge were a pretext for disability discrimination. As a result, the community college was entitled to judgment on the ADA claim. The court also rejected the FMLA claim, as **the employee did not provide adequate notice to the college regarding an intent to take FMLA leave**. *Wirey v. Richland Community College*, No. 10-CV-02216, 2012 WL 6681214 (C.D. Ill. 12/21/12).

◆ *A Florida community college did not violate the Americans with Disabilities Act (ADA), the Family and Medical Leave Act (FMLA) or state law by refusing to renew an instructor's contract and denying him tenure.*

The instructor worked under renewable full-time annual contracts. After three years of service, he would become eligible for tenure. At one point, the instructor was told he should become more involved in the college community to improve his chances of a continuing contract. An evaluation noted he had some deficiencies, and his supervisor determined the annual goals he set were unsatisfactory. A short time later, the instructor requested FMLA leave for surgery. The community college did not offer him tenure or a new contract.

The instructor sued the college in a federal district court, asserting violation of the ADA, the FMLA and a Florida civil rights act. The court held his disability discrimination claims under the ADA and state law failed because he did not show he had a disability. He did not prove his cervical spondylosis and headaches substantially limited a major life activity. Instead, the court found the ailments were temporary. Temporary conditions were not disabilities under either the ADA or state law. **The court rejected the instructor's FMLA claim because he did not show a causal connection between his taking of FMLA leave and the decisions to non-renew his contract and deny him tenure.** The court held the temporal proximity between his request for FMLA leave and the college's decision was not enough to prove an FMLA violation – especially since he had been placed on notice of performance issues well before he sought FMLA leave. *Trabulsky v. Polk Community College*, No. 8:08-cv-02271-T-33AEP, 2010 WL 1837909 (M.D. Fla. 5/3/10).

◆ *A Texas career services director could not pursue FMLA claims, as she did not prove she requested leave and was discharged for unprofessional conduct.*

The director injured herself at work and took a few days off to have back surgery. When she returned to work, she used a cane to walk. The director maintained that she advised her supervisor that her doctor suggested she take a medical leave, but the supervisor later denied any such conversation. A short time later, a staff member notified the supervisor that the director had engaged in unprofessional conduct with students and staff. This included counseling students to file complaints against the supervisor and seek tuition refunds because of his alleged management deficiencies. After the misconduct was corroborated by other employees, the supervisor discharged the director.

In a federal district court lawsuit against the supervisor and others, the director claimed interference with her FMLA rights, retaliation and various state law violations. The case reached the U.S. Court of Appeals, Fifth Circuit, which found her FMLA claims failed. **In order to succeed with a case for interference with FMLA rights, it must be shown that an employee took a leave that was protected by the FMLA.** There was no proof in this case that the supervisor even knew that the director had requested leave. The director's retaliation claim failed because she could not counter evidence of her unprofessional conduct. A lower court judgment against her was affirmed. *Burris v. Brazell*, 351 Fed.Appx. 961 (5th Cir. 2009).

◆ *A maintenance worker at a Seattle community college failed to show an FMLA violation or discrimination against him based on disability.*

After the worker compiled a record of chronic tardiness and absenteeism, he asked to change schedules. The college did not want to let him work the shift he sought because doing so would leave him unsupervised for three hours. However, the worker was permitted to work his desired shift on a trial basis. Even with the later start time, he continued to be late or absent and missed safety meetings. After the college reclassified the worker to a lower-paying position, he filed a federal district court action under the FMLA and the Americans with Disabilities Act (ADA). The court held he did not show he had a disability under the ADA. Even if he was disabled, he did not show the college failed to accommodate him, since he was offered a position with a later start time. The court rejected the worker's claim that the college violated the

FMLA by ending a period of FMLA leave without justification. **He never commenced an FMLA leave.** Although the worker said the college retaliated against him for filing a complaint under the state industrial safety and health act, he did not show the college was aware that he had filed the complaint or that it took action against him because of it. *Elkins v. North Seattle Community College*, No. C08-1466RSL, 2009 WL 3698516 (W.D. Wash. 11/3/09).

◆ *A college did not violate the FMLA or Americans with Disabilities Act (ADA) by denying a professor's request to work on campus three days a week.*

The professor typically worked only three days per week on campus. When his department changed its policy to require full-time staff members to be on campus for at least four hours a day for at least four days a week, the professor did not comply. He then took leave under the FMLA due to stress-related problems. He told the college that his department chair was "the source of his physical problems." When the professor returned to work, the college granted him a temporary transfer away from the department chair. He was also offered a transfer to a non-teaching position under a different supervisor. After the professor failed to report for this job, the college considered him to have resigned. He sued the college in a federal district court for violations of the ADA and FMLA. The court held for the college, and the professor appealed.

On appeal, the U.S. Court of Appeals, Third Circuit, held the professor did not show he had a disability under the ADA. Despite being treated for panic attacks and agoraphobia, he did not show he had a substantial limitation of a major life activity. The court also rejected the professor's claim that the college wrongly discharged him instead of granting him additional leave. **He was not eligible for FMLA leave because he did not have a "serious health condition"** as defined by the act. Even if he was FMLA-eligible, he took more leave than he was entitled to receive. As a result, the judgment was affirmed. *Lloyd v. Washington & Jefferson College*, 288 Fed.Appx. 786 (3d Cir. 2008).

◆ *A Vanderbilt University (VU) research assistant failed to prove a connection between her requests for leave and her discharge.*

The research assistant received several warnings about performance issues. After she told a supervisor she was pregnant, she was placed on performance improvement counseling (PIC). Her job performance continued to slip, and she took a leave of absence under the FMLA. While she was on leave, she and her husband were discovered using a lab computer after work hours. The research assistant filed an internal discrimination complaint while she was on leave, saying Vanderbilt issued the PIC because she was pregnant.

The research assistant's supervisors issued a final PIC for failing to follow instructions. The next day, she took another leave of absence under the FMLA. Her job performance did not improve upon her return to work, and her employment was terminated. The research assistant sued VU for retaliation based on taking her FMLA leave. She added claims for pregnancy and national origin discrimination. **The court held that to prevail in an FMLA claim for retaliation, the research assistant had to show a causal link between the leave and her discharge.** However, VU began counseling her about her work performance before she took FMLA leave, even before it learned she was pregnant. The evidence showed the discharge was due to poor work performance. As the research assistant could not show a link between the leave and the discharge, the case was dismissed. *Zhu v. Vanderbilt Univ.*, No. 3:06-0460, 2007 WL 2963980 (M.D. Tenn. 10/5/07).

◆   *A federal appeals court held FMLA posting requirements are met when the employer posts notices on its intranet site.*

A Massachusetts employee was involved in an accident and took a leave of absence from his supervisory job. The employer sent him a letter that provided information about the FMLA and told him the leave was being counted as FMLA leave. The employer also asked the employee to provide a medical certification regarding his condition. He provided a disability claim form signed by a physician and was given 15 weeks of leave. The employer later discharged the employee after he failed to return to work. He filed a federal district court action claiming the employer failed to post FMLA notices.

The court held for the employer, and the employee appealed. The U.S. Court of Appeals, First Circuit, noted the employer posted an adequate FMLA notice on its intranet website. This defeated the claim that employees did not receive notice of their FMLA rights. The site was accessible to all employees while they were at work, and the employee admitted he had used it at work. The court rejected the claim that the employer violated the FMLA because the site could not be accessed from home. **FMLA regulations only required that notice be posted at the workplace.** The district court's decision was affirmed. *Dube v. J.P. Morgan Investor Services*, 201 Fed.Appx. 786 (1st Cir. 2006).

◆   *An Illinois college did not retaliate against an employee who violated an employee dress code by discharging her after she sought time off.*

The employee was suspended for wearing maternity shorts in violation of the college dress code. The college president said her conduct was the grossest form of insubordination he had seen in 34 years at the college. The college board voted to approve the president's recommendation to fire the employee. She sued the college in a federal district court, which held that to prevail on her FMLA claim, she had to show the college fired her to prevent her from taking leave to which she was entitled. **Under the FMLA, an employee must provide sufficient notice to qualify for leave. Employees are not required to mention the FMLA by name.** They only need to put the employer on notice that FMLA leave would be necessary. For leave that is foreseeable, such as for the birth of a child, at least 30 days advance notice is required. The employee said she told the college months in advance that she was pregnant and intended to take leave. The court held she gave sufficient notice, but did not show she would not have been fired for other reasons. As there was evidence of other reasons for firing, the court dismissed the case. *Sample v. Rend Lake College*, No. 04-CV-4161-JPG, 2005 WL 2465905 (S.D. Ill. 10/5/05).

◆   *An Iowa university did not violate the Equal Protection Clause by allowing mothers, but not fathers, the benefit of paid leave after childbirth.*

The university's parental leave policy allowed biological mothers to take sick leave for any pregnancy-related temporary disability. A male employee alleged the policy violated the Equal Protection Clause. He filed a class action to represent biological fathers at the university. The case reached the U.S. Court of Appeals, Eighth Circuit. It found the policy did not allow mothers to use accrued sick leave after their disability ended. The time off was disability leave even though mothers often cared for a newborn during that time. The court held the university reasonably established a period of presumptive disability. **A distinction between biological mothers and fathers was rationally related to legitimate concerns**, and the policy did not violate the Equal Protection Clause. *Johnson v. Univ. of Iowa*, 431 F.3d 325 (8th Cir. 2005).

V. EMPLOYEE BENEFITS

Like their counterparts in the public sector, many private schools offer a broad range of employment benefits to employees. These benefit programs are subject to federal civil rights laws such as Title VII and the Equal Pay Act as well as income tax laws. Employer-employee disputes concerning benefits will generally be resolved according to contract law rules (see Section I).

A. Retirement Benefits

◆ *An Ohio university did not have to establish an early retirement incentive plan under state law based on the size of an employee's "state employing unit."*

A student affairs department employee who had worked for 26 years at the University of Toledo was one of 85 employees who lost their jobs due to layoff. She claimed the university had to establish an early retirement incentive plan under Ohio law. The case reached the Court of Appeals of Ohio, which held **the layoff was not large enough to trigger the legal obligation to establish an early retirement incentive plan** under Ohio R.C. Section 145.298 and state regulations. The law required a state entity to establish a plan based on the number of layoffs in an "employing unit." The number was the lesser of 350 or 40% of the employees in the employing unit. While the employee claimed this requirement was triggered by counting all 85 employees who lost their jobs, the court disagreed. It found the university correctly argued that the student affairs department was the relevant "employing unit" in this case. Only four employees in the department lost their jobs. As a result, the university did not have to establish an early retirement incentive plan. *State ex rel. Edgeworth v. Univ. of Toledo*, 185 Ohio App.3d 48, 923 N.E.2d 175 (Ohio Ct. App. 2009).

◆ *A professor could not enroll in an early retirement program because he waited too long to submit his application.*

An Ohio state university instituted an early retirement incentive program, which Ohio law authorized as long as enrollment did not exceed 5% of eligible employees. A professor/associate dean applied for the program but then withdrew his application. He later attempted to resubmit his application, but the university denied his request. After resigning, the professor sued, seeking an order that he be enrolled in the early retirement program. A state court ruled in his favor, but the Court of Appeals of Ohio reversed. Here, the university had improperly expanded the program to allow more than 5% of eligible employees to participate. As a result, even though the professor's initial application would have placed him in the eligible 5%, his resubmitted application came after the 5% threshold had already been met. He was ineligible for the program. *Bee v. Univ. of Akron*, No. 21081, 2002 WL 31387127 (Ohio Ct. App. 2002).

◆   *A New York professor could pursue a lawsuit for unpaid pension benefits.*

After 10 years teaching, a tenured assistant professor was notified that he would be reassigned to an administrative position. While trying to agree on a position, the professor performed no services for the university, which then stopped paying his salary and began dismissal proceedings against him. The university did not complete the proceedings because it determined that he had abandoned his job. When he sued for reinstatement and back pay, a New York court dismissed the case on the grounds that he should have filed an Article 78 proceeding. An appellate division court reversed the judgment, but the lawsuit was dismissed when he failed to appear. He later sued for unpaid salary and pension contributions, asserting the university had never formally fired him. A federal district court dismissed the case, but the U.S. Court of Appeals, Second Circuit, reversed the judgment in part, finding that **if his employment status claim was valid, he might be able to succeed on his pension claim**. However, his claim for unpaid salary had been properly dismissed. *Yoon v. Fordham Univ. Faculty and Administrative Retirement Plan*, 263 F.3d 196 (2d Cir. 2001).

◆   *Where a university reasonably modified a retirement plan, it was not liable for violating the Employee Retirement Income Security Act (ERISA).*

A professor employed by a New York private university retired in 1977 and began receiving benefits under the school's contributory retirement plan. The board of trustees amended the plan periodically to provide cost of living adjustments (COLAs) to plan members or their beneficiaries. Subsequently, the retirement committee amended the COLA, and the board of trustees amended the plan again to provide that "the retirement committee shall have exclusive authority and discretion to construe any disputed term." After the retirement committee denied the professor's claim for additional benefits, he filed suit against the retirement plan and the university under ERISA in a state trial court.

The case was ultimately transferred to a U.S. magistrate judge. The magistrate judge granted the university's motion for pretrial judgment, and the professor appealed to the U.S. Court of Appeals, Second Circuit. The retirement committee claimed it had properly modified the earlier increases by calculating what each retiree's monthly benefit would have been under the amended COLA, subtracting the value of increases actually given, and adding the difference to each retiree's monthly benefits. The professor contended that the base figure to which the above formula would be applied should include all prior COLAs. The court ruled that **the retirement committee had discretion to construe any uncertain or disputed term**. Consequently, the court applied the arbitrary and capricious standard of review. Because the retirement committee's interpretation of the statute was reasonable, the court affirmed the magistrate judge's ruling in favor of the university. *Jordan v. Retirement Committee of Rensselaer Polytechnic Institute*, 46 F.3d 1264 (2d Cir. 1995).

B. Other Benefits

◆ *A police instructor was not entitled to disability benefits because his injuries predated his membership in the state retirement system.*

The instructor was involved in two automobile accidents during his employment by a state university. He had been involved in an accident prior to his employment by the university that caused severe injuries to his spine, for which he underwent spinal fusion surgery and received psychiatric treatment for post-traumatic stress disorder. After going to work for the university, the instructor was involved in another motor vehicle crash and was diagnosed as having a sprain. His third accident occurred when he was going to work. After this accident, the instructor underwent a second cervical fusion operation. He applied for disability benefits based on his cervical injury and mental illness. A medical board denied his request, and a hearing officer upheld the denial.

The state retirement system adopted the hearing officer's findings, and the instructor appealed to the Court of Appeals of Kentucky. The court found medical testimony supported the hearing officer's finding that the instructor's physical and mental disabilities resulted from the first automobile accident and predated his university employment. The court rejected his argument that his injuries from the third accident occurred during the course of his employment because he changed his route to obtain water for use in his police training class. The record showed the instructor traveled just a mile out of his way and was not on campus when the accident occurred. **The university did not file an accident report or a workers' compensation claim, which would have indicated the accident was in the course of his employment.** The court affirmed the denial of benefits. *Morris v. Kentucky Retirement Systems*, No. 2002-CA-001570-MR, 2003 WL 21834980 (Ky. Ct. App. 2003).

◆ *Community college teachers who did not work during the summer were not entitled to state-paid health care benefits.*

Two teachers at community colleges in Washington worked under contract for each quarter they taught at more than 50% of a full-time schedule. They did not teach during the summer. When the teachers sued to get state-paid health benefits for the summer months, a state trial court held they were not employees during the summer.

The Washington Court of Appeals found that while **the teachers worked a nine-month period, they did so under quarterly contracts and did not qualify as career seasonal/instructional employees**. Also, despite the fact that they did not qualify for unemployment in the summer (because they received reasonable assurances of employment for the following quarter), they were not technically employed during that time. *Mader v. Health Care Authority*, 37 P.3d 1244 (Wash. Ct. App. 2002).

◆ *A New Hampshire college could provide less insurance benefits for mental illnesses than for physical illnesses.*

A college professor was treated for depression through medication and outpatient medical care. The college funded its own health care plan, which contained an annual limit of $3,000 for outpatient mental health benefits and a lifetime cap of $10,000. After the professor reached the lifetime cap, he filed a grievance, arguing that the cap violated a state statute and the collective bargaining agreement by providing less benefits for mental illnesses than physical illnesses. An arbitrator ruled that neither the state statute nor the bargaining agreement had been violated, and the Supreme Court of New Hampshire upheld that decision. **Because the college was not an insurer, the court held it was not subject to the statute requiring equal health insurance coverage for mental and physical illnesses.** *Marshall v. Keene State College*, 785 A.2d 418 (N.H. 2001).

C. Discrimination

◆   *A Michigan nonprofit corporation lacked standing to challenge a policy of providing benefits to same-sex domestic partners of state university employees.*

The corporation sued state entities to challenge the benefits policy, claiming it violated a state constitutional provision that required a marriage to be between a man and a woman. The corporation claimed the policy resulted in an illegal expenditure of state funds and violated state laws relating to marriage and divorce. Appeal reached the Court of Appeals of Michigan. It held that **to establish a right to bring a lawsuit, a party must have an injury that can be redressed by a favorable court decision**. The corporation did not show it suffered an injury that was different from any "injury" to the public at large. The only injury claimed was that the policy was "at odds with that which [it] seeks to promote." As this vague assertion was not enough to confer standing on the corporation, the court held for the state officials. *American Family Ass'n of Michigan v. Michigan State Univ. Board of Trustees,* 276 Mich.App. 42, 739 N.W.2d 908 (Mich. Ct. App. 2007).

◆   *An Ohio university employee lacked standing to challenge a university policy granting health insurance benefits to same-sex partners of employees.*

Miami University (MU) made health insurance benefits available to same-sex domestic partners of university employees. To receive benefits for a domestic partner, employees were required to submit an affidavit attesting to the existence of a same-sex domestic partnership. For the 2004-05 academic year, the university paid about $100,000 in premiums for domestic partner insurance coverage, which was about .5% of its total budget for faculty and staff compensation. Five months after the university adopted the policy, Ohio voters approved a state constitutional amendment recognizing only marriages between men and women. It also barred the state from creating or recognizing a legal status for unmarried couples that "approximate[d] the design, qualities, significance or effect of marriage." An MU employee sued the university and its board of trustees to challenge the same-sex benefits policy. A state court entered judgment for MU. On appeal, **the Court of Appeals of Ohio held the insurance premiums were funded by private party donations and not tax money**. Therefore, the employee could not claim a right to challenge the policy based on his status as a taxpayer. *Brinkman v. Miami Univ.*, No. CA2006-12-313, 2007 WL 2410390 (Ohio Ct. App. 7/27/07).

◆ *A California institute could not discontinue disability benefits to an employee who turned 65 because he was not receiving pension benefits.*

A research scientist at a California research and education institute was diagnosed with Parkinson's disease and took a medical leave. He became eligible for long-term disability benefits through the institute's insurance plan, but he retained his employee status and his right to return to work if his health improved. While still receiving his disability benefits, he turned 65 and became eligible for retirement. **Although he did not retire (and thus did not receive pension benefits), the institute offset his disability benefits with the amount of pension benefits he would have received by retiring, thereby reducing his income to zero.** The scientist filed suit against the institute, alleging violations of the Age Discrimination in Employment Act (ADEA) and a state statute. The institute cross-claimed for the amount of disability benefits it had inadvertently paid him after he turned 65 and filed a motion to dismiss.

The case reached the U.S. Court of Appeals, Ninth Circuit. In order to preclude an employee from receiving both long-term disability benefits and pension benefits for which he is eligible, the ADEA allows employers to offset the amount of disability benefits by the amount of pension benefits. As the employee had not retired, he was not receiving any pension benefits. The ADEA prohibits employee benefit plans from requiring or permitting involuntary retirement. The primary effect of the institute's policy was to leave an employee without an income unless he or she retired, and a reasonable person in the employee's position would believe he had no choice but to retire. Finding that **the offsetting of long-term disability benefits is allowed only when pension benefits are being paid concurrently,** the court held the institute's disability plan violated the ADEA. *Kalvinskas v. California Institute of Technology*, 96 F.3d 1305 (9th Cir. 1996).

VI. UNEMPLOYMENT AND WORKERS' COMPENSATION

A. Unemployment Benefits

The Federal Unemployment Tax Act (FUTA), 26 U.S.C. § 3301, et seq., establishes a federal program to compensate temporarily unemployed workers. Although the federal Department of Labor oversees the program, states meeting specific criteria administer it. A major exemption from coverage, in Section 3309(b)(1) of the act, states: "This section shall not apply to service performed ... in the employ of (A) a church or convention or association of churches, or (B) an organization which is operated primarily for religious purposes and which is operated, supervised, controlled, or principally supported by a church or convention or association of churches."

◆ *A tenured Idaho State University (ISU) professor who said he was fired for exercising his speech rights was instead found to have engaged in misconduct.*

After obtaining tenure in ISU's civil engineering department, the professor openly criticized the university and its administrators. He claimed unethical and criminal conduct by ISU administrators. Warnings did not stop the professor's comments, and ISU discharged him following a disciplinary proceeding. His application for unemployment benefits was denied by an appeals examiner who found he was discharged for employment-related misconduct. Appeal reached Idaho's highest court. It found misconduct was adequately shown in this case. Under state law, **disqualifying misconduct included "a disregard of the employer's expected standard of behavior."** In addition to misconduct, the court found the professor failed to be collegial and acted in an insubordinate manner. His conduct was not protected by the First Amendment. The decision to deny benefits was affirmed. *Sadid v. Idaho State Univ.*, 154 Idaho 88, 294 P.3d 1100 (Idaho 2013).

◆   *An adjunct professor was not justified in quitting work after a college paid her wages in an untimely manner four times.*

After four late paychecks, the adjunct quit working for the college and applied for unemployment compensation benefits. A state unemployment law judge found that the fourth late paycheck was caused by a miscommunication regarding the correct pay rate and held the adjunct did not have good reason to quit. On appeal, the state court of appeals explained that an employee who quits is eligible for unemployment benefits only if he or she had good reason to do so. A good reason is one that is directly related to employment and for which the employer is totally responsible – and would compel an average, reasonable worker to quit. An employee is not eligible for unemployment benefits unless he or she first gives the employer a reasonable opportunity to correct the adverse working conditions. **Evidence showed the adjunct had submitted her resignation after the college took steps to correct the problem that led to the fourth late paycheck.** The court upheld the finding that she did not provide the college a reasonable opportunity to correct adverse working conditions, and it affirmed the decision against her. *Jones-Schroyer v. Lake Superior College*, No. A11-1256, 2012 WL 1658893 (Minn. Ct. App. 5/14/12).

◆   *An Illinois college instructor was not entitled to unemployment benefits while working reduced hours during summer session classes.*

The instructor worked as an adjunct and part-time adult education teacher during fall, spring and summer terms. He was scheduled to teach during the next summer session at a reduction in work hours. He filed for unemployment benefits, which the college opposed on grounds of his part-time employment status. A claims adjudicator agreed with the college that the instructor was ineligible for benefits because he had a reasonable assurance of returning to work in the fall, as he had done the previous four years. The instructor appealed, arguing his claim was not filed "between successive terms" since higher education institutions do not consider summer session a "term."

Appeal reached the Appellate Court of Illinois, which noted the instructor was scheduled to teach during the summer months, in contrast to educators who are employed only during the spring and fall. He had applied for benefits between academic terms as opposed to during academic terms. An "academic year" included two semesters – fall and spring – and was differentiated from "summer session." For this reason, the court did not agree with the instructor that the summer session was intended to be included as an "academic term" under state law. **A key inquiry into eligibility for unemployment benefits is whether the instructor had a contract or reasonable assurances of future work.** Since he always had a reasonable expectation of returning for work in the fall, unemployment benefits were properly denied. *Kilpatrick v. Illinois Dep't of Employment Security*, 928 N.E.2d 545 (Ill. App. Ct. 2010).

◆ *An Ohio community college athletic director was not entitled to a name-clearing hearing after his unemployment compensation proceedings.*

The athletic director (AD) was accused of accepting $800 to rent space and failing to turn it over to the college. His employment was terminated, and a local television station reported he had been fired for embezzlement. When the AD applied for unemployment compensation benefits, the college opposed his application, maintaining that he was discharged due to theft, dishonesty and possible embezzlement. A hearing officer held the employee had been properly terminated, but noted he denied doing anything wrong and was not criminally charged. He sued the college in a federal district court, asserting a right to a name-clearing hearing. **The court held that to show entitlement to a name-clearing hearing, the AD had to show the college made public comments about his discharge.** Moreover, the comments had to be false and stigmatizing, not just statements about job performance, incompetence, neglect of duty or malfeasance. While the AD established these elements, the court found he had received an adequate name-clearing hearing in his unemployment compensation case, where he had enjoyed full procedural protections. *Welling v. Owens State Community College*, 535 F.Supp.2d 886 (N.D. Ohio 2008).

◆ *A New York university adjunct professor could keep his benefits despite improperly stating he had no reasonable assurance of continued employment.*

The professor filed for and received unemployment insurance benefits after the end of the spring semester of 2004. On his application for benefits, he denied that he was filing the claim between academic terms or years. The university rehired the professor for two courses in the fall 2004 semester. An administrative hearing law judge (ALJ) then found the professor received a reasonable assurance of continued employment and willfully misrepresented this on his application for benefits. The ALJ held he was ineligible to receive benefits, charged him with a recoverable overpayment and assessed a penalty.

The case reached the New York Supreme Court, Appellate Division. **The court held New York Labor Law Section 590(10) precludes an employee from receiving unemployment insurance benefits during the time period between two successive academic years, or terms, where he or she had received a reasonable assurance that he would perform services in the same capacity for those academic years or terms.** Because the professor taught three courses during the spring 2004 term and only two courses during the fall 2004 semester, the appellate court agreed with the board. The professor could not meet the economic standard of earning in the fall 2004 semester of at least 90% of what he earned during the spring 2004 semester. He therefore could keep the benefits he had already received. *In re Kendall*, 30 A.D.3d 863, 817 N.Y.S.2d 715 (N.Y. App. Div. 2006).

♦ *The Supreme Court of Hawaii held that a student, who was also a university employee, was not entitled to receive unemployment benefits.*

The student attended the University of Hawaii for five consecutive academic years. He was hired as a university peer counselor full time during a summer when he did not attend school. The student resumed his studies at the university that fall, then filed an unemployment insurance claim. The state Department of Labor and Industrial Relations determined the wages from his summer job could be considered for the purpose of unemployment benefits, since he was not enrolled or regularly attending classes during the summer session. A state trial court noted state law made students ineligible for unemployment benefits if they were enrolled or regularly attended classes while working for a university. It held the student's services were excluded from the unemployment statute's definition of "services." The Supreme Court of Hawaii held that **because the student attended classes full time for five consecutive academic years, his primary relationship was that of a student**. He would have been ineligible for summer work with the school without his status as a student. As the summer job was excluded from the term "employment," the court affirmed the judgment. *Univ. of Hawaii v. Befitel*, 100 P.3d 55 (Haw. 2004).

B. Workers' Compensation

An award of workers' compensation benefits is typically an employee's exclusive remedy for an injury in the course and scope of employment. This precludes personal injury suits by employees in most cases. A large group of cases in this area involves determining whether a student at a university may be deemed an "employee" based on performing on-campus jobs.

♦ *A Florida court held a college bookstore student-employee who was hit by a van while on campus could not file a negligence claim against the college.*

The student collided with a van on the college campus as she rode back to work on her bicycle. The college submitted a workers' compensation claim on her behalf. She filed a personal injury claim against the college, claiming it was responsible for the van driver's conduct. The case reached a Florida district court of appeals, which recited the general rule that **workers' compensation benefits generally are the exclusive remedy for employees who are injured during the course and scope of their employment**. The court found the student was an employee of the college. She had entered into a written contract with the college under which she agreed to work for affiliates of the college, such as the bookstore. Second, the court held the student was injured during the course and scope of her employment. The case was returned to a lower court with instructions to enter judgment for the college. *Pensacola Christian College v. Bruhn*, 80 So.3d 1046 (Fla. Dist. Ct. App. 2011).

♦ *A Pennsylvania State University employee who made insufficient efforts to regain employment lost his workers' compensation benefits.*

The employee received workers' compensation benefits for almost two years after injuring his shoulder. He then applied for a disability pension. The university petitioned for modification of the employee's compensation benefits, asserting work was available for him. A workers' compensation judge agreed with the university and substantially reduced the employee's benefits. Two years later, the university petitioned to suspend his benefits entirely based on voluntarily retirement and withdrawal from the work force. It presented the testimony of a vocational rehabilitation specialist, who identified several jobs the employee could perform. In response, the employee said he had registered with a career services organization and had checked websites and newspapers for job openings. Although there was no documentation to confirm these claims, the judge denied the university's suspension petition, finding he sought employment and did not voluntarily remove himself from the work force.

A workers' compensation board affirmed the ruling, and the university appealed. The Commonwealth Court of Pennsylvania held that a claimant who accepts a pension is presumed to have left the work force and the former employer is generally entitled to have benefits suspended. In this situation, the employee could avoid suspension by showing he was seeking employment or that his work-related injury forced his retirement. According to the court, **searching the Internet and newspaper ads was not enough** to show a good-faith effort to find employment. **The employee had to show he actually applied for work or did something to try to land a job.** Since he did not show good faith, he was not entitled to benefits. *Pennsylvania State Univ. v. Workers' Compensation Appeal Board*, 948 A.2d 907 (Pa. Commw. Ct. 2008).

◆ *A Michigan court reversed a grant of workers' compensation benefits to a university employee that was based on alleged harassment by her supervisor.*

The employee claimed psychological injury based on her supervisor's repeated harassment at work. A workers' compensation magistrate granted her application for benefits, finding she suffered a work-related psychiatric condition "that was significantly contributed to by actual events of her employment." The magistrate also found the employee showed she was disabled. The Court of Appeals of Michigan reviewed the case. It explained that to prove an entitlement to benefits based on a mental disability, the employee had to show a mental disability caused by an event that occurred in connection with her employment. Moreover, she had to show her perception of the event was "grounded in fact or reality," when viewed objectively. In awarding benefits, the magistrate had failed to address a crucial question of whether the employee reasonably perceived her supervisor's actions as racist, vindictive or discriminatory. So the court returned the case to the magistrate.

Any disability in this case ended when the employee's psychologist released her to return to work. Although the university refused to allow her to return to work because its own doctor had not cleared her, she nonetheless had the capacity to return to a job of a comparable salary as of the date of her release by her own psychologist. In the event that a magistrate found the employee was entitled to benefits, the award could not extend beyond the date on which her psychologist released her to return to work. *Swinton v. Michigan State Univ.*, No. 280135, 2008 WL 4604096 (Mich. Ct. App. 10/7/08). The state Supreme Court later denied the employee's appeal. *Swinton v. Michigan State Univ.*, 483 Mich. 922, 763 N.W.2d 280 (2009).

◆ *A resident assistant at a North Carolina university was limited to workers' compensation benefits for contracting asthma in a dormitory.*

A North Carolina State University student enlisted as a naval reserve and entered the Navy's Nuclear Propulsion Officer Candidate Program. A Navy physical did not reveal any significant abnormalities, and he was declared "fit for full service." The university hired the student as a resident advisor for a residence hall. Near the start of his second year of work, he resigned due to mold and mildew in living spaces of the hall. A month after resigning, the student was diagnosed with a permanent asthmatic and respiratory condition.

The student sought to recover $150,000 from the university under the state Tort Claims Act for exposing him to a substandard and unhealthy environment when he was a resident advisor. An administrative commission agreed with the university that the exclusive remedy was a claim for workers' compensation benefits. On review, the Court of Appeals of North Carolina held **the state workers' compensation act is the exclusive remedy for any employee who is injured in the course and scope of employment.** Since the student was an employee of the university while he attended classes there, his injuries arose out of the course of his employment. For this reason, the commission had correctly found the workers' compensation act was his exclusive remedy. *Christopher v. North Carolina State Univ.*, 661 S.E.2d 36 (N.C. Ct. App. 2008).

◆ *Columbia University could not avoid a worker's negligence claim on the basis that workers' compensation was his exclusive remedy.*

A temporary employment agency assigned the employee to kitchen work at Columbia. While working there, he was injured when he slipped and fell on a wet, greasy floor. The worker sued Columbia for negligence. Under state law, he would be unable to sue Columbia for negligence if it was his employer because negligence claims against employers are generally barred by the exclusive remedy provisions of the state's workers' compensation law.

The temporary agency was the worker's employer. It paid his salary and benefits, and it set his assignments. **A special employment relationship does not exist unless an entity has completely transferred control over the employee to another entity.** Columbia argued that it met this test, and it asked the trial court for judgment on this basis. The court denied the motion, and Columbia appealed. A state appellate division court held the evidence did not conclusively establish the existence of a special employment relation between the worker and Columbia. Uncontradicted evidence showed that no one at Columbia told him how to do his job or supervised him. There was a factual question as to whether the agency transferred control to Columbia to an extent that would justify the conclusion that Columbia became a special employer. Columbia was properly denied judgment on this issue. *Bellamy v. Columbia Univ.*, 50 A.D.3d 160, 851 N.Y.S.2d 406 (N.Y. App. Div. 2008).

◆ *A Minnesota appeals court upheld a decision for a college and a chemistry professor who were blamed for a student accident in a chemistry lab.*

The student was hurt while participating in a summer research program. He was paid a stipend and permitted to live in a campus dormitory at no charge. The student was seriously hurt when a chemistry flask exploded and chemical debris ignited his clothes. He sued the college, chemistry professor and several college officials for personal injury in a state court. The court noted that Minnesota law generally makes workers' compensation the exclusive remedy for employees injured on the job. It denied a motion for pretrial judgment.

The state appeals court said the facts related to the student's activities were not developed enough to support a determination regarding whether he was acting as an employee when hurt. The state workers' compensation act treated medical residents as employees but said nothing about how to treat other student workers. **The determination of whether an individual should be treated as an employee or a student depends on the context.** Deciding whether a student is an "employee" for purposes of the workers' compensation act required an analysis of purposes and character of the work performed. Because neither side offered detailed information about the nature of the work the student performed, the court upheld the trial court's decision. *Lindsay v. St. Olaf College*, No. A06-2137, 2008 WL 223119 (Minn. Ct. App. 1/29/08).

◆   *A Florida District Court of Appeal held a student who was injured while interning was not an "employee" under state workers' compensation law.*

A student at the University of Central Florida was injured when she was pushed into a wall. After the university advised her it was not responsible for her injuries, she sought workers' compensation benefits. A workers' compensation judge determined the student was entitled to benefits. Even though the student did not receive pay from the school board, the judge reasoned she was an employee because the internship was required for her to earn a degree. The board appealed to a state district court of appeal, which noted the workers' compensation statute defined "employee" as a person who received remuneration from an employer for performing work or a service.

Although the student received a benefit as a result of the internship, she was merely a participant in an internship course. This participation did not make her an "employee" under the state's workers' compensation law. Nor did a separate state law provision, which gave students in teacher preparation programs the "same protection of law" as certified educators, entitle the student to benefits. That provision did not supersede state workers' compensation law, which defined "employee" in a way that excluded the student from its coverage. The student was not covered under a workers' compensation law provision applicable to volunteers. She was at the school to complete a required course. The decision of the workers' compensation judge was reversed. *Orange County School Board v. Powers*, 959 So.2d 370 (Fla. Dist. Ct. App. 2007).

◆   *Missouri's labor and industrial relations commission erred in finding a sexual harassment incident could not trigger workers' compensation eligibility.*

The employee worked as a licensed practical nurse for about 21 years. Most of that time, she worked in the outpatient dialysis department. The employee was sexually harassed while administering dialysis treatment to a male patient. She notified the nurse in charge about the incident. After the employee left work that day, she broke down emotionally. She then took vacation time and began psychiatric treatment. The employee was diagnosed with depression and post-traumatic stress disorder. She took medication and received counseling. She resigned from her job because of the incident. A vocational expert found the employee permanently disabled due to emotional problems. The employee filed a claim for workers' compensation benefits.

The case reached the Missouri Court of Appeals, which explained that the employee's mental injury claim was based on a physical assault. Accordingly, it resulted from a traumatic incident, not work-related stress. The employee was not required to prove the stress was extraordinary or unusual. The Missouri Workers' Compensation Act requires compensation of employees for personal injury arising out of and in the course of employment. The court reversed the decision and returned the case to administrative levels to determine if the employee deserved compensation. *Jones v. Washington Univ.*, 199 S.W.3d 793 (Mo. Ct. App. 2006).

♦ *The Court of Appeals of South Carolina held an administrative assistant who was hurt on the job could collect lifetime workers' compensation benefits.*

In 2000, the administrative assistant hurt herself when she fell at work. She had a previous history of injury, including a 1973 spinal injury from a car accident. As a result of the 2000 work accident, the assistant began using a walker and lost her ability to control her bowels. Because of these problems, the assistant became able to carry out only menial tasks and was unable to pursue additional vocational training. She sought lifetime medical care and weekly compensation benefits for life. The workers' compensation commission determined the assistant was entitled to lifetime benefits. The decision was largely based on the testimony of a treating physician.

A state court affirmed the commission's decision, and the university appealed to the Court of Appeals of South Carolina. The court held **S.C. Code Section 42-9-10 provides that any person who is found totally and permanently disabled and is paraplegic from an injury is to receive workers' compensation benefits for life**. The university argued the circuit court was wrong in determining the assistant was paraplegic because the statute did not differentiate between complete and incomplete paraplegia. The court of appeals found the circuit court had reasonably relied on the physician's testimony. The university offered no evidence to refute the court's interpretation that the term "paraplegic" included incomplete paraplegia. *Reed-Richards v. Clemson Univ.*, 631 S.C. 304, 638 S.E.2d 77 (S.C. Ct. App. 2006).

CHAPTER SEVEN

Employment Discrimination

I. RACE AND NATIONAL ORIGIN DISCRIMINATION

Title VII of the Civil Rights Act of 1964, 42 U.S.C. § 2000e, et seq., prohibits discrimination in employment based upon race, color, sex, religion or national origin by any institution with 15 or more employees that effects commerce. Title VII exempts employment decisions based on religion, sex or national origin where these characteristics are bona fide occupational qualifications that are reasonably necessary to the operation of a particular business or enterprise.

Race discrimination lawsuits often include claims under 42 U.S.C. § 1981, which makes it unlawful for any person or entity to discriminate on the basis of race in the making and enforcement of contracts. Recently, the U.S. Supreme Court explained that a "ministerial exception" exempts religious employees from the coverage of anti-discrimination laws. See Hosanna-Tabor Evangelical Lutheran Church and School v. E.E.O.C., *Section V.B. of this chapter.*

A. Race Discrimination

◆   *A federal appeals court held a White woman could not show an Alabama community college denied her a full-time teaching job based on her race.*

After working for the community college as a full-time instructor and clinical coordinator, the employee was assigned to part-time work. Near this time, the college hired a black woman on a full-time basis. The employee sued the community college in a federal court, claiming she was more qualified for the full-time job. The court held for the community college, and appeal reached the U.S. Court of Appeals, Eleventh Circuit. Like the lower court, the appeals court held the employee could not show the reasons given for the decision were a pretext for unlawful discrimination. Evidence showed the community college faced serious financial problems. It was reasonable to believe the employee could successfully teach part time. **The only evidence presented to support the race discrimination claim was that the college concurrently hired an African-American on a full-time basis.** But an accrediting agency had required the college to take this action, and it was not enough to permit the claim to proceed. The decision for the college was affirmed. *Patrick v. Bishop State Community College*, 470 Fed.Appx. 797 (11th Cir. 2012).

◆   *An African-American campus police officer could proceed with federal race discrimination claims against a District of Columbia university.*

After an ankle injury limited the police officer's mobility, the university restructured his duties to include sedentary work such as manning dispatch or the front desk. He claimed a supervisor assigned him tasks outside his physical limits, told him he was insubordinate and lazy, and threatened to discipline him when he objected to walking or lifting. He said co-workers also made offensive remarks about his size and race almost daily. Claiming severe stress and anxiety, he took leave under the Family and Medical Leave Act and began to see a therapist. When his leave was up, the university discharged him, and he filed a race discrimination lawsuit. A federal court denied pretrial judgment to the university, finding the officer presented sufficient evidence to proceed to a trial. **He alleged discriminatory conduct that occurred on a nearly daily basis for almost three years.** In the court's opinion, a reasonable person could find this was enough to change the terms and conditions of his employment. *Leftwich v. Gallaudet Univ.*, 875 F.Supp.2d 81 (D.D.C. 2012).

◆   *An Indiana college basketball coach/maintenance assistant did not show his discharge was racially motivated.*

After serving as head men's basketball coach and a field maintenance assistant for some time, the coach told a supervisor he could not do Saturday maintenance work. He said he had conflicts with men's basketball, community service, church and family obligations. The coach neglected several warnings that he was to perform Saturday maintenance duties, and his employment was eventually terminated for not complying with this requirement. He sued the college in a federal court for race discrimination. As evidence, the employee claimed the athletic director had said recruiting basketball players from the inner city "created problems." He also asserted that another field maintenance employee of a different race was not similarly disciplined despite a similar performance record. The court held the employee could not proceed with his discrimination case. **He did not present sufficient evidence that he was meeting the college's legitimate expectations when he was discharged.** As a result, the college was entitled to pretrial judgment. *Helm v. Ancilla Domini College*, No. 3:11-CV-212 JVB, 2012 WL 4120006 (N.D. Ind. 9/19/12).

◆   *Texas community college employees were allowed to proceed with a federal action alleging an anti-Caucasian conspiracy in staffing.*

Seven female teachers or administrators at a Texas community college filed a federal court action alleging they "were victims of a plan on the part of the administration to discriminate against older, Anglo, female employees in an effort 'to turn the college into' a predominantly Hispanic institution." Saying they were targeted for employment termination and harassment, their suit alleged race, gender and age discrimination. The community college was also charged with due process and speech rights violations. In pretrial activity, the court granted partial judgment to the community college. It found the women could not show a due process violation. But one woman could show a speech rights violation, and **most of the discrimination claims were so factually complex and intertwined that they had to be resolved by a jury**. *Richmond v. Coastal Bend College Dist.*, 883 F.Supp.2d 705 (S.D. Tex. 2012).

◆   *An Indiana university avoided liability in a race bias case by showing it promptly investigated and addressed racial comments in the workplace.*

An African-American employee complained a co-worker used the N-word and boasted of family ties to the Ku Klux Klan. A supervisor investigated and substantially confirmed the report, and the university issued the co-worker a written warning and required her to meet with a compliance supervisor. But when the employee told the compliance supervisor that the co-worker had again used racial epithets, the university could not verify it, and the co-worker was not disciplined. Investigation of another incident involving the two produced conflicting accounts, so the university provided counseling for both.

After filing two administrative charges, the employee filed a federal case against the university for creating a racially hostile work environment. The court held for the university, and she appealed to the U.S. Court of Appeals, Seventh Circuit. It found no evidence that university supervisors were motivated by racial bias. **Evidence showed the university took prompt and appropriate action that was reasonably likely to prevent harassment from recurring.** Complaints were investigated promptly, and necessary discipline was imposed. No retaliation was shown, and there was no evidence of "adverse action" by the university. The court affirmed the pretrial judgment for the university. *Vance v. Ball State Univ.*, 646 F.3d 461 (7th Cir. 2011).

◆   *A Tennessee career college did not convince a federal court that it had legitimate reasons to discharge African-American admission representatives.*

Three African-American admission representatives at the college said their supervisor repeatedly made racially offensive remarks. They said she referred to African-Americans as "you people" and described their conduct as "ghetto." The representatives said the supervisor overwhelmingly assigned leads to white representatives, and that when they complained, they were fired. They sued the college in a federal court, asserting claims under Title VII, the state Human Rights Act and related laws. **The court held a reasonable jury could find that the college gave false reasons for firing the representatives.** The reason stated for firing two of the representatives was poor performance, but they countered this with evidence that leads had been distributed in a discriminatory way. They also presented evidence that white employees were not fired for not meeting quotas. Since the representatives were entitled to present their claims to a jury, the court denied a request for pretrial judgment. *Smith v. Draughons Junior College*, No. 3:10-00873, 2012 WL 86935 (M.D. Tenn. 1/11/12).

◆   *An Alabama federal court noted the Eleventh Circuit has held that claims under 42 U.S.C. § 1981 are analyzed the same way as Title VII claims.*

A white community college instructor repeatedly asked to be appointed chair of his division. He was not appointed as division chair, and two African-American women were appointed to replace departing chairs in other divisions. Noting that only one of the college's division chairs was white, the instructor sued the college in a federal court under Title VII and 42 U.S.C. § 1981. The court found the college was not seeking anyone to chair his division. **It held the appointment of two African-Americans as division chairs was not relevant to the instructor's case and was not evidence of racial bias.** As there was no inference of race discrimination, the university was entitled to judgment. *Thompson v. Bishop State Community College*, No. 1:10-246-KD-B, 2011 WL 1464846 (S.D. Ala. 4/15/11).

◆   *Discourteous and rude treatment of African-American campus safety officers did not support a claim of hostile work environment based on race.*

The officers said white supervisors gave them the "cold shoulder," used racial epithets, ignored them, and falsely accused them of sleeping on the job. They said the supervisors interfered with their radio transmissions, gave them unnecessary reprimands, assigned them difficult tasks and denied them backup in dangerous situations. After a college human resources officer investigated the complaints, she suggested brief suspensions and letters of discipline for the supervisors. She further recommended anti-discrimination training for the entire department and special training for the supervisors.

The African-American officers said the supervisors continued ignoring them, and they sued the college and supervisors in a state court. They claimed they were subjected to a hostile work environment in violation of the state Law Against Discrimination (LAD). The court found the evidence did not establish a claim and dismissed the case. On appeal, **a state appellate court noted that the test for liability under the LAD is virtually the same as the test under Title VII**. The officers not only failed to show a hostile work environment; they did not show any adverse employment action. The college promptly and thoroughly investigated their complaints and was shielded from any liability. As a result, the case had been properly dismissed. *Shockley v. College of New Jersey*, 2012 WL 996621 (N.J. Super. Ct. App. Div. 3/27/12).

◆   *Oklahoma university administrators were denied qualified immunity in a federal discrimination lawsuit by a business professor of Indian ancestry.*

According to the professor, the chair of his department said he was considered too "expensive" for an Asian Indian and that another Indian professor in their department was accepting less pay than the official salary schedule. At the end of the academic year, the university did not renew his contract. He sued the university and the four administrators who recommended his nonrenewal in a federal district court. His claim arose under 42 U.S.C. Section 1981, which prohibits race discrimination in the making of contracts.

According to the administrators, race had no part in the decision not to renew the contract and their decision was based on the professor's behavior problems. They said he started sleeping overnight in his office, left late night voice mails for a supervisor and sent her an inappropriate letter. The court denied the administrators' request for qualified immunity, and they appealed to the Tenth Circuit. It found the university president was entitled to pretrial judgment. His acceptance of a recommendation not to renew the professor's contract did not create an inference of intentional racial discrimination. But the court held the case against the other administrators should go forward. **Tenth Circuit decisions made it clear well before the time of their actions that employment discrimination on the basis of race violates Section 1981.** *Dasgupta v. Harris*, 407 Fed.Appx. 325 (10th Cir. 2011).

◆   *Finding the former department head of an Indiana religious university was a "ministerial employee," a federal court refused to hear her Title VII action.*

The department head said she was repeatedly exposed to discriminatory acts and harassed on account of her African-American race. She quit because of a dispute concerning a co-worker. The department head sued the university in a federal district court for racial bias under Title VII. But the court held she was a ministerial employee. Application of the ministerial exception to Title VII resulted in dismissal of certain federal claims by ministerial employees against religious employers. **The ministerial exception is based on a religious institution's First Amendment right to be free of government interference with employees who authoritatively interpret and preach its doctrine.**

According to the department head, her position did not make her the virtual equivalent of a minister. She argued the social work department was not designed to spread the faith, but instead had secular purposes. But the court noted that the Social Work Student Handbook declared one of the program's objectives was to "provide opportunities for the integration of Christian principles within the context of professional social work values and ethics." Finding the nature and character of her duties were ministerial, the court applied the ministerial exception and dismissed the case. *Adams v. Indiana Wesleyan Univ.*, No. 3:09-CV-468, 2010 WL 2803077 (N.D. Ind. 7/15/10).

◆   *A federal appeals court held Emory University did not discharge an employee based on his race in violation of 42 U.S.C. § 1981 and Title VII.*

In addition to his Section 1981 and Title VII claims, the employee alleged retaliation, wage bias, hostile environment and negligent retention. He asserted retaliatory action such as a demotion, denial of requests for office staff and space, and failure to award larger raises. To support his claims of wrongful termination and retaliation, the employee pointed to a Caucasian woman's rapid rise in job rank. He claimed the university did not truly discharge him for performance reasons and that the university did not place him into another position, as it had done for others. A federal district court held for the university, and the employee appealed to the U.S. Court of Appeals, Eleventh Circuit. The court found the **actions relied on to support the claims were not severe or pervasive enough to alter the terms or conditions of employment**. The court held a negligent retention claim could not survive, and the judgment for Emory was affirmed. *Hill v. Emory Univ.*, 346 Fed.Appx. 390 (11th Cir. 2009).

◆   *A single incident of racial discrimination was not enough to support a Title VII claim of hostile work environment.*

Appalachian State University (ASU) hired an African-American clerical worker. A Caldwell Community College (CCC) employee who was at ASU to pick up mail used a racial epithet in a conversation with an ASU secretary. The clerical worker said the secretary expressed agreement with the comment, and he claimed that ASU failed to take action to address the incident despite his complaints. The clerical worker later sued ASU and CCC in a federal district court for race discrimination under Title VII. He alleged no other incidents of discrimination. The court stated that to prove a hostile work environment exists, an employee must show harassment that is so severe or pervasive that it alters his or her working conditions and creates an abusive environment.

Hostile work environments generally result from repeated instances of harassment rather than single, isolated occurrences. Factors to consider in determining whether a hostile environment exists include the frequency of the conduct, whether the conduct is physically threatening or humiliating, and whether it unreasonably interferes with an employee's work performance. As the clerical worker was unable to show the hostility in his work environment was so severe that it altered his employment conditions or created an abusive atmosphere, the claims against both institutions failed. *Blue v. Appalachian State Univ.*, No. 5:07cv108, 2009 WL 703851 (W.D.N.C. 3/16/09).

◆   *A white assistant coach was allowed to go forward with a Title VII claim that he was discharged because he was married to an African-American woman.*

The coach claimed college athletic directors made numerous racially biased remarks, including disparaging comments about his African-American wife. The team was investigated for possible rules infractions. An athletic director's report criticized the coaching staff but proposed retaining the coaches under improvement plans. The college president and two other officials decided to fire the white assistant coach and an assistant of African-American heritage. The assistant coach claimed an athletic director referred to an African-American employee as a "jungle bunny" and to his wife as an "Aunt Jemima."

The assistant coach sued the college in a federal court, which held for the college. On appeal, **the U.S. Court of Appeals, Second Circuit, held Title VII's prohibition of race discrimination applied to claims based on a relationship with another person**. The court reasoned that an employee is subjected to discrimination based on race when an adverse job action is taken because an employer disapproves of interracial association. As the assistant coach was a member of a protected class, he could proceed with his Title VII claim. *Holcomb v. Iona College*, 521 F.3d 130 (2d Cir. 2008).

◆ *A Louisiana university football coach identified factual issues about the motive for his discharge that prevented pretrial dismissal of his lawsuit.*

The University of Louisiana at Lafayette (ULL) fired the coach after three losing seasons. He claimed ULL violated state law by removing him as coach because he is an African-American. ULL claimed he was fired for his losing record, a significant drop in attendance during his tenure, and a budget crisis.

The court held for ULL, and the coach appealed to the Court of Appeal of Louisiana. The court held the coach proved he was a qualified African-American who was removed from his post and replaced by a white male. He also offered evidence to rebut ULL's reasons for releasing him. As to the team's win/loss record during his tenure, the coach said ULL knew the team was weak and that it would take time to turn the program around. He also produced evidence showing attendance actually increased during his first year. Budget difficulties began long before the coach arrived. A previous coach was provided counseling when the administration disagreed with his decisions. Under the circumstances, **the coach raised a question regarding whether the reasons given for his removal were really a pretext for race discrimination**. As the trial court had improperly awarded judgment to ULL, the case was returned to the lower court for further proceedings. *Baldwin v. Board of Supervisors for the Univ. of Louisiana System*, 961 So.2d 418 (La. Ct. App. 2007).

◆ *Auburn University did not discriminate against an African-American employee by declining to reclassify her job.*

According to the employee, Auburn classified her position lower than for the same jobs performed by white employees. She said the university failed to promote her and retaliated against her for complaining about racial disparities in employee salaries and classifications. The employee sued Auburn in an Alabama federal district court, alleging it violated Title VII. In an attempt to support her claims, she compared herself to several other employees. The court found the other employees were not relevant for comparison as they had different job duties. **The court found no evidence to show any different treatment was based on race, and held the employee did not show a causal connection between her complaints about disparities and the failure to reclassify her position.** As the university offered legitimate nondiscriminatory reasons for its failure to reclassify the employee, the court held for Auburn. On appeal to the U.S. Court of Appeals, Eleventh Circuit, the court determined the decision by the district court was proper and affirmed the judgment for Auburn. *Johnson v. Auburn Univ.*, 193 Fed.Appx. 955 (11th Cir. 2006).

B. National Origin Discrimination

National origin discrimination cases are usually filed under Title VII. State anti-discrimination laws also include national origin as a protected class. In Delaware State College v. Ricks, 449 U.S. 250 (1980), the Supreme Court held the limitations period for a Title VII national origin discrimination case began to run on the date a teacher was denied tenure, not his final employment date.

In St. Francis College v. Al-Khazraji, 481 U.S. 604 (1987), the Supreme Court held that ethnic groups are not to be considered a single race under 42 U.S.C. Section 1981. For that reason, an Arab professor was entitled to prove that he was subjected to intentional discrimination because he was an Arab, rather than solely because of his place of origin or his religion. Persons of Arab descent were protected from discrimination under Section 1981.

◆　*A Texas college instructor's failure to prove he had the required credentials for his job was a valid reason to fire him.*

When the college audited its faculty qualifications, the instructor came under scrutiny. He held degrees from Addis Ababa University in Ethiopia and Odessa Civil Engineering Institute in Russia. To be qualified for his position, the instructor needed the equivalent of an advanced degree from a U.S. institution. The audit evaluated his degrees as only equivalent to an A.S. in Drafting Technology and a B.S. in Architecture. As a result, the instructor was let go as not properly credentialed. In a federal court, he asserted the real reason for dismissal was his race and national origin. **But the court found the college had a valid, nondiscriminatory reason for dismissing the instructor.** He lacked the credentials to be qualified for the job. Without evidence of an appropriate degree, the court found no reasonable jury would find the college dismissed the instructor for an unlawful purpose. *Tesso v. Westwood College*, No. 3:11-CV-0246-D, 2012 WL 3204916 (N.D. Tex. 8/8/12).

◆　*A Maryland community college responded to threats against a professor, defeating his national origin discrimination and retaliation lawsuit.*

After the professor received anonymous threats based on national origin, the community college investigated and reported the incidents to police. Emails were sent out soliciting evidence of hate crimes, and certain students were removed from his classes. The college provided the professor with on-campus escorts, and asked the police to check in with him at home. No perpetrator was ever identified, and the professor filed a charge against the college with the Equal Employment Opportunity Commission (EEOC). Meanwhile, a student accused him of sexual harassment and others told college investigators that he made inappropriate remarks to them. The community college learned he had viewed pornography and dating sites on a college computer in violation of its Internet policy. Based on a pattern of disruptive behavior such as accusing staff of forging documents and criticizing teaching evaluators, the college fired him.

The professor filed a federal district court action against the community college for hostile work environment and retaliation. The court held for the college, and the U.S. Court of Appeals, Fourth Circuit, affirmed the judgment. It held **the college was not liable for a hostile work environment based on**

the threats because it took reasonable action to address and correct the situation. Since the college had valid reasons for firing the professor that were unrelated to his EEOC charge, his retaliation claim also failed. He was unable to counter evidence that the reason for discharge was his own misconduct. *Latif v. Community College of Baltimore*, 354 Fed.Appx. 828 (4th Cir. 2009).

◆   *An Arizona community college faced a 42 U.S.C. § 1981 claim based on a decision not to promote an African-American advisor to a managerial job.*

The community college hired the advisor into its disability resources and services office. After 10 years, the office sought a manager, and the advisor applied for the job. He was not even interviewed, based on his alleged lack of qualifications. The advisor sued the college and several officials in a federal district court for race discrimination under Title VII, 42 U.S.C. § 1981 and 42 U.S.C. § 1983. **The court dismissed the Title VII claims against the officials, since "employees" cannot be held personally liable under Title VII.** Section 1981 and Section 1983 claims against two of the officials failed because the officials were not involved in the selection process. A community college manager who was a member of the hiring committee declared the advisor was the best candidate for the job and said a meeting was held just to exclude him because of his race. The court said her statement and the advisor's testimony were sufficient reasons to let a jury decide whether the college was being truthful about its decision. *McIntosh v. Maricopa Community College Dist.*, No. CV-07-0760-PHX-DGC, 2009 WL 364021 (D. Ariz. 2/12/09).

When the manager later gave more evidence at a deposition, she admitted she had only second-hand information about the meeting to decide whether to grant the employee an interview. The deposition testimony also revealed that the manager was removed from the hiring committee and never attended a meeting regarding the position. As the deposition did not yield direct evidence of a discriminatory motive, and the circumstantial evidence provided by the deposition was not specific or substantial, the court awarded pretrial judgment to the college. *McIntosh v. Maricopa Community College Dist.*, No. CV-07-0760-PHX-DGC, 2009 WL 1286197 (D. Ariz. 5/8/09).

◆   *A Hispanic candidate for an associate professor job failed to show his application was rejected based on his race, color or national origin.*

The candidate sought an associate professor position in the anthropology department at Montclair State University (MSU). Job announcements generated about 52 applications for the job, which were reviewed by a six-member hiring committee. A hiring committee narrowed the field to three. A Caucasian applicant was eventually chosen, and the Hispanic candidate filed a federal district court lawsuit against MSU for race, color and national origin discrimination under Title VII. The court held for MSU, and the candidate appealed to the U.S. Court of Appeals, Third Circuit.

Although the court found the candidate satisfied the preliminary elements of his case by showing he was qualified for the job and it was awarded to a non-Hispanic candidate, he failed to prove the reasons given by MSU for not hiring him were a pretext for discrimination. MSU said it chose another candidate because he did not have the qualifications it sought for the job. Specifically, the candidate's research focused on great apes, whereas the department was looking for someone who was an expert in the study of the social and cultural aspects of disease or health patterns. In addition, the candidate did not provide much evidence of past successful teaching performance. **Since MSU had legitimate and nondiscriminatory reasons for its decision, and there was not enough evidence to show a pretext, he did not prove MSU's decision was discriminatory**, and the judgment was affirmed. *Sarmiento v. Montclair State Univ.*, 285 Fed.Appx. 905 (3d Cir. 2008).

◆   *A Virginia university was not motivated by discrimination when it chose not to renew a temporary professor's contract.*

The professor was a Nigerian national who was hired under a nine-month contract for a non-tenure track position in the agriculture department. He was relocating from Australia, and he said the department chair emailed him about the possibility of reimbursement for moving expenses. But the written contract did not mention reimbursement. During his first semester of work, a colleague and students made repeated complaints about him. Despite the complaints, the department chair gave the professor a favorable evaluation. The next semester, another colleague began complaining about the professor. Students continued to complain about him, but the university again renewed his contract. However, it did not offer him a tenure-track position. Similar problems recurred the next year, and other faculty members complained about his condescending attitude.

After learning that his contract would not be renewed, the professor sued the university and officials in a federal district court, claiming his contract was not renewed based on his national origin and age. He also said the university breached a contract by disregarding a promise to pay his moving expenses. The court held for the university, and the professor appealed to the U.S. Court of Appeals, Fourth Circuit. It found **a reasonable jury could not find that the decision not to renew his contract was based on national origin or age discrimination**. Instead, the decision was based on the many problems the professor had at work. He did not dispute that colleagues who co-taught classes with him complained about him and said they would not work with him again. There was simply no evidence of national origin discrimination. The court also rejected the breach of contract claim and affirmed the judgment. *Ilozor v. Hampton Univ.*, 286 Fed.Appx. 834 (4th Cir. 2008).

◆   *A university that provided a research associate with an office, phone and business cards was not her employer under Title VII of the Civil Rights Act.*

The University of Utah granted the research associate a one-year appointment in its civil and environmental engineering department. She shared an office, phone and mailbox with other workers. However, the university did not pay her a salary or contribute Social Security or other taxes on her behalf. The associate used her own computer. The university did not monitor her day-to-day activities, but retained an ownership interest in the work she produced. After the university declined to renew the associate's contract, she claimed discrimination based on national origin and gender, and she sued the university in a federal district court. The court dismissed the case, finding the associate could not sue under Title VII because she was not a university employee.

On appeal, the U.S. Court of Appeals, Tenth Circuit, found that **the key inquiry was whether the university controlled "the means and manner by which the work [was] accomplished."** In affirming the conclusion that the associate was not an employee, the court relied heavily on the fact that the university exercised very little control over her daily activities. The associate was free to pursue any research activities she chose, and her research was not supervised. The university did not pay her a salary, and it provided only minimal supplies to her. The associate was different from faculty members because she had no teaching or administrative obligations. As the university exercised little control over her activities, she was not an employee and her Title VII claim failed. *Xie v. Univ. of Utah*, 243 Fed.Appx. 367 (10th Cir. 2007).

◆   *A Chinese-born professor failed to show he was denied tenure because of his race or national origin when a university did not select him for an award.*

The year before the assistant professor's tenure review, he won a teacher-of-the-year award. The next year, when the assistant professor was facing his tenure review, a tenured full professor said in a faculty meeting that he would no longer accept Chinese graduate students. The assistant professor claimed the department head retaliated against him by influencing faculty members to vote against him. The department head told the assistant professor he would not be granted tenure. The assistant professor sued the members of the board of trustees, alleging the university discriminated against him on the basis of race or national origin and violated his First Amendment speech rights.

A federal court held for the board members, and the assistant professor appealed. The Seventh Circuit held he could not prove the department head or the professor who made the anti-Chinese remark had a final say in the tenure decision. The assistant professor had insufficient evidence to warrant a trial based on indirect discrimination. The university showed that a Caucasian assistant professor had superior credentials in terms of funding and invited presentations. By contrast, **the assistant professor had several identifiable weaknesses related to funding, scholarship, and supervising grad students**. Judgment had been properly granted on the First Amendment claim. *Sun v. Board of Trustees of the Univ. of Illinois*, 473 F.3d 799 (7th Cir. 2007).

◆   *A Muslim job applicant failed to show an Ohio college based its decision not to hire him upon his race.*

The applicant was denied a full-time tenure-track position as an assistant professor of mathematics despite over 10 years of teaching experience and an extensive record of publishing. A hiring committee eliminated him from consideration because he had recently been denied tenure by another university and submitted outdated reference letters. One of the letters indicated concern about the applicant's performance. The college selected a white person for the position who had formerly studied under the department chair as a student. The applicant sued the college in a federal district court, alleging it violated Title VII of the Civil Rights Act and Section 1981. The court dismissed the case.

The applicant appealed to the Sixth Circuit, which held that **to prevail in a Section 1981 race discrimination case, there must be proof of intentional**

discrimination. The applicant argued the district court did not properly consider preferential treatment for the white applicant as proof of intent to discriminate. The court disagreed, finding the department chair's preference for the white applicant, whom he knew personally, did not prove discrimination. The court accepted the college's position – that the applicant was not one of the most qualified candidates and that the former student was the most likely to succeed – as legitimate, nondiscriminatory reasons for its actions. The judgment was affirmed. *Amini v. Oberlin College*, 440 F.3d 350 (6th Cir. 2006).

◆ *The removal of an instructor from a math course by a Kansas university was based on his inability to teach the course, not on his national origin.*

As part of his training, the instructor was assigned to teach a five-week math course under the mentorship of another instructor. When he began teaching, students began to complain about him almost immediately. The instructor improperly disclosed a student's personal academic information. As a result, he was removed from the course and told to retake an earlier portion of the training. The instructor sued the university in federal district court, alleging discrimination based on his Pakistani heritage. The court rejected his claim because he could not show he was able to teach the course in a satisfactory manner. **The university did not take an adverse action against the instructor when it instructed him that he needed to be retrained.** The retraining requirement did not significantly affect his employment status. Throughout the retraining, the instructor continued to receive pay. The court granted the university's motion for summary judgment. *Shinwari v. Univ. of Phoenix*, No. 05-1167-JTM, 2006 WL 3021116 (D. Kan. 10/23/06).

II.   SEX DISCRIMINATION

Sex discrimination is prohibited by Title VII, the Equal Pay Act, and state laws. These laws apply to public and private institutions of higher education. Colleges and universities may not engage in discriminatory employment practices. The First Amendment "ministerial exception" precludes discrimination claims by ministerial employees against religious institutions.

A. Different Treatment

◆ *A female law professor did not prove she was subjected to unlawful gender discrimination or retaliation by the University of Puerto Rico School of Law.*

During her five-year probationary period, the professor worked with a male professor who became romantically involved with a female student. At the time, there was no rule banning such relationships or requiring faculty to report them. While the professor's request for tenure was pending, the law school dean chastised her for failing to report the male professor's relationship. Later, the law school denied her request to extend her probationary period. The professor sued the university for gender discrimination and retaliation. A federal court held for the university, and she appealed. The U.S. Court of Appeals, First Circuit, held the professor was unable to show an adverse employment action based on failure to conform to gender stereotypes. **Nothing**

indicated she was held to a different standard based on her gender. Descriptions of the professor made during the tenure process were found to be gender neutral. Since these comments did not support a claim of unlawful gender discrimination under Title VII, the court affirmed the judgment. *Morales-Cruz v. Univ. of Puerto Rico*, 676 F.3d 220 (1st Cir. 2012).

◆ *A federal district court dismissed a New York professor's claim that a sexual harassment charge amounted to gender-based discrimination.*

University officials accused the professor of having a sexual relationship with a student. She denied the charge and reported to the university's human resources department that the accusation amounted to sexual harassment. After learning that her employment would soon be terminated, the professor sued the university and some of its officials in a federal court for Title VII sexual discrimination. She added claims for due process violations, speech rights violations, and retaliation. After dismissing the speech and due process claims, the court stated that a viable claim for sex discrimination under Title VII required adverse job action under circumstances suggesting unlawful discrimination. It held **"a false accusation of sexual misconduct is not sex discrimination merely because it deals with 'sex' as a topic."** A Title VII sex discrimination claim must allege discrimination based on sex. Even if the professor was wrongly accused and suffered an adverse employment action, nothing suggested the university was motivated by the fact that she was a woman. While her Title VII sex discrimination claim could not proceed, the court held she might have a viable Title VII retaliation claim. *Ying v. City Univ. of New York*, No. 10-cv-4990 (CBA)(SMG), 2011 WL 6337666 (E.D.N.Y. 12/19/11).

◆ *Gender discrimination claims brought by a male professor will go forward against a dean but not against a Pennsylvania community college.*

A male theater professor claimed a female faculty member was openly hostile to men and tried to get rid of him. After he received tenure, the female reported he had sexually harassed a student and given beer to others who were underage. His tenure was revoked, and he was fired. The male sued the college and dean in a federal district court, alleging he was fired and deprived of tenure because of his sex. The court held **the male could not show the college had a policy or custom that deprived him of his constitutional rights, acted deliberately and was the moving force behind the violation.** Nor could he show the college caused him injury via policy or custom. The court dismissed the claims against the college, but not the claims against the dean. The male alleged that the dean was the supervisor of the female faculty member who he charged with discrimination. *Heneghan v. Northampton Community College*, No. 09-04979, 2010 WL 2730638 (E.D. Pa. 7/8/10).

◆ *Michigan State University (MSU) defeated a gender bias claim by a male faculty candidate despite evidence that female candidates were preferred.*

After twice being denied tenured positions, the candidate filed an internal complaint for gender discrimination. A few months later, he claimed his work laboratory was substantially reduced in size. The candidate sued MSU in a state court for gender bias and retaliation. MSU conceded that a dean involved in the hiring process had shown a preference for female candidates, but argued this was irrelevant because the candidate was not qualified for either job. He did not hold a relevant doctoral degree, and was not an otherwise competitive applicant. MSU asserted that the candidate was also subject to discipline for assaulting a student. After the trial court held for MSU, the case came before the Court of Appeals of Michigan. **Despite the dean's bias toward females, the candidate was considered equally with other applicants in the early screening process.** MSU would have rejected him even if bias did not play a role in the hiring process. *Dybas v. Michigan State Univ.*, No. 281547, 2009 WL 2195110 (Mich. Ct. App. 7/23/09).

◆ *An Ohio community college did not commit age or gender discrimination by refusing to hire an overqualified candidate as an academic advisor.*

Sinclair Community College created and advertised two entry-level academic advisor positions. Nearly 200 women and more than 80 men applied for the jobs. Of nine finalists, the search committee chose to interview only one man, who was 59 years old at the time and had over 20 years of experience as a university director of academic advising. The new positions at Sinclair were entry level and paid much less than the director's current job. After Sinclair chose two women for the vacancies who were younger and less experienced than the director, he sued the community college in an Ohio court for sex and age discrimination. While the director stated a case of age discrimination, he could not pursue the claim because the college gave valid, nondiscriminatory reasons for not hiring him. The court found the gender disparity was not caused by favoritism, but because women dominate the field of academic advising.

The case reached the Court of Appeals of Ohio, which agreed with the director that he had a more impressive resume than the women who were hired. But his resume was not so impressive that an employer would have been compelled to hire him. **The college considered him overqualified for an entry-level job.** It had a good reason to hire the women, who had experience with Ohio community colleges. The court held the trial court had properly granted judgment to the college. *Silberstein v. Montgomery County Community College Dist.*, No. 23439, 2009 WL 3977080 (Ohio Ct. App. 11/20/09).

◆ *An Arizona community college could lawfully prohibit a transgendered instructor from using a women's restroom.*

The college received complaints about the instructor's use of a women's restroom and banned her from it until she completed sex reassignment surgery. Later, the college declined to renew her employment contract. The instructor sued the college in a federal district court for gender discrimination under Title VII. She also alleged a violation of Title IX and constitutional violations. After the court held for the college, appeal reached the U.S. Court of Appeals, Ninth Circuit. According to the court, gender stereotyping is direct evidence of sex discrimination. Transgender individuals can sue for sex discrimination based on the theory that they were subjected to discrimination because they did not conform to "socially constructed gender norms."

As a result, the court held **employers cannot discriminate against a transgender employee solely because the employee does not behave in a**

way that the employer believes is gender-appropriate. But the college produced evidence that it barred her from using the women's restroom for safety-related concerns. Since the instructor could not show this was pretextual and that its real reason for the ban was illegal gender discrimination, her Title VII claim failed. The court also affirmed the judgment on related Title IX and equal protection claims. *Kastl v. Maricopa County Community College Dist.,* 325 Fed.Appx. 492 (9th Cir. 2009).

◆ *A New York university employee did not show she was assigned a negative performance evaluation because she complained about sex discrimination.*

The employee received a poor job performance evaluation after she complained to supervisors about sex discrimination. As a result of the poor evaluation, her employment contract was not renewed, and she sued the university in a federal district court for retaliation under Title VII. The court awarded pretrial judgment to the university, and the employee appealed to the U.S. Court of Appeals, Second Circuit. It agreed with the lower court that **the university provided multiple, documented and nondiscriminatory reasons for the negative job evaluation**. Records showed the employee mismanaged programs and failed to meet revenue expectations. Since she did not show these reasons were a pretext for retaliation, the judgment was affirmed. *Malacarne v. City Univ. of New York,* 289 Fed.Appx. 446 (2d Cir. 2008).

◆ *The discharge of a North Carolina campus police officer for various insubordinate acts did not violate Title VII.*

The officer refused to comply with an instruction to wear a tie, which led to a written warning for unacceptable personal conduct. She filed a grievance but was told that she was not eligible to do so because she was not a permanent employee. The officer later struck a guard rail while driving her patrol car on campus. A report indicated she did not contact her superior until she realized he had learned about the accident. A week later, the officer met with a fellow officer at the university's cafeteria for breakfast during her shift, even though officers were prohibited from eating with other officers while on duty.

A university police captain ordered the officer not to charge a student for a misconduct incident as this would violate university policy. Because the officer refused his order, she was placed on administrative leave. After an investigation, the officer was discharged for unacceptable personal conduct and insubordination. She sued the university in a federal district court for sex discrimination. **The court held the officer did not show she was performing her job in a satisfactory manner at the time of discharge.** She failed to follow instructions, violated a rule against eating with other officers while on duty, and issued two criminal citations to a university student even though she knew it was against university policy. On appeal, the U.S. Court of Appeals, Fourth Circuit, affirmed the decision for the reasons stated by the district court. *Hooper v. State of North Carolina,* 222 Fed.Appx. 271 (4th Cir. 2007).

◆ *A 13-year veteran Indiana university tennis coach was allowed to pursue a claim that she was fired from her job based on her gender.*

In the coach's final year as head coach of the women's tennis team at

Indiana University-Purdue (Indianapolis), the team had its best season ever and qualified for the National Collegiate Athletic Association tournament for the first time. It also had the highest grade point average of all athletic teams at the school. Despite her performance, the university discharged the 53-year-old coach for violating rules requiring coaches "to treat others with dignity and respect" and to "exhibit a higher standard of behavior." About a month later, the university hired the 23-year-old sister of the men's tennis coach to replace her.

The coach sued the university in a federal district court for gender and age discrimination. The court held for the university, and she appealed to the U.S. Court of Appeals, Seventh Circuit. **The court found evidence that the university treated similarly situated male employees more favorably than the coach.** Specifically, there was evidence that the men's soccer coach and the men's tennis coach committed the same rules violations as the coach. The male coaches were provided with progressive discipline, while the female was not. The university never warned her she was in danger of losing her job and simply told her they were looking to move in a "new, different direction." Under these circumstances, it was improper to dismiss the gender discrimination claim. But the dismissal of her age discrimination claim was affirmed. *Peirick v. Indiana Univ.-Purdue Univ. Indianapolis Athletic's Dep't*, 510 F.3d 681 (7th Cir. 2007).

◆   *A professor who was turned down for a tenure-track position did not show the denial was based on her gender or ethnicity.*

The professor applied for a tenure-track professorship at the University of Texas-El Paso (UTEP). UTEP instead offered her a visiting professor position, which she accepted. The professor soon reapplied for the tenure-track position, but was not offered the job. She appealed unsuccessfully within the university, then sued UTEP in a federal district court. The professor claimed UTEP denied her a promotion on the basis of her Hispanic origin and gender.

The district court noted UTEP had stated nondiscriminatory reasons for its decision that were not shown to be false. Specifically, UTEP said it rejected the professor for the job due to her lack of experience in strategic management, level of potential for publishing, and level of collegiality with UTEP faculty during her employment as a visiting professor. As she did not convince the court that any of these reasons were false, the court held for UTEP. On appeal, the U.S. Court of Appeals, Fifth Circuit, noted that **UTEP set forth legitimate, nondiscriminatory reasons for declining to hire the professor for a tenure-track position. She could prevail only by showing these reasons were pretextual.** As the professor's own testimony was not enough to show UTEP's stated reasons were false, the court affirmed the judgment. *Alvarez-Diemer v. Univ. of Texas-El Paso*, 258 Fed.Appx. 689 (5th Cir. 2007).

◆   *A Pennsylvania chaplain's sex discrimination claims against a Catholic university were dismissed under the Title VII "ministerial exception."*

The chaplain worked as director of the university's Center for Social Concerns. She then became the university chaplain. Allegations surfaced that the university's president had an affair with a subordinate, and he took a leave of absence. Another female employee accused him of sexual harassment. The chaplain claimed the university attempted to cover up the president's misconduct. The university demoted the chaplain, took away many of her responsibilities and reduced her decision-making authority. The chaplain sued the university in a federal district court, alleging it retaliated against her based on her conduct and sex. The court stated the ministerial exception precludes courts from questioning the reason for a religious university's employment decision. The chaplain was a ministerial employee in light of how important her role was in supporting the school's spiritual and pastoral mission.

The court held she performed a "ministerial" function at the university, and declared it could not hear her Title VII claims. On appeal, the U.S. Court of Appeals, Third Circuit, joined seven other federal circuit courts that have recognized the ministerial exception. **Title VII exempts religious educational institutions from its anti-discrimination requirements to the extent that their decisions are based on religious preferences.** The chaplain's Title VII discrimination and retaliation claims were barred. As resolution of her fraudulent misrepresentation and breach of contract claims did not limit the university's free exercise rights, these claims were not precluded. However, the chaplain failed to plead fraud with sufficient particularity, and the claim was properly dismissed. The breach of contract claim required further consideration by the district court. *Petruska v. Gannon Univ.*, 462 F.3d 294 (3d Cir. 2006).

◆ *A Maryland university discharged a professor for professional misconduct and neglect of duty, not for discriminatory reasons.*

The head of the department considered the assistant professor to be a top-notch researcher. The university sometimes paid overload compensation, which must be recommended and approved by the dean's office and approved by the provost. It is paid when teaching or research exceeds the normal workload. The assistant professor asked the chair for overload compensation for overtime hours she claimed to have logged and for additional childcare expenses. The chair strongly endorsed her request and noted her extraordinary efforts in attracting research grants and contracts. The university rejected the request.

The assistant professor's relationships with university staff and faculty began to deteriorate. She accused the department head and other faculty members of sex discrimination. The university received allegations that the assistant professor had engaged in scientific misconduct in connection with the grant for which she sought overload compensation. After an investigation, the university discharged her for professional misconduct and willful neglect of duty. The assistant professor sued the university and others in a federal court for sex discrimination. The court found no evidence of discrimination. **The university had a legitimate, nondiscriminatory reason for every action it took.** The U.S. Court of Appeals, Fourth Circuit, affirmed the judgment. *Britton v. Univ. of Maryland at Baltimore*, 206 Fed.Appx. 282 (4th Cir. 2006).

◆ *The U.S. Supreme Court held that a Title VII "charge" did not have to be verified by oath or affirmation at the time it was filed with the Equal Employment Opportunity Commission (EEOC).*

Five months after a Virginia college denied tenure to a professor, he faxed a letter to an EEOC field office claiming he had been subjected to gender, national origin and religious discrimination. He then filed charges with the state and, 313 days after the denial of tenure, he filed a verified "Form 5 Charge of Discrimination." When he sued the college under Title VII, the college sought to dismiss the case on the grounds that he had failed to comply with the 300-day statute of limitations. A federal court found that the faxed letter was not a "charge" of discrimination within the meaning of Title VII and that the verification could not relate back to the letter. The Fourth Circuit agreed, but the U.S. Supreme Court reversed, finding that **the faxed letter to the EEOC could qualify as a "charge" under Title VII** and that the verification could relate back to the letter. Nothing in Title VII required the charge to be verified at the time it was made. The Court remanded the case. *Edelman v. Lynchburg College*, 535 U.S. 106, 122 S.Ct. 1145, 152 L.Ed.2d 188 (2002).

◆ *In an employment discrimination lawsuit filed under Title VII, the aggrieved party bears the burden of proving employer pretext.*

A federal district court ruled that a college had discriminated against a professor on the basis of sex. The U.S. Court of Appeals, First Circuit, affirmed the decision, ruling that Title VII of the 1964 Civil Rights Act, 42 U.S.C. § 2000e, *et seq.*, required the college to prove absence of discriminatory motive. The U.S. Supreme Court held that this burden was too great. It ruled that **in an employment discrimination case, the employer need only "articulate some legitimate, nondiscriminatory reason for the employee's rejection."** In other words, the employee has the burden of proving that the reason for the employee's rejection was a mere pretext. The Court vacated the court of appeals' decision and remanded the case for reconsideration under the lesser standard. *Trustees of Keene State College v. Sweeney*, 439 U.S. 24, 99 S.Ct. 295, 58 L.Ed.2d 216 (1978).

B. Harassment

Sexual harassment is a form of sex discrimination, which violates Title VII of the Civil Rights Act of 1964, Title IX of the Education Amendments of 1972 and state anti-discrimination laws. To pursue a harassment claim under Title VII, there must be "adverse employment action," which alters the terms and conditions of employment. In order to prove a harassment case under federal law, there must be severe or pervasive harassment based on gender, such as unwelcome sexual advances or requests for sexual favors.

Title IX of the Education Amendments of 1972 prohibits sex discrimination by all recipients of federal funding. In Davis v. Monroe County Board of Educ., 526 U.S. 629 (1999), the U.S. Supreme Court first held federal-funding recipients could be liable under Title IX for student-on-student harassment. The Court established a three-part test for institutional liability in Davis for peer-sexual harassment: (1) sexual harassment by peers; (2) deliberate indifference by officials who have actual knowledge of the harassment; and (3) harassment so severe, pervasive and objectively offensive it deprives the student of access to educational opportunities. A teacher's knowledge of peer harassment is sufficient to create "actual knowledge" that may trigger liability.

In Fitzgerald v. Barnstable School Committee, 129 S.Ct. 788 (U.S. 2009), the Court held Title IX does not bar students from advancing parallel gender discrimination claims under 42 U.S.C. § 1983. Section 1983 is a federal statute that creates no rights, but enforces rights created by federal laws and the Constitution. Sexual comments may be harassment if they affect a person's employment, or create an intimidating, hostile or offensive work environment.

◆ *A lesbian University of Washington (UW) program coordinator's sexual orientation discrimination claim will proceed in the state court system.*

The program coordinator accused her supervisor of maintaining a hostile work environment. She said he told her not to flaunt her sexuality around him. In addition, the coordinator claimed the supervisor often discussed his hatred of others and told her he kept a gun in his vehicle. After the supervisor learned of the coordinator's sexual orientation, she said he revoked her flexible work schedule, denied her overtime work, denied her advancement opportunities and tried to intimidate her. At a staff meeting before he was deployed for a military assignment, he announced that he was "going to come back a very angry man."

In a state court, the coordinator sued UW and the supervisor for creating a hostile work environment based on her sexual orientation in violation of state law. Washington did not amend its law against discrimination to include sexual orientation until after most of the relevant incidents in this case had taken place. The court held the coordinator could only rely on the "angry man" comment to support her claims because the amendment to the law was not retroactive. It held the comment was insufficient to prove sexual orientation discrimination. Appeal reached the Supreme Court of Washington, which held that conduct occurring before the effective date of the amendment was not actionable. But it found pre-amendment conduct was admissible as background evidence. And the "angry man" comment was sufficient to establish a preliminary claim of hostile work environment. **Since the coordinator established a preliminary claim for hostile work environment, she could pursue the lawsuit.** *Loeffelholz v. Univ. of Washington*, 175 Wash.2d 264, 285 P.3d 854 (Wash. 2012).

◆ *A federal court rejected harassment and discrimination claims filed by a California state university employee.*

According to the employee, a colleague repeatedly hugged and kissed her after she rejected her advances. She claimed the harassment went on for years and that her supervisor urged her not to report it. The employee claimed that when she reported the harassment to the human resources department, an investigator told her not to file a formal complaint. In a federal court, the employee sued the university for sexual harassment and sexual orientation discrimination. But the court held her claims under 42 U.S.C. § 1983 were barred by Eleventh Amendment immunity. Next, the court held the sexual orientation discrimination claim was too vague. The complaint did not indicate whether it was filed under federal or state law. Either way, it could not go forward. If the claim was filed under federal law, the employee was required to exhaust her administrative remedies before filing it in court. Since she did not do so, the claim could not proceed. **There was no basis to support the conclusion that complaints to a supervisor satisfied the administrative filing requirement.** *Brodie v. Board of Trustees of the California State Univ.*, No. CV 12-07690 DDP (AGRx), 2012 WL 6140205 (C.D. Cal. 12/11/12).

◆   *A federal court refused to dismiss a hostile environment case based on an employee's claim that a university did not protect her from sexual harassment.*

A university communications assistant said a business school finance director said, "I cannot control my feelings for you," made "moaning sounds" and told her he was obsessed with sex. She said he grabbed her arm so hard it left a bruise, told her he had been watching her and implied that she should keep her guard up or he might assault her. When the assistant complained to her supervisor, he doubted the report. She filed an administrative complaint, but she said the supervisor then ignored instructions to minimize her contact with the director. After being fired for unexcused absences, the assistant sued the university in a District of Columbia federal court for allowing a hostile environment based on sexual harassment. The court denied the university's request for judgment, finding the claims met the required standard for showing a hostile work environment. The assistant alleged that **sexual harassment had interfered with her work performance and created an intimidating, hostile, or offensive working environment**. There was evidence suggesting that the university knew about the harassment but did not promptly address it. As the assistant's factual assertions met the requirements for a hostile work environment claim, the court denied the university's motion for pretrial judgment. *Hoskins v. Howard Univ.*, 839 F.Supp.2d 268 (D.D.C. 2012).

◆   *A federal court rejected claims by a New York university football team manager because she did not prove bias, harassment or retaliation.*

The student worked as the football team manager and also dated a member of the team. She said players joked about the relationship and singled her out for being the only female on the team bus. Later, the student said players harassed her online and during a team camp. She said that a coach played a film with numerous sex scenes on a team bus, leading to many lewd comments by players. The next semester, a new team manager was hired, and the student was rejected for a graduate assistantship. She sued the university and a university vice president in a federal court for discrimination, harassment and retaliation under Title VII and the state human rights law. The court held the student was acting as a university employee in her role as the team manager and could pursue her Title VII claim. But it held a comment that she "stunk up the bathroom" and jokes when the film was shown on the team bus were gender neutral. Other incidents cited by the student were not severe or pervasive enough to create Title VII liability. **Since no reasonable jury could find a hostile work environment was created by the conduct, the court dismissed the claim.** The retaliation claim was also dismissed. *Summa v. Hofstra Univ.*, No. CV 08-0361 (WDW), 2011 WL 1343058 (E.D.N.Y. 4/7/11).

◆   *A New York court rejected a graduate student's claim that she was improperly disciplined after she sexually propositioned one of her professors.*

When the graduate student suggested a sexual affair, the professor asked her to stop contacting him. But the student did not, even after he said he would take formal action against her if she did not. Following that warning, the student did not contact the professor for two years, when she copied him on an email to the university president claiming the faculty of a college department violated her "institutional rights." The professor filed a sexual harassment complaint against the student, and she responded with her own complaint for sexual harassment and retaliation. The university rejected the student's complaint and determined she had harassed the professor. It issued a written reprimand and a no-contact order. A state supreme court upheld the university's decision, and later a state appellate division court reached the same result. **There was no indication that the university deviated from its disciplinary procedures with respect to the complaint against the student, and the decision was supported by the evidence.** There was clear and convincing evidence that she violated the university's conduct code. Nor did the university violate any procedural rules with respect to the discipline. *Hyman v. Cornell Univ.*, 82 A.D.3d 1309 (N.Y. App. Div. 2011).

◆ *Virginia's highest court upheld the firing of a university business manager after his second violation of a sexual harassment and discrimination policy.*

The business manager volunteered at a local youth boxing club that was seeking to raise funds by selling calendars with attractive young women posing in boxing settings. A supervisor who worked for the business manager at the university asked female students if they would be interested in posing. The two interviewed a student and asked her if she would be interested in posing in a bathing suit or short shorts. During the meeting, the manager told the student she should not eat a piece of candy she was reaching for because "you will look like a little refrigerator with your head on top." The comment upset the student, and she reported it. A formal investigation of the manager was begun for violating the university's sexual harassment and discrimination policy. He filed a grievance, but a hearing officer upheld the discharge on grounds that this was the manager's second harassment policy violation in three years.

A state court reversed the decision, and the case reached the Supreme Court of Virginia. It found that while the lower court found federal decisions persuasive, the hearing officer had rejected sexual harassment as a basis for the decision. **The hearing officer noted this was the business manager's second relevant offense in three years.** He had previously violated the policy when he used a university computer to access pornography. Since the business manager did not identify any applicable law that the hearing officer's decision contradicted, the lower courts lacked any basis for reviewing the decision. The court reinstated the hearing officer's decision. *Virginia Polytechnic Institute and State Univ. v. Quesenberry*, 277 Va. 420, 674 S.E.2d 854 (Va. 2009).

◆ *A federal district court held a sexual harassment claim cannot be based on conduct that is merely "bizarre."*

A New York college administrator was appointed to a regular, tenure-track position in 2003. A married, heterosexual female faculty member told others in her department that they "meant a lot to her" and were "very important to her." The administrator made several vague complaints to superiors about the faculty member, saying the two "did not always see eye to eye" and were involved in an "unhealthy relationship." She then told the faculty member of her intent to resign and seek a position elsewhere within the college. The faculty member stated she was unhappy as she was concerned about covering her teaching load.

The administrator moved to another department, but continued to collaborate with the faculty member on a grant. She later resigned as co-administrator of the grant, asserting her relationship with the faculty member affected her psychologically. The administrator sued the college in a federal district court, alleging a hostile work environment based on sex. The court found the incidents of allegedly harassing conduct were all facially neutral. The faculty member never made any sexual remarks to the administrator and did not touch her. **The administrator admitted that the faculty member's conduct toward her was not romantic in nature.** Instead, she characterized it as "bizarre." As there was not enough evidence to establish sexual harassment, the court dismissed the case. On appeal, the U.S. Court of Appeals, Second Circuit, found that while the faculty member's conduct was unwelcome or inappropriate, no reasonable jury could find that it took place because of gender. There was no evidence that her conduct was based on sex, and thus no hostile work environment under Title VII. No "adverse employment action" supported a retaliation claim, and the judgment was affirmed. *Guarino v. St. John Fisher College*, 321 Fed.Appx. 55 (2d Cir. 2008).

◆ *A court rejected a police officer's claim that a Pennsylvania university discriminated against her based on her need to produce breast milk at work.*

The university granted the officer's request for permission to express milk during breaks after she returned from maternity leave. However, supervisors refused to provide her a courtesy transport from her foot patrol to headquarters, where she expressed the milk. The officer claimed she was treated differently from colleagues in other ways and was assigned to menial tasks. She quit and sued the university in federal district court for race and pregnancy discrimination. The court held for the university, and the officer appealed.

The U.S. Court of Appeals, Third Circuit, explained that **to prove she was subjected to a hostile work environment, the officer had to show harassment that was so "severe or pervasive" that it changed the terms and conditions of her employment and created an abusive environment**. In addition, she needed to show she was subjected to conduct that was offensive both subjectively and objectively. It was clear that the conduct in this case was subjectively offensive. However, the officer did not show she was subjected to conduct that a reasonable person in her position would have found to be hostile or abusive. Other officers who were placed on light duty were also assigned menial tasks. The university provided breaks to express breast milk and switched the officer to a patrol route that was closer to headquarters. As no reasonable jury could conclude the university created a hostile work environment in violation of Title VII, the court upheld the judgment. *Page v. Trustees of the Univ. of Pennsylvania*, 222 Fed.Appx. 144 (3d Cir. 2007).

◆ *A Mississippi federal district court held an employee failed to establish a university did not promote her because of her sex.*

The university did not select the employee for the position of office manager. **She insisted that she was not chosen because she refused sexual advances by her supervisor.** The employee sued the university in a federal district court for discrimination based on her sex, claiming a violation of Title VII. The university argued the employee failed to establish sex discrimination because it selected another female applicant for the position. The supervisor testified that 20 applicants applied for the position and that he interviewed 16 females. The court rejected the employee's arguments. It said her alleged failure to accept the supervisor's advances were insufficient to support her claim that he sexually harassed her. *Turner v. Jackson State Univ.*, No. 3:04CV623LS, 2006 WL 1139931 (S.D. Miss. 4/25/06).

◆ *A federal district court declined to dismiss a Wisconsin university employee's sexual harassment claim.*

The employee claimed her manager harassed her repeatedly during the three years that she worked for a university bookstore. She sued the university in a federal district court, alleging his conduct violated Title VII. The university admitted there had been a touching incident but denied anything further. It argued the manager's conduct was not sexual harassment under Title VII. The court held each case must be analyzed on its own facts to determine whether the conduct is actionable. **Factors to consider include the frequency and severity of the discriminatory conduct, whether the conduct was physically threatening or humiliating or merely offensive, and whether the harassment interfered with the employee's job performance.** The court held the employee presented enough evidence to proceed to trial. While each incident may not have seemed physically or verbally abusive, the conduct continued for a considerable time. The court denied the dismissal motion and set the case for trial. *Gray v. Board of Regents of the Univ. of Wisconsin System*, No. 04-C-562, 2006 WL 314416 (E.D. Wis. 2/9/06).

◆ *An Illinois university did not subject an employee to a sexually hostile environment or treat her differently from her male counterparts.*

The employee worked for the university as a building services worker. She claimed male supervisors called her degrading and obscene names, although not to her face. The employee also asserted that a male employee asked her to join him on his boat for "a weekend of drinking and other things." School officials suspended her for insubordination and failure to follow departmental guidelines and practices. The employee sued the university in a federal district court, alleging it violated Title VII for allowing a sexually hostile environment.

The court found the employee did not present any evidence that the university treated her less favorably than the males. While there had been offensive conduct, there was no showing this was frequent, severe, threatening or humiliating. On appeal, the U.S. Court of Appeals, Seventh Circuit, held that **to establish a claim for Title VII sex discrimination, there had to be "adverse employment action."** Adverse employment action typically involves an economic injury, like suspension without pay. Because the employee voluntarily left her job, she was not subjected to economic injury. **An employment action is "adverse" only if it alters the terms and conditions of employment.** As the university did not change the terms or conditions of the employee's job, she could not prevail in a Title VII case and the judgment was affirmed. *Whittaker v. Northern Illinois Univ.*, 424 F.3d 640 (7th Cir. 2005).

◆ *An Alabama university did not violate Title VII when it declined to renew the contract of a former dean of students.*

The dean claimed her supervisor made indirect sexual advances and comments toward her. The supervisor told the dean he wanted to come visit her at home sometime, and that women sleep with their bosses to keep their jobs and get promotions. The supervisor denied he made sexual advances or comments toward the dean. After a poor performance evaluation, the supervisor told the dean the university was not renewing her contract.

The dean sued the college in a federal district court for violating Title VII. The court held sexual harassment is a form of sex discrimination which violates Title VII. **Unwelcome sexual advances, requests for sexual favors, and comments of a sexual nature may constitute sexual harassment if they affect an individual's employment, or create an intimidating, hostile or offensive work environment.** The court found the dean did not present evidence that the supervisor threatened to fire her if she refused to comply. She never let the supervisor know she was uncomfortable about his sexual remarks. No evidence supported the dean's contention that the decision not to renew her contract was connected to sexual advances. Even after the dean turned down her supervisor's advances, he appointed her dean of students. The court granted the university's motion for summary judgment. On appeal, the U.S. Court of Appeals, Eleventh Circuit, found the lower court had correctly held the dean did not satisfy the burden of proof framework established by *McDonnell Douglas Corp. v. Green.* It affirmed the judgment for the college. *Hammons v. George C. Wallace State Community College*, 174 Fed.Appx. 459 (11th Cir. 2005).

C. Equal Pay Issues

The Equal Pay Act (EPA) requires that employers pay males and females the same wages for equal work. Employees are protected by the EPA as long as the employer is engaged in an enterprise affecting interstate commerce. The EPA has been interpreted by the courts to require only that the jobs under comparison be "substantially" equal. Strict equality of the jobs under comparison is not required.

The EPA requires equal pay for jobs involving "equal skill, effort, and responsibility, and which are performed under similar working conditions, except where such payment is made pursuant to (i) a seniority system; (ii) a merit system; (iii) a system which measures earnings by quantity or quality of production; or (iv) a differential based on any other factor other than sex." Many cases alleging disparate pay rates based on sex include claims under Title VII and analogous state laws. If employers can prove that the difference in pay is for a reason other than the difference in sex, they do not have to provide the same pay and benefits. It is for the employer to show that such a factor exists and that it is the real reason for the difference.

◆ *A Wisconsin university lecturer earned a trial to determine if a university violated the Equal Pay Act by paying males more than she received.*

The lecturer was an untenured senior lecturer in the university's business school who was not on a tenure track. She taught business statistics, a required course for all business school students. Three of her male colleagues earned more money per course than she did. Two taught management courses and one taught a marketing course. The lecturer asked the department chair to perform a gender equity review of her salary. The dean concluded her pay was appropriate. The lecturer sued the university in a federal district court, alleging it violated the EPA by paying more money to the male lecturers.

The court explained that to determine whether the university violated the EPA, it must compare job requirements, not individuals. Under the EPA, the university could lawfully pay the male lecturers more than the female lecturer based on seniority, a merit system, a system which measured earnings by production, or another reason besides sex. The university argued that the difference between the lecturer's salary and the salaries of the other three lecturers was valid because she did not teach in the core area of the business school. According to the lecturer, the university failed to prove her skill, effort and responsibility were different from those of the male lecturers. The court found a genuine issue of fact concerning whether the lecturer and the male lecturers had the same skill and responsibility and put forth the same effort. For that reason, it denied the university's motion for dismissal and ordered that the case proceed to trial. *Mullins v. Board of Regents of the Univ. of Wisconsin System*, No. 05-C-581-S, 2006 WL 641079 (W.D. Wis. 3/10/06).

◆ *An Indiana university did not discriminate against a female professor who was denied a salary award given to some of her male peers.*

A university task force evaluated gender inequities at the university, with a particular focus on salary differences. After conducting a review, the task force reported that male professors tended to have higher mean salaries than female professors at all rank levels. It recommended a professional excellence program to reward tenured full professors who demonstrated excellence in scholarship, teaching and service. The professor was the only woman eligible in the college of liberal arts and sciences the first two years the awards were offered. The university made the awards only to male professors for both years. The professor filed a grievance with the faculty appeals committee, then sued the university for sex discrimination. A federal district court held for the university.

The professor appealed to the U.S. Court of Appeals, Seventh Circuit, which agreed with her argument that the denial of an award was an adverse employment action by the university. Adverse employment actions include denial of a raise, failure to promote, and termination. The court found the award was not a raise, but more closely resembled a bonus. The university contended it had a legitimate nondiscriminatory reason for not paying the award to the professor. For both years, it determined other professors exceeded her overall performance in the areas of teaching, scholarship and service. The professor alleged these reasons were a cover-up for sex discrimination. She said the existence of an "old boys' club" proved discrimination. **But the Seventh Circuit found the existence of an old boys' club did not in itself establish a cover-up. It accepted the university's reasons as legitimate and nondiscriminatory, and affirmed the judgment.** *Farrell v. Butler Univ.*, 421 F.3d 609 (7th Cir. 2005).

◆ *The U.S. Court of Appeals, Ninth Circuit, held a female professor failed to show a California university violated the Equal Pay Act.*

The professor claimed the university paid her male colleagues substantially more money than it paid her for the same kind of work. She sued the university in a federal district court for violating the EPA. The professor specifically pointed to a discrepancy between herself and the male employees in annual raises. The court dismissed the case, finding she did not show her total compensation was less than the average total compensation earned by her male colleagues for substantially equal work. **The court said the comparison of annual raises alone does not violate the EPA, which compares "wages." The act defines wages to include all payments made to an employee and all forms of compensation.** The professor appealed to the Ninth Circuit, which agreed with the reasoning of the district court and affirmed the judgment. *Ghirardo v. Univ. of Southern California*, 156 Fed. Appx. 914 (9th Cir. 2005).

◆ *A Minnesota assistant women's hockey coach lost his EPA and Title VII action because he did not prove he suffered any adverse employment action.*

The assistant coach learned the university paid him $13,000 per year less than a female assistant coach. He complained to the director of women's athletics, and then asserted the head coach retaliated against him and gave him a poor performance evaluation. The male assistant coach resigned and sued the university in a federal district court for EPA and Title VII violations. **The court noted the female assistant coach performed many job duties that the male assistant coach did not perform, such as recruiting and public relations. Their positions were not "substantially equal" under the EPA.**

The male assistant coach appealed to the Eighth Circuit, which upheld the EPA ruling. **It also rejected his Title VII retaliation claim because the performance evaluation was not an "adverse employment action."** The assistant's discomfort with the situation was not enough to create an adverse employment action under Title VII. As his working conditions were not so intolerable as to force his resignation, the court affirmed the judgment for the university. *Horn v. Univ. of Minnesota*, 362 F.3d 1042 (8th Cir. 2004).

◆ *An Ohio university did not discriminate or retaliate against a female professor who was paid less than a male counterpart.*

The university hired the professor at $2,000 less per year than a newly hired male professor in the same department. When she learned of the salary difference two years later, the university honored her request to begin to adjust her salary so it would eventually equal his pay. Three years later, the professor was promoted to full professor. She took sabbatical leave, and over the next three and a half years, she taught at the university only one semester. The professor then sued the university in a federal court, stating her salary was lower than eight other full-time professors in her department and $13,314 less than the male professor who was hired at the time of her hire. The court held for the university, and the professor appealed. The Sixth Circuit held that **to prevail under a Title VII sex discrimination claim, the professor had to prove she was treated differently from similarly situated members of a non-protected class.** The court found the university offered legitimate, nondiscriminatory reasons for paying her less than the male professor. The disparity was based on merit differences awarded during her absences and budgetary constraints. Because the professor had no evidence to counter the university's nondiscriminatory reasons, the court affirmed the judgment. *Harrison-Pepper v. Miami Univ.*, 103 Fed.Appx. 596 (6th Cir. 2004).

◆ *A Louisiana professor failed to show an EPA violation because she did not show her job was "substantially equal" to a male professor's.*

The professor worked as an adjunct for nine years before becoming a tenured associate. The university turned her down twice for a full professorship before doing so after 11 years. She claimed the university violated the EPA by paying her less than a male professor doing the same work she did and that she was more experienced than anyone else in her department. The professor sued the university in a state court for EPA violations. The case went before a jury, which rejected the university's evidence that the pay disparity reflected the different starting dates and annual performance reports of the two professors. The university appealed to the Court of Appeal of Louisiana, which held the **professor did not show her job was substantially equal to that of the male professor or involved the same skills**. Because of this, she failed to show an EPA violation, and the court reversed the judgment. *Ramelow v. Board of Trustees of Univ. of Louisiana*, 870 So.2d 415 (La. Ct. App. 2004).

D. Pregnancy Discrimination

Pregnancy discrimination is prohibited by the Pregnancy Discrimination Act (42 U.S.C. § 2000e(k)), which amended Title VII. The act specifies that discrimination "on the basis of sex" includes discrimination on the basis of pregnancy. It also requires employees to treat pregnant women the same as other employees for "all employment-related purposes" – including benefits.

◆ *A Mississippi college lab assistant was unable to convince a federal court that she was fired because of her pregnancy.*

The assistant became pregnant near the time of her hiring. After five months of work, she was fired due to performance problems. The assistant then sued the college in a federal district court for pregnancy discrimination. **Although she claimed she was fired to avoid the cost of placing her on maternity leave, the court noted she was not yet entitled to take leave.** Had the assistant kept the job, she would have been entitled to eight days of paid sick leave – about $923. The court held "it would be absurd for an employer to terminate someone just to avoid paying a mere $923, especially when that amount had already been budgeted as part of her salary." There was no merit to her case, so the college was entitled to pretrial judgment. *Healy v. Tougaloo College*, No. 3:10CV86TSL-FKB, 2011 WL 915050 (S.D. Miss. 3/15/11).

◆ *A federal district court refused to grant summary judgment to a university accused of retaliating against an adjunct professor for filing an earlier lawsuit.*

In a federal district court action filed in 1998, the adjunct professor claimed the university did not reappoint her because of her pregnancy. Her Title VII suit was settled in 2000, with the university agreeing to appoint the adjunct to teaching jobs for spring and fall in 2001. But as a result of a clerical error, she was not offered the fall assignment, and she threatened to sue to enforce the settlement agreement. Three years later, the adjunct did so, this time claiming the university declined to reappoint her in retaliation for the first action. The court found there was a possible causal connection between the first lawsuit and the decision not to reappoint her some time later. In addition, there was evidence that the professor who decided not to reappoint the adjunct played a role in evaluating her and had objected to the terms of the settlement.

There was enough evidence for a jury to infer retaliation in this case. Also, although the college claimed the decision not to reappoint the adjunct was based on student complaints, it did not produce any written records of complaints. **There was evidence that professors with equal or lower student evaluation scores were reappointed.** Thus, pretrial judgment was improper. *Rumain v. Baruch College of City Univ. of New York*, No. 06 Civ. 8256 (PKC) (MHD), 2008 WL 4866019 (S.D.N.Y. 11/6/08).

◆ *A pregnancy discrimination claim by an Oklahoma childcare employee could proceed to trial.*

The employee worked as a childcare attendant at a university childcare center. She claimed that after she became pregnant, her manager refused to consult with her and allowed other employees to harass her about her pregnancy. The employee gave her supervisors statements from a physician advising her to stop working because of pregnancy complications. She took FMLA leave and returned to work after the childbirth. The employee then gave her supervisors doctors' notes stating she could not lift more than 20 pounds, which meant she could pick up infants but not toddlers. The center told her she could not work with restrictions. The employee sued the university for pregnancy discrimination. The university argued she could not perform the job because lifting was required. The court held **the university did not conduct an independent evaluation to determine if the weight restrictions actually prevented the employee from performing her job duties**. It denied the university pretrial judgment and set the case for trial. *Borchert v. The State of Oklahoma*, No. 04CV0839 CVE/SAJ, 2006 WL 228913 (N.D. Okla. 1/30/06).

◆ *Columbia University did not subject an employee to "adverse employment action" by changing her supervisor.*

The employee worked as an associate director for the university until the associate dean decided to restructure her department. She suspected the restructuring was based on her pregnancy. She told the associate director she was having a high-risk pregnancy, and took disability leave. Meanwhile, the associate dean criticized her performance. The employee sued the university in a federal district court for pregnancy discrimination under Title VII, the Pregnancy Discrimination Act, and state law. The court found the employee did not prove the university subjected her to adverse employment action. It said **the assignment to report to a different supervisor was not a demotion or an "adverse employment action."** The executive director was senior to the employee in title and grade, and the change did not affect her title, grade, salary or benefits. The court explained that criticizing an employee was not an adverse employment action. **"Adverse employment actions" include demotion, termination, or a change that results in significantly diminished material responsibilities.** As the employee did not establish any of these, the court awarded summary judgment in favor of Columbia. *Palomo v. Trustees of Columbia Univ. in City of New York*, No. 03 Civ. 7853 (DLC), 2005 WL 1683586 (S.D.N.Y. 7/20/05).

III. RELIGIOUS DISCRIMINATION

Title VII generally prohibits religious discrimination. However, religious hiring preferences are permitted if the institution is substantially "owned, supported, controlled, or managed" by a religious organization or if the curriculum "is directed toward the propagation of a particular religion."

◆   *A Seventh-Day Adventist who worked as a University of Tennessee (UT) coordinator could have a trial concerning her religious accommodation request.*

Soon after she started working for UT, the coordinator told her supervisor her religion prevented her from working from sundown on Fridays to sundown on Saturdays. This created a problem because an emergency cell phone had to be monitored on weekends. The coordinator suggested that others cover the emergency cell phone on weekends while she worked more days during the week. But the proposal was rejected, and she refused other options. UT finally determined the coordinator could not fulfill her job duties, and her employment was terminated. She sued UT in a federal district court for Title VII violations. When the case reached the U.S. Court of Appeals, Sixth Circuit, it explained that **Title VII requires employers to accommodate employee religious practices unless doing so would create an undue hardship**. Whether a religious accommodation poses an undue hardship to the employer is generally a question for a jury. In this case, a fact question was present as to whether UT met its duty to attempt to provide reasonable accommodations for the coordinator. No evidence showed the requested accommodation would be so disruptive as to create an undue hardship for UT. As a result, the case was returned to the lower court for further proceedings. *Crider v. Univ. of Tennessee, Knoxville*, 492 Fed.Appx. 609 (6th Cir. 2012).

◆   *A federal court refused to grant an Ohio college pretrial judgment on a Muslim professor's abusive work environment claim.*

The professor became Imam and religious advisor for the college's Muslim student association. He accused his department head of excluding him from meetings and other events and calling him a terrorist. The two yelled at each other in a department meeting, and the professor emailed the dean, asking him to "resolve what has become a long and sustained pattern of workplace harassment." An investigative panel found no professional misconduct, but reported **years of miscommunication, staffing changes, and conflict had caused the department to become dysfunctional**. The panel recommended that the dean create a solution. The professor claimed the dean failed to do so and filed a federal district court action against the college, alleging it subjected him to a hostile work environment. The court held that if the claims were true, a jury would have to decide whether the behavior was sufficiently severe and pervasive to create an abusive working environment. For this reason, the court refused to dismiss the case. *Yedes v. Oberlin College*, No. 1-11 CV 465, 2012 WL 1004726 (N.D. Ohio 3/23/12).

◆   *A Texas community college groundskeeping employee could not convince the state court of appeals that he was fired because of his religion.*

The employee was a Catholic who had worked as a groundskeeper and foreman for 24 years at the community college. He said that when he applied for a promotion to be grounds manager, the department director asked if he was Catholic, then denounced Catholics as "a bunch of liars." Another employee received the promotion, and the employee said the director kept making anti-Catholic remarks to him. After repeated conflicts with the director and another groundskeeping foreman, the employee called the director a vulgar word and was promptly fired for insubordination. The employee sued the college in the state court system for discrimination, harassment and retaliation based on his religion. The case reached the Court of Appeals of Texas, which found the college had a valid nondiscriminatory reason for firing him. **The college had justified the insubordination charge because the employee had called his supervisor a vulgar word.** This was not a pretext for anti-Catholic discrimination. In addition, the employee acknowledged that calling his boss "pendejo" was a terminable offense. A lower court judgment for the community college was affirmed. *Leija v. Laredo Community College*, No. 04-10-00410-CV, 2011 WL 1499440 (Tex. Ct. App. 4/20/11).

◆   *A professor who refused to openly support gay students may pursue Title VII and equal protection claims against a Pennsylvania university.*

Faculty members in the university's department of social work asked the professor to express her support for the gay community. She declined, saying this would conflict with her religious beliefs. According to the professor, the other faculty members targeted her for discrimination, refused to collaborate on projects with her, and excluded her from meetings. She also said she was denied a tenure-track post as an assistant professor because of her stance. In a federal court lawsuit against the university, the professor claimed violation of Title VII. She added claims alleging speech and equal protection violations. The court dismissed the Title VII claims against the university officials, as there is no individual liability under Title VII. But **the claims against the university could proceed, as the professor claimed she was subjected to harassment due to her religious beliefs, not due to her heterosexual orientation.** On the other hand, the speech claims were dismissed, since they were based on employment grievances that were not protected by the First Amendment. Finally, the court refused to dismiss equal protection claims based on her assertion that an applicant for a position she sought did not share her religious beliefs and was treated more favorably than she was. *Gadling-Cole v. West Chester Univ.*, No. 11-0796 (JBS), 2012 WL 1075809 (E.D. Pa. 3/30/12).

◆ *A federal court held a trial was needed to decide if a Texas university violated Title VII by firing staff members who chanted at a colleague's cubicle.*

Three administrative support staff workers decided to stay after work one night to discuss a problem colleague. They rubbed olive oil on the metal doorway to the colleague's cubicle and chanted for demons to leave the area. They then said "I command you demons to leave [the colleague], you vicious evil dogs get the hell out of here in the name of Jesus, get the hell out of [the colleague]." They also said "amen" and "yes, Lord." One of the workers reported the incident to a supervisor, and the matter was investigated. The two workers who did not report the incident were discharged for harassment of a co-worker and for "blatant disregard for university property." They sued the university in a federal district court for religious discrimination under Title VII.

According to the university, there were valid, nondiscriminatory reasons to fire the workers. But the court found no disregard for university property, as the oil did not damage the cubicle. Any harassment claim was undercut by the fact that the colleague was unaware of the incident at the time and for two months afterward. **According to the court, praying for someone who did not know she was being prayed for was unlikely to constitute harassment.** And the university's nondiscrimination policy permitted religious expression, even if it might be offensive to others. There was evidence that the university only talked to employees for yelling at the colleague, but fired them for praying about her after hours. As a result, the court held a trial was necessary. *Shatkin v. Univ. of Texas at Arlington*, No. 4:06-CV-882-Y, 2010 WL 2730585 (N.D. Tex. 7/9/10).

◆ *An Illinois university defeated a religious discrimination claim by a Muslim professor, but a federal district court let his retaliation claim proceed.*

A probationary, tenure-track professor at Illinois State University (ISU) learned that another Muslim employee was not selected for a position, and became involved in an internal investigation. The professor believed his low student ratings were based on prejudice against him because of his color and national origin. When the professor learned he would not be offered another contract, he sued ISU in a federal district court. The court held for ISU on the professor's race, national origin and religious discrimination claims because he "failed to demonstrate a convincing mosaic of circumstantial evidence" indicating discrimination. He had a history of poor scores, and his ratings were below the school average. But the court found enough evidence of discrimination to proceed with the retaliation claim. **He complained of illegal discrimination and adverse employment action that was linked to his complaint.** As a result, the retaliation claim survived dismissal. *Abuelyaman v. Illinois State Univ.*, No. 07-1151, 2009 WL 3837012 (C.D. Ill. 11/13/09).

◆ *A physical altercation, not improper discrimination, motivated the discharge of a New York university employee.*

A supervisor accused the employee of punching the time card of a co-worker who was not at work. Their argument culminated in physical contact. The employee's union filed a grievance on her behalf but later declined to arbitrate it. The university determined the employee started the fight, but she denied this and sued the university in a federal district court for discrimination

based on her race, age, religion and color. The court held the employee did not
state a claim of age discrimination. Because the university concluded she had
struck the supervisor and that the supervisor had not struck her back, the two
were not subject to the same disciplinary standards. There was no evidence to
support the employee's claim that the person who investigated the incident was
biased against her for any reason. The employee admitted that she struck the
supervisor, and that act justified her termination.

The employee asserted she was discriminated against based on her
Christian faith, and claimed that religious materials she left on a break room
table were thrown to the floor. **The court found these incidents did not prove
religious bias by the university. It rejected the employee's remaining
claims and dismissed the case.** On appeal, the U.S. Court of Appeals, Second
Circuit, held the employee raised an inference of discrimination because she
claimed the supervisor had struck her first. However, even if this was true, she
did not show the reasons given for her discharge were false. There was also no
evidence of age discrimination, or any showing that an investigation of the
incident had been biased. As the employee did not show the explanation for her
discharge was a pretext for discrimination, the judgment for the university was
affirmed. *Mincey v. Univ. of Rochester*, 262 Fed.Appx. 319 (2d Cir. 2008).

◆   *A Texas court reinstated a former university librarian's claim that she was
discharged based on her Christian faith.*

The librarian claimed she was subjected to a hostile work environment
based on her religion. She stated she was asked to view a computer image of
"Jesus in a satan costume," and was subjected to anti-Christian comments such
as "Christianity is a 'cop out'" and "Catholics are paying for forgiveness."
According to the librarian, her supervisor instructed her to turn off her
Christian radio programs when others were present in the library. She
complained to a school dean about the supervisor's conduct, but about five
months later, the university discharged her. In a state court lawsuit against the
university, the librarian claimed she was fired based on her religion and in
retaliation for complaining about a hostile work environment. She also asserted
a claim for hostile work environment. The court held for the university.

On appeal, the Court of Appeals of Texas reversed the judgment on the
religious discrimination claim. Although the lower court had found it was
untimely filed, the court of appeals found this was error. On the other hand, the
hostile work environment claim failed because the administrative complaint
did not identify any acts of harassment occurring within 180 days from the date
of the complaint. **The court affirmed the judgment on the retaliation claim,
based on the delay of over five months between the time the librarian filed
a complaint with the dean and the date of her discharge.** Without more
evidence that her complaint caused her discharge, the retaliation claim failed.
Bartosh v. Sam Houston State Univ., 259 S.W.3d 317 (Tex. Ct. App. 2008).

◆   *A Jewish professor failed to show she was denied tenure by an Illinois
University on the basis of her religion.*

A university committee recommended the professor for tenure, but a dean noted a personality conflict and warned her not to politicize the tenure process. During a meeting, the dean told a university vice president that the professor had missed work and university events on Jewish holidays. The dean recommended against tenure, citing her lack of service on committees and negative comments by students. The dean also pointed to declining enrollment in her department. The university committee recommended against her tenure, and the university vice president and president agreed. The professor filed an unsuccessful grievance with the university, then commenced a federal district court action for discrimination. The court held for the university.

On appeal, the U.S. Court of Appeals, Seventh Circuit, noted that the professor had accused the dean of religious bias. However, no higher-ranking persons were accused of this. The dean explained that tenure was denied for nondiscriminatory reasons such as the professor's lack of committee service, negative student comments and declining enrollment in her program. The dean's allegedly biased comments did not show these reasons were false. **The dean was a subordinate participant in the tenure process, making it unlikely that there was a causal connection between a discriminatory motive and the denial of tenure.** There was not enough evidence to show the reasons given for the denial were a cover for discrimination. Finally, the court affirmed the rejection of a claim of tortious interference with prospective employment. No evidence showed the dean had acted recklessly or with an intent to injure the professor. The decision of the district court was affirmed. *Adelman-Reyes v. Saint Xavier Univ.*, 500 F.3d 662 (7th Cir. 2007).

◆ *A Missouri university did not discriminate against a doctor by refusing to rehire him because of license suspensions and criminal conduct.*

The doctor sued the university in a federal district court, alleging it violated Title VII when it did not hire him because the Catholic Church did not approve of his divorce. The university stated it did not rehire him because of medical license suspensions in Missouri and Illinois, criminal conduct, failure to provide a complete residency application, and past unprofessional conduct. **The court found the university had legitimate nondiscriminatory reasons for not rehiring the doctor.** He presented no evidence to show the decision was motivated by discrimination instead of the reasons it offered, and the case was dismissed. In a brief memorandum opinion, the U.S. Court of Appeals, Eighth Circuit, held that even if the doctor had shown discrimination, the university produced sufficient nondiscriminatory evidence to deserve pretrial judgment. The district court judgment was affirmed. *Kaminsky v. St. Louis Univ. School of Medicine*, 226 Fed.Appx. 646 (8th Cir. 2007).

◆ *A Georgia state university did not violate a Christian cheerleading coordinator's constitutional right to the free exercise of her religion.*

Two Jewish cheerleaders complained to the athletic department that the coordinator discriminated against them because of their religion. They said the coordinator treated them unfavorably and used her position to encourage students to pray, study the Bible and engage in other religious practices. The university placed the coordinator on probation, and it informed her she would be discharged if she continued to violate the university's policy on religious discrimination. She read a statement to the cheerleading squad, stating a Jewish cheerleader had accused her of religious discrimination and that the claim was without merit. The university fired the coordinator, who filed a federal lawsuit.

A federal district court held the university was entitled to Eleventh Amendment immunity. The terms of the coordinator's probation letter simply mandated that she keep her religious activities separate from the cheerleading program. **As the university did not compromise her religious beliefs or prevent her from doing anything essential to exercising her religion, the court dismissed the case.** *Braswell v. Board of Regents of the Univ. System of Georgia*, 369 F. Supp. 2d 1371 (N.D. Ga. 2005).

◆   *A Minnesota business college discharged an instructor for his poor performance, not his Muslim religion.*

The college hired the instructor to teach computer programming. There were soon complaints about his teaching. A student complained that the instructor did not respect students and refused to answer their questions. Several students claimed his presentation and lecture styles were ineffective. The college held an annual review and rated the instructor as "meeting expectations" in all categories. His next annual review was unfavorable. The university placed the instructor on probation and told him if he did not improve his performance, he would be discharged. After he failed to follow the conditions of his performance improvement plan, the college discharged him. The instructor sued the college in a federal district court, alleging it discriminated against him based on religion. The college argued the instructor failed to adequately perform his job. **The court agreed, finding evidence that he did not meet the legitimate employment expectations of the college. The college was entitled to summary judgment.** *Eldeeb v. Career Educ. Corp.*, No. Civ. 04-2932PAMRLE, 2005 WL 2105500 (D. Minn. 8/30/05).

◆   *An Orthodox Jewish professor's claims of religious discrimination, hostile work environment and retaliation were allowed to go to trial.*

An Orthodox Jewish professor at a New Jersey college said her department chair began to count days she missed for religious holidays against her sick time. She also was charged a sick day for observing a Jewish holiday that fell on a day she was not scheduled to teach. The professor was continually asked why she could not attend meetings on Friday nights and Saturdays, even though she said she wanted to observe the Sabbath. After her employment termination, she sued the college under Title VII and the New Jersey Law Against Discrimination for religious discrimination, hostile work environment and retaliation. A U.S. district court granted pretrial judgment to the university. On appeal, the U.S. Court of Appeals, Third Circuit, held the district court applied the wrong standard to the hostile work environment claim. The court should have asked **whether a reasonable fact finder could view the evidence as showing that the professor's treatment was attributable to her religion**. Although the college provided legitimate nondiscriminatory reasons for its decision not to retain the professor, she was able to cast doubt on the legitimacy of those reasons such that the lawsuit could proceed. *Abramson v. William Paterson College of New Jersey*, 260 F.3d 265 (3d Cir. 2001).

IV. AGE DISCRIMINATION

A. ADEA

The Age Discrimination in Employment Act (ADEA), 29 U.S.C. § 621, et seq., prohibits age discrimination against individuals who are at least 40 years old. As part of the Fair Labor Standards Act, it applies to institutions with 20 or more employees and which affect interstate commerce. State human rights acts may offer additional protection against discrimination on the basis of age.

◆   *The U.S. Supreme Court held employees may bring "disparate impact" actions under the ADEA. Disparate impact actions do not require proof of intentional age discrimination. Instead, they require an employee to show an employment policy has the effect of discriminating on the basis of age.*

The city of Jackson, Mississippi increased the salaries of all employees in 1999. Those with under five years of experience received comparatively higher raises than more experienced employees. The city justified the action as a way to remain competitive and "ensure equitable compensation to all employees."

A group of veteran police officers, most over 40 years old, claimed the city's action constituted discrimination on the basis of age. The officers sued the city in a federal district court for ADEA violations, alleging both disparate treatment and disparate impact. The court held for the city, and the U.S. Court of Appeals, Fifth Circuit, affirmed the judgment. The Supreme Court agreed to review the disparate impact claim. It compared the ADEA with Title VII of the Civil Rights Act of 1964. **Except for substitution of the word "age" for "race, color, religion, sex, or national origin," the language of the ADEA and Title VII was identical.** Title VII disparate impact claims have long been recognized by the Court. The Court stated the ADEA authorizes potential recovery for disparate impact cases, in a manner comparable to Title VII disparate impact claims for race, religion or sex discrimination. **Employees alleging an employer practice has a disparate impact on a class of employees need not show the practice is intentional.** While the Court held the officers were entitled to bring a disparate impact claim under the ADEA, they could not show the city violated the ADEA in this case. The Court noted the ADEA's coverage for disparate impact is narrower than that of Title VII. Under the ADEA, an employer can treat workers differently if the employer is motivated by reasonable factors other than age. Congress narrowed the ADEA's scope because there is often a connection between age and ability to perform a job. The city's decision to make itself competitive in the job market was based on a reasonable factor other than age. As the employees could not prove disparate impact, the Court affirmed the judgment. *Smith v. City of Jackson,* 544 U.S. 228, 125 S.Ct. 1536, 161 L.Ed.2d 410 (2005).

◆   *A veteran Texas college executive assistant who lost her job to a much younger employee made out a valid age discrimination claim.*

After 31 years as an executive assistant to five college presidents, the college reassigned the employee to an administrative associate position and cut her annual pay by more than $15,000. Her replacement was 15 years younger and had worked for the college for only two years. The employee sued the college in a federal court for age discrimination. The college said its action was needed because of her strong links to the previous administration. It said the current president distrusted the employee based on reports that she had complained about his policies and proposed changes. The court agreed with the employee that her service to five prior administrations undercut the college's defense. She also claimed she was more qualified than her replacement as she had a bachelor's degree, while her replacement did not. For these reasons, **the court found enough evidence for a jury to conclude that the college's stated reasons for the reassignment were a pretext for age discrimination.** The court denied the college's motion for judgment. *Robinson v. Jarvis Christian College*, No. 6:11-cv-073, 2011 WL 5080167 (E.D. Tex. 10/25/11).

◆   *A university administrative assistant failed to prove that the non-renewal of her contract was motivated by race or national origin discrimination.*

The administrative assistant began working for the university in 1995 when she was already over 40. She received good performance evaluations until a new dean arrived at her department in 2000. The dean later recommended that the university not rehire the assistant. She was replaced by a person of Hispanic origin. The administrative assistant sued the university in a federal district court for race, national origin and age discrimination. She also claimed officials retaliated against her and engaged in a conspiracy to discriminate against her.

The court held for the university, and the assistant appealed to the U.S. Court of Appeals, Third Circuit. The court held the allegations did not prove race discrimination. An assertion that the university wanted to diversify its staff was purely speculative, and the fact that the assistant dean and president were not Caucasian failed to prove racial discrimination. **There was no evidence that the university's affirmative action guidelines had been improperly applied or that the timing of the opening for the administrative assistant's old job was suspicious.** The age discrimination claim failed because the university produced evidence of unsatisfactory job performance. Despite the positive job evaluations from some supervisors, the court found the administrative assistant did not prove the negative ones from the other supervisor were a pretext for discrimination. The court affirmed the judgment for the university. *Hunter v. Rowan Univ.*, 299 Fed.Appx. 190 (3d Cir. 2008).

◆   *The U.S. Court of Appeals, Eighth Circuit, held that replacement by a substantially younger person is necessary to prove age discrimination.*

A Minnesota university promoted an employee to serve as a dean at the age of 62. He had a heart attack three years later, and learned of rumors indicating he wanted to retire and that a plan had been developed to replace him. The dean denied the rumors in a formal letter to the university president. He stated he was profoundly disturbed by the rumors and accused the president of trying to force his resignation. The next year, the university reorganized, and a newly hired provost/vice president soon recommended replacing the dean. The reasons stated were the dean's creation of a divisive environment, ineffective handling of conflicts, and favoritism and bias in personnel evaluations. The dean's permanent replacement was 64 years old at the time of his appointment. The dean sued the university in a federal district court for ADEA violations. The court held for the university, and the dean appealed.

The Eighth Circuit explained that the ADEA bars employers from taking age-based adverse employment actions against employees who are 40 or older. **The U.S. Supreme Court held in a 1996 case that the replacement of a 68-year-old by a 65-year-old was "very thin evidence" of discrimination.** The Eighth Circuit held the dean did not prove age discrimination based on his replacement by an employee who was only two-and-a-half years younger than he was. **The university had legitimate nondiscriminatory reasons for demoting him, and the court did not "sit as a super-personnel department and second guess" its decisions.** The dean's other discrimination and retaliation claims failed for the same reasons. The court affirmed the judgment for the university. *Lewis v. St. Cloud State Univ.*, 467 F.3d 1133 (8th Cir. 2006).

◆   *A federal district court held a 56-year-old professor was fired because he was not qualified and did not follow university procedures.*

The professor had taught night classes as an adjunct professor in the university's college of business (COB) since 1985. His academic background was in the field of education. In 2002, the university hired a new dean for its COB and prepared for an accreditation visit. The university took steps to ensure that adjunct faculty were teaching courses in which they had academic and professional credentials. As a result, the university stopped using the professor to teach courses at its COB. He was given the chance to teach marketing courses at the university, but he failed to comply with a policy that required students to purchase their books from the student bookstore.

The university then discharged the professor, and he filed a federal court action for violation of the ADEA. **The court held age was not a factor in the university's decision. Instead, the discharge was based on the professor's lack of qualifications to teach the classes he formerly taught.** He also failed to order course books through the university's book store, as required by university policy. There was no violation of the ADEA. *Anhalt v. Cardinal Stritch Univ.*, No. 04-C-1052, 2006 WL 3692631 (E.D. Wis. 12/12/06).

◆   *The Supreme Court held state employees could not sue their employers under the ADEA.*

Two associate professors at the University of Montevallo sued the university in an Alabama federal court under the ADEA. They alleged that the university had discriminated against them on the basis of their age, that it had retaliated against them for filing charges with the Equal Employment Opportunity Commission, and that its College of Business, where they were employed, used an evaluation system that had a disparate impact on older faculty members. The university sought to dismiss the action on the grounds of Eleventh Amendment immunity, and the district court agreed, finding that the ADEA did not eliminate the state's immunity. A group of current and former faculty and librarians of Florida State University and Florida International University filed suit against the Florida Board of Regents under the ADEA, alleging that the board refused to require the two state universities to allocate funds to provide previously agreed-upon market adjustments to the salaries of eligible university employees. They maintained that this failure had a disparate impact on the base pay of older employees with a longer record of service.

The court refused to dismiss the action. On appeal, the Eleventh Circuit consolidated the cases and held the ADEA did not abrogate (do away with) state Eleventh Amendment immunity. The U.S. Supreme Court noted that **although the ADEA contains a clear statement of Congress' intent to eliminate the states' immunity under the Eleventh Amendment, such action exceeded Congress' authority under Section 5 of the Fourteenth Amendment** (which grants Congress the power to enact laws under the Equal Protection Clause). Although state employees cannot sue their employers for discrimination under the ADEA, they are not without remedies. Every state has age discrimination statutes, and almost all of them allow the recovery of money damages from state employers. *Kimel v. Florida Board of Regents*, 528 U.S. 62, 120 S.Ct. 631, 145 L.Ed.2d 522 (2000).

◆   *The U.S. Court of Appeals for the Second Circuit held a New York university did not assign fewer courses to a professor because of his age.*

The university assigned the tenured professor a courseload of four courses for an academic year. He believed his tenure entitled him to teach at least five courses, and he sued the university in a federal court under the ADEA. The court ruled for the university, and the professor appealed. The Second Circuit held he did not establish adverse employment action. The assignment of four courses was not a "materially adverse change" in the terms and conditions of his employment. **Material changes include termination, a demotion evidenced by a decrease in wages, or a less distinguished title.** The average courseload for a tenured professor was fewer than four, and the professor claimed no wage loss. The court held that even if he had managed to show an adverse employment action, he submitted no evidence to support an inference that the assignment of classes was based on his age. The judgment for the university was affirmed. *Boise v. Boufford*, 121 Fed.Appx. 890 (2d Cir. 2005).

1. Applicability to Religious Schools

◆   *The ADEA did not apply to a pervasively religious Missouri seminary.*

A Missouri seminary allegedly dismissed an employee because of his age. He sued the seminary in a federal district court under the ADEA. The seminary brought a motion for pretrial judgment, stating that the ADEA was inapplicable because the institution was pervasively religious. The court agreed. It considered the U.S. Supreme Court's decision in *NLRB v. Catholic Bishop of Chicago*, 440 U.S. 490 (1979), in which the Court held the National Labor Relations Act (NLRA) inapplicable to church-operated schools. Although the ADEA was a remedial statute rather than a regulatory statute such as the NLRA, the ruling in *Catholic Bishop* applied here. Because application of the ADEA could implicate enforcement by the EEOC, government regulatory powers were involved. **As the potential existed for impinging the seminary's religious freedoms, the court ruled that the ADEA was inapplicable.** It held for the seminary. *Cochran v. St. Louis Preparatory Seminary*, 717 F.Supp. 1413 (E.D. Mo. 1989).

◆ *An Ohio federal court held that the ADEA could be applied to a religious institution.*

An employee at Xavier University, an institution operated by the Order of Jesuits, sued the university under the ADEA in an Ohio federal court. The university asserted that the court had no authority to rule on the case because the university, as a religious institution, was exempt from the ADEA's provisions. The court observed that because the ADEA gave no indication that religious institutions were exempt from its provisions, the issue became whether application of the ADEA to the university would violate the Free Exercise and Establishment Clauses of the First Amendment.

The court held for the employee, noting that the Fourth Circuit held in *Ritter v. Mount St. Mary's College*, 814 F.2d 986 (4th Cir. 1987), that **application of the ADEA to a religious institution did not present a significant risk of infringement on the institution's First Amendment rights.** Here, the facts gave no indication that enforcement of the ADEA would violate the religion clauses of the First Amendment. Accordingly, the university was not entitled to have the case dismissed. *Soriano v. Xavier Univ.,* 687 F.Supp. 1188 (S.D. Ohio 1988).

2. Defenses

The Eleventh Amendment protects state entities from private lawsuits but not from suits filed by the federal government. Thus, the U.S. Equal Employment Opportunity Commission (EEOC) may sue state entities for violating the Age Discrimination in Employment Act. See EEOC v. Board of Supervisors for the Univ. of Louisiana System, 559 F.3d 270 (5th Cir. 2009).

◆ *A federal court dismissed age discrimination claims against the University of Missouri because a lower court did not rule on a qualified immunity issue.*

A University of Missouri professor filed a lawsuit in federal court against the university, his department chair and department administrator, claiming age discrimination and hostile work environment. He added claims for federal due process and equal protection violations, and state law tortious interference with his employment contract. The defendants filed a motion to dismiss the case, arguing the professor did not state valid claims for due process or equal protection violations. They also argued they had qualified immunity from the due process and equal protection claims. Without addressing the issue of qualified immunity, the district court granted the defense motion to dismiss the equal protection claim. The chair and administrator appealed to the U.S. Court of Appeals, Eighth Circuit, arguing that the district court improperly rejected their qualified immunity defense.

The court explained that it could not grant the requested review because the lower court did not rule on qualified immunity. The district court did not even mention qualified immunity in its decision. **Since the district court did not make a finding with respect to the qualified immunity issue, there was nothing to review** and the appeal was dismissed. *Mitra v. Curators of the Univ. of Missouri,* 322 Fed.Appx. 467 (8th Cir. 2009).

♦   *A former women's basketball coach failed to show the decision to buy out the last year of her contract was motivated by age or gender discrimination.*

After the University of Miami exercised its contractual right to buy out the last year of the coach's contract, she filed a state court action for discrimination based on age and gender. A trial court held for the university, finding at least three legitimate business reasons for its decision. In addition, the court ordered the coach to pay the university's attorneys' fees. A Florida District Court of Appeal explained that once the university offered legitimate, nondiscriminatory reasons for its action, the burden shifted to the coach to show the claimed reasons for its actions were a pretext for discrimination. She tried to meet this burden with evidence about the university's treatment of other coaches, but the court found this evidence was insufficient. **Since the university provided a legitimate reason for its decision, the trial court had properly ruled for the university on the discrimination claims.** However, the court held the trial court should not have awarded attorneys' fees to the university, since the coach's claims were not "frivolous, unreasonable, or without foundation." *Labati v. Univ. of Miami*, 16 So.3d 886 (Fla. Dist. Ct. App. 2009).

♦   *Texas Tech University's decision to eliminate a college director's position was based on budgetary reasons, not age discrimination.*

The director had worked for Texas Tech since 1990, and earned outstanding job evaluations for several years. But some time later, several of her former and then-current subordinates filed written complaints stating she was an inflexible authoritarian who created an unpleasant work environment. When the director took a medical leave, her supervisor reassigned some of her job duties to others. The director claimed the changes constituted a demotion, and she filed an age, sex and disability discrimination claim with the Equal Employment Opportunity Commission (EEOC). After being reassigned to a different job that she also considered a demotion, the university informed her the job was being eliminated.

The director filed another EEOC charge, then sued the university in the state court system for age and sex discrimination as well as retaliation. The court awarded the university pretrial judgment, and the Court of Appeals of Texas agreed to review the case. On appeal, the court agreed with the lower court that the university had a legitimate reason for eliminating the director's position. She did not show this was a pretext for discrimination. **The university provided detailed information showing the decision to eliminate the position was made as part of an effort to reduce operating expenses.** The retaliation claim failed because the person who eliminated the position was unaware of the EEOC complaint. As a result, the judgment was affirmed. *Ptomey v. Texas Tech Univ.*, 277 S.W.3d 487 (Tex. Ct. App. 2009).

♦   *A federal court rejected a 57-year-old Illinois applicant's claim that she was not hired as a university enrollment counselor based on her age.*

The university sought applicants who had a general knowledge of the higher education market to contact and enroll prospective students. The applicant was invited to participate in a group assessment with about 10 other applicants, even though the university had already chosen two younger candidates, contingent on background checks. The university then filled other jobs by hiring people ages 31 or younger. The applicant sued the university in a federal district court for violating the Age Discrimination in Employment Act (ADEA). The university sought pretrial judgment, arguing she failed to show she applied for the four positions that opened after she initially submitted her resume. **The court found no age discrimination, because the university showed the individuals chosen for employment were better qualified than the applicant.** Each of the selected applicants held a bachelor's degree, which the candidate lacked. She also had no background in higher education. Because she did not present enough evidence to support her age discrimination claim, the court granted the university's motion for pretrial judgment. *Czubernat v. Univ. of Phoenix*, No. 07 C 2821, 2008 WL 2339570 (N.D. Ill. 6/4/08).

◆ *New York University (NYU) did not discriminate against a 70-year-old teacher by firing him for making inappropriate comments.*

NYU refused to reappoint the teacher after learning he made inappropriate comments during a class and was rude to the staff. The university presented evidence that he had commented during class that his phone number was "just for girls." This violated NYU's internal sexual harassment policy. The teacher claimed the reasons alleged for the employment decision were false. He insisted the remarks were merely jokes and did not offend the other female students. NYU replaced him with a teacher who was substantially younger. The teacher sued the university in a federal district court for age discrimination. **The court said whether female students found the comments offensive was irrelevant, since the teacher's remarks violated the harassment policy.** The teacher said the allegation he had been rude to members of the staff was a cover-up for unlawful age discrimination. He said he had always been polite and cooperative with staff. The court found the evidence supported the university's contention that the teacher was rude. It accepted NYU's legitimate, nondiscriminatory reasons for not reappointing him. As the teacher failed to prove the university's reasons were a cover-up for age discrimination, the court granted NYU's motion for summary judgment. *Chapkines v. New York Univ.*, No. 02CIV6355(RJH)(KNF), 2005 WL 167603 (S.D.N.Y. 1/25/05).

◆ *The U.S. Court of Appeals, Eleventh Circuit, held a Florida university did not reject an applicant because of his age.*

A 70-year-old white male applied for three positions at the university. The university rejected them all. The applicant sued the university in a federal district court, alleging it refused to hire him because of his age, in violation of the ADEA. The court dismissed the case, and the applicant appealed. The Eleventh Circuit found the university had legitimate, nondiscriminatory reasons for not hiring him. The university wanted to reduce turnover by filling the positions with faculty who had ties to the area. The applicant had no ties to central Florida, and one interviewer thought he was boring and unenthusiastic. **No evidence was presented to show the university lied about its reasons for not hiring him.** As the applicant failed to prove the reasons given by the university for not hiring him were untrue, the court affirmed the judgment. *Hillemann v. Univ. of Cent. Florida*, 167 Fed.Appx. 747 (11th Cir. 2006).

3. Evidence of Discrimination

◆   *An employee who lasted only three days at a Pennsylvania university failed to show discrimination based on her race or age.*

The employee claimed she was assigned to a small office with child-sized furniture and no phone or computer. The people she was supposed to supervise shared a larger office that had adult-sized furniture, a phone and a computer. The employee became sick and dizzy in her office because it was too hot. She told a supervisor about the problem, but when she reported for her third day of work, she was told she was being fired because she had complained about her office. The university later filled the post with a black female over age 40.

In a federal district court action against the university and supervisor, the employee alleged race-based claims of wrongful termination, disparate treatment and hostile work environment under Title VII. She also claimed age discrimination under the ADEA. The court explained that the employee did not show other employees were treated more favorably than she was. She did not identify circumstances indicating race played a role in the decision to discharge her. The court also rejected the age discrimination claim, as **the employee did not show she was replaced by someone who was younger than her by a margin that allowed an inference of discrimination**. She was either 43 or 44 at the time of her discharge, and she was replaced by someone over 40. This was not enough of an age difference to permit a finding of age discrimination. None of the evidence showed the employee was subjected to severe, extreme or pervasive discrimination, and the university was entitled to judgment. *Beaubrun v. Thomas Jefferson Univ.*, 578 F.Supp.2d 777 (E.D. Pa. 2008).

◆   *A candidate for a college instructor job failed to prove age discrimination.*

The college hired the candidate, who was in his 50s, as a sociology instructor under a temporary teaching appointment that was renewed on a semester-by-semester basis. A full-time, tenure-track appointment to teach sociology became available the next academic year. The position attracted 29 applicants, including the candidate. Applicants ranged in age from 27 to 55. The candidate performed poorly on a teaching demonstration and was not selected as a finalist. The position was awarded to a candidate in his early 30s who had teaching experience, a doctorate degree, and had presented an interactive technology-based teaching demonstration that impressed the college hiring committee. The candidate sued the college in a federal district court for violating the Age Discrimination in Employment Act. The court held the college offered a legitimate, nondiscriminatory reason for its decision.

Specifically, the college said it decided not to hire the candidate because he performed poorly during his teaching demonstration. The hiring committee believed he did not demonstrate qualities they believed to be important, including the ability to engage students and interact effectively with them. The candidate did not show these reasons were false. There was no other evidence showing the college decided not to hire him based on his age. Therefore, the college's motion for summary judgment was granted. *Salerno v. Ridgewater College*, No. 06-1717, 2008 WL 509001 (D. Minn. 2/8/08).

◆ *A Tennessee university did not violate the ADEA by changing a 69-year-old professor's position and decreasing his lab space.*

The professor had worked for the university for nearly 30 years when a newly hired pathology department chairman asked whether he would consider early retirement. The professor told him he had no intention of retiring any time soon, and claimed the chairman then began a series of retaliatory actions, including orders to vacate his lab and office space. The chairman offered him several employment options, but they all meant a lower salary and several included early retirement. The professor sued the university in a federal district court for age discrimination. The court dismissed the case, and he appealed to the Sixth Circuit. The court found no adverse employment action under the ADEA. The reduction in lab space did not affect salary or job status. **Any proposal to reduce the professor's salary was never carried out, and threats alone are not an adverse action.** The professor presented no evidence the job changes significantly decreased his responsibilities. As he could not prevail on his claim of age discrimination without evidence of an adverse employment action, the court affirmed the judgment for the university. *Mitchell v. Vanderbilt Univ.*, 389 F.3d 177 (6th Cir. 2004).

B. Retirement

◆ *The Alabama Legislature had the authority to set a mandatory retirement age of 70 for Alabama State University board members.*

An Alabama State University board member reached the age of 70 before his second 12-year term expired. The terms of an amended state law barred him from serving on the board for his full term. In an attempt to block his removal, the board member sued state and university officials in the federal court system for Equal Protection violations. He claimed the law discriminated on the basis of age without a rational basis and treated trustees at Alabama State University differently than trustees at other Alabama public universities. A district court held for the university, and the board member appealed. On appeal, the U.S. Court of Appeals, Eleventh Circuit, applied a deferential rational basis review. It found the law did not involve a fundamental right or suspect classification.

The court referenced *Gregory v. Ashcroft*, 501 U.S. 452 (1991), in which the Supreme Court upheld what the Eleventh Circuit said was "a remarkably similar retirement provision." **The court said that the age limit for trustees in this case satisfied rational basis review.** As for the claim that the law set an age limit for the trustees of some state universities but not others, the court held the legislature had leeway to do so. The court also upheld the finding that nothing prevented application of the mandatory retirement age rule. The lower court's ruling was affirmed. *Clark v. Riley*, 595 F.3d 1258 (11th Cir. 2010).

◆ *A federal district court held Cornell University did not discriminate against a professor because of her age.*

When the professor was 50 years old, the university told her she would not be offered a fourth five-year reappointment when her contract expired. Instead, it offered her a one-year assignment that would require travel between Ithaca and New York City. The university said the change was being made due to budget problems. Midway through the contract, the professor accepted the university's offer of early retirement. She continued to perform work for the university for several months. She then sent the university a $25,000 bill for her services. The university refused to pay the amount claimed by the professor, and she sued the university in a federal district court for ADEA violations. She claimed the university replaced her with a younger employee and that it fired six other females over 40 for budgetary reasons. The court said the professor failed to show the university subjected her to an adverse employment action.

Action must be "more disruptive than a mere inconvenience or an alteration of job responsibilities" to be "adverse." While termination is clearly an adverse employment action, the professor did not suffer adverse employment action because the university did not discharge her. Rather, it chose not to renew her appointment. The university extended the professor's employment for an additional year after the term of her reappointment expired. She terminated her employment when she volunteered to resign and accept early retirement. The court dismissed the case, and the employee appealed. The U.S. Court of Appeals, Second Circuit, applied the wrong standard in assessing the dismissal motion. The employee alleged an unofficial policy to guarantee her lifetime employment that was now being precluded on the basis of her gender and age. She also asserted a valid Equal Pay Act claim, arguing that male employees were paid more for similar work. While the employee had taken an early retirement package, she did so to preserve benefits she would have enjoyed if her job was secure. Two state law claims had been properly dismissed, but the discrimination claims were returned to the district court for further proceedings. *Leibowitz v. Cornell Univ.*, 445 F.3d 586 (2d Cir. 2006).

C. State Statutes

◆ *Two tenured business professors could proceed with their age discrimination case against St. John's University (SJU) under New York law.*

According to the professors, SJU practices led to systematic discrimination against older employees. They complained to SJU but claimed this led to retaliation. In a state court, the professors sued SJU for age discrimination in violation of the State Human Rights Law and the New York City Human Rights Law. SJU sought dismissal, claiming the action brought its academic judgment into question and was properly resolved as an administrative matter with only limited possibilities for court review. A state appellate division court agreed with SJU that decisions by educational institutions involve the exercise of highly specialized professional judgment. While the court agreed that higher education institutions are better suited to make final decisions concerning their internal matters, this case concerned age discrimination, not SJU policies. It held **the fact that the employer was an educational institution did not permit it to discriminate on the basis of age** or otherwise insulate it from liability for violations of state or city human rights laws. As these were not academic matters, a lower court properly refused to dismiss the case. *Wander v. St. John's Univ.*, 99 A.D.3d 891, 953 N.Y.S.2d 68 (N.Y. App. Div. 2012).

◆ *New Jersey's highest court held a community college dean could pursue a claim that her contract was not renewed because of age discrimination.*

In 2001, when the dean was 69 years old, she was informed by the college's acting president by letter that her contract might not be renewed for job performance. She had over 26 years of experience working for the community college at that time. The dean obtained a reprieve, but three years later she was informed that her contract would not be renewed when it expired for performance reasons. At the time, the dean was over 70 years old. She filed a state-law claim of age discrimination. The trial court ruled against her, and she filed an appeal. On appeal, the New Jersey Superior Court, Appellate Division, held the state Law Against Discrimination (LAD) does not allow employers to discriminate against employees who are age 70 or older.

Appeal then reached the Supreme Court of New Jersey, which held the LAD permits employers to refuse to accept for employment any person who is over the age of 70. **The court held the protection extended by the LAD applied to the non-renewal of an existing employee's contract.** It found that the refusal to renew the contract of an employee over 70, on the basis of age, was a prohibited discriminatory act under the LAD. For this reason, the appellate division's decision for the dean was affirmed. Although the parties advised the court that the case had been settled, the case was found not moot because it involved an important matter of public interest. *Nini v. Mercer County Community College*, 202 N.J. 98, 995 A.2d 1094 (N.J. 2010).

◆ *A New Jersey computer specialist's age discrimination case failed because he did not show that friction at work was due to age discrimination.*

At the time of the dispute, the specialist was 43 years old. His supervisor found he had poor interactions with co-workers and customers, and he had a string of unsatisfactory performance evaluations. The specialist was disciplined and twice suspended. He claimed his supervisor told him three times he was "too old." Following an investigation, the New Jersey Division of Civil Rights found the specialist did not prove age discrimination. He sought review by a state court, which upheld the civil rights division's ruling. It found that by choosing to file his complaint with the division instead of suing, the specialist chose his forum. The division did not act unfairly or unreasonably, and the evidence did not corroborate the claim of age discrimination. Instead, **the record showed the specialist was disciplined for legitimate reasons relating to his poor job performance.** *Bostanci v. New Jersey City Univ.*, No. EJ06WB-53199, 2009 WL 972673 (N.J. Super. Ct. App. Div. 4/13/09).

The specialist sued the university in a federal district court for wrongful discharge, retaliation and harassment under federal laws and the state Law Against Discrimination. The court considered the argument that a claim under the ADEA was barred by the Eleventh Amendment. While the court found sovereign immunity generally protects states from ADEA claims, sovereign immunity does not always protect state political subdivisions. To be entitled to Eleventh Amendment immunity, the university had to be an "arm of the state." The university did not present a detailed argument relating to why it should be considered an arm of the state. As a result, the court held it did not meet its burden to show it was immune to the ADEA claim. However, the court granted a motion to dismiss the Title VII claim. On appeal, the U.S. Court of Appeals, Third Circuit, upheld the district court's decision that the specialist failed to state a Title VII claim. It found the prior state age discrimination claim barred him from bringing a virtually identical claim in the federal court system. *Bostanci v. New Jersey City Univ.*, No. 11-2540, 2012 WL 164471 (3d Cir. 1/13/12).

◆   *The Court of Appeals of Missouri upheld an award of more than $1.2 million to a baseball coach for age discrimination.*

The coach was over the age of 40 at the time of his hiring. His team had a winning record every year, and 80% of his players graduated. After he pursued an administrative charge of age discrimination in 1998, the university reduced his job to a half-time position, cut his pay in half and eliminated his benefits. It also moved his office to a basement near a swimming pool. During the same time his position was cut to part time, the university classified a younger compliance officer who worked 5.5 hours per day as a full-time employee. An assistant basketball coach who was under 40 and had far less experience than the baseball coach received a higher salary. The baseball coach sued the university in the state court system for violating the Missouri Human Rights Act. A jury awarded him $1,275,000 in damages.

On appeal, the court upheld the punitive damage award, finding that state law specifically authorized it. The court found the evidence was sufficient to support the punitive damages award. **Evidence showed younger employees were treated better with respect to pay, hours and benefits.** The baseball field did not comply with National Collegiate Athletic Association requirements, and coaches who were hired after the baseball coach were given nicer offices in an athletic complex. The amount of scholarship money allotted for baseball was low compared with the amount allotted for other sports. **The university discontinued the coach's medical insurance with knowledge that he was a cancer survivor.** The court rejected the university's argument that the amount awarded exceeded reasonable compensation for any injury he suffered. The verdict against the university was upheld. *Brady v. Curators of the Univ. of Missouri*, 213 S.W.3d 101 (Mo. Ct. App. 2006).

◆   *A Pennsylvania law school did not violate a state anti-discrimination act when it discharged an employee who was over 40 years old.*

The law school asked the employee to resign shortly before it merged with a Pennsylvania university. The law school and employee entered into a separation agreement and general release placing him on administrative leave at full salary with full benefits. In return for signing the agreement and giving up his right to unemployment benefits, the employee agreed not to make any claims under the Pennsylvania Human Relations Act (PHRA). However, he filed age discrimination charges against the university with state and federal civil rights agencies. Later, the employee sued the university and law school in a state court, alleging they violated the PHRA. He argued the agreement was invalid because it did not meet the requirements of the Older Workers Benefit Protection Act. The court held for the university and law school. The employee appealed to the Superior Court of Pennsylvania. **The court held the agreement was binding unless the employee proved fraud, duress or other**

circumstances to invalidate it. Contracts are interpreted according to their plain language, and the court found this contract was clear. It affirmed the judgment for the university and law school. *Griest v. Pennsylvania State Univ. & Dickinson School of Law*, 897 A.2d 1186 (Pa. Super. 2006).

◆ *A graduate student could not sue for discrimination under Kentucky's employment laws because she was not an employee of the university.*

A 44-year-old graduate psychology student received a Regent's Fellowship that provided her with full tuition and a yearly stipend. She lost her fellowship after her third year of study due to her failure to have her thesis proposal approved by a department committee. She remained in the graduate program for another year, but was subsequently dismissed. The student filed an unsuccessful grievance, then sued for sex and age discrimination in violation of Kentucky law and the university handbook. A state court held the student had no claim under state discrimination law, because she was not a university employee. The Kentucky Court of Appeals found it clear that **nearly all of her duties and activities were in connection with her academic work** rather than providing a service to the university. It held no employer-employee relationship existed. *Stewart v. Univ. of Louisville*, 65 S.W.3d 536 (Ky. Ct. App. 2001).

V. DISABILITY DISCRIMINATION

Section 504 of the Rehabilitation Act of 1973, 29 U.S.C. § 794, prohibits discrimination against qualified individuals with disabilities in programs or activities receiving federal financial assistance. The Americans with Disabilities Act of 1990 (ADA), 42 U.S.C. § 12101, et seq., extends this protection to both private and public employees, and prohibits discrimination against employees who are associated with disabled individuals.

The 2008 ADA Amendments addressed the term "disability" – defined as "a physical or mental impairment that substantially limits one or more major life activities" of an individual. "Disability" under the ADA is to be construed in favor of broad coverage "to the maximum extent permitted by the terms of this Act." The term "substantially limits" is to be interpreted consistently with Congressional findings and purposes. U.S. Public Laws 110-325 (S. 3406), 110th Congress, Second Session. "ADA Amendments Act of 2008." 29 U.S.C. § 705, 42 U.S.C. §§ 12101-03, 12106-14, 12201, 12205a.

Guidance from the Equal Employment Opportunity Commission's ADA Enforcement Guide states that "if the employee's need for accommodation is not obvious, the employer may ask for reasonable documentation concerning the employee's disability and functional limitations."

In 2011, the U.S. Equal Employment Opportunity Commission (EEOC) issued regulations and interpretive guidance on the 2008 ADA Amendments. According to the EEOC guidance, the primary purpose of the 2008 ADA amendments was to make it easier for people with disabilities to obtain ADA protection. The EEOC states the primary issue in ADA cases should be whether an employer is meeting its legal obligations and whether discrimination has occurred, not whether an individual meets a qualifying definition of disability.

The guidance offers definitions of physical, mental and psychological impairment that include lists of qualifying impairments. Major life activities include caring for oneself, performing manual tasks, seeing, hearing, sleeping, walking, standing, speaking, breathing, learning, reading, concentrating, thinking, communicating, interacting with others and working.

The guidance indicates that it is unlawful for a covered entity to use qualification standards, employment tests or other selection criteria that screen out individuals with disabilities or classes of individuals with disabilities. A defense is offered in the guidance for employers who can show an individual's claimed impairment is both transitory and minor. Federal Register, *Vol. 76, No. 58, Page 16978, March 25, 2011. 29 C.F.R. Part 1630.*

A. Liability

◆ *A University of Illinois police officer who had a stroke did not show a federal court that the university discriminated against him based on disability.*

After suffering a stroke while off duty, the officer could not walk or care for himself. But he continued to improve to the point that the university stated in writing that he must return to work. The officer obtained medical clearance from the university health services department based on a cerebral angiogram showing his stroke-related injuries had healed. But he then refused to undergo a functional capacity examination and was not called back to work. After resigning, he found another job and sued the university in a federal court.

The court found the officer was not subjected to an adverse employment action because he had resigned and was not discharged. On appeal, the U.S. Court of Appeals, Seventh Circuit, rejected the officer's argument that the university should have proposed a reasonable accommodation once he agreed to return to work. **In ADA accommodation cases, employees have a duty to trigger the interactive process by telling their employers of their needs for accommodations.** In any event, the officer had insisted he was fully recovered and could do his old job. In seeking reinstatement, he did not say he needed any accommodations. The functional capacity evaluation was reasonable because it enabled the university to determine whether the officer could perform required job duties. As the lower court held, he did not suffer an adverse job action because he had voluntarily resigned. *Pamon v. Board of Trustees of the Univ. of Illinois*, 483 Fed.Appx. 296 (7th Cir. 2012).

◆ *A part-time Illinois college janitor with a mental disability was unable to show disability discrimination, as he had a record of poor job performance.*

The janitor's IQ was 67, which was in the range known as mild mental retardation. The community college rated his performance "unsatisfactory" in a job review. His supervisor noted that he "does only the bare minimum to meet job requirements." Other employees asked not to be scheduled with the janitor because they believed they had to make up for his poor performance. After he was turned down for three full-time jobs, the janitor filed an administrative charge of disability discrimination. He claimed that a college human resources officer said, "You should not be suing your employer." Within five months, the college fired the janitor after another evaluation determined his performance had not improved. He sued the community college board for disability discrimination and retaliation. After the court held for the board, the janitor appealed to the Seventh Circuit. While deeming the remark by the human resources officer "imprudent," the court found it irrelevant. **Since the janitor could not show he was meeting his employer's legitimate employment expectations, he could not pursue any disability claims.** *Dickerson v. Board of Trustees of Community College Dist. No. 522*, 657 F.3d 595 (7th Cir. 2011).

◆ *A federal court held a Louisiana professor with disabilities identified a potential ADA violation by his college that prevented the dismissal of his case.*

In addition to being diabetic, the professor had visual impairments. He used technology to enlarge print and convert text to speech, and he navigated the campus with the help of a cane. The professor said the college human resources director denied his request for accommodations. Two years later, he said the locks on his classroom were changed without notice, forcing him to cancel a class. The next year, an academic vice president suggested that the professor apply for disability benefits. Then, after the professor had completed 15 years of work for the college, he claimed that an official informed him his contract would not be renewed because of health concerns. The professor sued the college in a federal district court for disability discrimination. Although the college sought pretrial dismissal, the court denied it. It held that the professor stated a valid preliminary case under the ADA. In addition to showing evidence of a disability based on a visual impairment, the professor asserted he was still qualified for his position. In fact, **his performance had been considered satisfactory for 15 years, and he had demonstrated he could continue to perform his essential job functions**. Moreover, he produced evidence that he had not been rehired based on his disability. Because the professor's complaint was sufficient to state a plausible claim for relief, the court denied the college's request to dismiss his case at this point. *Fontenot v. Our Lady of Holy Cross College*, No. 11-1375, 2011 WL 4368836 (E.D. La. 9/19/11).

◆ *A Louisiana professor did not show an ADA violation when his request to limit faculty meetings to 20 minutes to accommodate his back pain was denied.*

The professor received poor evaluations for several years. Twenty years after being hired, he was subjected to a formal faculty performance review. A review panel found formal remediation was necessary. The professor asked the university to limit faculty meetings to 20 minutes to accommodate his chronic back pain. Instead, the university notified him it was initiating his termination for not cooperating with a remediation committee. After the professor was fired, he sued the university for violation of the Contracts Clause and his tenure rights. The court awarded pretrial judgment to the university, and he appealed.

On appeal, the U.S. Court of Appeals, Fifth Circuit, held the professor did not mention his constitutional and tenure claims in his brief and thus lost the right to appeal them. His ADA claims failed because his requests for a more accessible office were made so long before he filed suit that they were outside the statute of limitations. **An employee who challenges the denial of an accommodation must show why a requested accommodation is reasonable.** But the professor did not show his request to limit faculty meetings to 20 minutes was reasonable. As his ADA and other claims failed, dismissal was proper. *Windhauser v. Board of Supervisors for Louisiana State Univ. & Agricultural and Mechanical College*, 360 Fed.Appx. 562 (5th Cir. 2010).

◆ *A Kentucky court found Eastern Kentucky University (EKU) did not discriminate against a professor by refusing her an extension to earn her Ph.D.*

The professor told EKU she expected to get her Ph.D. almost immediately. She had to earn the degree by the end of the 1998-99 school year or face termination. But the professor was diagnosed with breast cancer at the start of her probationary period. She went through a mastectomy and chemotherapy. A few years later, with her deadline approaching, the professor asked EKU for more time to earn her Ph.D. She was granted one extension, but her request for another was denied. When the professor failed to complete her Ph.D. on time, EKU refused to give her another contract, and she sued EKU in a state court.

The court awarded EKU judgment on the professor's disability and gender discrimination claims. She appealed to the Court of Appeals of Kentucky, which found she could not make a case for disability or gender discrimination. **Both claims required the professor to be qualified for a position. She did not show this, as her job required the Ph.D. she had yet to earn.** The question of whether EKU had reasonably accommodated her disability (or whether a jury should decide that question) was moot. The court found the lower court had properly held for EKU. *Murray v. Eastern Kentucky Univ.*, 328 S.W.3d 679 (Ky. Ct. App. 2009). (Ky. review denied, Jan. 14, 2011.)

◆ *A Connecticut community college did not discriminate against an assistant professor when it declined to renew her teaching contract.*

A year after being hired to teach computer courses, the professor had major surgery and her mother died. She told a supervisor she was under psychiatric care, but she did not provide a diagnosis or other details. The college denied the professor's requests for only lower-level class assignments and that she not be required to teach both day and evening classes. Students began to complain that she had "stopped teaching" and was relying on a student to facilitate class discussions. A supervisor assigned the professor a poor performance evaluation, saying she was unprepared for class. After the college did not renew the professor's contract, she filed a federal district court action accusing it of disability discrimination under the ADA and sex discrimination under Title VII. **The court noted she only vaguely alleged having a mental impairment, and she failed to show she had a disability as defined by the ADA.** There was enough evidence to show her contract was not renewed due to her poor job performance. As no reasonable jury could conclude the decision was motivated by sex discrimination, the court held for the community college.

On appeal, the U.S. Court of Appeals, Second Circuit, found no evidence that the professor had an impairment that met the ADA definition of disability. She also did not show she had any record of a qualifying disability. Since the professor did not demonstrate that her contract was not renewed because of a disability, the judgment for the community college was affirmed. *Mastrolillo v. State of Connecticut*, 352 Fed.Appx. 472 (2d Cir. 2009).

◆ *A counselor at an Arizona community college could proceed with an ADA claim, even though she threatened her department chair.*

The counselor suffered a brain injury in a car accident. The injury impaired her ability to regulate her emotional responses. When the college tried to discharge her, she filed a disability discrimination claim that was eventually settled. Months later, a new department chair reminded the counselor that she was to work 35 hours each week. After the meeting, the counselor became upset and threatened the chair. She then called an associate dean of student services to say she had experienced a breakdown. The college placed the counselor on leave and asked her to submit to fitness-for-duty examinations. One of the examining psychologists concluded she was unable to function as a counselor. As all open positions at the college involved interaction with students, the counselor's employment was terminated.

The counselor sued the college in a federal district court for ADA violations. Although the college argued no accommodations would permit her to serve as a counselor, the court held a jury could find that a job coach would enable her to do this work. While the college argued the counselor had violated its violence policy by threatening the department chair, the court said conduct resulting from a disability is "part of the disability" and not a separate basis for discharge. Pretrial judgment was not allowed on the termination claim. **As an examination to determine whether a threat will be carried out is consistent with business necessity, the college could require one.** *Menchaca v. Maricopa Community College Dist.*, 595 F.Supp.2d 1063 (D. Ariz. 2009).

◆ *The U.S. Supreme Court concluded that Congress exceeded its authority by allowing monetary damage awards against states in ADA cases.*

According to a 2001 U.S. Supreme Court decision, Congress did not identify a history and pattern of irrational employment discrimination against individuals with disabilities by the states when it enacted the ADA. For this reason, the states were entitled to Eleventh Amendment immunity from such claims. As a result, **two state employees were unsuccessful in their attempt to recover money damages under the ADA from their state employer for disability discrimination**. *Board of Trustees of Univ. of Alabama v. Garrett*, 531 U.S. 356, 121 S.Ct. 955, 148 L.Ed.2d 866 (2001).

◆ *An American University driver may proceed with a disability discrimination lawsuit based on denial of permission to use a restroom.*

The driver claimed he was fired after being wrongfully denied the accommodation of using a restroom during a car trip between Washington, D.C., and Philadelphia. He sued the university and its president, claiming violations of the ADA and the District of Columbia Human Rights Act based on failing to accommodate his disability. A federal district court explained that the employee had to show he had a disability of which the university had notice, that he could perform the essential functions of his job with a reasonable accommodation, and that the university refused to provide the accommodation. The court held a reasonable jury could conclude he had an impairment. **Evidence showed the employee had a physiological disorder or condition that affected his digestive system.** A jury could find his condition substantially limited the major life activity of waste elimination, based on evidence that he needed to use a restroom up to 15 times a day. There was also evidence that the university had notice of this condition. As factual issues existed regarding whether he could perform the essential functions of his job, the court held it was up to a jury to decide if he was qualified for the job, and whether the university refused to accommodate his condition. *Green v. American Univ.*, 647 F.Supp.2d 21 (D.D.C. 2009).

◆   *A Harvard University staff assistant with bipolar disorder was permissibly discharged due to his egregious misconduct.*

The employee was diagnosed with bipolar disorder and sometimes had periods of mania on the job. He established a website where he criticized the pay scale. The employee updated his website at work on his personal laptop. Shortly after the employee created the website, he became severely manic. He was loud and animated as he told co-workers about Harvard's wage policies and invited them to view the website. In the university's main Museum lobby, he sang, clapped and danced to protest songs that were posted on his website. He was hospitalized for an episode of paranoia. Soon after that, staff members and police officers approached the employee and asked him to leave. When he refused, the officers arrested him, and the university later discharged him.

The employee sued Harvard in a state court for violating the ADA. Harvard relied on *Garrity v. United Airlines*, 421 Mass. 55 (1995), in which the state's highest court held if an employee's "egregious misconduct" is adverse to the interests of the employer and violates employer rules, the employee may not claim ADA protection. The court found the misconduct in this case was egregious and held for Harvard. On appeal, the supreme judicial court noted that its *Garrity* decision was consistent with the view adopted by the majority of courts facing the issue of egregious employer misconduct under federal law. This was so even though Congress only granted permission to employers to hold alcoholics to the same standard of conduct as other employees. **The court held disabled employees were not entitled to disability law protection if they engaged in egregious misconduct that would be sufficient to result in the discharge of a non-disabled employee.** *Mammone v. President and Fellows of Harvard College*, 446 Mass. 657, 847 N.E.2d 276 (Mass. 2006).

B. Defenses

In Hosanna-Tabor Evangelical Lutheran Church and School v. E.E.O.C., *below, the U.S. Supreme Court explained that there is a ministerial exception to the provisions of anti-discrimination laws, including Title VII and the ADA. This rule is rooted in the First Amendment rights of religious institutions to make decisions about the employment of those who carry out their missions.*

To be covered by the ADA, an employee must have a disabling condition that substantially limits the ability to engage in a major life activity such as work. In 2008, Congress broadened certain ADA provisions to correct Supreme Court decisions that interpreted the Act differently than Section 504. Congress expected the ADA's definition of "disability" would be interpreted consistently with how courts were interpreting the definition of "handicapped individual" under Rehabilitation Act Section 504. Congress singled out Sutton v. United Air Lines, Inc., *527 U.S. 471 (1999) and* Toyota Motor Mfg., Kentucky, Inc. v. Williams, *534 U.S. 184 (2002), as cases in which the Supreme Court interpreted "substantially limits" more restrictively than Congress intended.*

◆ *The U.S. Supreme Court held a Michigan Lutheran school could discharge a disabled teacher based on a "ministerial exception" that exempts religious employers from liability under state and federal anti-discrimination laws.*

A Michigan Lutheran school teacher became ill and took a disability leave for what was diagnosed as narcolepsy. Later, the school discharged her. She sued it in a federal court for violating the ADA. The court held the First Amendment prohibited it from considering claims involving the employment relationship between a religious institution and a ministerial employee. In dismissing the case, the court held the teacher was a ministerial employee. On appeal, the U.S. Court of Appeals, Sixth Circuit, reversed the judgment, finding she was not a ministerial employee because she spent most of her school day teaching secular subjects and using secular textbooks. Though she led a chapel service, she did so only twice a year. Appeal reached the U.S. Supreme Court, which said there is a ministerial exception to bias laws rooted in the First Amendment.

A court order requiring a church to accept or retain a minister, or imposing liability for failing to do so, would intrude upon church governance and deprive churches of the power to select those who would preach their beliefs, teach their faiths and carry out their missions. Declining to adopt a rigid formula for who may qualify as a "minister," the Court found significance in the teacher's title, which was "Minister of Religion, Commissioned." As a "called" employee, she had to complete extensive studies in church doctrine and ministry and become endorsed by the church synod and congregation. She could also claim an income tax break that was available only to ministers. In finding the teacher qualified for ministerial status, the Court noted her formal title of minister, the numerous requirements she performed to earn "called" status, and religious duties such as teaching religion and leading prayers and chapel services. As the teacher was covered by the ministerial exception, the Court reversed the judgment. *Hosanna-Tabor Evangelical Lutheran Church and School v. E.E.O.C.,* 132 S.Ct. 694 (U.S. 2012).

◆ *Georgia State University did not violate federal law by reducing the salary and later eliminating the position of a marketing director with a disability.*

After suffering a stroke, the director had to rely more on an administrative assistant to perform tasks that had become difficult for him. A budget reduction resulted in the layoff of the administrative assistant and a 20% reduction in the director's hours and salary. At his request, a part-time administrative assistant was provided for him. Soon, the director emailed an assistant dean and a human resources employee to complain that the reductions were made with knowledge that it would be hard for someone his age and with his disability to find a new job. He also met with the human resources employee and told him he believed the actions were related to his disability. A second round of budget cuts resulted in the elimination of the director's position, and he sued the university in a federal court. It held his request for a full-time administrative assistant was unreasonable. On appeal, the U.S. Court of Appeals, Eleventh Circuit, held the university did not unlawfully deny a disability-related job accommodation.

Although job restructuring was an available accommodation under federal disability laws, **the request for a full-time administrative assistant went beyond job restructuring and would have required the creation of a new position**. The court also held the director did not prove unlawful retaliation, as he could not show the budget cuts were a pretext. Similarly, the director could not show the elimination of his position was motivated by unlawful disability discrimination. As a result, the court held for the university. *Barton v. Board of Regents of the Univ. System of Georgia*, 478 Fed.Appx. 627 (11th Cir. 2012).

◆   *Generally, a seniority system takes precedence over ADA accommodation.*

In a case involving an airline employee with a bad back, who was seeking a mailroom position, **the U.S. Supreme Court held that as a general rule, an accommodation under the ADA is not reasonable if it conflicts with an employer's seniority rules**. However, employees may present evidence of special circumstances that make a "seniority rule exception" reasonable in a particular case. *US Airways, Inc. v. Barnett*, 535 U.S. 391, 122 S.Ct. 1516, 152 L.Ed.2d 589 (2002).

◆   *An Illinois college instructor with a hearing impairment did not convince a federal court that she was denied a tenure-track position due to her disability.*

Despite degenerative hearing loss in both ears, the instructor worked for the college for 13 years and received several teaching awards. She was a finalist for a new tenure-track position, but the college turned her down in favor of a candidate it considered to be a better fit. The instructor became disgruntled. She created offensive blog entries and sent bitter emails for almost a year after she did not get the job. Over the next two years, the department chair found it impossible to work with the instructor and decided not to renew her contract. In a federal court, the instructor sued the college for disability discrimination. The court accepted the college's nondiscriminatory reasons not hiring her into a tenure-track position. **The reasons given for selecting the other candidate were not shown to be a pretext for discrimination.** The college substantiated the decision not to renew the instructor's contract due to her unprofessional behavior. Since the instructor failed to show her lack of professionalism was not the real reason for contract non-renewal, her disability discrimination and related claims were rejected. *Craig v. Columbia College Chicago*, No. 09-CV-7758, 2012 WL 540095 (N.D. Ill. 2/16/12).

◆   *A federal court in Louisiana rejected a doctoral student's claim that a university unlawfully discriminated against her based on her depression.*

As a graduate assistant, the student earned a substantial stipend. She had a history of depression and anxiety, and she was hospitalized following a head injury. Her request for incomplete grades was denied, as was a request for retroactive withdrawal. The student sued the university's board of supervisors for ADA violations. A federal court rejected her ADA discrimination claim. **The student did not show she was qualified to perform the essential**

functions of her job or claim she suffered an adverse job action. In addition, the record showed the university allowed the student consideration for absences and gave her extra time for assignments. *Ladwig v. Board of Supervisors of Louisiana State Univ.*, 842 F.Supp.2d 1003 (M.D. La. 2012).

◆ *A federal court rejected a West Virginia university's defense that an employee could not pursue a disability action due to his own misconduct.*

A university information technology specialist had sleep apnea and sleep insomnia. He began to receive medical treatment and informed his supervisor and the human resources department. But the specialist was warned in writing about falling asleep on the job and eventually threatened with termination. The specialist responded by asking for accommodations, including a "doze alert" that would alarm him if his head tilted enough. After the accommodation was denied, the specialist sued the university in a federal district court for disability discrimination. According to the university, the specialist waited too long to ask for an accommodation and invoked it to excuse his prior misconduct. **The court agreed that the university was not required to excuse the specialist's past misconduct.** But the specialist had claimed that the university broke the law by rejecting his request for an accommodation. This claim was sufficient to survive pretrial dismissal. While it held for the specialist, the court held he would most likely not be qualified for his job under the law if he needed the "doze alert" to stay awake while at work. *Leschinskey v. Rectors and Visitors of Radford Univ.*, No. 7:11-cv-00189, 2011 WL 5029813 (W.D. Va. 10/24/11).

◆ *An Illinois college custodian did not show decisions not to promote and then to fire him were based on disability.*

The custodian worked for nine years as a part-time custodian at the college, despite having a mental impairment. He applied three times for full-time work without success. At a board of trustees meeting where new full-time custodial hires were expected to be approved, the custodian made a statement about college hiring practices and asked the board to delay the hiring decision until his application could be reviewed. Later, a supervisor issued the custodian's work evaluation and assigned him an overall rating of "unsatisfactory." The custodian filed an unsuccessful grievance and a disability discrimination claim with the U.S. Equal Employment Opportunity Commission (EEOC).

After six months on a correction plan, the college fired the custodian, and he filed a new grievance and EEOC complaint. An arbitrator reinstated him due to the college's failure to follow progressive discipline. The custodian sued the college in a federal district court for violating the ADA by denying him a promotion, firing him, and retaliating against him for addressing the board. The court held **the custodian's history of mediocre performance was a valid nondiscriminatory reason not to promote him**. He could not show retaliation because the supervisor who conducted the review testified he did not know about his board meeting comments. The court found the college used the same procedures it used for reviewing other part-time custodians, and dismissed the custodian's ADA claims. *Dickerson v. Belleville Area Community College Dist. 522*, No. 08-716-GPM, 2010 WL 3835781 (S.D. Ill. 9/24/10).

◆ *The University of Minnesota (UM) planned to eliminate an employee's position before he requested accommodations, defeating his retaliation claim.*

The employee worked in a four-person workers' compensation office. Shortly before a university restructuring eliminated his job, he went to the UM office of disability services to report his diagnosis of depression and panic attacks. As the disabilities were affecting his job performance, the employee asked for the accommodation of moving from an open cubicle to the private office he formerly occupied. He then learned his position was being eliminated and sued UM in a federal district court for violating the ADA and state law by firing him in retaliation for requesting a reasonable accommodation.

The court agreed with UM's claim to Eleventh Amendment immunity for the state law claim. And the ADA claim failed because **the employee could not show his request for an accommodation was the reason he was fired**. Evidence showed the restructuring was being planned at least two years before he knew about it, and that the decision to eliminate his position was made before he requested an accommodation. This sequence of events meant the decision could not have been retaliatory. UM showed it had a valid, nondiscriminatory reason to eliminate the employee's position. As UM had immunity to the state law claim, and the federal claim failed, UM was entitled to pretrial judgment. *Teachout v. Univ. of Minnesota*, No. 09-2140 (DWF/JSM), 2011 WL 916356 (D. Minn. 3/16/11).

◆ *A New York community college security guard with a foot injury was entitled to use a cane at work.*

For 29 years, the guard worked a 3:00 p.m. to 11:00 p.m. shift at the college. As the result of a work injury, he began to limp. The college sought medical documentation of the guard's disability. When he provided documents showing he had been diagnosed with reflex sympathetic dystrophy and a crush injury, the college denied that he was a person with a disability and said he did not need accommodation under the ADA. The guard sued the college in a federal district court for ADA, Title VII, equal protection and due process violations.

The court refused to award the college pretrial judgment on the ADA claim. There was evidence that the guard's foot injury was a disability under the ADA. **To prove the existence of a disability under the ADA, he had to show the injury substantially limited his ability to perform the major life activity of walking.** The court found evidence of substantial pain from the injury and that it was likely to be permanent. It also found enough evidence for a jury to find that using a cane would help the guard perform the essential functions of his job. His request to use a cane was "a plausible accommodation" with a negligible cost to the community college. For this reason, the college was denied pretrial judgment. *Schroeder v. Suffolk County Community College*, No. 07-CV-2060, 2009 WL 1748869 (E.D.N.Y. 6/22/09).

◆ *A Florida professor's claim that he was discharged because his employer thought he was an alcoholic will not be dismissed prior to a trial.*

The professor began teaching as an adjunct professor and soon became a full-time associate professor. A few years later, he began missing meetings and showing signs of alcohol abuse. His divorce became final near this time. An associate dean arrived unannounced at the professor's residence and concluded he was under the influence of alcohol. The professor was placed on medical leave. The university told him he would be deemed to have resigned if he did not submit a leave of absence form and physician's certification by a specified date. It then discharged him after he did not submit the forms on time.

The professor sued the university under the Rehabilitation Act, claiming it discharged him because it "regarded" him as an alcoholic. Alcoholism can be a disability under the Rehabilitation Act when the individual claiming protection is not currently abusing alcohol. The court rejected the university's claim that pretrial judgment should be granted based on the professor's failure to actively participate on a dissertation review committee. A factual dispute existed as to whether active participation on the committee was an essential job function and as to whether he adequately performed it. **The court also rejected the university's argument that it accommodated the professor by placing him on leave and making its employee assistance program available to him.** These steps did not conclusively establish it met its duty to reasonably accommodate him. *Gardiner v. Nova Southeastern Univ.*, No. 06-60590 CIV, 2006 WL 3804704 (S.D. Fla. 12/22/06).

C. Contagious Diseases

In 1998, the U.S. Supreme Court held that a person with HIV was protected by the Americans with Disabilities Act (ADA), despite the fact that she was not yet exhibiting symptoms of the disease. Since HIV substantially impaired her ability to reproduce, she could not be excluded unless her condition presented a direct threat to the health and safety of others. Bragdon v. Abbott, *524 U.S. 624, 118 S.Ct. 2196, 141 L.Ed.2d 540 (1998).*

◆　*An Ohio university police officer failed to show his employer violated the ADA by requiring him to undergo medical testing.*

After the university fired the officer for using excessive force, an arbitrator found no good reason for dismissal and ordered his reinstatement. When he returned to work, the chief required him to undergo pre-hire medical and psychological evaluations. According to the officer, he was ordered to be vaccinated for Hepatitis B, take a stress test, undergo an electrocardiogram and complete a psychological examination. He then sued the university in a federal court for violating the ADA by requiring testing, demanding a medical release, and disseminating confidential information. He added some state law claims.

Finding **Eleventh Amendment immunity barred money damage claims under the ADA**, the court dismissed those claims. Nor could any of the named university officials be held individually liable under the ADA. The court held the officer could not pursue his disability discrimination claims via 42 U.S.C. § 1983 because the ADA provides a comprehensive remedial scheme. Finally, the court rejected a group of state law claims. An invasion of privacy claim failed because the officer did not show his medical records were publicly disclosed. As a result, the case was dismissed. *Burnette v. Univ. of Akron*, No. 5:11CV2361, 2012 WL 3587568 (N.D. Ohio 8/20/12).

◆ *The Supreme Court held that a person with a contagious disease was entitled to the protections of the Rehabilitation Act.*

A Florida elementary school teacher was discharged because of her continued recurrence of tuberculosis. She sued the school board under Section 504 of the Rehabilitation Act. A federal district court dismissed her suit, but the Eleventh Circuit held persons with contagious diseases fall within Section 504's coverage. The case then reached the U.S. Supreme Court, which held that **tuberculosis was a disability under Section 504.** The disease attacked the teacher's respiratory system and affected her ability to work. It would be unfair to allow an employer to distinguish between a disease's potential effect on others and its effect on the afflicted employee in order to justify discriminatory treatment. Accordingly, she was entitled to reinstatement or front pay if she could show that despite her disability, she was otherwise qualified for her job with or without a reasonable accommodation. *School Board of Nassau County v. Arline*, 480 U.S. 273, 107 S.Ct. 1123, 94 L.Ed.2d 307 (1987).

VI. RETALIATION

A. Generally

Title VII prohibits an employer from retaliating against an employee for opposing an unlawful employment practice, or for making a charge, testifying, assisting, or participating in any manner in a discrimination investigation, proceeding or hearing. In Robinson v. Shell Oil Co., *519 U.S. 337 (1997), the Supreme Court held a former employee could bring a retaliatory discrimination lawsuit against a former employer after he was given a negative employment reference following his filing of a discrimination complaint.*

◆ *A federal court agreed with a private Pennsylvania college that a former employee presented insufficient evidence to proceed with a retaliation case.*

After serving the college as an associate dean for two years, the employee became a visiting assistant professor. She received negative reviews from her students and began having problems with a colleague. After the employee's contract expired, she was not rehired. She sued the college in a federal court for race discrimination and retaliation. In pretrial activity, the court found there was insufficient evidence of discrimination and retaliation to allow the case to proceed any further. Examples of racist comments by the colleague did not support either of her claims. **The college had valid, nondiscriminatory reasons for not rehiring the employee.** She conceded her supervisor had said her student evaluations were the worst he had ever seen. As a result, the court granted the college judgment without a trial. *Mosaka-Wright v. LaRoche College*, No. 11cv1139, 2012 WL 3060151 (W.D. Pa. 7/25/12).

◆ *A Michigan university employee did not prove retaliation based on complaints he made about a female co-worker.*

According to the employee, the female harassed him, followed him around, and gave him a Valentine's Day card and candy. She made a counter-complaint for staring at her, commenting about her breasts, standing near her, trying to engage her in sexual conversation, and simulating intercourse. After an investigation, the university found both employees acted unprofessionally but found that neither had violated the university's sexual harassment policy. Soon after filing his complaint, the employee took a medical leave. After granting him several leave extensions, the university eliminated his position. The employee sued the university in a federal court, claiming his employment was terminated in retaliation for his complaint about the co-worker. **The court held he did not suffer an adverse job action that would have prevented a reasonable employee from filing a sexual harassment complaint.** None of the actions in this case would dissuade a reasonable employee from filing a complaint. Nor did the employee show any causal connection between his complaint and his termination. As there was a legitimate reason for the action, the university was entitled to pretrial judgment. *Pines v. Board of Regents of the Univ. of Michigan*, No. 10-15106, 2012 WL 380242 (E.D. Mich. 2/6/12).

◆   *The U.S. Court of Appeals, Third Circuit, held a New Jersey university faculty member could proceed with his discrimination and retaliation claims.*

The faculty member claimed he was passed over for promotion twice based on his race and Filipino national origin. He filed two race and national origin discrimination claims with a federal agency and added a retaliation claim to the second charge. A federal district court awarded pretrial judgment to the university. On appeal, the Third Circuit held the lower court should have looked at the evidence in the light most favorable to the faculty member. **He made a valid preliminary case of employment discrimination by showing he was qualified for the promotions, and that colleagues who were not Asian or Filipino were promoted.** And the faculty member produced evidence that at least one of the colleagues was less qualified than he was for the promotion. At this stage, he did not have to prove his case, he only had to raise doubts about the reasons given for denying a promotion. He did this by presenting testimony from promotions committee members who said they had not reviewed or could not remember reviewing his application. As a result, the court vacated the judgment and returned the case to the lower court for reconsideration under the correct legal standard and based upon all the evidence. *Andes v. New Jersey City Univ.*, 419 Fed. Appx. 230 (3d Cir. 2011).

◆   *An African-American law professor at Louisiana State University (LSU) was unable to prove her discrimination claims, according to a federal court.*

According to the professor, LSU denied her a promotion and paid her less than a white professor. She said LSU retaliated against her with a bogus investigation after she filed a discrimination charge. The professor sued LSU in a federal district court, alleging racial discrimination and retaliation. After the court rejected both claims, appeal reached the U.S. Court of Appeals, Fifth Circuit. There, LSU claimed the professor's promotion request was untimely. She argued this was a pretext because LSU had accepted late applications from white applicants. The court found LSU showed the applications it accepted from white applicants were only slightly late. The professor's application, on the other hand, was so late it left insufficient time for faculty committee review.

According to the court, the only argument the professor had to fall back on was her personal belief that LSU discriminated against her. But that did not establish pretext. The court held the professor did not prove LSU retaliated against her by conducting what she called a "post-tenure review" of her teaching. It found **"a reasonable employee would not expect to be insulated from review of her questionable job performance simply because"** she had **previously filed a discrimination claim**. LSU showed the review was not prompted by the discrimination claim but by "vehement complaints from a number of students" about her performance. As the professor could not prove her claims, the court held LSU was entitled to judgment. *Goring v. Board of Supervisors of Louisiana State Univ.*, 414 Fed.Appx. 630 (5th Cir. 2011).

◆ *An Ohio university fundraiser whose position ended nine months after she made a complaint about a dean stated a valid preliminary case of retaliation.*

The fundraiser said a university dean used objectionable language, leered at her, inappropriately touched a female staffer and made comments about liking to "chase young women." She complained, and her office was moved twice. Eventually, her position was eliminated, and she sued the university foundation in a federal district court for retaliation in violation of Title VII. According to the court, a reasonable employee in the fundraiser's position might not report offensive behavior if the consequences included being moved to a different office, undergoing a job termination, being offered a lesser position, then being fired when she refused it. **The court held the fundraiser engaged in an activity protected by Title VII when she complained about the dean.** The university and the university foundation were aware of her protected activity and took adverse action against her following her complaints. As the fundraiser made out a valid preliminary case of retaliation, and showed the protected activity may have caused adverse employment action, the court allowed her case to proceed. *McCart v. Univ. of Cincinnati Foundation*, No. 1:08-CV-656, 2010 WL 1433309 (S.D. Ohio 4/7/10).

◆ *A federal court refused to dismiss retaliation claims brought by a former dean at Gallaudet University, a higher education institution for deaf persons.*

According to the dean, many Gallaudet students and staff espoused "Deaf Culture," which includes a belief that deaf persons should use only American Sign Language (ASL) to communicate. While the dean used ASL, she used other methods such as hearing amplification and lip-reading. When Deaf students staged protests over the appointment of a new university president, the board of trustees revoked the appointment. According to the dean, the only basis for this was the perception that the new president wasn't "Deaf enough." She suggested the movement was biased and later said Gallaudet faculty, staff and alumni supported the protesters while she stood behind the president. The dean claimed her responsibilities were reduced and that she was excluded from administrative decision-making. She claimed university staff retaliated against her and spread lies about her. After the dean sued the university in a federal court for retaliation under state and federal law, Gallaudet sought dismissal.

The court allowed a retaliation claim under Section 601 of Title VII. **Section 601 does not explicitly prohibit retaliation – but the court held Section 601 retaliation claims are implicitly allowed.** The court held the dean made a valid Title VII case by showing Gallaudet took adverse actions against her because of her advocacy for minority students. The court also found she stated a claim under the District of Columbia Human Rights Act, which prohibits retaliation for exercising civil rights, or for aiding or encouraging others to do so. The dean had supported a president whose appointment was revoked for what she alleged were discriminatory reasons. She also said that she suffered the same discrimination – being seen as not "Deaf enough." Finding the dean had stated valid retaliation claims, the court refused to dismiss the case. *Kimmel v. Gallaudet Univ.*, 639 F.Supp.2d 34 (D.D.C. 2009).

◆ *A Massachusetts general accounting director who complained about college financial practices could not claim retaliation under Title VII.*

The accounting director complained that a male co-worker's financial information was erroneous and in violation of state regulations. According to the director, illegal changes were made to the college's general ledger system. She said her supervisor retaliated against her for making these complaints and that instead of disciplining the co-worker, the supervisor discriminated against her and created a hostile work environment. The director took a leave of absence, claiming her supervisor had caused her to suffer a nervous breakdown. While she was on leave, an audit determined that her job performance was unsatisfactory. The college discharged the director, and she filed an administrative complaint for gender discrimination. She then filed a federal district court action against the college and some co-workers for gender discrimination and retaliation under Title VII. The court dismissed the case.

Appeal reached the U.S. Court of Appeals, First Circuit, which found the administrative complaint put the college on notice of possible gender discrimination. For this reason, the director's gender bias claim was reinstated. There is no individual liability under Title VII, so the lower court had properly disposed of the claims against the co-workers. **To prove her claim of unlawful retaliation under Title VII, the director had to show she opposed an unlawful employment practice under Title VII or participated in an investigation, proceeding or hearing under Title VII.** Since the financial improprieties she reported had nothing to do with Title VII, the court held this claim failed. *Fantini v. Salem State College*, 557 F.3d 22 (1st Cir. 2009).

◆ *No violation of Title VII occurred when a university employee was laid off after he complained that his supervisor was showing favoritism toward a lover.*

An Oklahoma State University (OSU) employee complained that his supervisor showed favoritism to a person he was having an affair with and then retaliated against him. After being laid off, he sued OSU in a federal district court for retaliation and age discrimination. OSU responded that the layoff was part of a restructuring. To prove retaliation, the court held the employee had to show he engaged in protected activity and suffered an adverse employment action as a result. However, he did not participate in a Title VII investigation, proceeding or hearing, and he could not show he opposed an unlawful employment practice. Since opposition to an affair is not protected conduct under Title VII, the employee could not proceed with his retaliation claim.

On appeal to the U.S. Court of Appeals, Tenth Circuit, the employee claimed he was subjected to a hostile work environment based on his reporting of the affair. The court held this was simply a re-hash of his invalid retaliation claim. **There was no evidence of a hostile work environment or unlawful discrimination.** As the supervisor's affair and favoritism were not enough to pursue a Title VII case, the court rejected the appeal. *Anderson v. Oklahoma State Univ. Board of Regents*, 342 Fed.Appx. 365 (10th Cir. 2009).

◆ *A university manager may pursue a claim that she was retaliated against for her complaints that a staff member was being treated unfairly due to race.*

The manager complained several times that she believed a refusal to implement a performance improvement plan for an African-American employee constituted race discrimination. The manager was told that the employee "had a history" with the university and that any action against her could result in a discrimination lawsuit. She felt the process followed for the employee was not equitable because it subjected her to such intense scrutiny. The manager filed a state court complaint alleging opposition to discriminatory employment practices. The case reached the Court of Appeals of Minnesota, which held she was not required to show that the employer's practices were actually discriminatory. **Instead, she needed to show only that she had a good-faith, reasonable belief that the employment practices she opposed were discriminatory.** The complaint set forth reasonable grounds for the belief that the university was treating the employee differently on the basis of her race. *Bahr v. Capella Univ.*, 765 N.W.2d 428 (Minn. Ct. App. 2009).

◆ *Two University of Denver professors did not show they were subjected to a hostile work environment or that they were retaliated against under Title VII.*

In their lawsuit against the university and several officials, the professors claimed retaliation after they engaged in more than 20 acts of protected conduct over a two-year period. They said they were subjected to public humiliation at a department meeting after they complained that they were treated unfavorably during a search for an assistant professor. The professors also said the Spanish section of their department was abolished after they complained about hostile work environment and discrimination. A federal district court dismissed the case, and the professors appealed to the U.S. Court of Appeals, Tenth Circuit.

The court held that to prove retaliation, the professors had to show they engaged in protected activity resulting adverse employment action. And there had to be a causal connection between the protected activity and the adverse employment action. The court held *Burlington Northern & Santa Fe Railway Co. v. White*, this chapter, required a showing that a reasonable person would have found the action was materially adverse in a way that dissuaded them from filing discrimination charges. The professors did not show this. The conduct they found humiliating consisted of colleagues rolling their eyes, laughing, snickering and making comments to one another while they talked. As this was insufficient to show they were subjected to an adverse action, the case was properly dismissed. **Title VII does not establish a workplace civility code.** *Somoza v. Univ. of Denver*, 513 F.3d 1206 (10th Cir. 2008).

◆ *A federal appeals court refused to disturb a verdict for a Grambling State University police chief who was fired after trying to hire a white job applicant.*

Grambling State University (GSU) is a historically black Louisiana institution. After reviewing the qualifications of four candidates for an assistant police chief position, he recommended a white applicant. A supervisor blocked the application, and the chief believed she was doing so based on race. Less than a week after the chief made a written inquiry about the status of the application, GSU fired him. He sued GSU in a federal district court for violations of Title VII and state law. GSU countered that the chief was discharged for not following proper hiring procedures, his rudeness at an interdepartmental meeting, and a harassment complaint by a co-worker.

A jury returned a unanimous verdict for the chief and awarded him $140,000 in compensatory damages. Appeal reached the U.S. Court of Appeals, Fifth Circuit, which upheld the compensatory damage award. **It found the chief's opposition to GSU's refusal to hire an applicant based on his race could be protected activity under Title VII.** There was also enough evidence for a jury to conclude GSU treated the applicant differently than others based on race. The compensatory damages award was justified, and the court held the lower court should have awarded the chief attorneys' fees. *Tureaud v. Grambling State Univ.*, 294 Fed.Appx. 909 (5th Cir. 2008).

◆ *Actions taken against a Nebraska professor did not form the basis of a retaliation claim.*

The professor had worked at Creighton University for 10 years when a colleague filed a sexual harassment claim against her. A four-person committee investigated the charge and recommended discharging the professor. Instead, the university's president placed her on probation under close monitoring. She was forbidden from contact with her accuser and required to undergo a year of psychological counseling and training. The professor filed discrimination charges against Creighton, claiming she was placed on probation based on her national origin. She then sued the university in a federal district court, alleging 21 counts of retaliation. The court ruled for the university, and the professor appealed to the U.S. Court of Appeals, Eighth Circuit. **The court found none of the actions noted by the professor were harmful enough to constitute a "materially adverse" job action.** For example, the decision to alter her teaching schedule did not cause any significant harm. Nor was the professor's allegation that she received "the silent treatment" and was ostracized by other faculty members sufficient to show retaliation. As no link between the charge and alleged retaliation was demonstrated, the judgment was affirmed. *Recio v. Creighton Univ.*, 521 F.3d 934 (8th Cir. 2008).

◆ *A Utah instructor failed to prove a university declined to renew her three-year teaching contract based on her gender, national origin or retaliation.*

The instructor claimed the university declined to renew her contract because she assigned some students poor grades. She said the failure to renew her contract was based on her gender and/or national origin, and she added a claim for hostile work environment. The instructor sued the university in a federal district court. It stated that to prove discrimination, she needed to show that she was doing satisfactory work. The instructor failed to satisfy this requirement. The facts showed she could not establish and maintain authority in her classroom. The instructor failed to respond to messages from the chair of her department. There were no facts showing the employment environment at the university was objectively hostile. **To prove retaliation, the instructor had to show she had engaged in a protected activity.** The instructor claimed she was retaliated against for academically penalizing students. The court held this was not protected behavior that can support a retaliation claim. *Mejia v. Univ. of Utah*, No. 1:05-CV-53 TS, 2007 WL 391586 (D. Utah 2/1/07).

◆ *The U.S. Supreme Court held the reassignment of a female to more arduous and dirtier work was evidence of retaliation by her employer.*

A Tennessee railway employee complained about her supervisor's sexually harassing comments. The company disciplined the supervisor but also transferred the employee to a less desirable position. A superior said her reassignment reflected complaints by co-workers that a "more senior man" should have the "less arduous and cleaner job of forklift operator." The employee filed a Title VII complaint, and the company suspended her without pay for insubordination. The employee sued, and the case reached the Supreme Court, which explained that Title VII's anti-retaliation provision was created to prohibit a wide variety of employer conduct intended to restrain employees in the exercise of protected activities. **Although Title VII does not create a general civility code for the workplace, the jury properly found that the reassignment and suspension amounted to retaliation.** The reassignment was "materially adverse" to the employee, who went unpaid for 37 days during which she was uncertain of her employment status. *Burlington Northern & Santa Fe Railway Co. v. White*, 548 U.S. 53, 126 S.Ct. 2405, 165 L.Ed.2d 345 (2006).

B. Defenses

In Univ. of Tennessee v. Elliot, *478 U.S. 788 (1986), the Supreme Court rejected the Title VII defense that a former employee's federal court lawsuit had to be dismissed because it already had been resolved in an administrative hearing. The court held that a state administrative proceeding on a Title VII discrimination claim filed in state court could be appealed to the federal court system when the state proceeding remained unreviewed by state courts.*

◆ *A Pennsylvania university defeated an African-American wrestling coach's retaliation lawsuit by showing he punched a student.*

The coach joked about a wrestler who executed a move he considered comical. He said the student rushed toward him in a rage and that he punched the student in the mouth. Within a few days, the coach was fired, and he sued the university in a federal court for retaliation. As evidence of retaliation based on race, the coach asserted that the university's athletic director "kept a file on him." While the court found this to be true, it noted the file documented misconduct such as the coach's refusal to follow university and NCAA rules. **The court held the university offered a legitimate nonretaliatory reason for firing him that was not a pretext for unlawful retaliation.** On appeal, the Third Circuit affirmed the judgment for the university in a brief memorandum. *Heard v. Waynesburg Univ.*, 436 Fed.Appx. 79 (3d Cir. 2011).

◆   *An appeal of a verdict on a New York college vice president's retaliation claim led to a $400,000 reduction in a punitive damage award.*

The college fired the vice president days after she filed a sex discrimination complaint. She sued the college in a federal district court for sex discrimination and retaliation. A jury found the discharge was in retaliation for her sex discrimination complaint, and it awarded her $75,000 in compensatory damages and $425,000 in punitive damages. The college sought to overturn the judgment or obtain a new trial, arguing that its president had discharged the vice president before he learned she had filed her complaint. Therefore, the college claimed the action could not have been in retaliation for the complaint.

The court found enough evidence for the jury to find the president fired the vice president after he learned of the discrimination complaint. He did not ask her for her keys or other college property before she left. Nor did the college prove the firing was based solely on dissatisfaction with the vice president's job performance. Although the court upheld the verdict, it found the punitive damage award was excessive. **The reasonableness of a punitive damage award depends largely on the reprehensibility of a defendant's conduct.** In this case, there was no violence, threats or evidence of repeated misconduct. Under the circumstances, the most a jury could reasonably award in punitive damages was $25,000. *Norris v. New York City College of Technology*, No. 07-CV-853, 2009 WL 82556 (E.D.N.Y. 1/14/09).

◆   *Four Illinois university police officers failed to prove claims that they were assigned to work at a particular university campus based on their race.*

The officers patrolled two university campuses, one of which was located in a predominantly black residential area in East St. Louis. Due to its smaller size, duties at the East St. Louis campus were deemed less strenuous than those at the Edwardsville campus. After the officers were denied promotions to sergeant positions, they were discharged for insubordination and other reasons. The officers sued the university in a federal district court, claiming the university violated Title VII by disproportionally assigning them to the East St. Louis campus based on race. The court held for the university, and the officers appealed. The U.S. Court of Appeals, Seventh Circuit, held **the assignments did not constitute a materially adverse employment action.** Three of the four officers had asked to work at the East St. Louis campus at some point, and their complaints regarding assignment location involved nothing more than subjective preference. There was no evidence that assignments were made with regard to race or in retaliation for complaining about discrimination. *Nichols v. Southern Illinois Univ.-Edwardsville*, 510 F.3d 772 (7th Cir. 2007).

◆ *A teaching assistant's retaliation claim failed because he did not engage in "protected activity" within the meaning of the law.*

An Iranian national began working as a graduate teaching assistant at a Missouri university while in a chemistry Ph.D. program. The student appealed a grade he received in an advanced inorganic chemistry course, accusing the professor of mismanaging the course and assigning grades capriciously. After a hearing, the grade was not changed. The teaching assistant later complained to a university international affairs office about compliance with Department of Homeland Security regulations regarding foreign nationals. He also complained to the university affirmative action office about an investigation into the transmission of anonymous emails to a female student.

The chemistry department dismissed the teaching assistant without stating a reason, and he withdrew as a student. He sued the university and its officials in a federal district court for retaliation. The court held for the university, and the assistant appealed to the U.S. Court of Appeals, Eighth Circuit. **The court held that to prove retaliation, he needed to show he had engaged in a protected activity, and that the university took adverse action against him on that basis.** The court held the assistant did not engage in any "protected activity." His complaints regarding grades, Department of Homeland Security regulations and the student affairs office related to his status as a student, whereas his retaliation claim related to his status as an employee. Because none of the activities related to his status as an employee, the assistant could not prove his retaliation claim. The decision for university officials was affirmed. *Bakhtiari v. Lutz*, 507 F.3d 1132 (8th Cir. 2007).

◆ *The U.S. Court of Appeals, Eleventh Circuit, reinstated an academic advisor's Title VII retaliation claim.*

The advisor claimed his direct supervisor began making unwanted sexual advances soon after he was hired. He said he rejected the advances and the supervisor then overloaded him with work and verbally abused him. He claimed that when he applied for a promotion, the supervisor verbally attacked him in his office, spit in his face, and knocked papers out of his hands. The advisor filed a formal written sexual harassment complaint, called campus police and filed a protection order against her. The advisor later gave the dean a copy of the police report and protection order, then claimed she withdrew her recommendation for the promotion and discharged him for unprofessionalism. A federal district court held the university did not violate Title VII, and the advisor appealed. **The U.S. Court of Appeals, Eleventh Circuit, held a call to police might qualify as protected activity under Title VII.** *Scarbrough v. Board of Trustees Florida A&M Univ.*, 504 F.3d 1220 (11th Cir. 2007).

◆ *The University of Kansas had legitimate, nondiscriminatory reasons for denying tenure to an adjunct professor and did not retaliate against her.*

A University of Kansas professor was denied tenure, then discharged. She sued the university in a federal district court for discrimination under Title VII. She was then appointed to an adjunct lecturer position, but was denied principal investigator (PI) status, which would have allowed her to act as a director of grant applications. A jury then ruled for the university. The professor applied for an administrative position with the university, but was not interviewed. Claiming retaliation for filing her Title VII lawsuit, she brought a second federal court lawsuit against the university for retaliation. The court held for the university, and the professor appealed. The U.S. Court of Appeals, Tenth Circuit, found the decisions to confer the adjunct lecturer title and deny her PI status were not significant changes in employment. The university's decision not to hire her as an administrator was not retaliation. **The university presented legitimate, nondiscriminatory reasons for declining to hire her for that position.** *Annett v. Univ. of Kansas*, 371 F.3d 1233 (10th Cir. 2004).

C. Causal Connection

To prove unlawful retaliation, the courts insist upon some showing of a causal connection between protected activity taken by the employee and the employer's decision to take adverse employment action.

◆ *A grants manager of Hispanic ancestry was allowed to proceed with a federal court retaliation claim against Hawaii Pacific University (HPU).*

According to the grants manager, HPU denied her a promotion because of her Hispanic origin. About one month later, HPU conducted an investigation that determined she had falsely stated a former HPU director destroyed files and misrepresented paperwork for a grant. Asserting multiple violations of the HPU employee handbook, the university discharged the grants manager. She sued HPU in a federal district court for race discrimination and retaliation. The court dismissed the discrimination claim, but it held the retaliation claim should go forward. It held **the proximity in time between the complaint of discrimination and the initiation of the investigation was short enough to raise a question of possible retaliation.** Although HPU presented a valid, nonretaliatory reason to discharge the grants manager, her evidence cast doubt on the investigator's finding that she had lied about the former director destroying files. As the employee had cast doubt on one reason given for firing her, the court found further proceedings were necessary to consider her retaliation claim. *Graciano v. Hawaii Pacific Univ.*, No. 11-00432 SOM/KSC, 2012 WL 3029587 (D. Haw. 7/25/12).

◆ *A sign-language instructor could not show he was denied a promotion by a Connecticut community college in retaliation for filing discrimination claims.*

After 13 years of working for the community college, the instructor filed two civil rights charges against it that were eventually settled. He then applied for promotion to an assistant professor position. But the college began to receive complaints from students about his class performance. The instructor filed a new charge of retaliation with the state civil rights agency, claiming the real reason he was denied promotion was his earlier charges of discrimination. He then sued the college board in a state court, which held for the board.

On appeal, a state appellate court found it is illegal to retaliate against an employee for filing a discrimination charge. While the instructor had filed a charge, and the college knew about it, he could not show the college refused to promote him because of the charge. Instead, **the lower court properly found** the college denied the instructor a promotion because of the numerous student complaints against him. *Ayantola v. Board of Trustees of Technical Colleges*, 116 Conn.App. 531, 976 A.2d 784 (Conn. App. Ct. 2009).

◆ *A federal court held a Louisiana university had a valid reason for firing an African-American employee who filed an internal discrimination claim.*

The employee was an assistant to the chancellor for equal opportunity, where her duties included ensuring compliance with Equal Employment Opportunity (EEO) requirements. She filed an internal grievance against the chancellor, claiming he subjected her to a racially hostile work environment after she returned to work following Hurricane Katrina. Her race-based claims included denying her an operating budget, staff and adequate raises. A year and a half later, the chancellor discovered the employee had not updated the university's EEO affirmative action plan for two years. He fired her for putting the university at risk of noncompliance with federal law. After being fired, the employee sued the university in a federal court for retaliation in violation of Title VII. The court found she was not fired on the basis of filing the internal grievance. Instead, **the university showed it had a valid, nonretaliatory reason for firing her, and she did not show this reason was a pretext to mask discrimination**. As the university showed it had a valid, nonretaliatory reason for firing her, the employee's retaliation claim failed. *Wall v. Univ. of New Orleans*, No. 09-3486, 2010 WL 1552730 (E.D. La. 4/16/10).

◆ *A New Jersey court rejected a professor's claims that a dean and a department chair discriminated against him because of his Indian origin.*

In a state court action, the professor alleged that the dean of the university's School of Business and the chair of the Department of Economics violated the state Law Against Discrimination by discriminating and retaliating against him based on his national origin. He claimed the chair refused to switch a summer course with him and that the dean examined a request for travel expenses "minutely." And the professor claimed the dean gave him poor employment evaluations. A trial court ruled against him, finding he had failed to prove the basic elements of his discrimination and retaliation claims. On appeal, a state appellate court found the record indicated that the professor's department chair declined the request to switch summer courses because the chair's schedule was already set. **The professor did not prove a causal connection between an earlier suit and the decision to decline his request for a switch.** The court found no evidence that the dean retaliated against him through his employment evaluations. It held the dean used the same standards for all faculty members, and the professor did not suffer an adverse employment action in connection with the evaluations. *Kant v. Seton Hall Univ.*, No. L-8638-07, 2010 WL 4007642 (N.J. Super. Ct. App. Div. 10/13/10).

◆ *An Illinois college instructor did not prove a causal connection between her complaint of sexual harassment and her discharge.*

A college vice president learned that the instructor used inappropriate language and gossiped with co-workers. Based on reports and observations, the supervisor issued a written warning and prepared a corrective action notice requiring her to immediately stop gossiping. However, the instructor refused to sign it. The next day, the supervisor learned she was spreading rumors that he was having a gay affair. Following an investigation, the regional vice president fired the instructor. A few days later, the instructor claimed that the supervisor had sexually harassed her. After filing an administrative complaint, the instructor sued the college in a federal district court for sexual harassment. She also claimed the college retaliated against her for reporting sexual harassment.

The court found the instructor did not assert any conduct so severe or pervasive that a reasonable person would find a hostile work environment. In addition, she did not show her supervisor's behavior toward her negatively affected her work. This defeated her sexual harassment claim. **To prove retaliation, the instructor had to show there was a causal connection between her post-discharge letter and the decision to fire her.** But there was no evidence that the vice president who made the termination decision was aware of any sexual harassment allegations at the time the decision to fire her was made. The court awarded pretrial judgment to the college. *Bozek v. Corinthian Colleges*, No. 07 C 4303, 2009 WL 377552 (N.D. Ill. 2/13/09).

◆ *A Tennessee community college discharged an African-American professor in retaliation for accusing the college of unlawful discrimination.*

The professor complained of racial discrimination during his 25-year career and filed several complaints. The college received criticism from the professor's students and colleagues about how he managed a psychology course. The department eventually relieved him of his teaching duties for unsatisfactory performance. He attempted to meet the requirements of a performance plan but was not given an entire term to complete it. The college discharged the professor, and he sued the college in a federal court, alleging it violated Title VII by opposing an unlawful employment practice. The court dismissed the action, but the U.S. Court of Appeals, Sixth Circuit, returned the case to the district court for further consideration. A jury awarded the professor $320,000, and the college appealed. When the case returned to the Sixth Circuit, it found sufficient evidence for a reasonable jury to have found the college unlawfully retaliated against him in violation of Title VII. **The professor presented ample evidence to support a causal connection between his termination and retaliation for his discrimination complaints.** Front pay was an appropriate way to compensate him for future loss. *Cox v. Shelby State Community College*, 194 Fed.Appx. 267 (6th Cir. 2006).

◆ *A Massachusetts university did not fire a professor in retaliation for supporting his wife's sexual harassment claim against a department head.*

The professor and his wife worked in the university's biochemistry and molecular biology department. A department head criticized the professor for certain fees charged by the research lab founded by the professor and his wife. The professor and wife filed a grievance, asking the university to remove the information from their personnel files. The grievance was resolved when the department head agreed his letter was a private communication. The university later reduced the professor's teaching assignments after he received negative comments on student evaluations. His evaluations remained poor for several years, and the university eventually held hearings and decided to fire him.

The professor sued the university and two department heads in a state court for retaliation in violation of Title VII and a Massachusetts anti-discrimination law. The court awarded judgment to the university and department heads, and the professor appealed to the Supreme Judicial Court of Massachusetts. He argued a court could infer the causal connection between support of his wife's complaint and the actions taken against him from the timing and sequence of events. **The court held the professor did not prove a causal link merely by showing that one event followed another. His performance and department funding problems began before his wife filed her complaint.** As the time span between endorsing the sexual harassment complaint and adverse employment action was too long, the court affirmed the judgment. *Mole v. Univ. of Massachusetts*, 442 Mass. 582, 814 N.E.2d 329 (Mass. 2004).

◆ *An Alabama university showed it did not fire an employee based on retaliation for turning her down for another job.*

The university discharged the employee, saying it wanted to achieve standardization and save money by outsourcing her tasks. It also denied her a job as an associate director of student housing, as she lacked relevant experience. The employee sued the university in a federal district court for discrimination based on gender and for retaliation. The court held for the university, and she appealed to the U.S. Court of Appeals, Eleventh Circuit. **The court held the gender discrimination claim failed because the university stated a legitimate and nondiscriminatory reason for the termination – saving costs and standardization.** Similarly, the retaliation claim failed because the individual who was chosen to fill the post had more relevant experience. The district court's ruling was affirmed. *Cashman v. Univ. of Alabama Board of Trustees*, 260 Fed.Appx. 216 (11th Cir. 2007).

CHAPTER EIGHT

Intellectual Property

I. COPYRIGHT LAW

State and federal copyright laws protect original works of authorship by creating exclusive rights for the owner to make copies of the work, prepare derivative works, distribute copies of the work, and perform or display the work publicly. See 17 U.S.C. § 106. Copyright protection for an original work exists even if no copyright is registered. See 17 U.S.C. § 408(a). Registration is required in order to initiate a copyright infringement action. Employers are presumed to own the copyright to works prepared by their employees within the scope of their employment, unless a specific written agreement says otherwise.

For further background, including an informative fact sheet on fair use, see the website of the U.S. Copyright Office at http://copyright.gov/.

A. Fair Use

Educators and others are entitled to make "fair use" of copyrighted works for the purposes described in 17 U.S.C. § 107. The statute lists four factors to assure such use is not for commercial purposes.

In Stewart v. Abend, 495 U.S. 207 (1990), the U.S. Supreme Court held the primary factor in fair use cases is the effect that use will have on the work's potential market or value.

17 U.S.C. § 107 states:

The fair use of a copyrighted work, including such use by reproduction in copies ... for purposes such as criticism, comment, news reporting, teaching (including multiple copies for classroom use), scholarship, or research, is not an infringement of copyright. In determining whether the

use made of a work in any particular case is a fair use the factors to be considered shall include –
(1) the purpose and character of the use, including whether such use is of a commercial nature or is for nonprofit educational purposes;
(2) the nature of the copyrighted work;
(3) the amount and substantiality of the portion used in relation to the copyrighted work as a whole; and
(4) the effect of the use upon the potential market for or value of the copyrighted work.

◆   *A federal court agreed with academic book publishers that the unlicensed posting to library e-reserves of excerpts from copyrighted books infringed the copyrights where the excepts were in excess of parameters set by the court.*

According to the publishers, the university allowed professors to post extensive tracts from copyrighted books in electronic formats for students. In response to a lawsuit filed in 2008, the university changed its copyright policy by requiring professors to use a copyright "checklist" to determine if a proposed use qualified as a fair use. Although the publishers claimed that copyright violations remained very significant at the university, the court later found only five of the challenged excerpts violated the "fair use" principle of federal copyright law. Significantly, the court found the excerpts were used for the purpose of teaching and scholarship, and for a noncommercial, nonprofit educational use. And the university was a nonprofit educational institution. For this reason, the first fair use factor weighed heavily in the university's favor.

Because all of the excerpts were informational and educational in nature and none were fiction, the second fair use factor favored the publishers.

The third fair use factor was variable, since the amount of the copying as a percentage of the book varied from book to book and by the individual professor's use of the excerpt. For this case, the judge determined that if a book was not divided into chapters or contained fewer than 10 chapters, unpaid copying of no more than 10% of the pages in the book was permissible under factor three. "In practical effect, this will allow copying of about one chapter or its equivalent." Where a book contained 10 or more chapters, the unpaid copying of up to but no more than one chapter (or its equivalent) was found permissible. Only five of the challenged excerpts were found in violation of these parameters. The fourth fair use factor involved the effect of the use in question on the potential market for or value of the copyrighted book. This factor depended upon the size of the excerpt, in the court's view. Unpaid use of a small excerpt would not harm the potential market for a copyrighted book. But where permissions were readily available from the publisher for small excerpts of copyrighted books, this factor favored the publishers. *Cambridge Univ. Press v. Becker*, 863 F.Supp.2d 1190 (N.D. Ga. 2012).

◆   *A Massachusetts federal court refused to find file-sharing falls under the fair use exception to the Copyright Act.*

The "fair use exception" is a limit on the virtual monopoly a copyright holder has over a work. The exception allows a limited, free use of the work for a worthy public purpose, such as education that does not harm the copyright holder's market interest. A student shared music files he downloaded even after court decisions clarified that file-sharing is a copyright violation. Applying the four fair use factors and weighing the equities, the court declined to find the student had made fair use of the files. His purpose and the character of his use of the music was personal enjoyment. **The court found music should enjoy "robust copyright protections."** The court held the effect of the student's use of music would be destructive to the market. No one would purchase iTunes songs if they could get them for free. The court implored Congress to amend the statute to reflect the reality of file-sharing in the face of this case and thousands of suits like it. The record companies were entitled to a judgment, and the student had to pay $675,000 in damages. *Sony BMG Music Entertainment v. Tenenbaum*, 672 F.Supp.2d 217 (D. Mass. 2009).

◆ *A Missouri teacher was unable to convince a federal appeals court that his materials deserved the protection of U.S. copyright and patent laws.*

The teacher designed an "Out of Area Program" for use by teachers to respond to student disruptions. He claimed he developed and implemented the program during his employment with the school district. The teacher asserted the school district continued using materials he developed after it discharged him. He sued the district in a federal district court for patent and copyright infringement. The court dismissed the case, finding the teacher's program was a "business idea" that was excluded from federal copyright protection.

The teacher appealed to the U.S. Court of Appeals, Federal Circuit, which noted that **general concepts and ideas are beyond the protection of copyright law. Copyright law protects the expression of an idea, but not ideas themselves.** The court found a hall pass used at the school during the relevant time period had the same language as the teacher's program. The school's hall pass was not otherwise like the teacher's materials. The court found the limited use of similar functional language did not constitute copyright infringement, even if the district had deliberately copied it. Fragmentary words and phrases were not protected by copyright law. **Forms of expression directed solely at functional considerations did not exhibit the minimal level of creativity to warrant federal copyright protection.** The teacher failed to provide any evidence that he had been issued a U.S. patent, and he could not maintain a patent infringement action without one. As the district court had properly dismissed the case, its judgment was affirmed. *Clark v. Crues*, 260 Fed.Appx. 292 (Fed. Cir. 2008).

◆ *The U.S. Supreme Court has held that publishing companies must obtain permission from freelance writers before reusing their works.*

In 2001, the U.S. Supreme Court determined that permission was required for inclusion of freelancers' works in electronic databases. Copyright law allows publishers to reuse freelancers' contributions when a collective work, such as a magazine issue or an encyclopedia, is revised, but the Court said that **massive databases such as NEXIS do not fit within that provision of the law because they are not revisions of previously published collective works.** The decision was the result of a lawsuit that was filed against New York Times Co., Newsday Inc., Time Incorporated Magazine Co., LEXIS/NEXIS and

University Microfilms International, alleging violation of freelance writers' copyrights in articles they wrote that were included in complete issues of the publishers' products. *New York Times Co., Inc. v. Tasini*, 533 U.S. 483, 121 S.Ct. 2381, 150 L.Ed.2d 500 (2001).

◆ *A New York university defeated a media foundation's claims for copyright infringement and breach of contract.*

The parties contracted to produce public service announcements. The foundation alleged the university breached the contract by refusing to pay additional compensation as a condition of producing the announcements. It also contended the university violated federal copyright law by displaying copyrighted material at a fundraiser for a commercial purpose. The foundation sued the university in a federal district court for breach of contract and violation of the "fair use" provision of copyright law. The court allowed the case to go before a jury, and after a trial, it found for the university. The foundation appealed to the U.S. Court of Appeals, Second Circuit.

The court held the foundation breached the contract with the university by demanding extra compensation. To determine if the university satisfied the fair use requirements of 17 U.S.C. § 107, the court considered: 1) the purpose and character of the use, including whether such use is of a commercial nature or is for nonprofit educational purposes; the 2) nature of the copyrighted work; 3) the amount and substantiality of the portion used in relation to the copyrighted work as a whole; and 4) the effect of the use upon the potential market for or value of the copyrighted work. The court determined the fair use issue was properly presented to the jury. **Copyright law permits the reproduction or distribution of a copyrighted work as long as it is not done for commercial reasons.** The judgment was affirmed. *New York Univ. v. Planet Earth Foundation*, 163 Fed.Appx. 13 (2d Cir. 2005).

◆ *Forcing a university to disclose the identities of students accused of illegally downloading copyrighted music did not violate student privacy rights.*

Several recording companies filed a federal copyright infringement lawsuit against 14 University of Kansas students for illegally downloading copyrighted music files. The companies discovered the Internet protocol addresses used to access the files but were unable to discover the names of the students. A university log enabled identification of the students. A federal district court allowed the companies to subpoena the university for student names, addresses, telephone numbers, email addresses and media access control addresses.

The court noted the university was free to try to quash the subpoena and avoid disclosing the information. Two students moved to quash the subpoenas, claiming disclosure would violate their privacy rights and FERPA. The court rejected the claim that student privacy interests outweighed the companies' interest in discovering their identities. **A person who uses the Internet to download copyrighted music without consent is engaging in the exercise of speech only to a limited extent.** Disclosing student identities would not violate privacy rights because the companies made a preliminary showing of copyright infringement, and the request for identifying information was specific enough to lead to disclosure of appropriate information. There was no other way to gain access to the requested information, and identifying the students was essential to a successful copyright infringement claim. In any event, the students could not reasonably expect a great degree of privacy, as they opened their computers to others for file-sharing. While FERPA generally bars federally funded educational institutions from disclosing specified student records, otherwise protected information may be disclosed pursuant to a valid court order. In this case, the limited scope of the subpoenas made it unlikely that information relating to student identities would become public. Therefore, the court held disclosing the information would not violate their privacy. *Interscope Records v. Does 1-14*, 558 F.Supp.2d 1176 (D. Kan. 2008).

♦ *An Illinois professor could pursue her copyright claims against a publisher, but could not pursue claims against a college that formerly employed her based on how her books were used after being sold.*

The professor taught the course "Smart Foreclosure Buying" at City Colleges of Chicago. She authored a book of the same name, which she copyrighted and used as a text. When the professor stopped teaching the class, the college offered it with a new instructor, but still used the professor's initials in a catalogue. The professor advised the text's publisher by phone, letter and fax to stop printing the book, but it continued printing and selling the text, and stopped paying her royalties. The professor sued the college in a federal district court to force it to stop offering courses using her book or its title as a course name. She added federal copyright and trademark claims against the publisher and an instructor, claiming the college engaged in false advertising, fraud and deceptive business practices. The court held the professor did not state a valid claim, and she appealed to the U.S. Court of Appeals, Seventh Circuit.

The court reversed the decision to dismiss the copyright claims against the publisher, noting the professor said she had mailed the publisher a letter of termination. Although the publisher claimed it never got the letter, **oral licenses and terminations are generally allowed**. A jury could reasonably determine the publisher had some notice of the professor's intent to withdraw her consent to publish the text, especially since it stopped paying her royalties. Although it reversed the decision on the copyright claims against the publisher, the court affirmed the ruling with respect to the copyright claims against the new instructor and the college. The professor could not pursue claims based on how the books were used after they were sold. **Once a copy of a work has been sold, the buyer may use it as he pleases so long as he does not create a new copy or derivative work.** The court also found a valid claim for trademark violation against the college. Finally, the professor stated a valid claim against the college for false advertising, fraud and deceptive business practices based on the continued use of her initials in the course catalog. *Vincent v. City Colleges of Chicago*, 485 F.3d 919 (7th Cir. 2007).

♦ *The U.S. Court of Appeals for the First Circuit rejected a Tufts University visiting lecturer's claims based on the terms of a publishing contract.*

The lecturer had co-authored the second and third editions of an undergraduate textbook with a professor and director of the graduate nutrition program at another college. The third edition agreement assigned all present and future copyrights of the third and future editions to the book's publisher. The lecturer and professor contracted with the same publisher for a fourth edition that increased the lecturer's share of royalties from 25% to 40%.

The professor failed to meet deadlines set by the agreement, and the publisher suggested she assign more work to the lecturer. The professor refused, and the lecturer notified the publisher she was withdrawing from the project. She also stated her revisions could not be used without her permission. The publisher sent the lecturer an acknowledgement that she would receive 12.5% of the fourth edition royalties – half her compensation under the third edition agreement. She signed the acknowledgement, but later discovered her revisions were included in the fourth edition and that the professor was listed as its sole author. The lecturer copyrighted her revisions and brought a federal court complaint against the publisher and professor for copyright infringement and breach of contract. The court held the lecturer assigned her copyright interest under the fourth edition revisions. The publisher was not obligated to terminate its contract with the professor when she failed to meet her deadlines. The First Circuit affirmed the decision, holding the lecturer could not claim a copyright interest in her fourth edition revisions. She had "assigned ... all present and future copyrights" of the third and future editions to the publisher. **The publisher was the sole copyright owner of the third edition, and consequently the fourth "revised edition." There was no breach of contract by the publisher, because it had the option to extend the deadlines and did so for legitimate financial reasons.** *Zyla v. Wadsworth*, 360 F.3d 243 (1st Cir. 2004).

B. Work-For-Hire

Employers are presumed to own the copyright to works prepared by their employees within the scope of their employment, unless they have agreed otherwise in writing. See 17 U.S.C. § 201(a), also referred to as Section 201(b) of the Copyright Act of 1976. The work of independent contractors is considered "work for hire" under a written agreement for specially ordered or commissioned work used as a contribution to a collective work, part of a motion picture or other audiovisual work, a translation, supplementary work, compilation, instructional text, test or test answer, or an atlas.

Agency principles help determine whether a professor's work is covered by the work-for-hire doctrine. Section 228 of the Restatement (Second) of Agency deems a work to be "for hire" only if the work is of the type the faculty member was hired to create, was created substantially within the space and time limits of the job, and was motivated at least partly by a purpose to serve the university. Professors are expected to produce intellectual property in the scope of their employment, and those who conduct research, write and publish scholarly articles and create other forms of intellectual property receive better performance evaluations, more promotional opportunities and higher pay.

◆   *A New York University (NYU) employee who helped design a logo selected as NYU's mascot could not overcome the "works made for hire" presumption.*

Although the employee began working for NYU as an equipment room aide, NYU also hired her as a graphic designer. Her artistic abilities were soon discovered, and she was invited to design a logo for use as the NYU mascot. For this work, the employee's compensation was doubled from $8 per hour to $16 per hour. When a final version of the logo emerged, she registered it with the U.S. Copyright Office, listing herself as the sole author. Although the employee claimed a supervisor reassured her that she would be compensated for use of the logo, NYU denied such conversations took place and maintained that the design had been a collaborative effort involving many NYU employees.

In a federal court, the employee sued NYU for copyright infringement. In pretrial activity, the court found that to prevail, she had to prove she owned a valid copyright and that NYU copied its constituent elements. Although the employee argued she owned the copyright because she registered it with the Copyright Office, the court held this only created a presumption of ownership. As NYU argued, **an employee's copyright is invalid if it was created within the scope of her employment**. This is known as the "works made for hire" exception to copyright ownership. In this case, the employee created the logo during the scope of her employment as a graphic designer. Evidence indicated NYU exerted control over her drafts of the logo and that she made changes on the basis of suggestions by NYU personnel. There was no written agreement assigning ownership to either party, and the works made for hire exception applied. Rejecting the employee's argument that creating the design was outside the scope of her duties as a graphic designer, the court held for NYU. *Fleurimond v. New York Univ.*, 876 F.Supp.2d 190 (E.D.N.Y. 2012).

◆ *Brown University retained its copyrights to photographs taken by a member of its staff under the "works-for-hire" doctrine.*

Brown University hired a full-time professional photographer to capture images of academic life and natural campus settings for its publications. He was also allowed to shoot pictures on his own initiative. The university purchased photographic equipment for him, arranged for student assistants, and provided him access to the university's darkroom. Brown's copyright policy contained a provision regarding the ownership of copyrightable materials.

After 24 years, Brown severed its relationship with the photographer as part of a reduction in force. He sued Brown in a federal district court, claiming ownership of 97 photographs in his possession. The court focused on the "Works Made for Hire" Section of the Copyright Act of 1976. The court explained that ownership rights of works by an employee typically vest with the employer. It held the photographs were "works for hire" owned by Brown. **The court distinguished between the photographs and the "faculty exception" from the works-for-hire rule.** Equitable considerations often mandate that a scholar retain the copyright to works, notwithstanding the works-for-hire doctrine. The faculty exception did not apply in this case because Brown officials often directed what images should be photographed. There was no document indicating a conveyance of ownership rights to the photographer. The language of the policy was too imprecise to support the photographer's claim of such a transfer. He did not think about copyright ownership in the photos until after his relationship with Brown was severed. As a result, the court held for Brown. *Foraste v. Brown Univ.*, 290 F.Supp.2d 234 (D.R.I. 2003).

◆ *The Supreme Court of Kansas held the work-for-hire doctrine did not prevent a state university and the employee association representing its faculty from entering into a memorandum of agreement on intellectual property rights.*

The university and Kansas Board of Regents proposed a policy to retain ownership and control over any intellectual property created by the faculty. The faculty association rejected the policy. The board responded it was not required to negotiate over the policy because intellectual property rights were not a "condition of employment." According to the board, the question of intellectual property rights was a management prerogative and was preempted by state and federal law. The board then adopted a policy giving some intellectual property rights to faculty, but without meeting and conferring with the association.

The state public employee relations board (PERB) held the university had no duty to meet and confer with the faculty association, because the subject was preempted by state and federal law. The case reached the Supreme Court of Kansas, which found neither state nor federal law preempted the subject of intellectual property from being included in a memorandum of agreement. **The work-for-hire doctrine was only a presumption regarding the ownership of copyrights, and it allowed parties to contract for particular ownership rights. The doctrine operated as a default provision, unless the parties agreed otherwise.** The court found Congress contemplated that parties could negotiate the ownership of a copyright. The federal Patent Act also allowed parties to assign patent ownership rights. Federal law did not preempt any kind of intellectual property rights from being covered by a memorandum of understanding or other written agreement. The court reversed the decision with directions to return the case to the PERB for further proceedings. *Pittsburg State Univ./Kansas National Educ. Ass'n v. Kansas Board of Regents/Pittsburg State Univ.*, 280 Kan. 408, 122 P.3d 336 (Kan. 2005).

C. Standardized Tests

◆ *A federal court agreed with four educational testing agencies, including the College Entrance Examination Board, that the required disclosure of test questions under a New York law violated federal copyright law.*

New York education law requires college testing services to file copies of their test questions and statistical reports with the state education commissioner. A number of testing agencies claimed that the statute violated federal copyright law, and filed a lawsuit against the governor and other state officials. In view of the result in a similar case filed by the Association of American Medical Colleges, the parties entered into a stipulation under which the testing agencies disclosed questions for only some of the tests administered in the state and were allowed to administer a fixed number of undisclosed tests. The court then considered a motion by the agencies for temporary relief. The agencies argued that the compelled disclosure of the test questions violated federal copyright law and did not meet the fair use exception to federal copyright law. The state argued that **the public had an interest in ensuring the fairness and objectivity of standardized admission tests** and had a strong need to evaluate the scoring process. It also claimed that disclosure did not violate copyright laws because of the lack of any commercial purpose.

The court agreed with the testing agencies that the disclosure of test questions violated federal copyright law and issued a preliminary injunction. The court also found that the agencies were entitled to the presumption of irreparable injury that normally accompanies a showing of infringement. But because of the many factual issues existing in the case, the court issued an order preserving the status quo, under which only some tests administered in the state would be subject to the disclosure law pending further proceedings. *College Entrance Examination Board v. Pataki*, 889 F.Supp. 554 (N.D.N.Y. 1995).

Three of the testing agencies sought an order completely barring enforcement of the state law or alternative relief. A fourth agency submitted a statement indicating that it would comply with the order by disclosing three testing forms administered in New York during the test year and an additional form traditionally administered in the state in low-volume administrations.

The testing agencies asserted that the wording of the preliminary order would prevent the Graduate Record Examination (GRE) program from offering at least one administration in the state, and that the status quo provision of the order did not account for changing circumstances in testing from year to year. They further asserted that the preliminary order contravened **the principle in copyright infringement cases that the status quo sought to be preserved is the state of non-infringement**. The court held that the preliminary order struck the correct balance between competing interests, including that of the students who would take the examinations. There was no need to strictly comply with the rule that the status quo to be preserved is a state of non-infringement, since the parties had agreed by stipulation to provide for limited disclosure of test forms. The court modified the order to accommodate the GRE program's phase-out of paper and pencil administrations. *College Entrance Examination Board v. Pataki*, 893 F.Supp. 152 (N.D.N.Y. 1995).

◆ *New York's Standardized Testing Act requires testing agencies to file reports on standardized tests with the Commissioner of Education and also requires the filing of copyrightable test questions.*

The American Association of Medical Colleges (AAMC), a nonprofit educational association, sponsors a medical school testing program, the central feature of which is the MCAT exam. The AAMC holds copyrights in the MCAT test forms, test questions, answer sheets, and reports. When the state of New York enacted the Standardized Testing Act, requiring disclosure of this copyrighted information, the AAMC sued to enjoin the application of the act. It claimed that the Act was preempted by the federal Copyright Act and moved for pretrial judgment, which the court granted. The court found that the purpose and character of the use was noncommercial and educational, and that disclosure of the test questions would prevent their reuse.

The Second Circuit Court of Appeals found issues of fact precluded pretrial judgment. If the disclosure of material were considered "fair use," then there would be no Copyright Act violation. However, if the state act facilitated infringement, then the Copyright Act would preempt it. **Here, the state's goal of encouraging valid and objective tests was laudable, and there was a question of fact as to whether the test questions could be used again after**

being disclosed. As a result, the fourth and most important fair use factor – the effect of the use upon the potential market for or value of the copyrighted work – did not necessarily weigh in favor of the AAMC. The court remanded the case for further proceedings. *Ass'n of American Medical Colleges v. Cuomo*, 928 F.2d 519 (2d Cir. 1991).

D. Due Process Issues

◆ *A University of Texas professor will not keep a six-figure verdict he had won based on the loss of notebooks after he was ordered to clear out of his lab.*

After 24 years of work at the University of Texas at San Antonio (UTSA), a research professor was told he was not keeping his office space and laboratory in good order and that they created a safety hazard. Two years later, UTSA followed through on its warnings and advised him by letter that it was going to close his lab and clean it out. According to the professor, some of his notebooks were lost or destroyed during the cleanout process, and he sued UTSA and an administrator for due process violations, based on depriving him of his property without notice and a reasonable opportunity to be heard.

After the professor initiated a state court action, UTSA removed the case to a federal district court. It held for UTSA and the administrator, and the professor appealed to the U.S. Court of Appeals, Fifth Circuit. Although the court affirmed the judgment for USTA, it returned a due process claim against the administrator to the district court for further consideration. The case was presented to a jury, which found the administrator had violated the professor's right to notice. The jury also found the professor had a property interest in the items in his lab. A verdict of $175,000 was awarded to him for the loss of his research notebooks. But following the verdict, the court granted the administrator's motion, finding the professor could not prevail under a due process claim because he did not have a protectable interest in the property that was lost. The case returned to the Fifth Circuit, which held the professor did not present enough evidence to show that he had a protectable property interest in notebooks that were lost in the cleanup. He argued he had a protectable property interest in his notebooks because they fell under an exception to the school's intellectual property policy applicable to "scholarly or educational materials." **But the court held the exception applies only to materials that are published, copyrighted or copyrightable.** In this case, the professor did not show the notebooks contained anything other than research data. For this reason, the judgment for the administrator was affirmed. *Stotter v. Univ. of Texas at San Antonio*, 369 Fed.Appx. 641 (5th Cir. 2010).

◆ *A tenured University of Michigan professor had an insufficient property interest in an idea to gain any protection of it as his intellectual property.*

In 1995, the professor wrote drafts for a design center in the university's Department of Aerospace Engineering. The drafts were revised by another professor and turned into an abstract. The first draft proposal listed two co-authors, and the second listed three others. The proposal identified a design center with resident visitors of different specialties, with a focus on Russian designers. The university obtained funding for the center and built it in 1999. The professor sued the university in the state court system asserting violation of his due process and intellectual property rights. The court held for the university, and he appealed. On appeal, the Court of Appeals of Michigan held the university had no fiduciary duty to the professor. A fiduciary relationship exists only "when there is confidence reposed on one side and a resulting superiority and influence on the other." The court disagreed with the professor's claim to a property interest in the design center. He prepared drafts for the center in 1995 with various others. The proposal indicated there were already programs for visiting designers. The university had previously hired retired designers to teach courses. The court held the protection of an idea under a property theory "requires that the idea possess property-like traits."

Moreover, "ideas themselves are not subject to individual ownership or control. They do not rise to the level of property and are not in themselves protected by law." The professor could not "own the idea" of a design center or a visiting designer program that already existed in other forms. The professor asserted the university's rules and policies made him "automatically the principal investigator" of the proposal. The court disagreed, finding no such rule or policy "promising or even hinting at how those benefits accrued to him." **In order to have a constitutionally protected interest, a person must have more than an abstract need or desire for it. There must be a legitimate claim of entitlement.** A party's unilateral expectation is insufficient to create a property interest protected by procedural due process. The court held that as the professor did not show any legitimate property interest in his idea, he could not allege a due process claim. *Kauffman v. Univ. of Michigan Regents*, No. 257711, 2006 WL 1084330 (Mich. Ct. App. 4/25/06). The Supreme Court of Michigan denied further review. *Kauffman v. Univ. of Michigan Regents*, 477 Mich. 911, 722 N.W.2d 823 (Mich. 2006).

II. PATENTS

A patent is a legally protected property interest that gives the owner the right to exclude others from making, using, selling, offering for sale, or importing the invention covered by the patent. Patents generally run for a period of 20 years from the effective filing date of the patent application. To be patentable, an invention must be useful, new or novel, and non-obvious.

Unlike copyright law, there is no federal patent law provision on work-for-hire. Patent ownership is instead resolved by common law. The federal Patent Act also allows parties to assign patent ownership rights. In determining who owns the patent rights to an invention, courts look at the nature of the relationship between the inventor and the employer. Where the inventor is hired to invent something, the employer retains all patent rights; and where the inventor is hired under a general contract of employment, the inventor will retain ownership rights. However, most cases fall somewhere in between these two: for example, where a university hires a professor or a graduate student to teach and do research. The ambiguity this creates has led colleges and universities to enter into pre-employment assignments of intellectual property rights that specifically lay out the rights of both parties. Sometimes this is done by written agreement – other times, by use of a faculty handbook.

With respect to patent rights, professors usually are required to assign creations and patent rights to the colleges and universities that employ them in exchange for a percentage of the royalties. The issue becomes trickier when dealing with graduate students. Some universities require graduate students to assign patent rights, while others do not.

A number of states have enacted statutes to limit the extent to which employers can claim an interest in employee inventions. However, those statutes generally provide that if the employer provides resources, or if the invention relates to the employer's business, the employer can require assignment of intellectual property rights. It is only where the employer has no involvement at all that the employee can claim full rights to an invention.

Literal infringement refers to the misappropriation of all essential elements in a patent. Infringement under the doctrine of equivalents results when a device performs the same function as the patented device in substantially the same way to achieve the same result.

A. Ownership and Inventorship

◆ *A federal court held the University of Massachusetts did not have to join an action filed by the University of Utah to name a Utah professor as an inventor or co-inventor of a "gene silencing process."*

Ribonucleic Acid (RNA) interference (RNAi), also known as "Gene silencing," is described as a process of great potential therapeutic value. It involves inserting a double-stranded RNA molecule into a cell to direct the destruction of messenger RNA before it can be translated into a protein. University of Utah officials sued research institutes, including the University of Massachusetts, asserting that a Utah professor should be named the sole or joint inventor on two patents directed to methods of preparing a particular type of double-stranded RNA molecule that could mediate RNAi. In a federal court, Utah requested an order correcting inventorship and a declaration of its rights that would require the research institutes to cease violating federal patent law.

In considering dismissal motions by the research institutes, the court held Massachusetts was not a necessary party. As other institutes and state officials would adequately represent its interests, Massachusetts was dismissed from the case. As for the merits of the claim, the court found **the complaint adequately stated that the Utah professor was the sole inventor of the patents at issue.** There was evidence that she had conceived the invention as a treatment for mammals, including humans. There was evidence that the Utah professor published an article explaining RNAi capabilities in mammals, which the other named inventors read and incorporated into their work. Since Utah presented a sufficient quantum of collaboration or connection with the other institutions to state a claim for joint inventorship, the court denied the dismissal motions. *Univ. of Utah v. Max-Planck-Gesellschaft Zur Forderung Der Wissenschaften E.V.*, 881 F.Supp.2d 151 (D.Mass. 2012).

◆ *Because an employment relationship alone is not sufficient to vest title to an employee's invention in the employer, Stanford University did not have exclusive patent rights to methodology in a joint venture with a company.*

In 1985, a small California research company began to develop methods to quantify blood-borne levels of HIV. Later, it began to collaborate with Stanford University to test the efficacy of new AIDS drugs. A doctor joined Stanford near that time and agreed to assign his "right, title and interest" in inventions resulting from his employment there. He conducted research at the company as part of the collaboration and signed an agreement by which he assigned his "right, title and interest" to it with respect to inventions made as a consequence of his working there. Along with employees of the company, the doctor devised a procedure for measuring the amount of HIV in a patient's blood.

Stanford secured three patents to the measurement process and received federal funding for the project. Roche Molecular Systems then acquired the company's assets and commercialized the HIV-quantification methodology developed at the company. Stanford sued Roche for patent infringement in a federal district court, and the case eventually reached the U.S. Supreme Court. The Court explained that the Bayh-Dole Act allocates rights in federally funded inventions between the federal government and federal contractors. In the Court's view, the Bayh-Dole Act did not automatically confer unilateral title to federal contractors. **Even though the doctor had developed the methods while working jointly for both Stanford and the company, Stanford did not have exclusive patent rights to the methodology.** Mere employment is not sufficient to vest title to an employee's invention in the employer. Roche was a co-owner of the procedure. Therefore, Stanford could not sue Roche for patent infringement. *Board of Trustees of Leland Stanford Junior Univ. v. Roche Molecular Systems, Inc.*, 131 S.Ct. 2188, 180 L.Ed.2d (U.S. 2011).

◆ *Vanderbilt University was unable to show that two of its scientists contributed to the invention of an erectile dysfunction treatment and method.*

Vanderbilt sued ICOS Corporation in a Delaware federal district court, asserting that two of its scientists should be added as joint inventors of patented compounds and methods for treating erectile dysfunction. These included tadalafil, a PDE5 inhibitor, which is the active ingredient in Cialis. According to Vanderbilt, its scientists were among the first to discover PDE5 in the late 1970s, and they continued to work on related research. Vanderbilt retained ownership of the intellectual property under an underwriting and license agreement with Glaxo, Inc. Glaxo later assigned all its rights, title and interest in the patented compounds to ICOS. Vanderbilt then sought to correct inventorship of the patents in a federal district court. The court found no evidence that Vanderbilt scientists conceived of tadalafil's specific chemical structure. Vanderbilt appealed to the U.S. Court of Appeals, Federal Circuit.

According to the court, federal patent law permits joint inventorship by one or more inventors who are not physically working together. Each inventor needs to perform part of the task and make some contribution to the inventive thought and the final result. **For persons to be joint inventors, there must be some element of joint behavior, such as collaboration or working under common direction.** Vanderbilt could not counter ICOS' evidence that an ICOS researcher independently discovered the compounds to be tested for PDE5 inhibition. While Vanderbilt claimed ICOS' research was done more than 10 years after Glaxo did the same work, the court found no evidence of joint collaboration on the invention. Vanderbilt failed to present clear and convincing evidence that the ICOS researcher could not have independently identified the compound. Since the parties' stories were equally plausible and there was no clear and convincing evidence of joint invention, the judgment for ICOS was affirmed. *Vanderbilt Univ. v. ICOS Corp.*, 601 F.3d 1297 (Fed. Cir. 2010).

◆   *A federal district court was instructed to reconsider a case that originally appeared before it in 1997 to determine whether certain products infringed on patents under the doctrine of equivalents.*

The University of California (UC) and Abbott Labs claimed patents for inventions to improve methods for identifying and classifying chromosomes to detect abnormalities associated with genetic disorders, degenerative diseases and cancer. They sought to employ a staining technique to allow rapid and highly sensitive detection of chromosomal abnormalities in both metaphase and interphase cells using standard clinical and laboratory equipment. The patent claims were directed at blocking, selectively removing or screening repetitive sequences. UC and Abbott Labs, as the owner and exclusive licensee of the patents, sued a manufacturer in a federal district court for a preliminary order to prohibit it from manufacturing and selling certain products. The court held UC and Abbott could not prevail on a patent infringement claim based on limitations for "morphologically identifiable chromosome or cell nucleus," and "heterogeneous mixture of labeled unique sequence nucleic acid fragments." They also did not show their product met a blocking nucleic acid limitation under the doctrine of equivalents. The court later issued pretrial judgment to the manufacturer as to two of its products.

On appeal, the U.S. Court of Appeals, Federal Circuit, considered UC and Abbott's claim that the district court misconstrued the phrase "heterogeneous mixture of labeled unique sequence nucleic acid fragments." The manufacturer's products contained repetitive sequences found in prior art, while the patents referred to unique sequence fragments. The court found it was erroneous to characterize the patent as prior art. However, the lower court correctly found the products did not infringe upon a second patent, which employed a mixture including repetitive sequences. The original patent claim did not include the phrase "unique sequence." This was a response to three separate enablement rejections by a claims examiner. **The prosecution history demonstrated how the inventor intended to limit the invention.** The non-infringement judgment was affirmed as to the first patent. However, as to the second patent, the lower court improperly applied prosecution history to the "blocking nucleic acid" limitation. The court returned this claim to the lower court for reconsideration of whether the manufacturer had infringed the patent under the doctrine of equivalents. *Regents of Univ. of California v. Dakocytomation Cal., Inc.*, 517 F.3d 1364 (Fed. Cir. 2008).

◆   *A patent licensee could pursue claims against a competitor under the California unfair competition law and the Lanham Act, but not the Florida*

Deceptive and Unfair Trade Practices Act.

Optivus Technology claimed to be the exclusive licensee of two proton beam therapy system patents. The University of Florida signed a non-binding letter of intent with Optivus regarding the proton beam therapy systems. After the letter expired, Florida considered other vendors and awarded a contract to Ion Beam Applications (IBA), which competed with Optivus in the same market. Optivus sued IBA in a federal district court for infringement of the patents. Loma Linda University Medical Center, as assignee of Optivus, became a party. Optivus added claims against IBA for unfair competition under California and Florida law, as well as violation of the Lanham Act. IBA counterclaimed against Optivus, seeking an order declaring the proton beam patents invalid in view of a neutron therapy facility in use at the University of Washington. The California unfair competition claim was based on the theory that IBA marketed a medical device that was not approved by the U.S. Food and Drug Administration (FDA). The district court refused to consider the California unfair competition law claim. The court held for IBA on the Florida Unfair Trade Act and Lanham Act claims, as well as a claim for intentional interference. The court found both patents invalid and ruled there was no patent infringement. Optivus appealed to the U.S. Court of Appeals, Federal Circuit.

The court agreed with Optivus that the district court should have ruled on the significance of an FDA letter. The district court had thus improperly dismissed the California state law unfair competition claim. The court considered the claim under the Florida Unfair Trade Act and noted the University of Florida had selected IBA as its vendor after the expiration of the letter of intent with Optivus. **At the time IBA was selected, only a "consumer" could bring a claim under the Florida Deceptive and Unfair Trade Practices Act.** For this reason, the district court properly awarded summary judgment to IBA on Optivus' Florida law claim. **The district court had found Optivus did not show a business relationship existed after the letter of intent expired.** The court of appeals found no error in this conclusion. Any business relationship between Optivus and Florida ended with the expiration of the letter. The court stated that to prevail on its Lanham Act claim, Optivus would have to show IBA made a false and material statement of fact that caused the University of Florida to award the contract to IBA. The court disagreed with the district court's findings in favor of IBA regarding false statements about financing. It reversed the judgment on the Lanham Act claim for further consideration of IBA's alleged statements. **The patent was invalid as obvious, in view of Washington's neutron therapy facility.** The patent for a safety system for a multi-room proton beam therapy facility was written with expansive, highly inclusive language. **As Loma Linda did not rebut this evidence, the judgment of patent invalidity was correct.** *Optivus Technology, Inc. v. Ion Beam Applications, S.A.,* 469 F.3d 978 (Fed. Cir. 2006).

◆   *A medical school student at a private New York university did not prove he contributed to a professor's patented treatment for glaucoma.*

The university owned a patent involving the use of prostaglandins in treating glaucoma. A long-time professor at the university was the named inventor of the patent. In 1980, the professor agreed to a proposal by the student to perform a one-semester ophthalmology research elective. He directed the student to begin his project by reviewing a faculty member's papers on prostaglandins and intraocular pressure (IOP). At the time, the professor had published several papers on the effects of prostaglandins on the IOP in animals such as rabbits and owl monkeys. The student conducted experiments in the lab that showed topical application of single doses of prostaglandin reduced IOP in rhesus monkeys and cats. After the student left the university, the professor conceived the patent while studying the effects of repeated prostaglandin application on the IOP in rhesus monkeys. He applied for the patent in 1982, and it was issued in 1986. When the student found out about the patent, he sued the university and professor in a federal district court, asking to be added as a co-inventor. The trial court granted summary judgment for the university and the professor. It found the student failed to present evidence of inventorship.

On appeal, **the U.S. Court of Appeals, Federal Circuit, held the student had to show he contributed to the conception of the invention in order to be considered one of the inventors of the patent**. The court found the student did not have an understanding of the claimed invention. He also did not discover that prostaglandins have an effect on IOP, or conceive of the idea of the use of prostaglandins to reduce IOP in primates. Furthermore, the student did not collaborate with the professor in developing a glaucoma treatment. **He simply carried out an experiment done previously by the professor on different animals.** The court held the student's contribution was insufficient to support his claim of co-inventorship and affirmed the judgment. *Stern v. Trustees of Columbia Univ. in the City of New York*, 434 F.3d 1375 (Fed. Cir. 2006).

◆ *A pharmaceutical company had to pay $54 million in damages for fraudulently obtaining a patent based on work by university researchers.*

Two University of Colorado researchers worked under an agreement with a pharmaceutical company. They discovered certain multivitamins were not supplying proper amounts of iron to pregnant women and published an article suggesting a reformulation to increase iron absorption. The researchers sent an advance copy to the doctor they had been working with at the company. The company then obtained a patent on the reformulation of the multivitamin without notifying the university. It copied and plagiarized portions of the article in the patent application. The university foundation sued the company in a federal district court for wrongfully obtaining the patent. The court found the company liable for fraudulent nondisclosure. It noted the company would have had to pay the university for the rights to the reformulation, and calculated the royalty rates at approximately $22 million. The court held the university could recover equitable damages for unjust enrichment of $23 million. It also ordered exemplary damages in the amount of $500,000 for each inventor, based on the company's "clandestine and deceptive conduct," and "fraud, malice, and willful and wanton misconduct." *Univ. of Colorado Foundation v. American Cyanamid Co.*, 216 F.Supp.2d 1188 (D. Colo. 2002).

The U.S. Court of Appeals, Federal Circuit, rejected the company's argument that the damage award for unjust enrichment created a state-based patent law that was inconsistent with the federal statutory scheme. The court held this was not the issue in this case. The unjust enrichment claim was based on the wrongful use of research and did not interfere with the federal patent scheme. The researchers satisfied state law requirements for unjust enrichment, as it would be unjust to allow the company to retain profits acquired through misconduct. **The district court had properly awarded damages based on incremental profits that were directly attributable to the misconduct. The court upheld the district court's findings establishing inventorship.** Clear and convincing evidence indicated the researchers were the sole inventors of the patent. Substantial evidence supported the damage award, including the award of exemplary damages, and the court affirmed the judgment for the researchers and university. *Univ. of Colorado Foundation v. American Cyanamid Co.*, 342 F.3d 1298 (Fed. Cir. 2003).

◆ *A university's patent policy validly required two researchers to assign all rights to their inventions to the university.*

The University of New Mexico's patent policy stated that all inventions developed during the course of research funded by the university or employment at the university belonged to the university. The policy also required the inventors to cooperate with the university in the patent process. Two researchers of chemical compounds completed work that led the university to submit 11 different patent applications regarding two compounds. The researchers assigned their rights in the patents to the university.

Two years later, the university submitted five continuation-in-part patent applications, and the researchers did not assign their rights under these applications to the university. When the university entered into a licensing agreement with a company regarding the two compounds, a dispute arose over the ownership of the patents. A New Mexico federal court assigned a special master, who concluded that the researchers had to assign their rights to one of the compounds to the university. With respect to the second compound, the court conducted a trial and determined that the university owned those patents as well. On appeal, the Federal Circuit largely affirmed. The researchers were to be listed as inventors, but **the university's patent policy, which was incorporated into the researchers' employment contracts, clearly made the university the owner of the patents**. *Regents of the Univ. of New Mexico v. Scallen*, 321 F.3d 1111 (Fed. Cir. 2003).

B. Validity of Patents

When competing applicants for a patent on the same invention cannot settle their differences privately, either party may seek to have the matter resolved by the U.S. Patent and Trademark Office via a procedure known as a patent interference proceeding. The purpose of these proceedings is to determine priority of invention between competing applicants. Sometimes, an applicant can ask that an interference proceeding be conducted even after the patent it seeks has been granted to another applicant.

◆ *A patent claimed by a New York university was invalid because it did not comply with the written description requirement of federal patent law.*

Researchers at the University of Rochester developed a method for identifying a prostaglandin synthesis inhibitor. The university received two U.S. patents, one of which was based on a method that inhibited PGHS-2 prostaglandins. After four pharmaceutical manufacturers began using the method, the university filed a federal district court action against them for patent infringement. The court held the patent did not meet statutory written description requirements and merely described a theory, not an invention. The patent did not satisfy statutory enablement grounds, as it did not allow those skilled in the art to make and use the invention without undue experimentation.

The university appealed to the Federal Circuit. It held **the patent failed the written description requirement, as its description was "vague." It did not disclose the structure or physical properties of any compounds**. While it was not necessary for the university to describe the exact chemical compound of an inhibitor, its description of a non-steroidal compound that inhibits the activity of the PGHS-2 gene product was insufficient for statutory purposes. It would not provide a researcher, skilled in this area, with sufficient information to understand what it claimed to accomplish and how to perform the method. The court affirmed the judgment for the manufacturers. *Univ. of Rochester v. G.D. Searle & Co.*, 358 F.3d 916 (Fed. Cir. 2004).

◆   *A university and its licensee could not patent a discovery about the best time to harvest and eat certain vegetables.*

Johns Hopkins University owned three patents based in part on the discovery of the beneficial effects of harvesting and eating broccoli and cauliflower at the two-leaf stage, when they contain the highest levels of glucosinates and Phase 2 enzymes, which reduce the risk of developing cancer. The patents also contained a method for preparing the sprouts in order to increase their protective properties. The university licensed the patents to a company, then joined the company in a lawsuit against competitors for violating the patents. The defendants asserted that the portions of the patents that referred to the eating and growing of sprouts should be invalidated by prior art. A Maryland federal court ruled in favor of the defendants. On appeal, the Federal Circuit Court of Appeals noted that under 35 U.S.C. § 101, a patent can be obtained for inventing or discovering any new composition of matter or any new improvement thereof.

The university and its licensee did not create a new kind of sprout or develop a new growing method. They merely discovered that the vegetables contained glucosinates and Phase 2 enzymes (anti-cancer agents). Those elements were inherent in the sprouts. Since prior art unquestionably included growing, harvesting and eating the sprouts, the patents were invalidated to the extent they tried to protect that activity. The judgment was affirmed. *Brassica Protection Products, LLC v. Sunrise Farms*, 301 F.3d 1343 (Fed. Cir. 2002).

◆   *Inventions by a pharmaceutical concern and a university were separately patentable as their molecules had different chemical structures.*

Eli Lilly and Co. filed a reissue application surrendering a patent covering deoxyribonucleic acid (cDNA), a sequence code for human protein C. At the same time, Lilly filed a patent interference claim against the University of Washington concerning a university-held patent that also related to the sequence of human protein C. The university denied any interference, asserting the cDNA molecules had different chemical sequences. The Board of Patent Appeals and Interferences agreed, finding Lilly's invention was not the same as the university's. Lilly was dissatisfied with the board's ruling and moved to define the interfering subject matter by proposing two alternative constructions of the cDNA: a narrow construction and a broad construction. The board applied a two-part test and rejected Lilly's contentions. Regardless of whether the claim was construed as a genus or a species, Lilly's reissue application and the university's claim did not define the "same patentable invention." There was no interference-in-fact, and the matter was dismissed. Lilly appealed to the Federal Circuit, which explained that under 37 C.F.R. § 1.601(n), the "'same patentable invention' means that the one invention of one party anticipates or renders obvious the other party's invention."

Since the claimed interference involved genus/species inventions, it was unclear whether the genus claim or the species claim was invented first. **The court found it possible that both a genus claim and a species claim could be separate, patentable inventions. The director resolved the issue by presuming that both Lilly's invention and the university's invention were "prior art."** This meant that the university's invention was assumed to be prior art of Lilly's invention and vice versa. Although the court acknowledged Lilly's assertion that a one-way test should be applied, it was within the director's discretion not to accept it. The court upheld the use of the two-way test and affirmed the board's decision. *Eli Lilly & Co. v. Board of Regents of Univ. of Washington*, 334 F.3d 1264 (Fed. Cir. 2003).

C. Defenses

The Eleventh Amendment to the U.S. Constitution generally bars claims against state defendants. States can waive immunity from suit.

◆ *A state university that voluntarily submits itself to the jurisdiction of the federal court system waives its Eleventh Amendment immunity.*

The University of Missouri filed an application for a patent of an unspecified invention. While the application was pending, a company filed an application to patent the same invention. The company's application proceeded more quickly, and it was granted while the university's remained pending. The university responded by instituting an interference proceeding. After a six-year interference proceeding, the U.S. Patent and Trademark Office held the company was not entitled to the patent. The university was awarded priority, and the office held it was entitled to the patent. The company appealed to a federal district court. The university moved for dismissal, arguing it was immune from suit in the federal courts under the Eleventh Amendment.

The district court agreed with the university, and the company appealed. The U.S. Court of Appeals, Federal Circuit, explained that a state does not waive its Eleventh Amendment immunity merely by participating in the federal patent system. In this case, however, the university asked the U.S. Patent and Trademark Office to conduct litigation-type activity, and it participated in that activity without claiming immunity. **When a state voluntarily submits itself** to the jurisdiction of the federal court system, it waives its state immunity with respect to the claims raised. In this case, an appeal to federal court was built into the U.S. Patent and Trademark Office proceeding by statute. Therefore, by instituting and participating in the proceeding, the university subjected itself to federal court jurisdiction. The appeals court reversed the decision and remanded the case for further proceedings. *Vas-Cath, Inc. v. Curators of the Univ. of Missouri*, 473 F.3d 1376 (Fed. Cir. 2007).

◆   *The Eleventh Amendment bars federal court lawsuits by private parties against states under the Patent Remedy Act and the Lanham Act.*

The Supreme Court held Congress overstepped its authority by enacting the Patent Remedy Act. It found no indication that the act was enacted under the authority of the Fourteenth Amendment. Rather, the legislation was authorized by Article I and thus improperly removed states' sovereign immunity. The case arose after College Savings Bank, which owned and marketed a patented investment methodology designed to finance the costs of college education, discovered that the state of Florida was selling a similar product. The bank brought separate actions against the state for patent infringement and false advertising under the Lanham Act. In the patent infringement action, the Court held Florida could not be sued without its consent where it engaged in interstate commerce. *Florida Prepaid Postsecondary Educ. Expense Board v. College Savings Bank*, 527 U.S. 627, 119 S.Ct. 2199, 144 L.Ed.2d 575 (1999).

In the false advertising action, the Court held that **the Trademark Remedy Clarification Act did not validly abrogate states' Eleventh Amendment immunity from a suit brought under the Lanham Act**. Although Congress may remove a state's sovereign immunity under Section 5 of the Fourteenth Amendment, there must be a property interest involved for it to do so. However, there was no property interest at stake in a false advertising suit under the Lanham Act. Further, the state of Florida had not constructively waived its immunity by engaging in interstate commerce. *College Savings Bank v. Florida Prepaid Postsecondary Educ. Expense Board*, 527 U.S. 666, 119 S.Ct. 2219, 144 L.Ed.2d 605 (1999).

III. TRADEMARKS

A trademark, defined at 15 U.S.C. § 1127, is any word, name, symbol or device, or any combination thereof used to identify and distinguish goods, including a unique product, from those manufactured or sold by others, and to indicate the source of the goods, even if the source is unknown.

Service marks are identical to trademarks in all respects except that they are intended to indicate the origin of services, rather than goods. Trade dress is defined as the total image of a product, and includes features such as size, shape, color, color combinations, texture, graphics or sales techniques.

Section 43(a) of the Lanham Act, 15 U.S.C. § 1125(a), creates a federal cause of action for unfair competition in interstate commercial activities. It forbids unfair trade practices involving infringement of trade dress, service marks or trademarks, even in the absence of federal trademark registration. See, for instance, Two Pesos, Inc. v. Taco Cabana, Inc., *505 U.S. 763 (1992).*

Under Section 43(a), civil liability exists in cases where a person "on or in connection with any goods or services, ... uses in commerce any word, term, name, symbol, or device, or any combination thereof, or any false designation of origin, false or misleading description of fact, or false or misleading representation of fact, which –

> *(A) is likely to cause confusion, or to cause mistake, or to deceive as to the affiliation, connection, or association of such person with another person, or as to the origin, sponsorship, or approval of his or her goods, services, or commercial activities by another person, or*
> *(B) in commercial advertising or promotion, misrepresents the nature, characteristics, qualities, or geographic origin of his or her or another person's goods, services, or commercial activities ... "*

According to one court, the "touchstone test" for a violation of Section 43(a) is the likelihood of confusion resulting from the defendant's adoption of a trade dress similar to the plaintiff's. See Original Appalachian Artworks, Inc. v. Toy Loft, Inc., *684 F.2d 821 (11th Cir. 1982).*

◆ *An artist did not violate the Lanham Act by portraying University of Alabama uniforms in paintings, calendars and prints. But a court would have to decide whether he could continue making mugs and "mundane objects."*

Since 1979, the artist painted University of Alabama football scenes, portraying uniforms, helmets, jerseys and school colors. He reproduced paintings as prints, calendars, mugs and other articles. By 1995, the parties had entered into licensing agreements for some of the artist's works. In 2002, the university told the artist he would need permission to continue producing trademarked material. He stated that he needed no permission to "realistically portray historical events." In a federal action, the university sued the artist for breach of contract, trademark infringement and unfair competition. A court held the artist could produce paintings and prints, but it held the university was entitled to judgment regarding calendars, mugs and other "mundane products."

Appeal reached the U.S. Court of Appeals, Eleventh Circuit. As for the paintings, prints and calendars, the court rejected the university's argument that the licensing agreements prohibited the artist from making unlicensed portrayals of its uniforms. As the agreements were ambiguous, the court upheld the lower court judgment regarding the paintings and prints. Under the university's interpretation of a 1995 agreement, the artist "would need to perpetually obtain permission to paint any historically accurate scenes from Alabama football games." Evidence indicated the parties did not intend that the artist's portrayal of uniforms in unlicensed paintings, prints and calendars would violate their licensing agreements. His **First Amendment interests in artistic expression outweighed any consumer confusion that might exist regarding university trademarks, so there was no Lanham Act violation.** But there was ambiguity in the licensing agreements regarding whether the artist needed permission to portray uniforms on mugs and other mundane items. As there was insufficient evidence about this aspect of the case, the lower court would have to engage in further fact-finding. *Univ. of Alabama Board of Trustees v. New Life Art, Inc.*, 683 F.3d 1266 (11th Cir. 2012).

◆   *A federal court denied an Indian tribe's action to stop the NCAA from ending the University of North Dakota's use of the "Fighting Sioux" nickname.*

In 1969, elders of the Standing Rock Tribe and one Spirit Lake elder ceremonially approved the use of the Fighting Sioux name by the University of North Dakota (UND). Later, the Standing Rock Tribe passed three resolutions requesting UND to stop using the name. In 2005, the NCAA prohibited Native American mascots, nicknames and images from championship events. UND and the state board of higher education sued the NCAA, which led to a settlement agreement under which UND could retain the name without sanctions if both tribes granted approval before November 30, 2010. But the Standing Rock Tribe never acted, and the state higher education board decided to retire the nickname. In a federal court, a Spirit Lake committee and elder sued the NCAA to enjoin any sanctions against UND for using the Fighting Sioux nickname. The action also sought non-economic damages of at least $10 million. After the court held for the NCAA, the committee and elder appealed.

The U.S. Court of Appeals, Eighth Circuit, held the committee and elder lacked standing to pursue the case. While they stated the NCAA's action would cause family turmoil, shame, humiliation, persecution and damage to Sioux youth self-esteem and educational opportunities, the court held this did not confer standing. Even if the court accepted the argument that the injury was sufficiently concrete and particularized, it was not shown that the NCAA acted with a discriminatory intent to "eradicate Sioux culture," as the committee and elder argued. **Nor did the court accept the claim that the NCAA interfered with a contract under the theory that a contract was created by the 1969 ceremony.** However meaningful the grant of the nickname may have been, there was no contract that could be enforced. Instead, the Tribes were free to withdraw their permission to use the nickname, and the state board was free to change it. As the ceremony was only a "statement of appreciation," it was not an enforceable contract. The judgment was affirmed. *Spirit Lake Tribe of Indians v. NCAA*, 715 F.3d 1089 (8th Cir. 2013).

◆   *A federal court rejected the University of South Carolina's bid to gain trademark rights in a mark resembling one that was already trademarked and was in use by the University of Southern California.*

The University of South Carolina filed an application to trademark its logo, which includes the letters "SC." South Carolina wanted to use the mark on hats, baseball uniforms, T-shirts and shorts. The University of Southern California opposed the registration of the mark, as it had previously registered a trademark that protects the letters "SC." It argued that allowing the proposed mark would create a likelihood of confusion. South Carolina filed a counterclaim seeking cancellation of Southern California's mark. South Carolina claimed the mark falsely suggested an association with the State of South Carolina. The Trademark Trial and Appeals Board refused to register South Carolina's proposed mark, finding it would create a likelihood of confusion among consumers. The board pointed out that the marks were identical and would appear on the same classes of goods and in the same channels of trade. South Carolina's counterclaim for cancellation of Southern California's mark was also rejected, as South Carolina did not show the initials "SC" are "uniquely and unmistakably associated" with South Carolina. On appeal, the U.S. Court of Appeals, Federal Circuit, held the evidence supported the board's conclusion.

Allowing registration of the mark would create a likelihood of confusion, since the marks were the same and would appear on the same kinds of goods and in the same channels of trade. The court upheld the decision to reject South Carolina's counterclaim for cancellation of Southern California's mark. To win on this claim, South Carolina had to show Southern California's mark was "unmistakably associated" with another person or institution. South Carolina did not make this showing, as "SC" refers to many entities other than the state of South Carolina. The initials "SC" do not uniquely point to the state of South Carolina. The Trademark Trial and Appeals Board's decision was affirmed. *Univ. of South Carolina v. Univ. of Southern California,* 367 Fed.Appx. 129 (Fed. Cir. 2010).

◆ *A federal district court retained an action by a former star basketball player who claimed the NCAA is unfairly profiting from the use of his image.*

Ed O'Bannon led the UCLA men's basketball team to the 1995 NCAA championship. According to O'Bannon, the NCAA required all student-athletes to sign a form authorizing the NCAA's use of their names and likenesses for promotional purposes. He claimed the forms were signed under duress and required student-athletes to give up all rights to the commercial use of their images, even after graduation. O'Bannon sued the NCAA for violation of federal antitrust law. He said the NCAA engaged in price-fixing by setting a price of zero for the use of his image. He added claims for unjust enrichment and an accounting. The Collegiate Licensing Company (CLC), described as the NCAA's licensing arm, was added as a party. The NCAA and CLC sought to dismiss the claims. The court explained that to prove a federal antitrust violation, O'Bannon had to show a contract, a combination or conspiracy that unreasonably restrained trade, and a restraint that affected interstate commerce.

The court found sufficient facts to avoid dismissal with respect to each of these elements. **O'Bannon alleged the existence of agreements among the NCAA, its members, CLC and distributors of products containing his images. He sufficiently alleged that a relevant collegiate licensing market existed, and that NCAA and CLC actions had significant anticompetitive effects.** There was an effect on interstate commerce. The court also preserved a claim of unjust enrichment. *O'Bannon v. National Collegiate Athletic Ass'n,* No. C 09-1967 CW, 2010 WL 445190 (N.D. Cal. 2/8/10).

◆ *A state court rejected a Michigan State University football team manager's attempt to challenge a decision to have the Nike logo appear on team apparel.*

The manager claimed the appearance of the logos on the uniforms created confusion as to whether Michigan State student-athletes were personally endorsing Nike products. A state court held for the university, and the manager appealed on his state consumer protection act claim. The state court of appeals explained that he lacked standing to act as a private attorney general, as he did not suggest any injury from a deprivation of constitutional rights to himself or student-athletes at Michigan State. **The manager did not identify any student-athlete who objected to wearing the Nike logo.** The court also rejected his challenge under the state consumer protection act. As the manager did not identify any loss, the judgment was affirmed. *Sternberg v. Michigan State Univ.*, No. 281521, 2009 WL 131737 (Mich. Ct. App. 1/20/09).

◆ *A federal appeals court affirmed a decision for four major universities that sued an apparel manufacturer for federal trademark infringement.*

Louisiana State University, Ohio State University, the University of Oklahoma, and the University of Southern California held registered trademarks for their names and abbreviations. However, the institutions had no trademarks specifically relating to their color schemes. A clothing manufacturer sold T-shirts in color schemes and logos that were associated with the universities. Retailers displayed them alongside officially licensed merchandise, and the universities sued the manufacturer for trademark infringement. A federal district court found that even though the universities did not hold trademarks for their color schemes, the colors were associated with them closely enough to be entitled to trademark protection.

The manufacturer admitted it used the colors with the intent of identifying the universities. Since there was a likelihood of confusion regarding the source of the shirts, the court held the manufacturer violated the universities' trademark rights. A jury awarded the universities about $10,500 in actual damages and nearly $36,000 in lost profits. On appeal, the U.S. Court of Appeals, Fifth Circuit, found the universities established ownership of legally protectable marks. While they did not hold trademarks in their color schemes, each had acquired a "secondary meaning." **Secondary meaning occurs when the main reason for a mark is to identify the source of a product.** The universities had used their respective color schemes since the late 1800s, and they demonstrated a likelihood of confusion for consumers. The court rejected the manufacturer's argument that it made fair use of the color schemes and was not liable for trademark infringement. **The fair use doctrine does not apply when the use creates a likelihood of confusion.** *Board of Supervisors for Louisiana State Univ. Agricultural and Mechanical College v. Smack Apparel Co.*, 550 F.3d 465 (5th Cir. 2008).

◆ *A federal district court approved a settlement involving a university that included too much personal information on credit card receipts.*

University of Pittsburgh students who had purchased sporting event tickets over the Internet filed a federal district court action asserting they had been given receipts displaying more than the last five digits of their credit cards and/or card expiration dates. At the time, the practice violated the Fair and Accurate Credit Transaction Act (FACTA). The parties executed a settlement agreement that called for each class member to receive a ticket to one of two University of Pittsburgh football games. The court granted preliminary approval of the agreement. **Congress then amended the FACTA to eliminate a private cause of action based on a seller's inclusion of an expiration date on a receipt.** The amendment said a party could not be deemed to have been in willful noncompliance with the statute simply by virtue of printing an expiration date on a receipt. The amendment applied to transactions that occurred between specified dates. The court rejected the university's petition to vacate the settlement agreement, since it was a binding contract. The amendment did not apply to any action that became final after Congress acted. *Colella v. Univ. of Pittsburgh*, 569 F.Supp.2d 525 (W.D. Pa. 2008).

◆ *The University of Texas at Austin (UT) will be allowed to proceed with several trademark violation claims against an electric company that used several logos resembling UT's familiar longhorn steer logo.*

UT first requested that the company stop using the logo in 2002, claiming it had a longtime registered trademark depicting the silhouette of a longhorn steer. The owner refused, noting he had used the silhouette with certain embellishments since 1998. UT sued the company in a federal district court in 2006 for state and federal trademark claims. The court found UT correctly argued that its trademark and unfair competition claims should not be dismissed prior to further court activity. Trademark infringement occurs when a person, without consent, uses in commerce any reproduction, counterfeit, copy or imitation of a registered mark in connection with the sale, distribution or advertising of goods or services, when the use is likely to cause confusion or deception. **The court found that for both trademark infringement and unfair competition purposes, a "likelihood of confusion" means that confusion is probable, not just possible.** The court refused to dismiss the case at this early stage, finding UT showed a likelihood that the company logo suggested a UT affiliation or endorsement. However, the longhorn logo was not sufficiently famous to establish a basis for monetary relief based on federal dilution under the Lanham Act. The mark was not a household name, despite evidence of retail sales of UT products near $400 million in 2005-06. Only the claim based on federal dilution was dismissed. *Board of Regents of University of Texas System v. KST Electric, Ltd.*, 550 F.Supp.2d 657 (W.D. Tex. 2008).

◆ *Texas Tech University won a $3.1 million judgment against a retailer who continued to sell unlicensed university merchandise after the termination of a longstanding contract between the parties.*

The retailer was one of 450 university licensees that sold a total of $8 million in licensed products annually. He failed to account for the university's share of royalties, and the license was terminated in 2003. However, the retailer continued selling unlicensed merchandise through 2005, when Texas Tech sued him in a federal district court for trademark infringement, unfair competition, breach of contract, trademark dilution and injury to business reputation.

The court held Texas Tech's marks were protectable under trademark law because they were distinctive and not functional. The color scheme of Texas Tech apparel and merchandise identified and distinguished it. The scheme was associated with the university since the 1920s. The products were easily recognized, and they signalled to the public that they were licensed by Texas Tech. The commercial impression created by the unlicensed products was identical to the impression created by the university's products. The strength of the marks was undeniable, and they deserved broad protection. In addition, the retailer sold licensed products right alongside unlicensed ones. Consumers were likely to be confused by the sales of similar goods at the same stores. Each of the factors regarding the potential confusion for consumers presented by the retailer's use of the trademarks weighed in favor of the university. Texas Tech was also entitled to judgment on the unfair competition claims. **Unfair competition occurs when an individual passes off the products of another by virtue of their substantial similarity.** The retailer clearly breached his contract with Texas Tech by continuing to sell licensed products after the contract was terminated. The Lanham Act permits the owner of a violated trademark to recover all the infringer's profits plus any damages and costs. Texas Tech showed the retailer's profits during 2004-05 totalled more than $2.8 million. The university was entitled to these profits as well as the royalties due under the contract. The court awarded the university a total of more than $3.1 million. *Texas Tech Univ. v. Spiegelberg*, 461 F.Supp.2d 510 (N.D. Tex. 2006).

◆ *The Nebraska Supreme Court denied an apparel store owner's claims against the University of Nebraska for wrongful use of a registered trade name.*

In late 1995, the Nebraska Athletic Department created an Authentic Shop, which would sell to the public apparel and equipment identical to that used by its teams and staff. That same year, the university's board of regents filed an application with the secretary of state to register the trade name "Husker Authentics" for licensed goods. But the university did not file necessary papers, and the registration was canceled without notice. Brent White, who had a license with the university, applied for registration of the trade name "Husker Authentics." Collegiate Licensing Company (CLC), the university's exclusive licensing agent, sent White a letter claiming he was in violation of his license agreement. The university then opened a store called Husker Authentic. Seven days later, White filed a petition requesting that the school be enjoined from using the disputed trade name. Later that month, White added a damages claim.

The university argued, among other things, that there had been a violation of common-law and statutory trade name and trademark rights. A state district court held White's registration had been improperly granted because he had not used the trade name prior to registration. White appealed. The Nebraska Supreme Court found the district court's decision to be correct, but on different grounds, citing the work the university had done in test-marketing the concept. It further concluded that this afforded the school the common-law right to the trademark and any subsequent registration was therefore invalid. **Because the university owned the common-law right to "Husker Authentics," White could not properly register the disputed trademark.** The lower court's cancellation of White's registration was upheld. *White v. Board of Regents of the Univ. of Nebraska*, 260 Neb. 26, 614 N.W.2d 330 (Neb. 2000).

CHAPTER NINE

Liability

I. NEGLIGENCE

Negligence results from a failure to use reasonable or ordinary care. To impose liability on a person or an institution there must be a legal duty. This is determined by the foreseeability of the risk of harm that caused injury. If an injury is a foreseeable result of negligent or intentional conduct, a legal duty exists, and liability may follow. Once a duty on the part of the institution is shown, liability exists if there was a breach of that duty, an injury or loss caused by the breach, and some damages. A pattern of negligence by schools and colleges that shows conscious disregard for safety may be "willful misconduct," a form of intentional conduct discussed in Section II of this chapter.

A. Duty of Care

◆ *A Utah student had a "special relationship" with a dance team instructor that created a legal duty to protect her from injury during a team rehearsal.*

A dance team instructor told the student and her partner they were doing a lift incorrectly. He warned them they would have to cut the lift from their routine if they could not do it properly. When the partner tried to lift the student over his shoulder as instructed, he lost his footing and dropped her, causing her injury. A state court held the student accepted a risk of injury because she had the option of eliminating the lift from the routine. On appeal, the state court of appeals explained that Utah law does not generally recognize a special relationship between a college and its students. But the Utah Supreme Court created an exception to this rule in *Webb v. Univ. of Utah*. Under *Webb*, students relinquished some autonomy to their instructors based on expertise.

In this case, **a special relationship was formed if the student was injured by following an instructor's directive that fell "within the scope of the academic enterprise."** As the student was hurt during a team rehearsal, she was relying on her instructor during an academic enterprise and a special relationship existed. As a result, the college could be liable if a jury found the instructor did not use reasonable care in instructing her. A jury would have to decide if the instructor's conduct was reasonable and whether it caused injury. *Cope v. Utah Valley State College*, 290 P.3d 314 (Utah Ct. App. 2012).

◆ *A Wisconsin college had no duty to prevent the rape of a student in her dorm room because she did not show the attack was foreseeable.*

The student was a freshman with a hearing impairment who lived in an all-female residence hall. She said that resident assistants encouraged residents to prop their doors open they while in their dorm rooms so they could get to know other residents. The student said that while she was in her dorm room with her door propped open as suggested, two males entered her room. She said one raped her while the other held her down. The student sued the college in a federal court for negligence, claiming that the assault was due to a failure to provide adequate security. The court explained that to prove negligence, the student had to show the college breached a duty of care. In pretrial activity, the student's expert tried to show that on-campus assaults at the college were increasing. But a study relied on by the expert did not address the likelihood that a female student with a hearing impairment would be raped in her dorm by a stranger. The expert testimony regarding the applicable standard of care was not admissible. As the expert's conclusion that the attack was foreseeable was deemed unreliable, **the student was unable to show the security at the residence hall should have been improved**. As a result, the court held for the college, finding she failed to establish a standard of care that was not met. *Lees v. Carthage College*, No. 10-C-86, 2011 WL 3844115 (E.D. Wis. 8/29/11).

◆ *A Massachusetts college was not liable for the death of a 20-year-old man who drank at a college party and then drove his car.*

The administrator of the man's estate sued the college for negligence in a state court, alleging that it failed to monitor its alcohol policy and prevent underage drinking. Before the Court of Appeals of Massachusetts, the administrator said the death was foreseeable because college students are known to behave irresponsibly. As an alternate argument, the administrator said social values and customs within the college community enabled the college to foresee and prevent the death. Noting that the man did not even attend the college, the court rejected any claim that the college owed him a duty to prevent his death. **While the college had policies relating to alcohol, they did not create a duty to someone outside the college community.** In addition, there was no special relationship between the man and the college that created a duty of care. The fact that the college owned the building where the party took place did not, by itself, create a special relationship and a resulting duty by the college. The man was in the best position to prevent the harm he suffered, as he could have decided not to drink and drive. The college was not responsible for his death. *Brody v. Wheaton College*, 74 Mass.App.Ct. 1105, 904 N.E.2d 493 (Table) (Mass. App. Ct. 2009).

♦ *A New York university could not be held liable for a slip and fall in a campus stairwell after a winter storm.*

A pedestrian slipped and fell on a stairwell, where she said there was a mix of water and icy snow on the stairs. In a state court personal injury action, the university argued that it was entitled to judgment because it did not know about or create the condition on the stairs. The court refused to award pretrial judgment, and the university appealed to a state appellate division court. An appellate panel found no evidence that the university knew students were tracking in snow and ice. **"A general awareness" that stairs become wet when ice and snow are tracked into a building was not enough to establish that the university knew of the particular condition that caused the fall.** As the university established it neither created nor knew of the condition that caused injury, the judgment was reversed. *Wartski v. C.W. Post Campus of Long Island Univ.*, 63 A.D.3d 916, 882 N.Y.S.2d 192 (N.Y. App. Div. 2009).

♦ *Parents of a University of Kansas (KU) freshman who fell to his death from a ledge outside his seventh-floor dorm room were unable to hold KU liable.*

The student fell to his death after removing window screens and going onto a ledge to smoke a cigarette. His blood alcohol level at the time was .16. The parents filed a wrongful death suit in a state court against KU, saying the ledge presented a dangerous condition that the university should have corrected.

After the court awarded pretrial judgment to KU, the parents appealed. The Court of Appeals of Kansas explained that a "discretionary function exception" insulates government entities from liability when harm results from an entity's performance of, or failure to perform, a discretionary duty or function. While the parents argued that the exception did not apply because KU was obligated to use reasonable care to protect their son, the court disagreed. Any duty of KU did not require it to warn of known and obvious dangers such as stepping out onto the ledge. KU was not required to take any extraordinary steps to minimize the obvious risk of danger from going out onto the ledge. **Universities are not required to protect their students from their own reckless and negligent acts and are not insurers of student safety.** The court affirmed the judgment for KU. *Wellhausen v. Univ. of Kansas*, 40 Kan.App.2d 102, 189 P.3d 1181 (Kan. Ct. App. 2008).

♦ *The University of the District of Columbia was not liable for injuries sustained by a student who was attacked in an on-campus parking garage.*

Two assailants demanded money from the student, and one of them stabbed her in the face. She was able to escape, but the criminals were never apprehended. The student and her husband sued the university for negligence, claiming it should have taken safety precautions to prevent the attack. After a jury awarded $300,000 to the student and $100,000 to her husband, the case went before the District of Columbia Court of Appeals. It explained that a party may be held liable for negligence when there is a duty, a breach of that duty causing injury, and proof that the injury was proximately caused by the breach. **When injury results from an intervening criminal act, the injured party cannot recover for negligence unless the criminal act is so foreseeable that it creates a duty on the part of the defendant to guard against it.** This required some evidence that the university had "an increased awareness" that there was a risk of a violent, armed attack in its parking garage.

It was not enough to show there was a general possibility that a crime could occur in the garage. Although there was some evidence of crime on campus, none of the incidents involved a weapon, and none were committed in a parking garage or caused serious injury. Finding the university could not have foreseen the attack, the court held for the university. *Board of Trustees of Univ. of District of Columbia v. DiSalvo*, 974 A.2d 868 (D.C. Ct. App. 2009).

◆ *A Mississippi university was required to defend a negligence claim alleging it was liable for the rape of a 14-year-old girl on its campus in 1993.*

The student claimed she was raped by two 15-year-old boys on the campus of Jackson State University (JSU) during a National Youth Sports Program. As part of the program, JSU leased a bus and transported participating children from their homes to the JSU campus. Both boys had prior histories of trouble in the program. One had been expelled from the program for fighting, and the other had been threatened with expulsion for fighting on a bus and on campus. The girl was dropped off at the wrong location on campus, where both boys raped her in a restroom. The boys later pled guilty to raping her. Her parents sued JSU and its officials in the state court system for negligence. The court awarded judgment to JSU, but the Supreme Court of Mississippi returned the case to the trial court in 2000. It again granted judgment to JSU.

The case returned to state's highest court in 2007. **The court focused on the question of whether the rape was foreseeable to JSU officials. If it was, then the university could be held liable for negligence.** The court held that a reasonable juror might conclude JSU could have foreseen that, by leaving the girl and two boys unattended and unsupervised, JSU placed her in danger of "some violent act or impermissible sexual act." A jury could find that JSU knew there were 63 crimes reported on campus in the 10 months preceding the rape, including other rapes. It could also find JSU was on notice that the girl had been in the boys' restroom prior to the date of the rape, and that the boys who committed the rape had violent tendencies. The court remanded the case for trial. *Glover v. Jackson State Univ.*, 968 So.2d 1267 (Miss. 2007).

◆ *An Ohio university was not liable for the rape of a student that took place in a university dormitory because the rape was not foreseeable.*

The student lived in a coed dorm with separate communal bathrooms for male and female students. She was raped while she was taking a shower in a dorm bathroom. Her attacker was never caught. The student sued the university in a state court for negligence, asserting it breached a duty of care by failing to install locks on the bathroom or shower doors. The court held for the university, but the Court of Appeals of Ohio reversed the judgment. It found the trial court had improperly admitted testimony by an expert witness. When the case was retried, the trial court held the university liable for negligence and awarded the student $100,000 for her injuries, pain and suffering. The university brought another appeal to the Court of Appeals of Ohio. According to the university, it did not owe the student a duty to protect her from rape by an unknown intruder. It claimed it was not liable because the attack was unforeseeable.

The court noted that while the university had a duty to warn or protect its students from the known criminal conduct of third persons, it was not an insurer of student safety. If the attack was not foreseeable, the university was not liable for negligence. The court of appeals found **the evidence was not specific enough to show the university could have foreseen the attack. The university did not breach its duty of care to the student**, and the court reversed the judgment. *Shivers v. Univ. of Cincinnati*, No. 06AP-209, 2006 WL 3008478 (Ohio Ct. App. 10/24/06).

◆   *The Supreme Court of Utah held a university was not liable for injuries to a student who fell on an icy sidewalk during a class field trip.*

As part of an earth sciences curriculum, the student attended a field trip to examine fault lines in Salt Lake County. An instructor told students to walk on icy and snowy sidewalks through a condominium complex. The student fell and was injured when a classmate slipped and grabbed him for support. The student sued the university in a state court for negligence. The case reached the Supreme Court of Utah, which reviewed whether the university had a special relationship with the student that created a duty of care. The court held that a special relationship can be created between an instructor and a student, because a college student will at times defer to an instructor's superior knowledge, skill, and experience. In this case, the instructor's directive that students cross the condominium sidewalk was not a command the student should have felt he had to obey. The court found it was unreasonable to believe the student would think his academic success could be affected if he refused to take a dangerous route so he could view fault lines. **The instructor did not exert the type of control in an academic setting required to create a special relationship.** As no special relationship existed, the court held the university had no legal duty to protect the student, and could not be held liable for his injuries. *Webb v. Univ. of Utah*, 125 P.3d 906 (Utah 2005).

◆   *A Minnesota university was not liable for injuries to a cheerleader who injured her spine while participating in a pyramid stunt during a practice.*

The cheerleader fell and suffered a cervical spine fracture when the squad tried to perform a pyramid stunt. She later admitted she knew the stunt was risky, but felt pressured to attempt it. The cheerleader sued the university for negligence in a state court. The court found the university had no duty to protect her and held for the university. The cheerleader appealed to the Court of Appeals of Minnesota. **The court held that to prevail on her negligence claim, the cheerleader had to establish first that the university owed her a duty of care. A university is not required to guarantee student safety.**

The court found that courts in Utah, Indiana and Louisiana have found no special relationship exists between a university and a student-athlete. While the university handled some administrative tasks for cheerleading programs, it exerted minimal control over cheerleaders. The university did not provide a coach to direct practices or otherwise impose rules on participants. The court noted the university did not profit from cheerleading programs. The university was not in a position to protect the student and could not have been expected to do so. Nothing suggested the cheerleader was vulnerable. Because there was no special relationship in this case, the university did not owe her a duty of care, and the court affirmed the judgment. *Vistad v. Board of Regents of Univ. of Minnesota*, No. A04-2161, 2005 WL 1514633 (Minn. Ct. App. 6/28/05).

◆ *A Delaware university was not negligent when its security officers responded to a student's 911 call within two minutes.*

The student heard someone outside the door of her dormitory room about 5:00 a.m. She called campus security, but by the time the security office picked up the call, she had hung up. The student was afraid the person would get in, so she jumped out her window, injuring herself. She crawled back into the building and hid in a men's room on the first floor. A university security officer arrived at the dorm room less than two minutes after the call was received.

When security arrived at the room, no one answered and there were no signs of an attempted break-in. Officers searched the grounds nearby. About an hour later, the student emerged from the men's room and the university quickly transported her to a hospital. The student sued the university in a Delaware trial court, alleging the school security personnel were negligent by failing to promptly respond to her 911 call. **The court held that to prevail on her claim of negligence, the student had to show the university owed her a duty of care and that it breached the duty.** While the university owed a duty to the student to protect her in her dorm, she failed to present any evidence of a breach of that duty. Evidence indicated university personnel acted professionally and effectively in responding to the incident. The court granted the university pre-trial judgment. *Pochvatilla v. Univ. of Delaware*, No. Civ.A. 03C-11-015 SCD, 2005 WL 434495 (Del. Super. Ct. 2/3/05).

◆ *The Court of Appeals of Tennessee held a state university was not liable to a non-student actress who fell during a rehearsal.*

In a state court lawsuit, the actress claimed the university negligently failed to place glow tape on the edge of a darkened stage, causing injury. The Tennessee Claims Commission found the actress 100% at fault for her injuries. She appealed to the Court of Appeals of Tennessee, which agreed with her argument that theaters owed a duty to actors and actresses to exercise reasonable care. However, that did not make them liable for risks that could not be reasonably foreseen. **The court found the actress did not prove the university knew or should have known she would fall because no glow tape was on the edge of the stage.** Another cast member's complaint that glow tape should be placed on set pieces did not put the university on notice there was a dangerous condition in another part of the stage. The court held the actress failed to establish the state was negligent. *Fox v. State of Tennessee*, No. E2003-02024-COA-R3-CV, 2004 WL 2399822 (Tenn. Ct. App. 10/27/04).

B. Premises Liability

Generally, an institution may be held liable if it either knew or should have known about a defective condition on its property. But a landowner has no duty to protect visitors or even warn them about a condition that is obvious and not inherently dangerous. When an injured party's presence on property is not reasonably foreseeable, the property owner cannot be held liable for injury.
   In Agnes Scott College v. Clark, *273 Ga.App. 619, 616 S.E.2d 468 (Ga. Ct. App. 2005), the Court of Appeals of Georgia held an institution is generally not liable for the unforeseen criminal acts of a third party.*

◆ *A New York appellate division court dismissed a negligence action by a college banquet guest, finding it was based on purely speculative claims.*
   During the banquet, the guest walked from a lavatory to the kitchen at least four times to talk to staff members. On his final trip, he slipped and fell. Later, the guest said he saw soapy water from dishwashing machines near the area where he fell. He sued the college in a state court for personal injury, claiming the college knew about a dangerous condition that caused his injury. The trial court held for the college. On appeal, a state appellate division court found that to prevail, the college had to show it maintained the premises in a reasonably safe condition and was not aware of water on the floor at the time of the fall.
   There was evidence that college wait staff had walked over the area of the fall without incident and without seeing any water. A supervisor explained that a college policy required wait staff to immediately attend to spills, slippery surfaces or liquid on the floor. Evidence indicated that college staff members routinely checked on dishwashing machines and had regular safety meetings. In the court's view, no evidence supported the guest's claim that there was water near the place of the fall due to negligence. **The guest's claim that the college created a danger of injury was based on speculation, not evidence.** As the trial court had ruled correctly, the judgment was affirmed. *Flahive v. Union College*, 99 A.D.2d 1151, 952 N.Y.S.2d 821 (N.Y. App. Div. 2012).

◆ *A South Carolina court upheld a jury verdict rejecting liability for negligence in a case filed by a parent who fell on university property.*
   The University of South Carolina leased an undeveloped island primarily for sea turtle research. The parent of a university intern was injured when she slipped on the stairs of a beach house and broke her ankle. She later sued the university in a state court for negligent design, construction and maintenance of the stairs. At trial, the judge explained to the jury the difference between an invitee and a licensee in a premises liability case. The jury was instructed to determine which category best fit the parent while she was on the island. The judge also told the jury that a state law limiting landowner liability applied.
   After the jury returned a verdict for the university, the parent appealed to the state court of appeals, arguing the judge should have decided she was an invitee. **Invitee status would have triggered a higher duty of care on the part of the university.** According to the court, there was enough evidence for the jury to conclude she was a licensee, not an invitee. The judge did not commit error by leaving this question for the jury. The court rejected the claim

that the judge, and not the jury, should have determined if the landowner liability statute applied. As the parent's other challenges to the jury instructions were not properly preserved for review, the judgment was affirmed. *Harris v. Univ. of South Carolina*, 706 S.E.2d 45 (S.C. Ct. App. 2011).

◆ *A New York college was denied pretrial dismissal in a slip-and-fall case due to evidence that it may have known about a defective condition in a shower.*

A New York woman and her friend visited the campus at Skidmore College to participate in a reunion planning meeting. They were assigned to stay in an on-campus apartment. The woman turned on a bathroom shower and stepped away while waiting for the water to heat up. When she returned to the bathroom, she slipped and fell on the floor, breaking her wrist. She sued the university in a state court for negligence, asserting that the showerhead had a clog that caused it to spray water over the top of the shower curtain and onto the floor. She claimed the defective showerhead led to the slippery floor and her fall. She also said the college made things worse by negligently applying a soap or polish to the surface of the floor. After the court entered pretrial judgment against her, an appellate division court reversed the decision. It found **the woman had presented evidence that the college either knew or should have known about the defective condition.** *Anderson v. Skidmore College*, 94 A.D.3d 1203, 941 N.Y.S.2d 787 (N.Y. App. Div. 2012).

◆ *An Ohio university was not liable for injuries to an elevator repairman because it did not control the building where he was hurt at the time of injury.*

An elevator repairman working in a Cleveland State University dormitory that was undergoing renovation was hurt when the elevator malfunctioned and fell eight stories. He sued the university in state court for negligence. The university asserted that it did not maintain, operate or control the dormitory on the day he was injured. Instead, it had leased the dormitory to a developer and did not possess or control it on the date of the injury. The case reached the Court of Appeals of Ohio, which stated the general rule is that **a lessee who manages and controls an elevator in a leased building is responsible for injuries caused by defects.** An exception says that owners can be held responsible if the defective condition existed at the time of the transfer of control and possession to the lessee. In this case, the elevator was not defective when the university transferred possession of it to the developer, and the university could not be held liable for the injuries. *Matteucci v. Cleveland State Univ.*, No. 10AP-576, 2011 WL 1744117 (Ohio Ct. App. 5/3/11).

◆ *A New York appellate court held City University of New York (CUNY) was properly granted pretrial judgment in a personal injury lawsuit.*

A visitor to the CUNY campus said she was injured going down steep steps that separated an upper patio from a lower patio. She also said it was the only available exit, meaning special rules of the New York City administrative code applied. CUNY sought pretrial judgment on the ground that the condition of the steps was open, obvious and not inherently dangerous. The court denied the motion and CUNY appealed. A state appellate division court held that in New York, landowners have a duty to maintain their premises in a reasonably safe manner. **But a landowner has no duty to protect visitors against or warn them about a condition that is both obvious and not inherently dangerous.** That was the case here. As CUNY breached no duty to the visitor, she could not hold it liable. The court also found that the administrative code provision concerning building exits did not apply to outdoor stairways. *Losciuto v. City Univ. of New York*, 80 A.D.3d 576, (N.Y. App. Div. 2011).

◆ *Boston University (BU) was not responsible for the death of a student who was struck by a train after she trespassed onto a railroad yard near campus.*

The student and a friend apparently gained access to the rail yard through a hole in a fence. They were struck from behind by a commuter train and killed. In a state court case against BU and several other entities, the student's parents asserted various tort claims. They included a contract claim against BU trustees premised on the theory that BU's website and police handbook obligated it to protect its students from harm. The court rejected the tort claims, finding no duty of care was owed the student. According to the court, any reasonable person could see that the rail yard was "an inherently forbidding place."

Where a danger is open and obvious, a landowner does not have a duty to warn of the danger, because it is not reasonably foreseeable that a person exercising reasonable care will fall victim. Nor was there any duty to remedy the risk posed by the yard, because the risk was "blatant and unequivocal" and could be easily avoided by a reasonable person. Both students were trespassing at the time they were killed, and state law made their presence on the tracks a criminal offense. Finally, the court held no reasonable jury could find BU breached a contractual duty to provide a safe environment. For this reason, BU was entitled to judgment on the contract claim. *Shattuck v. Trustees of Boston Univ.*, 27 Mass.L.Rptr. 288, (Mass. Super. Ct. 2010).

◆ *A woman who fell on a college campus could not recover damages because the college did not have notice of a dangerous condition where she fell.*

The woman was catering an event at the college when she slipped and fell in a restroom. She claimed she did not remember falling, but she said she heard others say the floor was slippery and that there was "something" on it. College employees examined the floor and found the texture of the tile in front of the sink smoother than the rest of the floor. When the woman sued the college in a state court, her expert witness offered the opinion that the college had maintained a hazardous condition due to the presence of glassware polish on the tile floor. The court entered an order that barred the woman's expert from testifying about the alleged existence of a foreign substance on the floor, since this was based on speculation. The court then awarded judgment to the college. On appeal, the court explained that **an expert cannot offer a mere conclusion. Instead, the expert must provide the "why and wherefore" of his opinion.** In this case, the conclusion that a foreign substance contributed to the fall was speculation. The lower court permissibly barred the expert from testifying that a foreign substance contributed to a slippery condition, and the college was entitled to judgment. *Byrd v. Salem Community College*, L-172-06, 2009 WL 2015128 (N.J. Super. Ct. App. Div. 7/14/09).

◆   *Morehead State University was not liable for injuries sustained by a blind student who slipped and fell on candy on the floor of an on-campus restroom.*

Four witnesses testified that pieces of candy the size of marbles were "strewn everywhere" on the restroom floor after the student fell. There was no evidence indicating how the candy got on the floor. A cleaning staff of 63 employees was responsible for maintaining 44 campus buildings. The building where the fall took place was cleaned twice a day. A maintenance worker testified that the bathroom where the fall took place was inspected and cleaned before the accident. A hearing officer dismissed the case, and appeal reached the Court of Appeals of Kentucky. It found substantial evidence supporting the decision for the university. **Evidence showed the restroom was cleaned before and after the fall. There was enough evidence to support a conclusion that the university reasonably maintained the property**, justifying a decision for the university. *Glass v. Morehead State Univ.*, No. 2008-CA-001018-MR, 2009 WL 2192739 (Ky. Ct. App. 7/24/09).

◆   *A Delaware college was not liable for injuries to a student who fell while stepping off a sidewalk, since it did not cause a defective condition.*

The student tripped on uneven pavement near the college campus and hurt himself. At the time, a construction company was working on the road and the abutting sidewalks and curbing. The student sued the college and construction company in a state court for negligence. He claimed the college knew or should have known that the pavement was unsafe. The court granted the college's motion for pretrial judgment. **Under state law, abutting landowners are liable for injuries caused by a defective sidewalk only if they cause the defect or have a statutory duty to repair it.** In this case, there was no evidence that any state law or local ordinance made the college responsible for maintaining the sidewalk. Instead, evidence showed the city was responsible to maintain the sidewalk. There was no evidence that the college caused the defect that led to injury. *Lawson v. Wilmington College of Delaware*, No. 07C-07-027 JTV, 2009 WL 27301 (Del. Super. Ct. 1/5/09).

◆   *A Tennessee university could be liable for injuries contractors sustained while performing repairs on the school's premises.*

A maintenance supervisor discovered a malfunctioning switchgear in an electrical equipment cabinet and called in outside help when he discovered unusually high voltage was present. He told the contractor's service manager that high voltage was present but did not relay this information to the two contractors who arrived to fix the problem. The two men began to work on the equipment and were injured when a high-voltage arc of electricity generated a flash of light and ball of fire. Both men sued the university in the state court system for negligence, claiming it misstated the voltage. They also faulted the university for failing to provide warning signs and failing to maintain its electrical equipment. The case reached the Supreme Court of Tennessee.

The court explained that a premises owner who hires an independent contractor and offers information regarding the repair has a duty to make sure the information is accurate. If the university employees told the contractors that the equipment carried only 480 volts, the university had a duty to make sure that information was correct. The university was also potentially liable to the contractors on a theory of negligent misrepresentation. Under that theory, a person or entity that supplies false information to others with respect to business transactions can be liable for losses suffered as a result of reliance on the information. Since a disputed issue remained as to whether university employees supplied false information to the contractors about the voltage in the equipment, the case was returned to a lower court for additional proceedings. *Bennett v. Trevecca Nazarene Univ.*, 216 S.W.3d 293 (Tenn. 2007).

◆ *A Texas student could not rely on a university safety manual to prove the university knew about the dangerous condition that caused his fall.*

While walking to a class on campus, the student tripped on a water hose and broke his knee. In his state court negligence lawsuit, the university claimed immunity under the state tort claims act. Under the act, the university was not liable for injuries caused by a premises defect unless it knew about a dangerous condition on its premises and failed to warn others about it. The court rejected the student's claim that a university safety manual, which required walking areas to be kept unobstructed, created a fact issue about whether the university had knowledge of the condition that caused his fall. A trial court agreed and denied the university's motion for summary disposition. The state appeals court affirmed the judgment, but **the Supreme Court of Texas held the manual was not evidence that the university knew about the hazard that caused the fall**. While the manual warned of the danger created when flexible cords were placed across paths of travel, it did so while discussing indoor safety. Nothing in the manual suggested that the hose created an unreasonable risk of harm. As a result, the lower court decisions were reversed, and the case was dismissed. *Univ. of Texas-Pan American v. Aquilar*, 251 S.W.3d 511 (Tex. 2008).

◆ *An Indiana college did not owe the parent of a student any duty to exercise reasonable care because he was not an "invitee" under state law.*

The parent slipped on some loose gravel on a campus walkway while walking toward a restroom. He severely injured his left arm and sued the college for negligence. A state court held for the college. On appeal, the Court of Appeals of Indiana explained that a landowner's duty in negligence cases depends on the legal status of the visitor. The duty owed varies depending on whether the visitor is an invitee, a licensee or a trespasser. The highest duty of care is owed to invitees, who are owed a duty of reasonable care. Licensees are those who enter premises for their "own convenience, curiosity or entertainment." The duty owed to licensees is the duty not to "willfully or wantonly" injure them or to "increase [their] peril." The law offers the least protection to trespassers. The court held that under the circumstances, "no reasonable person could conclude Ivy Tech extended an invitation" to the parent to use its public restrooms. **As a licensee, the parent needed to prove the college willfully or wantonly injured him or increased his peril.** However, he did not even allege that the college did so. Because the parent was aware of the loose gravel and it was not a latent danger, the judgment was affirmed. *Gilpin v. Ivy Tech State College*, 864 N.E.2d 399 (Ind. Ct. App. 2007).

◆ *A Utah student failed to produce expert testimony showing her fall was caused by defective stairs, defeating her negligence action.*

The student and her husband sued the university for negligence and loss of consortium, saying the student's fall was caused by a failure to maintain the stairs. They did not present any expert testimony and relied primarily on the student's account. A state trial court held an affidavit and report from a university emergency response team were admissible under state rules of evidence. It also held expert testimony was needed to prove causation. The Court of Appeals of Utah said the state rules of evidence took precedence in this case. The reviewing court also affirmed the finding that expert testimony was needed to show a causal link between the allegedly defective stairs and the injury. Only in "the most obvious cases" are plaintiffs excused from proving causation via expert testimony. **Without the benefit of expert testimony, a fact-finder would need to resort to speculation regarding what really caused the injury.** The trial court's decision for the university was affirmed. *Fox v. Brigham Young Univ.*, 176 P.3d 446 (Utah Ct. App. 2007).

◆ *The Court of Appeals of Mississippi held a university was not liable for a visitor's shooting of a student on campus.*

One evening, three non-students entered the university campus in a car. They were not asked to log in as required by a university policy. The non-students rode around the campus, threw beer bottles at students and became involved in a number of fights. One of the non-students drew a gun and shot into a crowd that had gathered to watch the fighting. A bullet hit a student and he underwent surgery to remove it. The student sued the university in a state trial court for negligence. The court held he could not prove a connection between alleged reckless disregard of the log-in policy by campus police officers and the shooting. The student appealed to the Court of Appeals of Mississippi, contending that had the police conducted log-in procedures, they would have become suspicious and would not have admitted the non-students. The court disagreed. It emphasized that because the log-in procedures did not require a search for weapons, the outcome would have been the same. **The court agreed with the trial court that the student failed to prove a causal connection between the police officers' conduct and his injuries.** As a result, the court affirmed the judgment for the university. *Johnson v. Alcorn State Univ.*, 929 So.2d 398 (Miss. Ct. App. 2006).

◆ *A Maryland university was not negligent when it assigned a student to live with a roommate who had a prior record of fighting.*

The student was in the process of moving out of the room when the roommate accused him of breaking a fish tank. The roommate hit the student in the jaw, requiring him to undergo surgery and have his mouth wired shut. The student sued the university for negligence in a state trial court. The case went before a jury. The student presented evidence of the roommate's disciplinary history at the university. He had been involved in fights with other students. The university had suspended the roommate and allowed him to return only after he completed a conflict resolution counseling program. The case reached the Court of Appeals of Maryland, which held **the university**

could not have reasonably foreseen what happened. The roommate had no history of violence under similar circumstances. Even the student did not believe the roommate was dangerous. He knew about the roommate's prior incidents and did not ask for a new room or roommate. As a result, the university was entitled to judgment. *Rhaney v. Univ. of Maryland Eastern Shore*, 388 Md. 585, 880 A.2d 357 (Md. 2005).

◆ *The Supreme Court of Montana held a state university was liable for injuries to a child who fell on library stairs.*

The child slipped between the stairway balusters of a second-story open stairwell and fell approximately 20 feet to the concrete floor. He suffered three skull fractures from the fall. The mother sued the state in a Montana trial court, alleging negligence. The court found the state had a duty of care to the child and breached that duty, so it was liable for the fall. The state appealed to the Supreme Court of Montana. **The court held the state had a duty to maintain the balcony and staircase at the university library so they were safe for ordinary public use.** The court found the risk of falling was foreseeable because the state knew the distance between the staircase balusters was 11 to 12 inches. As the state failed to cure, remove or warn the public about the stairway defect, the court affirmed the judgment. *Henricksen v. State of Montana*, 84 P.3d 38 (Mont. 2004).

C. Defenses

1. Immunity

State laws preclude liability in many tort cases against public institutions. Such laws confer immunity on public entities unless they cause injury through conduct that is willful, wanton or grossly negligent.

◆ *A man who was hurt while riding his bicycle on the campus of a Texas state university could not sue the university to recover for his injuries.*

Officials at the University of Texas at Austin (UT) closed off some areas of the campus to prepare for a football game. Workers stretched a metal chain across an entrance and placed an eight-foot orange-and-white barricade in front of the chain. While riding a bicycle on campus, the man crashed into the chain as he tried to avoid the barricade, suffering injuries. He sued UT for premises liability in a state court. As a state entity, UT would be immune to his claims unless he could show his injury resulted from either a premises defect or what Texas law refers to as a "special defect." After the trial court granted partial pretrial judgment to the man, appeal reached the Supreme Court of Texas.

On appeal, the court explained that state entities are not immune to tort claims that arise from premises defects or "special defects." In this case, **the condition that led to injury was not a special defect, such as an excavation or road obstruction**. Road users in the normal course of travel turn back or take another route when a barricade tells them a roadway is closed. The chain did not pose a threat because ordinary users would not have moved past the barricade. UT had closed the road and had no reason to know the chain was dangerous to users. There was no evidence that UT had any prior reports of injuries or accidents at the site of injury. As a result, the man failed to show the chain was a premises defect within the meaning of the state law, and the case was dismissed. *Univ. of Texas at Austin v. Hayes*, 327 S.W.3d 113 (Tex. 2010).

◆ *A spectator who slipped and fell in front of a stadium at the University of Texas could not recover damages for her injuries.*

The spectator was hurt when she slipped and fell on a removable drainage trench cover. The metal cover was slippery at the time of the fall because of rain. The spectator sued the university in a state court, claiming the trench cover was a premises defect. Under the tort claims act, state entities are immune from claims based on discretionary decisions. Despite an engineer's statement that the metal cover was used as the result of a discretionary design decision, the court refused to dismiss the case. The Court of Appeals of Texas held that the university had immunity if incorporating the cover into the sidewalk was a discretionary act. **A "discretionary act" requires the exercise of judgment and occurs when "the law does not mandate performing the act with such precision that nothing is left to discretion or judgment."** The engineer's statement established that the decision to place the cover in the sidewalk was discretionary. As a result, the university had state tort act immunity from the lawsuit. *Univ. of Texas v. Amezquita*, No. 03-06-00606-CV, 2009 WL 1563533 (Tex. Ct. App. 6/4/09).

◆ *A woman who was injured when she fell down a flight of stairs at Texas Southern University (TSU) could proceed with her lawsuit.*

The woman fell down stairs in an area where a work order had recently been issued to repair a loose handrail. A supervisor had signed off on the work order. The woman sued TSU in a state court for negligence. TSU responded by claiming state law immunity, but the court denied pretrial dismissal. TSU appealed to the Court of Appeals of Texas. It explained that state agencies such as TSU were immune from suit unless immunity was waived. An exception to immunity exists when a condition of personal or real property causes personal injury, or when an injury is caused by a premises defect. **To prove liability on a premises defect theory, the woman had to show TSU would be liable under the circumstances if it were a private person.** According to the court, she met this requirement by producing evidence that work orders were created for the handrail and that repairs were made to it. Since there was enough evidence to go forward with the claims, the judgment was affirmed. *Texas Southern Univ. v. Gilford*, 277 S.W.3d 65 (Tex. Ct. App. 2009). In 2010, the Supreme Court of Texas denied a petition to further review the case.

◆ *A personal injury action by the grandparent of a University of Michigan (UM) student was barred by state law immunity.*

The grandparent fell from a chair tethered to a riser in a UM auditorium after she watched a student performance. She sued the university in a state court, claiming the riser should have had guard rails to help prevent patrons from falling. The court noted **the state governmental immunity law provides a broad grant of immunity from tort liability to government agencies when**

they perform governmental functions. The court found a public building exception barred UM's claim to immunity. On appeal, the Court of Appeals of Michigan explained that the public building exception does not allow claims based on design defects. In this case, the grandparent claimed her injuries were caused by design defects. Therefore, the public building exception did not apply, and immunity barred her claims. *Hetherington v. Univ. of Michigan Regents*, No. 07-000036-MZ, 2009 WL 692444 (Mich. Ct. App. 3/17/09).

◆ *Immunity barred a claim by a Michigan community college student who tripped and fell over an electrical floor socket in a campus lab.*

In a state court lawsuit against the community college, the student asserted negligent maintenance of a dangerous and defective condition, failure to keep the floor free of improperly raised, protruding floor-mounted electrical boxes, and creation of a dangerous condition by failing to properly repair and/or maintain the premises. Under Michigan law, community colleges and other government entities are immune to such claims unless an exception applies. A state court held the public building exception applied since there was a claim based on a failure to properly repair or maintain public buildings. After the court denied the college's motion for summary disposition, appeal reached the Court of Appeals of Michigan. It reversed the judgment, finding that in reality, **the student was asserting a design defect claim**. Public building exception language relating to "dangerous or defective conditions" did not remove the requirement for claims to allege failure to repair and maintain premises. As a design defect was alleged, the court reversed the judgment. *Collins v. Oakland County Community*, No. 282351, 2009 WL 794686 (Mich. Ct. App. 3/26/09).

◆ *Eleventh Amendment immunity defeated a former student's claim that a community college violated the Constitution by dismissing her from campus.*

Students complained to a lab facilitator about a "chemical smell" surrounding the student caused by a hair product. She later argued with the lab instructor about closing a door, and he asked her to leave. When she refused, the instructor called campus security to escort her out. After a third incident of disruption, the college barred the student from campus. She sued the college in a federal district court, claiming the removal from campus violated her First and Fourteenth Amendment rights. The court held **the college was entitled to Eleventh Amendment immunity, as it was an entity that was an "arm of the state."** *Davis v. Cent. Piedmont Community College*, No. 3:07-cv-424-RJC, 2008 WL 5120616 (W.D.N.C. 12/4/08).

◆ *A Michigan university had immunity from liability for injuries to a high school student who fell and was injured at a university football stadium.*

The student participated in a band camp sponsored by her high school that was held on the campus of Central Michigan University (CMU). While watching a band performance at CMU's football stadium, she left her seat to use a restroom. She tripped and fell while walking up some steps, injuring her hand and wrist. The student sued CMU for negligence in a state court. The court held for CMU, finding it had government immunity under state law. On appeal, the state appeals court agreed that the university was immune and that no statutory exception applied. An exception requiring government agencies to repair and maintain public buildings did not apply. The band camp was not open to the public, so the stadium was not a "building" under the law. A proprietary function exception to immunity was also inapplicable, as there was no government activity designed to produce a profit in this case. CMU merely allowed the high school to use its facilities, and fees it charged the high school covered costs only. **Since neither exception applied, the university was immune to the student's suit, and the judgment was affirmed.** *Williams v. Cent. Michigan Univ.*, No. 276445, 2008 WL 942268 (Mich. Ct. App. 4/8/08).

◆ *A Texas recreational use statute barred claims by a bicyclist who was injured while riding on a university campus.*

Water from an oscillating sprinkler knocked the bicyclist to the ground, injuring her. She sued the university in state court for gross negligence. The university claimed immunity under the state tort claims act, which applied to claims arising out of discretionary decisions. It also asserted the claim was barred by the state recreational use statute. The court denied the university's motion to dismiss the case, and the university appealed. The Supreme Court of Texas held the state tort claims act did not bar the claim, as it was based on the university's implementation of a policy decision to irrigate its campus. However, **the claim was barred by the state's recreational use statute**. That law limited the liability of landowners who open their property to recreational use by immunizing them from claims unless there was gross negligence or intent to cause injury. As the bicyclist could not show the university intended to injure her or was grossly negligent, the lower court's ruling was reversed. *Stephen F. Austin State Univ. v. Flynn*, 228 S.W.3d 653 (Tex. 2007).

◆ *A Kentucky university was immune to a claim of negligence in the case of a student who was assaulted, raped and set on fire in her dormitory room.*

Three days after being brutally attacked in her dorm room at Western Kentucky University, the student died from her injuries. Two men who were not residents of the dorm were later charged in the case. The administrators of the student's estate filed negligence claims in a suit against the university in state court. The court dismissed the case, and the state appeals court affirmed the judgment. The case reached the Supreme Court of Kentucky.

The court explained that governmental immunity extends to state agencies that perform governmental functions. At the same time, immunity does not extend to state agencies that are not created to perform a governmental function. Officials of state agencies can also be entitled to immunity if the agency itself is immune to suit. When sued in their official capacities, these officials enjoy the same immunity as the state agency. The university operated the dorm as part of its statutory duty to provide college instruction, and therefore it was not performing a proprietary function. **As the dormitory operation was a discretionary function, the university was entitled to immunity.** Because the claims against the university were barred by immunity, the claims against the officials in their official capacities were also barred. *Autry v. Western Kentucky Univ.*, 219 S.W.3d 713 (Ky. 2007).

♦ *An immunity provision barred a personal injury action by a student who slipped and fell on a wet floor during a lifeguard training class.*

A University of Kansas (KU) student hurt her elbow and side when she fell on a wet floor in a health and education center. She sued KU and its Board of Regents for negligence in state court, seeking damages for medical expenses and pain and suffering. The board claimed immunity under a state recreational use exception to liability. The student argued that the exception did not apply because the health and education center was used primarily for the education of university students and only incidentally for public recreation.

The court held for the board. On review, the Court of Appeals of Kansas explained that the recreational use exception applied as long as the facility was intended or permitted to be used for recreational purposes. **The test for application of the exception was "whether the property has been used for recreational purposes in the past or whether recreation has been encouraged."** The exception could apply even if the injury did not result from purely recreational use of the facility. The court noted that the center was owned and operated by the university and located on its campus. Although students and faculty used the facility, it could also be rented out by general public groups. Under these circumstances, it was clear that the board intended and actually permitted the facility to be used for recreational purposes. As a result, the exception applied and the board was not held liable. *Marks v. Kansas Board of Regents*, 157 P.3d 1129 (Kan. Ct. App. 2007).

♦ *A Kansas state university was immune from liability in a case filed by a student who slipped and fell on an icy crosswalk.*

The student stated it was snowing lightly at the time of her fall. She testified that snow that had fallen earlier had been pushed off the crosswalk. She thought the snow had probably refrozen to form ice. The university had 13 landscaping employees responsible for snow removal. Most of them started work at 6:30 a.m. and were instructed to begin their shifts by walking the campus in search of any hazardous conditions needing immediate attention. Employees were to sprinkle ice melting compound on hazardous spots, remove the ice, or report the problem to a manager.

The student stated the employees negligently failed to inspect and treat the crosswalk on the morning she fell, and sued the university in a state court. The court granted summary judgment to the university, finding it was immune from liability under the Kansas Torts Claims Act. The student appealed to the Court of Appeals of Kansas. **The court agreed with the university that the only exception to state immunity is injury caused by an employee's affirmative act. By contrast, an employee's failure to act has no bearing on liability.** As the student did not allege any affirmative act by a university employee, the court held the university was immune from liability under the act and affirmed the judgment. *Owoyemi v. Univ. of Kansas*, 91 P.3d 552 (Kan. Ct. App. 2004).

♦ *A New Jersey state university was entitled to charitable immunity.*

A student at Montclair State University fell down an amphitheater staircase on campus, fracturing his ribs and elbow. He spent several days in the hospital and sued the university for damages. The university asserted that it was immune under the New Jersey Charitable Immunity Act, and a trial court agreed. Because the student was a "beneficiary" under the act, the university was entitled to charitable immunity. The appellate division court reversed that decision, but the New Jersey Supreme Court reinstated the trial court's ruling. Here, the university was formed for a nonprofit purpose; it was organized for educational purposes; and it was promoting those goals at the time the student (beneficiary) was injured. **Nothing in the act required that an entity be a private nonprofit institution in order to qualify for charitable immunity.** As a result, the public university was entitled to have the lawsuit against it dismissed. *O'Connell v. State of New Jersey*, 795 A.2d 857 (N.J. 2002).

2. Assumption of Risk

Assumption of risk is an affirmative defense to negligence. If the defense is proven, the claimant cannot recover on a negligence claim. To prove the defense, a university or college must show the claimant had knowledge of the risk, appreciated the risk, and voluntarily confronted it. Because the risk of injury is inherent and obvious in many sports, assumption of risk often bars recovery in negligence actions brought by student-athletes.

Institutions may further limit their liability in this area by requiring students to sign waivers and releases prior to engaging in hazardous activities. In Lemoine v. Cornell Univ., *769 N.Y.S.2d 313 (N.Y. App. Div. 2003), a New York Appellate Division, held that clearly stated release language pointing out the dangers of rock climbing barred negligence claims against a university.*

◆ *An employer's "hold harmless" agreement was sufficient to insulate a private Idaho university from liability in a negligence lawsuit.*

An employer scheduled a team-building exercise for its employees and held the event at the university. The program included a wall-climbing activity. The employer instructed its employees to sign a hold harmless agreement before participating. According to the agreement, the university, "its members, directors, administrators, representatives, officers, agents, employees, and assigns" were released from any and all present or future claims as the result of any injuries that might occur during the program. While on the climbing wall, an employee fell and was badly hurt. He sued the university in the state court system for negligence. The court held for the university, and the employee appealed. The Supreme Court of Idaho rejected his assertion that a disadvantage in bargaining power between him and his employer made the agreement unenforceable. In addition, **the language of the release clearly stated that the hold harmless clause applied to negligence and covered any loss or damage he might incur from participating in the program**. For this reason, the judgment for the university was affirmed. *Morrison v. Northwest Nazarene Univ.*, 152 Idaho 660, 273 P.3d 1253 (Idaho 2012).

◆ *A New York court summarized the general rule that voluntary athletic participants assume the commonly appreciated risks of a sporting activity.*

A freshman pitcher on Clarkson University's baseball team was hit by a line drive during an indoor practice. He was not using a protective screen. He sued the university in a state court, which held that he had assumed the obvious risk of getting hit by a line drive. On appeal, a state appellate division court noted the pitcher was an experienced baseball player who had encountered line drives hit at him some 50 to 100 times in the past. Moreover, the court found he had seen the conditions prior to stepping to the mound and engaging in the activity of pitching without a screen. Finding **the pitcher understood the risk of playing without a protective screen** and was not compelled to pitch without one, the court held the university was entitled to judgment. *Bukowski v. Clarkson Univ.*, 86 A.D.3d 736, 928 N.Y.S.2d 369 (N.Y. App. Div. 2011).

◆ *A New York appeals court allowed a student to proceed with a claim that his college was liable for his hand injury at the college fitness center.*

The student was hurt when 140 pounds on a jammed weight machine suddenly dislodged and fell onto his hand. He sued the college in the state court system. The college argued it could not be held liable because it did not have notice of any dangerous condition. But a college custodian admitted that jamming had been a recurring problem with the machine, which had been repaired several times. The court denied the college's request for pretrial judgment. On appeal, a state appellate division court found evidence that the college was on notice that the machine created a danger. There were relevant factual issues regarding whether an accessory weight was being used at the time of injury. There was a possibility that use of the accessory weight caused the jam that led to injury. **There would have to be further consideration of the college's claim that the student ignored a warning label on the machine by placing his hand underneath the weights.** This created the possibility that comparative fault principles applied. Since further consideration of the facts was warranted, the trial court's decision was affirmed. *Beglin v. Hartwick College*, 67 A.D.3d 1172, 888 N.Y.S.2d 320 (N.Y. App. Div. 2009).

◆ *A Georgia student who ran across a street to join a fight voluntarily assumed a risk of injury.*

A Morris Brown College student was killed after being struck on the head with a glass bottle during a fight. His parents sued the college in the state court system for wrongful death. The trial court denied judgment to the college. On appeal, the Court of Appeals of Georgia explained that **adults of ordinary intelligence are deemed to be aware that they risk injury to themselves when they voluntarily join a fight**. Even when a person enters an altercation with the intention of breaking it up, he is responsible for any injury he suffers. In this case, the student ran across a street to voluntarily join a fight that had already begun. Under a state law doctrine known as "the rescue doctrine," individuals may recover for their injuries even though they assumed a risk of harm – but only if the injured party was acting to rescue someone from harm and the rescue was made necessary by another party's negligence. The court held that the rescue doctrine did not apply in this case, because the student chose to interject himself into the fight. As he assumed the risk of injury, the judgment against the college was reversed. *Cornelius v. Morris Brown College*, 299 Ga.App. 83, 681 S.E.2d 730 (Ga. Ct. App. 2009).

◆ *An ice skater's claim that the University of Delaware failed to properly supervise skaters at its rink was not barred by the assumption of risk doctrine.*

After she began skating, the skater noticed others were frequently going in the wrong direction and "running into people." While trying to avoid another skater, the skater fell and was seriously injured. She later sued the university in a state court for negligently failing to supervise skaters, allowing an unsafe condition, and failing to adequately warn or protect her against a dangerous condition. The university sought pretrial judgment, arguing that the claims were barred because the skater assumed the risk of skating. The court explained that primary assumption of risk applies when an individual expressly consents to relieve the defendant of an obligation and to take the chance of being injured as a result of a known risk. Secondary assumption of risk applies when a person voluntarily encounters a known and unreasonable risk. **The court held that the primary assumption-of-risk doctrine did not apply because the skater never relieved the university of its duty to reasonably supervise the premises.** The university did not show she assumed the risk of reckless conduct by other skaters. Further consideration was required to determine whether the university could have prevented the fall. *Farrell v. Univ. of Delaware*, No. 07C-09-175 PLA, 2009 WL 3309288 (Del. Super. Ct. 10/8/09).

◆ *A federal district court rejected a college's attempt to dismiss a case filed against it by a student who was severely injured by a saw.*

While using a compound meter saw at the college, the student's shirt sleeve was pulled into the machine and his arm was partially amputated. Instructions from the manufacturer advised users not to operate the saw while wearing long sleeves, but the student did not read them. He sued the college in a federal district court, claiming it negligently failed to train and supervise his use of the saw. The court held the student did not show the saw's warning label proximately caused his injury. **Failure to provide adequate warnings cannot be said to cause an injury if the injured party admits he knew of the risks that caused injury.** Since the student admitted he knew of the risks associated with placing his hand in the path of a moving saw blade, he could not show the absence of any particular warning caused his injury. However, the court held the college had potential liability under ordinary negligence principles. Factual issues were present as to whether the student was negligent in operating the saw. The court found that the assumption of risk doctrine did not apply because it was not beyond question that he had "voluntarily and knowingly proceeded in the face of an open and obvious danger." *Hawkins v. Waynesburg College*, No. 07-5, 2008 WL 2952888 (W.D. Pa. 7/30/08).

◆ *The parent of a Maryland student was unable to pursue a negligence case because she assumed the risk of injury by trying to cross an icy parking lot.*

The parent drove to the university to deliver gas money and other supplies to her daughter after about 22 inches of snow had fallen in the vicinity. As soon as she drove into the parking lot near her daughter's dormitory, she noticed it had not been cleared of ice and snow. Although the parent made it to her daughter's room safely, she fell and broke her leg in the icy lot while returning to her car. She sued the university in state court for negligent failure to clear the lot of snow and ice. She also claimed negligent hiring, training and supervision based on the failure of university employees to clear the lot in a timely manner. A Maryland trial court held the parent voluntarily assumed the risk of injury by walking on the snow and ice. The state court of special appeals reversed the decision, finding that a jury should decide whether to bar her negligence claim.

On appeal, the Court of Appeals of Maryland held the parent had voluntarily assumed the risk of injury when she chose to cross the icy lot. There was no evidence that the parent was forced to confront the danger of walking on ice and snow against her will. She understood she was taking a chance when she chose to cross the lot. **It was clear that a person of normal intelligence would have understood the risk presented. In assumption of risk cases, the claimant relieves the defendant of its duty of care by voluntarily choosing to encounter a known risk.** For that reason, the university's failure to clear the lot was irrelevant. The decision against the university was reversed. *Morgan State Univ. v. Walker*, 397 Md. 509, 919 A.2d 21 (Md. 2007).

◆ *A California college was not liable to a student injured during a peace officer training class where he practiced arrest and control techniques.*

Three police officers taught the class. One of them demonstrated four maneuvers the students were to carry out. An officer saw the student perform each maneuver at least once. The student was injured when his partner pulled him down. He sued the college in a state court for negligence. The court held for the college, and the student appealed to the Court of Appeal of California.

The court discussed the doctrine of primary assumption of risk, which applies to activities or sports where "conditions or conduct that otherwise might be viewed as dangerous often are an integral part of the sport itself." The court explained that **during dangerous activities, the integral conditions of the sport or the inherent risks of careless conduct by others render the possibility of injury obvious and negate the duty of care usually owed for those particular risks.** The takeover maneuvers in the student's class bore a similar risk of injury inherent in many sports. The court found careless conduct by others was an inherent risk. Imposing a duty to eliminate the risk of injury from the activity in this situation would chill vigorous participation in learning the maneuvers. Because of the nature of the classroom activity and the lack of evidence that the college acted recklessly, the court held the action was barred by the doctrine of primary assumption of the risk. *Saville v. Sierra College*, 133 Cal.App.4th 857, 36 Cal.Rptr.3d 515 (Cal. Ct. App. 2005).

◆ *A Rhode Island university was not liable for injuries to a student who fell while walking at night on campus.*

The student lived in a university dormitory. He fell while on an unlighted pathway on an unpaved embankment on the side of a road on campus. The student sued the university in a state trial court for negligence. The case was heard by a jury. It ruled in favor of the university. The student filed a motion for a new trial. After the court denied the motion, he appealed to the Supreme Court of Rhode Island. The student argued the trial court overlooked evidence about defects in the asphalt where he fell. He also claimed the area was commonly used by students. The court held the trial court judge had properly reviewed the evidence and assessed the credibility of the witnesses. The judge had found the student was not credible. The court agreed with the trial court's finding that the student tripped on crumbled asphalt, not a defect in a campus walkway. **The trial court made a well-supported finding that the area of the fall was not an existing pathway and the student could have used an existing route instead of the one he chose.** The judgment for the university was affirmed. *Candido v. Univ. of Rhode Island*, 880 A.2d 853 (R.I. 2005).

D. Damages

Damage awards generally reflect the nature of the injury and the conduct of the parties. Compensatory damages compensate an injured party for his or her injuries such as medical expenses or pain and suffering. Punitive damages, on the other hand, are not designed to compensate for loss. Instead, they punish the offending party because of the party's willful and wanton conduct.

◆ *A Louisiana student who was injured on campus increased the amount of her personal injury recovery by appealing to the state court of appeal.*

A Louisiana university held an event at a ballroom for students to finalize the details of their graduation ceremony. Vendors were allowed to sell products and services on a three-tier stage in the ballroom. A student fell and was seriously injured as she left the station of one of the vendors. She later sued the state through the board of supervisors for the University of Louisiana in a state court for negligence. A jury decided the university was 66% at fault in causing the fall. It awarded the student more than $100,000 for her injuries.

On appeal, the state argued the evidence did not support the jury's finding that an unreasonably dangerous condition existed at the time of the fall. The Court of Appeal of Louisiana found **a university employee who was responsible for setting up and supervising student union activities acknowledged that the stage created a trip hazard**. Even though he was aware of the hazard, he did not take steps to reduce or eliminate it, such as by roping off certain areas or posting warning signs. Based on the testimony of the school employee and the student, the court held she met her burden to prove her case. It also noted that she had developed back and wrist problems, and it pointed to her husband's testimony that "she ceased to be her jovial self." In light of this evidence, the court increased the amount awarded for past, present and future pain and suffering by $85,000. *Antley v. State of Louisiana*, No. 10-316, 2010 WL 3903816 (La. Ct. App. 10/6/10, review denied 1/7/11).

◆ *A New York court preserved a $4 million verdict for a student who was injured when she fell into an open manhole on a college campus.*

The student stepped into an open manhole at 1:00 a.m. one morning and hurt her right leg. About three weeks after the fall, she experienced swelling and pain. She eventually was diagnosed with blood clots in both legs. In a state court action for negligence, a jury found negligence by the college had caused the student's injuries. The court substantially reduced a multi-million dollar verdict to reflect future pain and suffering in the amount of $1.5 million and future medical expenses of $3.36 million. The college appealed to a New York

Appellate Court,which found enough evidence for a jury to conclude that the fall caused a recurrence of the student's underlying medical condition.

The award of $3.36 million for future medical expenses was supported by testimony indicating the student would need to take blood-thinning medicine for the rest of her life, at a cost of about $5,000 per month. Since the college did not show these estimates were inaccurate, the award for future medical expenses was upheld. The court also upheld the decision to award $300,000 for past pain and suffering. But the $1.5 million awarded for future pain and suffering was not justified. After the student was released from a hospital, she was able to walk, exercise and go to the gym. **While she endured some long-term limitations and effects from the fall, her injuries were not debilitating, permanent or life-changing, and did not justify an award of $1.5 million.** A new trial on damages for future pain and suffering was required, unless the student agreed to accept only $450,000 for her future pain and suffering. *Nolan v. Union College Trust of Schenectady*, 51 A.D.3d 1253, 858 N.Y.S.2d 427 (N.Y. App. Div. 2008).

♦ *A Louisiana university was liable for failing to protect patrons from getting hit by foul balls when they entered a baseball park.*

A visitor went to a baseball game held on a university baseball field. She was struck in her right eye by a foul ball near the ticket booth along the third-base side of the field. The visitor suffered a fracture and permanent ocular blindness resulting in permanent 10/200 vision in her right eye. She sued the university in a state trial court for negligence. The court awarded the visitor $485,000, and the university appealed to the Court of Appeal of Louisiana. The court explained that ballpark owners cannot be held responsible for every foul ball in common areas. There are certain areas of a ballpark where protection is required. One such area is the main entrance, where people have to enter to buy a ticket. **The university could have reasonably anticipated there would be foul balls in the main entrance area.** There was sufficient evidence to support the jury's finding that the baseball park presented an unreasonably dangerous condition to those who entered and that the university had notice of the defect. The court affirmed the judgment. *Reider v. Louisiana Board of Trustees for State Colleges and Universities*, 897 So.2d 893 (La. Ct. App. 2005).

♦ *The Court of Appeals of Ohio held a university was liable for injuries to an operations manager of a mobile production unit.*

The manager got hurt when he was on the university's campus setting up for television coverage of a basketball game. He spoke to a university representative, who told him to run cables beside two large air conditioning units. The units were housed inside a dimly lit brick enclosure. Based on what the university representative told him, the manager thought the power was on the other side of the enclosure. He tossed the cable over a wall and over one of the air conditioner units, but it fell short. The manager entered into the darkness, took two steps and fell into a large pit. He injured his head, wrist and elbow. After two surgeries, the manager got a staph infection. He sued the university for negligence in a state trial court. The court found the university had breached its duty of care to the manager and caused his injuries.

The university appealed to the Court of Appeals of Ohio, arguing expert medical testimony was required to establish a connection between the manager's original injuries and the staph infection. The court of appeals disagreed. Expert testimony is needed only where the internal complexities of the body are at issue. The court found the staph infection was not internal or elusive, so the trial court needed to focus only on the location and nature of the infection to determine a connection. A court could sufficiently understand the infection and its connection to the surgery without expert medical testimony. **The court also rejected the university's contention that the operations manager played a part in getting hurt by stepping into the brick enclosure.** It was unclear whether a university representative lulled him into a false sense of safety by directing him to the area without warning him of the danger of the pit. The court affirmed the judgment. *Dixon v. Miami Univ.*, No. 04 AP-1132, 2005 WL 3316963 (Ohio Ct. App. 12/8/05).

II. INTENTIONAL CONDUCT

Institutions may be found liable for the intentional acts or omissions of their personnel. Courts have found colleges and universities liable for intentional acts of third parties on or near campuses. In those cases, courts may find the institution should have foreseen the potential for misconduct.

A. Instructor Misconduct

◆ *A federal court delayed its consideration of a civil action arising from the Jerry Sandusky sex abuse case pending the conclusion of criminal proceedings.*

After Penn State assistant football coach Jerry Sandusky was found guilty and sentenced for sexual abuse, a student charged him and other Penn State officials of violating his First, Fourth and Fourteenth Amendments rights in a federal court civil action. He also alleged state-law claims of premises liability, negligence, conspiracy, intentional infliction of emotional distress and sexual assault. The court found his complaint closely resembled the criminal charges against the officials. Their trials were not expected to begin until 2014. **Among the factors in favor of granting a stay was a risk of exposing the officials to self-incrimination for their criminal cases.** As the requested stay would not harm the public interest, it was granted. *Doe v. Pennsylvania State Univ.*, No. 1:12-CV-2068, 2013 WL 593415 (M.D. Pa. 2/14/13).

◆ *Five graduate students had no valid claim for infliction of emotional distress based on an Illinois university program director's misconduct.*

The students said a clinical exercise physiology program director touched their breasts, kissed them, trapped them, and suggested that they have group sex. According to the students, their complaints to university officials about the director went unheeded. They filed a multi-count federal court lawsuit against the director and university, and the university sought dismissal of claims for intentional infliction of emotional distress and punitive damages. The court stated that an intentional infliction of emotional distress claimant must show conduct that was extreme and outrageous, emotional distress so severe that no reasonable person could be expected to endure it, and offensive actions taken with a substantial certainty that severe emotional distress would result.

In this case, **any failure by the university to respond adequately to the complaints against the director was not outrageous enough to support a claim of intentional infliction of emotional distress**. Nor could any such failure be said to have been done with knowledge or substantial certainty that it would cause severe emotional distress. As the students did not state valid claims against the university for intentional infliction of emotional distress, and punitive damages were not available, the court dismissed the claims. *Krumlauf v. Benedictine Univ.*, No. 09 C 7641, 2010 WL 1418579 (N.D. Ill. 4/7/10).

◆   *A Tennessee court rejected a battery claim filed by a student against her instructor, who forcibly removed her from a nursing class.*

The student learned she would be removed from the program because of a D grade. She said a vice president of student affairs eventually phoned her to say her grade appeal had been granted. Based on this assurance, the student went to class on the first day of the semester. She said that when she got to class, the instructor asked her why she was there and then physically removed her from the room. In a state court lawsuit against the instructor and other university officials, the student asserted claims of battery, conspiracy to commit battery, and intentional infliction of emotional distress. The court dismissed the case, and the student appealed. The Court of Appeals of Tennessee rejected the student's battery claim. **Not every touching without consent amounts to a battery. Certain classes of employees, including police officers and teachers, "are expected to touch people at times in order to direct their movements."** In this case, the alleged touching of the student by the class instructor was not offensive enough to constitute a battery.

The instructor apparently believed the student was not supposed to be in his class. The student did not say she was injured as a result of the contact. Since her conspiracy claim was premised on the meritless battery claim, it failed as well. There was no evidence supporting the student's claim that the instructor had conspired with university administrators to keep her out of the classroom. An emotional distress claim failed, as it was based on conduct that was not extreme or outrageous. *Runions v. Tennessee State Univ.*, No. M2008-01574-COA-R3-CV, 2009 WL 1939816 (Tenn. Ct. App. 7/6/09).

◆   *Common lawsuits against university instructors include those claiming intentional infliction of emotional distress, defamation, or sexual misconduct.*

An Arkansas student claimed an anatomy professor performed a breast examination on her in his classroom. At the time, the rest of the class had left the room, and the door was closed. The student said she was "stunned, shocked and scared" when the professor performed the examination. After the student complained to a university official, the professor resigned. She sued him in a federal district court for violating her substantive due process rights. She added a state law claim based on outrage. Applying a "shocks the conscience" standard, the court found the complaint supported a substantive due process claim. The court also refused to dismiss the outrage claim. **To prove this claim, the student needed to show the professor caused her severe emotional distress through extreme and outrageous conduct.** The facts as alleged in her complaint were sufficient to avoid dismissal. Under the circumstances, a factual issue existed as to whether the professor acted with the intent necessary to prove a due process violation or the tort of outrage. The question of his intent was a matter of credibility that was best left for a jury. *Thompson v. Guntharp*, No. 3:07-CV-00010 GTE, 2007 WL 2769597 (E.D. Ark. 9/24/07).

B. Employee Misconduct

◆   *A New York student could proceed with a Fourth Amendment claim against college officials based on an incident in which she was involuntarily committed.*

An international honors student lived in an off-campus apartment. She told a college security officer that her roommates were defaming her on the Internet. The student also revealed that she suspected her landlord had installed a hidden camera in her bedroom. The security officer called the college honors academy coordinator and an assistant professor who also served as the school psychologist. The professor asked the student a series of questions about whether she had a history of mental illness, whether she ever heard voices and whether she ever thought about suicide. The professor and coordinator prevented her from leaving the office and then called an ambulance to transport her to a psychiatric hospital. As a result, the student was involuntarily committed for two weeks, which prevented her from taking her final exams. She later sued the college and several officials, alleging violation of her rights under the Fourth Amendment, among other claims. A federal court held that her Fourth Amendment claim could proceed to a trial even though no police were involved in her detention and transport to the hospital. But **the professor and coordinator could not be held liable for her involuntary commitment because neither was involved in the decision to commit her for inpatient treatment and evaluation**. *Eze v. City Univ. of New York at Brooklyn College*, No. 11-CV-2454 (JG)(CLP), 2011 WL 6780652 (E.D.N.Y. 12/27/11).

◆   *The sexual assault of a minor non-student by an Indiana university bus driver was not caused by negligence on the university's part.*

The university did not conduct a criminal history check when it hired the driver. He had been convicted of battery and furnishing alcohol to a minor, but he failed to reveal this information on his job application. On a day when he was not working for the university, the driver asked a minor to accompany him on a trip to a retail store. Using his own truck, the driver took the minor to a campus garage where the buses were parked, then molested him inside a bus.

The minor sued the university board of trustees in a state court for negligence. The court held for the university, and the student appealed. The Court of Appeals of Indiana held that to prevail on his claim of negligent hiring/retention, the minor needed to show the university breached a duty it owed to him. However, as he was not a university student, the university did not owe him a duty to exercise reasonable care in hiring the driver. The minor also failed to show the university owed all members of the public a duty to refrain from hiring individuals with criminal backgrounds. The driver was not acting within the scope of his employment at the time of the attack. **An employer can be liable for the criminal acts of an employee only if there is a sufficient association between the criminal acts and acts the employee is authorized by the employer to take.** The trial court's ruling was affirmed. *J.B. v. Board of Trustees of Vincennes Univ.*, 883 N.E.2d 229 (Ind. Ct. App. 2008).

C. Third-Party Misconduct

In Wheeler v. Ohio State Univ., *below, an Ohio court stated the general rule that "ordinarily no duty exists to prevent a third person from harming another unless a 'special relationship' exists between the actor and another." A special relationship may arise if the institution knows (or should have known) that a danger is present. Institutions cannot be held liable for unforeseen actions by third parties and are not the insurers of student safety.*

◆   *A federal court refused to dismiss claims filed by a student who claimed Duke University officials suggested she was raped through her own fault.*

When the student reported being raped, she said a Duke official issued a statement downplaying her report and suggesting she was at fault. The statement was broadcast nationwide, and the student claimed Duke discredited her report because she was a white woman accusing a black man of rape at a time when Duke was mired in negative press regarding its handling of an earlier rape case. According to the student, Duke did not adequately investigate the incident, and she said she was not allowed to register for the courses she wanted. In a federal court, the student sued Duke for negligence, infliction of emotional distress, hostile educational environment, and breach of contract.

The court found some of the negligence claims were untimely. But the student could pursue a claim based on a letter from Duke stating she had withdrawn from the university, as it was within the relevant three-year limitations period. **She could proceed with an intentional infliction of emotional distress claim, which was based on the charge that Duke suggested she was responsible for her own rape.** A breach of contract claim would also proceed, based on the charge that Duke breached its enrollment agreement by declaring the student ineligible for readmission. A hostile educational environment claim was sufficient to survive pretrial dismissal, as the student claimed she was subjected to harassment and humiliation on campus because she was a white woman who had accused a black man of raping her. She also claimed that Duke officials injured her by suggesting the rape was her own fault and then failing to investigate her report. *Rouse v. Duke Univ.*, No. 1:11-cv-549, 2012 WL 1150461 (M.D.N.C. 4/5/12).

◆   *Ohio State University avoided liability to a student who said classmates assaulted her, because it was not aware of any prior assaults or threats.*

The student was injured when a classmate pushed her chair forward from behind. She was not sure who pushed her, but she reported what happened to the university's chief student life officer. The university moved two classmates suspected of pushing the student to another area of the classroom. In addition, arrangements were made for the student and classmates to attend different laboratory classes. But the student claimed one of the classmates continued to harass her afterward, asserting that race may have been a factor. She sued the university in the state court system. The case reached the Court of Appeals of Ohio, which found the assault that caused the student's injuries was not reasonably foreseeable. For this reason, **the court held the university did not breach any duty of ordinary care by failing to protect her from being assaulted, and it could not be liable for her injuries**. *Wheeler v. Ohio State Univ.*, No. 11AP-289, 2011 WL 6147619 (Ohio Ct. App. 12/8/11).

◆ *A Tennessee court affirmed a $300,000 judgment for a student who was attacked while walking to her dorm.*

To get to her dorm, the student had to go down a stairwell in a parking garage. When she got to the bottom of the steps, she was attacked by a man who hit her on the head with a brick. The student suffered severe injuries, including permanent brain damage. Her family filed a state claims commission action against the university for negligently creating or maintaining a dangerous condition. The claims commissioner found the university created a dangerous condition by failing to provide and maintain adequate lighting on the steps. He awarded the student $300,000 – the maximum amount available. The case reached the Court of Appeals of Tennessee, which upheld the award. There was enough evidence to support a finding that the lighting on the stairwell was inadequate, creating a dangerous condition. In addition, **the history of crime near the garage justified a finding that the attack was foreseeable**. A university expert testified that there were 55 thefts at the garage in 2001-02. The university had breached a duty of care to the student, and the court affirmed the commission's decision. *Smith v. State*, No. E2007-00809-COA-R3-CV, 2008 WL 699062 (Tenn. Ct. App. 3/17/08).

◆ *A Massachusetts university was not liable for the murder of a student in his off-campus apartment because the risk of injury to him was not foreseeable.*

The student leased the apartment where he was murdered from a private landlord. On the day of the murder, another tenant let the perpetrators into the building. The student's estate sued the university for wrongful death and negligence. The court granted the university's motion for pretrial judgment on grounds that **the university had no duty to provide security for the student or to prevent his murder. Although there had been four burglaries at the building in the six months before the murder, there was no evidence that they involved violence or that any other violence occurred in the building.** The building was privately owned and managed, and the university was not in the best position to take the steps needed to ensure the student's safety. *Doyle v. Gould*, 22 Mass.L.Rptr. 373 (Mass. Super. Ct. 2007).

◆ *The Court of Appeals of Georgia reinstated negligence claims filed by a student who was beaten by a classmate with a baseball bat.*

The classmate attacked and beat the student in a dormitory shower, allegedly because he believed the student was a homosexual and "glanced at him in an inappropriate way." He was later convicted of assault and battery, and sentenced to prison. The student sued the college in a state court for negligence and related claims. The court dismissed the case, finding insufficient evidence of foreseeability. The court of appeals disagreed, finding that at this stage of the case, the student was not required to come forward with evidence that the harm he suffered was foreseeable. He was only required to allege facts which, if proven, created a factual issue on the question of whether the harm he suffered was foreseeable. In Georgia, **a college or university has a duty "to exercise ordinary and reasonable care for a student's safety and to take reasonable steps to protect against foreseeable acts of violence on its campus."** The student claimed the college should have been aware of a danger to him and that it had failed to address harassment of students believed to be homosexual. *Love v. Morehouse College*, 287 Ga.App. 743, 652 S.E.2d 624 (Ga. Ct. App. 2007).

◆   *The Supreme Court of Texas held a state university was not liable for the stabbing of a student actor during a school play.*

The university had no theater curriculum, but it offered a voluntary student drama club whose members received no grades or class credit for participating. The club director and his wife told actors to use a real knife in a play, in violation of a university policy prohibiting deadly weapons on campus. During the second performance of the play, an actor missed a stab pad worn by the student and drove the knife into the student's chest, puncturing his lung. The student sued the university in a Texas court, alleging the university was liable for his injuries. The court held for the student, and the university appealed. The state court of appeals reversed the decision, finding the director, his wife, and faculty advisors were not "employees" under the Texas Tort Claims Act. For that reason, the university was protected by governmental immunity. The Supreme Court of Texas found the advisors were university employees under the act. But the director and his wife had no employment contract with the university. **The university had only a minimal degree of control over them that did not indicate employee status. The court held the university was protected from liability by governmental immunity.** It reversed the judgment. *Texas A&M Univ. v. Bishop*, 156 S.W.3d 580 (Tex. 2005).

◆   *Lawsuits filed against Texas A&M after a tragic bonfire accident were allowed to continue by a federal appeals court.*

In 1999, a bonfire stack collapsed on the campus of Texas A&M University, killing 12 students and injuring 27 others. A university special commission report exonerated university officials, finding that their actions did not rise to the level of deliberate indifference. However, numerous lawsuits arose, alleging violations of 42 U.S.C. § 1983 under a state-created danger theory. A federal district court dismissed the lawsuits, but the Fifth Circuit reversed and remanded the case. The court held **the record supported a finding of deliberate indifference**. The plaintiffs presented evidence that university officials allowed the bonfire stack to increase over the years to a pile of burning trash weighing more than 3 million pounds.

A university official had described the stack as the "most serious risk management activity at the university." Nevertheless, university officials did not use their authority to control the stack's building or destruction. The plaintiffs even asserted that the university encouraged students to add to the stack as a "marketing tool to lure prospective students" and to gain alumni donations. Based on all this evidence, the Fifth Circuit found that the plaintiffs established their Section 1983 claim. The district court's decision was reversed, and the case was remanded. *Scanlon v. Texas A&M Univ.*, 343 F.3d 533 (5th Cir. 2003).

◆ *An Alabama district court found a state university was not liable for the murder of a freshman residing in a dormitory.*

The student was a freshman at the university and lived in a dormitory room. A stranger entered the dormitory without authorization and murdered her in her room. Her parents sued the university in a federal district court for civil rights violations. They argued the student's relationship with the university was involuntary, such that it had a "special relationship" to her. This meant the university would have a duty to protect her from violence by a third party. The parents argued this relationship arose from a university requirement that all freshmen live on campus. The court disagreed. The student voluntarily attended the university and was not in its custody. She was able to retain her liberty and therefore had no special relationship to the university. The court also rejected the parents' due process claim based on deliberate indifference to a risk of serious injury to the student. **The university did not know about or disregard a risk to the student's health and safety.** The court found the university was entitled to qualified immunity and dismissed the case. *Griffin v. Troy State Univ.*, 333 F. Supp.2d 1275 (D. Ala. 2004).

◆ *The University of Maine may have been negligent in failing to prevent a sexual assault that occurred in one of its dorms.*

A student participated in a pre-season summer soccer program at the University of Maine. The university allowed participating students to live on campus during the program. The student stayed in a dorm and attended a fraternity party, after which a young man offered to escort her back to her dorm. When she reached her room, the man followed her in and sexually assaulted her. The student and her parents sued the university for negligence and breach of an implied contract. The court granted pretrial judgment to the university. On appeal, the Supreme Judicial Court of Maine reversed the dismissal of the negligence claim. It found that the university owed a duty of care to the student. Under Maine law, **a business (such as the university) has a duty to protect its "invitees" from reasonably foreseeable danger**.

A sexual assault in a college dormitory is foreseeable and is one of the reasons the university went through the trouble of establishing safety measures in the dorms. In this case, the student had never seen or met with the resident assistant on her floor; there were no group meetings offering instruction on rules and regulations regarding safety within the dorms; and there were no signs posted in the dorms informing residents who should or should not be allowed in. The negligence claim was allowed to proceed, but the court affirmed the dismissal of the contract claim. *Stanton v. Univ. of Maine System*, 773 A.2d 1045 (Me. 2001).

III. BREACH OF CONTRACT

Colleges and universities can be liable for breach of contract even where they have immunity from lawsuits for negligence or other torts. In order for a contract to exist, there must be some enforceable promise, not just general representations of the kind typically found in student handbooks.

◆ *A University of Miami (UM) graduate and medical student did not show a breach of contract based on failure to follow UM student handbook provisions.*

The student co-authored and published an article with his department chair. An investigation by the graduate school raised questions about the data used for the article, prompting a scientific misconduct investigation. After a hearing, the graduate school dismissed the student for misconduct and unethical behavior. The medical school also investigated him and then dismissed him for unprofessional conduct. He sued UM in a federal court for race discrimination and breach of contract, claiming UM did not follow its honor code and student handbook procedures. But the court held the procedures were neither exclusive nor mandatory. On appeal, the U.S. Court of Appeals, Eleventh Circuit, held the student did not show he was treated differently than similarly situated colleagues of another race. The court held UM was entitled to judgment on the breach of contract claim. It found **Florida courts do not interfere with a private university's interpretation of its own rules unless its actions are arbitrary, fraudulent or illegal**. As a result, the court affirmed the decision for UM. *Sirpal v. Univ. of Miami*, 509 Fed.Appx. 924 (Table) (11th Cir. 2013).

◆ *A Tennessee restaurant owner, who claimed she lost revenue because she closed shop for two nights based on incorrect information, was unable to pursue a breach of contract claim against a private university.*

Informed that the sidewalk in front of her two Nashville restaurants would be closed for a 2008 presidential debate at Belmont University (BU), the owner closed her restaurants for that evening. After it turned out the sidewalks were not closed, the restaurant owner sued BU and the local government in the state court system, seeking reimbursement for lost revenue and alleging negligent misrepresentation. The court held for BU, and the owner appealed to the Court of Appeals of Tennessee. It held that to claim negligent misrepresentation under Tennessee law, the owner had to show she relied on information that was false and not carefully communicated about a past or present fact. But the court found the information about the planned sidewalk closing was a representation of a future event. At the time, it was only a "present intention" – and could not be a present fact. The breach of contract claim failed because the restaurant owner could not show she and the restaurants were intended beneficiaries of an indemnification agreement between a local government agency and BU. A third-party beneficiary is someone for whose benefit the contract was entered. **Though not a party to the contract, a third-party beneficiary has a legal right to sue if the contract is breached.** But this contract was only for the benefit of the local government agency and BU. Tennessee Law only recognized citizens as third-party beneficiaries to a government contract if a contract specified this. This contract contained no such specification. As both of the restaurant owner's claims failed, the court affirmed the judgment. *Int'l Market and Restaurant, Inc. v. Belmont Univ.*, No. M2010-00005-COA-R3-CV, 2010 WL 4514980 (Tenn. Ct. App. 11/9/10).

◆ *Since they failed to present evidence of a specific promise, two Minnesota students failed to prove breach of contract by their university.*

The students were accepted into the Master of Arts in Instruction program at St. Mary's University of Minnesota. The program is designed for students who want to teach but have not obtained an undergraduate education degree. The students had to complete a number of prerequisites before they could be recommended for licensure as teachers. They said that the program director promised them that all the courses they needed would be offered. However, the university did not offer the courses they needed at their campus. Instead of pursuing alternative options, one student applied for a teaching license, which was denied. The other student also failed to secure a license, and they sued the university in a state court for breach of an educational contract.

Appeal reached the Court of Appeals of Minnesota. It stated a general rule for breach of contract claims by students against educational institutions. **Breach of contract claims are available only if the institution failed to perform on specific promises to a student, and only if the claims would not involve "an inquiry into the nuances of educational processes and theories."** The court rejected a claim based on failure to provide the students all math classes they needed for licensure. Course requirements vary from student to student and are subject to change. The evidence showed that the program director said only that she would request that the courses be offered. Nor did the college breach a contract by declining to accept life experience as an alternate for course requirements. Review of the decision to reject life experiences as an acceptable substitute would involve an impermissible inquiry into the nuances of educational process and theory by the court. There was no evidence that the university promised the pair it would recommend them for licensure even if they failed to satisfy all applicable program requirements. *Clem v. St. Mary's Univ. of Minnesota*, No. A09-1231, 2010 WL 773596 (Minn. Ct. App. 3/9/10).

◆ *Representations to incoming students in a university's medical department brochure were not sufficiently definite to form an enforceable contract.*

A Massachusetts Institute of Technology student overdosed on Tylenol with codeine during her freshman year. She was hospitalized and admitted to a psychiatric hospital for one week. While receiving treatment there, the student revealed she suffered from mental health problems and had cut herself when she was in high school. A psychiatrist at the university's mental health services department diagnosed the student with adjustment disorder. He recommended further therapy when she returned for her sophomore year. When the student returned after summer break, she told a dean she was thinking about suicide.

The dean sent her to the mental health department for an immediate assessment. The psychiatrist stated the student had passive suicidal ideation, but he did not believe she was at risk of hurting herself. Her mental health problems resurfaced about five months later. The psychiatrist decided the student should be admitted for observation at the university infirmary. After she was examined, she was allowed to return to the dorm. Shortly thereafter, the student died from self-inflicted thermal burns. Her parents sued the university in a state court, asserting representations in the university's medical department brochure and in its medical department bylaws created an enforceable contract. **The court held the representations in the brochure and bylaws were only generalized representations of the purpose and medical services available to the school community. Such statements are not definite and are too vague to form an enforceable contract.** There was no evidence of specific promises made by the university. The court held there was no contract and awarded the university pretrial judgment. *Shin v. Massachusetts Institute of Technology*, 19 Mass. L. Rptr. 570 (Mass. Super. 2005).

◆ *A North Carolina university could be sued for breach of contract, but not for an intentional tort.*

The dealer for a piano manufacturer entered into a contract with a North Carolina university to loan the university a number of pianos in exchange for the right to service the university's other pianos. When the contract ended, the dealer and the manufacturer sued the university for breach of contract, conversion and property damage, claiming that the university returned the pianos in damaged condition and that the university improperly retained 14 pianos. The university sought to dismiss the lawsuit on grounds of sovereign immunity. The North Carolina Court of Appeals noted that the state's tort claims act allows state entities to be sued for negligence. However, conversion is an intentional tort (wrongfully depriving another of it property) and that action had to be dismissed. The breach of contract action, on the other hand, could continue because **when the university entered into the contract, it impliedly agreed to be sued for damages if it breached the contract.** Also, the property damage claim was a breach of contract claim that could proceed. The court remanded the case. *Kawai America Corp. v. Univ. of North Carolina at Chapel Hill*, 567 S.E.2d 215 (N.C. Ct. App. 2002).

◆ *The U.S. Supreme Court held that the doctrine of substantial performance applied to contracts in an academic setting.*

An overweight Rhode Island student joined a college nursing program in her sophomore year. During her junior year, the college began pressuring her to lose weight. She received a failing grade in a clinical nursing course, for reasons related to her weight rather than her performance. By school rules, the failing grade should have resulted in expulsion from the program. However, the college offered her a contract that allowed her to stay in the program if she lost at least two pounds per week. She failed to lose the weight, was asked to withdraw from the program, and transferred to another nursing program. She sued the college in a federal district court, alleging that it had violated the Rehabilitation Act and that it had breached an implied contract to educate her. She was awarded damages for breach of contract. The jury determined that the student had substantially performed her obligations under the contract so as to enable her to prevail on her claim against the college. Appeal reached the U.S. Supreme Court. The Supreme Court held that the court of appeals should have reviewed the case *de novo* (as if hearing it for the first time). The appellate court should not have deferred to the district court's determination of what state law would be. Instead, **it should have examined the doctrine of substantial performance to ascertain whether it ought to be applied to a contract in an academic setting**. The Court reversed and remanded the case. *Salve Regina College v. Russell*, 499 U.S. 225, 111 S.Ct. 1217, 113 L.Ed.2d 190 (1991).

IV. INSURANCE

Insurance policies may provide coverage for both first- and third-party claims. Third-party claims generally involve liability policies and lawsuits for negligence by employees. Unless an exclusion in the policy specifically exempts a claim from coverage, an insurer may be required to defend and indemnify the policyholder in any lawsuit arising from an injury to a third party.

◆ *Insurers were obligated to defend and indemnify a New York college that was sued by a man who was injured at a volleyball tournament.*

The man was hurt when a referee's platform collapsed. He sued the college and the tournament sponsor for his injuries. The college asserted cross-claims against the sponsor, which was obligated to indemnify the college by contract. Although the college was listed as an additional insured party on the sponsor's liability policies, the insurers denied a request by the college for defense and indemnification. The college sued the insurers in a state court, which held for the college, ruling that the sponsor had contracted to defend and indemnify it. The insurers were also required to defend and indemnify the college.

On appeal, a state appellate division court noted that the injured party had settled his case for $75,000. Despite the settlement, the case was not moot because the settlement reserved the right to pursue an appeal regarding the college's responsibilities. **The court found the parties had expressly agreed that the sponsor would indemnify the college against all claims for damages based on injuries during the tournament.** The fact that the college was named as an additional insured on the policy created a duty on the part of the insurers to provide a defense. The trial court's ruling was affirmed. *Balyszak v. Siena College*, 63 A.D.3d 1409, 882 N.Y.S.2d 335 (N.Y. App. Div. 2009).

◆ *The U.S. Court of Appeals, Third Circuit, held a private college's breach of contract claim against its insurance carrier could proceed to trial.*

The college purchased a policy that covered repairs necessary to return property to pre-fire condition. It bought a separate "Ordinance and Law Endorsement" that covered loss to the undamaged portion of a building if it had to be fixed to comply with any ordinance or law. The insurance carrier denied coverage for fire damage caused to the upper floors of a dormitory. The college sued the carrier in a federal district court for breach of contract, contending the endorsement provided coverage for repair and renovation costs required by the Americans with Disabilities Act (ADA). It asserted that the endorsement covered numerous accessibility upgrades made to the building because they had to be done to comply with the ADA. The court held the protections of the

ADA did not apply to dormitory space on the second, third and fourth floors of the building. It found they were akin to apartments. The court held for the carrier, and the college appealed to the U.S. Court of Appeals, Third Circuit.

The court held the repairs to the dormitory were alterations within the meaning of the ADA because they included remodeling, renovation or reconstruction. **The court agreed with the college's contention that because dorms are part of boarding colleges, they are places of education.** The ADA prohibited denying disabled students reasonable accommodations that would allow them to live in its dorms. The court held the ADA applied to all four floors of the dormitory. It reversed the judgment. *Regents of Mercersburg College v. Republic Franklin Insurance Co.*, 458 F.3d 159 (3d Cir. 2006).

◆ *A liability insurer did not have to defend a university accused of fraud.*

A Florida university did not disclose in its catalog that its physical therapy program's accreditation status was probationary. When the applicable accrediting organization withdrew the program's certification, students who had enrolled in the program became ineligible for a physical therapy licensing examination. They sued the university in a state court for breach of contract, fraud, and violation of the Florida Deceptive and Unfair Trade Practices Act. The university sought to have its liability insurer defend and indemnify it in the action, but the Florida District Court of Appeal held for the insurer. Here, **the insurance policy covered any bodily injury caused by an occurrence, and defined "occurrence" as an accident**. However, the students were alleging intentionally fraudulent conduct by the university, not anything accidental. Fraud in the inducement could not be accidental. The university would have to defend itself in the action. *Barry Univ. v. Fireman's Fund Insurance Co. of Wisconsin,* 845 So.2d 276 (Fla. Dist. Ct. App. 2003).

◆ *A North Dakota university was entitled to coverage for flood damage in a case that reached the state's supreme court.*

After a record rainfall, the Red River flooded, and the city of Grand Forks shut down two sanitary sewer lift stations that serviced the University of North Dakota campus. As a result, water entered 22 campus buildings through the sewer system and damaged boiler and machinery equipment. The university's insurer denied coverage on the grounds that the sewer backup actually was caused by flooding, which was excluded by the policy. The university asserted that the damage was caused instead by the sewer backup, and that the policy therefore provided coverage. In the lawsuit that followed, a jury ruled in favor of the university, finding that the flood was not the efficient proximate cause of the damage. (Efficient proximate cause is the predominating cause of the loss, though not necessarily the last act in the chain of events, nor the triggering cause of the loss.) **The jury determined that the sewer backup, not the flood, was the efficient proximate cause of the damage.** The North Dakota Supreme Court affirmed, noting that the jury had properly considered the evidence before finding that the sewer backup caused the loss. Accordingly, the court upheld the jury's award of $3.35 million to the university. *Western National Insurance Co. v. Univ. of North Dakota,* 643 N.W.2d 4 (N.D. 2002).

◆ *An insurer had to contribute to a Colorado university's defense costs.*

A Colorado professor sued a university in state court for denial of tenure, wrongful termination, defamation and breach of contract, among other claims. Eighteen months later, she filed a second lawsuit against the university in federal court, but chose not to include the defamation claim. The lawsuits were consolidated in federal court, and a question of insurance coverage then arose – namely, which insurer (primary or excess) had to pay the costs of defending the university. The primary insurer was held to have the responsibility for defending the first lawsuit because of the defamation claim – the only claim it was potentially liable for paying. **The excess insurer had to contribute $50,000 to the second lawsuit** (where no defamation claim was presented and the primary insurer could not be liable) even though the two cases were consolidated. Here, even though the cases were consolidated and the primary insurer had the primary obligation to defend the lawsuit, the second lawsuit retained its separate identity for purposes of allocating defense costs. *Farmington Casualty Co. v. United Educators Insurance Risk Retention Group, Inc.*, 36 Fed.Appx. 408 (10th Cir. 2002).

◆ *A Missouri medical school could not obtain reimbursement from its insurer for a settlement.*

The medical school agreed to buy land from an energy company that it intended to convert into a parking lot. Before the sale closed, the school's contractor began working on the site, struck and ruptured an underground storage tank, and caused the release of coal tar wastes. The company sued the school and contractor for negligence and trespass, and the school's insurer initially defended it. It withdrew from the defense after a federal court concluded it had no duty to defend. That decision was later reversed. After a court found that the contractor had not trespassed because it had implied permission to work on the site, a settlement was reached. The school then sued its insurer for indemnification. A federal court ruled in favor of the insurer, and the Eighth Circuit affirmed. Here, the policy excluded environmental contamination claims, and the contractor was found not to have trespassed (the only claims for which the insurer could have been liable). Thus, **even though the insurer breached its duty to defend the school, it did not have to indemnify the school for the settlement**. *Royal Insurance Co. of America v. Kirksville College of Osteopathic Medicine*, 304 F.3d 804 (8th Cir. 2002).

◆ *City University of New York (CUNY) did not have to compensate Carnegie Hall Corporation for damages resulting from a student fall at graduation.*

CUNY's licensing agreement with Carnegie Hall allowed CUNY to use the hall for the 1994 graduation ceremony of the university's technical college. The agreement required CUNY to obtain comprehensive general liability insurance to cover any claims arising out of the event, but CUNY never obtained the required coverage. During the ceremony, a graduating student fell on a staircase and sued Carnegie Hall for failing to keep the staircase in a reasonably safe condition. The hall's insurance company ultimately paid $41,987 in settlement fees and defense costs. Carnegie Hall and the insurance company sued CUNY for reimbursement because the university failed to get insurance coverage, as mandated by the license agreement. A state appellate division court held neither Carnegie Hall nor the insurer had any basis for recovery against CUNY. Carnegie Hall had no ground to seek damages from CUNY because it did not incur any financial loss – its insurer paid the expenses related to the student's lawsuit. In addition, **the insurer was not entitled to recover settlement and defense costs. It was not a party to the license agreement, and it did not claim to be a third party to the agreement.** Therefore, any basis for recovery was based on its status as the subrogee of Carnegie Hall. New York's high court previously has ruled that recovery for the breach of a contract requiring the purchase of insurance is limited to the cost of obtaining substitute coverage, and not defense costs. Accordingly, the case was dismissed. *Carnegie Hall Corp. v. City Univ. of New York*, 729 N.Y.S.2d 93 (N.Y. App. Div. 2001).

V. PRIVATE INSTITUTIONS

Like their public counterparts, private colleges and universities are liable for negligence if they breach a legal duty. In most situations, institutions have a duty to exercise only "reasonable care" in their activities. A claimant in a tort case must show a legal duty, breach of the duty that proximately caused an injury, and damages. Institutions organized exclusively for religious, charitable, or educational purposes may claim charitable immunity.

In Bloom v. Seton Hall Univ., *704 A.2d 1334 (N.J. Super. Ct. App. Div. 1998), a New Jersey court held nonprofit corporations, societies or associations organized exclusively for religious, charitable, or educational purposes could not be held liable for negligence under the state charitable immunity statute, where the injured party was a beneficiary of the works of the nonprofit corporation, society or association. But in* Mooring v. Virginia Wesleyan College, *514 S.E.2d 619 (Va. 1999), the Supreme Court of Virginia denied charitable immunity to a professor who was not acting on behalf of a charitable institution at the time he injured a beneficiary.*

◆ *The Mississippi Supreme Court held an arbitrator, not a court, had to consider a challenge to the validity of enrollment contracts.*

Virginia College (VC) is a private chain of institutions that offers online study options. VC enrollment and tuition agreements for surgical technology students had an arbitration clause. Thirty-one surgical technology students sued VC in a Mississippi court, claiming it falsely represented to them that its program was or would be accredited for appropriate professional licensure. VC asked the court to compel the students to arbitrate their claims, but the court held the enrollment contract and arbitration clause were both invalid because VC had fraudulently induced the students to sign them. On appeal, the Mississippi Supreme Court held the claims had to be arbitrated. Arbitration agreements are severable from a contract in which they might appear. **Under established law, courts leave challenges to the validity of a contract to an arbitrator.** Since the students did not claim VC fraudulently induced them to enter the arbitration agreement, their claim had to be heard by an arbitrator. *Virginia College LLC v. Blackmon*, 109 So.3d 1050 (Miss. 2013).

◆ *A federal district court upheld an Alabama college's decision to expel a student who sent a series of harassing messages to college officials.*

The student sent anonymous letters to a college vice president and the college president. The letters included harassing and threatening language. After an investigation, the student admitted writing the letters. The president decided to expel her immediately. She sued the college for First Amendment and due process violations, negligence, and breach of contract. The court rejected the First Amendment and due process claims. **As the college was a private institution, it could not be subjected to constitutional liability.** The court found no breach of contract based on student handbook violations. The handbook was not a binding contract, and it had language declaring it was subject to revision at the discretion of the college. Even if the handbook was considered a contract, it allowed for the immediate expulsion of students who engaged in conduct that might violate the law. As college officials were confident that the student's conduct could be prosecuted, the court held in its favor. *Cook v. Talladega College*, 908 F.Supp.2d 1214 (N.D. Ala. 2012).

◆ *Seattle University avoided liability in a slip-and-fall case because the injured party did not show a repaired walkway was unreasonably dangerous.*

A Seattle University student fell on a walkway that had been damaged by plant roots. The university had patched the walkway, but the student apparently failed to recognize the unevenness of the pavement. As a result of the fall, she injured her hand, wrist, knee, chin and mouth. In a state court action, the student sued the university for negligence, claiming that despite the repair work, the condition of the walkway created an unreasonable risk of harm. A trial court ruled in favor of the university, and the state court of appeals affirmed. In the court's view, **the university's efforts to repair the walkway did not prove the presence of an unreasonable risk of harm at the time of the fall**. As a result, the judgment for the university was affirmed. *Webert v. Seattle Univ.*, 161 Wash.App. 1018 (Wash. Ct. App. 2011).

◆ *A New York court rejected a personal injury claim because evidence showed a sidewalk where a pedestrian slipped and fell had been regularly shoveled.*

A pedestrian slipped and fell on a sidewalk on a university campus. He claimed that the fall took place during a snowstorm, and he had a meteorologist prepare a statement that the ice that caused the fall was there before the storm. A state court held for the university, and appeal went to a state appellate division court. In the court's view, no evidence supported the meteorologist's statement. **A building custodian testified the area of the fall was shoveled and salted at least twice per weekday during the relevant time.** Based on this evidence, the court affirmed the judgment for the university. *Rand v. Cornell Univ.*, 91 A.D.3d 542, 937 N.Y.S.2d 49 (N.Y. App. Div. 2012).

◆ *Under New York law, students could not be liable for injuries to another student at a party unless it was foreseeable that she would get drunk.*

A 19-year-old Ithaca College sophomore drank alcohol at a party. She then fell from a balcony and was seriously hurt. Her parents sued Ithaca in a state court, claiming the college was liable because the balcony and railings were unsafe and negligently designed. Ithaca sought contribution from five students who shared the apartment and from the architect who designed the balcony and railings. The college claimed the injuries were caused, at least in part, by the fact that the students who hosted the party supplied the student with alcohol. The trial court denied pretrial judgment to a student who had provided alcohol. But another who did not know the student was at the party until after the accident avoided liability. On appeal, a New York Appellate Division Court affirmed the judgment. Under state law, the students could not be liable unless it was foreseeable that someone at the party would get drunk, engage in a fight, and cause an injury. That showing was not made. **There was no common law claim based on negligent provision of alcohol to underage drinkers.** *O'Neill v. Ithaca College*, 56 A.D.3d 869, 866 N.Y.S.2d 809 (N.Y. App. Div. 2008).

◆ *Private institutions must exercise reasonable care to protect students from foreseeable criminal or dangerous acts by third persons.*

A New York private college student was punched in the face by a classmate during a classroom altercation. He sued the college in the state court system for negligently failing to prevent the attack. The court held for the college, and the student appealed. The New York Supreme Court, Appellate Division, held that to prove negligence, there must be a breach of a legal duty that proximately caused damages. **The court noted that colleges generally have no duty to shield students from dangers presented by other students.** However, **they must exercise reasonable care to protect students from reasonably foreseeable criminal or dangerous acts committed by others**, including other students. In this case, the college did not breach any duty, because the injury was the result of a "sudden, unexpected, and unforeseeable act." Because the attack was not foreseeable, the college's failure to prevent it was not negligent. The judgment was affirmed. *Luina v. Katharine Gibbs School New York, Inc.*, 830 N.Y.S.2d 263 (N.Y. App. Div. 2007).

◆ *A discharged female employee could not proceed with a claim of intentional infliction of emotional distress against university officials.*

The employee discovered a male university employee was earning nearly $10,000 more annually than she was for doing essentially the same job. She filed administrative claims of discrimination against the university, then sued the university, supervisors and a human resources representative in a federal district court. The employee claimed violations of the Equal Pay Act, the Fair Labor Standards Act, Title VII, and the state fair employment practices act. She added a state law claim for intentional infliction of emotional distress, saying supervisors continuously harassed her for filing the administrative complaint.

The employee claimed supervisors denied her access to files she needed to do her job and took away significant job responsibilities. She said they had a "shadow" follow her around at work and subjected her to discipline without cause. According to the employee, these actions caused her to suffer from sleeplessness and anxiety. **The court held that to prevail on an emotional distress claim, the employee had to show conduct that was extreme and outrageous, and that it caused her to suffer severe emotional distress.** The court rejected the claim, because she did not show the conduct was extreme or outrageous. The employee's allegations did not indicate conduct that "transcended the bounds of civilized society," and she did not allege she was subjected to any public ridicule or humiliation. In short, she did not allege facts sufficient to support her claim of intentional infliction of emotional distress. The motion to dismiss the claim was granted. *Jamilik v. Yale Univ.*, No. 3:06 CV 0566 (PCD), 2007 WL 214607 (D. Conn. 1/25/07).

◆ *A private Connecticut university was not liable for harassment of a student based on his religion.*

The student attended a doctoral program in management systems. He claimed one of his professors suggested he adopt some Chinese heritage and culture, and that another remarked that he had a "mind like a computer." The student told the professor his mental abilities came from God. The professor responded, "It doesn't come from God, it comes from David, from the Jewish religion." A third professor allegedly made a remark about the student being Catholic. The student claimed several other faculty members also harassed him, delayed his presentation of his doctoral thesis, and prevented him from taking classes. He sued the university, claiming it violated state and federal laws when it harassed him based on his religion. The student alleged the university violated his federal civil rights, as protected by 42 U.S.C. § 1983. **The university argued it was a private entity that could not be sued for federal civil rights violations.** The student contended that as the university received some federal funding, the court should further determine if its acts or decisions would be considered functions of the state. The court agreed with the university and granted its motion for summary judgment. *Martin v. Univ. of New Haven*, 359 F.Supp.2d 185 (D. Conn. 2005).

◆ *A university was determined to have breached its agreement with a philanthropist; it could not claim that the money was a gift.*

A private California university asked a philanthropist to endow a professional chair at one of its research centers. After a number of conversations and the exchange of several letters, the philanthropist agreed to endow the chair. However, the university later selected an existing faculty member for the chair in violation of the endowment terms and also failed to fund the chair. The philanthropist sued for breach of contract, promissory fraud and misappropriation. A state trial court dismissed the action, finding that no contract existed and that the philanthropist made a gift to the university. The California Court of Appeal reversed, finding that **the contract (partially verbal and partially written) existed**. The letters confirmed the verbal agreement; they did not make up the agreement exclusively. The philanthropist could sue the university. *Glenn v. Univ. of Southern California*, No. BC 236256, 2002 WL 31022068 (Cal. Ct. App. 2002).

◆ *A student who was shot could proceed with his lawsuit against a college and a fraternity for negligence.*

A Missouri student enrolled in a private college for the summer semester and moved into a fraternity house. After a confrontational phone call, the student attempted to lock the front door, but the latch malfunctioned and popped open. Ten minutes later, two men entered the house and shot him. He sued the college and the fraternity for negligence, asserting that they breached a duty to maintain the premises in good repair. The college and fraternity maintained that they had no duty to prevent a third person from performing an intentional criminal act, and that even if they had a duty to maintain and repair the house, the student could not show that a breach of that duty caused his injuries under the law. A state court granted pretrial judgment to the defendants, but the Missouri Supreme Court reversed. It found issues of fact as to **whether the student was in a landlord-tenant relationship with either of the defendants so as to impose a duty of care**. There also was a jury question as to whether the breach of that duty was the proximate cause of the student's injuries. *Letsinger v. Drury College*, 68 S.W.3d 408 (Mo. 2002).

◆ *A Vermont university was liable for over $2 million in damages for hazing.*

A five-year veteran of the Navy enrolled in the Military College of Vermont of Norwich University under a Navy Reserve Officer Training Corps scholarship. He lasted for only 16 days, during which he was subjected to, and observed, repeated instances of hazing by upperclassmen. After withdrawing from school, he sued the university for assault and battery, infliction of emotional distress and negligence, asserting that it was vicariously liable for the actions of the upperclassmen. A jury returned a verdict in the student's favor, awarding him almost $500,000 in compensatory damages and $1.75 million in punitive damages. The Supreme Court of Vermont affirmed the compensatory damage award against the university, but reversed the award of punitive damages, finding no evidence of malice on the university's part. Here, **the university had charged the upperclassmen with "indoctrinating and orienting"** the student. As a result, this was not a simple case of student-on-student hazing for which the university could not be held liable. Because the upperclassmen were acting as agents of the university, it breached its duty of care toward the student. The court also found that the nearly $500,000 in compensatory damages awarded by the jury was not clearly erroneous. *Brueckner v. Norwich Univ.*, 730 A.2d 1086 (Vt. 1999).

◆ *An errors and omissions policy did not provide a private Texas college coverage for losses caused by a board member's misrepresentations.*

A Texas Christian College purchased a "school leaders errors and omissions" policy that insured it against wrongful acts committed by directors and officers of the school. Subsequently, a member of the board of trustees convinced the board to invest $2 million of its endowment funds in a company that accepted accounts receivable as security for short-term loans. However, he did not disclose that the company had a negative net worth, that he was a 49% owner of the company, or that he also was a salaried employee of the company.

When the investment failed, the college obtained the board member's resignation, then sued him and his company for misrepresentation of certain facts and for making false statements. The college obtained a judgment against the board member for $1.8 million and against the company for $2 million. Unable to collect on the judgments, it sought to collect under its errors and omissions policy. The insurer denied coverage under the "fraud or dishonesty" exclusion and the "personal profit or advantage" exclusion. A Texas federal court held that the two exclusions applied to bar coverage, and the college appealed to the U.S. Court of Appeals, Fifth Circuit. The appellate court affirmed. It noted that **the exclusion for "any claim arising out of the gaining in fact of any personal profit or advantage to which the Insured is not legally entitled" applied to bar coverage**. Here, the board member clearly gained a personal advantage by his company's receipt of the $2 million in endowment funds from the college. Despite the fact that the board member did not ultimately make a profit, he did gain a personal advantage by his wrongful acts. As a result, the insurer had no obligation to pay out under the policy. *Jarvis Christian College v. National Union Fire Insurance Co.*, 197 F.3d 742 (5th Cir. 1999).

◆   *A New York college could declare an alumnus "persona non grata" and bar him from campus.*

Over the course of his nine years at a college, a student exhibited disruptive behavior on campus and began receiving psychiatric treatment. His mother allegedly warned a nurse that he might act violently at his graduation ceremony, and security guards questioned him shortly before the ceremony began. However, the ceremony took place without any trouble. A month later, the student was declared "persona non grata" by the college and was barred from the campus. He eventually sued the college and the nurse. A state court ruled for the defendants, and the New York Supreme Court, Appellate Division, affirmed. Here, **since he had graduated, he was no longer a student and was not entitled to due process as a result of the college barring him from campus**. Further, his claims against the nurse could not succeed because he could not show that she breached a duty to keep information confidential. *Godinez v. Siena College*, 733 N.Y.S.2d 262 (N.Y. App. Div. 2001).

CHAPTER TEN

University Operations

I. GOVERNMENT REGULATION

A. Public Records and Freedom of Information

Enacted in 1966, the federal Freedom of Information Act (FOIA) 5 U.S.C. Section 552, provides that any person has a right, enforceable in court, to obtain access to federal agency records, except as protected by an exemption such as law enforcement, personnel records and other confidential items. States have analogous freedom of information and data practices acts that govern the disclosure of government data and create procedures for requesting records.

◆ *Connecticut's highest court denied a freedom of information act request for databases containing information that could be considered trade secrets.*

A private individual sought database information from the University of Connecticut relating to season ticket buyers, subscribers, individual event ticket buyers, library donors and others. The university claimed the information was exempt from disclosure under the state's freedom of information act. It said the databases were trade secrets that qualified for an exemption for "contact and/or other information related to students." A state commission found the databases were not "customer lists" protected by the trade secret exemption. The commission held the university was not required to disclose the library list with respect to people who had requested anonymity or information that would personally identify students, it said the university otherwise had to comply with the request. Appeal reached the Supreme Court of Connecticut.

The court held the university could create a trade secret that was entitled to an exemption under the state's freedom of information act. **The state law definition of "trade secrets" focused on the nature and accessibility of the information, not whether the entity holding the information was engaged in a trade.** In fact, there was no requirement that an entity be engaged in a trade before claiming entitlement to the trade secret exemption. As the information sought in this case met the statutory criteria for trade secrets, a lower court ruling denying the request for access was affirmed. *Univ. of Connecticut v. Freedom of Information Comm'n*, 303 Conn. 724, 36 A.3d 663 (Conn. 2012).

◆   *The Florida public records law did not shield the NCAA from disclosing to the media documents from investigation reports it kept on a secure website.*

Florida State University (FSU) learned that staff members gave improper assistance to student-athletes. It conducted an investigation, then turned over its findings to the NCAA. Months later, the NCAA issued FSU a formal notice of allegations to initiate disciplinary proceedings for the reported misconduct. An NCAA committee issued an infractions report and imposed penalties for academic misconduct, including the forfeiture of some games. To prepare an appeal, FSU lawyers viewed documents posted on a secure NCAA website. The Associated Press (AP) sought disclosure of the NCAA documents in a state court action. A state court held for the AP, finding the documents were "public records" as they were received by a state agency and not exempt under federal laws (they contained no information directly related to a student).

A Florida District Court of Appeal noted Chapter 119 had a public policy of keeping public records open for personal inspection and copying. It held **the Public Records Law applied to documents maintained on a computer in the same way that it would apply to those kept in a file cabinet**. A document may qualify as a public record if it was prepared by a private party, if it was received by the government and used in the transaction of public business. The term "received" referred to examination of a document on a remote computer, as had taken place in this case. The requested documents did not reveal the identity of any student, so federal law did not prohibit disclosure. Since the documents were "received" by FSU lawyers in connection with public business, the Public Records Law applied, and the documents had to be disclosed. *NCAA v. Associated Press*, 18 So.3d 1201 (Fla. Dist. Ct. App. 2009).

◆   *Two Wisconsin veterans could not proceed with a court challenge to a proposal to change the name of a university football stadium.*

In 1945, the city of La Crosse chose the name Veterans Memorial Stadium for the football facility at the University of Wisconsin-La Crosse (UWL). Between 2000 and 2005, the name of the facility was changed three times. The veterans said the 2000 and 2001 name changes violated Wisconsin's open meetings and public records laws and UWL policies. They claimed the changes resulted from "malfeasance" by UWL's board of regents. A state circuit court dismissed the case, finding that the veterans failed to show they had suffered any injury and thus lacked standing to pursue their claims.

The Court of Appeals of Wisconsin agreed with the trial court that the veterans lacked standing to challenge the name change. **To have standing, or the legal right to bring an action, a party must show he has suffered an injury or has been threatened with an injury as a result of the other party's conduct.** In addition, the injury must be to a legally protectable interest. The veterans did not allege any direct personal injury as a result of the name changes. Their concern that the name changes did not sufficiently honor veterans was not a "direct personal injury" that gave them the right to bring an action against UWL. The court affirmed the judgment for UWL. *Nedvidek v. Kuipers*, No. 2006AP3077, 747 N.W.2d 527 (Table), 2008 WI App. 51, 2008 WL 516781 (Wis. Ct. App. 2/28/08). The Supreme Court of Wisconsin dismissed a later appeal. *Nedvidek v. Kuipers*, 766 N.W.2d 205 (Wis. 2009).

◆ *A Michigan university police report had to be reviewed by a trial court judge in chambers to consider if parts of it were exempt from public disclosure.*

Three men were arrested in connection with an assault on the campus of Michigan State University (MSU). A news organization asked MSU for a copy of its police incident report related to the incident. The request was filed under the state freedom of information act (FOIA). The organization had already published a story with the names of three men who were arrested for the assault, but it wanted additional information from the report, such as personally identifiable information relating to victims, witnesses, and police officers. The report also included photographs and statements from the responding officers and others. MSU officials denied the request, saying disclosure would violate individual privacy rights and interfere with the law enforcement investigation.

The case reached the Michigan Court of Appeals, which held MSU did not show FOIA privacy and law enforcement exemptions applied. It held the trial court had wrongfully failed to review the report to decide if parts of it could be separated and disclosed without violating privacy rights or interfering with the investigation. Appeal reached the Supreme Court of Michigan, which held that unless a FOIA exemption provided otherwise, the relevant time to consider was when the public body asserted the exemption. **The passage of time and the course of events after asserting a FOIA exception did not affect whether a public record was initially exempt from disclosure.** This part of the appeals court decision was reversed, and the case was returned to the trial court. Upon return to that court, the judge was to inspect the police incident report in chambers to determine what information was exempt from disclosure, to make particularized findings regarding disclosure or nondisclosure, and to separate any exempt material from nonexempt material. *State News v. Michigan State Univ.*, 481 Mich. 692, 753 N.W.2d 20 (Mich. 2008).

◆ *A federal district court found a Montana student had no constitutional right to his school transcripts and or continued enrollment at a state university.*

A sophomore at Montana State University (MSU) enrolled in a program that would enable him to study in England. After leaving his studies in England early, officials at the school in England informed officials at MSU that he had left without completing his exams and that he owed rent at his residence hall. MSU responded by suspending the student for the remainder of the summer term, terminating his financial aid, and placing a hold on all of his academic records. After his grievance was denied, he sued university officials in federal court, claiming they unconstitutionally deprived him of his property interest in continued enrollment and transcripts without due process. A federal magistrate judge recommended dismissing the case. The court adopted the recommendation. **Legal precedent established that a student has no property interest in a transcript, which is owned by the school and not the student.** As to the other claim, there is no clearly established right to continued enrollment. Summary judgment was granted to the university officials. *Comer v. Meyers*, No. CV-06-65 BURFC, 2007 WL 1810684 (D. Mont. 6/20/07).

◆ *Massachusetts' highest court held incident reports and other documents held by a private university police department were not "public records."*

A student newspaper asked two municipal police departments and Harvard University's police department for all records related to certain incidents listed on the university department's weekly log of complaints, including incident reports and correspondence. The municipal police departments supplied the documents to the newspaper, but the university asserted it did not have to comply with the public records law because it was not a public entity.

The newspaper asked a state court for an order requiring the university to release the documents. The court dismissed the case, ruling that private university officers were not governmental employees. Accordingly, documents they made or received were not "public records." The newspaper appealed to the Supreme Judicial Court of Massachusetts, arguing the appointment of some university officers as special state police officers or deputy sheriffs vested them with broad police powers. Under this theory, they were subject to public records law requirements. **The court held the university records were not covered by the state public records law and did not have to be disclosed.** The judgment for Harvard was affirmed. *Harvard Crimson v. President and Fellows of Harvard College*, 445 Mass. 745, 840 N.E.2d 518 (Mass. 2006).

◆ *The Supreme Court of Iowa held a state university could not shield its financial records from public view by outsourcing certain university functions.*

University financial records were managed by a private nonprofit foundation that had been incorporated by the university in 1958. In 2002, the university and foundation renewed an elaborate service agreement. In the agreement, the university expressed its desire to engage the expertise of the foundation as an independent contractor to provide advice, coordination, and assistance in fundraising, development, and in the operation, accounting and fund investment management of those areas.

A group of citizens sought a state court order to view university tax and financial records under the Iowa Freedom of Information Act, I.C.A. § 22.1, *et seq.* The act creates a public right to view governmental records. The court held the foundation was not a government body under the act, so its documents were not "public records." On appeal, the Supreme Court of Iowa stated "public records" included documents or other information belonging to the state, school corporation, or nonprofit corporation whose facilities are supported with property tax revenue, and relate to the investment of public funds. **The court held the foundation was performing a government function through the contract with the university, so its records were subject to public disclosure.** It said a government body may not outsource its functions to a private corporation and then keep the information from the public. In executing the service agreement, the university, a government body, contracted away its ability to raise money and manage its finances to what was assumed to be a nongovernment body. The university had attempted to do indirectly what it could not do directly – avoid disclosure of what would otherwise be public records. The court held the act prevented this result and reversed the judgment. *Gannon v. Board of Regents of State of Iowa*, 692 N.W.2d 31 (Iowa 2005).

B. Aliens and Immigration

A federal immigration law, 8 U.S.C. § 1623, bars the states from providing "any postsecondary education benefit" to illegal aliens "on the basis of residence within a state" – unless U.S. citizens are also eligible for the benefit. Another federal law, 8 U.S.C. § 1621, generally makes illegal aliens ineligible for state or local public benefits. In Martinez v. Regents of the Univ. of California, *this chapter, the Supreme Court of California upheld a state law provision making illegal aliens eligible for an in-state tuition rate as long as they satisfied certain criteria. These are: attendance at a high school in the state for at least three years, graduation from a high school in the state, registration at an accredited California higher education institution, and an affidavit indicating the intention to seek legalized immigration status.*

◆ *Florida regulations denying in-state tuition rates to children of undocumented residents were held invalid under the Equal Protection Clause.*

A Florida law disqualified from resident status any dependent child whose parents were not state residents. Any dependent child who could not show his or her parents were in the country legally was disqualified from resident status under a state regulation. Five high school graduates who were born in the U.S. and resided in Florida sued state officials under the Equal Protection Clause. Although they could not provide proof of their parents' federal immigration status, they were not aliens. According to the state, the classification was needed to prevent the loss of $200 million a year in tuition revenue. The court rejected this argument, finding that the state would not be required to offer in-state tuition to all U.S. citizens. The state could still distinguish between in-state and out-of-state residents. **By classifying the students as aliens, the state created a second tier of citizenship that depreciated the historic values of citizenship.** The court found the classification was not reasonably related to any state interest in ensuring that in-state tuition rates were provided only to those who intended to stay in Florida. The state's definition of "legal resident" and the state regulation violated the Equal Protection Clause. *Ruiz v. Robinson*, 892 F.Supp.2d 1321 (S.D. Fla. 2012).

◆ *A New York university that disenrolled a Nigerian engineering student after his arrest by federal agents had to provide him with his official transcript.*

The university disenrolled the student after U.S. State Department special agents arrested him on campus because they suspected that he had fraudulently obtained his F-1 student visa. The university never conducted a hearing into the matter, but it deemed the charges against him to be true. The expulsion led to the student's deportation and cut short his higher education. He sought a copy of his official transcript to help him continue his education elsewhere, but the university refused to provide it on the grounds that he owed various fees. When the student sued the university for due process violations, a federal district court held in his favor. However, a hearing would not benefit him because he could not presently re-enter the country. As a result, **the court ordered the university to provide the student with his official transcripts, despite the fact that withholding them was not related to the due process violation**. The university also had to convene a new hearing, when and if he was ever able to re-enter the United States and request one. *Oladokun v. Ryan*, No. 06 cv 2330(KMW), 2011 WL 4471882 (S.D.N.Y. 9/27/11).

◆ *A foreign student was unable to obtain relief in a federal court action asserting constitutional violations when her name was accidentally removed from a Utah university's international student list.*

The student sued Weber State University in a federal court, claiming a computer glitch caused the removal of her name from the university's list of international students. She raised several state law and constitutional claims, asserting her legal status to be a student in the U.S. had been accidentally taken away. A federal magistrate judge found the university was immune from suit because it was an arm of the state of Utah. **The student's constitutional claim failed because she did not assert discrimination by any individual**, and her claim of cruel and unusual treatment failed because the case did not involve prison officials or penological responsibilities. Since the court lacked jurisdiction over the state law claims, the case was recommended for dismissal. A federal district court adopted the recommendation, and the student appealed to the U.S. Court of Appeals, Tenth Circuit. It affirmed the district court's decision, concluding that the student had failed to identify any reversible error. *Sethunya v. Weber State Univ.*, 382 Fed.Appx. 793 (10th Cir. 2010).

◆ *The Supreme Court of California upheld a state law allowing illegal aliens to pay in-state tuition rates at state public universities and colleges.*

A number of out-of-state U.S. citizens sued the Regents of the University of California in a state court, alleging a state law allowing illegal aliens to pay in-state tuition rates violated federal immigration law. After the court dismissed the case, the state court of appeal reversed the judgment, finding the state law was preempted by federal law and that the citizens could pursue Equal Protection and Privileges and Immunities challenges. On appeal, the Supreme Court of California found the state law conditioned in-state tuition to those who had attended a California high school for at least three years, graduated from a high school in the state and met certain other requirements. According to the court, the state law did not violate 8 U.S.C. § 1623, which is a federal immigration law. Section 1623 bars the provision of education benefits to illegal aliens only when a benefit was provided on the basis of state residence. **The court found California was not providing an education benefit to illegal aliens on the basis of state residency**, but was offering in-state tuition rates based on satisfaction of the other criteria. The court also found the state law did not violate 8 U.S.C. § 1621. While that section generally made illegal aliens ineligible for state or local public benefits, it also said **states may enact laws negating the ineligibility and extending benefits to illegal aliens**, as California had done. The court found no legal authority for a Privileges and Immunities Clause claim by the citizens asserting a privilege "of being treated no worse than an illegal alien in the distribution of public benefits." The court rejected the citizens' other arguments and reversed the judgment. *Martinez v. Regents of the Univ. of California*, 50 Cal.4th 1277, 241 P.3d 855 (Cal. 2010).

◆ *A Muslim scholar was entitled to further consideration of a claim that he was improperly denied a visa without an opportunity to show he did not knowingly support an organization that gave support to terrorist groups.*

The federal Immigration and Nationality Act (INA) makes an alien who has afforded material support to terrorist organizations ineligible for a visa. The American Academy of Religion and the American Association of University Professors sued the Department of Homeland Security in a federal court, challenging the exclusion of a well-known Muslim scholar who shuns violence and has spoken out against terrorism and radical Islam. However, the U.S. revoked his visa because he admitted making donations to an organization that supported terrorist groups. This was a direct violation of the INA. Finding the government excluded him for legitimate reasons, the court held for the U.S.

The organizations appealed to the U.S. Court of Appeals, Second Circuit, arguing that the visa was improperly rejected in violation of a First Amendment right to hear the scholar's views. The court upheld a statutory provision making contributors to terrorist organizations ineligible for visas. **A knowledge requirement provision of the INA required a consular officer to find that the scholar knew his contributions provided material support to a terrorist organization, and to confront him and afford him an opportunity to deny this.** Since the record did not establish that the consular officer who denied the visa confronted the scholar with the claim that he knowingly gave support to Hamas, the court returned the case to the district court. The scholar would be entitled to an opportunity to demonstrate by clear and convincing evidence that he did not know he was supporting a terrorist organization. *American Academy of Religion v. Napolitano*, 573 F.3d 115 (2d Cir. 2009).

◆ *A federal court ordered the University of Pittsburgh to retain a research assistant while she pursued administrative charges of unlawful discrimination.*

The research assistant worked at the university until her supervisor told her that her contract would end due to insufficient funding. If the contract ended on the stated date, the research assistant's visa would expire and she would be forced to return to Russia. She claimed that the decision to end her employment was motivated by national origin discrimination. To support this claim, she noted that her supervisor had hired and/or retained similarly situated Korean employees while non-renewing her contract. A federal district court granted the research assistant's request for an injunction and ordered the university to retain her while she filed administrative charges of discrimination. She showed a reasonable probability of succeeding on the merits of her discrimination claim since she was let go while similarly situated Korean employees were retained. **In addition, if relief was denied, she would either have to return to Russia voluntarily or be subject to immediate deportation.** *Karakozova v. Univ. of Pittsburgh*, No. 09cv0458, 2009 WL 1652469 (W.D. Pa. 6/11/09).

◆   *The right to rebut a presumption of nonresidence extends even to aliens with visas living in state.*

The University of Maryland granted "in-state" tuition status only to students domiciled in Maryland, or, if a student was financially dependent on the student's parents, to students whose parents were domiciled in Maryland. The university also could deny in-state status to individuals who did not pay the full spectrum of Maryland state taxes. The university refused to grant in-state status to a number of students, each of whom was dependent on a parent who held a "G-4 visa" (a nonimmigrant visa granted to officers and employees of international treaty organizations and members of their immediate family). The university stated that the holder of a G-4 visa could not acquire Maryland domicile because the holder was incapable of showing an essential element of domicile – the intent to live permanently or indefinitely in Maryland.

After unsuccessful appeals at the administrative level, the students brought a class action lawsuit in federal court seeking declaratory and injunctive relief. The students alleged that university policy violated the Equal Protection Clause. A federal district court granted relief, stating that the G-4 visa could not create an irrebuttable presumption of nondomicile. On appeal, the U.S. Supreme Court stated that the case was controlled by the principles announced in *Vlandis v. Kline*, this chapter, that **when a state purports to be concerned with domicile, it must provide an individual with the opportunity to present evidence bearing on that issue**. Federal law allows aliens holding a G-4 visa to acquire domicile in the United States. However, the question of whether such domicile could be acquired in Maryland was a question of state law. Since no controlling precedent had been decided by the state's highest court, the Supreme Court declined to rule and certified the question to the Maryland Court of Appeals for resolution. *Elkins v. Moreno*, 435 U.S. 647, 98 S.Ct. 1338, 55 L.Ed.2d 614 (1978).

◆   *The Supreme Court struck down a university policy that restricted an alien's right to acquire domicile in a state and thus qualify for in-state tuition.*

The University of Maryland's student fee schedule policy denied students whose parents held nonimmigrant alien visas in-state status, even if they were domiciled in the state, thus denying them preferential fee and tuition schedules. The U.S. Supreme Court found the policy to be in violation of the Supremacy Clause of the U.S. Constitution. The Court stated that the university's policy conflicted directly with the will of Congress as expressed in the Immigration and Nationality Act of 1952. In passing the Immigration and Nationality Act, Congress explicitly decided not to bar nonimmigrant aliens, such as these, the right to acquire domicile in the United States. **The university's policy denying these aliens "in-state" status, solely on the basis of their immigration status, amounted to a burden not contemplated by Congress** in admitting them to the United States. Thus, the University of Maryland's student fee schedule, as applied to these aliens, was held to be unconstitutional. *Toll v. Moreno*, 458 U.S. 1, 102 S.Ct. 2977, 73 L.Ed.2d 563 (1982).

C. Residency and Tuition Issues

State laws creating favorable in-state tuition rates are valid insofar as they create a presumption of residency based on reliable indicators. However, an inflexible or improperly applied presumption is open to challenge.

◆ *State residency requirements for favorable tuition rates are subject to the due process right of students to present evidence about their residency.*

Connecticut required nonresidents enrolled in the state's university system to pay tuition and other fees at a higher rate than state residents. It also created an irreversible and irrebuttable statutory presumption that if the legal address of a student, if married, was outside the state at the time of application for admission or, if single, was outside the state at some point during the preceding year, the student remained a nonresident as long as the student remained enrolled in Connecticut schools. Two resident students, one married, one single, challenged the presumption, claiming it violated the Fourteenth Amendment's guarantee of due process and equal protection. A panel upheld the students' claim. The U.S. Supreme Court held that **the Due Process Clause does not permit states to deny a student the opportunity to present evidence that the student is a bona fide resident of the state, and thus entitled to in-state tuition rates**, on the basis of an irrebuttable presumption of nonresidence. Such a presumption is not necessarily true, and the state had alternatives in making residency determinations. *Vlandis v. Kline*, 412 U.S. 441, 93 S.Ct. 2230, 37 L.Ed.2d 63 (1973).

◆ *A student who failed to show she had established residency in Oregon was not entitled to the in-state tuition rate at a state university.*

An Oklahoma student moved to Oregon at the age of 22, at a time when she was financially independent. More than a year later, she enrolled at a state university and sought to qualify for the in-state tuition rate. Her request was denied by a university committee, which found she was not a resident of Oregon for tuition purposes. The state board of education upheld the determination, ruling that to prove residency, students must establish and maintain a domicile in Oregon for at least 12 straight months and be primarily engaged in activities other than those of being a college student. A state circuit court then held the second requirement for establishing entitlement to the in-state tuition rate was unconstitutional, as it created an irrebuttable presumption against residency for students who attended school in the state within 12 months of moving there.

On appeal, the Court of Appeals of Oregon found **the student did not give up her residency in Oklahoma and failed to establish and maintain a domicile in Oregon for at least 12 straight months**. It held reviewing courts should not address constitutional challenges when a case can be resolved otherwise. In this case, the court held the circuit court should have affirmed the board's decision on the domicile issue. The judgment was reversed, and the case was returned to the lower court with instructions to reinstate the board's decision. *Deatherage v. Pernsteiner*, 239 Or.App. 161, 243 P.3d 865 (Or. Ct. App. 2010). The Supreme Court of Oregon denied review in *Deatherage v. Pernsteiner*, 249 Or. 664, 249 P.3d 1282 (Or. 2011).

◆   *A state court upheld a determination by Florida Atlantic University (FAU) that a student did not qualify for resident tuition rates.*

After graduating from a Michigan high school, the student went to Florida to attend a community college. Three years later, she transferred to FAU. After a year at FAU, the student took steps to qualify as a resident of the state for in-state tuition rates. She obtained a Florida driver's license and executed a declaration of domicile. FAU denied the student's application to reclassify her as a Florida resident for tuition purposes, and she commenced a state court action against FAU. A Florida district court of appeal explained that a student seeking to qualify for resident tuition rates must show Florida residency for the previous 12 months, and that Florida is the student's permanent domicile. In this case, there was sufficient evidence to support FAU's conclusion that residency in Florida was merely incident to the student's school enrollment.

Although the student had been in the state for the previous 12 months, she did not produce enough evidence to show she intended to reside in Florida permanently. **She did not own real property in the state or have a vehicle registered there, and she did not work there on a full-time basis.** In addition, the student did not get her Florida driver's license or execute a declaration of domicile until just a month before she applied for residency reclassification. When she initially applied to FAU in 2007, she said she was not a Florida resident. This statement contradicted the student's later claim that she intended to become a resident in 2005. There was enough evidence to support FAU's decision, and the court affirmed it. *Hallendy v. Florida Atlantic Univ.*, 16 So.3d 1057 (Fla. Dist. Ct. App. 2009).

◆   *A student did not present sufficient evidence of residence to overcome a presumption that he was in the state just to attend law school.*

The student completed a graduate degree program in Indiana, then moved to Virginia. During his first year at a Virginia law school, he paid an out-of-state tuition rate while taking steps to establish residency in Virginia. He registered his car in Virginia, obtained a state driver's license, and registered as a voter. Before the start of his second year, the student asked the school to reclassify him as a state resident. While over a year had passed since he moved to the state, the law school said he failed to prove he had established and maintained a Virginia domicile for a year before the start of his second year.

The student's internal appeals failed, but a state circuit court reversed its decision. The case reached the Virginia Supreme Court. The court held that to qualify for in-state tuition in Virginia, students must prove they have been domiciled in the state for at least a year and have abandoned any previous domicile. Importantly, **the law specifies that an out-of-state student who**

attends school in Virginia is presumed to be in the state for the purpose of attending school and not a resident of the state. Students cannot prove they have become Virginia residents simply by "performing acts which are auxiliary to fulfilling educational purposes" or acts that are "required or routinely performed by temporary residents." State law sets out a number of factors to be considered in determining whether a student has established residency for tuition purposes, including income taxes, driver's license, motor vehicle registration, voter registration, employment, property ownership, sources of financial support, military records and employment offers following graduation. After reciting these factors, the court found the university had reasonably concluded the student was in Virginia primarily to attend law school. *George Mason Univ. v. Floyd,* 654 S.E.2d 556 (Va. 2008).

◆ *A New Jersey university wrongly denied its in-state tuition rate to an applicant based solely on the residence of her out-of-state parents.*

Rutgers University denied a student's request for the in-state tuition rate because she was financially dependent on her parents and they resided outside the state. The student provided information detailing her ties with the state and her intention to stay there. She also noted that under state law, any individual who has lived in the state for 12 months is presumed to be entitled to the in-state rate. The university rejected her arguments. The student appealed to a state court, which held for Rutgers.

Appeal reached the Supreme Court of New Jersey, which held that state law established a presumption of residency for anyone who lived in the state for 12 months. Because the student had lived in the state for over four years when she enrolled at Rutgers, she was entitled to the presumption. While Rutgers argued that its interpretation established a counter-presumption of non-domicile when an individual is financially supported by out-of-state parents, this was plainly at odds with the statute. **The court said the regulation merely neutralized the presumption of domicile when a student is financially dependent on out-of-state parents.** Instead of tipping the presumption against residency, financial dependence on out-of-state parents eliminated the presumption of residency. It did not create a contrary presumption of nonresidency. The case was remanded so that Rutgers could more fully consider the evidence relating to whether the student was entitled to the in-state tuition rate. *Shim v. Rutgers,* 191 N.J. 374, 924 A.2d 465 (N.J. 2007).

◆ *Arizona's highest court refused to address a constitutional challenge to the state's decision to substantially raise tuition rates at state universities.*

The Arizona Constitution requires state universities to provide instruction "as nearly free as possible," and provides for the state board of regents to set tuition and fees. The board approved a request from state universities to increase tuition rates by over 39% for the 2003-2004 academic year. Four students at the University of Arizona sued the board and the state legislature to challenge the increase, saying it violated the "as nearly free as possible" constitutional provision. A state court dismissed the claims, finding the board and legislature had state law immunity. The case reached the Arizona Supreme Court, which held the case presented a nonjusticiable political question that was not suited for resolution by the judicial branch. **Decisions about setting university tuition were entrusted by the state's constitution to other government branches, and there were no manageable standards a state court could apply to determine whether tuition was being provided "as nearly free as possible."** As neither case law nor statutes provided adequate guidance, the supreme court held the case had been properly dismissed. *Kromko v. Arizona Board of Regents*, 216 Ariz. 190 165 P.3d 168 (Ariz. 2007).

◆ *A Maryland state university's presumption against in-state residency for all students who depended upon out-of-state sources did not violate equal protection principles. However, university administrators may not have applied the presumption in a constitutional manner.*

Four students who were enrolled in professional and post-graduate degree programs at a state university sued the university board of regents in a state court, claiming the board violated their constitutional rights by refusing to classify them as in-state residents. This decision denied them a substantial tuition reduction offered to Maryland residents, which the students claimed was a violation of equal protection principles. The university system presumed that students who were not financially independent were residing in the state primarily for the purpose of attending a college or university, if they remained financially dependent upon a nonresident. A state court held for the board and the students appealed to the Court of Special Appeals of Maryland.

The court stated no single definition could mechanically determine a person's domicile. The most important factors for determining domicile were where a person actually lived and where he or she voted, although a number of other factors also had weight. **The court held the university system's presumption was valid. The source of a student's financial support was related to the issue of residence.** However, there was evidence that some administrators did not allow students to challenge the presumption by treating the financial dependency presumption as irrebuttable. **The absence of uniformity in standards or criteria under the tuition policy violated equal protection principles.** The students were in the state during the time they attended the university, and each satisfied many other traditional domicile factors. The court vacated the lower court order for the board and remanded the case for further activity. *Bergmann v. Board of Regents of the Univ. System of Maryland*, 167 Md. App. 237, 892 A.2d 604 (Md. Ct. Spec. App. 2006).

◆ *The Court of Appeals of Kansas held that a student who moved to Kansas to attend law school could not claim resident tuition status.*

The student, who was born in England, came to Kansas in May 1999 and moved to Colorado in July 1999. He lived there until March 2002. He signed a contract to build a house in Kansas, contingent on his acceptance to the law school there. He was accepted, and he and his wife finalized the purchase of a house in Kansas in June 2002. The university denied the student's application to be reclassified as a Kansas resident for the 2003 fall semester. The residence committee denied his appeal. A state court agreed, and the student appealed.

The court of appeals noted several state law factors determined if a student was a Kansas resident. **These included a continuous presence in**

Kansas, employment in the state, payment of resident income taxes, reliance on in-state sources of financial support, commitment to an education program indicating an intent to remain permanently, and owning a home in Kansas. The committee found the purchase of the house was contingent on the student's acceptance to the law school. This did not demonstrate an intent to remain in Kansas permanently. All of the other factors could be considered routinely performed by temporary residents of Kansas. The court found the committee's decision supported by substantial competent evidence and affirmed the judgment. *Lockett v. The Univ. of Kansas, Residence Appeals Committee*, 33 Kan. App.2d 931, 111 P.3d 170 (Kan. Ct. App. 2005).

D. Zoning and Land Use

◆ *A Rhode Island municipal ordinance was upheld in the face of a constitutional challenge by university students and others.*

A resort town attempted to keep disturbances by college students to a minimum by passing an ordinance making it a public nuisance to "conduct a gathering" of at least five people in a way that "constitutes a substantial disturbance of the quiet enjoyment of private or public property in a significant segment of the neighborhood, as a result of conduct constituting a violation of law." The ordinance authorized police to post a bright orange sticker at the front of any residence found to have hosted an "unruly gathering." Further offenses called for fines of up to $500. The University of Rhode Island's Student Senate, a group of students and a group of landlords sued the town in a federal district court to challenge the constitutionality of the ordinance. After the court held for the town, the students appealed to the U.S. Court of Appeals, First Circuit.

First, the court held that the ordinance was not preempted by the state landlord and tenant act. Next, it rejected a procedural due process claim, which was focused on the posting of orange stickers on a dwelling before a hearing was held. The court found this did not result in harm to any legally recognized liberty or property interest. **An asserted right of association did not encompass purely social gatherings**, and the ordinance did not reach a substantial amount of constitutionally protected conduct. As a result, the court rejected a claim that the ordinance was overbroad. While it used vague terms like "substantial disturbance" and "significant segment of the neighborhood," when viewed in context, the court found it clearly indicated the conduct it banned. The district court's decision to uphold the ordinance was affirmed. *URI Student Senate v. Town of Narragansett*, 631 F.3d 1 (1st Cir. 2011).

◆ *The Supreme Court of Vermont upheld the state environmental court's approval of a college building project over the objections of several neighbors.*

The college proposed to renovate an existing building in Burlington and build a new 18,000 square-foot building on the same lot to create 49 new student rooms that could house 94 students. A development review board conditionally approved the project and neighbors appealed to the Vermont Environmental Court. After a hearing and a site visit, the court approved the application with conditions, finding the project satisfied city density and setback requirements. On appeal, the Supreme Court of Vermont considered a claim by the neighbors that the lower court order had permitted a project exceeding the city's maximum allowable density and setback requirements.

The court deferred to the city's approach of treating each group of four dormitory rooms as a "single dwelling unit." Using this approach, the court upheld the environmental court's conclusion that the project complied with city density requirements. While neighbors complained that the lot was not a "corner lot" and thus violated setback requirements, the court disagreed. It found that **the neighbors sought to have the court "rewrite the zoning ordinances to declare that large lots cannot be corner lots under the City's definition of that term."** Since the lot was a "corner lot" as defined by the city, the environmental court did not commit error in allowing the project with conditions. *In re Champlain College Maple Street Dormitory*, 186 Vt. 313, 980 A.2d 273 (Vt. 2009).

◆ *A New Jersey court rejected claims that a zoning board improperly approved a university's plan to build a dormitory in a residential area.*

A group of neighbors objected to the construction of a three-story dormitory at Monmouth University. The local board of adjustment granted several variances for the project, which was planned in an area zoned for low-density residential uses. The neighbors sued Monmouth in the state court system, claiming several board members should have been disqualified from the application based on their financial or personal involvement with the university. The court upheld the decision, and the neighbors appealed.

A New Jersey appellate division court acknowledged that **the state Municipal Land Use Law has a conflict of interest provision that bars board of adjustment members from acting on any matter on which they have any personal or financial interest**. But none of the board members in this case came within the scope of this law. Some members were alumni of the university, but they were inactive and did not contribute substantially to Monmouth. No board members or any of their family members were currently students at the university. As none of the connections noted by the neighbors could reasonably be expected to impair the independence or objectivity of a board member, the judgment was affirmed. *Hughes v. Monmouth Univ.*, 394 N.J. Super. 193, 925 A.2d 741 (N.J. Super. Ct. App. Div. 2007).

◆ *The Court of Appeals of North Carolina upheld a decision to grant a university's request for an order to close a road running along its property.*

The university asked the Town of Chapel Hill to close part of Laurel Hill Road to promote safety, unify the grounds of the North Carolina Botanical Garden, and provide better teaching and visitor experiences. The town council adopted an order to permanently close a section of the road. A nearby property owner filed a state court petition to vacate the order. The court dismissed the petition and affirmed the order of the town council. The owner appealed to the Court of Appeals of North Carolina. He contended the trial court erred in failing to conduct an evidentiary hearing and in refusing to allow him to present evidence at the hearing on his petition.

The court noted the owner did not contest the procedures at the town hearing and did not contend the trial court violated other applicable local requirements. **The town held three public hearings on the proposed road closing in two months. Those hearings were the proper place for the owner to present evidence, not the trial court.** The court affirmed the judgment upholding the town's decision. *Houston v. Town of Chapel Hill*, 177 N.C.App. 739, 630 S.E.2d 249 (N.C. App. 2006). The state's highest court denied review in *Houston v. Town of Chapel Hill*, 639 S.E.2d 449 (N.C. 2006).

◆ *A federal district court upheld a District of Columbia zoning board order concerning a campus plan.*

The District zoning board approved the university's campus plan for 2000-2010, but imposed conditions including a cap on student enrollment. The university had already admitted a substantial number of its students for the next semester. The order also directed that if the university failed to meet a requirement to house 70% of buildings on campus, it would be barred from erecting nonresidential buildings on campus while it was noncompliant. A federal district court granted the university's request to prevent enforcement of the order. The board then issued a corrected final order that also imposed a cap on housing with certain housing requirements for undergraduates. The university amended its federal district court complaint to include a due process claim. The court found the board's order was not rationally related to its legitimate purpose and violated due process. The U.S. Court of Appeals, D.C. Circuit, reversed in part, noting that **the zoning board did not violate the university's substantive due process rights by imposing the housing restrictions.** Since students are not a suspect class deserving of heightened protections, the board's zoning regulations would be constitutional if they were rationally related to a legitimate governmental interest. Preservation of the residential character of an adjoining neighborhood was a legitimate governmental interest, and the zoning restrictions were upheld. *George Washington Univ. v. Dist. of Columbia*, 318 F.3d 203 (D.C. Cir. 2003).

The case returned to the district court, which found the final order did not deprive the university of all economic benefits. The university did not show the order diminished the property value. The court held the order did not interfere with the university's reasonable investment-backed expectations because it knew the property was subject to regulation. Because of the potential impact on the neighborhood, the court held the board's order advanced a common good or public purpose. The conditions imposed by the order did not constitute a taking of property, and the complaint was dismissed. *George Washington Univ. v. Dist. of Columbia*, 391 F.Supp.2d 109 (D.D.C. 2005).

◆ *A Massachusetts zoning board's density regulation was invalid as applied to a college campus under state law.*

Boston College (BC) applied to the Newton Board of Aldermen for special permits to construct three buildings. It also sought an exemption from the parking requirements of a local zoning ordinance. The purpose of the construction project was to provide additional space for academic functions, faculty offices and dining facilities. The board denied the application, and BC sued the board in a state court, alleging violation of the Dover Amendment, a state law barring zoning ordinances that prohibit or restrict the use of land for educational purposes. The court held the board unreasonably applied its dimensional and density regulations to the building project, but was reasonably justified in denying a parking waiver. The parties appealed.

The Court of Appeals of Massachusetts noted that **a municipality could reasonably regulate parking, open spaces, and buildings used for educational purposes**. The floor area ratio density requirement of the local zoning ordinance was invalid as applied to the BC middle campus. The entire middle campus was "nonconforming" under the ordinance, with the practical result that enforcement would require BC to always secure a special permit to construct any building there. Strict compliance with the density requirement would thwart an "educational use" and was invalid. The trial court correctly found the denial of a waiver for more parking spaces was unreasonable. The court affirmed the decision. *Trustees of Boston College v. Board of Aldermen of Newton*, 793 N.E.2d 387 (Mass. App. Ct. 2003).

◆ *The U.S. Supreme Court found the Religious Freedom Restoration Act (RFRA) unconstitutional as applied to state actions.*

The case involved a building permit for the enlargement of a church. It was denied on the ground that the church building was part of a historical district. The Supreme Court held that the church could not use the RFRA to obtain the permit because the RFRA proscribed state conduct that the Fourteenth Amendment did not even prohibit. However, the Supreme Court did not address the question of whether the RFRA was unconstitutional in all respects. It limited its analysis to state actions. Accordingly, the RFRA still may provide protections against federal actions. *City of Boerne, Texas v. Flores*, 521 U.S. 507, 117 S.Ct. 2157, 138 L.Ed.2d 624 (1997).

E. State and Local Regulation

In Valley Forge Christian College v. Americans United for Separation of Church and State, *454 U.S. 464, 102 S.Ct. 752, 70 L.Ed.2d 700 (1982), the Supreme Court explained that Courts were not available to taxpayers to vent generalized grievances about government conduct or spending. Litigants were entitled to bring a lawsuit only by showing some actual or threatened injury. As a result, the Court held a Pennsylvania taxpayer group lacked standing to challenge a governmental sale of surplus property to a religious college.*

◆ *Oregon's State Board of Higher Education lacked authority to create a rule prohibiting firearms on university property, as this was a legislative matter.*

The state board of higher education adopted a rule penalizing anyone who used or possessed firearms on institutionally owned or controlled property without express authorization. A firearms group challenged the rule, asserting that the board had exceeded its statutory authority in creating it. According to the challengers, the state legislature had the exclusive authority to regulate firearms. The case reached the Court of Appeals of Oregon, which agreed with the group that the board's rule exceeded its authority under state law. **The board had only the general authority to control and manage its property.** This general authority did not extend so far as to regulate an area that was specifically reserved to the state legislature by statute. As a result, the court invalidated the board's rule. *Oregon Firearms Educ. Foundation v. Board of Higher Educ.*, 244 Or.App. 713, 264 P.3d 160 (Or. Ct. App. 2011).

♦ *Virginia's highest court upheld a regulation banning possession of firearms inside school buildings and at educational events.*

A non-student patronized George Mason University (GMU) resources and libraries. He objected to a GMU regulation prohibiting weapons possession on campus in academic office buildings, student housing, dining facilities, and from on-campus sporting, entertainment and educational events. In a state court action, the non-student claimed the regulation violated the Second Amendment and a corresponding provision of the Virginia Constitution. A state trial court held the regulation was consistent with the requirements of the state and federal Constitutions. It relied on a U.S. Supreme Court ruling that said local laws can legally forbid the carrying of firearms in "sensitive places" such as schools.

On appeal, the Supreme Court of Virginia held the right to carry a firearm is not unlimited. Second Amendment jurisprudence does not ban laws that bar the carrying of firearms in "sensitive places." GMU had some 30,000 students. Another 50,000 high school and elementary students attended GMU summer camps, and 130 attended a preschool on campus. **There was no question that the university qualified as a "sensitive place" under the Supreme Court's ruling.** The regulation did not impose a total ban of weapons on campus, and it was tailored to keep weapons out of places where people congregate and are most vulnerable. As the university was a "sensitive place" and its firearms regulation did not violate the Second Amendment or the corresponding state constitutional provision, the court held for the university. *DiGiacinto v. Rector and Visitors of George Mason Univ.*, 281 Va. 127, 704 S.E.2d 365 (Va. 2011).

♦ *A weapons-control policy banning firearms and other dangerous or illegal weapons from the University of Colorado may be in conflict with state law.*

The University of Colorado enacted a weapons-control policy banning firearms and other dangerous or illegal weapons on any campus without written permission from the chief of police or UC chancellor. Students for Concealed Carry on Campus sued the regents in a state court, claiming the policy violated the state Concealed Carry Act (CCA) and a state constitutional provision. The court dismissed the case, and the case came before the Court of Appeals of Colorado. It noted the CCA allowed permit holders to carry guns in all areas of the state, with a list of exceptions that did not include public universities. **Since the legislature did not indicate an intent to exempt universities from the CCA, the court found the students had a potentially valid claim that the university policy violated the CCA.** Therefore, the trial court had wrongfully dismissed the CCA claims. The court also reversed the decision to dismiss the constitutional claims. It held that the lower court applied the wrong test to determine whether the policy violated the Colorado Constitution. As these claims required further consideration, the case was returned to the trial court. *Students for Concealed Carry on Campus, LLC v. Regents of the Univ. of Colorado*, No. 09CA1230, 2010 WL 1492308 (Colo. Ct. App. 4/15/10).

◆ *Wisconsin taverns that banned drink specials in response to pressure from municipal officials could claim immunity in an antitrust suit.*

Concerned about binge drinking by its students, officials at the University of Wisconsin, Madison pressured city officials to prohibit taverns from using weekend drink specials to lure customers. When officials threatened to pass an ordinance that would ban the practice by all taverns, a group of tavern owners announced at a news conference that they were giving in to the demands and would no longer offer drink specials. Some students at the University of Wisconsin accused the taverns of unlawful price-fixing and brought a state court antitrust action against them. The court held that the antitrust claim was barred based on the city's public health and safety concerns.

Appeal reached the Supreme Court of Wisconsin, which held the taverns were immune to the antitrust claim. **When legislators enacted the antitrust law, they intended to permit municipalities to take anti-competitive actions.** It was reasonable to find the regulation was intended to supersede competition in alcohol sales. Cities can regulate alcohol, as long as doing so serves an important public interest. Municipal immunity extended to the taverns because it was essentially the city that was responsible for the taverns' decision to "voluntarily" end the weekend drink specials. Since the lower courts correctly held for the taverns, the court affirmed the judgment. *Eichenseer v. Madison-Dane County Tavern League*, 748 N.W.2d 154 (Wis. 2008).

◆ *A Texas law violated the First Amendment by requiring private postsecondary schools to obtain a certificate of authority or accreditation before granting degrees or using the name "seminary."*

In an effort to stop "diploma mills," Texas passed a law that barred schools from using the words "college," "university," "seminary" and other specified terms in their names unless they first obtained a certificate of authority from the state. The law also restricted the designations schools could use regarding educational attainment. HEB Ministries, Inc., which operated a school it called the Tyndale Theological Seminary and Bible Institute, was assessed an administrative penalty of $173,000 for violating the state law. In response, it sued the state for a declaratory judgment that the law violated the Establishment Clause and the Free Exercise Clause of the First Amendment.

An intermediate court ruled for the state, and HEB Ministries appealed. The Supreme Court of Texas held **the state law violated the Establishment Clause by requiring private postsecondary institutions to obtain a certificate of authority or accreditation before granting degrees or using the word "seminary" in their names**. In addition, the law violated the Free Exercise Clause because it forced a party to either comply with state standards and compromise its religious mission or forgo the use of restricted terms. The decision of the intermediate court was reversed. *HEB Ministries, Inc. v. Texas Higher Educ. Coordinating Board*, 235 S.W.3d 627 (Tex. 2007).

◆ *The Court of Appeal of California held a community college was required to perform an environmental study before moving a campus shooting range.*

The college proposed a new site for a shooting range used for firearms courses offered in its criminal justice programs. It obtained approval by county and city governments, but a report indicated high levels of lead contamination at the new site. A public interest group alleged violation of state Environmental Quality Act requirements for an environmental study. A state superior court disagreed, finding the site change was not a "project" under the act.

The Court of Appeal of California stated that under the act, **a "project" is defined as "an activity which may cause either a direct physical change in the environment, or reasonably foreseeable indirect physical change in the environment" by a person or agency receiving public funds**. Even though dismantling and removing the range would be accomplished incrementally, these actions were all part of a single project. The college argued the lead abatement aspect of the move was exempt from the act, as the cleanup would cost less than $1 million. The court held that while lead abatement was exempt, this did not relieve the college of its responsibility to conduct an initial study of the project. **The decision was reversed and remanded with instructions for an environmental study.** *Ass'n for a Cleaner Environment v. Yosemite Community College Dist.*, 10 Cal.Rptr.3d 560 (Cal. Ct. App. 2004).

F. Licensing

◆ *Wyoming's amended Private School Licensing Act did not violate the rights of a private educational institution.*

A Wyoming corporation offered post-secondary degrees to students in 17 international learning centers. It operated under a license granted in 2003. In 2006, amendments to the Private School Licensing Act significantly changed state licensing requirements. Prior to the change, institutions could obtain licensure by paying fees and posting a bond. Under amended law, all private post-secondary institutions had to become accredited within five years unless they obtained a good cause extension. The amended law imposed minimal standards for institutions and provided for state investigation and evaluations to implement state rules. An emergency rule required all private post-secondary degree-granting institutions to submit applications to the state and provide proof of an application for accreditation from an association approved by the U.S. Department of Education. The corporation attempted to renew its license under the old law, but the department rejected its application.

Appeal reached the Supreme Court of Wyoming, which denied each of the corporation's constitutional claims. There was no differentiation among new state regulations, as the corporation argued, defeating an equal protection claim. As the lower court found, the new law did not create classes of institutions that were accredited or not. Instead, the law required all trade, correspondence, distance education, technical, vocational, business or other private schools to be accredited. There was no improper delegation of legislative authority based on the requirement of accreditation by an approved association. The amended law was not so vague as to be constitutionally void. The court held that **the state had authority to regulate private institutions under its police powers**. As none of the corporation's arguments had merit, the court held for the department. *Newport Int'l Univ. v. State of Wyoming, Dep't of Educ.*, 186 P.3d 382 (Wyo. 2008).

◆   *The Michigan Department of Education could deny a license to operate to the owner of a trade school teaching casino gambling.*

A Michigan resident applied to the proprietary school unit of the department of education for a license to operate a private trade school teaching casino gambling. The board denied his application because gaming was considered criminal behavior in Michigan. The applicant appealed to a Michigan trial court. The trial court reversed, and the board of education appealed to the Court of Appeals of Michigan. The court of appeals noted that public policy did not completely prohibit casino gambling as evidenced by the legislature's decision to legalize millionaire parties and to allow casino gambling on Indian reservations. On further appeal, the Supreme Court of Michigan reversed. It adopted the dissenting opinion from the lower court, which stated that **licensing the proposed school would violate public policy**. If the school were allowed to teach casino gambling, it would be teaching behavior that was currently defined as illegal under Michigan law. *Michigan Gaming Institute v. State Board of Educ.*, 547 N.W.2d 882 (Mich. 1996).

◆   *A corporation that provided review courses for nursing school graduates had to pay an annual renewal licensing fee for each location.*

The corporation offered courses that prepared nursing school graduates for state certification exams. It operated at five different locations in the state. The review courses were held in hotel meeting rooms, college auditoriums or hospital conference rooms. The California legislature modified the Private Postsecondary and Vocational Education Reform Act to increase the annual renewal fee for nondegree-granting institutions from $225 to a range of $600 to $1,200, depending on size. The corporation made a single $1,200 payment but refused to make a separate payment for each of its course sites.

A lawsuit arose, and a California trial court found that a separate fee could be charged for each location. The California Court of Appeal, First District, noted that because the corporation's educational sites were 50 miles from corporate headquarters and were held in places such as hotel conference rooms, they were neither branches nor satellites subject to separate annual fees under the act. However, since the legislature provided that each site be inspected by the governing council, the court inferred a legislative intent to require separate annual fees for each site. **As long as the governing council used some "reasonable method" of estimating the administrative costs of the entire program, its annual fee interpretation was reasonable.** Thus, the court of appeal required the corporation to pay an annual fee for each site. *RN Review for Nurses, Inc. v. State*, 28 Cal.Rptr.2d 354 (Cal. Ct. App. 1994).

◆   *A board for community colleges should have provided an occupational school with a hearing prior to terminating the school's license.*

A private Colorado occupational school was licensed to do business by the State Board for Community Colleges and Occupational Educations. A new statute revised licensing requirements, and the school was required to renew its license. The board's vice president rejected the school's application because it had not employed an independent accountant or utilized accepted accounting procedures as required by the new statute. The school filed a 42 U.S.C. § 1983 action in a Colorado district court against the vice president and the board. It alleged that both had failed to provide a hearing prior to terminating the school's license and had failed to provide an impartial tribunal.

A trial court determined that neither the board nor its vice president could be sued under 42 U.S.C. § 1983 and dismissed the case. The Colorado Court of Appeals found that the board was a state regulatory body that was entitled to immunity from suits for damages. Next, the court determined that **the vice president's failure to grant the school a pre-deprivation hearing was not a clear violation of its constitutional rights**. The vice president therefore had immunity on the claim for damages under Section 1983. However, the board's refusal to grant the school a pre-deprivation hearing potentially violated its statutory rights. On remand, the school could sue for injunctive relief. *National Camera, Inc. v. Sanchez*, 832 P.2d 960 (Colo. Ct. App. 1991).

G. Desegregation

◆ *A longstanding court battle to end racial segregation in Alabama colleges and universities could not be used to force changes in state K-12 funding.*

The suit was filed in 1981, when a group of black citizens claimed the state perpetuated a segregated university system. They said admissions standards at historically white institutions disqualified disproportionate numbers of black applicants. The citizens claimed historically black institutions were plagued by unfair funding and facility policies. In 1991, a federal district court ordered the state to encourage greater racial integration at its colleges and universities. Four years later, it entered a decree that ordered numerous additional changes to the state's higher education policies. Among other things, it required more flexible admissions policies and increased integration of faculty and administration at all state colleges and universities. The court also required the state to increase its funding of historically black institutions. Over the next eight years, the state and the plaintiffs "worked tirelessly" to make the changes required by the court. From 1990-2004, the state increased its annual funding of higher education by $340 million. During this time, undergraduate and graduate degrees awarded to black students increased by over 96%. In 2009, the plaintiffs filed a motion to require the state to provide better funding for K-12 schools. They sought an order invalidating property tax limitations imposed by the state constitution.

The plaintiffs said a funding crisis in the state's K-12 schools resulted in segregation at its colleges and universities. The district court denied the motion, and the plaintiffs appealed. On appeal, the U.S. Court of Appeals, Eleventh Circuit, explained that the case had always been about segregation in the state's higher education system. The plaintiffs' motion was about reforming the state's K-12 school funding system. Because the motion raised a claim relating to school finance rather than desegregation, it could not be pursued. The plaintiffs tried to link the inadequacy of K-12 funding with segregation at higher levels by proposing a chain of causation. Property tax limitations resulted in underfunded public schools, leading to the diversion of higher education funds to lower education. This diversion resulted in higher tuition rates and decreased black student enrollment at state colleges and universities. **Under *U.S. v. Fordice*, below, race-neutral state policies governing higher education can**

be challenged under the Constitution if they are traceable to a system of segregation. The court found the asserted relationship between the underfunding of the state's K-12 schools and segregation in Alabama colleges and universities was too attenuated and based on too many unpredictable premises. The judgment for the state was affirmed. *Knight v. Alabama*, 476 F.3d 1219 (11th Cir. 2007).

◆   *Where a state perpetuates policies and practices that can be traced to a segregative system and that have segregative effects, the policies will be considered unconstitutional unless there is sound educational justification for them and it is not practical to eliminate them.*

Mississippi maintained a dual system of public education at the university level – one set of universities for whites, and another set for blacks. In 1981, the State Board of Trustees issued "Mission Statements" to remedy this, classifying the three flagship historically white institutions (HWI) as "comprehensive" universities, redesignating one of the historically black institutions (HBI) as an "urban" university and characterizing the rest as "regional" institutions. However, the universities remained racially identifiable. A federal court found that state policies need merely be racially neutral, developed in good faith, and not contribute to the racial identifiability of each institution. It held that Mississippi was currently fulfilling its duty to desegregate. The U.S. Court of Appeals, Fifth Circuit, affirmed.

On appeal, the U.S. Supreme Court held that the district court had applied the wrong legal standard in ruling that Mississippi had brought itself into compliance with the Equal Protection Clause. **If a state perpetuates policies and practices traceable to its prior dual system that continue to have segregative effects, and such policies are without sound educational justification and can be practicably eliminated, the policies violate the Equal Protection Clause.** This is true even if the state has abolished the legal requirement that the races be separated and has established neutral policies. The proper inquiry is whether existing racial identifiability is attributable to the state. Applying the proper standard, several surviving aspects of Mississippi's prior dual system were constitutionally suspect. First, the use of higher minimum ACT composite scores at the HWIs, along with the state's refusal to consider high school grade performance was suspect. Second, the unnecessary duplication of programs at HBIs and HWIs was suspect. Third, the mission statements' reflection of previous policies to perpetuate racial separation was suspect. Finally, the state's policy of operating eight universities had to be examined to determine if it was educationally justifiable. *U.S. v. Fordice*, 505 U.S. 717, 112 S.Ct. 2727, 120 L.Ed.2d 575 (1992). On remand, a federal court **entered a remedial decree prohibiting the state from maintaining remnants of the prior segregated system** and mandating specific relief in areas of admissions and funding. However, the court refused to order the relief requested by the complaining parties, which would significantly increase the number of African-Americans accepted for regular admission at state universities. The complaining parties claimed that the district court order's reliance on a summer remedial program to boost African-American admissions was inappropriate, and the parties appealed to the Fifth Circuit. The court held the district court's order affirming the elimination of many remedial courses had to be reconsidered, along with its finding that use of college entrance scores as a criterion for scholarships was not traceable to the illegal system of segregation. The court remanded for clarification the status of a proposal to merge two universities to eliminate unnecessary program duplication, as well as questions of increasing the other-race presence at two HBIs and issues of accreditation and funding. The court affirmed many aspects of the district court decision as consistent with the *Fordice* decision, significantly affirming its decision to maintain admissions standards that ensured educational soundness. *Ayers v. Fordice*, 111 F.3d 1183 (5th Cir. 1997).

II. ACCREDITATION

Regional and other accrediting institutions have been sued by private schools upon withdrawal of accreditation. The cases suggest: 1) actions of accrediting institutions do not constitute "state action" triggering due process requirements, 2) a school may maintain a breach of contract lawsuit against an accrediting institution if the institution fails to follow its own rules and procedures, and 3) if an accrediting institution's procedures are fair, its decision to revoke accreditation will likely be upheld.

A. Grants of Accreditation

◆   *Where an accreditation foundation's denial of accreditation to a college of art and design was supported by substantial evidence, it did not qualify as arbitrary or unreasonable.*

In 1995, Savannah College of Art & Design sought accreditation for its interior design program from the Foundation for Interior Design Education Research. Although a team of evaluators' report generally praised the program, it recommended the denial of accreditation. The foundation's board of trustees accepted the recommendation. Savannah College appealed, and a second on-site evaluation also recommended denial of accreditation for poor student achievement. Believing it had been treated unfairly, Savannah turned to the foundation's appeals panel, which determined that the denial of accreditation was supported by substantial evidence and consistent with other schools' accreditation reports. After the college threatened legal intervention, the foundation sued for a declaration that its decision to reject accreditation was lawful. In response, the college filed counterclaims against it. A federal court granted pretrial judgment to the foundation and dismissed all of the counterclaims. The school appealed to the Sixth Circuit.

The court held the foundation's denial of accreditation was neither arbitrary nor discriminatory. Savannah College argued that the foundation's method of evaluation deviated from the usual evaluative process and was therefore discriminatory. The court agreed that the process in this case differed, but to the college's favor. The foundation would not normally send a second evaluation team, but it did so in this case to ensure fairness. Savannah's final argument claimed the foundation acted arbitrarily because the college's interior design program closely resembled other accredited programs. The court disagreed and affirmed the judgment, finding the foundation's decision was based on substantial evidence. *Foundation for Interior Design Educ. Research v. Savannah College of Art & Design*, 244 F.3d 521 (6th Cir. 2001).

◆   *A federal court refused to force the American Bar Association (ABA) to provisionally accredit a law school.*

After a religious university acquired a non-accredited law school, it applied for provisional accreditation from the ABA. The ABA rejected the application. The following year, the university applied again, and again was rejected. A group of graduates, students and instructors then sued the ABA seeking a preliminary injunction to force provisional accreditation. The university also filed a third application for provisional accreditation. A Florida federal district court refused to grant the injunction, finding no evidence that irreparable harm would befall the plaintiffs if the injunction was not granted. While the third application was pending, **graduates still could be admitted to practice in other states, and they could seek a waiver of the 12-month rule on sitting for the Florida Bar Exam** from the state supreme court. *Staver v. American Bar Ass'n*, 169 F.Supp.2d 1372 (M.D. Fla. 2001).

◆   *An Oregon law allowing certain schools to be exempted from requirements that out-of-state schools were not exempted from, was struck down.*

A private Washington university with a branch campus in Oregon was accredited by the Northwest Association of Schools and Colleges (NASC). Following NASC accreditation, the Oregon Office of Educational Policy and Planning (OEPP) continued to review non-Oregon schools every three years. The statute provided that "no school ... shall confer ... any degree ... without first having submitted the requirements for such degree to the [OEPP] and having obtained the approval of the director." However, an amendment exempted Oregon schools in good standing with the NASC from OEPP review. The university filed suit in an Oregon circuit court, seeking a declaration that the statute violated the Commerce Clause. The circuit court held for the university and severed a portion of the amendment. The court of appeals affirmed but invalidated the exemption in its entirety. The Oregon Supreme Court allowed the university's petition for review solely on the issue of remedy.

The university contended that the entire amendment had been improperly invalidated. The supreme court disagreed, ruling that the statute as severed was not capable of being executed in accordance with legislative intent. The legislature had intended both to continue the exemption from OEPP authority for Oregon schools that were members of the NASC and to remove the exemption from OEPP authority for out-of-state schools, even if those schools were NASC members. However, the dominant intent of the amendment was to ensure that Oregon branch campuses of the out-of-state schools had the same level of faculty and facilities as their main campuses. **As partial severance would subject these out-of-state schools to lesser scrutiny, the court ordered the amendment severed in its entirety.** The court of appeals' ruling was affirmed. *City Univ. v. Office of Educ. Policy*, 885 P.2d 701 (Or. 1994).

B. Claims of Fraud

◆ *A Georgia court refused to certify a class action by students who alleged fraud by a private university, because it found their claims required a case-by-case review.*

According to the students, the education they received was "not worth the cost." They claimed the university engaged in fraudulent recruiting practices. Although the university was continuously accredited during the time in question, the students asserted that the accreditation was obtained through false representations including inflated employment rates for university graduates. They filed a state court action against the university and its parent corporation, seeking damages because they had paid tuition and incurred loans but were unable to find employment in their respective fields of study. The court found no reason to certify the case as a class action, and on appeal, the Court of Appeals of Georgia agreed. **The students had introduced a great deal of individualized evidence that required a case-by-case review.** For this reason, the court found their claims not suitable for class certification. As determining whether each student was adversely affected by some aspect of the university's operation would "require a separate mini-trial," the court affirmed the judgment denying class certification. *Diallo v. American Intercontinental Univ.*, 301 Ga.App. 299, 687 S.E.2d 278 (Ga. Ct. App. 2009).

◆ *A law school graduate who could not take a bar exam after attending an unaccredited Massachusetts law school could not proceed with fraud claims.*

At the time of the student's admission, the school was not accredited by the American Bar Association (ABA). This meant graduates could not sit for a state bar examination. Upon learning that the ABA was recommending a provisional accreditation, the school sent prospective students a letter expressing confidence that accreditation was forthcoming. But a disclaimer was included in the law school catalogue, which stated that it did not represent it would be approved prior to the graduation of any matriculating student. The ABA denied the school accreditation near the time the student enrolled.

Further attempts to gain accreditation failed, and the student was unable to transfer to another school. He graduated but was unable to sit for a state bar examination due to the school's lack of accreditation. The student sued the school for fraudulent misrepresentation in a federal district court. The case reached the U.S. Court of Appeals, First Circuit, which held that to prevail, **the student had to show he relied on a false representation and acted on it to his detriment. He also had to show his reliance on the false statement was reasonable.** But the student did neither. His claim that he relied on statements regarding accreditation was contradicted by his transfer attempt after the school indicated its difficulties gaining accreditation. The student's transfer application strongly suggested he did not believe the assurances regarding accreditation. Even if the student did rely on the statements of assurance regarding the school's chances at accreditation, reliance was not reasonable. As a result, the court affirmed a lower court judgment for the law school. *Rodi v. Southern New England School of Law*, 532 F.3d 11 (1st Cir. 2008).

◆   *A university's failure to gain accreditation for its Master of Social Work program did not violate students' due process rights.*

Governor's State University instituted a Master of Social Work Program in 1997. Three years later, university officials informed graduate students enrolled in the program that the National Council of Social Work Education had denied the university's application for accreditation. As a result, graduates were not permitted to sit for a licensing examination in Illinois. Graduating students discussed the accreditation problem with university officials at a board meeting. Additional students remained outside, protesting. A month later, graduate students were invited to an alumni fundraising dinner. The university limited the number of entrances and exits and permitted the students to picket only in the vestibule area. Security guards removed the students from the premises and refused to allow them to re-enter the grounds.

A group of students sued the university, its president and trustees in a federal district court for due process and speech rights violations. The court held for the university, and the students appealed. The U.S. Court of Appeals, Seventh Circuit, held the students did not show any arbitrary government action in violation of the Due Process Clause. **While the university was responsible for ensuring its programs were accredited, the students had adequate remedies at law to resolve their complaints.** The trustees were not involved in the dinner event and did not prevent the protesters from attending. The university president did not retaliate against the students for their protests. The actions of security guards were merely a response to overcrowding. The court held summary judgment was properly entered for the university and its officials. *Galdikas v. Fagan*, 342 F.3d 684 (7th Cir. 2003).

C. Withdrawal of Accreditation

◆   *A Pennsylvania immunity statute did not block claims against a community college that lost its certification.*

Students attending a police training program at a Pennsylvania community college learned the college had lost its certification and that their credits were jeopardized. A group of students filed a lawsuit against the college for breach of contract, breach of warranty, and violation of the state Unfair Trade Practices and Consumer Protection Law (UTPCPL). According to the community college, the UTPCPL did not apply to local governmental entities, and it was immune to any UTPCPL claim. The court denied pretrial judgment for the community college on the UTPCPL claims. It held the immunity statute was intended to block claims based in tort, not contract claims such as the ones the students were advancing. Appeal reached the Supreme Court of Pennsylvania, which agreed with the students that the governmental immunity afforded by the statute did not extend to all statutory causes of action. Instead, **the court held the statute granted immunity based on conduct that caused "injury to a person or property."** These terms indicated to the court an intent to grant immunity with respect to tort claims. As a result, the court returned the case to the trial court for further proceedings. *Meyer v. Community College of Beaver County*, 606 Pa. 539, 2 A.3d 499 (Pa. 2010).

◆ *A small college in Tennessee failed in its attempt to reverse an accrediting agency's decision to remove its accreditation.*

Hiwassee College lost its accreditation by the Southern Association of Colleges and Schools (SACS) based on its troubled financial condition. The college sued the SACS in a federal district court, claiming that SACS failed to meet its own requirements relating to removal of accreditation. It asserted that SACS denied it due process of law under the Higher Education Act (HEA) and the Due Process Clause of the Fifth Amendment. The court held the SACS was entitled to judgment as a matter of law, and the college appealed.

The U.S. Court of Appeals, Eleventh Circuit, held the college could not bring a claim against SACS under the HEA statute. **Nothing indicated Congress intended to create a private right of action in the HEA. The court held the SACS was not a government actor and therefore was not required to comply with Fifth Amendment due process requirements.** Nor did SACS fail to meet any common law duty to provide the college with due process in connection with the accreditation decision. The college never asserted that it was in compliance with the agency's accreditation criteria. The judgment was affirmed. *Hiwassee College, Inc. v. Southern Ass'n of Colleges and Schools*, No. 07-13033, 2008 WL 1701694 (11th Cir. 4/14/08).

III. CONSTRUCTION AND OUTSIDE CONTRACTS

◆ *A New Jersey court revived a claim against a company that provided snow and ice removal services to Rider University (RU).*

A student slipped and fell on a patch of black ice after leaving a piano lesson on campus. She was about 16 feet from the building she had exited. A private contractor was responsible for clearing building entrances and the perimeter of campus buildings to a distance of eight feet. Typically, arrangements to remove snow and ice beyond the eight-foot perimeter were made informally by the contractor and RU. An RU facilities director said he told the contractor that de-icing was needed in various areas of the campus beyond the eight-foot perimeter on the morning of the student's fall. He said this included the area where she later fell and that the contractor had previously agreed to provide de-icing for the entire campus when conditions were icy.

The student sued the contractor in a state court for negligence based on its failure to remove the black ice. In response, the contractor filed a third-party complaint against RU for contribution and indemnification. RU sought dismissal under a state law immunity provision, but the court instead granted the contractor pretrial judgment. A New Jersey Appellate Division Court reversed the decision, finding that the lower court had to resolve a number of fact issues. **The case was returned to the lower court so it could determine if the area where the student fell was within the scope of the oral agreement.** It would also have to consider if the ice was reasonably observable and whether the time period between notice of the need for additional services and the fall was sufficient to allow de-icing. *Besner v. UNICCO Service Co.*, No. A-4804-07T2, 2009 WL 483225 (N.J. Super. App. Div. 1/29/09).

◆   *A federal district court refused to find an American university breached a contract to enter into an affiliation agreement with an Israeli college.*

In 1994, the college began partnering with American institutions to offer courses at a campus in Israel. It began a search to replace New England College. The search led it to Southern New Hampshire University (SNHU), which initially decided not to go forward with the affiliation. Two years later, negotiations proceeded to a point where the parties signed affiliation and academic supervision agreements. The agreements outlined the responsibilities of each party with respect to curriculum, faculty, admission criteria and other details. They also outlined contractual obligations. The president of SNHU signed the documents, and the Israeli college president then signed them. Five months later, SNHU's president decided not to move ahead with the affiliation. The college then sued SNHU for breach of contract in a federal district court.

SNHU claimed that the parties had a memo of understanding but not a contract. The court denied the college pretrial judgment. **There were disputed facts about what happened at meetings leading up to the signing of the two documents, and it was unclear whether an agreement to enter into a binding contract was conditioned on SNHU's completion of due diligence.** *Israel College-Educational Horizons, Ltd. v. Southern New Hampshire Univ.*, No. 05-cv-392-JD, 2008 WL 187606 (D.N.H. 1/17/08).

◆   *A university that did a thorough environmental impact evaluation of a construction project did not have to file an environmental impact statement with New York state officials.*

A New York state university planned five separate campus housing projects, including a 116-unit building for which it filed a full environmental assessment form that was supported by an environmental site assessment report. A lawsuit nevertheless ensued, seeking to compel the university to file an environmental impact statement and seeking a temporary injunction to prevent construction until such statement was filed. The New York Supreme Court, Appellate Division, ruled that the university did not have to file an environmental impact statement because its thorough study of the environmental effects of construction concluded that there would not be an adverse impact on wetlands, cultural resources, groundwater, air quality, solid waste, removal of vegetation, wildlife or open space such that the project should be stopped. **In light of the university's thorough evaluation, the project could proceed.** *Forman v. Trustees of State Univ. of New York*, 757 N.Y.S.2d 180 (N.Y. App. Div. 2003).

◆   *Alaska's highest court held a state university was entitled to money from a contractor who underbid a project and then sought to recoup its losses as additional work.*

The University of Alaska solicited bids for fixing a drainage problem involving an access road and gravel pad surfaces at a research facility. **It accepted the lowest bid but then experienced problems with the contractor.** The contractor first obtained a one-week extension, then sought approval for extra materials, extra work and the payment of additional money. The university rejected the claims. When the contractor failed to finish the project on time, the ground froze, and it was unable to complete the project. Both the university and the contractor sought financial reimbursement, and a hearing officer determined that the contractor underbid the project, then sought to recover its losses as additional work. However, the university also owed some additional monies to the contractor. The case reached the Supreme Court of Alaska, which largely upheld the hearing officer's determinations. It refused, however, to grant the university liquidated damages because the university had entered into an agreement with the contractor's bonding company regarding the hiring of another contractor to finish the project. *Lakloey, Inc. v. Univ. of Alaska*, No. 5-9690, 2002 WL 1732561 (Alaska 2002).

◆ *Fact issues prevented a New York court from granting pretrial judgment to a university on a breach of contract claim involving an electrical contractor.*

A New York university hired an electrical contractor to perform work on a biomolecular medicine and residential tower. Shortly after the contract was signed, the project fell behind schedule. The electrical contractor blamed the construction manager and inadequate security, which led to vandalism and theft, forcing the electrical contractor to redo some work. Eventually, a lawsuit was filed, with the electrical contractor asserting that the university breached the contract by failing to pay for work performed, and the university asserting that it had to correct and complete work the electrical contractor was supposed to finish. A New York court granted pretrial judgment to the university, but the Supreme Court, Appellate Division, reversed. **Evidence existed indicating that the electrical contractor performed its obligations under the contract.** The court remanded the case for further proceedings. *F. Garofalo Electric Co. v. New York Univ.*, 754 N.Y.S.2d 227 (N.Y. App. Div. 2002).

◆ *West Virginia's highest court set forth five factors to be used in determining whether a construction project is a public project.*

West Virginia University and the West Virginia University Foundation (a private, nonprofit corporation) began planning and developing a layout for the construction of a building to be known as the University Services Center. After a bidding process, a developer agreed to build the center at its own cost and risk. The foundation would then purchase the site and lease the building to the university. When an affiliation of construction trades sued for a declaration that the proposed construction was a public project governed by state wage and competitive bidding laws, the university and the nonprofit foundation moved for pretrial judgment. A state court granted the motion, finding that the foundation was not a state agency, and its connection to the university did not convert the construction into a public project.

On appeal, the West Virginia Supreme Court of Appeals listed five factors to be used in determining whether a construction project is a public project. It held **the lower court record was not sufficiently developed to determine whether public funds had been used on the project**. Further, the building was now completed, and there was no indication of wage violations. *Affiliated Construction Trades Foundation v. Univ. of West Virginia Board of Trustees*, 557 S.E.2d 863 (W. Va. 2001).

◆ *A university could not recover from a contractor for an explosion and fire several years after the construction of a power plant.*

The University of Colorado contracted with a construction company to build a co-generation power facility on its Boulder campus. The contract contained a provision stating that **acceptance of the work would constitute a release of all claims against the company**, and also contained a 12-month warranty period. However, the university purchased an extended five-year warranty from the subcontractor that furnished the gas turbine engines for the facility. After the facility had been in operation for three and a half years, a combination of events caused a backup in one engine, resulting in an explosion and fire. The university sued the contractor and subcontractor for breach of contract, breach of warranty, negligence and strict liability. A state court ruled for the defendants, and the Colorado Court of Appeals affirmed. Here, the contractor's warranty and the release clearly protected it from liability. Also, with respect to the subcontractor, the jury's ruling was not unsupported by the evidence. *Regents of the Univ. of Colorado v. Harbert Construction Co.*, 51 P.3d 1037 (Colo. Ct. App. 2001).

◆ *The U.S. Supreme Court held a choice of law clause in a construction contract entered into by Stanford University superseded arbitration rights found in the Federal Arbitration Act.*

An electrical contractor contracted with a California university to install conduits. The contract contained a clause in which the parties agreed to arbitrate disputes relating to the contract. The contract also contained a choice-of-law clause that stated that it would be governed by the law of the place of the project's location. A dispute arose concerning overtime compensation, and the contractor made a formal request for arbitration. The university sued the contractor in a California trial court for fraud and breach of contract. **The contractor claimed that it was entitled to arbitration under the contract and the Federal Arbitration Act (FAA).** The court granted the university's motion to stay arbitration under a California statute that permits a stay when arbitration is the subject of pending court action. The contractor appealed to the California Court of Appeal, which affirmed the trial court's decision. The court of appeal acknowledged that although the contract affected interstate commerce, the California statute applied because of the contractual choice-of-law clause. The California Supreme Court denied the contractor's petition for discretionary review, but the U.S. Supreme Court agreed to hear its appeal.

On appeal, the contractor reiterated its argument that the court of appeal's ruling on the choice-of-law clause deprived it of its federally guaranteed right to arbitration under the FAA. The Supreme Court ruled that **the FAA did not confer a general right to compel arbitration. Rather, it guaranteed the right to arbitrate according to the manner provided for in the parties' contract.** The court of appeal had correctly found that the contract incorporated California law. The FAA was not undermined by the state law that permitted a stay of arbitration. The Court affirmed the court of appeal's decision for the university. *Volt Information Sciences v. Board of Trustees of Leland Stanford Junior Univ.*, 489 U.S. 468, 109 S.Ct. 1248, 103 L.Ed.2d 488 (1989).

IV. CAMPUS SAFETY AND SECURITY

A. Search and Seizure

The Fourth Amendment to the U.S. Constitution prohibits unreasonable searches and seizures by states, including state institutions of higher education. A "seizure" does not occur every time police stop and question a person. Officers may use reliable reports from staff to make investigatory stops.

◆   *A federal appeals court upheld a drug testing program for students who were training to perform safety-sensitive jobs at a Missouri technical college.*

The college's mandatory drug screening policy required students in certain areas to take a urine test or face withdrawal. A number of students sued college officials in a federal court, claiming the policy violated the Fourth Amendment. The court granted their request for a temporary order, barring the college from implementing the policy. On appeal, **the U.S. Court of Appeals, Eighth Circuit, held the public has an interest in deterring drug use among students who are engaged in programs that pose a significant safety risk**. It found the college's testing methods were relatively non-intrusive, as testing was conducted in accordance with federal regulations and not done randomly. Testing did not reveal any medical condition beyond the presence of certain drugs, and results were not shared with law enforcement agencies. As the students did not show they were likely to succeed in the case, the court vacated the temporary order. *Barrett v. Claycomb*, 705 F.3d 315 (8th Cir. 2013).

◆   *Massachusetts private college security officers could inspect dorm rooms and turn over items they found to the police. But the police were not allowed to use such items in a criminal case if they lacked a warrant or student consent.*

While inspecting a dorm for safety compliance, a college security officer smelled marijuana. He entered a room and saw drugs and paraphernalia in plain sight. The security officer called municipal police and took them to the room. The student consented to a police search, and they charged him with drug crimes. During the same inspection, college security officers saw marijuana and a pipe in plain view in a second student's room. They called the police and took the officers into this student's room. Later, the police obtained a warrant and searched the room. Based on their findings, they charged the student with drug possession. A state court granted requests by both students to suppress the evidence in their criminal cases. On appeal, the state court of appeals held the evidence could be used against the first student but not the second.

Massachusetts law bound the students to a college handbook provision by which they had consented to security officers entering and inspecting their rooms. In the first student's case, private security officers had simply shown the police what they had discovered in plain view. But **the warrant for searching the second student's room described what the police officers had seen – not what the college security officers saw**. This made the search warrant invalid. The court held the evidence against the second student could not be used against him. *Comwlth. v. Bair*, 82 Mass.App.Ct. 1107 (Mass. App. Ct. 2012).

◆   *A Texas student was unable to show a search by University of Texas at San Antonio (UTSA) campus police violated his constitutional rights.*

A UTSA officer smelled marijuana in an apartment. From the hallway, he saw marijuana on a table in a room. The officer conducted a protective sweep of the apartment. In a bedroom, he saw drug paraphernalia and a lockbox. After the student's parents arrived, the student consented to a search. Police found a handgun, ammunition, a stun gun, cocaine and $517. In criminal proceedings, the UTSA officer said he saw marijuana on a table in the student's room from the hallway. In response, the student said this would have been impossible. But photographs showed it was possible to see the table from where the officer stood. The student was convicted of possession with intent to deliver cocaine. On appeal, he argued the evidence seized from the search should have been suppressed and excluded from the case. But the Court of Appeals of Texas held that **the jury was entitled to determine which witnesses were the most believable.** Marijuana odor alone might not have been enough to justify a warrantless search. The court held it would defer to the jury verdict, as the jury had relied on the testimony it found the most believable. *Clark v. Texas*, No. 04-10-00540-CR, 2012 WL 3025685 (Tex. Ct. App. 7/25/12).

◆   *A federal court upheld the seizure of marijuana and drug paraphernalia from a student's dorm room after safety inspectors observed the contraband.*

Indiana University student housing contracts allowed university personnel to enter dorm rooms to perform safety inspections. During a routine health and safety inspection, two resident specialists saw a clear tube of what looked like marijuana in plain view on a desk in a student dorm room. They called university police, who saw the container on the desk and detected a strong odor of marijuana. An officer entered the room and confiscated the container. When a resident specialist continued on with the safety inspection, she found what looked like a large marijuana plant inside a closet. She told one of the officers, who re-entered the room and saw the plant. The officer then obtained a search warrant. After further searching of the room, the officer seized an additional 89 grams of marijuana and assorted drug-related paraphernalia.

The student was arrested, and two days later he was suspended from school. He sued the university in a federal court, claiming the search violated his Fourth Amendment rights. The court disagreed, finding **the resident specialists went into his room solely to perform a health and safety inspection, not to gather evidence for a criminal proceeding.** Once the specialists lawfully entered his room and saw marijuana, they were justified in allowing access by the university police. *Medlock v. Trustees of Indiana Univ.*, No. 1-11-cv-00977-TWP-DKL, 2011 WL 4068453 (S.D. Ind. 9/13/11).

◆   *A Pennsylvania university avoided liability for civil rights violations based on the security stop of a high school student who resembled a criminal suspect.*

Temple University officers stopped a high school student who fit the description of a shooting suspect. They took him to the police station, where he was arrested and charged with attempted murder, aggravated assault and firearms offenses. He spent time in jail and missed his senior prom and graduation. After the student was cleared, he sued the university for violation of his constitutional rights under the Fourth and Fourteenth Amendments. Among other things, he claimed that Temple University officers intentionally provided false information to the Philadelphia Police Department and failed to investigate his alibi. A federal court dismissed the lawsuit, holding that **Temple University was a municipal subdivision that could not be held responsible for the conduct of its employees on vicarious liability grounds**. The student did not allege that the Temple officers acted at the direction of a Temple official or pursuant to a policy or custom. *Franks v. Temple Univ.*, No. 11-879, 2011 WL 1562598 (E.D. Pa. 4/26/11).

◆ *A community college in New Mexico did not violate the constitutional rights of a former student when it briefly detained him.*

After being disenrolled by the college, the student went to the financial aid office, where he got into a heated argument with an employee. Before he left campus, several officials detained him and questioned him about the argument. After the questioning, the student left campus without further incident. He sued the community college and several officials in a federal district court for Fourth Amendment violations. He added a breach of contract claim based on the decision to disenroll him. The court dismissed the complaint, finding no unreasonable seizure. The student appealed to the U.S. Court of Appeals, Tenth Circuit. According to the court, **the brief detention was reasonable under the circumstances**. Thus, the district court had properly dismissed the Fourth Amendment claim. The court also affirmed the district court's decision to decline jurisdiction over the state law contract claim. *Reyes v. Cent. New Mexico Community College*, 410 Fed.Appx. 134 (10th Cir. 2011).

◆ *Massachusetts roommates who consented to the search of their dorm room by a campus police officer could not later claim to have been illegally searched.*

After a report that one of the roommates had been bullying other students and "waving a knife around," campus police went to his dorm room. An officer told the roommates he was there because of a report of a gun in the room. He found a plastic gun under the bed. Upon further searching, two knives and a spiked martial arts weapon were found. The roommates signed *Miranda* waiver forms and forms consenting to further searching of the room, which yielded cocaine, psilocybin and marijuana. The roommates were arrested and charged with various drug crimes. A trial judge granted their motion to suppress evidence retrieved during the search. The officer's initial entry into the dorm room was held unlawful because he did not wait for an invitation to enter.

On appeal, the Court of Appeals of Massachusetts found the officer's entry into the room was authorized under the college's conditions of residency. **The officer did not need a warrant or consent to enter the room, as he acted in reliance on a credible report from two students that one of the roommates had a knife.** Campus police did not act in a manner offensive to the dignity of the roommates. They voluntarily consented to the search of the room. As the request to conduct a search was not ambiguous, and they were old enough to know they could have refused to allow a search, the lower court's decision was reversed. *Comwlth. v. Carr*, 918 N.E.2d 847 (Mass. App. Ct. 2009).

◆ *A mentally disabled African-American woman did not prove she was unlawfully excluded from a Northwestern University library.*

Although not affiliated with the university, the woman used its law school library to research disability law. After the law school revoked her permission to use its facilities, she researched elsewhere. The woman accused a student in a computer lab of assaulting her, and she was escorted from the building. Later, she claimed campus security told her to leave another library. In a federal district court action against Northwestern, the woman claimed race and disability discrimination under federal laws. After the court dismissed her case, she appealed to the U.S. Court of Appeals, Seventh Circuit. It found the claims relied on laws requiring proof of differential treatment based on race or disability. **But as the woman did not allege any facts that could reasonably lead to the belief that the university excluded her on either basis, the district court was correct in dismissing the action.** *Gillard v. Northwestern Univ.*, 366 Fed.Appx. 686 (7th Cir. 2010).

◆ *A "seizure" does not occur every time police stop and question a person. Officers may rely on trustworthy reports from staff to make investigatory stops.*

An African-American library patron was using a computer in a library at the New Jersey Institute of Technology. An assistant librarian called the security department to report him for taking a stapler. The patron agreed to answer questions by the police and let them search his bag. After they did not find the stapler, the patron left the building. He sued the officers, institute and library staff in a federal district court for constitutional rights violations. The court held for the institute and staff, and the patron appealed to the U.S. Court of Appeals, Third Circuit. While he admitted consenting to the questioning and the search of his bag, he claimed the consent was invalid because one officer failed to inform him that he had a right to refuse the search. The court found no such requirement. The patron's consent was valid, as the investigation lasted only seven minutes, took place in public, and was not threatening or intimidating. The district court had properly held that no jury could have found a Fourth Amendment violation. The U.S. Supreme Court has held a seizure does not occur every time police approach someone to ask a few questions.

The court found the patron obviously did not feel coerced or threatened into remaining in the library or responding to questions. After the brief search of his bag, he walked out of the library without responding to the officer's request for his name. In any event, **officers may rely on a trustworthy secondhand report and need not base an investigatory stop on personal observation**. The court rejected the patron's additional arguments and affirmed the judgment. *Only v. Cyr*, 205 Fed.Appx. 947 (3d Cir. 2006).

◆ *The U.S. Supreme Court held a school search must be reasonable at its inception, and not overly intrusive under the circumstances.*

A New Jersey high school teacher found two girls smoking in the lavatory in violation of school rules. She brought them to the assistant vice principal's office where one of the girls admitted smoking in the lavatory. The other denied even being a smoker. The assistant vice principal then asked the latter girl to come to his private office, where he opened her purse and found a pack of cigarettes. As he reached for them he noticed rolling papers and decided to thoroughly search the entire purse. He found marijuana, a pipe, empty plastic bags, a substantial number of one dollar bills and a list of "people who owe me money." He then turned her over to the police. After a juvenile court hearing, the girl was found delinquent. Appeal reached the U.S. Supreme Court.

The Supreme Court held the search did not violate the Fourth Amendment. When police conduct a search, they have to meet the probable cause standard. But school officials are held to the lower "reasonable suspicion" standard. In determining the reasonableness of a search, the search must be justified initially by reasonable suspicion. Second, the scope and conduct of the search must be reasonably related to the circumstances that gave rise to the search, and school officials must take into account the student's age, sex and the nature of the offense. **The Court upheld the search of the student in this case because the initial search for cigarettes was supported by reasonable suspicion.** The discovery of the rolling papers then justified the further searching of the purse since such papers are commonly used to roll marijuana cigarettes. The "reasonableness" standard was met by school officials in these circumstances. *New Jersey v. T.L.O.*, 469 U.S. 325, 105 S.Ct. 733, 83 L.Ed.2d 720 (1985).

B. Other Police Matters

To help assure campus security, some of the states have empowered state universities and their campus police to exercise their authority off campus.

◆ *Finding an employee's right to bear arms trumped a university ban on weapons, Kentucky's highest court held a university unlawfully discharged him.*

Co-workers expressed concern that the employee had a gun in his locker, and administrators contacted university police. The employee told officers he had a state permit for a concealed weapon and had a gun in a vehicle parked on university property. After an investigation, he was fired for violating a university policy banning the possession of a deadly weapon on university property or while conducting university business. In a state court, the employee sued the university for violating a public policy that was inconsistent with his Second Amendment and state law rights. The Supreme Court of Kentucky held there is an exception in the state to the rule of at-will employment. This exception applies to a violation of a fundamental, well-defined public policy as evidenced by law. While the court found the university had the authority to control its property, there was also a fundamental, well-defined public policy limiting its authority to control the possession of deadly weapons on campus. **State law provided that no organization could ban a person from keeping a deadly weapon in the glove box of a vehicle.** As the employee held a valid license, the university would be in violation of state law if his gun was in the glove box. The court resolved ambiguous state laws in the employee's favor. Concluding the state legislature's intent was to support a right to bear arms, the court held he proved his discharge was contrary to a fundamental, well-defined public policy. The case was returned to a lower court for further proceedings. *Mitchell v. Univ. of Kentucky*, 366 S.E.3d 895 (Ky. 2012).

♦   *A Pennsylvania student who withdrew from school after being arrested for a firearms offense could not pursue a federal case against the university.*

When the student began a graduate program, she brought along an unregistered .22-caliber revolver. Knowing she was not allowed to keep the gun in her dorm, she asked another student, during class, where she should keep it. She was then called out of class by the university's chief of campus police and a police officer. She told the chief that her estranged husband had been harassing her. The chief told her to let him know if she received further harassing messages from her estranged husband. The police chief and the university's dean of student affairs later told her she had committed a crime by having an unregistered gun on campus. The student insisted she had done nothing wrong, but she signed a withdrawal form and was conditionally banned from the campus. She claimed that the police chief and dean of student affairs reacted to her gun possession the way they did because she had appealed the issuance of an earlier parking ticket. In a federal district court action against the university, the student asserted a host of claims. However, **the court agreed with the university that some of the laws she cited were not privately enforceable.** Others were time-barred or subject to the defense of immunity. In any event, the student did not present sufficient evidence to support any of her claims, and the case was dismissed. *Lewen v. Edinboro Univ. of Pennsylvania,* No. 10-164, 2011 WL 4527348 (W.D. Pa. 9/28/11).

♦   *A rule that gave West Virginia University (WVU) campus police too much discretion to issue trespassing forms was held unconstitutional.*

A person wearing a trench coat disturbed others at the WVU student union building because of his mannerisms and because he sat down with a yellow bag near his feet. Campus officers detained the person, searched him, and forced him to empty his pockets. Though nothing inappropriate was found, the officers issued him a "trespassing form" that said he had "interfered with the peaceful or orderly operations" of the university. The person was escorted from the campus and told he would be arrested if he returned. He sued WVU officials in a federal court for constitutional violations. The court held **WVU's trespassing policy was unconstitutionally vague because it was based on a state law that provided for the removal of individuals from campus based on no standards at all.** There were no guidelines or standards for issuing the forms. In addition, the failure to provide an appeal process for the trespassing forms violated due process. The court granted the person's motion for pretrial judgment and declared the trespassing policy unconstitutional. It barred WVU from enforcing the policy, but declined to rule on the issue of damages pending its receipt of further information. *Williams v. West Virginia Univ. Board of Governors,* 782 F.Supp.2d 219 (N.D. W. Va. 2011).

♦   *The arrest of a job applicant by California university campus police did not violate his rights because he matched the description of a criminal suspect.*

A sergeant in the university police department was called by a Florida sheriff's investigator about a suspect wanted in Florida for aggravated battery with a deadly weapon. After contacting a university department, the sheriff confirmed that a person matching the description of the Florida suspect had applied for employment at the university. The applicant had the name and birth date of the suspect, was the same race and gender, had the same hair color and eye color, and was similar in height and weight to the suspect. Based on this information, the sergeant orchestrated an arrest. The applicant later sued the university, sergeant and others in a federal district court. The court applied an objective standard to determine if there was probable cause for the arrest. This involved determining whether a reasonable officer would believe the applicant was the same person named in the warrant based on information available to the sergeant at the relevant time. **The court found the sergeant reasonably believed he was arresting the right person, defeating the false arrest and negligence claims.** *Garcia v. Univ. of California at Los Angeles*, No. CV 09-8193-R, 2010 WL 3814551 (C.D. Cal. 9/27/10).

◆ *A federal court ordered a Pennsylvania state university to let a student take her finals pending the completion of her challenge to drug possession charges.*

University police officers arrested the student after discovering 12 ecstasy pills in her dorm room. At a disciplinary hearing a month later, the university refused to let a lawyer represent her. The only witness at the hearing was the university police chief, who read out the arresting officer's report. The student declined to cross-examine him, called no witnesses and did not testify on her own behalf. The hearing body recommended immediate suspension, academic probation, a drug and alcohol evaluation, and a ban from campus housing. The student sued the university and its president in a federal district court for due process violations. The court granted her request for a preliminary order preventing her expulsion and allowing her to attend classes and take exams. **The court found the university violated her due process rights by refusing to let her attorney speak for her at the hearing.** Since this could lead to a one-sided hearing and wrongful discipline, the court ordered the university to let the student take her finals. *Coulter v. East Stroudsburg Univ.*, No. 3:10-CV-0877, 2010 WL 1816632 (M.D. Pa. 5/5/10).

◆ *A federal district court rejected a man's claim that Marquette University safety officers violated his rights when arresting him for aggravated battery.*

Marquette University Department of Public Safety (DPS) officers assisted the Milwaukee police in arresting the man for aggravated battery. He claimed a DPS employee and Milwaukee police officers held him "hostage" for about two hours and placed him in a "bogus" lineup. After the man was convicted for aggravated battery, he sued the DPS in a federal district court for false imprisonment and violation of his due process rights. **The court explained that to prevail, the man had to show an intentional deprivation of a constitutionally protected right "under color of state law."** He further had to show any constitutional deprivation was caused by an official DPS policy, ordinance, or regulation. A single employee who was not named as a party was the only person from DPS who had anything to do with the arrest. As the claims were insufficient to hold the DPS or any employees liable, DPS received pretrial judgment. *Scott v. Marquette Univ. Dep't of Public Safety*, No. 06-C-0384, 2009 WL 2240234 (E.D. Wis. 7/27/09).

◆   *A Florida university did not violate a student's due process rights when it relied on an unsworn police report as a basis for imposing discipline on him.*

The student asserted the use of the police report in his disciplinary hearing violated his due process rights. He said the police report was unsworn hearsay evidence and that its use violated the university's code of student conduct. The court held the use of an unsworn report did not violate this code provision, which applied only to witnesses who testified at disciplinary hearings. Since the challenged evidence related to a report and not to witness testimony, there was no violation of the code provision. Even though hearsay evidence was used, the court held the student was given all the process he was due. **He was confronted with the report and had a chance to rebut the charges against him.** Also, the student made no attempt to call witnesses or present evidence. He refused to answer questions and relied on his right not to incriminate himself. Under the circumstances, there was no due process violation. *Heiken v. Univ. of Cent. Florida*, 995 So.2d 1145 (Fla. Dist. Ct. App. 2008).

◆   *University of Virginia campus police had authority to act within a statutorily prescribed distance from the jurisdictional limits of Charlottesville.*

A University of Virginia campus police officer observed a vehicle being driven erratically. The officer pulled over the vehicle, and the driver failed a series of field sobriety tests. The driver was arrested and later convicted of driving while intoxicated. By statute, University of Virginia police have concurrent jurisdiction with the City of Charlottesville police department. When the campus officer pulled over the vehicle, he was 200 yards outside the city limits. The driver challenged his conviction on this basis, saying the officer was outside of his jurisdiction when he pulled him over and arrested him. A Virginia trial court rejected this claim and upheld the conviction.

The relevant statute gave both the Charlottesville police and University of Virginia campus police the authority to act "within a statutorily prescribed distance from the jurisdictional limits" of the city. On appeal, the Court of Appeals of Virginia upheld the conviction. *Boatwright v. Comwlth. of Virginia*, 50 Va.App. 169, 647 S.E.2d 515 (Va. Ct. App. 2007).

◆   *A Michigan court properly entered a personal protection order (PPO) against a student who was accused of stalking one of her professors.*

A professor at Wayne State University filed a petition for a PPO against a student who sent her inappropriate emails of a sexual nature. She said the student left a magazine at her office that included an article about love with her picture pasted on it with disturbing comments. The professor said the student then continued to contact her after she was told not to. The court granted the petition, taking into account three prior PPOs issued against the student in other cases, including one that involved another instructor. The Court of Appeals of Michigan held the evidence relating to the other PPOs was admissible because it was relevant to show a scheme or plan of harassing college instructors. Even without the evidence relating to the prior PPOs, there was enough evidence to support the entry of a PPO. **On at least two occasions, the student engaged in acts of what the state harassment law called "unconsented contact" that caused emotional distress to the professor.** Under applicable provisions of state law, this was enough to show the student stalked the professor. As a result, the lower court had properly entered the PPO, and its judgment was affirmed. *Hilgendorf v. Lee*, No. 270335, 2007 WL 1713114 (Mich. Ct. App. 6/14/07).

C. Liability

University police officers sometimes have to make split-second decisions under stressful conditions. Because of the discretionary nature of their work, the law gives officers immunity from civil liability when they act in good faith. But immunity was denied to officers who used pepperballs to disperse a crowd.

◆ *University of California at Davis (UCD) police faced constitutional liability after shooting pepperballs into a crowd of partygoers.*

Police responded to a gathering of about 1,000 people at an apartment complex. When some of the people started rocking a car and setting off bottle rockets, a property owner asked the police to disperse the crowd for trespassing. Municipal police called UCD police for backup. Officers in riot gear moved through the crowd, but the partygoers did not disperse. When officers shot pepperballs, a student was hit in the eye. He lost visual acuity, eventually lost his athletic scholarship and withdrew from UCD. In a federal court, the student sued UCD for seizing him in violation of his civil rights. The case reached the U.S. Court of Appeals, Ninth Circuit, which held it was not relevant that the injury was inadvertent. In the court's opinion, **the incident was an unreasonable Fourth Amendment seizure because the police used unjustified force**. It held the general disorder of the complex could not be used to legitimize the use of pepperballs against non-threatening individuals. As a result, the court held university police officers were not entitled to pretrial judgment. *Nelson v. City of Davis*, 685 F.3d 867 (9th Cir. 2012).

◆ *A parent who was injured by campus police when she visited Indiana University did not convince a court that she had viable constitutional claims.*

The parent visited her undergraduate son on campus. She claimed she was hurt when a campus police officer ran into her while pursuing a fleeing suspect. In a federal court, the parent accused the university of violating her right to bodily integrity and her Fourth Amendment right to be free from unreasonable seizures. The court found police officers have to make quick decisions when pursuing suspects. The evidence did not show the officer acted with malicious intent. Instead, he simply knocked the parent down while chasing a suspect. This behavior did not violate any constitutional provision. **An accident is different from an intentional detention, and the parent was not "seized."** In any event, the university had qualified immunity. The court dismissed the federal claims while allowing the parent to file state law claims in a state court. *Bean v. Indiana Univ.*, 855 F.Supp.2d 857 (S.D. Ind. 2012).

◆ *North Carolina's highest court rejected an arrestee's argument that a private university could not maintain campus police officers.*

A Davidson College campus police officer pulled over a speeding vehicle that was weaving on roads near campus and, after administering two alcohol tests, arrested the driver for reckless driving and driving while impaired. The driver later filed a motion to suppress the evidence against her, asserting that since Davidson was a religiously affiliated college, it should not have campus police officers or there would be a violation of the Establishment Clause. When the case reached the state supreme court, it held that the evidence could be used against the driver. **The state's Campus Police Act (CPA) had a secular purpose and did not foster excessive state entanglement with religion.** The CPA provided substantial protections to ensure neutrality and guard against excessive church-state entanglement. In particular, the CPA made it clear officers could only enforce secular laws – not campus policies or religious rules. As a result, the court denied the driver's challenge. *State v. Yencer*, 365 N.C. 292, 718 S.E.2d 615 (N.C. 2011).

◆   *Police departments of a South Carolina public university and municipality were entitled to dismissal of a town resident's excessive force claim.*

Due to a previous run-in with the resident, university police knew his drivers license was suspended, and they stopped him when they saw him driving a van. They arrested him and put him in the back of the patrol car. His cooperation ended when an officer began to discuss having the van towed. Then the resident stuck out his legs, kicked, and yelled to bystanders that he was being beaten. When municipal officers arrived, they saw him kicking the patrol car windows and threatening to cause damage. A "hobble cord" was put on the resident's legs but he continued resisting, and he kicked an officer's chest and neck. Two officers hit the resident with their batons. He sued both departments and three officers in a federal district court for excessive force and injury.

A federal magistrate judge filed a report and recommendation to dismiss the case. **To decide if police used excessive force, courts must balance the intrusion on a suspect's rights against the reason for using force.** Police decisions are often made under stressful, rapidly changing circumstances. The resident's conviction for resisting arrest defeated his excessive force claim. A Fourteenth Amendment claim based on use of the hobble cord also failed. After the district court adopted the magistrate's recommendation for dismissal, appeal reached the U.S. Court of Appeals, Fourth Circuit. It affirmed the judgment for the university in a brief order. *Alston v. Winthrop Univ. Police Dep't*, 431 Fed.Appx. 226 (4th Cir. 2011).

◆   *Nevada university officials were entitled to immunity in an action by a student who was arrested by campus police and later disciplined.*

A University of Nevada, Las Vegas (UNLV) student reported to a campus residential life coordinator (RLC) that her roommate had harassed and threatened her. She later said the RLC breached her confidentiality by telling the roommate about her report. The roommate called campus police to report the student had threatened her with scissors. Police arrested the student, and UNLV found she violated the student code. She sued UNLV, the RLCs and campus police in a federal court for unlawful arrest and due process violations.

After the court dismissed the case, the student appealed to the U.S. Court of Appeals, Ninth Circuit, claiming campus police violated the Fourth Amendment by arresting her without a warrant or probable cause. The court disagreed, finding **a reasonable officer would decide there was probable cause for arrest if two university employees and a victim said a student had committed a violent attack**. The court also dismissed a claim that UNLV officials violated the student's due process right by making a false disciplinary charge to her transcript. Since no law, regulation or official opinion established clear law in this area, the court held UNLV officials had qualified immunity. Unlike a legal entitlement created by a law or state constitution, reputation is not the kind of "liberty" or "property" interest that may be protected by the Fourteenth Amendment. As the lower court had correctly dismissed the case, the judgment was affirmed. *Krainski v. Nevada ex rel. Board of Regents of Nevada System of Higher Educ.*, 616 F.3 963 (9th Cir. 2010).

◆   *Students who said California community college police attacked them and used unreasonable force avoided pretrial judgment in their federal lawsuit.*

The students were married to each other and attending separate classes at the community college. When the wife began to experience extreme anxiety during a class, she went to her husband's class, where the instructor escorted them to a private classroom. The wife then knocked items from a desk and said she was "looking for something to hurt somebody." Campus police were called, and they restrained the couple, who claimed the campus police made racial comments. The couple sued the community college and officers, raising claims including battery, unreasonable seizure, infliction of emotional distress, false imprisonment, and disability discrimination. The court found a viable claim for battery against one officer and declined to dismiss the case.

The court refused to dismiss a claim based on detention without probable cause and use of excessive force. **Any reasonable officer would know he lacks a right to drag and pin someone to the ground when there are no exigent circumstances.** A claim of intentional infliction of emotional distress was rejected because an unprovoked attack could be considered extreme and outrageous conduct. But two claims of intentional infliction of emotional distress were dismissed because they were unsupported. False imprisonment claims against one officer survived because factual issues existed on these claims. *Newman v. San Joaquin Delta Community College Dist.*, No. CIV. 2:09-3441 WBS KJN, 2010 WL 2179964 (E.D. Cal. 5/27/10).

◆   *A student who involuntarily withdrew from a Texas college based on his juvenile criminal history was not allowed to further pursue a federal case.*

In his federal lawsuit, the student sued the college, its parent organization and two college officials. He claimed due process violations, breach of contract, intentional infliction of emotional distress, and negligent hiring, training and supervision. A federal magistrate judge issued a report and recommendation to dismiss the case. Claims for punitive damages were not authorized against a Texas governmental unit. **The college and its parent were immune to claims for negligent hiring, negligent training, negligent supervision and intentional infliction of emotional distress.** Similarly, the claims of intentional infliction of emotional distress against the individual defendants in their official capacities were barred by immunity. In addition, the magistrate found expulsion from the program was not extreme or outrageous. There was no cause of action allowing the student to pursue monetary damages under the due process clause of the state constitution. *Kimbrough v. Alamo Colleges*, No. SA-09-CV-0738 XR (NN), 2010 WL 841368 (W.D. Tex. 3/8/10).

◆ *A New York federal court dismissed a student's federal claims against New York University (NYU) for making a false police report about him.*

A university security employee accused the student of stealing a wallet in a locker room. Although the student denied this, the employee called NYU's public safety administrator, who in turn called municipal police. A municipal police officer arrested and jailed the student. After the student was acquitted of all charges, he accused NYU of refusing to let him return as a student. He sued NYU in a federal court. The court found the federal claims were all based on conclusory allegations and did not state necessary facts. The race discrimination claim failed because the student did not claim he was mistreated because of his race. There was no evidence that NYU conspired with the police to frame him, defeating the conspiracy claim. **The court dismissed all the federal claims against NYU as they were based on conclusory allegations.** *Johnson v. City of New York*, 669 F.Supp.2d 444 (S.D.N.Y. 2009).

◆ *An Arkansas federal judge refused to dismiss a private security contractor and an employee from a lawsuit brought by a university chief of police.*

According to the chief, the security contractor was volatile and dangerous. The chief stated that the contractor and some of his private security guards were involved in "several instances of disturbing and abusive conduct." This culminated when the contractor fought with university police officers and the chief unsuccessfully tried to arrest him. The chief stated the contractor resisted so violently that the chief suffered arm and shoulder injuries requiring surgery and rehabilitation, stress bad enough to trigger a heart condition, and severe and persistent emotional distress. When the contractor sought to dismiss the case, the court refused. Arkansas law requires "substantial evidence" that a contract was intended to benefit a person before a judge can determine if there is a third-party beneficiary. The judge decided it was too early in the proceedings to make this determination. **He also refused to dismiss the excessive force claim, since enough facts were presented to support it at this stage of the lawsuit.** *Weatherspoon v. Univ. of Arkansas Board of Trustees*, No. 4:08CV00635 JLH, 2009 WL 3765916 (E.D. Ark. 11/10/09).

◆ *An Oregon public university did not violate the First Amendment by expelling a student who threatened a university administrator.*

The student kept guns and ammunition in his dorm room and told acquaintances that he wanted to kill or hurt an assistant director of residence life. University officials told the assistant director about the comments and recommended that he and his family move off campus for a few days. The assistant director followed the recommendation and also obtained a restraining order against the student. The school then held a hearing at which a committee recommended expulsion for violating the student conduct code and standards relating to residence housing. The university adopted the recommendation, and the student sought court review, claiming the expulsion violated his free speech rights. **The court held that it was reasonable for school officials to expel him since the threats disrupted university activities.** *Hagel v. Portland State Univ.*, 228 Or.App. 239 (Or. Ct. App. 2009).

◆ *A student identified as a safety threat was properly dismissed from a Pennsylvania nurse anesthesia program.*

The university said the student constantly needed assistance, and nurse anesthetists who supervised him said he had clinical performance issues. The university placed the student on probation and later dismissed him from the program for jeopardizing the health or safety of patients. He sued the university in a federal district court for breach of contract and related claims. The court rejected the student's claim that his contract called for progressive discipline prior to dismissal from the program. **A university handbook separately provided that it could dismiss any student who jeopardized the safety or welfare of a patient.** There was no evidence that the student was dismissed for any reason other than patient safety. The court upheld the action. *Kimberg v. Univ. of Scranton*, No. 3:06cv1209, 2009 WL 222658 (M.D. Pa. 1/29/09).

◆ *The criminal prosecution of a temporary instructor charged with making email and phone threats to college personnel was allowed to proceed.*

Based on his poor job performance, the college decided not to renew the temporary instructor's contract. But he continued to threaten faculty and administrators. The college responded by barring him from campus. However, the instructor sent several emails and made phone calls in which he threatened to kill faculty and administrators, as well as members of their families. Threats were made to professors, a department chairman, the vice president of the college, and the dean of the college. After the FBI executed a search warrant at the instructor's residence and seized evidence relating to the case, a grand jury indicted him on nine counts of transmitting an interstate email threat to kill or injure another person. It also indicted him on three counts of interstate threats via telephone. The instructor sought dismissal, claiming the indictment did not sufficiently allege that he transmitted a "true threat," as the applicable statute required. **The court found a "true threat" exists if the recipient is familiar with the context of the communication and would interpret it as a true threat.** Each count of the indictment in this case met the test. *U.S. v. Li*, 537 F.Supp.2d 431 (N.D.N.Y. 2008).

◆ *A federal district court refused to grant pretrial judgment to a university accused of negligently allowing a student to stab another student to death.*

The deceased student's estate sued the university in a federal district court for premises liability, fraudulent misrepresentation and negligence. In denying the university's motion for pretrial dismissal, the court found the fraudulent misrepresentation claim was based on university recruitment materials and a website claiming its campus was a "safe, peaceful environment." Advertising claimed campus security personnel worked closely with state and local police agencies, and that campus security promptly reported all criminal activity. While the university argued that these statements were opinion rather than fact, the court held reasonable jurors might disagree on this. Fact issues existed as to whether the student relied on university representations about campus safety, and **the estate raised a question about notice to the university of the slayer's mental health history during his admission process**. *Estate of Butler v. Maharishi Univ. of Management*, 589 F.Supp.2d 1150 (S.D. Iowa 2008).

◆ *A Florida court held that in an emergency, a university can exclude a student and provide a hearing afterward to protect the campus.*

A graduate of Florida Atlantic University (FAU) returned to FAU for a graduate program but was dismissed for receiving a failing grade. She then enrolled in continuing education classes. Faculty members became fearful of the student, saying she made veiled threats. FAU issued a "no trespass warning" that barred her from campus. The student was arrested three times for violating the warning and was convicted of trespassing. After several more incidents, the student was banned from FAU indefinitely. She sued FAU in a state court, claiming it violated her due process rights. The court held for FAU, and the student appealed. A Florida District Court of Appeal found that due process protection can extend to interests in specific benefits created by state laws or state university rules and policies. It was a mistake for the trial court to rule the student had no interest in continued enrollment. FAU could not permanently deprive her of access to its campus without notice and an opportunity for a hearing. **However, the court recognized that in emergencies, a university can exclude a student and provide a hearing afterward.** *Lankheim v. Florida Atlantic Univ.*, 992 So.2d 828 (Fla. Dist. Ct. App. 2008).

◆ *A Connecticut college did not violate a student's due process rights as he received notice and a chance to be heard regarding the charges against him.*

The university held a disciplinary hearing, after which a hearing officer found the student had stalked a female classmate. He was suspended for 15 months, barred from student activities and prevented from earning credits. After an unsuccessful internal appeal, the student filed an action in state court, seeking an order that would require the university to reinstate him as a full-time student in good standing. The court found he was entitled to the requested order only if he could show the suspension proceeding did not meet due process requirements. He failed to make this showing as he could not prove a violation of any due process rights. **There is no fundamental right to attend college. The student received notice of the charges against him, and neither the form nor content of the notice prejudiced his ability to defend the charges.** As he was not denied due process with respect to the university's procedures, the court denied his request for a preliminary injunction. *Danso v. Univ. of Connecticut*, 50 Conn.Supp. 256, 919 A.2d 1100 (Conn. Super. Ct. 2007).

CHAPTER ELEVEN

School Finance

I. PUBLIC ASSISTANCE TO SCHOOLS

A. Federal Funding

1. Compliance

The U.S. government distributes funds to higher education institutions under Title IV of the Higher Education Act (HEA), 20 U.S.C. § 1094, to assist with the costs of secondary education. In order to receive federal funds under the HEA, institutions must enter into Program Participation Agreements with the U.S. Department of Education. In doing so, the institutions agree to various statutory, regulatory, and contractual requirements. Among these requirements is a recruiter-incentive compensation ban, which prohibits institutions from paying recruiters "incentive payments" based on the number of students they enroll. This provision was considered by a District of Columbia federal court.

◆ *In December 2012, a federal appeals court held a group of religious colleges could not challenge the federal Affordable Care Act's requirement that employers provide health insurance coverage for contraceptives.*

In separate federal court actions, Wheaton College and other religious institutions challenged the Affordable Care Act's mandate that group health plans and health insurers cover preventive care and screenings for women. This has been defined by the U.S. Health Resources and Services Administration (HRSA) to mean plans must cover contraception. But the HRSA acknowledged that requiring coverage for contraceptives might interfere with the religious beliefs of some employers. In March 2012, federal agencies implementing the law announced that they would create a rule that would not require cost-sharing for contraceptives among all participants in religious employers' health plans.

A federal district court dismissed the cases, finding the colleges lacked standing and the claims were not yet ripe for judicial review. On appeal, the U.S. Court of Appeals, District of Columbia Circuit, held the lower court had erred on the standing issue. But the court held the claims by the religious colleges were not ripe for court review. Noting the federal government's indication that **a rule relating to contraceptive coverage requirements was forthcoming**, the court held the cases were not ready for review. *Wheaton College v. Sebelius*, 703 F.3d 551 (D.C. Cir. 2012).

Note: On July 2, 2013, the federal government issued final regulations concerning the Coverage of Certain Preventive Services under the Affordable Care Act. See 78 FR 39870-01. The rule protects certain nonprofit religious organizations with religious objections to providing contraceptive coverage from having to contract, arrange, pay or refer women for such coverage.

◆   *The U.S. Court of Appeals, District of Columbia Circuit, allowed an action to proceed that asserts violation of Higher Education Act (HEA) regulations aimed at preventing employee compensation that is based solely on recruiting.*

Two individuals filed a federal court action against a California vocational college operator that received billions of federal dollars under HEA Title IV. They claimed the college violated HEA regulations "as a matter of corporate practice." According to the complaint, the college maintained enrollment quotas for recruiters and paid them bonuses of up to 10% of their pay based on their recruiting numbers. It was further asserted that the college made false statements to obtain Title IV loan funds and falsely represented compliance with the HEA prohibition against using incentive payments for recruiters.

A federal district court found no violation of the regulations, ruling that the corporate practices fell within a regulatory "safe harbor." This was because recruiter salaries were not awarded "solely on the basis of the number of new enrollees that the recruiter achieved." On appeal, the District of Columbia Circuit noted that the action asserted knowing violations of the federal False Claims Act. It rejected the lower court's ruling on the "safe harbor" issue, as further information could lead to the conclusion that the corporation was attempting to subvert HEA requirements in its compensation policies. The complaint asserted that recruiters who did not meet enrollment quotas were disciplined, demoted or discharged. While this by itself did not prove an HEA incentive compensation violation, it was possible that college achievement ratings for recruiters might be solely based on the number of students enrolled. Since **it was possible that the recruiter performance rating system was "merely a proxy for employee recruitment numbers,"** the court returned the case to the district court for more proceedings on the safe harbor issue and other aspects of the case. *U.S. v. Corinthian Colleges*, 655 F.3d 984 (9th Cir. 2011).

◆   *A conservative advocacy group lacked standing to enforce the Solomon Amendment on behalf of its student-members in a federal court.*

Under the Solomon Amendment, a college or university can lose federal funds if the U.S. Secretary of Defense determines the institution does not allow military recruiting on campus on terms at least equal to those allowed other employers. The Young America's Foundation (YAF) informed the Secretary of Defense that some students and faculty prevented or disrupted military recruiting at the University of California at Santa Cruz (UCSC) and prevented YAF members from meeting with military recruiters at campus job fairs. When the Secretary took no action under the Solomon Amendment, the YAF asked a federal court to order him to withhold funds from UCSC. The court dismissed the case, and the YAF appealed to the U.S. Court of Appeals, D.C. Circuit. The court held the YAF lacked standing to bring the action. Organizations may sue to enforce the rights of members if at least one member has the right to bring the lawsuit on her own behalf. But since none of these member-students did, the YAF lacked standing. **The YAF could not demonstrate that ordering the Secretary of Defense to withhold funds from UCSC would provide student-members greater access to military recruiters** at job fairs. *Young America's Foundation v. Gates*, 573 F.3d 797 (D.C. Cir. 2009).

◆   *Federal assistance may be conditioned on compliance with federal law.*
     Section 12(f) of the Military Selective Service Act denied federal financial assistance under Title IV of the Higher Education Act to male students between the ages of 18 and 26 who did not register for the draft. Applicants for assistance were required to file a statement with their institutions attesting to their compliance with the Selective Service Act. A group of students who had not registered for the draft sued the selective service system to enjoin enforcement of Section 12(f). A federal district court held that the act was a bill of attainder (a law that imposes a penalty on a group of people without a trial) because it singled out an identifiable group that would be ineligible for Title IV aid based on their failure to register. The court also held that the compliance requirement violated the Fifth Amendment. On appeal, the Supreme Court rejected the claims that the law was a bill of attainder and upheld the law.
     The law clearly gave non-registrants 30 days after receiving notice of ineligibility for federal financial aid to register for the draft and thereby qualify for aid. Furthermore, the bill of attainder prohibition in the Constitution applies only to statutes that inflict punishments on specified groups or individuals such as "all Communists." The Court also held that the denial of aid based on these requirements was not "punishment." The Court stated that **if students wish to further their education at the expense of their country, they cannot expect the benefits without accepting their fair share of governmental responsibility**. Finally, the law did not violate the Fifth Amendment because there was nothing forcing students to apply for federal aid. *Selective Service System v. Minnesota Public Interest Research Group*, 468 U.S. 841, 104 S.Ct. 3348, 82 L.Ed.2d 632 (1984).

◆   *Private schools whose students receive federal funds are deemed to be recipients of federal assistance. Therefore, even a college with an unbending policy of rejecting all forms of government assistance was required to comply with federal laws because its students received federal grants and loans.*
     A private college, which had an "unbending policy" of refusing all forms of government assistance in order to remain independent of governmental

restrictions, was asked by the Department of Education (DOE) to supply "assurance of compliance" with Title IX, which the college refused to do on the ground that it was receiving no federal funding. The DOE disagreed, saying that because the school enrolled large numbers of students receiving federal Basic Educational Opportunity Grants (BEOGs), it was receiving financial assistance for purposes of Title IX. The DOE then cut off student financial assistance based on the college's failure to execute assurances of compliance.

Students and the college brought suit challenging the termination of financial assistance. **The Supreme Court held that the college was a recipient of federal financial assistance and was thus subject to Title IX.** This was so despite the fact that only some of the college's students received BEOGs and even though the college did not receive any direct federal financial assistance. The college was obliged to submit assurance of compliance, but only with regard to the administration of its financial aid program, in order for students to continue to receive federal aid. *Grove City College v. Bell*, 465 U.S. 555, 104 S.Ct. 1211, 79 L.Ed.2d 516 (1984).

◆ *A federal law that cuts off financial aid to students convicted of drug-related offenses did not violate the Fifth Amendment.*

A federal statute located at 20 U.S.C. § 1091(r) cuts off federal grant, loan or work assistance to any student who is convicted of an offense involving the sale or possession of a controlled substance. A student advocacy group sued the U.S. Department of Education Secretary, claiming the law was unconstitutional because it punished them criminally a second time for the same offense in violation of the Double Jeopardy Clause of the Fifth Amendment.

A federal district court rejected the group's arguments. On appeal, the U.S. Court of Appeals, Eighth Circuit, analyzed whether punishment imposed by the statute was civil or criminal in nature. **The fact that the law suspended eligibility and did not impose penalties, and the fact that an administrative agency determined eligibility indicated that Congress intended a civil sanction, not a criminal one.** The court also found the statute's scheme was not so punitive that it could be deemed to levy a criminal penalty. Application of the relevant factors weighed in favor of a finding that the statute did not impose criminal punishment. Therefore, there was no violation of the Double Jeopardy Clause, and the judgment was affirmed. *Students for Sensible Drug Policy Foundation v. Spellings*, 523 F.3d 896 (8th Cir. 2008).

◆ *The Supreme Court held a violation of Title IV of the Higher Education Act may be shown without proving specific intent to injure or defraud.*

A private, nonprofit technical school in Indiana participated in the Guaranteed Student Loan (GSL) program authorized by Title IV of the Higher Education Act. The program required the school to make refunds to the lender if a student withdrew from school during a term. If the school failed to refund loans to the lender, the student – and if the student defaulted, the government – would be liable for the full amount of the loan. The treasurer of the school conferred with the school's owners and initiated a practice of not making GSL refunds. As a result, the school owed $139,649 in refunds. After the school lost its accreditation, a federal grand jury indicted the treasurer for "knowingly and willfully misapplying" federally insured student loan funds in violation of 20 U.S.C. § 1097(a). A federal district court dismissed the indictment because it lacked an allegation that the treasurer intended to injure or defraud the U.S. The Seventh Circuit reinstated the prosecution, and the U.S. Supreme Court affirmed the decision. The Court held Section 1097(a) did not require the specific intent to injure or defraud. **If the government can prove the defendant misapplied Title IV funds knowingly and willfully, that is sufficient to show a violation of Section 1097(a).** *Bates v. U.S.*, 522 U.S. 23, 118 S.Ct. 285, 139 L.Ed.2d 215 (1997).

2. Government Authority

To participate in HEA Title IV programs and accept federal funds, a postsecondary institution must satisfy several statutory requirements. These requirements are intended to ensure that participating schools actually prepare their students for employment, such that those students can repay their loans.

◆ *Months after the University of Phoenix (UP) paid $78.5 million to settle a case charging the institution with breaching HEA student aid requirements, two former employees filed a new case stating that UP fraud was continuing.*

To participate in federal student loan programs, an institution must agree not to base compensation for admissions staff on the number of students they enroll or financial aid awards they obtain. In December 2009, UP paid $78.5 million to settle a lawsuit alleging it had violated this provision. About nine months later, two former UP admission counselors filed a new action in a federal court against UP, alleging it was still committing the same offenses.

Both the U.S. government and the state of California intervened in the case, alleging UP violated federal and state false claims acts. Former UP admission counselors said UP's policies would continue to disguise the unlawful practice of basing salaries on enrollment numbers. The court found the prior case was not a bar to the second action. It held the first case was no longer "pending," as it had been settled. UP also argued the suit was blocked by a federal rule that an action based on already-disclosed allegations or transactions is barred unless the person bringing the action was an original source of the information. **The court held the employees in the present case based their action on the claim that UP adopted procedures to cover up a continuation of the fraud.** As a result, the court held the case could proceed. *U.S. ex rel. Hoggett v. Univ. of Phoenix*, No. 2:10-cv-02478-MCE-KJN, 2013 WL 875969 (E.D. Cal. 3/7/13).

◆ *A federal court challenge to 2009 HEA Title IV regulations governing compensation practices in higher education, state authorization requirements for institutions of higher learning, and distance education will proceed.*

In 2009, the U.S. Department of Education (DOE) proposed new HEA regulations to address concerns that its regulations governing several areas of Title IV administration were lax. The DOE's 2010 regulations concerned state authorization, compensation, misrepresentation, and other statutory requirements. One regulation required states to authorize specific institutions by name, and to maintain a process to review and act upon complaints concerning these institutions. Another rule required institutions offering distance or correspondence education (including online courses) to obtain state authorization. One regulation eliminated a "safe harbor" provision for compensation practices to eliminate incentive payments.

An association representing private colleges sued the DOE's secretary in a federal court to challenge certain requirements of the 2010 regulations. The federal court upheld the provision regarding compensation and misrepresentation by higher education institutions. The federal court also found the group lacked standing to challenge the regulation regarding state authorization of institutions. It also upheld the provision on distance education. On appeal, the U.S. Court of Appeals, District of Columbia Circuit, upheld the compensation regulations. But it sent two aspects of the compensation issue to the lower court for further consideration. While the challengers had standing to bring a lawsuit challenging the school authorization regulation, the court upheld it as valid. **A challenge to a distance education regulation was struck down because it was "not a logical outgrowth of the Department's proposed rules."** *Ass'n of Private Sector Colleges and Univ. v. Duncan*, 681 F.3d 427 (D.C. Cir. 2012).

◆ *A private college was not covered by the Privacy Act because participation in a student financial assistance program did not make it a federal agent.*

An Illinois student's father died, and her mother was unable to comply with her college's requests for verification of income. As a result, she did not receive federal financial aid for one school year. The college allowed the student to register for classes and treated her tuition as an "unpaid debt." Although she qualified for federal aid, the college's financial aid office refused to issue her funds because she was not in good standing. The student's mother then took out private loans to cover her tuition. The student completed the requirements for her bachelor's degree that year – but the college refused to grant her a degree because her tuition for the previous year remained unpaid.

The student and her mother sued the college and the U.S. Department of Education (DOE) in a federal district court for violating the federal Privacy Act. **The court found the Privacy Act is intended to protect citizens from the improper disclosure of personal information by government agencies.** The court awarded pretrial judgment to the college because it is not a government agency. The DOE was also entitled to judgment because it had not maintained the financial information in this case. Instead, the college kept it. The court rejected the argument that the college was a DOE agent that could be held liable for record-keeping. *Lengerich v. Columbia College*, 672 F.Supp.2d 599 (N.D. Ill. 2009).

◆ *A Florida law restricting state universities from spending funds on travel to "terrorist states" was an impermissible embargo on the exchange of ideas, culture and academia that also intruded on federal authority.*

An Act Relating to Travel to Terrorist States restricted state universities from spending both "state" and "nonstate" funds on activities related to travel to "terrorist states" as designated by the U.S. Department of State. A sponsoring Florida legislator declared the act was intended to prevent public funds from assisting Cuba's communist regime. A group of university faculty members claimed the act violated the Constitution and filed a federal district court action against state officials to bar its enforcement. Some of the faculty members argued that the act would hamper their research in nations such as Cuba and Iran. The court noted that the act restricted the use of both "state" and "nonstate" funds. It found the design and intent of the law took in more than spending, as it made a political condemnation of the designated countries.

A spending limitation on "state funds" could be justified as within the legislature's discretion. State officials claimed the funding restrictions for travel to designated countries did not prevent individuals from traveling "on their own dime." The court disagreed, finding the act not only prevented use of private and federal funds for travel, it effectively foreclosed travel to, and research in, the designated countries by preventing universities from disbursing funds and conducting other travel and research activities. The act made it impossible for individuals to travel to Cuba. **Characterizing the act as "essentially an impermissible 'embargo' on the exchange of ideas, culture and academia," the court found it was outside the realm of permissible state activity.** Restrictions on the use of "nonstate" funds for activities related to travel to the designated countries was also an obstacle to federal authority in international relations. The faculty members were entitled to pretrial judgment regarding the restrictions on the use of "nonstate" funds. *Faculty Senate of Florida Int'l Univ. v. Roberts*, 574 F.Supp.2d 1331 (S.D. Fla. 2008).

◆ *A private university did not meet the eligibility requirements for student financial assistance programs under Title IV of the Higher Education Act.*

In 1991 and 1992, the DOE found the university system, Sistema Universitario Ana G. Mendez, was not eligible for Title IV programs dealing with Pell grant programs. As a result of the DOE's finding, **the university system was responsible for refunding to the federal government $1,712,540 in student grant funds** that were disbursed from 1989 to 1991. The secretary of education's determination was based on the fact that the university system failed to license its additional campuses. When filling out its Title IV application forms, the university system did not report these campuses under the "additional locations" section. It also failed to obtain prior approval from the Puerto Rico Commission on Higher Education for most of the satellite locations. The university system filed an administrative challenge, but a DOE administrative law judge affirmed its $1.7 million liability. The university system appealed to a federal district court, which reversed the administrative decision, finding the satellite campuses were licensed. However, it also found that the certifications did not necessarily constitute legal authorization under the Higher Education Act. On remand, the DOE determined that the certifications did not constitute legal authorization. The district court affirmed.

The university system then asked the U.S. Court of Appeals for the First Circuit to determine whether the Higher Education Act gives the secretary of education the final word on whether a university program is legally authorized by a state under the act and is therefore eligible for Title IV funding. The First Circuit held that **the Higher Education Act does not explicitly give either the secretary of education or the states the exclusive right to determine "legal**

authorization." However, the court reasoned that it is not impermissible or unreasonable to allow the secretary to make that determination. The DOE's finding of liability was affirmed. *Sistema Universitario Ana G. Mendez v. Riley*, 234 F.3d 772 (1st Cir. 2000).

B. State Funding

◆ *A Wisconsin federal judge refused to order the University of Wisconsin (UW) to fund a conservative student group from student fees.*

UW student fees funded registered student organizations. "Collegians for a Constructive Tomorrow-Madison" (CFACT) missed an application deadline for funding set by the student services finance committee (SSFC), and the application was rejected. CFACT appealed, arguing its conservative viewpoint was the real reason SSFC denied it eligibility. After a student government panel upheld the decision, CFACT filed a federal district court action against UW, alleging denial of equal access to UW's student activity fee forum based on its viewpoint. The court denied the organization's request for a preliminary order requiring UW to fund it. It found a limited pool of money for student groups meant both sides faced equal harm. **Denying the injunction would hinder the group's ability to convey its expressive message on campus, but granting it would cause the same harm to other student groups.** UW successfully refuted the claim that SSFC granted eligibility to other groups that missed the deadline. The court denied the injunction. *Collegians for a Constructive Tomorrow-Madison v. Regents of Univ. of Wisconsin System*, 698 F.Supp.2d 1058 (W.D. Wis. 2010).

◆ *The New York Supreme Court, Appellate Division, held that the state could review a nonpublic educational institution's certification of a student's eligibility for a state grant.*

A New York private college accepted and certified a group of students who had previously attended a local community college as eligible for state Supplemental Tuition Assistance Program (STAP) grants. The STAP grants provided tuition assistance to New York students whose educational deficits were so great that they would not be considered admissible to a college-level program. The state denied the college's request for STAP award, and a New York trial court affirmed the denial. On appeal by the college, the appellate division court held that **the state had both the authority and the obligation to review a nonpublic educational institution's certification of a student's eligibility for a STAP grant**. The regulatory scheme did not contemplate awards to students with successful college experience who had previously received funds pursuant to the Tuition Assistance Program. The appellate court affirmed the trial court's denial of STAP funds. *Touro College v. Nolan*, 620 N.Y.S.2d 558 (N.Y. App. Div. 1994).

◆ *A university could not maintain a race-based scholarship program where past discrimination did not justify it.*

The University of Maryland maintained a merit scholarship program open only to African-American students. It alleged that the program redressed prior constitutional violations against African-American students by the university, which had formerly been segregated by law. A student of Hispanic descent attempted to obtain a scholarship under the program, but was denied on the basis of his race. He filed a lawsuit against the university and a number of its officials in the U.S. District Court for the District of Maryland. The court granted summary judgment to the university, and the student won reversal from the U.S. Court of Appeals, Fourth Circuit. On remand, the parties again filed cross motions for summary judgment, and the district court again awarded summary judgment to the university.

The case was again appealed to the court of appeals. It determined that the district court had improperly found a basis in the evidence for its conclusion that a remedial plan of action was necessary. It also had erroneously determined that the scholarship program was narrowly tailored to meet the goal of remedying past discrimination. The court had misconstrued statistical evidence presented by the parties and had erroneously found a connection between past discrimination and present conditions at the university. **The reasons stated by the university for maintaining the race-based scholarship – underrepresentation of African-American students, low retention and graduation rates and a negative perception among African-American students – were legally insufficient.** The court reversed the summary judgment order for the university and awarded summary judgment to the student. *Podberesky v. Kirwan*, 38 F.3d 147 (4th Cir. 1994).

C. Student Default

Section 523(a)(8) of the U.S. Bankruptcy Code does not allow the discharge of student loans in bankruptcy. However, a bankruptcy court may permit the discharge of student loan debt if the student can show it would impose an undue hardship to repay the loans. In addition to the test for "undue hardship," a bankruptcy court may consider exceptional circumstances that strongly suggest a continuing inability to repay, such as a disability, and a student's failure to take advantage of forebearances or deferments.

The bankruptcy code does not define "undue hardship," and the courts have struggled with its meaning. In the case of In re Frushour, *433 F.3d 393 (4th Cir. 2005), the U.S. Court of Appeals, Fourth Circuit, held that having a low-paying job does not in itself cause undue hardship, especially when the debtor has not tried to get a job that pays more. Government-backed student-loan debt is ordinarily not discharged in Chapter 7 proceedings.*

◆   *Finding a student owed Middle Tennessee State University (MTSU) $9,000 in student loans, a court held he had to pay the debt plus costs and interest.*

From 1988 through 1993, the student earned 136 credit hours at MTSU. According to the university, he received $9,000 in Perkins Loans during this time. MTSU produced documents showing the student had signed eight Perkins Loan promissory notes, seven Perkins Loan Program forms, two pre-loan counseling forms, a loan repayment schedule, and a Truth-in-Lending letter. Despite this evidence, the student said that he never borrowed any money from MTSU. He claimed all the documents were forgeries and that he never received any notice advising him of delinquent loan status. The university sued the student in a state court to recover $9,000 in loans, more than $6,460 in interest and $7,728 in attorneys' fees. A handwriting expert examined the loan documents and concluded that the student had signed them. After the court entered a judgment of $24,099.71 for MTSU, the student appealed. The state court of appeals rejected all of his arguments, including his claim that the trial court should have let another handwriting expert look at the documents.

The trial court was justified in assigning great weight to the MTSU handwriting expert's testimony. Other evidence showed the student had signed the documents. Loan recipients had to appear personally and produce identification before signing for and receiving loan funds. Finally, the trial court did not abuse its discretion when it awarded discretionary costs and attorneys' fees. *Middle Tennessee State Univ. v. Simmons*, No. M2011-00825-COA-R3-CV, 2012 WL 2244821 (Tenn. Ct. App. 6/15/12).

◆ *An African-American student at a South Carolina technical college did not convince a federal court that his financial aid was withheld based on race.*

The student claimed in his federal lawsuit that the college held back financial aid money because of his race. He asked for an order requiring the college to pay him $5 million in damages for pain and suffering. He also asked the court to order the college to provide him with "passing grades of (C) and above." A magistrate judge recommended that his complaint be dismissed, and a federal court adopted the magistrate judge's recommendation. In ruling for the technical college, **the student failed to allege that the financial aid disbursement policy applied only to him or only to members of his racial group**. *Logan v. Greenville Technical College*, No. 6:11-467-TMC, 2011 WL 5082230 (D.S.C. 10/26/11).

◆ *A disabled student borrower's request to have her student loan debt discharged was rejected by a federal appeals court.*

A former Illinois college student took out federal loans totalling $13,250. She later defaulted on them and filed a series of applications with the U.S. Department of Education (DOE) to discharge her debt on the basis of her disability. Although the former student produced letters from her physician declaring her inability to work, the DOE denied the application for discharge.

When the student sought judicial review of the denial, her doctors provided 10 years of medical records. Based on the new evidence, the court sent the case back to the DOE. But the DOE found her physician failed to explain why she was completely unable to work, and the DOE again denied discharge. A federal district court upheld the decision, and appeal went before the U.S. Court of Appeals, Seventh Circuit. It found that **to discharge a student loan debt on the basis of disability, the student had to show she was "permanently and totally disabled."** To do so, she had to establish she was unable to work because of an injury or illness that was expected to continue indefinitely or result in death. The student did not meet this standard. Her physician provided few details about her condition, and the DOE was not required to accept his conclusory assertions. *Boutte v. Duncan*, 348 Fed.Appx. 151 (7th Cir. 2009).

◆ *An Ohio court reversed a decision that excused a suspended student from repaying student loan funds he had received.*

The student compiled a history of using profanity and raising his voice when calling the university's financial aid office. He received repeated warnings about his behavior. The university approved a financial aid package on the assumption that the student would be taking a certain number of courses. When officials learned he would not be taking all the classes, his financial aid was decreased. The student called the financial aid office and used profanity. He told a financial aid office employee that "if he could reach through the phone, he would slap her." Shortly after his outburst, the student received a student loan check of $2,600. The university suspended him for misconduct.

The student's appeal was denied, and the university adjusted his account and sued him in a state court to recover $1,700 of the financial aid it gave him. He said he was not required to pay back the money because the suspension was unjust. The court agreed, saying the university had "demanded full payment for classes never given." The university appealed to the Court of Appeals of Ohio, which reversed the judgment. It found **the student had undisputedly received a loan check and spent the money**. Some of the funds were used to purchase a computer. Under the circumstances, the trial court abused its discretion, and the case was returned to it for more proceedings. *Franklin Univ. v. Ickes*, 181 Ohio App.3d 10, 907 N.E.2d 793 (Ohio Ct. App. 2009).

◆ *A Wisconsin university violated federal law by denying a transcript to a teacher whose tuition debt had been discharged in a bankruptcy proceeding.*

An art teacher stopped making payments midway through the first year of her master's degree program. By the time she completed the program, she owed the university over $6,000 in tuition. A federal bankruptcy court discharged this debt. During and after the bankruptcy proceeding, the university denied the teacher's requests for a copy of her transcript. **Under the U.S. Bankruptcy Code, creditors cannot take actions to collect a debt until a bankruptcy proceeding ends.** The code also bars creditors from taking action to collect debts that have been discharged. The teacher said the university violated both provisions when it denied her requests for her transcript. A bankruptcy judge ordered the university to provide the teacher a copy of her transcript, and to pay her damages and attorneys' fees. On appeal, **the U.S. Court of Appeals, Seventh Circuit, said students have a right to receive copies of their transcripts**. It found a right to receive a transcript "is essential to a meaningful property right in grades." Finding the university violated the Bankruptcy Code by refusing to provide the teacher with a copy of her transcript, the court affirmed the judgment. *In re Kuehn*, 563 F.3d 289 (7th Cir. 2009).

◆ *A New York court rejected a graduate's claim that a college wrongfully intercepted his state tax refunds to recoup money he owed for tuition.*

A college intercepted the graduate's state tax refunds after obtaining a civil court judgment against him for failing to pay his tuition. He filed a state court action to force the return of the intercepted refunds. The graduate claimed he had already paid back his student loans and did not owe more tuition. He claimed the college failed to apply the intercepted refunds to his loans. After a trial, the court dismissed the case, and the graduate appealed. On appeal, a New York Appellate Division Court agreed with the lower court's decision that the case was meritless. The judgment authorizing interception of the graduate's state tax refunds was obtained in a suit to recover sums previously awarded to him as federal Pell grants and state awards. **Those sums were used to pay his tuition, and the college was obligated to repay them to state and federal agencies.** As a result of this obligation, the college was entitled to recoup tuition amounts, which the graduate did not pay. The graduate failed to show the civil court judgment that served as the basis for intercepting the funds was not properly entered. As a result, the court affirmed the judgment for the college. *Onitiri v. CUNY*, 55 A.D.3d 808, N.Y.S.2d 294 (N.Y. App. Div. 2008).

◆   *A Utah college graduate was not entitled to have about $88,000 in student loan debt discharged during bankruptcy proceedings.*

The graduate had a degree in Middle East studies and formerly worked as an interpreter. As a single parent, she did not apply for a job for over 10 years, and received $1,100 per month in government benefits. When the graduate filed for bankruptcy, she asked the court to discharge her student loan debt. A bankruptcy court instead held the debt was not dischargeable in bankruptcy because requiring her to repay it would not impose an undue hardship on her.

A federal district court affirmed the decision. The graduate appealed to the U.S. Court of Appeals, Tenth Circuit, arguing she had medical conditions precluding full employment. But the only evidence she offered regarding her condition was her own testimony, and she admitted that no doctor had ever told her she was unable to work. **Instead, the court focused on her failure to apply for a job in more than 10 years and her failure to repay any portion of the debt when she received lump sums of cash.** Her decision to use $1,000 of that money for dance lessons and $4,000 of it for orthodontic work indicated she did not act in good faith. In addition, she had turned down an opportunity to consolidate her student loan debt. Because the graduate failed to meet the applicable test, the court affirmed the denial of her request for discharge of her student loan debt. *In re Roe*, 295 Fed.Appx. 927 (10th Cir. 2008).

◆   *The U.S. Department of Education could intercept a 67-year-old disabled Washington man's Social Security benefits to offset a delinquent student loan.*

The man failed to repay federally reinsured student loans he incurred between 1984 and 1989 under the Guaranteed Student Loan Program. The loans were reassigned to the Department of Education, which certified the debt to the U.S. Department of Treasury through the Treasury Offset Program. The U.S. began withholding a portion of the man's Social Security benefits to offset his debt, part of which was over 10 years delinquent. He sued the U.S. in a federal district court, alleging the offset was barred by the 10-year statute of limitations contained in the Debt Collection Act of 1982. The federal district court dismissed the case, and the U.S. Court of Appeals, Ninth Circuit, affirmed. The U.S. Supreme Court agreed to review the case.

The Court noted the Debt Collection Act permits U.S. agency heads to collect an outstanding debt by "administrative offset." However, Section 407(a) of the Social Security Act limits the availability of benefits to offset a debt. The

Court explained that the Higher Education Technical Amendments of 1991 "sweepingly eliminated time limitations as to certain loans." This included the student loans in this case. The Debt Collection Improvement Act of 1996 clarified that, notwithstanding any other law, including Section 407, all payments due under the Social Security Act were subject to offset. **The Court held the Debt Collection Improvement Act clearly made Social Security benefits subject to offset. Moreover, the Higher Education Technical Amendments removed the 10-year limit that would otherwise bar an offset of Social Security benefits.** The Court rejected the man's argument that Congress could not have intended in 1991 to repeal a statute of limitations as they concerned Social Security benefits that were not made available for offset until 1996. Congress does not need to foresee all the consequences of a statutory enactment. It was also unnecessary for Congress to explicitly mention Section 407 in the Higher Education Technical Amendments. The Debt Collection Improvement Act gave the U.S. the authority to use Social Security benefits to offset debts. The retention of the 10-year limit on debt collection in the Higher Education Technical Amendments did not apply in all contexts, including this administrative offset. It affirmed the judgment for the U.S. *Lockhart v. U.S.*, 546 U.S. 142, 126 S.Ct. 699, 163 L.Ed.2d 557 (2005).

◆ *A federal court denied a Pennsylvania law school graduate's request to have her student debt discharged in bankruptcy.*

At the time of her bankruptcy filing, the graduate had accumulated over $150,000 in student loan debt and repaid only $622. She was 36 years old, in good health and earning more than $51,000 a year. The graduate sought discharge of her student loan debt on grounds of undue hardship. **The court found the graduate failed to show she would be unable to maintain a minimal standard of living if she had to repay the debt.** Her net income at the time of the proceedings exceeded her monthly expenses by almost $500. In addition, she had the option of reducing her expenses. The court noted that the graduate had indulged in luxuries beyond her basic needs. She was young and healthy, and she had marketable skills. Therefore, she did not show she would be unable to repay her student loans in the future. As the graduate's efforts to repay her student loan debt had been "negligible," her request to discharge the debt was denied. *Johnson v. Access Group*, 400 B.R. 167 (M.D. Pa. 2009).

◆ *A husband and wife who failed to make a good-faith effort to repay their student loans could not discharge their student loan debt.*

The couple received student loans in connection with their studies at several North Carolina universities. The husband had a degree in information systems and obtained work as a programmer. He was later laid off, then went to work at a home improvement store. The store fired the husband because of "excessive daytime sleepiness." The wife worked as a music teacher at a middle school. In 2002, 2003 and 2004, the couple earned about $75,500, $78,300 and $64,100, respectively. In December 2004, they asked a court to discharge their student loan debt in connection with their ongoing bankruptcy proceedings. At the time, they had a combined total debt of about $120,500. The bankruptcy court considered whether they showed they would not be able to maintain a minimum standard of living if they had to repay the loans; whether their current state of financial affairs was likely to continue for a significant part of the loan repayment period; and whether they made a good-faith effort to repay the loans.

The court found that the pair satisfied each part of the test, and it discharged their student loan debts. The case reached the U.S. Court of Appeals, Fourth Circuit, which determined the couple did not make a good-faith effort to obtain employment and maximize their income. The wife did not work during the summer, and the husband did not show that his medical condition completely prevented him from working. The monthly budget they submitted to the court showed $75 for Internet service, $80 for cell phones, $60 for satellite television and $68 for a YMCA membership. In the three months prior to their bankruptcy filing, the couple spent a combined total of $4,600 on consumer expenditures. These expenditures were not necessary to maintain a minimal standard of living and were evidence that the couple did not make a good-faith effort to minimize expenses. **The record also showed the pair failed to make loan payments for a period of time when they were financially able to do so, and they did not adequately pursue loan consolidation options.** The decision to discharge the student loan debt was reversed. *In re Mosko*, 515 F.3d 319 (4th Cir. 2008).

◆   *A debtor was not required to present expert medical evidence to support his claim for discharge of his student loans due to his medical condition.*

The student accumulated nearly $95,000 in student loan debt while earning master's degrees from Saint Louis University. His student loans became due while he underwent chemotherapy for Hodgkin's disease. The treatments made him too weak to work, and he was approved for economic hardship deferments in 2000 and 2001. The student filed for bankruptcy and was then diagnosed with vascular necrosis. The condition caused him to suffer severe pain in his hips, shoulders and knees. He underwent two shoulder surgeries and began taking multiple pain medications. He also expected to undergo surgery on both hips and his other shoulder. The student was the only witness at his bankruptcy proceeding, where he said he performed computer jobs that required him to do nothing more than move a computer mouse with his left hand. In addition, he claimed his condition was getting worse. The bankruptcy court considered records indicating the student had a monthly income of $868 and monthly expenses of $3,575. Based on the evidence presented, the bankruptcy court found it would be an undue hardship for him to repay his student loans.

The creditor sought review by the U.S. Court of Appeals, Sixth Circuit. It argued the student was required to provide expert medical evidence showing his condition was likely to last throughout the repayment period of the loans. It also claimed he had failed to show he made a good-faith effort to repay his loans. **The court rejected the argument that expert medical evidence was needed to show entitlement to discharge.** Under the circumstances, requiring corroborating medical evidence would only serve to place an additional, unnecessary burden on the student. His account of his medical status and history was not disputed. The court also rejected the argument that the student did not make a good-faith effort to repay the loans based on his failure to apply for a particular repayment option. *In re Barrett*, 487 F.3d 353 (6th Cir. 2007).

II. ESTABLISHMENT CLAUSE ISSUES

The Establishment Clause of the First Amendment prohibits Congress from making any law respecting an establishment of religion. It was construed by the U.S. Supreme Court through the 1980s as prohibiting financial assistance by government agencies to religious schools and colleges.

In 1997, the Court decided Agostini v. Felton, *521 U.S. 203, 117 S.Ct. 1997, 138 L.Ed.2d 391, an important private school finance case in which the Court abandoned the presumption that the presence of public employees on parochial school grounds creates a symbolic union between church and state that violates the Establishment Clause. Under* Agostini, *government assistance to private schools must not result in government indoctrination or endorsement of religion. The recipients of government assistance must not be defined by reference to their religion, and the assistance must not create excessive entanglement between church and state.*

◆ *State appropriations for a pharmacy school at a Baptist college and a scholarship program violated the Kentucky Constitution.*

Kentucky legislators appropriated $10 million to build a pharmacy school building on the campus of a Baptist college. In the same budget bill, $1 million was appropriated for a pharmacy scholarship program to benefit students who attended a four-year higher education institution located in a designated area encompassing the site of the new school. Taxpayers sued the governor, university and others in a state court, claiming the appropriations violated the state constitution. The court declared both appropriations unconstitutional.

On appeal, **the Supreme Court of Kentucky explained that Section 189 of the state constitution bars any portion of any tax raised or levied for educational purposes to aid any church, sectarian or denominational school**. Since the university was "precisely the type of school referenced in Section 189," the appropriation was unconstitutional. The court rejected a claim that Section 189 violated the First Amendment. Construing Section 189 to ban the pharmacy school appropriation did not constitute illegal viewpoint discrimination. The court also rejected an argument that Section 189 violated the Equal Protection Clause. The scholarship program violated the state constitution because it was intended only for students who would attend the new pharmacy school. It was "special legislation" that violated Section 59 of the Kentucky Constitution. By restricting scholarships to those who would attend a particular school, the legislature failed to treat all members of the relevant class equally. As a result, the judgment for the taxpayers was affirmed. *Univ. of Cumberlands v. Pennybacker*, 308 S.W.3d 668 (Ky. 2010).

◆ *Colorado violated the Establishment Clause by denying scholarship funding to state colleges it deemed to be "pervasively sectarian."*

Colorado provided scholarships to in-state students who attended private colleges except for those that were "pervasively sectarian." Some confusion existed among state officials regarding eligibility criteria. When the state law provision excluding pervasively sectarian schools was enacted in 1977, U.S. Supreme Court precedents indicated the states could not provide financial aid to pervasively sectarian schools. But the Supreme Court modified its Establishment Clause jurisprudence in cases such as *Agostini v. Felton*, above.

Colorado never repealed the statutory provision that barred funding to pervasively sectarian schools, and state officials determined Colorado Christian University (CCU) was "pervasively sectarian." CCU filed a federal district court challenge to the denial of its application for public funding, claiming religious Free Exercise, Establishment Clause and Equal Protection violations. The court held for state officials, and CCU appealed to the U.S. Court of Appeals, Tenth Circuit. **The court explained that the Establishment Clause permits "evenhanded funding" of education through student scholarships.** Federal law did not require the state to discriminate against CCU with respect to funding, and it also prevented the state from permissibly doing so. Instead, religions must be treated neutrally and without discrimination or preference by the state. **Making scholarships available to students who attended "sectarian" but not "pervasively sectarian" schools discriminated among religious institutions.** Proof of discriminatory intent was not required to invalidate the challenged provision as unconstitutional. The state law required intrusive judgments by officials relating to questions of religious belief or practice. This type of entanglement between government and religion violated the Establishment Clause, requiring reversal of the judgment for state officials. *Colorado Christian Univ. v. Weaver*, 534 F.3d 1245 (10th Cir. 2008).

◆   *An Arkansas city bond issue to finance a Christian university building project was upheld as a neutral benefit available to any entity seeking funding.*

An Arkansas city issued bonds to fund building projects at a private Christian university. Before issuing the bonds, a local housing board required the university to agree that the facilities being financed would not be used for sectarian instruction or religious worship. The university agreed to repay the bonds and all expenses, operate and maintain the financed facilities as a four-year, degree-granting institution, and maintain its nonprofit status. After the city approved the bonds, several residents sued the university in a federal district court for constitutional violations. They claimed the bond issue violated the Establishment Clause and provisions of the Arkansas Constitution.

The court held the city did not act to advance or inhibit religion. The bond issue had a secular purpose and did not have the effect of advancing or inhibiting religion. There was no risk that issuing the bonds would result in any religious indoctrination, and no evidence supported the residents' claim that the bonds had the primary effect of promoting or fostering religion. Moreover, no evidence showed government funds were being used for religious purposes. The tax benefits of the bonds were neutrally available. Issuance of the bonds did not create an excessive entanglement with religion. The bonds were issued to finance buildings that were to be used for the nonsectarian purpose of buildings for higher education. **The court cited U.S. Supreme Court decisions indicating that the government may provide aid to religiously affiliated institutions of higher learning.** The court also concluded that the issuance of the bonds did not violate the state constitution. *Gillam v. Harding Univ.*, No. 4:08-CV-00363BSM, 2009 WL 1795303 (E.D. Ark. 6/24/09).

◆ *The U.S. Supreme Court approved of the state of Washington's choice to exclude devotional theology candidates from a state scholarship program.*

Washington law created the Promise Scholarship Program, which made state funds available to qualified students for their educational costs. To be eligible, students had to meet certain performance standards and income limits, and enroll at least half-time in an eligible postsecondary institution in the state. The program excluded scholarships for theology majors, but students who attended religiously affiliated schools could still obtain scholarships so long as they did not major in theology and the institution was accredited. A student who received a Promise Scholarship enrolled as a double major in pastoral ministries and business at a private Christian college. A college financial aid administrator advised him he could not use the scholarship to pursue a devotional theology degree and could only receive program funds by certifying he would not pursue a theology degree. The student sued state officials in a federal court for violating the Free Exercise, Establishment, Speech and Equal Protection Clauses. The U.S. Supreme Court held **the program was not a state expression of disfavor against religion**, as the student argued. The program did not impose civil or criminal sanctions on any type of religious service or rite.

There was no Free Exercise Clause violation, as the program did not require students to choose between their religious beliefs and a government benefit. The state had only chosen not to fund a distinct category of instruction. The training of ministers was essentially a religious endeavor that could be treated differently than training for other callings. There was no evidence of state hostility toward religion. **The program permitted funding recipients to attend pervasively religious schools, and nothing in its text or the state constitution suggested anti-religious bias.** The state interest in denying funds to theology majors was substantial, and the program placed only a minor burden on recipients. *Locke v. Davey*, 540 U.S. 712, 124 S.Ct. 1307, 158 L.Ed.2d 1 (2004).

◆ *A federal appeals court held taxpayers could not sue to force a Catholic university to repay federal funds it received for a teacher quality initiative.*

The federal Department of Education (DOE) awarded the University of Notre Dame a one-time, $500,000 grant for a program called Alliance for Catholic Education. The program trained and placed teachers in underserved Catholic schools. Two private taxpayers sued the secretary of the DOE to block payment of the grant money, claiming it would violate the Establishment Clause. But they did not file a motion for a preliminary injunction, and by the time the district court heard the case the money had already been paid. As a result, the district court dismissed the case as moot. On appeal to the U.S. Court of Appeals, Seventh Circuit, the taxpayers agreed any request for injunctive relief was moot. But they argued they could still seek to force Notre Dame to repay the money by having the court order the DOE to seek recoupment.

The court rejected the taxpayers' argument on the basis that it was up to the DOE to decide whether to file an enforcement action to recoup the money. The DOE's decision was not judicially reviewable. However, the district court could order Notre Dame to repay the money if the disbursement violated the Establishment Clause. In the meantime, the U.S. Supreme Court made it clear in *Hein v. Freedom from Religion Foundation*, 127 S.Ct. 2553 (U.S. 2007), that **taxpayers who claim a congressional appropriation violates the Establishment Clause can sue for injunctive relief only**. When the Notre Dame case later reached the Supreme Court for review, the Court vacated the decision and returned it to the Seventh Circuit for reconsideration. On remand, the appeals court held the district court had properly dismissed the case as moot. *Laskowski v. Spellings*, 546 F.3d 822 (7th Cir. 2008).

◆   *Missouri's highest court held the city of St. Louis could constitutionally fund the construction of an arena at a Jesuit university.*

St. Louis University's philosophy is "to teach young men and women ... to follow their Judeo-Christian conscience." The president is a Jesuit, as are nine of its 42 trustees. However, the university is not owned or controlled by any church. When the university decided to construct a new 13,000-seat arena, it sought financial assistance from the city under a state law that authorizes the provision of assistance to encourage urban renewal. Since the proposed site for the arena was in a blighted area, the city authorized funding for the project. The Masonic Temple Association of St. Louis filed a federal court action against the city, claiming it violated the establishment clauses of the state and federal constitutions by providing public aid to a religious institution.

After Masonic's suit was dismissed, the university filed a state court action, seeking a declaration that the funding was valid. The court granted summary judgment for the university. On appeal, the Supreme Court of Missouri rejected the argument that university bylaws proved it was a religious institution. **Mere affiliation with a religion does not prove a college or university is controlled by a religious creed.** Although they clearly indicated a religious affiliation, neither the bylaws nor the university's mission statement showed the school was controlled by a religious creed. The university convinced the court that its primary mission was education and not indoctrination. Moreover, the purpose of the arena was not to advance religion. Instead, its purpose was to provide a venue for secular student and community events in a blighted area of the city. Because Masonic did not show the university was controlled by a religious creed, the city did not violate the state constitution. *Saint Louis Univ. v. Masonic Temple Ass'n of St. Louis*, 220 S.W.3d 721 (Mo. 2007).

◆   *The U.S. Supreme Court held the First Amendment did not prevent the state of Washington from providing financial assistance directly to an individual with a disability attending a Christian college. However, the Supreme Court of Washington held on remand that the assistance violated the state constitution.*

A visually impaired Washington student sought vocational rehabilitative services from the Washington Commission for the Blind pursuant to state law. The law provided that individuals with visual disabilities were eligible for educational assistance to enable them to "overcome vocational handicaps and to obtain the maximum degree of self-support and self-care." However, because the plaintiff was a student at a Christian college intending to pursue a career of service in the church, the Commission for the Blind denied him assistance. The Washington Supreme Court upheld this decision on the ground that the First Amendment to the U.S. Constitution prohibited state funding of a student's education at a religious college. The U.S. Supreme Court took a less restrictive view of the First Amendment and reversed the Washington court. The operation of Washington's program was such that the Commission for the Blind paid money directly to students, who could then attend the schools of their choice. The fact that the student in this case chose to attend a religious college did not constitute state support of religion because "the decision to support religious education is made by the individual, not the state." The First Amendment was therefore not offended. *Witters v. Washington Dep't of Services for the Blind*, 474 U.S. 481, 106 S.Ct. 748, 88 L.Ed.2d 846 (1986).

On remand, the Washington Supreme Court reconsidered the matter under the Washington State Constitution, which is far stricter in its prohibition on the expenditure of public funds for religious instruction than is the U.S. Constitution. **Vocational assistance funds for the student's religious education violated the state constitution because public money would be used for religious instruction.** The court rejected the student's argument that the restriction on public expenditures would violate his right to free exercise of religion. The court determined that the commission's action was constitutional under the Free Exercise Clause because there was no infringement of the student's constitutional rights. Finally, denial of the funds to the student did not violate the Fourteenth Amendment's Equal Protection Clause because the commission had a policy of denying any student's religious vocational funding. The classification was directly related to the state's interest in ensuring the separation between church and state as required by both state and federal constitutions. The court reaffirmed its denial of the student's tuition. *Witters v. State Comm'n for the Blind*, 771 P.2d 1119 (Wash. 1989).

◆ *For more than a generation, courts have analyzed Establishment Clause cases under the framework established by the following decision.*

In *Lemon v. Kurtzman*, the Court invalidated Rhode Island and Pennsylvania statutes that provided state money to finance the operation of parochial schools. The Rhode Island statute provided a 15% salary supplement to parochial school teachers who taught nonreligious subjects using public school teaching materials. The Pennsylvania statute authorized payment of state funds to parochial schools to help defray the cost of teachers' salaries, textbooks and other instructional materials. Reimbursement was limited, however, to the costs of secular subjects, which also were taught in the public schools. The Supreme Court evaluated the Rhode Island and Pennsylvania programs using its **three-part test: First, the statute must have a secular legislative purpose; second, its principal or primary effect must be one that neither advances nor inhibits religion; finally, the statute must not foster "an excessive government entanglement with religion."**

Applying this test to the two state programs in question, the Court held that the legislative purpose of the programs was a legitimate, secular concern with maintaining high educational standards in both public and private schools. The Court did not reach the second inquiry because it held that the state programs failed under the third inquiry. The Rhode Island salary supplement program excessively entangled the state with religion because of the highly religious nature of the Catholic schools that were the primary beneficiaries of the program. The teachers who received the salary supplements provided instruction in classrooms and buildings containing religious symbols such as crucifixes. In such an atmosphere, even a person dedicated to remaining religiously neutral probably would allow some religious content to creep into the ostensibly secular instruction. Similar defects were found in the Pennsylvania program. The Court also observed that in order to ensure that the state-funded parochial school teachers did not inject religious dogma into their instruction, the state would be forced to extensively monitor the parochial school classrooms. This would result in excessive state entanglement with religion. Consequently, **the salary supplement programs were held to violate the Establishment Clause of the First Amendment**. *Lemon v. Kurtzman,* 403 U.S. 602, 91 S.Ct. 2105, 29 L.Ed.2d 745 (1971).

◆   *The Supreme Court held that the "secular side" of a college could be distinguished from sectarian programs, making it permissible for a state to provide funding to a religiously affiliated college's secular side.*

The state of Maryland enacted a program that authorized annual, noncategorical grants to religiously affiliated colleges. The program was challenged by taxpayers who alleged that state money was being put to religious uses by the schools, which had wide discretion in spending the funds.

The Supreme Court held that (1) no state aid at all may go to institutions that are so "pervasively sectarian" that secular activities cannot be separated from sectarian ones, and (2) if secular activities can be separated out, they alone may be funded. The colleges involved in this case were not found to be pervasively sectarian even though they were affiliated with the Catholic Church. The Court held that the "secular side" of the colleges could be separated from the sectarian and found that **state aid had only gone to the colleges' secular side**. It was admittedly somewhat difficult to ensure that the colleges and the Maryland Council for Higher Education would take care to avoid spending state funds on religious activities, but the Court expressed its belief that those entities would spend the money in good faith and avoid violating the First Amendment. *Roemer v. Board of Public Works*, 426 U.S. 736, 96 S.Ct. 2337, 49 L.Ed.2d 179 (1976).

◆   *The Supreme Court held that the receipt of Higher Education Facilities Act funds by four religious colleges did not violate the Establishment Clause.*

The Higher Education Facilities Act of 1963 contained an exclusion for any facility used for sectarian instruction or as a place of religious worship or any facility that is used primarily as part of a school divinity department. Federal education officials had powers to enforce the statute for a 20-year time period during which they could seek to recover funds from violators. A group of Connecticut taxpayers filed a federal district court action against government officials and four religious colleges that received Higher Education Facilities Act funds, seeking an order against the release of funds to sectarian institutions that used federal funds to construct libraries and other facilities. The court held the act did not have the effect of promoting religion.

The U.S. Supreme Court reviewed the case and held that the statute had been carefully drafted to ensure that no federal funds were disbursed to support the sectarian aspects of these institutions. **The four colleges named as defendants in this case had not violated any of the restrictions in the statute, as they had placed no religious symbols in facilities constructed with the use of federal funds, and had not used the facilities for any religious purposes.** There was no evidence that any of the colleges maintained a predominantly religious atmosphere, and although each of them was affiliated with the Catholic Church, none excluded non-Catholics from admissions or faculty appointments, and none of them required attendance at religious services. The receipt of funds by the colleges did not violate the Establishment Clause. The Court held, however, that the 20-year limit on federal oversight created the potential for religious use of the facilities after the 20 years expired. Because of the risk of use of the facilities for advancing religion, the court invalidated this portion of the legislation. *Tilton v. Richardson*, 403 U.S. 672, 91 S.Ct. 2091, 29 L.Ed.2d 790 (1971).

◆ *A Tennessee city development board could issue tax-exempt bonds to a sectarian university for a building project without violating the Constitution.*

A Christian university began a renovation project and sought $15 million in low-interest loans from the Industrial Development Board for Nashville, Tennessee. The board approved the loan and issued tax-exempt bonds to the university. A group of taxpayers sued, asserting that the bond issuance impermissibly benefited a religious university in violation of the Establishment Clause. A federal court ruled that the university was so pervasively sectarian that no state aid could go to it. The Sixth Circuit Court of Appeals reversed, noting that **the tax-exempt bonds did not violate the Establishment Clause**. First, public funds were not used to issue the bonds; the university had to arrange for private financing; and bond purchasers only had recourse against the university. Second, the bonds were issued in a neutral manner to nonprofit organizations. Third, the bonds advanced the secular objective of promoting economic development. The university was entitled to receive the tax-exempt bonds. *Steele v. Industrial Development Board of Metropolitan Government of Nashville*, 301 F.3d 401 (6th Cir. 2002).

◆ *A Wisconsin program allowing unrestricted telecommunications access grants to sectarian schools and colleges violated the Establishment Clause.*

A 1997 Wisconsin law created the Technology for Education Achievement (TEACH) Board, which administered the Education Telecommunications Access program. The TEACH board approved access for data lines and video links under a heavily subsidized program in which both public and private schools participated. A taxpayer group objected to the program on constitutional grounds because $58,873 of the program's annual total of over $1.9 million was awarded to nine religiously affiliated Wisconsin schools and private colleges. The taxpayers sued state education officials, including the TEACH board, challenging the program as unconstitutional.

The case reached the Seventh Circuit. It noted that **the Wisconsin law violated the Establishment Clause. In the absence of any restriction on the expenditure of public funds by the schools, the expenditures had a primary effect that advanced religion**. The subsidies could easily be used for maintenance, chapels, religious instruction, or connection time to view religious websites. The law did not bar schools from using the grants for these and other constitutionally impermissible purposes. Because direct aid from the government to a sectarian institution in any form is invalid, the court held the direct subsidies to religious schools were unconstitutional. *Freedom From Religion Foundation Inc. v. Bugher*, 249 F.3d 606 (7th Cir. 2001).

III. PRIVATE SCHOOL TAXATION

In Camps Newfound/Owatonna, Inc. v. Town of Harrison, Maine, *520 U.S. 564, 117 S.Ct. 1590, 137 L.Ed.2d 852 (1997), the Supreme Court found no reason why nonprofit status should exempt a private entity from laws regulating commerce, including local property tax laws.*

A. Federal Income Taxation

◆ *The U.S. Supreme Court upheld a federal regulation requiring colleges and universities to make employment tax payments on behalf of employees who are normally scheduled to work at least 40 hours a week.*

Under federal law, no Federal Insurance Contributions Act (FICA) employment tax payments are due for "service performed in the employ of ... a school, college, or university" if the service is "performed by a student who is enrolled and regularly attending classes [at the school]." In 2004, the U.S. Treasury Department clarified an implementing regulation said the exemption did not apply to those who normally worked at least 40 hours a week for a school. The department cited medical residents as an example of employees who were not exempt. Medical school graduates typically worked 50-80 hours a week in a medical residency program offered through the Mayo Foundation of Medical Education and Research, the Mayo Clinic and the University of Minnesota. The programs lasted from three to five years, and residents received annual stipends of $41,000 to $56,000 with health and malpractice insurance and vacation time. Mayo sued the federal government to recover a refund of FICA tax it had withheld and paid on resident stipends. It claimed the residents were exempt under the statute and asserted that the regulation was invalid.

A federal district court held for Mayo, and after an appeals court reversed the judgment, the case reached the U.S. Supreme Court. The Court found the relevant statute did not define the term "student" or address whether medical residents were subject to FICA. But it held the regulation was a reasonable interpretation of the statute. **The Court rejected Mayo's argument that the Treasury Department should have to determine what each resident does and why before deciding whether the exemption applied.** The Court affirmed the decision upholding the regulation. *Mayo Foundation for Medical Educ. and Research v. U.S.*, 131 S.Ct. 704, 178 L.Ed.2d 588 (U.S. 2011).

◆ *A strong public policy against racial discrimination was held sufficient to deny tax-exempt status to an otherwise qualified private college.*

Section 501(c)(3) of the Internal Revenue Code (IRC) provides that "corporations ... organized and operated exclusively for religious, charitable ...

or educational purposes" are entitled to tax-exempt status. The Internal Revenue Service routinely granted tax exemption under IRC Section 501(c)(3) to private schools regardless of whether they had racially discriminatory admissions policies. In 1970, however, the IRS concluded it could no longer grant tax-exempt status to racially discriminatory private schools because such schools were not "charitable" within the meaning of Section 501(c)(3). In *Bob Jones Univ. v. U.S.*, two private colleges whose racial admissions policies were allegedly rooted in their interpretations of the Bible sued to prevent the IRS from interpreting the federal tax laws in this manner. The Supreme Court rejected the colleges' challenge and upheld the IRS's interpretation.

The Court's ruling was based on a strong federal public policy against racial discrimination in education. **Because the colleges were operating in violation of that public policy, the colleges could not be considered "charitable" under Section 501(c)(3). Thus, they were ineligible for tax exemption. The Court held that in order to fall under the exemption of Section 501(c)(3) an institution must be in harmony with the public interest.** It also held that the denial of an exemption did not impermissibly burden Bob Jones' alleged religious interest in practicing racial discrimination. *Bob Jones Univ. v. U.S.*, 461 U.S. 574, 103 S.Ct. 2017, 76 L.Ed.2d 157 (1983).

B. State and Local Taxation

◆ *A Maryland local tax on admissions and amusements did not apply to gate receipts from Johns Hopkins University lacrosse games, because the funds were used exclusively for educational purposes.*

Maryland law authorizes counties and municipalities to impose admissions and amusement taxes. But no admissions and amusement taxes may be imposed by a county or municipality on gross receipts that are used exclusively for charitable, educational, or religious purposes. Johns Hopkins University earned substantial revenue from its men's lacrosse program. It paid an admission's and amusement tax to the comptroller of the treasury for several years. The university then sought a refund from Baltimore City, asserting it was entitled to the exception for receipts used exclusively for an educational purpose. The Maryland Tax Court granted the university's request for a refund, and the comptroller appealed to the Court of Special Appeals of Maryland.

The court considered evidence that lacrosse game revenues were used to cover the costs of games and to contribute to the maintenance of the field and surrounding jogging track. The comptroller had already deemed the university field exempt from real property tax, and the university was exempt from federal tax under 26 U.S.C. § 501(c)(3). The court found substantial evidence to support the tax court's conclusion that receipts from the lacrosse games were used exclusively for an educational purpose. **The evidence showed that gross receipts were used to benefit the university, intercollegiate athletes, other non-participating students, and spectators.** About 50% of university students were involved in athletics of some sort. The field was used by all students and their families for commencement exercises, and it was also used by some students for ROTC and intramural games. As intramural athletic contests had always been treated by the Maryland taxing authorities and the

Tax Court as "educational" in purpose, the court affirmed the judgment for the university. *Comptroller of Treasury v. Johns Hopkins Univ.*, 186 Md.App. 169, 973 A.2d 256 (Md. Ct. Spec. App. 2009).

◆   *Office space leased by a bank from a university was exempt from property taxation because it was used for a "school purpose."*

The University of Delaware contracted with a bank to develop a student identification card that could also be used as a debit card for services. The university provided office space to the bank for the project. The local land use department discontinued the university's property tax exemption for the space and assessed taxes on it. A county board of assessment review upheld the assessment, but its decision was reversed by a state superior court, which found the space was used for a school purpose under state law.

The Supreme Court of Delaware noted the term "school purpose" was undefined by 9 Del. C. Section 8105. Under that section, college or school property used for educational or school purposes was not subject to taxation. The court rejected the county's argument that Section 8105 must be read narrowly. Statutes exempting educational institutions from taxation are generally "construed more liberally than other tax exempting statutes." The trial court had correctly determined the bank served a "school purpose." The court held "school purposes" included use of school-owned property that contributed to the legitimate welfare, convenience, and/or safety of the school community or its members. The judgment was affirmed. *New Castle County Dep't of Land Use v. Univ. of Delaware*, 842 A.2d 1201 (Del. 2004).

◆   *A university's bus service was not entitled to a credit for fuel taxes for its campus bus service.*

An Ohio public university owned a campus bus service that provided free transportation within the university campus. It also transported disabled students to and from the airport, and serviced the city of Kent and neighboring townships. However, it did not operate under a contract with the city or any other regional transit authority. When it applied for reimbursement of motor vehicle fuel taxes, claiming eligibility for the credits because its buses were transit buses, the tax commissioner and the Board of Tax Appeals ruled that its buses did not meet the statutory definition of "transit buses." The Supreme Court of Ohio upheld that determination. Here, even though the buses benefited non-students as well as students, **the bus service did not meet the requirement that it be operated by or for a municipal corporation**. The bus service was not entitled to the tax reimbursement. *Campus Bus Service v. Zaino*, 786 N.E.2d 889 (Ohio 2003).

◆   *A city was allowed to proceed in its lawsuit against a Catholic university for back taxes.*

The city of Scranton and its school district sued the University of Scranton, a Roman Catholic institution, for payment of back business privilege and/or mercantile taxes since 1995. The city asserted that the university gained income in those years from the sale of books and food, from parking lot revenue and from other sources. Since those income-generating activities took place in the city, the university ought to have to pay mercantile taxes. The university sought to dismiss the suit, **asserting that it was a charitable institution under the state's Purely Public Charity Act**, and the court of common pleas agreed. However, the Pennsylvania Commonwealth Court reversed, finding issues that required the lawsuit to proceed. As a result, the university had to answer the city's complaint. *School Dist. of City of Scranton v. Univ. of Scranton*, No. 2345 C.D. 2001, 2002 WL 876980 (Pa. Commw. Ct. 2002).

◆   *An office building owned by teaching doctors of Midwestern University did not qualify for real estate tax exemptions.*

The primary activities taking place at the property constituted billing, collection, data processing, accounting, administration, management, payroll and related functions for the physician group. When a state court held that the physician group did not qualify for the "charitable purposes" or "school" exemptions under Illinois law, appeal reached the Appellate Court of Illinois. **Under Illinois law, a property entitled to an exemption must be used exclusively for charitable purposes and owned by a charitable organization.** Here, the group failed to meet either requirement. The Appellate Court did not allow the group to use its relationship with the university to cast itself as a charitable organization. No patient care, medical research or instructional classes took place on the property. *Midwest Physician Group, Ltd. v. Dep't of Revenue of Illinois*, 711 N.E.2d 381 (Ill. App. Ct. 1999).

◆   *A university could not claim tax-exempt status for a parking garage or parts of a building leased to for-profit companies.*

A university owned a four-story building with an attached parking garage, and leased space to five tenants. Two tenants were nonprofit organizations, and the other three tenants were for-profit companies. The Board of Tax Appeals found that the building and the land under it were exempt from taxation, but the garage and land under it were not. The Cleveland Board of Education filed a notice of appeal, wanting the whole property to be taxed. The Supreme Court of Ohio affirmed the Board of Tax Appeals decisions regarding the tax exemption for the space leased by the two nonprofit organizations, and the non-tax-exempt status of the garage and the land under it. It reversed exemptions given to the university for the space held by the for-profit tenants and vacant areas in the building. **The garage did not qualify for tax-exempt status because it was not an essential and integral part of the university's or nonprofit tenants' charitable and/or educational activities.** *Case Western Reserve Univ. v. Tracy*, 84 Ohio St.3d 316, 703 N.E.2d 1240 (Ohio 1999).

◆   *Land used by a seminary for recreational purposes and as a buffer zone was exempt from taxation.*

A North Carolina county reviewed several parcels of land owned by a seminary and determined that they were not eligible for tax exemptions because they were not used for educational or religious purposes. After the state property tax commission held that exemptions applied to three parcels, the county appealed. The North Carolina Court of Appeals affirmed the decision in favor of the seminary. **Although the land was used essentially for**

recreational purposes, and as a buffer between the campus and commercial development surrounding the campus, it served to provide and maintain a relaxed campus atmosphere. Further, the seminary's attempt to rezone one of the parcels for commercial development so that it could sell the land for a profit was a planned future use, which did not change the present exempted use of the land. *In the Matter of Southeastern Baptist Theological Seminary,* 135 N.C.App. 247, 520 S.E.2d 302 (N.C. Ct. App. 1999).

◆   *The Commonwealth Court of Pennsylvania held that property owned by the private college in the following two cases was tax exempt because the college was a public charity under state law and the property was regularly used for the purposes of the college.*

A Pennsylvania nonprofit private college owned a house occupied by its grounds crew leader. The college charged the grounds crew leader a discounted rent that averaged about 70% of the fair market value. In exchange for the discount, the grounds crew leader agreed to be available on a 24-hour basis to respond to emergencies and nighttime calls. He was allegedly called to campus after-hours six times in both 1991 and 1992 for snow and ice removal, and to remove fallen tree limbs. The Delaware County Board of Assessment Appeals determined that the house was not exempt from property taxes. On appeal by the college, a Pennsylvania trial court reversed, finding the house exempt from taxation. A local public school district appealed the finding to the Commonwealth Court of Pennsylvania.

Article VIII of the **Pennsylvania Constitution provides that the general assembly can exempt real property of public charities "regularly used for the purposes of the institution."** Section 204 of the General County Assessment Law exempts all college property "necessary for the occupancy and enjoyment of the same." The commonwealth court stated that the college need not prove that the property was absolutely necessary to its needs for the exemption to apply. Rather, it was required to show only that it had a reasonable need for the property. Here, emergency personnel were essential to the college community. The grounds crew leader was able to respond much quicker to an emergency than personnel who were living off campus. The college properly chose to forgo the additional rental revenues to provide these needed services. Further, the alleged infrequency of emergency situations did not render the house incidental to the college's purposes. **Because emergency services were directly related to the proper functions of the college, the trial court did not err in concluding that the house was tax exempt.** *In re Swarthmore College,* 645 A.2d 470 (Pa. Commw. Ct. 1994).

The college also owned a large house designed for entertaining. The college's vice president for alumni development lived in the house rent-free and was not charged for utilities. The house was used for meetings, special events, receptions and to entertain potential donors from whom one-third of the college's yearly income was derived. The county Board of Assessment Appeals determined that the house was not exempt from property taxes. The Commonwealth Court of Pennsylvania stated that the **college was not required to prove that the property was absolutely necessary to its needs for the exemption to apply. Rather, it was required to show only that it had**

a reasonable necessity for the property. Here, the vice president was required to live in the house, use it to cultivate personal relationships with donors, and utilize it for numerous college functions. These uses were directly related to the proper functions of the college. Consequently, the vice president's house was tax exempt. *In re Swarthmore College*, 643 A.2d 1152 (Pa. Commw. Ct. 1994).

◆ *The Court of Appeal of Louisiana held that state law does not require private colleges to substantiate their tax-exempt status except as set forth by the state legislature.*

A Louisiana church operated a private university that offered a variety of secular undergraduate and graduate programs. The Louisiana Board of Regents notified the university that it had failed to complete and submit the required licensure application and was therefore in violation of state law. Consequently, it sought to close the school. **Although degree-granting institutions were generally required to be registered and licensed by the board, institutions granted a tax exemption under the Internal Revenue Code were exempted from these requirements.** Previously such private universities were required to supply only basic information to obtain a license. The state attorney general filed suit in a Louisiana trial court, seeking to enjoin the church's operation of the university based on its noncompliance with the board's procedural requirements. The trial court found that because the Internal Revenue Code does not require churches to obtain recognition of their exempt status, the board was prohibited from requiring the organization to do so. It denied the state's request for injunctive relief, and the state appealed.

The Court of Appeal of Louisiana affirmed the decision, noting that the state legislature chose to defer to federal law in this procedural area. Federal law, pursuant to the Internal Revenue Code, granted churches automatic exempt status without the necessity of paperwork. Absent a contrary directive from the state legislature, the court refused to read additional requirements into the law. *Ieyoub v. World Christian Church*, 649 So.2d 771 (La. Ct. App. 1994).

IV. PRIVATE ASSISTANCE TO SCHOOLS

Generally, when private parties donate money to schools, they have to be careful to specify how that money will be used or the schools will be able to put the money into their general operating funds. Colleges and universities often rely on financial boosters to support their athletic programs. But when questions arise as to how money is being raised and spent, relationships between booster organizations and schools can go sour. In the following case, an Iowa court rejected a college's claim that the head of a booster club mishandled funds and engaged in other unauthorized activities.

◆ *The departure of a prominent researcher from a university led to a dispute regarding whether donors could authorize a transfer of donated materials.*

A highly respected urologist and researcher had worked at Washington University, a private institution in Missouri, since 1976. His area of specialty was prostate cancer, and he performed thousands of surgeries and spearheaded research activities. The urologist was particularly interested in the genetic basis of prostate cancer, and he focused his research efforts in this area. In 1983, he began collecting samples of biological materials consisting of blood and tissue that were removed during surgery. The storage facility he helped create for biological samples eventually became the largest of its kind in the world. Donors who became research participants by allowing their samples to be used were required to complete an informed consent form, which used the term "donation" to describe the transfer of biological samples from the participant to a university physician or medical technician. The forms also specified that participants agreed to waive any claim to donated body tissues. In early 2003, the urologist accepted a new position at Northwestern University. Soon after he arrived there, he sent a letter to donors, asking them to release their samples to him. Washington University filed a federal court lawsuit seeking a declaration that it owned them and was not required to honor any transfer request. The urologist filed a counterclaim, seeking a declaration that the donors had a right to transfer their samples to him. The court held Washington owned the samples. It also found that neither the urologist nor the donors had an ownership interest in them, and that none of the urologist's forms transferred their ownership.

The U.S. Court of Appeals for the Eighth Circuit affirmed the district court's ruling, finding the donors did not retain an ownership interest allowing them to transfer the samples to a third party. **All of the donors transferred their samples to the university as gifts.** The university established that a gift was made by showing the donors intended to make a gift. The samples were delivered by the donors, and the university accepted them. The consent form and brochure language supported the conclusion that the sample transfers were gifts, and the university retained "absolute possession" over them, while at Washington. The urologist signed agreements acknowledging the university's ownership of the samples. Although he claimed that the donors retained an ownership interest, he also regularly ordered the destruction of donated samples to create more storage space. This activity was inconsistent with his claim that the donors retained an ownership interest. In addition, both federal and state regulations bar the return of donated body tissue and blood to donors. *Washington Univ. v. Catalona*, 490 F.3d 667 (8th Cir. 2007).

◆ *Members of nonprofit organizations are not liable for the debts of an organization unless they engage in intentional misconduct.*

Over the course of his long tenure as a benefactor, Charles Talbot personally donated more than $45,000 and helped raise more than $97,000 for Indian Hills Community College. Talbot approached the school to discuss the creation of a more formal tax-exempt booster club in 2001. The school told Talbot it would need to endorse such a move, but he went ahead and formed a nonprofit corporation without asking for approval. The relationship between Talbot and the school began to sour. The president told the group they needed to run the booster club funds through a school-audited account, but the group refused to do so. They also refused to provide the college access to the club's financial records. In April 2004, the college sued Talbot and the booster club in a state court. The suit accused Talbot and the club of conversion, and it claimed he had engaged in unauthorized acts. The trial court held for Talbot, relying on state law immunity for members of nonprofit organizations and corporations. On appeal, the Court of Appeals of Iowa held the trial court had correctly applied state law immunity provisions to block the college's claims. **Members of nonprofit organizations were not liable for debts or obligations of the organization unless they engaged in intentional misconduct, knowingly violated the law, or derived an "improper personal benefit" from a transaction.** There was no showing that any actions taken by Talbot were illegal or inappropriate Therefore, he could not be held liable for any of the allegedly improper actions taken on behalf of the booster club. The trial court decision against the college was affirmed. *Indian Hills Community College v. Indian Hills Booster Club*, No. 06-0392, 734 N.W.2d 486 (Table), 2007 WL 911890 (Iowa Ct. App. 3/28/07).

◆ *Vanderbilt University could not change the name of its dormitories in violation of an agreement with a donor organization.*

In 1905, trustees of the Peabody Education Fund voted to direct $1 million to create a permanent endowment for a college of higher education for teachers in the southern states. Trustees of the college voted to buy several properties adjacent to Vanderbilt University. The United Daughters of the Confederacy (UDC) entered into a contract with college trustees to raise $50,000 to construct the women's dorm on the new campus. In return for the gift, the college had to allow female descendants of Confederate soldiers nominated by the UDC to live in the dorm rent-free. In 1927, the college and UDC entered into a second contract specifying that a Confederate Memorial Hall be constructed on the campus. From 1935 until the late 1970s, female descendants of Confederate soldiers nominated by the UDC lived in the dorms rent-free. The college started experiencing financial difficulties. To raise money, college trustees leased two dorms, including Confederate Memorial Hall, to Vanderbilt. When the college's financial situation became worse, it merged with Vanderbilt. A year after the renovation of Confederate Memorial Hall, some Vanderbilt students, faculty and staff expressed dissatisfaction with the building name. They emphasized demographic changes over the years. The chancellor of Vanderbilt decided to change the name to "Memorial Hall" without consulting the UDC. The UDC sued Vanderbilt in a state court for breach of contract. The court awarded summary judgment to Vanderbilt. It found it impractical and unduly burdensome for Vanderbilt to continue to perform the terms of the contract. The UDC appealed to Court of Appeals of Tennessee.

Vanderbilt argued it already had substantially fulfilled its obligations because it had allowed many women to live in the dorms rent-free over the years and had kept the building's original name for almost 70 years. Moreover, the university should no longer be obligated to keep the name because it would be inconsistent with laws prohibiting racial discrimination. **The court held the intent of the UDC was for the funds to be a conditional gift. Generally, if the university failed to comply with the conditions, the donor would recover the gift.** However, since the value of a dollar was different now from when the money was given, returning the gift would be unfair to the UDC. The court held that as Vanderbilt had refused to abide by the conditions of the gift, the present value of the gift must be returned, or the university would have to agree to abide by the conditions. The court reversed the judgment and returned the case to the trial court to calculate the gift's present value. *Tennessee Division of United Daughters of the Confederacy v. Vanderbilt Univ.*, 174 S.W.3d 98 (Tenn. Ct. App. 2005).

◆   *The Court of Appeals of Kentucky denied a claim to property by a college under a property owner's will.*

A Kentucky property owner bequeathed property to a relative. However, the will stated that if the relative died without children, the property was to pass to the relative's younger sister and her heirs. The will also provided Georgetown College would receive the proceeds from the sale of 71 acres of farmland, to be used to fund a permanent endowment at the college. Any additional money would be paid to the college for the endowment fund. Both the relative and her sister died without children. A state court distributed $1.3 million from the estate in three equal shares to the sister's heirs, finding the college was only covered under a specific item in the will. The state appeals court rejected the college's argument that the devises to the sisters were substitutional. **When the property owner died, the court explained, the interest in her property vested in the sister's heirs. The college's reasoning would lead to a finding that the property owner had died without heirs.** As this result was disfavored, the court affirmed the judgment for the heirs. *Georgetown College v. Alexander*, 140 S.W.3d 6 (Ky. Ct. App. 2003).

◆   *A university hospital could not get money bequeathed to another institution even though a condition of the will was illegal.*

A doctor associated with the Keswick Home in Baltimore provided for four annuitants in his will and, after the death of the last of them, directed that the remainder of his estate (nearly $29 million) go to the Keswick Home for the acquisition or construction of a new building in his name for "white patients who need[ed] physical rehabilitation." If Keswick found the bequest unacceptable, the money was to pass to the University of Maryland Hospital to be used for physical rehabilitation. A lawsuit developed over the funds, with the university hospital arguing that the illegal racial restriction required the money to be awarded to it. A trial court agreed, but the Maryland Court of Appeals reversed. It excised the illegal condition attached to the will and awarded the money to Keswick. *Home for Incurables of Baltimore City v. Univ. of Maryland Medical System Corp.*, 797 A.2d 746 (Md. 2002).

UNITED STATES CONSTITUTION

Provisions of Interest to Higher Educators

ARTICLE I

Section 1. All legislative Powers herein granted shall be vested in a Congress of the United States, which shall consist of a Senate and House of Representatives.

* * *

Section 8. The Congress shall have Power To lay and collect Taxes, Duties, Imposts and Excises, to pay the Debts and provide for the common Defence and general Welfare of the United States; but all Duties, Imposts and Excises shall be uniform throughout the United States;

To borrow money on the credit of the United States;

To regulate Commerce with foreign Nations, and among the several States, and with the Indian Tribes;

To establish an uniform Rule of Naturalization, and uniform Laws on the subject of Bankruptcies throughout the United States;

* * *

To promote the Progress of Science and useful Arts, by securing for limited Times to Authors and Inventors the exclusive Right to their respective Writings and Discoveries;

* * *

To make all Laws which shall be necessary and proper for carrying into Execution for the foregoing Powers, and all other Powers vested by this Constitution in the Government of the United States, or in any Department or Officer thereof.

* * *

Section 9. * * * No Bill of Attainder or ex post facto Law shall be passed.

* * *

Section 10. No State shall * * * pass any Bill of Attainder, ex post facto Law, or Law impairing the Obligation of Contracts, or grant any Title of Nobility.

ARTICLE II

Section 1. The executive Power shall be vested in a President of the United States of America. * * *

ARTICLE III

Section 1. The judicial Power of the United States, shall be vested in one supreme Court, and in such inferior Courts as the Congress may from time to time ordain and establish. The Judges, both of the supreme and inferior courts, shall hold their Offices during good Behaviour, and shall, at stated Times, receive for their Services a Compensation, which shall not be diminished during their Continuance in Office.

Section 2. The judicial Power shall extend to all Cases, in Law and Equity, arising under this Constitution, the Laws of the United States, and Treaties made, or which shall be made, under their Authority; - to all Cases affecting Ambassadors, other public Ministers and Consuls; - to all Cases of admiralty and maritime Jurisdiction, - to Controversies to which the United States shall be a party; - to Controversies between two or more States; - between a State and Citizens of another State; - between Citizens of different States; - between Citizens of the same State claiming Lands under the Grants of different States, and between a State, or the Citizens thereof, and foreign States, Citizens or Subjects.

* * *

ARTICLE IV

Section 1. Full Faith and Credit shall be given in each State to the public Acts, Records and judicial Proceedings of every other State. * * *

Section 2. The Citizens of each State shall be entitled to all Privileges and Immunities of Citizens in the several States.

* * *

Section 4. The United States shall guarantee to every State in this Union a Republican Form of Government, and shall protect each of them against Invasion; and on Application of the Legislature, or of the Executive (when the Legislature cannot be convened) against domestic Violence.

ARTICLE V

The Congress, whenever two thirds of both Houses shall deem it necessary, shall propose Amendments to this Constitution, or, on the Application of the Legislatures of two thirds of the several States, shall call a Convention for proposing Amendments, which, in either Case, shall be valid to all Intents and Purposes, as part of this Constitution, when ratified by the Legislatures of three fourths of the several States, or by Conventions in three fourths thereof, as the one or the other Mode of Ratification may be proposed by the Congress; Provided that no Amendment which may be made prior to the Year One thousand eight hundred and eight shall in any Manner affect the first and fourth Clauses in the Ninth Section of the first Article; and that no State, without its Consent, shall be deprived of its equal Suffrage in the Senate.

ARTICLE VI

* * *

This Constitution, and the Laws of the United States which shall be made in Pursuance thereof; and all Treaties made, or which shall be made, under the Authority of the United States, shall be the supreme Law of the Land; and the Judges in every State shall be bound thereby, any Thing in the Constitution or Laws of any State to the Contrary notwithstanding.

The Senators and Representatives before mentioned, and the Members of the several State Legislatures, and all executive and judicial Officers, both of the United States and of the several States, shall be bound by Oath or Affirmation, to support this Constitution; but no religious Test shall ever be required as a Qualification to any Office or public Trust under the United States.

* * *

AMENDMENT I

Congress shall make no law respecting an establishment of religion, or prohibiting the free exercise thereof; or abridging the freedom of speech, or of the press; or the right of the people peaceably to assemble, and to petition the Government for a redress of grievances.

* * *

AMENDMENT IV

The right of the people to be secure in their persons, houses, papers, and effects, against unreasonable searches and seizures, shall not be violated, and no Warrants shall issue, but upon probable cause, supported by Oath or affirmation, and particularly describing the place to be searched, and the persons or things to be seized.

AMENDMENT V

No person shall be held to answer for a capital, or otherwise infamous crime, unless on a presentment or indictment of a Grand Jury, except in cases arising in the land or naval forces, or in the Militia, when in actual service in time of War or public danger; nor shall any person be subject for the same offence to be twice put in jeopardy of life or limb; nor shall be compelled in any criminal case to be a witness against himself, nor be deprived of life, liberty, or property, without due process of law; nor shall private property be taken for public use, without just compensation.

AMENDMENT VI

In all criminal prosecutions, the accused shall enjoy the right to a speedy and public trial, by an impartial jury of the State and district wherein the crime shall have been committed, which district shall have been previously ascertained by law, and to be informed of the nature and cause of the accusation; to be confronted with the witnesses against him; to have compulsory process for obtaining witnesses in his favor, and to have the Assistance of Counsel for his defense.

AMENDMENT VII

In Suits at common law, where the value in controversy shall exceed twenty dollars, the right of trial by jury shall be preserved, and no fact tried by jury, shall be otherwise re-examined in any Court of the United States, than according to the rules of the common law.

AMENDMENT VIII

Excessive bail shall not be required, nor excessive fines imposed, nor cruel and unusual punishments inflicted.

AMENDMENT IX

The enumeration in the Constitution, of certain rights, shall not be construed to deny or disparage others retained by the people.

AMENDMENT X

The powers not delegated to the United States by the Constitution, nor prohibited by it to the States, are reserved to the States respectively, or to the people.

AMENDMENT XI

The Judicial power of the United States shall not be construed to extend to any suit in law or equity, commenced or prosecuted against one of the United States by Citizens of another State, or by Citizens or Subjects of any Foreign State.

* * *

AMENDMENT XIII

Section 1. Neither slavery nor involuntary servitude, except as a punishment for crime whereof the party shall have been duly convicted, shall exist within the United States, or any place subject to their jurisdiction.

Section 2. Congress shall have power to enforce this article by appropriate legislation.

AMENDMENT XIV

Section 1. All persons born or naturalized in the United States, and subject to the jurisdiction thereof, are citizens of the United States and of the State wherein they reside. No State shall make or enforce any law which shall abridge the privileges or immunities of citizens of the United States; nor shall any State deprive any person of life, liberty, or property, without due process of law; nor deny to any person within its jurisdiction the equal protection of the laws.

* * *

Section 5. The Congress shall have power to enforce, by appropriate legislation, the provisions of this article.

APPENDIX B

Subject Matter Table of United States Supreme Court Cases Affecting Higher Education

Note: Please see the Table of Cases (located at the front of this volume) for Supreme Court cases reported in this volume.

Academic Freedom
Univ. of Pennsylvania v. EEOC, 493 U.S. 182, 110 S.Ct. 577, 107 L.Ed.2d 571 (1990).
Epperson v. Arkansas, 393 U.S. 97, 89 S.Ct. 266, 21 L.Ed.2d 228 (1968).
Sweezy v. New Hampshire, 354 U.S. 234, 77 S.Ct. 1203, 1 L.Ed.2d 1311 (1957).
Meyer v. Nebraska, 262 U.S. 390, 43 S.Ct. 625, 67 L.Ed.2d 1042 (1923).

Arbitration
Volt Information Sciences v. Board of Trustees of Stanford Univ., 489 U.S. 468, 109 S.Ct. 1248, 103 L.Ed.2d 488 (1989).

Athletics
NCAA v. Smith, 525 U.S. 459, 119 S.Ct. 924, 142 L.Ed.2d 929 (1999).
NCAA v. Tarkanian, 488 U.S. 179, 109 S.Ct. 454, 102 L.Ed.2d 469 (1988).

Attorneys' Fees
Webb v. Board of Educ., 471 U.S. 234, 105 S.Ct. 1923, 85 L.Ed.2d 233 (1985).
Smith v. Robinson, 468 U.S. 992, 104 S.Ct. 3457, 82 L.Ed.2d 746 (1984).

Civil Rights
Farrar v. Hobby, 506 U.S. 103, 113 S.Ct. 566, 121 L.Ed.2d 494 (1992).
St. Francis College v. Al-Khazraji, 481 U.S. 604, 107 S.Ct. 2022, 97 L.Ed.2d 749 (1987).
Grove City College v. Bell, 465 U.S. 555, 104 S.Ct. 1211, 79 L.Ed.2d 516 (1984).
Rendell-Baker v. Kohn, 457 U.S. 830, 102 S.Ct. 2764, 73 L.Ed.2d 418 (1982).

Collective Bargaining
Davenport v. Washington Educ. Ass'n, 127 S.Ct. 2372 (U.S. 2007).
Cent. State Univ. v. American Ass'n of Univ. Professors, Cent. State Univ. Chapter, 526 U.S. 124, 119 S.Ct. 1162, 143 L.Ed.2d 227 (1999).

Compulsory Attendance

Wisconsin v. Yoder, 406 U.S. 205, 92 S.Ct. 526, 32 L.Ed.2d 15 (1972).

Pierce v. Society of Sisters, 268 U.S. 510, 45 S.Ct. 571, 69 L.Ed. 1070 (1925).

Continuing Education

Austin ISD v. U.S., 443 U.S. 915, 99 S.Ct. 3106, 61 L.Ed.2d 879 (1979).

Harrah ISD v. Martin, 440 U.S. 194, 99 S.Ct. 1062, 59 L.Ed.2d 248 (1979).

Corporal Punishment

Ingraham v. Wright, 430 U.S. 651, 97 S.Ct. 1401, 51 L.Ed.2d 711 (1977).

Court Intervention in School Affairs

Epperson v. Arkansas, 393 U.S. 97, 89 S.Ct. 266, 21 L.Ed.2d 228 (1968).

Criminal Activity

Bates v. U.S., 522 U.S. 23, 118 S.Ct. 285, 139 L.Ed.2d 215 (1997).

Desegregation

U.S. v. Fordice, 505 U.S. 717, 112 S.Ct. 2727, 120 L.Ed.2d 575 (1992).

Freeman v. Pitts, 503 U.S. 467, 112 S.Ct. 1430, 118 L.Ed.2d 108 (1992).

Disabled Students

Florence County School Dist. Four v. Carter, 510 U.S. 7, 114 S.Ct. 361, 126 L.Ed.2d 284 (1993).

Zobrest v. Catalina Foothills School Dist., 509 U.S. 1, 113 S.Ct. 2462, 125 L.Ed.2d 1 (1993).

Dellmuth v. Muth, 491 U.S. 223, 109 S.Ct. 2397, 105 L.Ed.2d 181 (1989).

Honig v. Doe, 484 U.S. 305, 108 S.Ct. 592, 98 L.Ed.2d 686 (1988).

City of Cleburne, Texas v. Cleburne Living Center, 473 U.S. 432, 105 S.Ct. 3249, 87 L.Ed.2d 313 (1985).

Honig v. Students of California School for the Blind, 471 U.S. 148, 105 S.Ct. 1820, 85 L.Ed.2d 114 (1985).

Burlington School Committee v. Dep't of Educ., 471 U.S. 359, 105 S.Ct. 1996, 85 L.Ed.2d 385 (1985).

Smith v. Robinson, 468 U.S. 992, 104 S.Ct. 3457, 82 L.Ed.2d 746 (1984).

Irving Independent School District v. Tatro, 468 U.S. 883, 104 S.Ct. 3371, 82 L.Ed.2d 664 (1984).

Board of Educ. v. Rowley, 458 U.S. 176, 102 S.Ct. 3034, 73 L.Ed.2d 690 (1982).

Univ. of Texas v. Camenisch, 451 U.S. 390, 101 S.Ct. 1830, 68 L.Ed.2d 175 (1981).

Pennhurst State School and Hospital v. Halderman, 451 U.S. 1, 101 S.Ct. 1531, 67 L.Ed.2d 694 (1981).

Southeastern Community College v. Davis, 442 U.S. 397, 99 S.Ct. 2361, 60 L.Ed.2d 980 (1979).

Discrimination, Generally

Fisher v. Univ. of Texas at Austin, 133 S.Ct. 2411 (U.S. 2013).

Edelman v. Lynchburg College, 532 U.S. 106, 122 S.Ct. 1145, 152 L.Ed.2d 188 (2002).

Raygor v. Regents of Univ. of Minnesota, 534 U.S. 533, 122 S.Ct. 999, 152 L.Ed.2d 27 (2002).

Alexander v. Sandoval, 531 U.S. 1049, 121 S.Ct. 1511, 141 L.Ed.2d 517 (2001).

Board of Trustees of the Univ. of Alabama v. Garrett, 531 U.S. 356, 121 S.Ct. 955, 148 L.Ed.2d 866 (2001).

Kimel v. Florida Board of Regents, 528 U.S. 62, 120 S.Ct. 631, 145 L.Ed.2d 522 (2000).

Texas v. Lesage, 528 U.S. 18, 120 S.Ct. 467, 145 L.Ed.2d 347 (1999).

Lane v. Pena, 518 U.S. 187, 116 S.Ct. 2092, 135 L.Ed.2d 486 (1996).

Jett v. Dallas Independent School Dist., 491 U.S. 701, 109 S.Ct. 2702, 105 L.Ed.2d 598 (1989).

Carnegie-Mellon Univ. v. Cohill, 484 U.S. 343, 108 S.Ct. 614, 98 L.Ed.2d 720 (1988).

School Board of Nassau County v. Arline, 480 U.S. 273, 107 S.Ct. 1123, 94 L.Ed.2d 307 (1987).

Hazelwood School Dist. v. U.S., 433 U.S. 299, 97 S.Ct. 2736, 53 L.Ed.2d 768 (1977).

DeFunis v. Odegaard, 416 U.S. 312, 94 S.Ct. 1704, 40 L.Ed.2d 164 (1974).

Due Process

Gilbert v. Homar, 520 U.S. 924, 117 S.Ct. 1807, 138 L.Ed.2d 120 (1997).

Univ. of Tennessee v. Elliot, 478 U.S. 788, 106 S.Ct. 3220, 92 L.Ed.2d 635 (1986).

Memphis Community School Dist. v. Stachura, 477 U.S. 299, 106 S.Ct. 2537, 91 L.Ed.2d 249 (1986).

Cleveland Board of Educ. v. Loudermill, 470 U.S. 532, 105 S.Ct. 1487, 84 L.Ed.2d 494 (1985).

Perry v. Sindermann, 408 U.S. 593, 92 S.Ct. 2694, 33 L.Ed.2d 570 (1972).

Board of Regents v. Roth, 408 U.S. 564, 92 S.Ct. 2701, 33 L.Ed.2d 548 (1972).

Employment

Hosanna-Tabor Evangelical Lutheran Church and School v. E.E.O.C., 132 S.Ct. 694 (U.S. 2012).

City of Ontario v. Quon, 130 S.Ct. 2619 (U.S. 2010).

Burlington Northern & Santa Fe Railway Co. v. White, 126 S.Ct. 2405 (U.S. 2006).

Smith v. City of Jackson, 125 S.Ct. 1536 (U.S. 2005).

Corporation of the Presiding Bishop of the Church of Jesus Christ of Latter-Day Saints v. Amos, 483 U.S. 327, 107 S.Ct. 2862, 97 L.Ed.2d 273 (1987).

O'Connor v. Ortega, 480 U.S. 709 (1987).

Franklin & Marshall College v. EEOC, 476 U.S. 1163, 106 S.Ct. 2288, 90 L.Ed.2d 729 (1986).

NLRB v. Catholic Bishop of Chicago, 440 U.S. 490, 99 S.Ct. 1313, 59 L.Ed.2d 533 (1979).

Federal Aid

Traynor v. Turnage, 485 U.S. 535, 108 S.Ct. 1372, 99 L.Ed.2d 618 (1988).

Selective Service System v. MPIRG, 468 U.S. 841, 104 S.Ct. 3348, 82 L.Ed.2d 632 (1984).

Bell v. New Jersey and Pennsylvania, 461 U.S. 773, 103 S.Ct. 2187, 76 L.Ed.2d 312 (1984).

Grove City College v. Bell, 465 U.S. 555, 104 S.Ct. 1211, 79 L.Ed.2d 516 (1984).

Valley Forge Christian College v. Americans United for Separation of Church and State, 454 U.S. 464, 102 S.Ct. 752, 70 L.Ed.2d 700 (1982).

Board of Educ. v. Harris, 444 U.S. 130, 100 S.Ct. 363, 62 L.Ed.2d 275 (1979).

Wheeler v. Barrera, 417 U.S. 402, 94 S.Ct. 2274, 41 L.Ed.2d 159 (1974).

Tilton v. Richardson, 403 U.S. 672, 91 S.Ct. 2091, 29 L.Ed.2d 790 (1971).

Freedom of Religion

City of Boerne, Texas v. Flores, 521 U.S. 507, 117 S.Ct. 2157, 138 L.Ed.2d 624 (1997).

Edwards v. Aguillard, 482 U.S. 578, 107 S.Ct. 2573, 96 L.Ed.2d 510 (1987).

Ansonia Board of Educ. v. Philbrook, 499 U.S. 60, 107 S.Ct. 367, 93 L.Ed.2d 305 (1986).

Freedom of Speech

Christian Legal Society Chapter of the University of California, Hastings College of the Law v. Martinez, 130 S.Ct. 2971 (U.S. 2010).

Garcetti v. Ceballos, 126 S.Ct. 1951, 164 L.Ed. 2d 689 (U.S. 2006).

Board of Regents of Univ. of Wisconsin System v. Southworth, 529 U.S. 217, 120 S.Ct. 1346, 146 L.Ed.2d 193 (2000).

Board of Educ. of Westside Community School v. Mergens, 496 U.S. 226, 110 S.Ct. 2356, 110 L.Ed.2d 191 (1990).

Board of Trustees of the State Univ. of New York v. Fox, 492 U.S. 469, 109 S.Ct. 3028, 106 L.Ed.2d 388 (1989).

Hazelwood School Dist. v. Kuhlmeier, 484 U.S. 261, 108 S.Ct. 562, 98 L.Ed.2d 592 (1988).

Rankin v. McPherson, 483 U.S. 378, 107 S.Ct. 2891, 97 L.Ed.2d 315 (1987).

Bethel School Dist. v. Fraser, 478 U.S. 675, 106 S.Ct. 3159, 92 L.Ed.2d 549 (1986).

Wayte v. U.S., 470 U.S. 598, 105 S.Ct. 1524, 84 L.Ed.2d 547 (1985).

Connick v. Myers, 461 U.S. 138, 103 S.Ct. 1684, 75 L.Ed.2d 708 (1983).

Board of Educ. v. Pico, 457 U.S. 853, 102 S.Ct. 2799, 73 L.Ed.2d 435 (1982).

Givhan v. Western Line Consolidated School Dist., 439 U.S. 410, 99 S.Ct. 693, 58 L.Ed.2d 619 (1979).

Mt. Healthy City School v. Doyle, 429 U.S. 274, 97 S.Ct. 568, 50 L.Ed.2d 471 (1977).

Papish v. Board of Curators, 410 U.S. 667, 93 S.Ct. 1197, 35 L.Ed.2d 618 (1973).

Grayned v. City of Rockford, 408 U.S. 104, 92 S.Ct. 2294, 33 L.Ed.2d 222 (1972).

Police Dep't v. Mosley, 408 U.S. 92, 92 S.Ct. 2286, 33 L.Ed.2d 212 (1972).

Tinker v. Des Moines, 393 U.S. 503, 89 S.Ct. 733, 21 L.Ed.2d 733 (1969).

Pickering v. Board of Educ., 391 U.S. 563, 88 S.Ct. 1731, 20 L.Ed.2d 811 (1968).

Whitehill v. Elkins, 389 U.S. 54, 88 S.Ct. 184, 19 L.Ed.2d 228 (1967).

Keyishian v. Board of Regents, 385 U.S. 589, 87 S.Ct. 675, 17 L.Ed.2d 629 (1967).

Elfbrandt v. Russell, 384 U.S. 11, 86 S.Ct. 1238, 16 L.Ed.2d 321 (1965).

Baggett v. Bullitt, 377 U.S. 360, 84 S.Ct. 1316, 12 L.Ed.2d 377 (1963).

Cramp v. Board of Public Instruction of Orange County, 368 U.S. 278, 82 S.Ct. 275, 7 L.Ed.2d 285 (1961).

Shelton v. Tucker, 364 U.S. 479, 81 S.Ct. 247, 5 L.Ed.2d 231 (1960).

Slochower v. Board of Educ., 350 U.S. 551, 76 S.Ct. 637, 100 L.Ed. 692 (1955).

Adler v. Board of Educ., 342 U.S. 485, 72 S.Ct. 380, 96 L.Ed. 517 (1952).

Intellectual Property

New York Times Co. Inc. v. Tasini, 533 U.S. 483, 121 S.Ct. 2381, 150 L.Ed.2d 500 (2001).

Florida Prepaid Postsecondary Educ. Expense Board v. College Savings Bank, 527 U.S. 627, 119 S.Ct. 2199, 144 L.Ed.2d 575 (1999).
College Savings Bank v. Florida Prepaid Postsecondary Educ. Expense Board, 527 U.S. 666, 119 S.Ct. 2219, 144 L.Ed.2d 605 (1999).

Labor Relations

Lehnert v. Ferris Faculty Ass'n, 500 U.S. 507, 111 S.Ct. 1950, 114 L.Ed.2d 572 (1991).

Fort Stewart Schools v. Federal Labor Relations Authority, 495 U.S. 641, 110 S.Ct. 2043, 109 L.Ed.2d 659 (1990).

Minnesota State Board for Community Colleges v. Knight, 465 U.S. 271, 104 S.Ct. 1058, 79 L.Ed.2d 299 (1984).

NLRB v. Yeshiva Univ., 444 U.S. 672, 100 S.Ct. 856, 63 L.Ed.2d 115 (1980).

NLRB v. Catholic Bishop of Chicago, 440 U.S. 490, 99 S.Ct. 1313, 59 L.Ed.2d 533 (1979).

Abood v. Detroit Board of Educ., 431 U.S. 209, 97 S.Ct. 1782, 52 L.Ed.2d 261 (1977).

Maternity Leave

Richmond Unified School Dist. v. Berg, 434 U.S. 158, 98 S.Ct. 623, 54 L.Ed.2d 375 (1977).

Cleveland Board of Educ. v. La Fleur, 414 U.S. 632, 94 S.Ct. 791, 39 L.Ed.2d 52 (1974).

Cohen v. Chesterfield, 414 U.S. 632, 94 S.Ct. 791, 39 L.Ed.2d 52 (1974).

Private School Funding

Agostini v. Felton, 521 U.S. 203, 117 S.Ct. 1997, 138 L.Ed.2d 391 (1997).

Board of Educ. of Kiryas Joel Village School Dist. v. Grumet, 512 U.S. 687, 114 S.Ct. 2481, 129 L.Ed.2d 546 (1994).

Witters v. Washington Dep't of Services for the Blind, 474 U.S. 481, 106 S.Ct. 748, 88 L.Ed.2d 846 (1986).

Aguilar v. Felton, 473 U.S. 402, 105 S.Ct. 3232, 87 L.Ed.2d 290 (1985).

Grand Rapids School District v. Ball, 473 U.S. 373, 105 S.Ct. 3216, 87 L.Ed.2d 267 (1985).

Mueller v. Allen, 463 U.S. 388, 103 S.Ct. 3062, 77 L.Ed.2d 721 (1983).

Valley Forge Christian College v. Americans United for Separation of Church and State, 454 U.S. 464, 102 S.Ct. 752, 70 L.Ed.2d 700 (1982).

Committee for Public Educ. and Religious Liberty v. Regan, 444 U.S. 646, 100 S.Ct. 840, 63 L.Ed.2d 94 (1980).

New York v. Cathedral Academy, 434 U.S. 125, 98 S.Ct. 340, 54 L.Ed.2d 346 (1977).

Wolman v. Walter, 433 U.S. 229, 97 S.Ct. 2593, 53 L.Ed.2d 714 (1977).

Roemer v. Board of Public Works, 426 U.S. 736, 96 S.Ct. 2337, 49 L.Ed.2d 179 (1976).

Meek v. Pittenger, 421 U.S. 349, 95 S.Ct. 1753, 44 L.Ed.2d 217 (1975).
Wheeler v. Barrera, 417 U.S. 402, 94 S.Ct. 2274, 41 L.Ed.2d 159 (1974).
Sloan v. Lemon, 413 U.S. 825, 93 S.Ct. 2982, 37 L.Ed.2d 939 (1973).
Committee for Public Educ. and Religious Liberty v. Nyquist, 413 U.S. 756, 93 S.Ct. 2955, 37 L.Ed.2d 948 (1973).
Hunt v. McNair, 413 U.S. 734, 93 S.Ct. 2868, 37 L.Ed.2d 923 (1973).
Levitt v. Committee for Public Educ. and Religious Liberty, 413 U.S. 472, 93 S.Ct. 2814, 37 L.Ed.2d 736 (1973).
Lemon v. Kurtzman, 403 U.S. 602, 91 S.Ct. 2105, 29 L.Ed.2d 745 (1971).
Flast v. Cohen, 392 U.S. 83, 88 S.Ct. 1942, 20 L.Ed.2d 947 (1968).

Racial Discrimination

Grutter v. Bollinger, 539 U.S. 306, 123 S.Ct. 2325, 156 L.Ed.2d 304 (2003).
Gratz v. Bollinger, 539 U.S. 244, 123 S.Ct. 2411, 156 L.Ed.2d 257 (2003).
St. Francis College v. Al-Khazraji, 481 U.S. 604, 107 S.Ct. 2022, 97 L.Ed.2d 749 (1987).
City of Pleasant Grove v. United States, 479 U.S. 462, 107 S.Ct. 794, 93 L.Ed.2d 866 (1987).
Wygant v. Jackson Board of Educ., 476 U.S. 267, 106 S.Ct. 1842, 90 L.Ed.2d 260 (1986).
Regents of the Univ. of California v. Bakke, 438 U.S. 265, 98 S.Ct. 2733, 57 L.Ed.2d 750 (1978).
Runyon v. McCrary, 427 U.S. 160, 96 S.Ct. 2586, 49 L.Ed.2d 415 (1976).
Lau v. Nichols, 414 U.S. 563, 94 S.Ct. 786, 39 L.Ed.2d 1 (1974).
Norwood v. Harrison, 413 U.S. 455, 93 S.Ct. 2804, 37 L.Ed.2d 723 (1973).

Recognition of Student Organizations

Bender v. Williamsport Area School Dist., 475 U.S. 534, 106 S.Ct. 1326, 89 L.Ed.2d 501 (1986).
Healy v. James, 408 U.S. 169, 92 S.Ct. 2338, 33 L.Ed.2d 266 (1972).

Release Time

Zorach v. Clauson, 343 U.S. 306, 72 S.Ct. 679, 96 L.Ed. 954 (1952).
McCollum v. Board of Educ., 333 U.S. 203, 68 S.Ct. 461, 92 L.Ed. 649 (1948).

Religious Activities in Public Schools

Rosenberger v. Rector and Visitors of Univ. of Virginia, 515 U.S. 819, 115 S.Ct. 2510, 132 L.Ed.2d 700 (1995).
Lamb's Chapel v. Center Moriches Union Free School District, 508 U.S. 384, 113 S.Ct. 2141, 124 L.Ed.2d 352 (1993).
Lee v. Weisman, 505 U.S. 577, 112 S.Ct. 2649, 120 L.Ed.2d 467 (1992).

Karcher v. May, 484 U.S. 72, 108 S.Ct. 388, 98 L.Ed.2d 327 (1987).
Wallace v. Jaffree, 472 U.S. 38, 105 S.Ct. 2479, 96 L.Ed.2d 29 (1985).
Widmar v. Vincent, 454 U.S. 263, 102 S.Ct. 269, 70 L.Ed.2d 400 (1981).
Stone v. Graham, 449 U.S. 39, 101 S.Ct. 192, 66 L.Ed.2d 199 (1980).
Chamberlin v. Dade County Board of Public Instruction, 377 U.S. 402, 84 S.Ct. 1272, 12 L.Ed.2d 407 (1964).
Abington School Dist. v. Schempp, 374 U.S. 203, 83 S.Ct. 1560, 10 L.Ed.2d 844 (1963).

Residency

Martinez v. Bynum, 461 U.S. 321 103 S.Ct. 1838, 75 L.Ed.2d 879 (1983).
Toll v. Moreno, 458 U.S. 1, 102 S.Ct. 2977, 73 L.Ed.2d 563 (1982).
Elkins v. Moreno, 435 U.S. 647, 98 S.Ct. 1338, 55 L.Ed.2d 614 (1978).
Vlandis v. Kline, 412 U.S. 441, 93 S.Ct. 2230, 37 L.Ed.2d 63 (1973).

School Liability

Gebser v. Lago Vista Independent School Dist., 524 U.S. 274, 118 S.Ct. 1989, 141 L.Ed.2d 277 (1998).
Regents of Univ. of California v. Doe, 519 U.S. 425, 117 S.Ct. 900, 137 L.Ed.2d 55 (1997).

Sex Discrimination and Harassment

Fitzgerald v. Barnstable School Committee, 129 S.Ct. 788 (U.S. 2009).
Jackson v. Birmingham Board of Educ., 125 S.Ct. 1497 (U.S. 2005).
United States (Brzonkala) v. Morrison, 529 U.S. 1062, 120 S.Ct. 1740, 144 L.Ed.2d 658 (2000).
Davis v. Monroe County Board of Educ., 526 U.S. 629, 119 S.Ct. 1661, 143 L.Ed.2d 839 (1999).
U.S. v. Virginia, 518 U.S. 515, 116 S.Ct. 2264, 135 L.Ed.2d 735 (1996).
Franklin v. Gwinnett County Public Schools, 503 U.S. 60, 112 S.Ct. 1028, 117 L.Ed.2d 208 (1992).
Ohio Civil Rights Comm'n v. Dayton Christian Schools, 477 U.S. 619, 106 S.Ct. 2718, 91 L.Ed.2d 512 (1986).
Mississippi Univ. for Women v. Hogan, 458 U.S. 718, 102 S.Ct. 3331, 73 L.Ed.2d 1090 (1982).
Cannon v. Univ. of Chicago, 441 U.S. 677, 99 S.Ct. 1946, 60 L.Ed.2d 560 (1979).
Trustees of Keene State College v. Sweeney, 439 U.S. 24, 99 S.Ct. 295, 58 L.Ed.2d 216 (1978).

Student Loans

Lockhart v. U.S., 126 S.Ct. 699 (U.S. 2005).

Student Privacy

Owasso Independent School Dist. No. I-011 v. Falvo, 534 U.S. 426, 122 S.Ct. 934, 151 L.Ed.2d 896 (2002).
Gonzaga Univ. v. Doe, 536 U.S. 273, 122 S.Ct. 2268, 153 L.Ed.2d 309 (2002).

Student Searches

Vernonia School Dist. 47J v. Acton, 515 U.S. 646, 115 S.Ct. 2386, 132 L.Ed.2d 564 (1995).

New Jersey v. T.L.O., 469 U.S. 325, 105 S.Ct. 733, 83 L.Ed.2d 720 (1985).

Student Suspensions

Regents v. Ewing, 474 U.S. 214, 106 S.Ct. 507, 88 L.Ed.2d 523 (1985).

Board of Educ. v. McCluskey, 458 U.S. 966, 103 S.Ct. 3469, 73 L.Ed.2d 1273 (1982).

Carey v. Piphus, 435 U.S. 247, 98 S.Ct. 1042, 55 L.Ed.2d 252 (1978).

Board of Curators v. Horowitz, 435 U.S. 78, 98 S.Ct. 948, 55 L.Ed.2d 124 (1978).

Wood v. Strickland, 420 U.S. 308, 95 S.Ct. 992, 43 L.Ed.2d 214 (1975).

Goss v. Lopez, 419 U.S. 565, 95 S.Ct. 729, 42 L.Ed.2d 725 (1975).

Taxation

Camps Newfound/Owatonna, Inc. v. Town of Harrison, Maine, 520 U.S. 564, 117 S.Ct. 1590, 137 L.Ed.2d 852 (1997).

Allen v. Wright, 468 U.S. 737, 104 S.Ct. 3315, 82 L.Ed.2d 556 (1984).

Bob Jones Univ. v. United States, 461 U.S. 574, 103 S.Ct. 2017, 76 L.Ed.2d 157 (1983).

Mueller v. Allen, 463 U.S. 388, 103 S.Ct. 3062, 77 L.Ed.2d 721 (1983).

Ramah Navajo School Board v. Bureau of Revenue, 458 U.S. 832, 102 S.Ct. 3394, 73 L.Ed.2d 1174 (1982).

California v. Grace Brethren Church, 457 U.S. 393, 102 S.Ct. 2498, 73 L.Ed.2d 93 (1982).

Gordon v. Lance, 403 U.S. 1, 91 S.Ct. 1889, 29 L.Ed.2d 273 (1971).

Askew v. Hargrave, 401 U.S. 476, 91 S.Ct. 856, 28 L.Ed.2d 196 (1971).

Doremus v. Board of Educ., 342 U.S. 429, 72 S.Ct. 394, 96 L.Ed. 475 (1952).

Teacher Termination

Patsy v. Board of Regents, 457 U.S. 496, 102 S.Ct. 2557, 73 L.Ed.2d 172 (1982).

Chardon v. Fernandez, 454 U.S. 6, 102 S.Ct. 28, 70 L.Ed.2d 6 (1981).

Delaware State College v. Ricks, 449 U.S. 250, 101 S.Ct. 498, 66 L.Ed.2d 431 (1980).

Beilan v. Board of Public Educ., 357 U.S. 399, 78 S.Ct. 1317, 2 L.Ed.2d 1414 (1958).

Textbooks

Norwood v. Harrison, 413 U.S. 455, 93 S.Ct. 2804, 37 L.Ed.2d 723 (1973).

Board of Educ. v. Allen, 392 U.S. 236, 88 S.Ct. 1923, 20 L.Ed.2d 1060 (1968).

Cochran v. Louisiana State Board of Educ., 281 U.S. 370, 50 S.Ct. 335, 74 L.Ed.2d 1929 (1930).

Transportation

> *Kadrmas v. Dickinson Public Schools*, 487 U.S. 450, 108 S.Ct. 2481, 101 L.Ed.2d 399 (1988).
>
> *Wolman v. Walter*, 433 U.S. 229, 97 S.Ct. 2593, 53 L.Ed.2d 714 (1977).
>
> *Everson v. Board of Educ.*, 330 U.S. 1, 67 S.Ct. 504, 91 L.Ed. 711 (1947).

Weapons

> *U.S. v. Lopez*, 514 U.S. 549, 115 S.Ct. 1624, 131 L.Ed.2d 626 (1995).

The Judicial System

In order to allow you to determine the relative importance of a judicial decision, the cases included in ***Higher Education Law in America*** identify the particular court from which a decision has been issued. For example, a case decided by a state supreme court generally will be of greater significance than a state circuit court case. Hence a basic knowledge of the structure of our judicial system is important to an understanding of higher education law.

Almost all the reports in this volume are taken from appellate court decisions. Although most education law decisions occur at trial court and administrative levels, appellate court decisions have the effect of binding lower courts and administrators so that appellate court decisions have the effect of law within their court systems.

State and federal court systems generally function independently of each other. Each court system applies its own law according to statutes and the determinations of its highest court. However, judges at all levels often consider opinions from other court systems to settle issues that are new or arise under unique fact situations. Similarly, lawyers look at the opinions of many courts to locate authority that supports their clients' cases.

Once a lawsuit is filed in a particular court system, that system retains the matter until its conclusion. Unsuccessful parties at the administrative or trial court level generally have the right to appeal unfavorable determinations of law to appellate courts within the system. When federal law issues or constitutional grounds are present, lawsuits may be appropriately filed in the federal court system. In those cases, the lawsuit is filed initially in the federal district court for that area.

On rare occasions, the U.S. Supreme Court considers appeals from the highest courts of the states if a distinct federal question exists and at least four justices agree on the question's importance. The federal courts occasionally send cases to state courts for application of state law. These situations are infrequent and, in general, the state and federal court systems should be considered separate from each other.

The most common system, used by nearly all states and also the federal judiciary, is as follows: a legal action is commenced in district court (sometimes called trial court, county court, common pleas court or superior court) where a decision is initially reached. The case may then be appealed to the court of appeals (or appellate court), and in turn this decision may be appealed to the supreme court.

Several states, however, do not have a court of appeals; lower court decisions are appealed directly to the state's supreme court. Additionally, some states have labeled their courts in a nonstandard fashion.

In Maryland, the highest state court is called the Court of Appeals. In the state of New York, the trial court is called the Supreme Court. Decisions of this court may be appealed to the Supreme Court, Appellate Division. The highest court in New York is the Court of Appeals. Pennsylvania has perhaps the most complex court system. The lowest state court is the Court of Common Pleas. Depending on the circumstances of the case, appeals may be taken to either the Commonwealth Court or the Superior Court. In certain instances the Commonwealth Court functions as a trial court as well as an appellate court. The Superior Court, however, is strictly an intermediate appellate court. The highest court in Pennsylvania is the Supreme Court.

While supreme court decisions are generally regarded as the last word in legal matters, it is important to remember that trial and appeals court decisions also create important legal precedents. For the hierarchy of typical state and federal court systems, please see the diagram below.

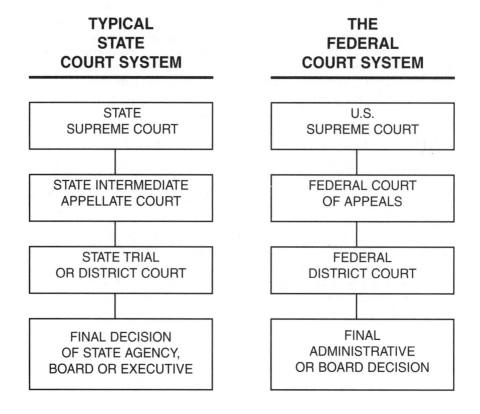

TYPICAL STATE COURT SYSTEM

| STATE SUPREME COURT |
| STATE INTERMEDIATE APPELLATE COURT |
| STATE TRIAL OR DISTRICT COURT |
| FINAL DECISION OF STATE AGENCY, BOARD OR EXECUTIVE |

THE FEDERAL COURT SYSTEM

| U.S. SUPREME COURT |
| FEDERAL COURT OF APPEALS |
| FEDERAL DISTRICT COURT |
| FINAL ADMINISTRATIVE OR BOARD DECISION |

Federal courts of appeals hear appeals from the district courts that are located in their circuits. Below is a list of states matched to the federal circuits in which they are located.

First Circuit — Puerto Rico, Maine, New Hampshire, Massachusetts, Rhode Island

Second Circuit — New York, Vermont, Connecticut

Third Circuit — Pennsylvania, New Jersey, Delaware, Virgin Islands

Fourth Circuit — West Virginia, Maryland, Virginia, North Carolina, South Carolina

Fifth Circuit — Texas, Louisiana, Mississippi

Sixth Circuit — Ohio, Kentucky, Tennessee, Michigan

Seventh Circuit — Wisconsin, Indiana, Illinois

Eighth Circuit — North Dakota, South Dakota, Nebraska, Arkansas, Missouri, Iowa, Minnesota

Ninth Circuit — Alaska, Washington, Oregon, California, Hawaii, Arizona, Nevada, Idaho, Montana, Northern Mariana Islands, Guam

Tenth Circuit — Wyoming, Utah, Colorado, Kansas, Oklahoma, New Mexico

Eleventh Circuit — Alabama, Georgia, Florida

District of Columbia — Hears cases from the U.S. District Court for the District of Columbia.

Federal Circuit — Sitting in Washington, D.C., the U.S. Court of Appeals, Federal Circuit hears patent and trade appeals and certain appeals on claims brought against the federal government and its agencies.

How to Read a Case Citation

Generally, court decisions can be located in case reporters at law school or governmental law libraries. Some cases also can be located on the Internet through legal websites or official court websites.

Each case summary contains the citation, or legal reference, to the full text of the case. The diagram below illustrates how to read a case citation.

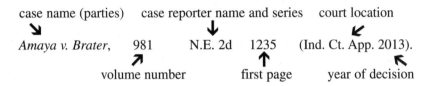

Some cases may have two or three reporter names, such as U.S. Supreme Court cases and cases reported in regional case reporters as well as state case reporters. For example, a U.S. Supreme Court case usually contains three case reporter citations.

first reporter   third reporter

U.S. v. Lopez, 514 U.S. 549, 115 S.Ct. 1624, 131 L.Ed.2d 626 (1995).

second reporter

The citations are still read in the same manner as if only one citation has been listed.

Occasionally, a case may contain a citation that does not reference a case reporter. For example, a citation may contain a reference such as:

case name   year of decision   first page   date of decision

Maltbia v. Coffie, No. H-06-834, 2007 WL 43793 (S.D. Tex. 1/5/07).

court file number   WESTLAW[1]   court location

The court file number indicates the specific number assigned to a case by the particular court system deciding the case. In our example, the Texas Court of Appeals has assigned the case of *Maltbia v. Coffie* the case number of "H-06-834," which will

---

[1]WESTLAW® is a computerized database of court cases available for a fee.

serve as the reference number for the case and any matter relating to the case. Locating a case on the Internet generally requires either the case name and date of the decision, and/or the court file number.

Below, we have listed the full names of the regional reporters. As mentioned previously, many states have individual state reporters. The names of those reporters may be obtained from a reference law librarian.

P.　　　　**Pacific Reporter**
　　　　　　　Alaska, Arizona, California, Colorado, Hawaii, Idaho, Kansas, Montana, Nevada, New Mexico, Oklahoma, Oregon, Utah, Washington, Wyoming

A.　　　　**Atlantic Reporter**
　　　　　　　Connecticut, Delaware, District of Columbia, Maine, Maryland, New Hampshire, New Jersey, Pennsylvania, Rhode Island, Vermont

N.E.　　　**Northeastern Reporter**
　　　　　　　Illinois, Indiana, Massachusetts, New York, Ohio

N.W.　　　**Northwestern Reporter**
　　　　　　　Iowa, Michigan, Minnesota, Nebraska, North Dakota, South Dakota, Wisconsin

So.　　　　**Southern Reporter**
　　　　　　　Alabama, Florida, Louisiana, Mississippi

S.E.　　　**Southeastern Reporter**
　　　　　　　Georgia, North Carolina, South Carolina, Virginia, West Virginia

S.W.　　　**Southwestern Reporter**
　　　　　　　Arkansas, Kentucky, Missouri, Tennessee, Texas

F.　　　　**Federal Reporter**
　　　　　　　The thirteen federal judicial circuits courts of appeals decisions. *See The Judicial System, p. 495* for specific state circuits.

F.Supp.　**Federal Supplement**
　　　　　　　The thirteen federal judicial circuits district court decisions. *See The Judicial System, p. 495* for specific state circuits.

Fed.Appx.　**Federal Appendix**
　　　　　　　Contains unpublished decisions of the U.S. Circuit Courts of Appeal.

U.S.　　　**United States Reports**
S.Ct.　　　**Supreme Court Reporter**　⟩ U.S. Supreme Court Decisions
L.Ed.　　　**Lawyers' Edition**

GLOSSARY

Ad Valorem Tax - In general usage, a tax on property measured by the property's value.

Age Discrimination in Employment Act (ADEA) - The ADEA, 29 U.S.C. § 621, *et seq.*, is part of the Fair Labor Standards Act. It prohibits discrimination against persons who are at least 40 years old, and applies to employers that have 20 or more employees and that affect interstate commerce.

Americans with Disabilities Act (ADA) - The ADA, 42 U.S.C. § 12101, *et seq.*, was signed into law on July 26, 1990. Among other things, it prohibits discrimination against a qualified individual with a disability because of that person's disability with respect to job application procedures, the hiring, advancement or discharge of employees, employee compensation, job training, and other terms, conditions and privileges of employment. The act also prohibits discrimination against otherwise qualified individuals with respect to the services, programs or activities of a public entity. Further, any entity that operates a place of public accommodation (including private schools) may not discriminate against individuals with disabilities.

Bill of Attainder - A bill of attainder is a law that inflicts punishment on a particular group of individuals without a trial. Such acts are prohibited by Article I, Section 9 of the Constitution.

Bona fide - Latin term meaning "good faith." Generally used to note a party's lack of bad intent or fraudulent purpose.

Claim Preclusion - (see Res Judicata).

Class Action Suit - Federal Rule of Civil Procedure 23 allows members of a class to sue as representatives on behalf of the whole class provided that the class is so large that joinder of all parties is impractical, there are questions of law or fact common to the class, the claims or defenses of the representatives are typical of the claims or defenses of the class, and the representative parties will adequately protect the interests of the class. In addition, there must be some danger of inconsistent verdicts or adjudications if the class action were prosecuted as separate actions. Most states also allow class actions under the same or similar circumstances.

Collateral Estoppel - Also known as issue preclusion. The idea that once an issue has been litigated, it may not be re-tried. Similar to the doctrine of *Res Judicata* (see below).

Due Process Clause - The clauses of the Fifth and Fourteenth Amendments to the Constitution which guarantee the citizens of the United States "due process of law" (see below). The Fifth Amendment's Due Process Clause applies to the federal government, and the Fourteenth Amendment's Due Process Clause applies to the states.

Due Process of Law - The idea of "fair play" in the government's application of law to its citizens, guaranteed by the Fifth and Fourteenth Amendments. Substantive due process is just plain *fairness*, and procedural due process is accorded when the government utilizes adequate procedural safeguards for the protection of an individual's liberty or property interests.

Employee Retirement Income Security Act (ERISA) - Federal legislation that sets uniform standards for employee pension benefit plans and employee welfare benefit plans. It is codified at 29 U.S.C. § 1001, *et seq.*

Enjoin - (see Injunction).

Equal Pay Act - Federal legislation that is part of the Fair Labor Standards Act. It applies to discrimination in wages that is based on gender. For race discrimination, employees paid unequally must utilize Title VII or 42 U.S.C. § 1981. Unlike many labor statutes, there is no minimum number of employees necessary to invoke the act's protection.

Equal Protection Clause - The clause of the Fourteenth Amendment that prohibits a state from denying any person within its jurisdiction equal protection of its laws. Also, the Due Process Clause of the Fifth Amendment that pertains to the federal government. This has been interpreted by the Supreme Court to grant equal protection even though there is no explicit grant in the Constitution.

Establishment Clause - The clause of the First Amendment that prohibits Congress from making "any law respecting an establishment of religion." This clause has been interpreted as creating a "wall of separation" between church and state. The test now used to determine whether government action violates the Establishment Clause, referred to as the *Lemon* test, asks whether the action has a secular purpose, whether its primary effect promotes or inhibits religion, and whether it requires excessive entanglement between church and state.

Ex Post Facto Law - A law that punishes as criminal any action that was not a crime at the time it was performed. Prohibited by Article I, Section 9, of the Constitution.

Exclusionary Rule - Constitutional limitation on the introduction of evidence that states that evidence derived from a constitutional violation must be excluded from trial.

Fair Labor Standards Act (FLSA) - Federal legislation that mandates the payment of minimum wages and overtime compensation to covered employees. The overtime provisions require employers to pay at least time-and-one-half to employees who work more than 40 hours per week.

Federal Tort Claims Act - Federal legislation that determines the circumstances under which the United States waives its sovereign immunity (see below) and agrees to be sued in court for money damages. The government retains its immunity in cases of intentional torts committed by its employees or agents, and where the tort is the result of a "discretionary function" of a federal employee or agency. Many states have similar acts.

42 U.S.C. §§ 1981, 1983 - Section 1983 of the federal Civil Rights Act prohibits any person acting under color of state law from depriving any other person of rights protected by the Constitution or by federal laws. A vast majority of lawsuits claiming constitutional violations are brought under § 1983. Section 1981 provides that all persons enjoy the same right to make and enforce contracts as "white citizens." Section 1981 applies to employment contracts. Further, unlike § 1983, § 1981 applies even to private actors. It is not limited to those acting under color of state law. These sections do not apply to the federal government, though the government may be sued directly under the Constitution for any violations.

Free Exercise Clause - The clause of the First Amendment that prohibits Congress from interfering with citizens' rights to the free exercise of their religion. Through the Fourteenth Amendment, it also has been made applicable to the states and their sub-entities. The Supreme Court has held that laws of general applicability that have an incidental effect on persons' free exercise rights are not violative of the Free Exercise Clause.

Incorporation Doctrine - By its own terms, the Bill of Rights applies only to the federal government. The Incorporation Doctrine states that the Fourteenth Amendment makes the Bill of Rights applicable to the states.

Individuals with Disabilities Education Act (IDEA) - 1990 amendment to the Education of the Handicapped Act (EHA) that renames the act and expands the group of children to whom special education services must be given.

Injunction - An equitable remedy (see Remedies) wherein a court orders a party to do or refrain from doing some particular action.

Issue Preclusion - (see Collateral Estoppel).

Jurisdiction - The power of a court to determine cases and controversies. The Supreme Court's jurisdiction extends to cases arising under the Constitution and under federal law. Federal courts have the power to hear cases where there is diversity of citizenship or where a federal question is involved.

Labor Management Relations Act (LMRA) - Federal labor law that preempts state law with respect to controversies involving collective bargaining agreements. The most important provision of the LMRA is § 301, which is codified at 29 U.S.C. § 185.

Mill - In property tax usage, one-tenth of a cent.

National Labor Relations Act (NLRA) - Federal legislation that guarantees to employees the right to form and participate in labor organizations. It prohibits employers from interfering with employees in the exercise of their rights under the NLRA.

Negligence per se - Negligence on its face. Usually, the violation of an ordinance or statute will be treated as negligence per se because no careful person would have been guilty of it.

Occupational Safety and Health Act (OSHA) - Federal legislation that requires employers to provide a safe workplace. Employers have both general and specific duties under OSHA. The general duty is to provide a workplace that is free from recognized hazards that are likely to result in serious physical harm. The specific duty is to conform to the health and safety standards promulgated by the Secretary of Labor.

Overbroad - A government action is overbroad if, in an attempt to alleviate a specific evil, it impermissibly prohibits or chills a protected action. For example, attempting to deal with street litter by prohibiting the distribution of leaflets or handbills.

Per Curiam - Latin phrase meaning "by the court." Used in court reports to note an opinion written by the court rather than by a single judge or justice.

Preemption Doctrine - Doctrine that states that when federal and state law attempt to regulate the same subject matter, federal law prevents the state law from operating. Based on the Supremacy Clause of Article VI, Clause 2, of the Constitution.

Prior Restraint - Restraining a publication before it is distributed. In general, constitutional law doctrine prohibits government from exercising prior restraint.

Pro Se - A party appearing in court, without the benefit of an attorney, is said to be appearing pro se.

Remand - The act of an appellate court in returning a case to the court from which it came for further action.

Remedies - There are two general categories of remedies, or relief: legal remedies, which consist of money damages, and equitable remedies, which consist of a court mandate that a specific action be prohibited or required. For example, a claim for compensatory and punitive damages seeks a legal remedy; a claim for an injunction seeks an equitable remedy. Equitable remedies are generally unavailable unless legal remedies are inadequate to address the harm.

Res Judicata - The judicial notion that a claim or action may not be tried twice or re-litigated, or that all causes of action arising out of the same set of operative facts should be tried at one time. Also known as claim preclusion.

Section 504 of the Rehabilitation Act of 1973 - Section 504 applies to public or private institutions receiving federal financial assistance. It requires that, in the employment context, an otherwise qualified individual cannot be denied employment based on his or her handicap. An otherwise qualified individual is one who can perform the "essential functions" of the job with "reasonable accommodation."

Section 1981 & Section 1983 - (see 42 U.S.C. §§ 1981, 1983).

Sovereign Immunity - The idea that the government cannot be sued without its consent. It stems from the English notion that the "King could do no wrong." This immunity from suit has been abrogated in most states and by the federal government through legislative acts known as "tort claims acts."

Standing - The judicial doctrine that states that in order to maintain a lawsuit a party must have some real interest at stake in the outcome of the trial.

Statute of Limitations - A statute of limitation provides the time period in which a specific cause of action may be brought.

Summary Judgment - Also referred to as pretrial judgment. Similar to a dismissal. Where there is no genuine issue as to any material fact and all that remains is a question of law, a judge can rule in favor of one party or the other. In general, summary judgment is used to dispose of claims that do not support a legally recognized claim.

Supremacy Clause - Clause in Article VI of the Constitution that states that federal legislation is the supreme law of the land. This clause is used to support the Preemption Doctrine (see above).

Title VI, Civil Rights Act of 1964 (Title VI) - Title VI prohibits racial discrimination in federally funded programs. This extends to admissions, financial aid, and virtually every aspect of the federally assisted programs in which private schools are involved. Codified at 42 U.S.C. § 2000d.

Title VII, Civil Rights Act of 1964 (Title VII) - Title VII prohibits discrimination in employment based upon race, color, sex, national origin, or religion. It applies to any employer having 15 or more employees. Under Title VII, where an employer intentionally discriminates, employees may obtain money damages unless the claim is for race discrimination. For those claims, monetary relief is available under 42 U.S.C. § 1981.

Title IX - Enacted as part of the Education Amendments of 1972, Title IX prohibits sexual discrimination in any private school program or activity receiving federal financial assistance. Codified at 20 U.S.C. § 1981, *et seq.*

U.S. Equal Employment Opportunity Commission (EEOC) - The EEOC is the government entity that is empowered to enforce Title VII (see above) through investigation and/or lawsuits. Private individuals alleging discrimination must pursue administrative remedies within the EEOC before they are allowed to file suit under Title VII.

Vacate - The act of annulling the judgment of a court either by an appellate court or by the court itself. The Supreme Court generally will vacate a lower court's judgment without deciding the case itself, and remand the case to the lower court for further consideration in light of some recent controlling decision.

Void-for-Vagueness Doctrine - A judicial doctrine based on the Fourteenth Amendment's Due Process Clause. In order for a law that regulates speech, or any criminal statute, to pass muster under the doctrine, the law must make clear what actions are prohibited or made criminal. Under the principles of the Due Process Clause, people of average intelligence should not have to guess at the meaning of a law.

Writ of Certiorari - The device used by the Supreme Court to transfer cases from the appellate court's docket to its own. Since the Supreme Court's appellate jurisdiction is largely discretionary, it need only issue such a writ when it desires to rule in the case.

INDEX